JUDICIAL POWER, DEMOCRACY AND LEGAL POSITIVISM

JUDICIAL POWER, DEMOCRACY AND LEGAL POSITIVISM

Edited by
TOM CAMPBELL
Professor of Law, The Australian National University

and

JEFFREY GOLDSWORTHY
Associate Professor of Law, Monash University, Melbourne

Ashgate

DARTMOUTH

Aldershot • Brookfield USA • Singapore • Sydney

Published by
Dartmouth Publishing Company Limited
Ashgate Publishing Ltd
Gower House
Croft Road
Aldershot
Hants GU11 3HR
England

Ashgate Publishing Company
Old Post Road
Brookfield
Vermont 05036
USA

Ashgate website: http://www.ashgate.com

British Library Cataloguing in Publication Data
Judicial power, democracy and legal positivism. – (Applied legal philosophy)
1. Legal positivism 2. Justice (Philosophy) 3. Judicial power – Philosophy
I. Campbell, Tom, 1938– II. Goldsworthy, Jeffrey
340.1'12

Library of Congress Cataloging-in-Publication Data
Judicial power, democracy and legal positivism / edited by Tom Campbell and Jeffrey Goldsworthy.
p. cm. – (Applied legal philosophy)
Includes index.
ISBN 0-7546-2061-1
1. Legal positivism. 2. Judicial review–Philosophy. I. Series.
II. Campbell, Tom, 1938– III. Goldsworthy, Jeffrey Denys.

K331.J83 2000
340'.112 21–dc21

99-046651

ISBN 0 7546 2061 1

Typeset by Manton Typesetters, Louth, Lincolnshire, UK.

Printed and bound in Great Britain by MPG Books Ltd, Bodmin, Cornwall

Contents

PART II ASSEMBLIES VERSUS COURTS IN DEMOCRATIC THEORY AND PRACTICE

List of Contributors

Tom Campbell has been Professor of Law in The Australian National University since 1990. He was formerly Professor of Jurisprudence in the University of Glasgow and Professor of Philosophy in the University of Stirling. His publications include *The Left and Rights* (Routledge, 1983), *Justice* (Macmillan, 1988), and *The Legal Theory of Ethical Positivism* (Dartmouth, 1996).

John Daley, a graduate of the University of Melbourne, has been an Associate to Justice Daryl Dawson of the High Court of Australia and a policy adviser to the Victorian government. He recently completed a doctorate in law at the University of Oxford, investigating sources of authority for the Australian Constitution.

Tim Dare is a Senior Lecturer in philosophy, and coordinator of the postgraduate Diploma in Professional Ethics at the University of Auckland. His doctorate is in philosophy and he also holds postgraduate qualifications in law. He has taught law, and been a researcher for the High Court of New Zealand. He has published on applied and theoretical ethics, the philosophy of law, and political philosophy, and is currently writing a book on legal ethics.

Margaret Davies is a Senior Lecturer in Law at Flinders University. She is the author of two books on legal theory, *Asking the Law Question* (Law Book Co/Sweet & Maxwell, 1994) and *Delimiting the Law* (Pluto Press, 1996). Her research centres on the intersections between many areas, including jurisprudence, feminist legal theory, postmodernism, queer theory, and the philosophy of property. She is currently working with Dr Ngaire Naffine on the relationship between the philosophy of property and legal personality.

Arthur Glass is a member of the Faculty of Law at the University of New South Wales. He has written in the areas of legal theory, public law and immigration law. He is the co-author of books on Federal Constitutional Law and has published articles in *Rechtstheorie, Ratio Juris*, the *Sydney Law Review* and *Text/Law/Culture*.

Jeffrey Goldsworthy is an Associate Professor of Law at Monash University in Melbourne, where he teaches constitutional law and legal philosophy. He has published widely in both fields, and is the author of *The Sovereignty of Parliament, History and Philosophy* (Clarendon Press, 1999).

Martin Krygier is Professor of Law at the University of New South Wales. He has edited *Marxism and Communism: Posthumous Reflections on Politics, Society and Law* (Rodopi, 1994), and co-edited *Bureaucracy: The Career of a Concept* (Edward Arnold, 1979) (with Eugene Kamenka) and *The Rule of Law after Communism* (1999) (with Adam Czarnota). He delivered the Boyer lectures for the Australian Broadcasting Commission in 1997, subsequently published as *Between Fear and Hope: Hybrid Thoughts on Public Values* (ABC Books, 1997).

Nicola Lacey is Professor of Criminal Law at the London School of Economics, and a former Professor in Law at Birkbeck College, London and Fellow of New College, Oxford University. Her publications include *State Punishment: Political Principles and Community Values* (Routledge, 1988), *Reconstructing Criminal Law* (2nd edn, Butterworths, 1998) (with Celia Wells), *The Politics of Community* (Harvester Wheatsheaf/University of Toronto Press, 1993) (with Elizabeth Frazer), and *Unspeakable Subjects: Feminist Essays in Legal and Social Theory* (Hart Publishing, 1998).

Neil MacCormick holds a Leverhulme Research Professorship in the University of Edinburgh, where he has been Regius Professor of Public Law since 1972. His most recent books include *Interpreting Precedents* (Ashgate/Dartmouth, 1997) and *Interpreting Statutes* (Dartmouth, 1991), both co-edited with Robert Summers. His current research is on the theme 'law, state and practical Reason', and his forthcoming book deals with sovereignty, legal reasoning, and the institutional theory of law.

Frederick Schauer is Academic Dean and Frank Stanton Professor of the First Amendment in the Kennedy School of Government at Harvard University. His books include *The Law of Obscenity* (Bureau of National Affairs, 1976), *Free Speech: A Philosophical Inquiry* (Cambridge, 1982), and *Playing By The Rules: A Philosophical Examination of Rule-Based Decision-Making in Law and Life* (Clarendon Press, 1991).

Walter Sinnott-Armstrong is Professor of Philosophy at Dartmouth College, where he teaches ethics, philosophy of law, theory of knowledge, and informal logic. His books include *Moral Dilemmas* (Basil Blackwell, 1988), *Understanding Arguments* (5th edn, Harcourt, 1996) (with Robert J. Fogelin), *Contemporary Perspectives on Constitutional Interpretation* (Westview, 1993) (with Susan Brison), *Modality, Morality, and Belief* (Cambridge, 1995) (with Diana Raffman and Nicholas Asher), *Philosophy of Law* (Harcourt, 1996) (with Fred Schauer); and *Moral Knowledge?* (Oxford, 1996). He is currently working on a monograph on limited moral scepticism.

Helen Stacy is a Senior Lecturer in the Faculty of Law at Queensland University of Technology, Brisbane. Her work analyses the broader social catalysts of legal regulation utilizing comparative and critical methodology. She has published in legal theory, feminist legal theory, semiotics and environmental law. Her most recent work is *Beyond the Adversarial System* (Federation Press, forthcoming) (with M. Lavarch).

Natalie Stoljar is a Senior Lecturer in philosophy at Monash University. She has published articles in the areas of legal philosophy, feminist philosophy and philosophy of mind. She is co-editor (with Catriona Mackenzie) of *Relational Autonomy: Feminist Essays on Autonomy, Agency and the Social Self* (Oxford, 1999), and is working on a book on legal and literary interpretation.

Margaret Thornton is Professor of Law and Legal Studies at La Trobe University in Melbourne. Her publications include *The Liberal Promise: Anti-Discrimination Legislation in Australia* (Oxford, 1990) and *Dissonance and Distrust: Women in the Legal Profession* (Oxford, 1996), together with an edited collection *Public and Private: Feminist Legal Debates* (Oxford, 1995). She is presently engaged in a study of citizenship and contractarianism.

Jeremy Waldron is the Maurice and Hilda Friedman Professor of Law, and Director of the Center for Law and Philosophy, at Columbia University. His many books include *The Right to Private Property* (Clarendon Press, 1988), *Liberal Rights: Collected Papers 1981–91* (Cambridge, 1993) and *Law and Disagreement* (Clarendon Press, 1998).

George Williams teaches and writes in the areas of constitutional law and human rights at the Australian National University. He is the author of books including *Human Rights Under the Australian Constitution* (Oxford, 1999) and *Australian Constitutional Law and Theory: Commentary and Materials* (2nd edn, Federation Press, 1998) (with Tony Blackshield). He also practises as a barrister and has appeared in constitutional cases before the High Court of Australia.

Leslie Zines is Emeritus Professor of Law, and Visiting Fellow in the Law Program of the Research School of Social Sciences, at the Australian National University. His books include *Federal Jurisdiction in Australia* (2nd edn, Oxford, 1978) (with Zelman Cowen), *Constitutional Change in the Commonwealth* (Cambridge, 1991) and *The High Court and the Constitution* (4th edn, Butterworths, 1997).

Series Preface

The objective of the Dartmouth Series in Applied Legal Philosophy is to publish work which adopts a theoretical approach to the study of particular areas or aspects of law or deals with general theories of law in a way which focuses on issues of practical moral and political concern in specific legal contexts.

In recent years there has been an encouraging tendency for legal philosophers to utilize detailed knowledge of the substance and practicalities of law and a noteworthy development in the theoretical sophistication of much legal research. The series seeks to encourage these trends and to make available studies in law which are both genuinely philosophical in approach and at the same time based on appropriate legal knowledge and directed towards issues in the criticism and reform of actual laws and legal systems.

The series will include studies of all the main areas of law, presented in a manner which relates to the concerns of specialist legal academics and practitioners. Each book makes an original contribution to an area of legal study while being comprehensible to those engaged in a wide variety of disciplines. Their legal content is principally Anglo-American, but a wide-ranging comparative approach is encouraged and authors are drawn from a variety of jurisdictions.

TOM D. CAMPBELL
Series Editor
The Faculty of Law
The Australian National University

Preface

'Judicial activism' is on the rise throughout the world, for reasons that are somewhat obscure although clearly related to growing international concern with the protection of human rights.[1] Judges are increasingly interested more in doing justice as they see it, than in merely applying laws previously laid down by other decision-makers. In common law jurisdictions, this phenomenon is evident in a much greater judicial willingness to reform the common law, and to restrain or correct actions of the legislative and executive branches of government. Since 1992, for example, the High Court of Australia has radically changed the common law relating to property rights, in order to accommodate a previously unrecognized form of native title to land, and has also purported to discover 'implied rights' in the Constitution whose existence was hitherto unsuspected.[2]

These developments, in Australia and elsewhere, have reinvigorated debates concerning the role of judges, and the relationship between the legislative and judicial branches of government, in modern democracies. The legitimate role of judges cannot be properly examined without considering the nature and form of law, and therefore debates concerning judicial activism have become intertwined with debates between critics and defenders of legal positivism. Ronald Dworkin, for example, has spent his career vigorously defending what critics decried as the judicial activism of the USA's Warren Court, by way of a sophisticated critique of legal positivism. Dworkin argues that law in a genuinely democratic community is most fundamentally a matter not of rules authoritatively laid down by legislators, but of abstract principles of political morality. He claims that, at least in the USA, judges are the ultimate oracles and guardians of these principles, which govern the interpretation of statutes as well as the development of the common law, and in addition are enshrined in the US Constitution.[3]

Another theory principally concerned with the nature and form of law, and with the judicial function, is expounded in Tom Campbell's recent book, *The Legal Theory of Ethical Positivism*.[4] But Campbell's position is about as far from Dworkin's as one could get: he defends legal positivism and advocates judicial subservience to democratically elected and accountable legislatures. He argues that, ideally, the law would consist of relatively clear rules enacted by such a legislature, which judges would confine themselves to expounding and enforcing. But whereas Dworkin's anti-positivism is 'interpretive' rather than purely prescriptive – he argues that his theory is the best available interpretation of the law as it already is – Campbell's 'ethical' legal positivism is prescriptive – the law should accord with his recommendations, insofar as it does not now do so.

The essays in this volume deal with these questions concerning the nature of law and the proper role of judges. They are divided into two parts, Part I dealing with legal positivism as either a descriptive or prescriptive theory of law, and Part II with the respective roles of legislatures and judges in modern democracies. The essays originated in a Workshop on 'Judicial Activism and Judicial Review in Australian Democracy' held at the Australian National University in July 1998. Despite that title, the essays are not concerned solely, or even principally, with Australia. Their authors come from England, Scotland, New Zealand and the United States, as well as Australia, and discuss issues common to all common law jurisdictions. Another strength of the Workshop was its inclusion of representatives of different theoretical perspectives – analytical, feminist, postmodernist, and sociological – leading to the wide variety of contributions included in this book. Participants at the Workshop engaged in vigorous but friendly exchanges, and left with an enhanced understanding and appreciation of one another's perspectives. We hope that readers will derive the same benefit from reading this collection of their essays. In what follows, I introduce the essays very briefly, touching on only some of the main points, and without attempting to summarize all the issues which they canvass. In every case, my description of their contents should be prefaced by the words '*inter alia*'!

In the first essay, Tom Campbell elaborates on some of the main themes of his book, *The Legal Theory of Ethical Positivism* emphasizing the way in which rule governance enhances democracy. Some of his arguments are queried or challenged in subsequent essays by Neil MacCormick, Martin Krygier and Arthur Glass. Drawing on the 'institutional' theory of law that he has defended in other writings, in Chapter 2 MacCormick argues that, in interpreting statutes, judges should pay more attention than Campbell allows to statutory coherence with the pre-existing body of law. Following on from this, Martin Krygier advocates an empirical approach to the benefits of rule governance, pointing out that, in some contexts, a regulatory regime of general standards may be preferable to one of more concrete rules. Glass, in Part II (Chapter 15), argues that Campbell pays insufficient attention both to the inevitability of administrative discretion in modern states and the desirability of its being subjected to judicial supervision guided by broad standards rather than precise rules.

Nicola Lacey, Margaret Davies and Helen Stacy (Chapters 4–6) scrutinize legal positivism from feminist and postmodernist perspectives. Lacey identifies a variety of different feminist objections to legal positivism and considers their applicability to Campbell's version of 'ethical' positivism. Davies criticizes legal positivists' separation of law from other aspects of the personal, political and cultural realms and complains that they are insufficiently attentive to the inherently political nature, and oppressive potential, of this separatism. Stacy accuses modern legal theories of erroneously assuming that there is a single, universal human nature and experience and advocates a postmodern jurisprudence based on the recognition of 'a multiplicity of identities and a host of complexities and contradictions within individual and collective identities'.

In Chapter 7 Natalie Stoljar discusses an issue that must be central to any form of legal positivism: how statutory rules should be interpreted. She argues that, even if statutes are attempts by legislators to communicate norms of conduct, it does not logically follow that statutory interpretation must be governed by their intentions. In the following chapter Walter Sinnott-Armstrong proposes a reconciliation of legal positivism and its traditional rivals – natural law and legal realism – by arguing that each of them accurately expresses the point of view of a particular group of actors within legal systems. Frederick Schauer, in Chapter 9, pinpoints the relevance of legal positivism to judicial review by pursuing the question of what distinguishes legal institutions from other institutions. This leads him to surmise that the virtues of judicial review lie in the procedural differentiation which provides legal institutions with comparative immunity from majoritarian forces, while one of its vices lies in the information differentiation which cuts courts off from receiving and using information of great relevance to the policy decisions which are inseparable from judicial review and judicial activism.

Part II begins with my own essay, devoted to a philosophical analysis and defence of the constitutional doctrine of parliamentary sovereignty, which holds that in Britain, and some other countries influenced by British tradition, legislatures have unlimited law-making authority. I attempt to refute arguments that, in these countries, judges necessarily have authority to invalidate legislation that they believe violates fundamental human rights. In Chapter 11 Jeremy Waldron also argues against judicial supremacism. He asks why representative legislatures are typically so much larger, numerically, than courts and executives and concludes that it is because decision-making processes in which all interested parties can participate are more authoritative than those restricted to small elites. John

Daley (Chapter 12) analyses the concept of judicial restraint (and therefore, by implication, its opposite – judicial activism), criticizing, in the process, previous attempts at clarification.

In his second contribution to the book, Walter Sinnott-Armstrong (Chapter 13) asks whether judges should have constitutional authority to enforce their own understandings of broad moral standards, instead of deferring to the decisions of a legislature. He concludes that there is no single, generally applicable answer to this question and identifies five factors that determine whether or not, with respect to particular kinds of question, judges should be able to do so. In Chapter 14 Margaret Thornton discusses ways in which resort to civil litigation, rather than political agitation, can enhance active participation in citizenship by members of subordinated groups, such as indigenous people, who are discriminated against in the legislative process. Tim Dare then shifts the focus of the book from the role of judges to that of lawyers, defending what he calls the 'standard conception' of legal ethics, characterized by neutrality, non-accountability and partisanship. He argues that this conception is more consistent than its rivals with the principal function of law in a pluralist community, which is to mediate between inconsistent moral views. The concluding essays, by Leslie Zines and George Williams, describe the recent judicial decisions in Australia which have generated unprecedented complaints and debates about judicial activism.

I conclude by expressing my thanks to my co-editor, Tom Campbell, for inviting me to help organize the Workshop and edit this book, and for doing the lion's share of the work in both cases, to the authors of the essays for their stimulating presentations at the Workshop and prompt submission of manuscripts, and to the Australian Research Council for awarding Tom and myself a large grant, part of which made the Workshop, and this volume of essays, possible. Thanks are also due to Dr Andrew Gleeson for his substantial editorial assistance.

Jeffrey Goldsworthy

Notes

1 C.N. Tate and T. Vallinder (eds), *The Global Expansion of Judicial Power* (New York: New York University Press, 1995).

2 These developments are described in the essays by Zines and Williams (Chapters 17 and 18 in this volume).

3 R. Dworkin, *Law's Empire* (London: Fontana Press, 1986) and *Freedom's Law, The Moral Reading of the American Constitution* (Cambridge, Mass.: Harvard University Press, 1996).

4 Aldershot: Dartmouth, 1996.

PART I
REORIENTING LEGAL POSITIVISM

1 Democratic Aspects of Ethical Positivism

TOM CAMPBELL[1]

This book deals with constitutional questions about the role of judiciaries and legislatures in contemporary democracies. These issues are discussed in the context of the suggestion that the tradition of legal positivism has an important bearing on the formulation of principles specifying how judges and legislatures ought to carry out their tasks.

This is a formidable undertaking. It requires the articulation and deployment of both a theory of law and a theory of democracy, and this in an age in which theories of any sort are suspect. It is a particularly formidable task because the theory of law in question is legal positivism, a paradigm which has been systematically questioned as a result of developments in philosophy and the social sciences. Today, legal positivism is widely regarded as intellectually, empirically and morally untenable, and legal positivists no longer have the confidence which arises from espousing what used to be the reigning orthodoxy of leading practitioners.

The intellectual problems of legal positivism arise principally from the role that legal positivists ascribe to rules as a means of controlling conduct, including the conduct of governments, which runs counter to contemporary views on the indeterminacy of language. The empirical problems of legal positivism centre on their perceived failure to identify the boundaries between law, morality and politics in actual legal systems. Morally, legal positivism is frequently portrayed as bankrupt, having in the past tolerated slavery,[2] Hitler's democratic socialism[3] and South Africa's apartheid system,[4] and currently resisting the progressive institutionalization of the human rights movement. It is also held responsible for the failure of legal systems to adapt to changing circumstances, the insensitivity of judges to the personal and social realities affecting the litigants who pass through their courts, and the amorality or immorality of lawyers whose professional conduct is often regarded with contempt.[5]

Democracy gets a rather better press, although its almost universal popularity makes it harder, rather than easier, to find our way through to a satisfactory theory of democracy. Beyond the conceptual link between democratic government and political equality and a high level of agreement that it is desirable that governments be subject to periodic popular elections, accompanied by a minimum threshold of civil liberties and political rights, there is no single coherent theory of democracy which can both guide us as to what sort of democratic system we should have and, at the same time, elicit the general support of specialist participants and ordinary citizens which would be required to put it into practice. We seem doomed to operate with an uneasy mixture of incompatible democratic ideals with, on the one hand, a market model according to which political power is a commodity and voters as consumers are out to satisfy their individual desires by purchasing the political package that seems to offer them most of what they want and, on the other hand, a participatory or deliberative theory which relies on the unlikely prospect of giving a controlling political influence to a public discourse which is directed to the achievement of a consensus as to what constitutes justice and the common good.

Notwithstanding these difficulties, this chapter suggests a framework for deriving some tentative answers to some rather familiar questions – answers which have some prospect of commanding general approval and generating practical guidance. These answers and guidance are designed to be relatively neutral in terms of the particular substantive matters which divide citizens as to the content of first-order political and legal decisions but enable them to set up democratically acceptable legal processes and procedures for the resolution of such disagreements and direct those who operate such institutions as to how they should conduct their business.

I call the politico-legal framework of principles proposed 'democratic positivism'. Democratic positivism is positivistic in the tradition of a legal positivism that is wedded to the political significance of channelling governmental power through specific unambiguous conduct-governing mandatory rules, with genuine exclusionary force, capable of being applied without recourse to contentious moral and political judgements – rules which have their source in empirically identifiable and constitutionally defined human acts.[6] Democratic positivism is democratic in that it affirms that the source of these authoritative rules is empirically identifiable institutional acts which are the outcome of democratic procedures. Democratic procedures are taken to be procedures which serve to maximize the involvement of all those affected by the rules which bind them in a way which approximates to the ideal of giving their choices equal weight with respect to rules and decisions which are binding on them. This confines the term democracy to those systems of government which seek to approach equality of individual self-determination, either through direct participation in the legislative and executive process or through the election of representatives whose role is to legislate and govern on their behalf, subject to periodic election ongoing opportunities for criticism and systems of answerability which require public responses to criticism, both prior and subsequent to electoral accountability.[7]

Democratic Positivism

Democratic positivism is a theory in tension in so far as the positivist aspects involved can come into conflict with its democratic elements. For instance, a democratic political process may come up with a decision to depart from the rule of positive law in favour of more particular and less formal outcomes. Or the requirement of the rule of positive law may prevent elected governments from exercising judicial functions or passing laws embodying vague moral standards.

We can reduce this tension between democracy and positivism by excluding, from the normal democratic process, those rules which constitute the electoral procedures and the systemic prerequisites, such as freedom of speech, which give legitimacy to putatively democratic decision-making. These prerequisites, which could even include the governance of rules as a means of promoting political equality, may be exempt from democratic change on the grounds that they are constitutive of democracy and cannot therefore be dispensed with without undermining the democratic credentials of the system. This move does not solve that core problem of democratic theory which concerns the appropriate decision procedures for determining precisely what these untouchable democratic fundamentals should be, but it is an indispensable part of any genuinely democratic theory that self-destructive 'democratic' decisions are not democratic at all. And, in so far as it can be shown that legal positivism is itself a democratic prerequisite, and therefore partially constitutive of any acceptably democratic system, the tension between legal positivism and democracy is eliminated. Moreover, it is arguable that a system of law and government which embodies the norms of prescriptive legality is part of the presuppositions which constitute democratic systems. On this view, the issue of whether government must be conducted in accordance with a system of positive law is not open to democratic disposal.

To follow through this analysis, we must move from clarification of terms enabling empirical descriptions of political and legal institutions to the substance of the rationales and justifications of democracy and legal positivism which are indispensable to the further specification of both concepts. In relation to legal positivism, the main justificatory task relates to the social utility and moral significance of societal rules, as opposed to unfettered individual autonomy or the discretionary power of officials, and the moral appropriateness of rule governance in the distribution, exercise and control of political power. In *The Legal Theory of Ethical Positivism*,[8] I explore such instrumental virtues of rule governance with respect to predictability, regularity, coordination, conduct control, conduct facilitation, dispute resolution, individual autonomy, economic efficiency, power allocation, the formal preconditions of substantive justice and the focus of democratic dialogue. There I argue that these are the principal reasons why it is good for a society to have systems of specific mandatory rules which preclude individual members from exercising their own judgement over certain matters with respect to their own conduct.

I do not rehearse all these rationales here, although they are central to the understanding of democratic positivism, including its account of legal authority and legal obligation. However, it is worth highlighting those justifications of rule governance which are particularly germane to democracy. These rationales focus on the thesis that empowering officials with wide-ranging discretion, although it holds out the prospect of utilizing expert opinion and making fine-tuned decisions in the light of the particular circumstances of each situation, is inappropriate where the decisions call for value judgements whose content depends both on the personal or collective outlook of those exercising that discretion and their susceptibility to the influence of interested parties, so that what varies is not so much the circumstances of the case as the personal beliefs and interests of the officials who have the discretionary power and the pressures which are brought to bear on them.

In the arena of political conflict and evaluative disagreement, the advantages of expertise and particularized justice promised by the wise deployment of such discretionary power are negated, for the democratic positivist, by the scope provided thereby for the impact of opinions and influences which have no legitimacy within the system. Abstracting from the content of rules, which may or may not be themselves embodiments of class, gender and racist attitudes, the absence of rules increases the vulnerability of parties to controversial political or discriminatory attitudes and beliefs which are as endemic within legal institutions as they are in society at large. The contention is that rule governance can be an effective way to promote the neutralization of unauthorized ideology, prejudice and illegitimate self-interest in the exercise of power.

Pointing out the various benefits of rule governance does not imply that social life as a whole should be strictly rule-based or that there should be a system of positivistic rules covering every aspect of social life. The thesis is, rather, that where there is government – that is non-optionality enforced by punishment and detriment – then it must be rule-governed. Indeed, legal positivism fits neatly with a political theory which favours a limited domain for government along the few simple rules model developed by Epstein.[9] However, in the light of the pervasive role of unjustifiable domination in social relations, in most complex societies the domain of law should be far more extensive than anything envisaged by libertarians.

Further, it is important to note that, in practice, rules and democracy converge in so far as rules are a powerful instrument for bringing about predictable change and democracy is justified in part by self-determination in the strong sense in which people can collectively achieve their goals in and through the public sphere. If rule governance has a positive correlation with effective governance, defined in terms of meeting the objectives of those with legitimate power, then it makes for a more effective democracy (if that is the system in operation) just as it can make for a more effective tyranny.[10] Arguments based on the alleged effectiveness of rules in producing desired outcomes are vulnerable to evidence that they do not do so either in general instances or contexts. Why, then, is the democratic process not a source of legitimate decision-making as to whether positive rule governance is or is not desirable in this or that circumstance? After all, there is much interesting, and apparently evenly balanced, discussion about whether certain policy objectives are better served by setting general standards rather than enacting specific rules.

The answers to this essentially empirical challenge to the paramountcy of rules directs us towards less contingent rationales for rule governance which have more to do with the issues of political authority which generate theories of democracy. It can be argued, for instance, that any exercise of political power must have its substance approved by the consent of the governed and that this can only be achieved prospectively by the democratic authorization, not just of rulers but of rules. Anything less subjects the citizen to a degree of illegitimate coercion. The system violates the principle of political legitimacy that no one should be subject to the democratically unconstrained will of another to the precise extent that state officials – that is, persons whose decisions are backed by coercive sanctions or non-voluntary detriments – have discretionary power. If rules are a necessary element in the control of government officials, it follows that exclusionary rules are necessary conditions of democratic coercive authority.

A version of this thesis is to be found in those aspects of Rousseau's social contract model[11] which relate to the problem of securing equality of self-determination in the democratic process. Rousseau dissociates himself from what we now call the populist majoritarian vision of democracy where the decision that is made is the one which attracts the majority of self-interested endorsements. Such a process might elicit the rule of all but it would not realize the general will – a will aimed at the common good. It is unnecessary to base democratic positivism on something so intangible and idealistic as an electorally-based process that realizes the common good, whatever that might be.[12] But we can go as far as a modified version of the model and claim that an assembly formulating a choice of rules is intrinsically more acceptable than one making singular decisions. This thesis can be supported on three grounds. One is that, potentially, all members of the assembly are affected by the rule and are therefore going to scrutinize it carefully. Rousseau made this contingently true by insisting on economic and social homogeneity in his republic so that all rules did impact on all citizens in the same way – something to which we might seek to approximate but can hardly require.

A second reason why we might restrict assemblies to the choice of rules – that is, norms relating to categories of person and types of situation – is that dealing with these types of rule guards against decisions being made purely on the basis of the identity of individuals or named groups who would thereby be vulnerable to the exploitation of self-interested majorities. Although such restraints as rules might place on victimization and discrimination can be evaded formally by the selection of general rules which uniquely or disproportionately identify the targeted persons or groups, this requirement does institutionalize the unacceptability of victimization and discrimination, and serves to reduce their incidence by requiring the legislative debate to be about types and categories rather than particulars.

This takes us to the third and more basic ground for restricting democratic assemblies to the choice of rules, which is that the moral legitimacy of coercive power depends on the exercise of that power conforming with a normative form which is capable of being morally justified. This form must be general not particular. A minimum requirement of morality is treatment in accordance with an acceptable reason which the person concerned is committed to applying to similar circumstances on different occasions, or at least until such time as they change their moral beliefs. The political version of this universalizability requirement is that government's treatment of citizens be in accordance with reasons relating to the characteristics of persons and circumstances, and this can be done systematically only through treatment in accordance with rules. Rule governance, therefore, is a precondition, although by no means a guarantee, of morally justified political authority. A system which does not frame its choices in this way is simply not a candidate for moral legitimacy.

This third ground for preferring rules, which I call the moral form advantage, can be further developed in the context of deliberative democracy which makes actual debate a prerequisite of legitimate democratic process. It can be argued that such a debate is moralized by being confined to a choice of rules which requires principled reasons to be given to justify the categories which feature in the alternative rule formulations. If the rationale for the debate requirement is epistemological, in that it is grounded on the claim that public discourse involving all those affected by a decision promotes the development of morally just outcomes, then we are close to full-blown Rousseauism.[13]

If we put these arguments together then we have a powerful combination of moral and political reasons for rule governance as an essential part of democracy – some demonstrating that a choice of rules enhances the power of populations and some demonstrating it helps moralize majoritarianism, either by increasing the size of the majority or by subjecting the substance of the choices to moral scrutiny. This is comforting to the extent that it shows an affinity between positivism and democracy and reduces the scope of the tension between democracy and positivism which is latent in democratic positivism.

The force of such arguments is limited in so far as they establish only the practically necessary conditions for political legitimacy and can offer no guarantees of acceptable outcomes with respect to the content of the rules and the overall efficacy of rule governance in terms of the ideas it is intended to serve. On the other hand, given the inherent difficulty not only of dealing with the pervasive social and economic forces which generate inequality and injustice, but also the fundamental epistemological problems over establishing the content of the moral and political values through which we can evaluate political outcomes, they do constitute a powerful *prima facie* case for democratic positivism.

All this clears the way for addressing some of the apparently intractable problems – philosophical, empirical and evaluative – which are routinely used as a reason either to bury positivism or to demonstrate that there is no theory of democracy which both describes democracies as they are or might be and offers convincing justifications for systems that are compatible with rule governance. In doing this, some orienting principles for good legislating and good adjudication emerge.

Philosophical Problems of Legal Positivism

The philosophical problems of legal positivism relate mainly to the epistemology and ontology of rules. The epistemological problem is that rules have no meaning in themselves but acquire meaning through the conceptual and linguistic apparatus that people within particular cultures bring to the texts which constitute their verbal formulations. It is not just that rules have a core meaning that can be interpreted differently at the margins by different individuals and groups. The core meaning is itself relative to the cognitive contribution brought by the individuals and groups who give their meanings to the symbols in question, and this cognitive contribution varies both between groups and between individuals. Traditionally, it has been possible to work with a distinction between the undeniably correct reading of a text in so far as it is clear and precise, and the areas of uncertainty which require us to deploy various techniques of interpretation to arrive at a reasonable, but not conclusively correct, reading of a text which is not entirely clear and precise.

However, on the radical epistemological critique, there is no distinction between understanding and interpretation. Every linguistic act is a matter of ascribing meaning. Moreover, interpretation is irredeemably creative and subjective. There are no fixed meanings 'out there', only what individuals, in the light of their personal and cultural constitution, make of the signs and signifiers that, in abstraction from the linguistic practices of specific groups and individuals, are the only things that enable us to identify a rule as the same rule. This relativity of meanings seems to undermine the idea that rules can impose significant limits on conduct, even with good-faith commitment to understanding the rules. There is always an in-built flexibility to all readings of all texts which renders such concepts as plain, natural or ordinary meaning, which are central to traditional expositions of legal positivism, suspect to the point of ridicule.

This philosophical problem for positivism opens up an enormous and difficult terrain. Here I address not the substance of the philosophy of language but its relevance to the credibility of legal positivism. The strength of philosophical scepticism about human communication is such that we might feel forced to conclude that we only think that we understand each other, whereas in fact, for the most part, we do not. Perhaps we are protected from the emotionally devastating loneliness of this subjectivity by the illusions of shared understandings. But, in fact, it is argued on philosophical grounds that we have no justification for such no doubt life-enhancing beliefs beyond the explanations provided by evolutionary epistemology or psychoanalysis.

It is tempting, however, to take the line that the alleged inability of philosophers to justify our claims to shared understandings capable of being communicated verbally demonstrates the failure of philosophy rather than the failure of communication. If the philosophical theories cannot account for the palpable experience of mutual understanding based on verbal exchanges, often mediated by texts, then it is the theories rather than the experience which are found wanting. In general we might say that the philosophy of language seems to leave us where we began – namely, with a sense that we have no real understanding of the mysteries of our existence and the nature of our capacities. All philosophical theories of language do no more than scratch the surface of the awesome experience of interpersonal communication. It would therefore be foolish, to stop trying to communicate on the grounds that no one has given a satisfactory explanation of how we manage to do this.

While there might be even some philosophical strength to this reaffirmation of common sense, which is itself a cyclical occurrence in the history of philosophy, the trouble with such a no-nonsense approach to the perceived failure of the philosophy of language is that this failure is more a manifestation than a cause of communication scepticism. We do have many real doubts about our capacity to transcend quite limited cultural confines by way of discourse and shared texts, and sceptical theories of meaning may serve to explain why we could be right to have these doubts rather than undermine an otherwise confident and successful process.

Moreover, if we take a more positive approach to the philosophical argument we will see that their critiques do not all point to the futility of attempting to improve the level of shared understanding. Indeed the core Wittgensteinian position, linking language to shared ways of life, can be read as a vindication, implicit in his endeavour to provide an explanation for genuine communication within its proper contexts. Further, if we regard communication not as a given which is there to be enjoyed but as a possibility to be more or less achieved, then we can view the critiques as providing signposts for improvement rather than reasons for retreat.

In the case of law, for instance, we may theorize the whole enterprise as involving a systematic exercise in mass communication. Law, involving, as it does, the audacious objective of regulating whole societies through clarifying what is required, permitted and institutionally enabled is evidently a grandiose project which invites communicative failure. On the positivist model, law has particularly ambitious communicative goals in that it requires attempts to state general rules in a relatively context-free manner so that they can be understood by large numbers of people in approximately the same way. This is far removed from the situations in which we learn to speak and where we have the greatest sense of our communicative achievements – namely, where we are engaged in a practical activity with a small number of people with similar life experiences.

Our confidence that we can achieve some success with such communicative feats in which there are agreed rules with agreed meanings governing large populations may be bolstered by the claim that this population of persons already has other rules of language which they share and by reference to which they can all end up with something like the same reading of the same text. So we explain the communicability of some rules, legal rules, by the prior existence of other rules, language rules. It is, however, at the level of linguistic rules that the philosophical critique which undermines the communicability of legal rules has its greatest impact. We cannot account for linguistic rules by bringing in yet other rules, and so on into an infinite regress. At this level of explanation language rules must be seen as simply attempts to give incomplete and inadequate expression to a set of skills which are learned in concrete social situations by people with shared experiences involved in face-to-face interactions. However, if language itself is not a matter of applying rules and thereby deducing a correct meaning, we can still maintain that law is a matter of applying other rules, rules of conduct, which have acquired meanings prior to, and independently of, the description of conduct in question.

The suggestion is that, if we regard human communication as a fragile and even endangered achievement which requires constant renewal and reinforcement and view the rules of language as principally attempts to formulate these achievements rather than create them, then we will, as practical theorists, look to the philosophy of language as a source of ideas of how to achieve the seemingly impossible and transcend the convention of our immediate social networks by successfully communicating with a wider range of persons. The crucial questions in legal philosophy then become who should have the tasks of formulating these communications and how should they go about the processes of creating and/or applying them.

In this case it makes sense to see law as a process of communication between law-maker and legal subjects mediated, in cases of dispute and enforcement, by adjudicators whose task is to discern the intentions of the law-maker in so far as they are expressed in the authorized text, these intentions not being the ulterior purposes, if any, that the legislation is designed to achieve, but the meaning that the text is intended to convey to its audience. Such a process has to proceed on the basis of an infinity of shared assumptions which, for all their contingency, enable us to think in terms of what we may call the intended plain meanings of legal enactments as legal enactments. This is not because there are such things as plain meanings automatically attached to particular words and sentences. The role of the notion of plain meaning in legislative communication is by way of a paradigm assumption that what legislators intend to communicate is what they have reason to believe the selected text will be taken to mean, which relates to what will seem the 'plain' or 'natural' meaning to the audience addressed – an assumption on which subjects, including judges, are entitled and required to rely. Legislators could try to communicate in code and this might do if the code was clearly understood and universally known. However, it so happens that the mutual focus on 'plain meaning' is the best practicable basis for maximizing communicative success over time.

The priority of plain meaning in statutory interpretation can thus be seen as a contingent device required for the successful communication of rules. Plain meaning represents a 'common ground' on the basis of which disputes can be resolved and conduct controlled and facilitated.[14] It is the presuppositions of successful communication to a large and diverse audience that dictate the function of the idea of plain or ordinary language as the primary and default criterion for a correct reading of a legal text. Where there is no basis for communication of this sort because of the absence or inadequacies of shared systems of meaning, then other criteria, such as stipulative definition, enter the picture.

Further, plain meaning can be contextualized in at least two senses without undermining the communicative objects of legislation. In the first place, fixing on a common meaning has to start with shared assumption about, and experiences of, types of social situation in which that discourse is active. The fact that law seeks to transcend particular contexts does not mean that it can be decontextualized in relation to types of situation. Second, legislation has to be read in the context of the practice of legislation itself – that is, with an understanding of the function of legislation and the particular form of legislative institutions that are in operation. This does not require that the meaning of a positive rule be subject to significant revision in the light of earlier legislation and case law but it does enable rules to be read as modifications of existing bodies of law. Thus, democratic positivism allows that the ideal of plain meaning has to be related to particular conceptions of the roles of legislation and the historically contingent devices for improving communications between legislatures and subjects adopted in that jurisdiction.

However, considerable difficulties arise in adopting plain meaning where the legislation is intended to counteract assumptions and patterns of conduct accepted as normal in a society or parts thereof, for language embodies the existing outlooks and ideologies of the people whose language it is. This is why it is plausible to argue that no rules can be read in an ideologically neutral manner and that there is no way in which legal reasoning can be autonomous in the sense of being entirely cut off from the (always problematic) cultural assumptions of the society in question. However, what a political system can do is select from the variety of socially available discourses those which embody the beliefs and assumptions that the legislature chooses to favour. This is largely a matter of piecemeal changes to, or clarifications of, pre-existing socially accepted meaning.

On such a basis we may formulate the basic positivist principle of adjudication as applying a pre-existent rule in accordance with the plain or stipulated meaning of the authorized text in relation to the intended audience in the context of the legal enterprise, positivistically conceived. This does not mean that this goal is always achievable. Some rules may not have plain or stipulated meaning. Rules which do have such meanings may not be readily applied to unforeseen situations. The basic principle does make clearer, however, what legislators ought to be trying to do and is required as a basis for a working distinction between the application, non-application and the creation of law in the process of adjudication, thus enabling us to give some cognitive content to the rather emotive term 'judicial activism', the cognitive content being judicial determinations which do, or do not, seek to have as their primary and overriding objective the application of laws in accordance with such plain and stipulated meaning as they may have.

Within this broad definition we may distinguish negative judicial activism, which is the failure to apply law in its plain and stipulated meaning, and positive judicial activism which is making a judicial decision, either in a particular instant or through the creation of a ruling which becomes a precedent, which is not warranted by existing authoritative legal texts. Negative judicial activism is failure to apply the law; positive judicial activism is the creation of new law. The two forms of judicial activism may operate together but may be identified and evaluated separately.[15] For instance, it may be argued that negative judicial activism is harder to justify than positive judicial activism when the latter is directed to supplementing, rather than overriding, existing rules. The concept of judicial activism presupposes that it makes sense to seek to identify the specific content of pre-existing law, and may have little application where there is no such law. I take it that legal positivism seeks to maximize the extent to which it does make sense to speak of judicial activism, giving it a prime focus on law-making.

No assumption is being made here that everyday discourse is replete with plain meanings, and such positivistic objectives must take into account the fact that everyday plain meanings usually depend on the occurrence of communication within a social context familiar to the participants. Rather, the language of positivistically good legislation is selected because of its suitability to communicating across contexts and communities, which involves, amongst other things, a reluctance to use broad evaluative language, a preference for empirically verifiable properties and a willingness to offer definitions where terminology is in doubt.

The difficulties which arise in achieving communication of this sort can sometimes be overcome by conventional devices for reading texts which are designed to reduce lack of clarity and ambiguity – devices which, if known to the legislature, enable it to make its intended meaning more transparent. Hence the various techniques of statutory interpretation, sometimes presented as systemic gatekeepers whose function is to preserve the autonomy of law, can be seen as a natural extension of those many conventions of language that are designed to promote mutual communication.

This approach immediately undercuts the standard caricature of legal positivism as an approach to law which assumes that words have intrinsic meanings which are simply there for all to see and follow mechanically without regard to context and social differences. Rather, if large-scale communication in general terms is a socially achieved goal which has little that is mechanical about it, plain meaning is as much an object than a supposition of the law, although law is not alone in pursuing such goals but in fact rides on the back of the ongoing processes of socially constructed meanings on whose success the feasibility of the legal enterprise depends.

Indeed, the role of adjudication in such a process must be quite limited and has to be seen in the context of a general political process which is geared to articulating choices between different existing and potential patterns of shared activities to the point where certain alternatives can be clarified and identified as authoritative norms within the system. Political dialogue and the process of legislating may not readily be seen as an exercise in improving communication (although they are more readily seen as the articulation and making of choices) but the idea of law as a communicative process with the objective of clearly articulating the general requirements and permissions of social and economic activity depends on just such a context. Positivism needs, before a theory of adjudication, a theory of legislation which focuses on, and renders coherent, what we are doing when we arrive at a text which is to serve as an authoritative instrument for mandatory and coercive order.

In this way, the philosophical problems of positivism may be deconstructed, or perhaps reconstructed, until they represent more of a practical challenge for the achievement of large-scale interpersonal communication in a world in which there are powerful vested interests (lawyers and their clients included) operating against such a goal.

This leaves open the question of precisely who is communicating with whom. The Benthamite model assumes the centrality of a legislative sovereign distinct from the administrators of law, which leaves the courts a law-making function only with respect to the clarification of statutes, essentially by rendering them more specific and unambiguous. But positivism has also been used as the basis for common law legal developments through extrapolation of rules from individual decisions using the basis of precedent. Precedents too may be exclusionary if decisions, once made, restrict the range of factors that a court may take into account when making subsequent decisions on similar cases.

It may be thought that the choice between statute and common law depends on democratic, rather than positivist, norms. Common law judgments can have all the specificity that derives from a clear decision on a particular case, although there is room for continuing scepticism about the precision of the way in which individual decisions come to have legal authority and how the rules alleged to be implicit in these precedents are articulated with respect to the form of their generality and specificity. Yet it is not clear that common law and statute law have equal claims to embody positivist ideals for there is an internal contradiction in a system which depends on precedents which were not themselves the outcome of precedential reasoning to identify the pre-existing law. The idea of the development of the common law necessarily embodies elements of both negative and positive judicial activism. This can largely be overcome by confining judicial activism to the highest court and redescribing it as sharing in legislative sovereignty, although this could have problems for jurisdictions which have a constitutional commitment to the separation of legislative and judicial power.[16]

This, then, requires us to explicate the highest courts' law-making methodology as something other than fully precedential. The end result of these conceptual manoeuvres may satisfy the positivist norms in principle, and the issue of whether or not judge-made law is desirable then becomes a matter to be determined by reference to the democratic ingredients of the democratic positivism. Currently it is probably correct to say that common law reasoning aspires more to a Dworkinian model than a positivist one, with an ever increasing use of generalized moral principles and a widening range of possible sources of new common law being brought into play, so that legal positivism is becoming increasingly inadequate as a description of common law reasoning in relation to these fluid, revitalized and diffuse common law approaches. This does not exclude, however, a reassertion of the Benthamite critique of the common law on both positivistic and democratic grounds. To the legal positivist, there is an unfortunate lack of precision, clarity and predictability in common law and statutory interpretation modelled on common law methods. To the democrat there is something alarming in a common law system with increasingly more open-ended sources, drawing on whatever jurisdictional innovations seem attractive to the judiciary and including a variegated transnational human rights jurisprudence which threatens to entrench judicial law-making in a way which makes it less democratically accountable.[17]

Empirical Problems of Legal Positivism

Having reconstructed some of the philosophical problems of positivism as stimuli to renewed efforts at communicative development, our critical focus must be turned to legal process, positivistically conceived, and the implications for legal positivism of the evidence that, in the area of the social construction of agreed meanings, positivist ideals are not realized in legal practice. Traditionally, legal positivism has claimed primarily to describe and explain the nature of all developed legal systems. The empirical critique is that it fails lamentably in these respects.

Thus, with respect to the goal of large-scale communication, is the function of the lawyer in an adversarial system not to undermine such agreed meanings as may appear to be established? If one reading does not help her client is the lawyer not bound to commend a different reading? And do not judges – particularly appellate judges in postmodern jurisdictions – openly use the flexibility of communicative process to produce individualized justice and provide constructive solutions to social and economic disputes without seeking to follow, or even create, specific rules, which are widely seen as a distraction from the political choices that have to be made in the application of any pre-existing law? Moreover, is there not evidence that the required process of justifying decisions by reference to precedent and statute in fact misrepresents the reality of the forces which lead to particular decisions which are better explained in terms of ideological assumptions, class, ethnic and gender affiliations and the realities of what courts can achieve in given political and economic circumstances?

This is the domain of the empirical problems which beset legal positivism. Law, it is contended, simply has little resemblance to what legal positivists would have us believe. Legal rules are seldom clear, and judges do not always follow them even when they are clear: they change the law in the process of adjudication, and give reasons in their judgments which underdetermine the result and are often no more than rationalizations for decisions taken on other grounds, so that there is endless scope in the system, through the manipulation of process and the purchase of technical expertise, to achieve a result which is in no way evident on a rule-centred analysis.

The short answer to such points is to say that they do not apply to legal positivism in its currently vital mode as a prescriptive legal theory which sets standards against which to assess and – if the allegations above are correct – criticize existing practice. Hence the label 'ethical positivism' which serves to indicate that we are dealing with those elements of legal positivism which are aspirational with respect to a formally good system of law which is not derived from any analysis of the concept of law or description of current practice, but rather from a political philosophy that is conscious of the paradox of political life – namely, that we need states but have reason to fear them – whose partial solution depends on establishing the rule of positive law. In brief, showing that actual legal systems do not operate positivistically does not negate the claim that they ought to do so. It is therefore wrong to assume that legal positivism is either purely a descriptive or an inherently conservative approach.[18]

The legal theory of ethical positivism is ethical in a further sense, in that it is accepted that no system of rules can in itself produce any beneficial results or protect from any of the evils of government without the ethical commitment of functionaries of the system and its subjects and citizens. If subjects routinely seek to evade their legal obligations wherever possible, if citizens take no interest or part in the creation of law through the democratic process, if lawyers successfully work to subvert the application of law and judges are practising legal realists, then no system of rules will operate effectively with respect to the values posited in the rationales of rule governance. Indeed, the sins that are often placed at the door of legal positivism, such as gender, race and class bias, are perhaps better seen as unwarranted departures from rules which exclude such factors as irrelevant than as failures of rule governance to combat such improper partialities.

That said, however, we have to note that there are two types of empirical test for a theory – one relates to actualities and the other to potentialities. The argument that existing systems are not positivistic may be deemed irrelevant to ethical positivism, but the argument that no system can conform to the ideal of ethical positivism is less readily dismissed. There is no point in extolling an ideal which is idealistic in the pejorative sense that it is unattainable to the extent that no useful progress can be made towards its implementation.

Legal positivism is so vulnerable to this line of attack that, historically, the theory may have evaded the issue by making the coincidence of the existence of law and conformity to law a matter of definition. Thus the thesis that the existence of a sovereign, and hence the existence of legal obligation, depends on efficacy (or general obedience to authoritative commands) makes the existence of law depend on the existence of a certain level of conformity to identifiable human authority. Hence the slogan that validity presupposes efficacy.[19]

This rather circular contention can be reinterpreted on the basis of the Hobbesian distinction between laws which oblige *in foro interno* and those which oblige *in foro externo* – a distinction which can be illustrated by saying that our commitment to keep our promises is conditional on others doing so as well, the argument being not one of moral reciprocity or fairness, but the basic fact that the benefits of promising are not to be had unless people in general keep their promises. We can generalize this line and say that the rule rationales which play such a substantial part in the justification of legal positivism presupposes that there can be such conformity to rules as is necessary for the promised benefits of rules to be realized.

In some cases of conduct-controlling rules there are benefits to almost every single act of conformity and harms to almost every contravention. The law of homicide is an example in point. The moral form advantage, also, may not be undermined by patchy conformity. But in many other types of rationale – such as rules of cooperation, coordination, dispute avoidance and resolution – the benefits do not come from individual conformity but from general, and sometimes near universal, conformity, as in the case of most road traffic rules.

In so far as the rule rationales on which ethical positivism depends involve consequentialist assumptions about the effects of rule-following, its general appeal is vulnerable to empirical study and its relevance may vary according to the areas of social and economic life in question and the type of society to which it is applied. This means that it is important for legal positivism to identify the various thresholds of conformity at which the benefits of rule governance kick in with respect to the different consequentialist rule rationales. Questions requiring answers include: what are these thresholds, are they attainable, and what should we do if conformity falls short of these thresholds? And who are 'we'? These issues are explored further below.

Ethical Positivism in an Imperfect World

The analysis of some of the empirical presuppositions of ethical positivism brings us to a fundamental issue in the articulation of democratic positivism – namely, its response to positivist shortfalls in actual systems, including the failure to meet coordination thresholds, the non-existence of appropriately positivistic laws, the failure of legal and judicial ethics and the absence of realistic mechanisms for constitutional change. Considering each of these in turn, I suggest how the practical implications of ethical positivism vary with different types of defect. What emerges is something like a strong form of Schauer's presumptive positivism[20] in which the adjudicative norms of ethical positivism emerge as defeasible in the light of positivist shortfalls. This approach threatens to undermine the whole logic of exclusionary rules by providing bases on which citizens and judiciaries can opt out of their obligations, but accepting practical limitations to the applicability of exclusionary rules need not lead to the introduction of generalized discretion within a legal system.

Coordination Thresholds

In a perfect positivist world no law would be promulgated which cannot attain an efficacy threshold of conformity. In the real world compliance can be a major problem. In this real world, it may be argued, there is no obligation on the subject to conform to any rules that are promulgated without attaining that threshold. Such a response is within the positivist tradition of making efficacy a condition of validity and hence of obligation. On the other hand, condoning individuals choosing not to conform to mandatory rules on the basis of their own assessment of efficacy thresholds threatens the achievement of the necessary threshold conformity. The idea of law as mandatory relates to such matters as law's function in solving coordination problems as set out in the various versions of the Prisoners' Dilemma. Permitting the subject the right to make up her own mind is to give up the compulsory coordination strategy which seeks to overcome the Prisoners' Dilemma. Permitting individual judgement makes coordination vulnerable to the self-partiality of those who are prone, even in good faith, to delude themselves as to the consequences of their conduct, to say nothing of those who follow their immediate self-interest. For such reasons there are good grounds for staying with a very sticky form of presumptive positivism in order to maximize conformity so that, for instance, administrators and judiciaries should not fail to enforce a law on the basis of perceived non-conformity in other instances. Enforcement agencies have duties to avoid selective enforcement which threatens the non-discrimination goals of legal positivism. However, legislatures have a political duty not to enact and retain certain types of laws when these fail the test of practical conformity necessary for their efficacy.

Despite the critical significance of compliance thresholds for the justification of coordination rules, decisions about what these levels are and whether they have been met are not best taken at the point of assessing what is to be done in particular cases. Responses to the ineffectiveness of coordination rules as a result of failures of compliance is a law enforcement and political problem – not a matter for individual agents or courts of law.

The Absence of Positivistically Good Law

What are subjects and judges to do when there is a dispute to be settled but no rule to apply, or where the apparently relevant rule is vague or in other ways unclear? A traditional answer, favoured by Kelsen, is that they, or judges at any rate, should do nothing. No criminal conviction should follow in such circumstances, and in civil disputes the loss will have to lie where it falls, for there can be no remedy on the basis of judicial invention.

This seems unsatisfactory in the light of at least some of the values which underpin the case for having rules. If we are to have rules to aid dispute resolution, what are we to do when such rules are not available and we are faced by a dispute that needs to be resolved? In this context it seems inadequate to depend on the principle of 'no rule, no resolution', although it may be defensible to draw back from coercively imposed solutions to disputes if we take on board all the negative arguments about discretion as a vehicle of bias and arbitrariness.

On balance, where disputes threaten serious injustice or social disorder, it is tempting to underwrite, in such second-best situations, positive judicial activism in the sense of making decisions without specific legal authority and even creating new law through the system of precedent. This may aid the existing dispute settlement, avoid future conflicts and be compatible with democracy, provided such precedent-setting decisions are subject to legislative review.

The questions which arise here relate principally to variations in the appropriateness of judicial activism in relation to imperfect positive law according to the areas and types of law concerned and the feasibility of effective legislative review of such developments. Problems of inaction focus on the substantive injustice of providing no remedies for what are apparently evident wrongs and having no acceptable alternative way of settling damaging disputes. Problems of action lie more in the opportunities it gives for those with ready access to the courts to use their economic power to thwart the legitimate expectations and interests of others.[21]

In the case of gaps in existing law, something may depend on the reason for these gaps. Advocates of positive judicial activism will point to the failure of legislatures to address important issues whose solution involves making choices that will, however they are decided, lose electoral support or bring out divisions within political parties, thus creating a legislative vacuum which it is proper for courts to fill. However, the counterargument is that legislation lacks democratic legitimacy where it is opposed by intense minorities and that picking and choosing between proper and improper inaction on the part of legislatures involves illegitimate value judgements as to the importance of the neglected issue and the proper response to disagreement about how they should be addressed.

Failures in Legal and Judicial Ethics

The legal and judicial ethics I have in mind here relate to the proper perception and execution of the legal and judicial roles with respect to the application of positive law. This conception of legal ethics relates directly to the role of legal participants with respect to the rule of law and therefore depends on the value judgements required to select appropriate judicial method and litigation norms as well as conformity to such methods and norms as are chosen. For the ethical positivist, the prime ethical duty of judges, for instance, is to apply positivist methods of judicial determination to such positive law as is available to them.

The initial plausibility of legal realism rests substantially on the evident truth that, at least in the short term, the law in any particular case is the finding of a court with respect to that case. This departs from the positivist model in so far as that decision does not apply the relevant rules in the light of an accurate finding as to the relevant facts of the case as identified by the rules in question. The failure of the positivist model in a particular case may be due to the inappropriate theory of judging utilized by the court, or by a failure to follow an acceptably positivistic model for some other reason, including departures from the appropriate norms of litigation. Such matters concern the ethics of lawyering and, in particular, of judging because they cannot be easily controlled from outside the confines of peer pressure and systems of judicial appeal to which the legal realist truism also applies.

While, in many onslaughts on the performance of legal systems, it is difficult to distinguish criticisms of the content of law from criticism of its administration, many of the failures identified by those who see legal systems as favouring the economically powerful and culturally dominant groups in a society relate not to the inadequacies of positivistic models of proper process but to the failure of those who operate the system.

Dealing with deficiencies in judicial ethics is one of the least tractable problems with respect to rule governance. Internally, to the system, the hierarchy of courts and possibility of appeals are of paramount importance. But where the legal culture accepts legal realism as a liberating norm rather than as an unpleasant fact there are real difficulties in rectifying the situation. Courts must be given the power ultimately to determine particular cases; otherwise, the separation of powers collapse. On the other hand, if courts have the last word on the methods they use, then they can clearly usurp the powers which rightfully belong to a legislature under any theory of democracy by choosing to ignore or revise any rules with which they are presented, by using the techniques of free-ranging interpretative methods.

There is no clearly optimal response to unethical judging, for any attempt to rectify the matter, except, perhaps, by way of public discourse, tends to undermine the very independence of the judiciary which is required for positivist systems of law. Legal positivism may rely on ethics in this sphere simply because there is no acceptable alternative. In theory, ethical positivism holds to the view that legal method is a legitimate matter of concern for the entire polity, including the legislature. Further, there is no good reason to give the judiciary the power to determine its methods other than that there is good reason not to give such power to legislatures. Perhaps there is a constitutional need for a workable system of calling judges to account for their operative methodology. However, even if we do not have to trust judges to set the proper standards for judicial process and judgment, policing conformity to these standards has to be largely a matter of judicial self-regulation.

The problem of having to rely on judicial ethics is reduced by the possibility of legislative review of judicial action, but the practicalities of legislative review, with packed agendas and powerful pressure groups, are such that unethical judicial reasoning often rules by default. In this context positivists may argue for the political propriety and efficiency of the routine legislative review of judicial activism as a normal and acceptable device, with judicial activism being explicitly signalled and then subjected to legislative scrutiny. Such transparencies can be viewed as part of the ideology of democratic positivism.

Constitutional Constipation

The final category of second-best scenarios relates to the problem of what constitutional courts are to do when there is no effective mechanism for legitimate constitutional change – a problem which arises in an acute form if we are looking for a legitimate source of positivist rules for the judicial review of legislation.

If we assume that constitutions should be interpreted in the same way as any other piece of positive law, then we encounter the problem that there is no legislative review of constitutional decisions by courts, other than constitutional amendment. This can be seen as a problem both with respect to the discipline of constitutional courts and the difficulty of keeping constitutions up-to-date.

For reasons such as this it is argued that legal positivism is particularly inappropriate in the constitutional area. For functional reasons, constitutions, as the basis for historically long-term political association, tend to include some highly imprecise terminology. The very idea of constitutionality restricts the role of executives and legislatures in determining constitutional matters. The problems of intergenerational communication render the plain meaning ideal of legal positivism less applicable. No wonder, then, that courts feel bound to develop constitutions in line with their perception of current needs, particularly when the formal procedures of constitutional change stack the cards against change. Of course, it can be argued that this is precisely what constitutions are meant to do, otherwise there would be no point in entrenchment. On the other hand, it is easy to be persuaded that flexibility of interpretation is more appropriate in constitutional than in other areas of law.[22]

This is a problem which could be greatly reduced were it feasible to redraw the rules for constitutional changes so as to provide for frequent constitutional amendment through plebiscites, subject to whatever entrenchment procedures are consider appropriate. This would enable politics to move towards some precision and contemporary relevance with respect to the rules governing contentious constitutional institutions and concepts such as representation, equality and judicial power. If regular amendment can be institutionalized, there is no reason, in principle, why constitutions should not be reasonably specific, clear and up-to-date.

In the nature of the case, such change is not normally attainable – hence the phenomenon of constitutional constipation accompanied by incurable imprecision of terminology. In these circumstances second-best solutions are called for, but what they should be is far from clear. To take just one example, from examination of the Australian constitutional cases which are so central to questions of judicial activism in that jurisdiction, it seems evident that any system of constitutional interpretation which depends on the judicial unpacking of such broad concepts as representative government, and the social and political preconditions of their instantiation, are potentially so sweeping as to undermine the operation of ordinary law when conceived on the positivist model by making large areas of ordinary law vulnerable to unending constitutional challenge.[23]

The prospects for containing this form of second-best judicial activism through restricting it to some working conception of human rights or fundamental values are not good, partly because, in many jurisdictions, constitutional interpretation extends to federal matters and cannot therefore be confined to individual rights, but also because the scope and range of human rights, democratic and otherwise, are either inherently controversial or far too extensive to remove from legislative oversight. It is salutary to note that, despite the ever increasing role of the concept of human rights in world politics and the undeniable importance for any political system to identify the priority human interests that require to be defended and promoted, the powerful philosophical arguments against the existence of any privileged knowledge of what these rights might be, both in content and form, have not been adequately answered. If there was a list of specific universal rights which could be known to be true or correct by any rational person then the rationale for placing the administration of these rights in the hands of a small group of specialist adjudicators would be strong although, due to problems of selecting the specialists and insuring against their human frailties, not overwhelming.

However, as things are, all the points about diversity and difference which features in the justification of having a system of democratically derived positive law to provide a framework for economic and social life apply *a fortiori* to the basic value judgements involved in concretizing human rights. Shared reflection may produce agreement with respect to an affirmation of the principle of equality, but this does not mean that agreement will be forthcoming as to what similarities and differences between individuals and groups are proper grounds for similar and different treatment. All the questions of relevance and degree which arise in decisions about rulings, and which have sufficient specificity to affect people's actual situations, are inherently controversial in that there is no basis for removing their resolution from whatever political processes we think best suited to arrive at politically authoritative determinations.

All this becomes progressively clearer as covenants, charters and declarations of rights become more concrete. It is not being hostile to the value commitments which underpin the development of human rights, conceived of as the priority interests to be protected and furthered in a political community, to hold that the articulation and specification of the applicable content of these rights is properly a matter for the political, rather than judicial, process. But this still leaves us with the question as to what that political process should be and the problem of what to do if we do not have a usable process for constitutional change.

This survey of reasons why we might seek to depart from the model of ethical positivism prompts a change of focus towards political reforms which will reduce the incidence of such pressures but does not suggest that the presumption of positivism need be systematically overridden. This leads us on to the democratic ingredients of democratic positivism which have to be examined further before we can come to a final view on the various second-best solutions to the positivistic deficits of actual legal and political systems.

The Democratic Setting

While there may be, as I have argued, more than a mere affinity between legal positivism and democracy, one further factor which may require courts to depart from their duties to positive law is the absence of proper democratic process. Even those who accept that it undermines positivism to give courts wide powers to review legislation in the light of broad value standards, which they use to crystallize vaguely worded fundamental rights, nevertheless look to courts to conserve the democratic framework that is a precondition of the political legitimacy of law, if only by scrutinizing the formal or procedural validity of putative laws.

As we have noted, democratic positivism is directed as much at the legislative and general political process as it is at the activities of courts. In this sphere, deficits can arise both from failures with respect to the enactment of positivistically good laws, and with respect to inadequate democratic process which may proceed the enactment of what may be formally satisfactory laws. Just as it seems inadequate to make judiciaries the arbiters of their own conduct with respect to adjudication, so it seems inadequate to entrust democratic decision-making to the self-scrutiny of legislatures.

Legislation may be undemocratic either in its origins (perhaps because it was not adequately debated) or in its content (perhaps because it restricts freedom of assembly). Both defects give rise to the prospect of judicial review as a response to second-best situations of this sort where legislatures are undemocratic in their composition or procedures, or, while being democratic in these respects, enact substantively undemocratic laws. These are the prime, but not the only, circumstances in which judicial review of legislation, with the power to declare undemocratic legislation invalid, is held to be a proper constitutional device and a legitimate part of the separation of powers. For instance, with democratic positivism, there is scope for making the constitutional validity of ordinary laws dependent on sufficient specificity and clarity.

At one level there is no positivist difficulty with judicial review provided this is governed by specific procedural and substantive rules. Thus, courts may have the power to apply certain tests to all legislation, provided these tests are clearly set out and can be applied without recourse to contentious moral and political opinions. Indeed, some such powers are inevitable in enabling courts to recognize the putative sources of law as authoritative; hence the role of rules of recognition in legal positivism.

Judicial review of legislative action, when it goes beyond questions of federal power, may seem particularly straightforward in the case of legislation which is undemocratic in the first sense – that is, it is the product of a procedurally undemocratic process – provided these procedural requirements are uncontentious in their meaning, although there are immense problems in requiring anything more than the fulfilment of formalities of due democratic and legislative process.

Judicial review is not much more problematic in the case of legislation which is undemocratic in content provided that content relates to changes in the democratic process as identified in the constitution – for instance, by electoral boundary changes which do not take account of population distribution. Again, there could be concerns about the precision of such review rules which may be no more than broad standards of political equality, but this can be dealt with within the theory by rendering the review rules more precise. Indeed, it is difficult to see why judicial review of a democratic positivist sort – namely, judicial review governed by clear and specific rules – should, in principle, be confined to matters of democratic form and substance, for there is nothing anti-positivist or anti-democratic is establishing rules which are lexically prior to other laws. Objections arise only when these are entrenched in a non-democratic manner or include vague conceptions, such as equality or non-discrimination which can be used to override just about any legislation with which the judges involved disagree.[24] Objection to judicial review of legislative action must be based on the constitutional illegitimacy or the substantive vagueness of the rules for review rather than the institutional fact of there being such rules.

This is not to legitimate, however, systems of judicial review of legislation which are the creations of courts and which courts seek to make fireproof against legislative revision by claiming an inherent constitutional priority to judicial review on the basis of a political philosophy rather than an historical constitution or statute. Neither the nature of judging nor the concept of the separation of powers, for instance, gives a sufficient basis for requiring judiciaries, by constitutional default, to be the guardians of either formal or substantive democracy. *Marbury* v. *Madison* is a clever piece of politics but not a watertight piece of reasoning.[25] It seems right to argue that Congress cannot be judge in its own case if its actions are under constitutional scrutiny, but the same logic applies to a Supreme Court making a judgment as to its own powers. No political system can deal with the problem of who guards the guardians except by the inculcation of appropriate ethics. There is simply no institutionalizable answer to the ultimate political conundrum as to who is to judge the constitutionality of the actions of any branch of government at the highest level, in the absence of express constitutional provision. However, there is nothing within democratic positivism to reject the idea of judicial review of legislative action in principle. The problems lie in how to specify what these rules might be and how they are to be authorized and applied.

The realities of judicial reviews of legislation is that their standards are rarely democratically authenticated, and where they are so authenticated, they take such unspecific form as to remove from the normal democratic process matters whose determination are at the heart of self-determination. This is particularly evident where the democratic content is extended to include a range of fundamental rights which go beyond the sort of democratic process to which clear content can be given. If we have an expansive idea of what is involved in democracy, and the fundamental democratic rights are stated in broad and by no means purely procedural terms, then to remove judgments about the proper content of democratic laws from legislatures and give it to judges on the ground that they are guardians of democracy is to remove most of the most important political issues from the democratic process and thus to undermine the possibly more basic right – the right to self-government.[26]

This conclusion may not be unwelcome to the majority of citizens in contemporary jurisdictions, for legislatures and democratic politicians do not currently have a good reputation as sources of law, particularly where their self-interest is at issue. The more checks the better, it may be thought, in the case of a class of persons whose role obliges them to act in unprincipled, unreliable and partisan ways. To many people impartial judiciaries seem to be better sources of law than populist assemblies, particularly with respect to democratic process where there are reasons within democratic theory to distrust political practitioners. If the articulation of democratic positivism does provoke such a patently anti-democratic response, this may indicate that some such sentiments underlie both the enthusiasm for giving further discretionary power to judges and the willingness to acquiesce in the increasing power of judicial review over legislative enactments.

The thesis that judges are better placed to make good law than politicians takes us to the core of the democratic debate, which is addressed below. First, there are two arguments to be considered. One is the argument derived from the impartiality of judges. The other is the argument derived from the veniality of politicians.

While philosophy may be ineffectual in accounting for communicative realities, it can be self-referentially very powerful in cutting down the pretensions and claims of its own practitioners. Thus analytical and critical philosophy effectively counter the claims that information and impartiality are sufficient bases for claims to such superior moral knowledge as to justify the imposition of obligations on others. Before and since the founding father of legal positivism, Thomas Hobbes, tried to deduce the authority of the state and the validity of core social and legal obligations from enlightened self-interest, philosophers have been trying to prove alternative and more exalted channels for the justification of morality and the provision of guidance as to how we should criticize and develop our moral convictions without resorting to untestable appeals to human 'reason'. The core modern example is Kant's contention that an act is right if all rational persons are willing to see it universalized – or, in other words, applied to all similar persons in similar circumstances. More recently, the liberal philosopher John Rawls has drawn this together with other enlightenment insights about the moral point of view as being one which is impartial in that it does not give any preference to one individual or type of person over another.

These theorists have taught us much and, while they have all undoubtedly provided tests which can help us not only identify moral questions but also improve the quality of moral judgements, it has been decisively shown, again and again, that they do not enable us to settle genuine moral disagreements in a manner which gives satisfactory grounds for systems of mandatory rules backed with coercive sanctions. In particular, defining impartiality, as we normally do, in terms of absence of personal attachment to the individuals involved in the dispute in question and an ability not to make an exception of oneself or another person simply because we are ourselves or have particular attachments to other person, is a sound basis for determining some issues of public morality. But such tests are perfectly compatible with unending value disagreements – that is, disagreements about what is worthwhile, important and significant in human life. Given diversities of cultures, individuals and tastes, impartiality does not solve the problems involved in adopting shared values, although it may be helpful in deciding how what we value should be shared.

Impartiality, in a judicial context where positivistic rules are available, is able to generate objectively justifiable decision-making but only because the available rules make it possible for judges to approximate to a position of value neutrality. Such institutionalized value neutrality, however, renders proper judicial method ineffectual in dealing with substantive moral disagreements. Further, requiring judges to abandon value neutrality threatens their capacity to act in those matters where impartiality is of the essence – namely, in the ethically proper interpretation of rules and their accurate implementation to specific fact situations without recourse to contentious personal opinions.

Curbing the pretensions of judicial impartiality leaves us with the problem of the partialities and ignorance of parliaments, the selfishness of majorities, and the often greater selfishness of powerful minorities. If we are not to encourage constitutional change which enables judges to make major value choices for us, then how are we to reorient and reinvigorate democratic processes so that they produce rules which are not only positivistically good but also tolerable in content. On some (market-style) democratic theories, it is to be expected and welcomed that politicians are unprincipled or adaptive, in that it is their job to respond to changes in popular opinion, and it is to be expected and welcomed that politicians are self-interested at least with respect to being motivated by the desire for re-election, for this is what makes government responsive to general opinion. But can such creatures also fulfil the role of legislators and leaders without a framework that forces them to act against their politically-oriented roles in such a way as to manipulate the majorities that support them and neglect the minorities who do not? This leads us to the issue of what do about democratic deficits.

We may restart the overview of the democratic setting of ethical positivism by working through the consequences of accepting the argument that informed impartiality is insufficient to vindicate a right to make value judgements on behalf of others. What does the rejection of such an epistemology of values imply for the theory of democracy? One possibility is that it amounts to a form of moral relativism which requires us to abandon anything beyond contingent agreement as to shared values and ideals of social justice, accepting the individual's assessment of what he or she considers worthwhile and providing a system which gives as many as possible of these individuals what they want. Democracy is, then, the aggregation of desires – the ideal of desire maximization.

This is the model of democracy historically associated with legal positivism in its classical utilitarian manifestation. For any theory that retains an emphasis on individual autonomy it remain a telling element in favour of individuals having an equal say in government that this maximizes the realization of desires. In this model the crucial element is an effective political market with good information on the proffered packages, freedom of choice in the expenditure of votes and equality of opportunity between potential political candidates.

However, our scepticism over reaching objectively justified agreement on values means that we may endorse, but cannot justify, the utilitarian principle on which the classical theory depends. The principle that we ought to maximize the greatest happiness of the greatest number is simply one amongst the many principles that have been commended by those who have striven to attain the required standpoint of informed, but sympathetic, impartiality. We can bypass this difficulty to some extent if we can obtain intersubjective agreement and if that agreement includes agreement as to the desirability of achieving such agreement. But does this give us the basis for coercing those who do not share in the hoped-for consensus? Probably not, but then, in a world where values cannot be objectively justified, there can be no establishable objection to the coercion of a minority by a majority or vice versa. In this context the idea of maximizing preferences may seem a pragmatic approach to the problem of disagreement, and we may proceed with the utilitarian justification of democracy that, by making rulers subject to re-election, we make it more likely than with any other method of government that rulers will rule in the interests of the majority.

A significant flaw in this pragmatic market approach is that, in purchasing a package for themselves, the individual voters are at the same time selecting the same package for others. Hence the problem of the absence of consensus leading to the rule of majorities and the incompatibility of that with the initial premise of political equality. Hence also the temptation to modify the pure market approach and say that voting in a political election is giving an opinion as to what is in the common good rather than expressing a preference related to individual self-interest. Add the contestable premise that the view of the common good which is shared by the largest number of people is epistemologically superior, in that majority voting is actually a guide to correctness in the determination of what is the common good and what will best promote that objective, and we have a more promising basis for justifying majority decision-making because the losing minorities can be assured that the outcome is the one most likely to serve the common good.

For the purpose of this chapter, normative democratic positivism involves a commitment to maximizing individual autonomy subject to a democratic override. This implies that, other things being equal, government should maximize negative liberty and provide for equal political power in relation to the determination of whether other things *are* equal and, if not, what legislation is warranted, while at the same time seeking to mitigate the unfortunate side-effects of the majoritarianism which gives practical effect to equal political power by introducing as much as possible of the mechanisms and culture which render individual preferences more oriented towards conceptions of the common good.

This may be considered inconsistent, since one model requires individuals to vote and perhaps debate in accordance with their self-interest so that the results maximize the sum of self-interest, while the other model requires the voter to select and debate according to an ideal in which his or her interests play only a small part. However, there is no formal difficulty here, as people can take satisfaction in the well-being of others, thus rendering their self-interest inclusive of the interests of others. Problems do arise, however, when some vote on a purely self-oriented basis and others on a more altruistic assessment of the common good, thus skewing the aggregate decision towards those with a narrow conception of self-interest.

Assuming this problem can be contained, what sorts of device might suffice to channel democratic process towards the common good model and how do these impact on issues of judicial activism and judicial review? I have already suggested one tactic: the governance of positivistically good rules. We have seen that this approach does not favour judicial activism (except perhaps as a rectificatory or second-best technique). What rule governance does suggest, however, is the propriety of formal judicial review of legislative action with respect to the clarity and specificity of law. In such a system, courts would be required to declare invalid putative laws which are directed at named individuals, perhaps even named groups, such as bills of attainder, and also, more controversially, putative laws which are seriously unclear or too general to provide genuine guidance for subjects and courts (the issue of constitutional vagueness). We may call this type of formal judicial review of legislation 'rule-testing'.[27]

Another common good device which is more usually used when seeking to improve the acceptability of majority voting is the requirement of effective deliberation and public criticism as an essential part of the democratic process. This is particularly interesting because it is the model which is thought to lead us towards a broad-ranging system of judicial review which, with its emphasis on universal knowledge of fundamental rights, seems to derive from the natural law tradition. Yet deliberation, as such, features also in classical utilitarian market models of democracy, principally as a source of information which enhances consumers' capacity to get what they really want, and hence what will satisfy their desires. Such information may also, of course, be relevant to discussions aimed at the discovery of a common good, but deliberation is given to other functions, such as the pursuit of consensus, which reduces the problem of minority oppression or, more ambitiously, to obtaining collectively an improved conception of the common good. The latter makes an epistemic claim for deliberation on the basis that the outcome of genuine deliberation between all parties affected by a decision as to the terms of collective existence is more likely to provide a correct apprehension or construction of the common good.

If this has sufficient plausibility, then there is good reason to require that democratic legitimacy includes a public discussion requirement not only in the electoral phases of democracy but also in the ongoing processes from which legislation emerges. However, the constructive criteria of any form of deliberative democracy – particularly one that makes claims to epistemic authority – are such that they would be very difficult to capture in a set of positivistically good rules that could be applied in a satisfactory scheme of judicial review.

The norms which courts apply to their own deliberations, such as giving their reasons in terms of preceding authorities, are inappropriate for deliberative democracy, as they have a more limited function and are designed in part to restrict the range of arguments that can be introduced. In some ways, courts may be expert reasoning forums, but the constraints of reasoning within the domain of law, and the restrictions on who may participate in the deliberations, mean that courts do not have the sort of open dialogue with respect to available arguments and available sources of argument that discourse theory requires. Further, as we have seen, there is no reason to think that any form of deliberative method enables us to delegate our moral reasoning to any restricted group of people, with or without legal qualifications and experience. Indeed, the most persuasive forms of deliberative democracy are those which see the requisite discussion as diffuse within a society, with deliberation leading up to, but itself part of, the decisions which embody the reflective preferences of those liable to be affected by the group decision in question.[28]

Nevertheless, it is possible to conceive of specific formal requirements for public debate and consultation, disclosure of relevant information and explicit reference to a checklist of factors which must be considered in the course of legislative drafting, parliamentary process and enactment. It is consonant with the deliberative democratic positivist critique of substantive judicial review to have a system whereby a pre-enacted convention or charter of specific rights is used by a constitutional court to review legislation in the light of its implications for these specified rights and either provisionally override, refer back, reinterpret or simply give a declaratory opinion on legislation which appears to conflict with such rights, thus establishing a dialogue between courts and legislatures in which legislatures, nevertheless, have the last word. Such processes can contribute to the articulation and implementation of basic rights without returning to the political authority of elected legislatures, thus providing a form of judicial review without positive judicial activism.[29]

In democratic positivism these basic rights might include those democratic rights which relate to adequate public discussion, information and consultation regarding new legislation. If weight is given to the deliberative aspects of democratic theory, these democratic rights could be cashed out in part as requirements which must be met in the enactment of new legislation, going beyond formal rights of political participation to require actual processes of communal debate beyond the legislative assembly itself. Such requirements could be supplemented by the proposed interactive process for the development of legislation whereby some judicially dominated body has the power to return to the legislatures enacted laws which seem to violate defined fundamental positive rights. Democratic positivists might also explore ways in which the legislative assemblies are better focused on their legislative task and more open and orderly in their deliberative procedures. These are radical suggestions, and are made primarily to illustrate the point that there are responses to positivistic and democratic deficits other than looking to the remedial activism of courts, the nature of whose impartiality is inadequate to settle value disagreements and ought to be preserved for other important and more specialist tasks, particularly the application of existing law, with all its controversial embodiments of value commitments, to specific situations, which, it is argued, is a necessary ingredient of a genuinely democratic system.

Notes

1 This chapter benefited greatly from the enthusiastic participation of everyone who attended the Workshop on 'Judicial Activism and Judicial Review in Australian Democracy', particularly Fred Schauer who has been highly supportive of the project at every stage.

2 Robert Cover, *Justice Accused* (New Haven: Yale University Press, 1975).

3 See H.L.A. Hart, 'Positivism and the Separation of Law and Morals', *Harvard Law Review*, **71** (1958), p. 593; and L.L. Fuller, 'Positivism and Fidelity to Law: A Reply to Professor Hart', *Harvard Law Review*, **71** (1958), p. 630.

4 See David Dyzenhaus, *Hard Cases in Wicked Legal Systems: South African Law in the Perspective of Legal Philosophy* (Oxford: Clarendon Press, 1991).

5 See William Simon, *The Practice of Justice: A Theory of Lawyers' Ethics* (Cambridge, Mass.: Harvard University Press, 1998).

6 More technically, democratic positivism is a form of prescriptive hard positivism which presupposes soft positivism (the thesis that a legal system may, with conceptual propriety, incorporate morality as a criterion of the rule of recognition) but contends that no legal system ought to incorporate such criteria. See T. Campbell, 'The Point of Legal Positivism', *King's College Law Journal*, **9** (1998), pp. 61–87 at pp. 68–70.

7 A more familiar term than democratic positivism would be constitutional democracy, but this does not sufficiently capture the fact that the constitutions in question are concerned to establish governance through rules or, more specifically, governance through positive rules. Another description for my politico-legal ideal might be democracy within the rule of law, but this is apposite only if we give a positivistic interpretation to the rule of law whereby the law in question fits the positivist model of the application of pre-existing specific rules capable of being understood and implemented without direct recourse to contentious value judgements.

8 T. Campbell, *The Legal Theory of Ethical Positivism* (Aldershot: Dartmouth, 1996). See also F. Schauer, *Playing by the Rules: A Philosophical Examination of Rule-Based Decision-Making* (Oxford: Clarendon Press, 1991).

9 R.A. Epstein, *Simple Rules for a Complex World* (Cambridge, Mass.: Harvard University Press, 1995).

10 Moreover, it can be argued that democracy, as the rule of the many, is more dependent than other systems on rule governance for it is easier to institutionalize the shared power of all citizens in the choice of rules than it is in the aggregate of decisions on a case-by-case basis. Of course, democracy could consist only in the election of fixed-term dictators, and some will argue that this is the system that many democratic systems resemble, but that is to make the scope of the democratic

choice less than it need be. At the other extreme all citizens could decide on each particular matter, but that is impractical. A choice of rules seems to be a compromise which maximizes efficiency by reducing input costs and maximizes the impact of the decisions.

11 J. Waldron, 'Rights and Minorities: Rousseau Revisited' in J. Chapman and R. Wertheimer (eds), *Majorities and Minorities* (New York: New York University Press, 1991).

12 For the classic critique of this approach, see J. Schumpeter, *Capitalism, Socialism and Democracy*, 5th edn (London: Allen & Unwin, 1976).

13 The debate requirement can also be interpreted in the context of a consumer model of democracy as having to do with the pooling of information, in which case we are not saddled with quite such an idealistic theory of democracy. This latter option puts more weight on the second reason for rule democracy – namely, that it reduces the likely impact of selfish majorities or, even worse, selfish minorities or individuals.

14 See F. Schauer, 'Statutory Construction and the Coordinating Function of Plain Meaning', *Supreme Court Review* (1990), p. 231; and David A Strauss, 'Why Plain Meaning?', *Notre Dame Law Review*, **72** (1997), p. 1565.

15 For the purpose of clarification it may be necessary to distinguish judicial activism, in any form, from the sort of decisions that have to be made in applying a general term to any particular thing, however clear and specific these general terms may be – what may be called the process of concretization.

16 See T. Campbell, 'Legal Positivism and Political Power' in A. Vincent, *Political Theory: Tradition and Diversity* (Cambridge: Cambridge University Press, 1997), pp. 172–92.

17 This may apply to both the current defamation law regime in Australia (see Chapter 16) and the Human Rights Act (1998) in the UK. See T. Campbell, 'Human Rights: A Culture of Controversy', *Journal of Law and Society*, **26** (1999), pp. 6–26.

18 A point well made in A.J. Sebok, 'Misunderstanding Legal Positivism', *Michigan Law Review*, **92** (1995), p. 2054.

19 H.L.A. Hart, *The Concept of Law* (Oxford: Clarendon Press, 1962), pp. 100–1.

20 See F. Schauer, 'Rules and the Rule of Law', *Harvard Journal of Law and Public Policy*, **17** (1991), p. 645.

21 Many legal positivists have seen such second-best scenarios as potentially beneficial opportunities which enable helpful developments of law to be made by wise judges, benefits which provide welcome flexibility to meet individual circumstances in the interests of justice, or make the law as a whole more coherent. This leads to an interesting argument about whether law is better made in response to individual situations known in detail to hopefully impartial judges, or in the light of policy goals articulated by legislative bodies who are often far removed from knowledge of individual circumstances.

22 But, see F. Schauer, 'Constitutional Positivism', *Cornell Law Review*, **25** (1993), p. 797.

23 For a discussion of these cases, such as *Australian Capital Television Pty Ltd* v. *Commonwealth* (1992) 177 CLR 106 and *Theophanous* v. *Herald & Weekly Times Ltd* (1994) 182 CLT 104, see Chapters 17 and 18 of this book.

24 Thus, in a minority opinion in *Leeth* v. *Commonwealth* (1992) 174 CLR 455 at 502, Gaudron J takes the judicial power which is entrenched in the Australian Constitution to include 'the concept of equal justice' along the lines of substantive interpretations of the 14th Amendment of the Constitution of the United States which guarantees every citizen the equal protection of the law.

25 See Carlos Nino, *The Constitution of Deliberative Democracy* (New Haven, Conn.: Yale University Press, 1996).

[26] See J. Waldron, 'A Right-Based Critique of Constitutional Rights', *Oxford Journal of Legal Studies*, **13** (1993), p. 18.

[27] For a recent Australian example, see *Polyukhovich* v. *Commonwealth* (*War Crimes Case*) (1991) 172 CLR 501 at 535, in which there was majority support for the view of Mason CJ that the Commonwealth could not enact a law 'adjudging a specific person or specific persons guilty of an offence constituted by past conduct and imposing punishment in respect of that offence'.

[28] Particularly, J. Habermas, *Between Facts and Norms* (London: Polity Press, 1996).

[29] Numerous actual alternatives are on offer in Sweden, New Zealand, Canada and, most recently, in the UK in relation to the Human Rights Act 1998.

2 Ethical Positivism and the Practical Force of Rules

NEIL MACCORMICK

Tom Campbell's *Legal Theory of Ethical Positivism*[1] goes back to the real roots of the positivist tradition, to the reforming impulses of Jeremy Bentham and his disciples. By Campbell as by Bentham, the division between expository and censorial jurisprudence is drawn with no view to concentrating on the former at the expense of the latter. On the contrary, it is made in the context of an insistence on the need for a practically critical attitude to law and legal institutions and their performance. The demands arising from, and the values of, a democratic political system are also in the forefront of attention. The difference here between discussions of law *de lege ferenda* and discussions *de lege lata* is vital.

There is a strongly value-oriented element in any piece of legislation, but in Campbell's view this value element should, as far as possible, be exhausted at the legislative stage. Later, disputes may arise concerning the meaning and application of a piece of legislation, and these disputes may call for adjudication. At this adjudicative stage, judicial activity should, as far as possible, be confined to the factual inquiry into what was enacted and what the words of enactment mean in context, into the facts that are provable by evidence and, finally, into the question whether these facts satisfy or do not satisfy the operative facts stipulated in generic terms in the enacted rule.

From this point of view rules extracted from precedents (to whatever extent rules can truly be extracted from precedents) are a very second-rate species of the genus 'rule', since, at best, they are too malleable and unclear and moreover they are made by judges – officials whose role is ideally to apply rules rather than to make them. Judge-made law is required only when legislator-made law is excessively complex or ambiguous, or lacking altogether. Ideally, legislatures should settle to the task of making clear and intelligible rules that courts can understand and apply with a minimum of controversy.

Law in the real world is not always like this, of course. There may be many situations in which judges are too activist in their approach, legislators are paralysed by party division or ineptitude and legislative drafters are ill-trained for their work. But the theory of ethical positivism sets the ideal not only of a real separation of powers, but also an independent and willingly cooperative judiciary backed up by an efficient, well-purposed and well-serviced legislature. In terms of democratic theory, Campbell's case is that only where a legal system approximates to formal characteristics of this sort can representative democracy be made to work adequately. Under such circumstances, the people's representatives in the legislature then really do determine the content of the law and, if they do so in accordance with the legislative programmes for which they were elected, the ideal of popular self-government is realized. So long as the judges conduct themselves (in the celebrated phrase) as mere 'mouthpieces of the law', the people's will is the true determinant of the content of the general rules of the law.

Legal positivism in its descriptive, analytical, mode is thus a description of a possible social state of affairs. Not everything that we might be willing to call 'law' – for example, a governmental regime that confers very wide discretionary powers on decision-makers – would match the 'positivistic' system envisaged by Campbell. But, provided the possible world depicted really is a possible one, the argument for the ethical ideal of 'ethical legal positivism' is one that can be taken seriously. Others might disagree about its desirability, and that would be an important argument. But if the picture of legal system advocated by Campbell is in truth chimerical, there is nothing for the ethical argument to get its teeth into. Fairyland might be a nice place in theory, but there is no point in planning to live in fairyland or launching political programmes aimed at setting it up as a framework for human society. Since Tom Campbell regards me as a fellow subscriber to ethical positivism – and, indeed, is kind enough to regard me as its co-founder, despite the fact that we differ on some important points as will appear below, I hope the 'fairyland' reproach is fallacious – but we shall have to see about that.

Certainly, this cautionary thought leads us to consider whether the world could be as ethical positivism (hereinafter EP) invites us to make it. Can there be a legal system of clear, hard rules such that judges could confine themselves mainly to a neutral rule-applying task, guided simply by the plain meaning of the rule-texts issued by the legislature? Two counterpositions immediately suggest themselves. The view from the standpoint of critical legal studies (CLS) is that language is simply so indeterminate, and legal systems have built up such a battery of approaches to interpreting language in its legal applications, that the ideal set by EP is simply chimerical.[2] By contrast, the view from the standpoint of Ronald Dworkin and his followers is that law is an interpretive enterprise guided by a vision of the integrity of the political society to which the law belongs.[3] Sometimes, it might accord with that integrity to follow a 'plain meaning' approach, but it need not always be so. The best interpretation is that which is most faithful to a whole view of the law in the light of constructive interpretation. In a Dworkinian perspective, EP would be more sharply criticized for posing a misplaced ideal than for presupposing an impossible state of affairs.

In what follows, I shall write from a fourth point of view, not that of EP, or CLS, nor that of Dworkin, but my own – the point of view that Ota Weinberger and I call an 'institutional theory'. I shall accept the thesis that interpretation and interpretive argument about rules is an inevitable feature of an institutionalized normative order such as we see in a modern state or federation. To that extent I acknowledge that EP may tend to overstate the possible determinacy of law. But in recommending that steps be taken to maximize determinacy and therefore reduce interpretative leeway to a reasonable minimum, it makes a perfectly reasonable proposal that could, over time, be implemented to a reasonable extent. On the other hand, I do consider that the legal context is one in which interpretation must take place in the whole context of legal order, and in that context it is indeed true that a 'plain meaning' approach to interpretation is only one component of well-ordered legal argumentation. The proponents of EP may wish, on reflection, to adopt more of the Dworkinian approach than they seem inclined to do at present.

Institutional Theory of Law: Law as Institutional Normative Order

All human life is implicitly normative, in the sense that whatever a person is doing at any time, either as an individual or in common with others, it is an open question whether she or he is doing the right thing, or doing it in the right way. To put it the other way, one may be doing the wrong thing, or doing an acceptable thing incorrectly, in the wrong way. There are many grounds of judgement against which these questions can arise – autonomously held moral principles, conventional social morality, grammatical rules, rules of a game or of a competition, professional ethics, company by-laws or college code of discipline, the positive law of a state, and so on.

Much of our understanding of activity is suffused with an assumed normative framework, so that descriptions of activity are intelligible only in the relevant normative context. Is Jane gyrating meaninglessly, or dancing? Is Hugh making strange noises or practising for his Mandarin Chinese class? Is Helen waving her hand at another driver, or making a traffic signal according to the Highway Code? Is Hector piling rock upon rock or rebuilding his boundary wall? An example that I have recently[4] developed at some length is this: you see people standing in a certain mutual relationship spatially, one in front, the next one behind facing the back of number one, the next behind the second, and so on. One inference that such an arrangement seems naturally to evoke, among people acculturated as I have been acculturated, is that the individuals are standing in a queue. This presupposes that the front person is at or near the point at which some service is available, and all are waiting in the expectation of receiving the service in the order in which they have lined up, which in turn represents the order of their arrival at the point of service.

In some situations, queues form, as it were, spontaneously. This requires a general acknowledgement that everyone ought to 'wait their turn'. Hence spontaneous queuing can occur only where there is a fairly strong social morality of turn-taking, enforced by common or overlapping opinion, and under a broadly shared (not necessarily identical) interpretation of the way people ought to behave in queuing contexts. But in other contexts, there is non-spontaneous queuing – for example, at a railway ticket counter with roped-off lines, or an airport check-in, or at a supermarket fish counter where there is a numbered ticket-roll and an electronic display calling forward number-holders in order. Non-spontaneous queuing happens where some person is put in charge of providing a service with instructions to provide it in a particular way, or with a general authority to manage the service in what she or he deems an orderly and efficient way that is satisfactory to customers. This can work effectively even where the individuals seeking the service would not, of their own free will, act in the kind of cooperative turn-taking way involved in spontaneous queuing.

This distinction between spontaneous and non-spontaneous may be used as a simple illustration of the dividing line between informal normative order and institutional normative order. Informal normative order depends on implicit norms which lack any single authoritative formulation, although they may be subject to much discussion and attempts to establish agreed interpretations of what is required. Institutional normative order creates the possibility of establishing articulate and authoritatively formulated norms of conduct – for example, 'persons are to take a numbered ticket off the roll and are to be served in the order in which their number comes up'. Furthermore, they create the possibility of authoritative interpretations of the articulated norms in contexts of doubt or dispute. They also create the possibility of establishing revised or expanded versions of the norm or norms if it seems that too much has been left implicit and subject to common-sense assumptions in earlier versions.

The difference between institutional and informal order is that, in the former, there is more than one tier of norms. Informal normative order requires only a common understanding of what one ought to do in given circumstances. Institutional normative order requires an arrangement in which some person or group has some authority to maintain or manage a situation in which there is some norm or norms about what one ought to do in given circumstances. Decisions about what ought to be done generate authoritative versions of first-tier norms; and managerial authority may explicitly include, or by usage come to acquire, the capability to issue authoritative general statements of binding first-tier norms.

Of course, the manager of the queue may be appointed and given authority by the director of the airline, and the director by the board, and the board by the chief executive of the holding company, and so on. Institutional normative order has at least two tiers, but often many tiers. Informal normative order need have no more than a single tier; institutional normative order has (1 + *n*) tiers. However, if we are to avoid an infinite regress, we shall have to conclude that the *n*th tier is inevitably itself informal. All institutional order has in fact a customary foundation, in the sense that the ultimate reason for accepting some ultimate source as authoritative must be a shared sense of the normative among those who acknowledge the ultimate authority.

Authority both depends on, and is a source of, interpersonal power in the non-normative sense – non-normative power is the ability to affect the interests of other persons in such a way as to shape or change their prudential reasons for action. Hence institutional normative order is always intimately connected to power relations among humans and is thus a focus of political interest, concern and action. Analytically, its character as normative order is explicable in terms distinct from those necessary to elucidate the political as a discourse of (non-normative) power, but the analysis reveals that there is always an interaction between politics and institutional normative order, and explains why this is so.

States and Non-States: Normative Pluralism

The contemporary world is still dominated by the system of states that emerged in Renaissance Europe, as kingdoms (France and England in particular) established independence from emperor and pope and, over time, shifted sovereignty from the personal monarch to people or parliament under some form of more or less articulate Constitution. States are essentially territorial, with governments exercising power over, and claiming legitimacy in respect of, a demarcated territory and its inhabitants. Governmental claims to legitimacy make necessary reference to some Constitution that grants authority and that has itself some ground of legitimacy in supposed popular choice or immemorial usage. The maintenance of some degree of civil order is the mark of an effective exercise of territorial power, and this depends on upholding and policing laws governing the citizens of the state and any non-citizens present in the territory.

Institutional normative order thus finds its most elaborate and (hitherto) prestigious manifestation in the laws of the state. A state's law comprises Constitution, public law, criminal law, commercial law and private law. In turn, the legal system is upheld (and in one sense constituted) by the agencies empowered through constitutional and sub-constitutional norms to take authoritative decisions on the norms that govern conduct and create normative institutions, on the pursuit of policy within the normative framework, and on the proper interpretation, application and enforcement of the system's norms in the case of detected breaches or disputes of various kinds among persons or between persons and state agencies. The common acknowledgement of the normativity of the Constitution – that is, a custom or informal normative order[5] that makes observance of the power relations legitimated by the Constitution obligatory – is what sustains states and makes possible their persistence in time. It is sufficient for such a custom to be shared among those active in the superior agencies of a state, provided they can dispose of sufficient power to maintain the state order through the compliance, including coerced compliance, of citizens and inhabitants. But it is a mark of stable democracies that customary respect for the Constitution, whether or not one originally chosen by some form of popular vote, is widespread and can therefore impose significant, though never absolute, limits on the freedom of action of those in power.

The tendency among practical lawyers, legal scholars and jurisprudents has been to treat as either the only or the paradigmatic form of law the institutional normative orders of independent states, together, perhaps, with the norms considered binding among states as interacting and potentially mutually hostile entities – 'international law'. The present account does not deny that law in these forms has great practical importance, nor that the law schools in our universities have quite properly a primary concern with state law, and indeed particularly with the law of their own state. But it does deny the unexamined assumption that 'law' is just state law, and the related assumption that use of the term in relation to anything that is in some way similar to state law is a kind of analogical or metaphorical extension of the term 'law'. On the contrary, once we clarify the concept of institutional normative order, we are able to see that state law is simply one species of this genus, and we can explore its particularities and specific differences in a more intelligent way.

This makes possible a pluralistic account of law. Nothing in the concept of institutional normative order as analysed here and elsewhere requires us to suppose (with Hans Kelsen[6]) that there is a deep unity in all genuine normative order. There can be a plurality of normative orders, none of which from the viewpoint of its partisans depends for validity on satisfying conditions set by another. Different churches and organized religious sects can have their own bodies of law ('canon law' or whatever), and these can be independently valid; states can have their law, and can purport to constitute state churches, *inter alia*. Sporting organizations and international sporting federations have their own institutional order, and may or may not look to some parent state to give them validity. Trades unions, professional associations and all kinds of similar organizations have their own normative order. It is an empirical, not a conceptual, question to determine whether these are offshoots of state law or have their own self-referential grounds of validity.

Above all, in Europe since 1958 there has emerged a body of law that its own authoritative judicial organ states to be a new legal order *sui generis*. This did, indeed, originate in international treaties, but is declared to have evolved into a position apart from international law, while being also distinct from state law and being in its own proper sphere supreme over state law. This, of course, is European Community law, directly applicable and effective in relation to citizens as well as states, and overriding member-state law within its own material sphere of validity. It is an interesting and discussible question whether the best account of the relationships between the laws of the states and the law of the Community is monistic, in the sense that one derives from, or is subordinate to, the other, and how one factors into this account the relationship of these to public international law.[7] But at least it is clear that there is no conceptual obstacle to a radically pluralistic account of these relations, and this seems at first sight to do better justice than a monistic account to the respective views of their own law held by the European Court of Justice and the supreme judicial or constitutional tribunals of the member states.

Sovereignty and Post-sovereignty

A further upshot of the development of Community law in Europe has been to curtail fundamentally the sovereignty of states as this has traditionally been understood.[8] For example, in the UK, the fundamental doctrine of the Constitution, in its classical nineteenth- and twentieth-century understanding, has been that of the sovereignty of parliament. This doctrine implies that parliament can, at any time, make any law it thinks fit and can repeal wholly or in part any previously enacted law – for 'Parliament cannot bind its successors'.[9] Moreover, it implies that no authority can sit in judgement on the question of the validity or applicability of an Act duly enacted by parliament, assented to by the monarch, and authenticated as the Queen's Printer's copy of such an Act. In 1991, however, in the case of *Factortame* v. *Secretary of State for Transport*, the House of Lords, following an interpretative ruling laid down by the European Court of Justice (ECJ), held that it was obliged to 'disapply' certain offending provisions of the Merchant Shipping Act 1988 on the ground that they were incompatible with the UK's Community obligations.[10] Other cases in other member states and other decisions by the ECJ have likewise cast doubt on the tenability of traditional conceptions of sovereignty in respect of member states.[11] Conversely, however, there has been a strong body of judicial opinion, especially from the German Constitutional Court, that denies the possibility of ascribing sovereignty to the European Community or Union as these are presently constituted, and that denies their capability to assume sovereignty over the democratically constituted member states without violating fundamental constitutional principles of democratic government.[12]

These European developments have been particularly striking in relation to the transcendence of old-style state sovereignty, but they are not an isolated phenomenon. Throughout the world, the emergence of a jurisprudence of human rights around such international instruments as the Covenant on Civil and Political Rights, or regional conventions such as the European Convention on the Protection of Human Rights and Fundamental Freedoms, has set limits on the pretensions of states to legal omnipotence in their own territories. The principle of non-intervention has been found to admit of exceptions in the face of violations of human rights in their contemporary positivized versions. In place of the sovereign states of classical theorizing, we have the emergence of a condition that we might call 'post-sovereignty'.[13] Today's states are post-sovereign states, and the life of human beings comes to be referable to a number of interacting normative orders, with the old simplicity of the absolute internal supremacy of a state's law now heavily qualified.

Positivism and Statism

Many contemporary legal scholars have taken exception to legal positivism as an analytical–descriptive theory about law[14] (in contradistinction to ethical positivism which belongs to normative rather than analytical legal theory). I suspect, however, that the main odium should attach not to analyses of law that show how legal order can be differentiated conceptually from moral order, according to certain conceptions of morality. It ought to attach rather to the implicit statism of much that has been presented as positivist legal theory, and as legal scholarship carried out under the broad aegis of an assumed 'positivism'. Exegetical legal scholars have considered their proper task, both in scholarly writing and in teaching, to be that of giving an objective account of the law as it exists in a given state at a given time.

Whereas states are one form of political order, comparatively recent in origins and remarkable for their effective centralization of coercive power,[15] their presence behind the forms of law and legal study cultivated by law schools – themselves elements within state financed and state-governed institutions – has been taken for granted as unquestioned reality. States and their law have been considered as though they are part of the furniture of the universe rather than as contestable constructs of human thought, and legitimating frameworks of coercive government.[16] Institutional normative order in the form of state law has been given an unquestionable pride of place, and all too often the kind of critical distance that ought to separate scholars from the object of their study has been lost, as the activists of critical legal studies movement have loudly complained.[17]

But the exponents of postmodernist legal theory seem to have remained captivated by the same paradigm. Jacques Derrida's essay 'Devant la loi' is one seminal text for postmodernists.[18] We notice that Derrida places his essay in front of '*la loi*', not '*le droit*', and his discussion of the underlying violence of legal institutions is conducted in this spirit. Thus does French statism flourish even in the critique of it, for, of course, *la loi*, statute law, is law as it is produced by the state, law enacted by *la nation française* through its legislative organ. There is no denying that all modern states emerged – each in its own way – from violent struggles, violent overthrowing of earlier régimes in favour of a new order. Even the reasonable force that may be used to enforce law must have behind it the capability to outface and overwhelm the most violent of resistance. So the peace and order achieved by states, to the extent that they do achieve it, has real violence in its history and potential violence in its present and future. But this is not intrinsic to the idea of law as such – *le droit*, institutional normative order in all its manifestations – but only state law, and it is the state, not the law, that is the agency of coercion and even of violence.[19]

In the context of a discussion of ethical positivism and its bearing on the utility or disutility of judicial activism in the setting of Australian constitutional jurisprudence, this may be thought a rather useless refinement, even if true. For the issue here is the proper use of state law and its institutions, not the question whether law has manifestations other than in state law. Ethical positivism is a theory about the proper use of state law in the contemporary state; hence it at least shares assumptions, even if not conclusions, with postmodernism.

The Value of the 'Institutional': Making Norms Determinate

Taking that point, let us continue with the question why – especially in the context of the state, but not necessarily in that context alone – people may find value in institutional normative order. What is the point of order's being 'institutional'? The earlier discussion of the gap between informal and institutional normative order already contains the answer to this question. The difference between the informal and the institutional, the move from the single-tier to the multi-tier normative order, creates the possibility of the explicit and authoritative articulation of norms in the form of norm-texts pronounced or issued textually by persons in authority, this authority depending on higher-tier norms of the relevant order. Informal queues rest on informal mutual understandings, and on some sufficient overlapping consensus about the inarticulate norm that each regards as governing conduct in the relevant activity of queuing and turn-taking. Institutionalized queues have people appointed to be in charge of them (and perhaps also of the service for which persons are queuing). By refusing to give service except in accordance with what they assume to be, or articulate as, the queuing rule for this service, they can make determinate, and indeed progressively ever more determinate, what are the rules by which this queue is governed.

At least two consequences follow from this. The first is that there can be greater interpersonal clarity and consensus as to the exact terms of the rule that governs people who join this line. Mutual beliefs grounded in implicit interpretations of an assumed common norm are superseded by a third-party articulation of a rule in express terms. To the extent that these terms are vague they can be made more exact and concrete through a process of express decision-making carried out over time. As a truism: rules expressly articulated by persons in authority are more determinate interpersonally than implicit informal norms, even where the subject matter of the regulation is substantially similar. Quite simply, institutionalization yields the possibility of making rules more determinate and explicit in their terms than informal or customary rules can possibly be. Indeed, a progressively greater determinateness is facilitated, to the extent that new rules or rulings can be issued to cover interpretational doubts or regulatory gaps as these arise in practice. This process of rendering determinate, *'determinatio'* as the Thomists call it,[20] has real importance both in law and in the handling of problems of mutual coordination in society. Jeremy Waldron also stresses this point in Chapter 11.

The second consequence is that there exists in the institutional case an extraneous motive to compliance. This need not be a sanction in the positive sense of a distinct threat of adverse consequences that will be imposed in the event of non-compliance. It can simply arise from the explicit or implicit commitment of the service provider to give service only to persons who queue up in the appropriate way, and to provide it to such persons each at her or his due turn in the queue. Observance of the rule becomes a necessary condition of achieving that which one has set out to achieve. If you don't stand in the appropriate line and take your turn, you will simply not be able to board the aircraft or catch your train.

The fact that institutionalization can generate motives to compliance in this way (and also, in some cases, by the deployment of coercively enforced penal or remedial sanctions) strengthens the normative order in an obvious way, for it strengthens mutual beliefs and expectations. One reason for not forming an orderly queue is a lack of belief that others will wait their turn. Trying to get on to a bus at a busy time in Florence is a daunting experience, and those who wait their turn never get on board a bus at all or at least not until well after rush-hour. It is different at Florence airport where a queuing system to board the plane is managed by the airport and airline staff. The belief that others will (by and large) wait their turn is a condition for the rationality of waiting my turn. If 'waiting one's turn' does not occur on an informal and voluntary basis, the relevant belief is lacking in us all. Some kind of institutionalization can make good this deficiency.

There are elements in critical feminism that attack the hegemony of legal rules and the element of entrenched social, presumptively patriarchal, hierarchy that this hegemony reinforces.[21] This is for some, perhaps many, contexts a more than fair point to make, given the content and genesis of many rules and institutions currently observed or in function among us. But the determinateness of rules, and their institutionalization in a way that reinforces motives to observe them, has an important aspect that ought not to be overlooked: the protection of weaker parties. The Florentine struggle to board a bus inherently favours larger, stronger and more aggressive people (although, to some extent, small lithe and nippy ones, too), leaving behind the old, the weak and the disabled, whereas institutionalized queue-keeping gives weaker persons a fairer opportunity. This seems generally applicable to many coordination rules and, indeed, the domains covered by criminal law and parts of civil law, too. Some of the concerns properly advanced by critical feminism point towards, rather than away from, the value of institutional normative order and, indeed, state-enforced order in a number of relevant domains.

Heteronomy and Autonomy: The So-called 'Autonomy of Law'

One conception of morality places the idea of 'autonomy' at its heart.[22] One acts morally when one acts as a 'law unto oneself', pursuing good rules and principles of conduct for their own sake, and because one adopts them freely as one's own governing laws of conduct. Being bribed, cajoled or coerced into doing the right thing may, in a certain sense, be desirable (for the right thing is, in fact, done), but here there is neither moral merit nor a fully functioning moral agency. From this point of view, any move towards institutional order is, at least, suspect. The independent moral agent falls under the authority of rules made (in ever more determinate terms) by agencies and authorities set over her or him, not effectively controllable by or answerable to her or him. The human being in the institutional setting is then pushed into a situation of heteronomy and, for all the potential advantages of institutionalization, there may be a heavy moral price to be paid. This is all the more so, in so far as the organs and agencies of institutional order might indeed have been captured by sectional interests or powerful elites.

If ideal morality is characterized (as I believe it to be) by its conceptual dependence on the autonomy of moral agents, then it follows that there is a contrast between moral order and institutional normative order. For the latter brings with it the heteronomy, rather than the autonomy, of the people subjected to it. Positive law – the law of the state – being a prime instance of institutional normative order, there is accordingly a profound conceptual distinction between morality and law (in this sense of the term). That conceptual distinction is sometimes rather pompously, but most misleadingly, referred to as engaging the 'autonomy of law',[23] meaning the disciplinary independence of the study of law from related departments of practical philosophy such as ethics and politics. But if 'autonomy' is held as a concept to its etymological foundations, it means self-rule, not conceptual differentiation. And the point is that law is not a self-ruling entity, institution or activity. State law is the law of a state, and a state is a political organization in which governmental power is secured coercively within a territory. The political process determines the content of law through legislation, and the personnel of law through judicial appointments and professional regulation. The 'rule of law' is a political value or imperative that demands restrictions on the political process – in particular, through a separation of the judicial from the other powers of the state, the subjection of the executive and military powers of the state to general rules of law substantially the same as those that govern ordinary citizens in their mutual interactions, and fidelity to law and the Constitution among all office-holders. There cannot be good legal order without substantial operational independence of the law enforcement agencies and courts, but this is a truth obscured, rather than captured, in describing the law itself as 'autonomous'.

This is a line of argument fully in sympathy with the ideas of ethical positivism. Judicial independence is independence from illegitimate political interference with, or pressure concerning, law interpretation and law application on individual cases. Ethical positivism argues for the subordination of law to the democratic process, is so far as it concerns determination of the content of the enacted rules of law. It argues for this determination to proceed at the level of relatively detailed rules expressed in clear terms, and for judicial interpretation to be guided primarily by the 'plain meaning' of the words and sentences enacted into rules of law. Such rules, coercively enforced, address the citizen heteronomously, for they are binding regardless of the citizen's will in the matter. Yet the legal order envisaged by EP does favour autonomy in a qualified sense, for the clarity of the rules and the predictability of their interpretation and application by judges mean at least that citizens can plan and direct their own lives provided only that they avoid infringing laws and incurring whatever sanctions are involved.[24]

Many might be inclined to go further and deny that the citizen of a democratic polity is heteronomously subject to law, since each citizen is a participant in the political process and part author, in however small a part, of the laws that are enacted. Even if opposed to any particular enactment, the citizen can take the view that he or she is a willing participant in the process and be ready to embrace the outcome voluntarily even when it is counter to his or her preferences or considered moral judgements. This is a stance with which I myself am comfortable, at any rate so far as concerns the broad run of legislation. But this is a matter of my moral judgement, and there is no logical compulsion on others to pass the same judgement about the highly flawed democratic processes exhibited by contemporary states. Moreover, as not all states are, or have been, even imperfectly democratic, there is nothing in the concept of state law as such that secures, or even tends to secure, a coincidence between autonomous morality and enforced law.

The Practical Force of Legal Rules

Let us, however, take it that the argument from qualified autonomy does favour a legislative process with the characteristics suggested by EP, and that a good judicial style would be a somewhat restrained one in face of statutes of the desired quality, relying chiefly on a 'plain meaning' approach to interpretation. To return now to a point mentioned in the introductory section of this chapter, this implies ascribing to enacted rules of law the practical force of being 'rules of absolute application'.

What does this mean? Earlier, it was suggested that institutional normative order involves a multi-tier hierarchy of norms, though always with conventional (informal) norms at the apex level. This hierarchical structuring enables us to contemplate the possibility of empowering both law-making agencies or individuals and law-applying agencies or individuals. At the same time, it makes possible the adoption of higher-level rules prescribing how lower-level rules ought to be used by those responsible for applying them. In a recent paper I have suggested that there are three possibilities: rules can be treated as being 'rules of absolute application', as being 'rules of strict application', or as being 'rules of discretionary application'.[25] My explanation of these is as follows:

> A rule is of **absolute application** if it is to be understood and applied on the footing that each and every occasion of the occurrence of stipulated facts (the 'operative facts' stipulated in the conditioning hypothesis of the rule) must be attended unfailingly by the normative consequence specified by the rule as following from these facts. Moreover, this normative consequence may not be put into effect except when either these operative facts obtain or some other rule independently providing for this is satisfied by virtue of the ascertained presence of its operative facts. Typical example of rules of absolute application are those of the rules of essentially mathematical and closed-ended games like chess.[26]
>
> A rule is of **strict application** if it is to be understood and applied on the footing that circumstances bearing on the values secured by it may occasionally arise such that there will be very considerable derogation from those values if on a particular occasion the stipulated normative consequence is invoked just because of the present instantiation of the given operative facts. By its spirit, the rule should not be applied, but by its letter it should. The person charged with applying the rule and

managing the activity within which the rule has application is accorded some degree of guided discretion to make exceptions, or to override the rule, in special, or very special, cases.

A rule is of **discretionary application** if the decision-maker is expected to consider every case in the light of all factors that appear relevant given the values and goals of the relevant activity or enterprise, and to decide in accordance with the clear balance of factors, but when all things are equal, or when the balance of factors is rather fine and difficult to judge, the decision-maker is expected to use the rule as a fall-back way of deciding the case.

Rules of absolute application and rules of discretionary application belong at opposite ends of a spectrum. Rules of strict application occupy the intervening range on the spectrum and are more or less strict according to how they approximate to one or other limiting case.

Certain rules and maxims of equity may approximate to the 'discretionary application' end of the scale. But in general, within positive law, rule creation proceeds on the assumption that, at the very least, enacted rules are to be treated as of very strict application, and even rules of case law laid down in precedents are of fairly strict application.[27] The case made by EP suggests that statute law ought to be treated by courts as being of absolute application, in order to prevent undue judicial activism eroding the supremacy of the legislature and, with that, the democratic legitimacy of the legal process. EP further suggests that this will be effectively undermined unless fairly strict canons of interpretation are followed by, and, if necessary, imposed on judges.[28] The point of this is fairly clear: if a broad and freewheeling style of interpretation is adopted, the interpreted rule may be said to be of absolute application, but the courts will in fact use just as much discretion in applying it as they would under a regime of strict interpretation (in which they would be free in an appropriate case to exercise a discretion not to apply the rule in cases where the values implicit in it would be more damaged by application than by non-application).

On Interpretation

With certain apparent exceptions, statute law in the legal systems of contemporary states (and in such partly analogous systems as that of the European Community) ought to be deemed of absolute application, at any rate in countries with reasonably democratic institutions. On this I am fully at one with EP, but I cannot follow Tom Campbell the whole way in his arguments concerning interpretation. The advocacy of overriding reliance on 'plain meaning' considerations is not acceptable given the character and complexity of contemporary legal systems. A flexible approach to interpretation does substantially blur the line between strict application and absolute application, or rather indicates the absence of any clear line of demarcation towards that end of the spectrum.

Together with colleagues from several other legal traditions, over the past 15 years I have engaged in the comparative study of legal interpretation – interpretation of both statutes[29] and precedents.[30] The fruits of that study suggest strongly to me that, in the conditions of contemporary legal systems, interpretation has to be broader-based than EP concedes and, in particular, has to take into account such values as the internal coherence of statutes considered as wholes or, sometimes, as parts of a group of interrelated statutes, particular branches of law, the coherence of the relevant branch of law to which the statute or group of statutes belongs, and the overall coherence of the legal system as a totality, especially with regard to the matching of lower-level law with constitutional provisions, including any entrenched or non-entrenched provisions about human rights or fundamental constitutional rights.

The best way of contemplating forms of interpretative argument in law seems to be one that divides them in the first place into three broad categories:[31]

1. There are arguments that deal predominantly with the meanings of words and sentences in the natural language in which legislation is cast, or in special registers of it, especially with regard to technical vocabularies in specialist areas of activity.
2. There are arguments, or types of argument, that focus on the significance of the (legal) system context of the statutory sentences under consideration and take account of such factors as:
   - the need for a harmonious reading of a statute as a whole
   - the need to have regard to precedents, so that the statute is applied according to one received reading in all courts
   - the legitimacy of having regard to analogy in reading similar words and phrases in statutes of similar bearing
   - the need to have regard to established legal understandings of technical legal concepts as these occur in different statutes
   - the relevance of general principles of law to the reading of a statute – for example, the 'principles of natural justice' in their bearing on a statute that empowers an official to take decisions affecting important interests of citizens
   - the relevance of history, especially in the case of older statutes that have come to be understood as embodying some overall scheme or system of values.
3. There are arguments concerning justice and utility, in the sense that a reading of a statute which generates what seems a serious

injustice should not be preferred to one that seems more compatible with justice, and a reading that generates what seems like undesirable consequences should not be preferred to one which avoids or minimizes such consequences, in either case perhaps leading to acceptance of a more strained reading of the act (judged in pure 'plain meaning' terms) to avoid injustice or undesirable consequences.

Ethical Positivism and the Critique of Interpretation

It is, of course, just at this point that the proponent of EP may well leap into the argument to ask, 'But who is the judge of what is unjust or undesirable? Why should unelected judges superimpose their judgements of such deeply contestable values on the interpretation of acts whose plain meaning reveals that the legislature acted on a different view of what is just or desirable? The problem, however, is that this is usually not just a question, but a question-begging argument, for it assumes that we are able to ascribe to the legislature the intention not only to use language in a particular way, but also to pursue whatever ends follow from implementing the legislation according to that reading. The appropriate response to this is that one can quite as readily impute to legislatures intentions about the values and ends that an Act ought to realize as intentions about the 'plain meaning' of its terms according to a rather decontextualized conception of ordinary language semantics. This means that the issue is which of the imputations seems the more reasonable overall in the given interpretational dilemma. Furthermore, any of the 'systemic' arguments listed can be appealed to as also disclosing a legislative intent, for the legislature cannot be supposed to have legislated without regard to the consideration of 'fit' between the newly enacted law and the whole body of the law that it amends – and it also must be taken into account that the types of systemic argument noted may themselves pull in different directions in a specific instance.

Since appeals to legislative intent can thus range over all three other categories of 'linguistic', 'systemic' and 'justice or utility', the argument from intention has what we call a 'transcategorical' quality.[32] How far it can be crystallized in a given case as a matter of history is a contingent question, complicated by the well-known conceptual difficulties about identifying anything legitimately describable as 'the intention' of a collective agency like a parliament. The upshot, it seems to me, is that we have to figure out grounds for the rational imputation of intentions to legislatures, having regard to the legislative record, the contemporary conditions of the country and the state of political debate, the purport of committee reports and the like, and, above all, the text of the enacted statute taken as a whole. Thus it is impossible to get the genie back into the bottle and rely on pure 'plain meaning' argumentation unless there are arguments of a 'justice-and-utility' kind that suggest this is the least troublesome interpretational approach over the long run. For myself, I do not believe that such considerations exist or, if they did, that they would have the kind of persuasive weight that would be needed. This leads me to a departure from full-strength EP.

There are two lines of reasoning for my position. The first concerns the idea of maintaining overall coherence in a legal system. The reason for favouring this is not mere elegance in law, but rather justice and the reasonable securing of legal expectations. If different and mutually opposed rules or principles cut across each other and one or other is applicable in a quite arbitrary way, there is a real difficulty from the standpoint of formal justice – that is, from the 'like alike' principle. The state that exhibits no care to avoid this is one which, as Dworkin[33] has powerfully argued, manifests a defect in 'integrity' in the way it treats its citizens. This is objectionable.

It is not, of course, in any case a decisive, knock-down objection. A recently elected reforming government with a well-advertised commitment to a programme of law reform set out in a clear election manifesto is entitled to argue that temporary incoherence in law is the inevitable price you pay for the fact that a legislative reform programme may take several sessions to complete. Reformers are usually animated by conceptions of justice different at least in significant detail from the conception(s) to be found in existing law. Against the early phases of a reform programme, the argument from coherence might well be no more than a cloak for illegitimate conservatism, frustrating the fair outcome of a democratic election.

Observe, however, that this is itself an interpretative argument based on the injustice and disutility of interpretations that uphold existing legal principles in face of a democratic mandate for change. As such, it is a good argument, but not a plain-meaning argument. Moreover, it does not show that legal coherence has no value, merely that it does not, at all times and in all contexts, have overriding value. The reforming administration is, after all, not engaged in a programme of rational law reform if it does not envisage some new equilibrium in the law at the end of the programme, when a new constellation of principles has been given determinate form in a body of enacted statute law that can now be read as a coherent whole, partly overriding prior principles, partly outweighing them and partly confining them to more narrowly circumscribed fields than previously. So arguments from coherence are always relevant and significant, but may have variable weight according to context.

In this respect, they are similar to other types of interpretative argument.

Finally, the Napoleonic or Justinianic argument may be raised: abolish interpretative argument altogether. Statutes should be clear, and *interpretatio cessat in claris* ('where matters are clear, there is no place for interpretation'). The trouble is that, in part, the law demarcates a terrain of competing interests. The clarity of a law may depend on the position from which you are looking at it and how it affects your interest. To deny someone affected by law the opportunity to dispute the issue of whether or not it really is clear in its impact on the case in hand is quite unreasonable. To give the opportunity is to open the door to the whole panoply of interpretative arguments and to their adversarial deployment as between people who press rival readings of the same text on the court, aiming to secure an outcome favourable to their interest or their conception of justice and public policy. *Interpretatio cessat in claris* is better viewed as a kind of conclusion about a failed interpretative argument than an available barrier to admitting such arguments to the seat of justice.

I do not deny that the admission of parties' arguments for and against their interpretations and the great sprawl of interpretative argument that takes place in law can have their own unfair effects. It is true that those with deep purses have less to fear than the poor from protracted litigation since they can hire highly skilled lawyers to deploy all the possible arguments in their most persuasive form: this draws attention to the fact that, in grossly inegalitarian societies, the value of the rule of law is substantially less than in those that achieve greater equality of resources for their citizens. It is too late in the day, however, to argue that the rule of law should be ignored where there is inequality, for there is no better recipe for further exacerbating inequality. On this, as on very many points, Tom Campbell and I are fully at one.

Notes

1 Aldershot: Dartmouth, 1996.

2 See, for example, Duncan Kennedy's *Critique of Adjudication: Fin de Siècle* (Cambridge, MA: Harvard University Press, 1997), pp. 275–81.

3 See R. Dworkin, *Law's Empire* (Cambridge, MA: Harvard University Press, 1986), chs 6 and 7.

4 N. MacCormick, 'Norms, Institutions, and Institutional Facts', *Law and Philosophy*, **17** (1998), pp. 301–45.

5 In an ideal world, no doubt, the common acknowledgement of the Constitution would be a moral endorsement of it, and reciprocal or mutual commitment to it, by each citizen as an autonomous moral agent. But the world is not always or everywhere ideal in these respects, and a merely customary or conventional or even oppressively exacted acknowledgement is enough to make a constitutional

order, including the system of positive law validated by the Constitution, viable. Compare N. MacCormick, 'The Relative Heteronomy of Law, *European Journal of Philosophy*, **3** (1995), pp. 69–85.

6 See H. Kelsen, *The Pure Theory of Law*, trans. M. Knight (Berkeley and Los Angeles: University of California Press, 1967) at pp. 328 ff.

7 For an outstandingly clear and thorough discussion, see C. Richmond, 'Preserving the Identity Crisis: Autonomy, System, and Sovereignty in European Law', *Law and Philosophy*, **16** (1997), pp. 377–420.

8 See N. MacCormick, 'Beyond the Sovereign State', *Modern Law Review*, **56** (1993), pp. 1–18.

9 See Sir W. Wade, 'Sovereignty – Revolution or Evolution?, *Law Quarterly Review*, **112** (1996), pp. 568–75. The classical statement remains Dicey's; see A.V. Dicey, *An Introduction to the Study of the Law of the Constitution*, 10th edn, ed. E.C.S. Wade (London: Macmillan, 1960), p. 27.

10 *Factortame* v. *Secretary of State for Transport* [1991] AC603.

11 Cf. N. MacCormick, 'The *Maastricht-Urteil*: Sovereignty Now', *European Law Journal*, **1** (1995), pp. 553–67.

12 Cf. D.R. Phelan, *Revolt or Revolution: The Constitutional Boundaries of the European Community* (Dublin: Round Hall/Sweet and Maxwell, 1997), esp. pp. 98–120.

13 See N. MacCormick, 'Liberalism, Nationalism, and the Post-Sovereign State', *Political Studies*, **44** (1996), pp. 553–67.

14 See, for example, R. Cotterrell, *The Politics of Jurisprudence: A Critical Introduction to Legal Philosophy* (London: Butterworth, 1989); V. Kerruish, *Jurisprudence as Ideology* (London and New York: Routledge, 1991), pp. 47–56; M. Davies, *Delimiting the Law: 'Postmodernism' and the Politics of Law* (London & Chicago: Pluto Press, 1996), pp. 80–87.

15 See G. Poggi, *The State: Its Nature, Development, and Prospects* (Cambridge: Polity Press, 1990).

16 Cf. Roger Cotterrell's plea for a more pluralistic vision of law: *Law's Community; Legal Theory in Sociological Perspective* (Oxford: Clarendon Press, 1995), pp. 306–10.

17 For example, Kennedy, *Critique of Adjudication op. cit.*, pp. 8–20.

18 I owe this to Margaret Davies' discussion in *Delimiting the Law, op. cit.*, pp. 70–1; see J. Derrida, 'Devant la loi' in A. Phillips Griffiths (ed.), *Philosophy and Literature* (Cambridge: Cambridge University Press, 1984).

19 It seems to me that Derrida and his followers (for example, Davies, *Delimiting, op. cit.*, p. 120) tend to overstretch the concept of 'violence'. The reasonable use of force is not always and necessarily violent, and the concept of 'violence' is implicitly evaluative, implying an injurious and illegitimate use of force.

20 See J. Finnis, 'On "The Critical Legal Studies Movement"', *American Journal of Jurisprudence*, **30** (1985), pp. 21–42 at 23–5.

21 See, for example, E. Kingdom, *What's Wrong with Rights* (Edinburgh: Edinburgh University Press, 1991), pp. 26–45.

22 The idea, of course, comes from Kant; for my conception of it, see N. MacCormick 'The Concept of Law and *The Concept of Law*', *Oxford Journal of Legal Studies*, **14** (1994), pp. 1–23 and 'The Relative Heteronomy of Law', *European Journal of Philosophy*, **3** (1995), pp. 69–85.

23 See J. Raz, *Ethics in the Public Domain* (Oxford: Clarendon Press, 1994), ch. 13 'On the Autonomy of Legal Reasoning'; and R.P. George (ed.), *The Autonomy of Law* (Oxford: Clarendon Press, 1996), this latter being a volume of essays about legal positivism to which I contributed. But it seems to me highly dubious to treat legal positivism as being about law's 'autonomy', since the whole point of what is known as the 'social sources' thesis is to show that the content of law derives from various forms of political decision-making. That law is not the same as morality,

because morality distinctively engages the autonomous subject, is very unhappily captured in propositions about law itself having some spurious 'autonomy'.

[24] See J. Raz, *The Authority of Law* (Oxford: The Clarendon Press, 1979) ch. 11, and cf. T. Campbell, *Legal Theory of Ethical Positivism*, (Aldershot: Dartmouth, 1996), pp. 97–120.

[25] MacCormick, 'Norms, Institutions', *op. cit.*, pp. 301–45 at 311–18.

[26] Fernando Atria in *The Powers of Application* (Edinburgh: Edinburgh University PhD. thesis, 1998) draws a distinction between what he calls 'autonomous institutions' like games and 'regulatory institutions' like law, which would account for the prevalence of my 'rules of absolute application' in games and the like.

[27] Typically, precedents have a binding force dependent on the level of the deciding court in a hierarchy of courts. The practical force attaching to a precedent depends on the hierarchical relationship obtaining between the now-deciding court and the court that laid down the precedent.

[28] Campbell, *Ethical Positivism, op. cit.*, pp. 129–48.

[29] D.N. MacCormick and R.S. Summers (eds), *Interpreting Statutes: A Comparative Study* (Aldershot: Dartmouth, 1991).

[30] D.N. MacCormick and R.S. Summers (eds), *Interpreting Precedents: A Comparative Study* (Aldershot: Dartmouth, 1997).

[31] What follows is a somewhat abbreviated account of the view stated with greater elaboration in MacCormick, 'Argumentation and Interpretation in Law', *Ratio Juris*, **6** (1993), pp. 16–29.

[32] MacCormick and Summers, *Interpreting Statutes, op. cit.*, pp. 515–16.

[33] Dworkin, *Law's Empire, op. cit.*, chs 6 and 7.

3 Ethical Positivism and the Liberalism of Fear[1]

MARTIN KRYGIER

Tom Campbell has observed that '[e]very legal theory requires a political setting and no political philosophy should lack a theory of law'.[2] His own recent work seeks to make good these requirements by recommending ethical positivism as a 'highly political theory of law'[3] – a response not only, but above all, to what he calls 'the tragic paradox of politics, according to which states are both highly necessary and extremely dangerous'.[4] In this chapter I explore this paradox, as setting and source of a political philosophy from which ethical positivism gains plausibility, and discuss some implications that have been drawn from it. I endorse some of these implications and question others.

I do not seek to draw a genealogy of ideas – Tom Campbell's or any others' – nor, except where I cite him, am I concerned to attribute to Campbell any explicit commitment to the broader views of the political domain which are outlined below. Briefly, I believe his argument echoes many of those views, but not all of them and not them alone. More generally, although the ideas which I discuss have distinguished exemplars and I will frequently refer to other authors, what follows is less plausibly their version, or fault, than mine. This caveat is entered not merely to protect me from the erudite, but also because, among those who betray signs of the disposition I want to flesh out, there are many who have not engaged directly with the writers I mention or the arguments that interest me, and would not admit to being – indeed, may not actually be – influenced by them. What they share is as much a certain *disposition of thought* as a particular theory or the influence of a particular theorist.

I wish to characterize that disposition, one of whose manifestations is a normative conception of the role of law greatly resembling what Campbell calls ethical positivism. Whether or not Campbell would feel flattered or slandered to be put in the company I mix him with, his theory exemplifies many of the views of that company, shares in their strengths, and is subject to some of their weaknesses.

The Liberalism of Fear

Much has been asked of public institutions and actors – among them, fulfilment, liberation, justice, mercy, prosperity and social equality. The list is long and it can be inspiring. There is, however, a strain of thought which appears to ask for little, and for something quite austere, but does so insistently. It asks for security from the evils that flow from unrestrained power. People of this disposition might ask for more than such security, but they insist that it is central. Judith Shklar, one of the most recent, uncompromising and eloquent exponents of this way of thinking about politics, has aptly named it the 'liberalism of fear'.[5] It is only one strand within the larger liberal tradition,[6] often combined with other strands, but it is a profoundly important one. I want to investigate some of the implications of taking fear seriously, to explore its logic, some of its tendencies and some of its limitations.

Fear underlies and informs many of our central institutional arrangements and thoughts about them, although it weighs more heavily on some than others. In thought about public affairs, fear is more associated with a sceptical temper, than with optimistic, sunny expectations or ideals. Those who fear fear are likely to be impressed more by history and memory than by hope,[7] are aware of the 'crooked timber' of which we are all made,[8] take the first duty of public arrangements to be 'damage control'[9] rather than the pursuit of perfection, dream less about attaining the best than avoiding the worst, and indeed prefer talk of the least worst to that of the very best.

Acknowledged and unacknowledged, this concern to tame major sources of fear has had deep resonance among thinkers about public affairs over several hundred years. It is expressed, among other places, in the writings of Montesquieu which greatly influenced the American Founding Fathers. They, in turn, influenced us all, even if nowadays restraint of fear commonly finds more eloquent partisans among those who have suffered its absence than those who live off the fruits of its presence.

This disposition has a distinctive concern with the character of public *institutions*, rather than, say, of public persons, for political thinkers of a fearful disposition are reluctant to leave too much in public affairs to individuals' propensity for virtue or other good traits. They believe that, in such matters, while we might (or might not) want to *encourage* individual virtue, for example, we would be unwise to *rely* on it and certainly to rely solely on it. There are two reasons for this. One is that we might not find enough of it, and we need safeguards against its absence. The other is that we might find too much of it and we need safeguards against its presence. For we have good reasons to fear not only fiends but saints as well – particularly if they are powerful fiends or saints. We need security against excess of zeal from either source – indeed, excess or abuse of power from *any* source.

For such security to be enduring and reliable, institutions are necessary, particularly those that restrain the exercise of power, channel it through established pathways, divide it, check it, tame it and thus help us keep fear, at least of the power so exercised, at bay. Many of our most valuable legal and political institutions are intended to serve as barriers against, or antidotes to, some of the most dangerous public sources of fear. It is important to keep that in mind, particularly when the institutions work effectively and the fear is hard to recall.

A classical first move in the argument is the claim that (at least in modern large societies) life will be literally and necessarily frightful, at the very least disorderly, without institutions which can keep the peace, adjudicate disputes and restrain and disarm potentially combative citizens. In different ways, thinkers such as Hobbes and Locke made this move. As they, and particularly Hobbes, knew, not only does the existence of public institutions make it possible to disarm people who can make each others' lives 'solitary, poore, nasty, brutish, and short', but, where they are effective, such institutions can reduce fears that might otherwise impel people to behave in abominable ways. At least on some readings, the ghastliness that has overtaken so much of the former Yugoslavia confirms this insight. In response to clichés about primordial ethnic hatreds, for example, Michael Ignatieff has recently observed that the slide into savagery in that tragic country followed a particular trajectory, which he thinks is generalizable, and which he explicates in the following terms:

> Note here the causative order: first the collapse of the overarching state, then Hobbesian fear, and only then nationalist paranoia, followed by warfare. Disintegration of the state comes first, nationalist paranoia comes next. Nationalist sentiment on the ground, among common people, is a secondary consequence of political disintegration, a response to the collapse of state order and the interethnic accommodation that made it possible. Nationalism creates communities of fear, groups held together by the conviction that their security depends on sticking together. People become 'nationalistic' when they are afraid; when the only answer to the question 'Who will protect me now?' becomes 'my own people'.[10]

To avert such tragedies, and lesser ones too, so it is reasoned, we need law-makers who can issue binding, generally applicable laws and who have sufficient power and resources to be able to enforce the laws they make. This spawns the next problem, and the one that Locke identified in opposition to Hobbes. If we have so much reason to fear our neighbours who are just individual humans, how should we avoid terror of that 'mortal God', the state, which Hobbes called Leviathan?[11] This is a question Kosovon Albanians might well put to Ignatieff. It underlies the 'tragic paradox' which Campbell, among others,[12] has identified.

One very old answer – central to liberalism though not its invention – is that rulers must be constrained to operate in accordance with an overarching legal ideal: the framework ideal for law known as the rule of law. At least since Aristotle, Western legal and political traditions have known ideals of 'the rule of law and not of men', even though no one imagined that law could rule without men. Why should people be so attracted to this ideal, and why should they think it so important? One very good reason has to do with fear of the arbitrary exercise of power. Quite apart from the particular *aims* of any exercise of power, law is looked to as a means of restraining the *ways* in which power can be exercised. Locke put the point thus:

> Absolute Arbitrary Power, or Governing without *settled standing Laws*, can neither of them consist with the ends of Society and Government, which Men would not quit the freedom of the state of Nature for, and tie themselves up under, were it not to preserve their Lives, Liberties and Fortunes; and by *stated Rules* of Right and Property to secure their Peace and Quiet. ... And therefore whatever Form the Common-wealth is under, the Ruling Power ought to govern by *declared* and *received Laws*, and not by extemporary Dictates and undetermined Resolutions ... For all the power the Government has, being only for the good of the Society, as it ought not to be *Arbitrary* and at Pleasure, so it ought to be exercised by *established and promulgated Laws:* that both the People may know their Duty, and be safe and secure within the limits of the Law, and the Rulers too kept within their due bounds ...[13]

Similarly, Judith Shklar considers escape from arbitrary power the fundamental virtue to be sought from legal and political arrangements and insists that it cannot be achieved without the rule of law. The choice, according to Shklar, is simple and stark. As she explicates Montesquieu's institutional recommendations, designed to ensure what he described and valued as 'moderation' in government, '[t]his whole scheme is ultimately based on a very basic dichotomy. The ultimate spiritual and political struggle is always between war and law. ... The Rule of Law is the one way ruling classes have of imposing controls upon each other.'[14]

In a similar vein, in the conclusion of his book, *Whigs and Hunters*, the eminent Marxist historian, E.P. Thompson scandalized many other Marxists, who traditionally had little time for law, by insisting that:

> ... the rule of law itself, the imposing of effective inhibitions upon power and the defence of the citizen from power's all-intrusive claims, seems to me to be an unqualified human good. To deny or belittle this good is, in this dangerous century when the resources and pretentions of power continue to enlarge, a desperate error.[15]

What Shklar, a lifelong liberal, and Thompson, a somewhat rueful Marxist or ex-Marxist, share is the insistence that the value of the rule of law lies primarily in what it shields us against. When they warn complacent beneficiaries of the rule of law to value what they have – what *we* have – it is by comparison with the perils that they know flow from its lack.

But, as Locke, Shklar and Thompson knew all too well, despots have laws too, so not just any sort of law will do. And important as ideals are, no sceptic will want to trust to them alone. They need support, and if the support is to be robust and lasting, it needs to be built into enduring structures, among which legal structures are crucial. The trick is to arrange an institutional order in such a way that it manages to restrain precisely those with the most power – law-makers, as well as other significant power-holders. That's quite a trick.

One way of elaborating Locke's theme is to try to spell out the institutional implications of rule of law values – values that, above all, seek to ensure that power cannot catch us unawares. Note that in the passage quoted above, Locke is not insisting merely that government be by something that can be called 'law'. Nor does he say anything in this passage about the *content* of the law. He insists, rather, on the need for laws of a particular – clear, stable and knowable – *character*, on '*settled standing Laws* ... *stated Rules* of Right and Property ... *declared* and *received Laws*, and not ...extemporary Dictates and undetermined Resolutions ... '. The reason for this emphasis on the medium rather than the message is plain. The vice he is most concerned to condemn is not the exercise of power itself but 'Absolute Arbitrary Power', 'Government ... Arbitrary and at Pleasure'. And, as anyone who has suffered such power will confirm, he is right to condemn it.

Laws that conform to the rule of law are not retrospective, secret, incomprehensible and contradictory. They do not require anything that is impossible to perform. On the basis of them, one can make plans. To the extent that a legal order approximates the rule of law ideal, citizens have, or can obtain, clear advance understanding of their legal obligations and they can reasonably have faith that the law will constrain other citizens and officials of state in ways that, under the rule of law, they can predict.

This is not just a question of the formal character of the written laws, for citizens must also be able to have reasonable faith that the interpreters and enforcers of the law will construe it with fidelity to its publicly known terms and independently of extra-legal pressures to bend or ignore it. That, in turn, will require institutional safeguards for the independence of those who interpret the laws. It will also benefit from a host of – apparently 'soft' but actually crucial – cultural supports, including socialization into the values of the rule of law, at least of the professionals who have to administer it and, commonly less self-consciously and explicitly, among large numbers of citizens. For a crucial aspect of the rule of law which only partly depends on the law itself is that, in the society at large, laws can, do and should significantly *count* as part of the normative fabric of everyday life. The extent to which any of these features exists is highly variable among and within societies and so, therefore, is the salience of the rule of law.[16]

To the extent that the ideals and conditions of the rule of law are honoured in practice, citizens have some means of knowing where they, and others, stand. This helps reduce their reasons for fearing what others might do, or at least clarifies what they have to fear. And it also puts others in the same position when they seek to anticipate what we will do.

The various strands of thought that Shklar characterizes as the 'liberalism of fear' can be understood as moments in an extended meditation on ways to institutionalize restraint on power, consistent with the rule of law ideal. The products of such meditations are various. Different rule of law regimes have often embodied different judgments about how to implement rule of law ideals, and have different legal and other histories and traditions which have influenced the particular shape of their institutions. These differences are not automatically fatal, since the rule of law is not a recipe for detailed institutional design. It represents rather a cluster of values which might inform such design, and which might be – and have been – pursued in a variety of ways.[17]

Still, among liberal arrangements which have often been adopted are forms of separation and division of powers, and more generally attempts to check power by institutionalizing countervailing powers. Since the American Revolution, a written and binding Constitution has stood as a symbol and instrument of many endeavours in this direction, and, since shortly thereafter, judicial review of the legality of the exercise of power has become its common accessory. Many motives feed these arrangements, but one important among them is trenchantly, if perhaps uncharacteristically, expressed by Thomas Jefferson:

> ... free government is founded in jealousy, and not in confidence; it is jealousy, not confidence, which prescribes limited constitutions, to

> bind down those whom we are obliged to trust with power; ... in questions of power, then, let no more be heard of confidence in man, but bind him down from mischief by the chains of the Constitution.[18]

None of this can completely *eliminate* fear, of course. Nothing could do that, and particularly not law, since its association with force renders it, for many people in many circumstances, inevitably a source of fear itself. But it helps tame some of the worst things we have reason to fear from public power, and it helps us know what, and in what circumstances, we have to fear. All it needs to make one take this kind of thinking seriously is the concession that the world can be a dangerous place. And all it needs to make that concession seem sensible is a cursory knowledge of history, or even a glance at a newspaper. The less cursory that knowledge, the longer the glance, the more sensible the concession will appear.

The legal recommendations so far discussed are devoted to providing frameworks for the containment, and channels for the safe transmission, of political energies. But what of the animating sources of these energies, where politics and law meet? Politics is, after all, not a frictionless motion of actors bounded and insulated by faithfully applied and unchanging laws. And laws are not neutral or eternal frameworks. They are *made* by people with purposes and ambitions. How do we domesticate those purposes and tame those ambitions? Moreover, laws have effects, so one is not merely concerned with what goes into the political machinery, but with what comes out. How can we make those who make and enforce laws accountable to those whom they will affect?

Central to most modern answers to these questions is democracy. In modern times, the rule of law has been intertwined with political democracy to the extent that we speak routinely of liberal democracy. Yet these two elements were not always linked historically and on one view[19] they have no special conceptual connection either, since one can imagine a benign and liberal prince who respects legal constraints[20] or an elected demagogue who does not. Nevertheless, quite apart from the many independent reasons to value democracy, their connection makes a great deal of sense.

One principal reason for democracy – certainly not the only reason but one which allies it with the liberalism of fear – is that it puts ultimate control, over those with their hands immediately on the levers of power, in the hands of those who will be affected by the exercise of that power. But what stops the people themselves from being unruly? After all, politics is a domain of passions, contests, ambitions, interests and values. How do we contain the consequences of these often tempestuous forces? Here the liberal democrat folds politics back into the restraining web of institutions and the rule of law. Political power should be exercised by way of laws within a system that conforms to the rule of law, and social power should also be contained within the framework of such laws.

To simplify complex theory and different and unevenly successful practice, the political process has the task of liberating, but then containing, what emerges from the agitation of politics and then *funnelling* it through legislative institutions which distil it into laws. Some laws come out of this process to affect us directly, others through the activities of officials. If there are disputes about the meaning and bearing of laws, other officials interpret those laws and adjudicate those disputes.

On this view, it is important to distinguish between the mouth of the funnel, where new matter appropriately enters to become law, and these ancillary points of official intervention, which are to be limited to enforcing and applying the law and not be additional sources of that law. For the ambition is to fix the location of political decision to where the people are or can be, so that from the time it leaves them to be distilled into laws it can emerge to affect them as untainted and unaltered by alien material as can be contrived. From this perspective the application of the law by unelected officials should not be another inlet; it should not itself be the occasion for fresh political agitation or law-making. For that one must return to the funnel mouth, where politics rightly happens and the people can control what is decided.

Now with respect to the liberalism of fear, the complex arrangements that I have merely sketched are at once indispensable and fragile. They are indispensable because they limit the sway of unaccountable power. They are fragile both because they are subject to external threats and also because the complex intedependencies and balances on which they rely are so easily upset. Each of the elements might become stronger or weaker than it needs to be to cooperate with and to limit the others. Popular passions might overflow or erode the channels intended to restrain them, or they might be led astray. Power might seep or flood from the elected government to its bureaucracy as unelected officials contrive to render oversight by the people or their representatives nugatory. And what also of unelected and virtually irremovable judges, particularly senior judges? These are strategically located in the whole design of control over other institutions and the law, but they themselves escape the circles of control because of their institutionally protected independence which itself has impeccable liberal foundations. Here the liberal component in liberal democracy tends to strain against its partner: the former often biased in favour of institutions that limit law-makers, such as courts; the latter favouring those that are accountable to the people, such as legislatures. And I have not even mentioned the arguments of radical critics of liberalism, who suggest that the whole enterprise of constraining social power by legal means is doomed to fail or at least systematically to serve some elements of society at the expense of others, while masking this systematic bias under the universalist rhetoric of the rule of law.[21]

At each of these and other points of suspected vulnerability, the logic, the *grain*, of the liberalism of fear will tend towards strengthening accountability, finding ways of controlling controllers, guarding guardians, cabining, confining and balancing every position and every moment where power can be exercised: legislatures by citizens; governments by legislatures, courts and tribunals; courts by the law. This, of course, makes adjudication a very sensitive and delicate business *in principle*, since, although the judges are the exemplary officers of the rule of law, responsible for maintaining it against all comers, they are – at least in constitutional matters – formally controllable by no one. If fear is what motivates you, that is a worry, and I will return to it. But it is only one of many.

Ethical Positivism

The logic of the liberalism of fear leads naturally, then, to concern for systematic restraint on state power. But it is important to recognize that that is one *consequence* among others of that logic, not its originating source. To forget the distinction between source and consequence, as many fearful liberals have, often leads to exaggeration of the importance of that consequence. It also tends to obscure the fact that a feature of the 'paradox of politics' is that *restraint* on the state comes into play only after the first – sometimes only dimly remembered – move of the liberals' own argument. That, after all, was to stress the importance of having a state with, in Madison's terms, 'regular powers commensurate to its objects'.[22] That in turn requires a state that is sufficiently strong and effective to do what states need to do. That, as I have tried to show elsewhere, is quite a lot.[23] It also requires states, and public institutions more generally, to do what they do effectively. That, too, is no small matter. For what must be avoided is not state power *per se*, but arbitrary, capricious and despotic exercise of that power. What must be nurtured is not state weakness, but sufficient strength of the right sort to enable the state to act fairly and usefully, spend effectively and deploy its power to good ends.

Not only must states and public institutions be *strong* enough to do what they should but they must also be *competent* to do what they are peculiarly suited to do, even whilst they must be restrained from doing what they are ill-suited to do well, or well suited to do badly.

Even those who understand the need for state strength do not always understand the character and imperatives of competence. To ensure it we must understand what it involves. This will be complex and variable, as competence varies from institution to institution. Then there remains the small matter of achieving it. Fearful liberals are not incapable of addressing these issues, but they are not always their central interest, nor always their special strength.

There is, of course, nothing startling about recommending that public institutions be competent. Who wants anything else? Nevertheless the recommendation is not as banal as it might seem, for there are several contexts in which the natural and laudable implications of the liberalism of fear, untempered by other concerns, tend to pinch and strain against certain kinds and sources of institutional competence. They do so, I would maintain, even when, like Tom Campbell, one recognizes a large and important role for public power and is firmly committed to a competent and active state.

One context of crucial importance is that of law. Here there are strong liberal, and perhaps even stronger democratic, reasons to insist that the law be solely or as much as possible a 'law of rules',[24] where rules are understood to act as 'exclusionary reasons'.[25] Where such reasons for decision are in play, they exclude recourse, by all but authoritative law-makers, to extra-rule considerations which might otherwise be considered relevant, whether these be considerations of politics, morals, consequences or whatever. On a strict interpretation of this view, that might even exclude direct consideration of, say, the purposes which might have, or be thought to have, led to the rules in the first place,[26] and it would certainly exclude any considerations which lie further afield. That, so this view insists, is what is meant by *applying* the law that you have, rather than speculating about why you have it or making a new law, different from the one in front of you. For a rule to have the signal attribute of 'ruleness', then, it must act at the point of application as an unambiguous, mandatory and exclusionary rule, to be preferred to non-rule considerations, and not be a mere rule of thumb, simply to be taken into account along with them.

There are authoritarian 'top-down' versions of such a model of rules which emphasize the subordination of officials and citizens to rules but leave prerogatives untrammelled at the centre. Here the law is seen as above all an *instrument* of authoritative command, and 'ruleness' is assessed in terms of its efficacy in transmitting central commands. It will be associated with weak political and legal accountability of power-wielders and a merely instrumental and contingent commitment on the part of the centre to abide by the rules. There may well also be circumstances where open-ended discretions or extra-rule exercise of power will be preferred by the rulers instead of, or as well as, insistence on rules. Citizens will not be empowered to insist that rules bind rulers as well.

When combined with liberal democracy, however, the significance of rules in the model is different. Their point is to segregate the legislative level at which politics, interests and clashes of value have legitimate play from the executive and adjudicative levels where they do not, on the grounds that the former are controlled democratically, while the latter are not. Only this, and the associated *autonomy* of law application from the world of politics, interests and clashes of value, gives democratic legitimacy to the former, since the *demos* is there, and to the latter, since it isn't. Moreover, unless the law observes such segregation, the rule of law itself might be imperilled, since any alterations at the stage of application would mean that the law could not have been known beforehand. Its effect will be retrospective. So it is also with any softening of the 'ruleness' of law. If law comprises of open-ended 'standards' which are only made concrete at the point of 'application', if it can be outweighed by the decision-makers' views of morals, politics or consequences, then again the rule of law threatens to degenerate into the rule of men.

It is easy to see the attractiveness of this understanding to the liberalism of fear, and to liberal democrats influenced by it. It would seem to keep the consideration of politics and values where, in their scheme of restraint, they should lie – at the properly *political* stage of the process, where laws are made by representatives answerable to the people. If the laws so made can be ignored, revised and remade by unelected officials, whether bureaucrats or judges, or if their terms are so vague that their particular scope and meaning must await an interpreter's decision, the whole ambition to *funnel* values into a set of institutions constrained by law begins to disintegrate. Such a situation seems calculated to puncture holes in the legal funnel, through which legitimate (because under democratic control) purposes and values might seep out, and illegitimate ones (because uncontrolled either by legality or democracy) might be injected. Moreover, the whole notion of clarity, non-retrospectivity and stability of law would seem to be up for grabs, at the mercy of the next decision. If this is the case, doesn't that rob citizens of precisely what the rule of law was intended to ensure them?

It is parallel considerations that lead many people to decry the consequences of the welfare state for the rule of law. The modern active state relies heavily on open-ended laws, expanding official discretions, ballooning and hard-to-ascertain regulations. How can we know them in advance? How can we interpret them? How can we rely on them? How can we keep them from favouring some at the expense of others? Many thinkers have warned against the consequences of these developments for the maintenance of the rule of law,[27] and their fears, though often exaggerated, are not without foundation.

One response to such developments is to favour tight legislative definition of administrative action and limitations on administrative discretion,[28] clear and precise legislative rules rather than vague standards, statutes rather than the common law,[29] 'judicial restraint' rather than 'judicial activism',[30] precise legislative definition of rights rather than vague constitutional bills of rights,[31] especially not constitutionally entrenched bills of rights. These latter, it might be observed from this viewpoint, are falsely considered difficult to amend, because, although citizens have difficulty in amending them, judges are free to do so whenever they come to 'interpret' them. This would seem to offend the principles of democracy and liberalism simultaneously.

Fear of uncontrollable judges might, then, lead some to spurn bills of rights, even though it might have been fear of only loosely controlled legislatures which led others to embrace them. And this is an instance of a wider difficulty or source of tensions within attempts to realize the liberalism of fear. There are so many potential sources of fear that attempts to institutionalize antidotes to one such source might themselves build up powers in another, which one has in turn reason to fear. This, as we saw earlier, is where democratic and liberal commitments might strain against each other. A strong court might neutralize a strong legislature or executive, but then what about the court? So long as courts keep their heads down and can convince people that they are merely applying laws made elsewhere, this fear might lie dormant. However, many find it disquieting as soon as they seem to show some initiative, since there is no obvious way to impose extra-judicial control over that initiative without destroying the independence so precious to the role that fearful liberals require courts to play. This is where the attack on judicial activism has its most potent source, for if the defences of fearful liberalism are to be rigorous they should leave no unguarded guardians – and that is precisely what law-making judges seem to be.

The foregoing account has deliberately been cast broadly, since the considerations advanced in it have persuaded many people who have never heard either of the liberalism of fear or of ethical positivism. But there is no doubt that an ethical positivist of Campbell's sort would find many of them compelling, and it is not surprising that, while they are not the only considerations that move Campbell, he himself emphasizes many of them. After all, ethical positivism, like the liberalism of fear, is an attempt to deploy law to deal with 'the tragic paradox of politics'. And like the fearful liberal, the ethical positivist considers that:

> ... the paradox is tragic in so far as both the need for and the dangers of government stem from the same features of the human condition: the vulnerability of individuals and small groups in situations where scarcity, or perhaps human nature itself, generates the drive to dominate and control others.[32]

And so, ethical positivism 'sets out a rule-based framework for mitigating the tragic dilemmas arising out of the paradox of politics',[33] designed, above all, to funnel decisions into law and separate the activities and personnel engaged in making the law from those involved in its interpretation and application. As Campbell explains:

> The point of legal positivism – understood as an ethical theory concerning the legally relevant conduct of citizens, legislators and judges – can be seen as the provision of a model and a justification for the construct of a legal system which approaches as far as is practicable to the realisation of an autonomous system of rules as a necessary part of any acceptable legal system. The autonomy in question relates not to the inputs to legal system which, on the democratic model of legal positivism at least, are the rules emanating from legislatures, but to the court-centred processes whose function is to apply legal rules to particular circumstances and resolve the question of law and fact which are brought to their attention. The point of legal positivism, so understood, is to commend that legal systems be developed in such a way as to maximise the social and political benefits of having a system of readily identifiable mandatory rules of such clarity, precision and scope that they can be routinely understood and applied without recourse to contentious moral and political judgments.[34]

These are weighty considerations. It is certainly no answer to them to favour judicial or administrative activism simply on the grounds that one prefers the results in particular cases. For there will be other cases, and institutions are in for the long haul. Nor can a sceptic be happy to 'let justice be done though the heavens fall'. People who advocate that are unlikely to have experienced falling heavens. And demands that 'justice' should invariably triumph over 'blind adherence to rules' ignore at their, or our, peril just how contentious justice can be and how important the work of rules is. Liberals, democrats and ethical positivists are right to emphasize the importance of rules, and they are equally right to insist that a serious political theory must reckon not merely with what results institutions should generate but equally with what institutions should generate them. They must have a theory of what institutions should have *authority* when values are in dispute, not merely what values they think should win.[35] There *are* strong democratic reasons to favour legislative sources for fundamental value decisions, strong liberal reasons for 'ruleness', and strong reasons to worry about unfettered discretions in the hands of unfettered decision-makers. But are they always and everywhere overwhelming, and more particularly should they uniformly override any other considerations? For such considerations do exist.

First, one must reckon with the impossibility, now almost universally acknowledged among lawyers, of a gapless regime of totally, mechanically, applicable rules. No legal theorist, and certainly not Tom Campbell, pretends that such a regime can exist in practice, for there are so many unavoidable factors about law and about life that militate against the perfect ruleness of rules. Just to mention one: rules, expressed in words, have to be interpreted and they cannot dictate the interpretation they receive. That comes from outside them, from those who interpret them.[36] It does not follow that meaning is necessarily unstable, at least among lawyers, since there is usually considerable consensus within interpretive communities on how they are to be interpreted. But that in turn depends, among other things, on canons of interpretation within such communities, which in turn are controversial, are often inconsistent and change, for the proper grounds, means and ends of interpretation are themselves complex and matters of dispute. And then rules of interpretation, even when agreed upon, have themselves to be interpreted, and so on. None of this is news to any legal theorist, although different theorists draw different conclusions from it, and popular polemics often ignore it. Other chestnuts of legal theory concern questions of what decision-makers should do if their understanding of the meaning of the rule, as applied in a particular case, contradicts what they understand the purpose of the rule to have been. Or what if the rule seems to dictate a conclusion out of line with values deep in the larger body of law? Or manifestly unjust? It is not obvious that such considerations should invariably trump respect for rules, but nor is it obvious that they should always lose.

The real dispute about the role of officials is rarely between those who think the law is, or can always be, plain and officials shouldn't ignore it and those who deny these things. Rather, it is a dispute of political morality as to what officials should do in those many cases when there is no simple and uncontroversial way of reading off a univocal result from the words of the legal rules. What approach by officials, at that point of decision, best serves democracy, fidelity to law, justice, institutional competence and whatever other values are nominated, and then – if these values point in different directions – which should have what priority? These questions are particularly insistent at appellate levels, since the odds are that the case would not be there is the answer were simple. And to such questions, as to most questions of institutional design, there is no one-size-fits-all answer that will do.

Thinkers who still are primarily concerned to confine official acts often modify their original injunction that the law should simply be applied to say that officials should stick as close to the rules as they can when they apply them, and add as little of their own as they can. They should be systematically 'restrained', not 'activist', deferential to legislatures and cautious in any extensions of the law they might be driven to suggest. And, given the democratic deficit under which judges labour, there is much to be said for judicial restraint in many, perhaps most, circumstances, for judges' settling for 'incompletely theorised agreement'[37] short of the fully theorized 'moral reading' that some[38] demand from them. Modesty is, after all, a virtue, particularly from incumbents of an institution which is deliberately cut off from democratic accountability, systematic training in anything other than law, and systematic access to information other than law. However, modesty is not the only virtue and where it is disingenuous it might not even be virtuous. That aside, the demand for 'restraint' rather than simple rule application already suggests that the legal funnel is leaking. And if the leakage proves unstoppable, one might reconsider whether to try all measures to stem the flow. Instead, it might be worth thinking whether it could be directed to good ends.

The 'England Problem'

Among the primary virtues of the rule of law is that it allows us to know what the law is in advance, and therefore place reliance on it. Potentially, these are remarkable contributions that a stable and coherent legal order bestows on a society. However, *how much* predictability a legal order needs to successfully undergird a civil society, what sorts of law produce it, and what besides law is needed, are less simple questions than they appear. They are sociological, rather than philosophical, questions and ones on which evidence bears. There is therefore no reason to believe that philosophers are particularly well equipped to answer them, although they have not been too shy to try. And the answers of many fearful liberals – namely, the more predictability the better, and a tight rule-based legal order – are less obviously compelling than they might seem.

An example might help here. Max Weber argued powerfully that modern 'sober bourgeois capitalism' could not have developed in the absence of a highly predictable order of politics, administration and law. Where the ruler's prerogative was constantly threatened, or the administration was unsystematic and not based on rules, or the law was unclear or unascertainable or liable to arbitrary change, various forms of 'adventurous and speculative capitalism and all sorts of politically determined capitalisms are possible, but no rational enterprise under individual initiative, with fixed capital and certainty of calculations'[39] and, with it, the enormous dynamism which the Western capitalist order uniquely displayed. Such an economic order needed 'a calculable legal system and an administration in terms of formal rules'.[40] The key, Weber insisted, was the sovereignty of predictable rules.

This is a sociological thesis and a highly plausible one. Without at least a reliable threshold of predictability of political action and of restraint on the arbitrary exercise of significant power, sober bourgeois capitalism won't develop, although snatch-and-grab capitalism might. That is a lesson that contemporary Russia confirms. However Weber went further. As a trained German lawyer and legal philosopher, Weber identified the continental civil law order, which had as its regulative ideal a gapless, coherent system of formal general rules, as the most predictable and hence the most suitable for capitalism. Weber knew that the ideal was unrealizable in practice, but he seemed to think that the determined attempt to approximate it would generate more predictability than could any alternative. Tom Campbell favours statute law to common law, apparently for similar reasons.

That, however, left Weber with a notorious difficulty, often simply called his 'England problem'. The common law as developed in England and its offshoots, among them the United States, had altogether messier, inductive, case-by-case methods; English legal thought, Weber wrote, 'is essentially an empirical art ... One can also still observe the charismatic character of lawfinding, especially, although not exclusively in the new countries, and quite particularly the United States'.[41] Indeed:

> ... [a]ll in all, the Common Law... presents a picture of an administration of justice which in the most fundamental formal features of both substantive law and procedure differs from the structure of Continental law as much as is possible within a secular system of justice.[42]

This is an embarrassment for Weber's legal thesis, because it was precisely these common law countries which were the great engines of capitalism, not Germany and France with their far more systematic sets of rules. Worse still, Weber – who was nothing if not honest (and a genius besides) – acknowledged that where the two systems competed, as in Canada, 'the Common Law has come out on top and has overcome the Continental alternative rather quickly'.[43] He might also have acknowledged that the English system of political rule was not obviously more arbitrary than the German, for all the latter's formality and rules, nor – to address the liberals' preoccupation – did the English have more reason to fear abuse of political power than the German or French.

Weber made a variety of ad hoc attempts to reconcile his thesis about Continental technical superiority with the facts of English and American success. These brief hypotheses were unsuccessful in that aim because they each undercut the special significance of formal rationality, but each was fertile. I will recall one here, and one later. The first was that English law 'while not rational [roughly: derived from a coherent system of general rules] ... was calculable, and it made extensive contractual autonomy possible'.[44] This saves the sociological thesis that capitalism requires predictable law, but not the legal one that it requires 'formally rational' law on the Continental model. It appears that law can be predictable *enough* – perhaps more than enough – even in cases where predictability matters a great deal, although it is, by some standards, quite unruly.

This suggests two important points for fearful liberals and ethical positivists committed to a law of rules. First, the attempt to realize an unrealizable ideal is not necessarily the best strategy for anchoring one's values in the world. That is perhaps an illustration of the economists' 'theory of the second best'. As I understand it, this theory holds that if, in an ideal theoretical model, a combination of factors and circumstances would produce a particular optimal result, but some of these factors are missing in actuality, you won't necessarily do best by simply seeking to maximize those of the stipulated factors that remain, in the circumstances that you have. Or to adapt an illustration made by Avishai Margalit,[45] imagine that you are desperate to fly for a holiday in Hawaii, but only have enough fuel to drop you a few hundred miles short, somewhere in the Pacific Ocean. Rather than try to fly as close to your goal as you can, you might do better to settle for somewhere closer, particularly if there are other benefits in doing so. In our context, also one of inevitable shortfall – in this case from formalistic perfection – it might not prove sensible relentlessly to urge approximation to an unattainable ideal. There is evidence that it is not necessary for what you want, and where other considerations are also important. This is even more the case, since, as I will argue later, legislators are neither in control nor have much knowledge of many of the factors which will ultimately determine the effects of the laws they launch into the world.

Second, the liberalism of fear can only distinguish itself from paranoia, and ethical positivism can only make plausible claims about the effects of laws in the world, if they are prepared to take circumstances, and variations in institutional strength, support and resilience into account. Many who understand the power of evil and corruption in the world are genuinely and rightly reluctant to compromise on the rule of law and the autonomy from other pressures which a law of rules promises. Comparing relatively autonomous legal orders with repressive and arbitrary ones, they quite rightly prefer the former. However, these are not the only alternatives, for legal orders differ greatly in the extent to which the values and practices of the rule of law are strongly embedded within them. In strong legal orders, such as those of the Western liberal democracies, there are large cadres of people trained within strong legal traditions, disciplined by strong legal institutions, working in strong legal professions and socialized to strong legal values. Western legal orders are bearers of value, meaning and tradition laid down and transmitted over centuries, not merely tools for getting jobs done. Prominent among the values deeply entrenched in these legal orders over centuries are rule of law values, and these values have exhibited considerable resilience and capacity to resist attempts to erode them. Not every legal order is so strong. That suggests that not every legal order is equally at risk from limited incursions on its 'ruliness': some will be much threatened, others less so.

Philip Selznick insists on this point, in arguing for a legal order more 'responsive' to changing needs, particular circumstances, principles of justice embedded in legal traditions but often not formulated as hard and fast rules, and considerations of justice more broadly. Responsive law, in Selznick's theory, is not a horse for all courses; it is not equally salutary in every time and every place. On the contrary, he points out that it is sinister (or frivolous) to demean the values and institutions committed to restraining power and that a system of 'autonomous' law, which gives a high priority to rules, is a potent complex of such values and institutions. However, he also observes that just as people exhibit what he calls 'moral development', so can institutions, systems and communities.[46] For example, at certain stages in the career of an institution, particularly during the formative stages, certain values rightly rank high because they are not yet established or institutionalized, or because they are at risk, or because they face strong threats. Such values must be secured and it is dangerous to compromise them. When, however, they *are* secure, the balance of emphasis in our moral ambitions can change, and striving towards aspirations can more safely supplement the establishment of baselines of security. We can even take some risks. This is not because the baselines become less important; it is just that they are more firmly in place and the risks are less risky. Thus:

> For many institutions, a large measure of autonomy is especially important in its *formative* stages. When policies and perspectives must be nurtured – given a chance to become established and secure; in a word, institutionalized – they need the protection autonomy can give. Once the system or policy is secure, that need becomes less compelling. Then more precision is required as to *what kind of* autonomy and *how much* is required or desirable.[47]

One can, then, agree with Campbell's 'modest but important claim ... that, given the appropriate political and legal culture, specific rule governance can have an important role to play in moving societies towards the attainment of general prosperity, effective humanity and social justice',[48] without agreeing that rule governance should be always the only legal game in town. But why would one want to compromise the ruleness of law?[49] Basically because, while we need institutions and the rule of law to protect us, we might need to enlist them for other purposes as well, and characteristics apt for one purpose might not be equally apt for others, however legitimate they both are. And so Selznick insists on the importance of attending to both baselines, conditions of survival, on the one hand, and aspirations, conditions of flourishing, on the other.

Fears and Hopes

We ask many things of law as of life, and not all of them are consistent with each other. After all, judges are sworn to do justice according to law, so there is something poignant when the two demands come apart. Sometimes our fondness for ruleness might seem outweighed by our wish to do justice in a particular case, sometimes simply by our wish to act sensibly in particular circumstances, and sometimes by our wish to serve the purposes of a statute, even if that involves setting aside the implications of what we understand its words to require, because in a particular case the result of their application would lead to a foolish result. And judges are not the only officials who are bound by rules and bound to apply them. Throughout the society regulators are sent, authorized by law, to check on the performance of industries, hospitals, schools and so on. How should they do their important jobs? Our fears lest such sources act poorly will often point in different directions from our hopes that the same sources might act well. Fear is important enough to have considerable priority – possibly important enough to raise a presumption in favour of moves to counteract it. But it should not always be our only concern.

This is something Weber hints at in another attempt to explain the embarrassing English advantage. In English law, he writes,

> ... [s]afety valves are ...provided against legal formalism. ... the institution of the civil jury imposes on rationality limits which are not merely accepted as inevitable but are actually prized because of the binding force of precedent and the fear that a precedent might thus create 'bad law' in a sphere which one wishes to keep open for a concrete balancing of interests. ... It does in any case represent a softening of rationality in the administration of justice.[50]

Such 'safety valves', which allow escape from the excessive rigidity often associated with a single-minded devotion to rules, might be useful in other contexts as well. Paradoxically they might even deliver us more reliable legal consequences.

There are at the same time important sociological and moral dimensions to all this, and I will take them in turn. A confidence in the real-world consequences of precise rules, tight discretions, crisp definitions, judicial restraint and so on assumes much about the ways that laws in the books and in the courts affect lives in the world. But much of this advocacy, whether by lawyers, legislators, economists, philosophers or even Max Weber, betrays a remarkable sociological innocence. First, few of us are simply waiting to hear from officials and their law. This law competes with many other signals, pressures and sources of normative guidance and dispute resolution in our life – such as Petrazycki's 'intuitive' and Ehrlich's 'living' law – many of them closer and more salient to us and the groups within which we move than the laws on which lawyers and legal philosophers concentrate. Not only will they compete with the law for our attention, and often win, but they will be part of the context in which the law is understood, used or not used, heeded or ignored.[51] Since people live most of their lives in such 'semi-autonomous social fields'[52] of which legislators know little, it is not surprising that the life of the 'law in action' is difficult if not impossible for the legislator, or anyone who merely relies on lawyers' folk understandings of human behaviour, to predict. So if we are concerned with how law actually affects people's lives and what is made of it there, any simple extrapolation from the technical character of laws, and their official interpretation in particular hard cases, to their systematic effects in the world, is simply uninformed guesswork. One has to look at the play of law in the world.

When one does look, much that one finds would surprise those who imagine that the virtues of a law of strict and strictly applied rules is self-evident. For example, the literature of regulatory theory is full of accounts of the pathologies generated by attempts to 'fix' rules as precisely as possible. In their splendid and splendidly named work, *Going by the Book*,[53] Bardach and Kagan point to the 'site unreasonableness', unresponsiveness and ineffectiveness which systematically occur when overinclusive rules are applied inflexibly to complex, variable and changing circumstances. They stress the 'perverse effects of legalism', among which are the dumbing-down effects of formal rules which 'by their nature ... are enforceable only if they specify *minimum conditions* of performance or quality or whatever. They cannot be designed to bring about higher levels of *aspiration* or continuous improvement or concern about quality'.[54]

This is a theme echoed by the American sociologist, Carol Heimer who explores regulation in a variety of contexts where there is reason for concern both to eliminate abuses and encourage excellence. Typically, regimes of legalistic rules are aimed at the former goal, and not only don't serve, but undermine, support for the latter. As Heimer writes:

> Ideally, two different sets of incentives should address the analytically separate problems of discouraging and punishing dishonesty and wrongdoing and encouraging and rewarding high-quality performances. Ideally these two incentive systems would be quite independent since incentive effects get distorted when the two problems are addressed by a single set of rewards and punishments. One doesn't want rules designed to curb the abuses of the worst 1% to become the guidelines for an entire system.[55]

Or, as she remarks in the same piece, '[w]e would not have great symphony orchestras if conductors focused only on keeping musicians from playing out of tune'.[56]

One overriding danger of such officious negatively inclined regulation, emphasized by Bardach and Kagan, is that *'accountability replaces responsibility'*,[57] a theme which Heimer's studies vividly illustrate. This suggests, and it has suggested to Geoffrey Brennan – no enemy of rules – that there might be point in discriminating among the targets of regulatory regimes and varying the mode and character of regulation accordingly.[58] If your principal aim is to catch criminals, one sort of regime might be the regime of choice. If, on the other hand, among one's aims are improving the competence, talents, application, care and loyalty of actors in the institutions that one is regulating, a system of inflexible rules might be dramatically counterproductive.

Indeed, even if it is bad performance which worries you, such a system might still serve you badly, for strict rules lend themselves to what Heimer elsewhere calls 'creative compliance, in which people or organizations follow the letter but not the spirit of the law' and 'feigned compliance [where people] do not even bother with the letter of the law except to use it as a guide for creating an appearance of compliance'.[59] John and Valerie Braithwaite, for example, compared the regulation of nursing homes in the United States and Australia. The former is based on a large number of very precise and detailed rules; the latter on a small number of vague and value-laden standards. The Braithwaites demonstrate that, contrary to their initial intuitions, the Australian system of 'wishy washy and blunt' standards turns out to be far more reliable than the American law of detailed rules. There are many reasons for this, the most important being that conscientious staff are empowered and involved in the activity of particularizing and satisfying the standards, rather than alienated and tempted to avoid or simply formally to conform to the host of detailed rules while ignoring the goals which the rules were intended to serve. But there is a negative pay-off as well:

> Detailed laws can provide a set of signposts to navigate around for those with the resources to employ a good legal navigator ... Marching under the banner of consistency, business can co-opt lawyers, social scientists, legislators and consumer advocates to the delivery of strategically inconsistent regulation of limited potency.[60]

Standards are often harder to evade.

The point here is not that rules serve no purpose, or that standards should always be preferred or that administrators and judges should do what they like. And it is certainly not that political authority should abandon the mediation of rules and be 'simply a matter of ad hoc particularistic decrees or discretions'.[61] This 'are you still beating your wife?' way of posing the alternatives is unhelpful and is no necessary implication of scepticism with regard to lawyers' and philosophers' speculations about the ways of law in the world. Two things are suggested, however, by even this cursory sketch. The first, and more general, point is that Campbell's salutary and effective critique of the division of labour between legal and political philosophy should be extended. The disciplinary apartheid which often divides philosophical from empirical and social theoretical enquiries is also unfortunate, since not everything on which legal philosophy depends – particularly philosophy that is committed to understanding law in its 'political setting' – is discoverable by philosophy.[62] More specifically, there is little that is self-evident about the ways laws percolate into social life, about how much and in what circumstances they matter, about what about them matters, about what is made of them, about what effects they have and about what in them has effects. Much that seems self-evident, including some of the ethical positivist's confidence in the comparative efficacy of rules, might well be false. And even where it is not false, it might simply exaggerate the importance of what it advocates and underrate the importance of considerations that it overlooks or overrides.

There are many dimensions to this – one of them moral. I will conclude with it. Again and again, the language of the law, and aspirations people have for it, include distinctions which we should not ignore when considering what might be gained from our institutions: the letter and the spirit of the law; legality and justice; rules and principles; baselines and aspirations; negative and affirmative ambitions; fears to be allayed; and hopes to be realized. Ideally, we would serve them all, and practically we need security from fear to be able to pursue hopes with confidence. But securing the first is not the same as securing the second, and a single-minded devotion to one might undermine our chances to gain the other.

Since my wrestling with these problems is so deeply indebted to Philip Selznick's wise, uncomfortable and relentless determination to hold on to both horns of important dilemmas, I will quote him at length:

> Positivism is not indifferent to legal values. On the contrary, from positivism we gain a steady focus on *clarity*, *certainty*, and institutional *autonomy*. These virtues serve the ends of justice. They uphold the expectations of citizens, limit the abuse of official discretion, and determine the reach of binding obligations. By insisting on a definite boundary between the legal and the nonlegal, they sustain the independence of judges and the separation of law from politics. They thereby enhance, in some respects at least, the integrity of legal institutions ...
>
> The truth in legal positivism is, however, a limited truth. The virtues of clarity, certainty, and institutional autonomy are contingent, not absolute. They do not always serve justice; indeed, they often get in its way. Precise rules, accurate facts, and uniform administration are elements of *formal* justice, which equalizes parties, restrains partiality, and makes decisions predictable. These surely contribute to the mitigation of arbitrary rule. But legal 'correctness' has its own costs. Like any other technology, it is vulnerable to the divorce of ends and means. When this occurs, legality degenerates into legalism. Substantive justice is undone when there is too great a commitment to upholding the autonomy and integrity of law. Rigid adherence to precedent and mechanical application of rules hamper the capacity of the legal system either to take new interests and circumstances into account or to remedy the effects of social inequality. Formal justice tends to serve the status quo. It therefore may be experienced as arbitrary by those whose interests are only dimly perceived or who are really outside the 'system'.[63]

Australians have a local example, which has engaged the country in a welter of legal, moral and political debate over several years. In *Mabo* v. *Queensland No. 2*,[64] the Australian High Court acknowledged what no Australian court had ever acknowledged before: that Aborigines had original title over their lands, which the common law recognized, even though statute might override it. The reaction of most public commentators to this decision, as to the later *Wik*[65] decision, which held that native title was not automatically destroyed by grants of land use to pastoralists, could be read off simply from where they stood on the issue of native title. If they approved its recognition, they approved the decision; if not, then not. However, there was also an institutional issue which formed a strong theme in the debate. What was the proper role of the High Court in such a case? Opponents of the decision adopted the 'law of rules' approach to judicial decision. There was an established legal understanding (though never enunciated by the High Court) that Australia had been *terra nullius* when white people arrived, and in consequence there were no rights to recognize. On this view, that is where the Court should have stopped. If the law were to be changed, the legislature should be the body to do it.

That seems to me an inadequate response to the Court's predicament. Certainly the Court is not a legislature, but nor did it act as one. It recognized the previous understanding of Australian courts. It carefully considered the available law of property, the history of settlement, and in particular the empirical falsity of the doctrine of *terra nullius* on which non-recognition of native title had been legally based. It noted that, on the evidence before it, the claim that this country was uninhabited or inhabited by peoples without laws, was false. It noted too, that the law governing settlement in the United States, Canada and New Zealand – all members of the common law family of nations to which Australia belongs – had not categorized the countries they occupied, and consequently the legal status of the indigenous occupiers, in this way. The Court was without doubt also clearly moved by the injustice of non-recognition, its injustice at the time of settlement and the tragic injustices that ensued. Many of the values which led to this recognition – such as equality before the law, and others – are often-repeated principles of our legal tradition itself. Others they took to be values of our contemporary community. These entered, and perhaps motivated, the decision, but they were not the whole of it. It was suffused with consideration of law which was far from merely ceremonial. Indeed, the ultimate modesty of the scope of that decision was derived from the existing law. The Court did not treat the modification of the law as a simple matter of invoking morality – as a legislature might – but wrestled with the bearing of the law as it was supposed to be, knowing that even in its own terms it had been based for 200 years on a mistake of fact and had authorized shocking injustice. Certainly the Court did not simply apply an existing rule, but it did not invent it out of thin air either. It did something noble and appropriate to a court, particularly a High Court. It did justice, not as the crow flies but in the context of existing law and as mediated by the law and legal values – and moral ones too. And, happily, although they shook a little, the heavens didn't fall.

Conclusion

Life and legal philosophy would be easier if one could identify a comprehensive and exceptionless set of mandatory meta-legal rules, such as those of ethical positivism, to allocate and determine the precise scope, limits and character of decision-making authority, wherever it occurs. The caricatured legal positivist (Keen, J) and legal realist (Handy, J) among the judges in Lon Fuller's *Case of the Speluncean Explorers*[66] subscribe to such meta-rules: one that the written law is all that matters in the tragic case before them, and the other that it doesn't matter at all. This makes their decisions easier than those of some of their more tortured fellow judges, but it also makes them less interesting and it doesn't necessarily make them more wise.

More generally, few of the real and difficult questions of institutional decision-making can be disposed of by such simple choices. They demand more complex combinations of textual and other considerations, and, since people disagree on what should be combined and how, these questions are destined to remain controversial. I suspect these controversies are, in principle, inescapable, since our institutional ambitions are not all of a piece. In any event, whatever the case in principle, one can confidently predict that such controversies will be perennial. We don't yet know much about how law best fulfils what we want of it, and even if we did we want many different things. The demands on our most significant institutions often pull in different directions. For example, even if – and it is a very big 'if' – it was clear that the requirements of institutional restraint and accountability were always best served by an order in which all non-elected institutions deferred fully and unexceptionally to unambiguous laws emanating from a centralized legislature, and even if we knew how to engineer such an exceptionless order, the character and conditions of competence of particular institutions faced with particular problems would remain more complex and variable. And in that domain, as Selznick has observed, 'in the contemporary situation, separation of spheres is no longer the key to political wisdom. The community needs all the help it can get, from institutions capable of making up for one another's deficiencies.'[67] It is unlikely that this need will diminish soon.

Notes

1 This chapter builds on an Australian Senate Occasional Lecture that I delivered in November, 1998 ('Fear, Hope, Politics and Law', *Papers on Parliament*, no. 33 (Canberra: Department of the Senate, Parliament House, 1999)). I am grateful to David Anderson, Arthur Glass, Owen Harries, Philip Pettit and Philip Selznick for their comments on that lecture and to the students in my class on 'Law between Fear and Hope' for helping me to work through some of the issues raised here. Tom Campbell's comments assisted me in reworking that lecture for inclusion in this book.

2 *The Legal Theory of Ethical Positivism* (Aldershot: Dartmouth, 1996), p. 13. See also at p. 41: '[w]hat we take law to be, and how we relate it to other aspects of society, is largely determined by a wider political philosophy.'

3 Ibid., p. 2.

4 Ibid., p. 41.

5 J. Shklar, 'The Liberalism of Fear', in N.L. Rosenblum (ed.), *Liberalism and the Moral Life* (Cambridge, MA: Harvard University Press, 1984), p. 5.

6 And arguably beyond liberalism, properly so-called. It figures centrally in a tradition that liberalism largely supplanted from the seventeenth century – republicanism. See Philip Pettit, *Republicanism: A Theory of Freedom and Government* (Oxford: Oxford University Press, 1997) and Quentin Skinner, *Liberty Before Liberalism* (Cambridge: Cambridge University Press, 1998). With one exception (below n. 19) in what follows I have not discussed the crucial distinction that Pettit and Skinner see between the republican (or, for Skinner, neo-roman) and liberal understandings of freedom and its relation to law. I don't believe that that distinction affects the arguments presented here, although a historically more scrupulous discussion might have to abandon Shklar's capacious notion of the 'liberalism of fear' and distinguish between republican and liberal approaches to fear and when, how and why it needs institutional containment.

7 See Shklar, 'The Liberalism of Fear', *op. cit.*, p. 8, citing Emerson's distinction between the 'party of memory' and the 'party of hope'.

8 Isaiah Berlin renders Kant's aphorism in these terms: 'out of the crooked timber of humanity no straight thing was ever made.' See his *The Crooked Timber of Humanity* (New York: Alfred A. Knopf, 1991).

9 Shklar, 'The Liberalism of Fear', *op. cit.*, p. 5.

10 Michael Ignatieff, *The Warrior's Honor. Ethnic War and the Modern Conscience* (New York: Metropolitan Books, 1998), p. 45.

11 Cf. John Locke, *Two Treatises of Government*, rev. edn, with introduction and notes by Peter Laslett (Cambridge: Cambridge University Press, 1965), p. 405.

12 Brennan and Hamlin characterize 'a central problem of politics – indeed, the central problem of politics ... as a form of principal-agent problem. Society must delegate powers to agents, but the agents cannot be trusted fully to act in the interests of the principals.' Geoffrey Brennan and Alan Hamlin, 'Constitutional Political Economy: The Political Economy of *Homo Economicus*', *The Journal of Political Economy* **3** (3) (1996), p. 296.

13 John Locke, *Two Treatises*, *op. cit.*, pp. 405–6.

14 Judith N. Shklar, 'Political Theory and the Rule of Law', in J.N. Shklar, *Political Thought and Political Thinkers*, ed. Stanley Hoffmann (Chicago: University of Chicago Press, 1998), p. 25.

15 E.P. Thompson, *Whigs and Hunters. The Origins of the Black Act* (Harmondsworth: Penguin), p. 266.

16 I have sought to explore the nature, complexity and consequences of some of these conditions in 'Institutional Optimism, Cultural Pessimism and the Rule of Law' in Martin Krygier and Adam Czarnota (eds), *The Rule of Law after Communism*, (Aldershot: Ashgate, 1999), pp. 77–105.

17 See Philip Selznick, 'Legal Cultures and the Rule of Law' in Martin Krygier and Adam Czarnota (eds), *The Rule of Law after Communism*, *op. cit.*, pp. 23–40.

18 Quoted in Philip Selznick, *The Moral Commonwealth*, (Berkeley: University of California Press, 1992) pp. 279–80.

19 This is the classical position of such writers as Benjamin Constant and Isaiah Berlin, for whom '[t]he answer to the question "Who governs me?" is logically distinct from the question "How far does government interfere with me?"': 'Two Concepts of Liberty', reprinted in *Four Essays on Liberty* (Oxford: Oxford University Press, 1969) p. 130. The first question, according to Berlin has to do with 'positive',

the second with 'negative' liberty. And, Berlin believes, the liberal is first of all committed to negative liberty. According to Pettit and Skinner, on the other hand, republican or 'neo-roman' thought saw liberty not merely as absence of interference, but *secure* absence; the opposite not merely of coercion by another but of domination by another, whether coercive or not and whether benign or not. That, so the argument goes on, is why slavery is always inconsistent with freedom, even if a slave-owner treats his slaves well. For he *could* do otherwise. Republican freedom requires that no one else have dominion over me, and for this to be possible I must have the right to control over decisions that affect me, however indirect practical constraints make that right. As Skinner expresses the neo-roman argument: 'From the perspective of the individual citizen, the alternatives are stark: unless you live under a system of self-government you will live as a slave': *Liberty Before Liberalism, op. cit.*, p. 76. See also Pettit, *Republicanism, op. cit., passim*.

20 This was implicit in the non-democratic ideal of the *Rechtsstaat* in nineteenth-century Prussia.

21 I have discussed one version of this criticism, that of the Critical Legal Studies movement, in 'Critical Legal Studies and Social Theory. A Response to Alan Hunt', *Oxford Journal of Legal Studies*, 7(1) (1987), pp. 26–39, and others, from within the Marxist tradition, in 'Marxism, Communism, and the Rule of Law', in Martin Krygier (ed.), *Marxism and Communism. Posthumous Reflections on Politics, Society, and Law*, Poznan Studies in the Philosophy of Sciences and the Humanities (Amsterdam and Atlanta, GA: Rodopi, 1994), pp. 135–68.

22 *The Federalist Papers*, no. 38, (New York: Mentor, 1961), p. 240.

23 *Between Fear and Hope: Hybrid Thoughts on Public Values* (Sydney: ABC Books, 1997), ch. 5.

24 Cf. Antonin Scalia, 'The Rule of Law as a Law of Rules', *University of Chicago Law Review*, **56** (1989), p. 1175. This is the central theme of Tom Campbell's *The Legal Theory of Ethical Positivism*. Campbell's 'ethical positivism' is 'an aspirational model of law according to which it is a presumptive condition of the legitimacy of governments that they function through the medium of specific rules capable of being identified and applied by citizens and officials without recourse to contentious personal or group political presuppositions, beliefs and commitments' (p. 2).

25 Joseph Raz, *Practical Reasons and Norms* (London: Hutchinson, 1975), pp. 15–84. Although this is Raz's conception of mandatory rules, what follows is not his conception of the role of the judge. However, it is Tom Campbell's (see *Ethical Positivism, op. cit.*, chs 1 and 3), since he insists on the '"prescriptive separation thesis" according to which the identification and application of law ought to be kept as separate as possible from the moral judgments which go into the making of law' (p. 3). And see also p. 5: 'a system of law ought to be a system of rules. Further, the rules in question must be "real" rules, that is rules which have, in Raz's term, "exclusionary force".'

26 Although this is not precisely Campbell's view. *Ethical Positivism* does not allow recourse to purposes 'ulterior' to those which emerge from the words of legislation or the 'intent' such words convey, and certainly not purposes which could conflict with those words. However, Campbell does condone judges, in circumstances of ambiguity or uncertainty, interpreting those words in the light of 'overt and publicly stated purposes' (p. 9) which can be drawn from 'a contextual understanding of the rules themselves' (p. 7), 'the purpose as stated in the legislation or the politically authenticated statement of the legitimating purpose of the law in question' (p. 143). Nevertheless, '[o]nly when there is a failure of communication between legislator and subject is a direct use of legislative purpose relevant to the regulatory process' (p. 147). See also pp. 87–91, esp. 109–17 on the 'technique and ... ethic of judging' and Chapter 6.

27 See F.A. Hayek, *Law, Legislation and Liberty*, vol. 1 (Chicago: University of

Chicago Press, 1973); vol. 2 (1974); vol. 3 (1979); Eugene Kamenka and Alice Erh-Soon Tay, 'Beyond Bourgeois Individualism – The Contemporary Crisis in Law and Legal Ideology' in Eugene Kamenka and R.S. Neale (eds), *Feudalism, Capitalism and Beyond* (Canberra and London: ANU Press, 1975), pp. 127–44; Theodore J. Lowi, 'The Welfare State, the New Regulation, and the Rule of Law', in Allan C. Hutchinson and Patrick Monahan (eds), *The Rule of Law. Ideal or Ideology* (Toronto: Carswell, 1987), pp. 17–58; Geoffrey de Q. Walker, *The Rule of Law* (Melbourne: Melbourne University Press, 1988).

28 See Campbell, *Ethical Positivism*, *op. cit.*, p. 9: 'LEP is opposed to the extensive use of judicial or administrative discretion directed only by general standards.'

29 See ibid., pp. 8–9; Tom Campbell, 'The Point of Legal Positivism', *The Kings College Law Journal*, **9** (1998–99), pp. 63–87.

30 Ibid., p. 134.

31 'The Point of Legal Positivism', 85–6, *op. cit.*, pp. 63–7; Campbell, *Ethical Positivism*, *op. cit.*, pp. 4, 29, ch. 7.

32 Campbell, *Ethical Positivism*, *op. cit.*, p. 20.

33 Ibid., p. 69.

34 'The Point of Legal Positivism', *op. cit.*, pp. 65–6.

35 For a forceful argument on this and related points, see Jeremy Waldron, 'A Rights-Based Critique of Constitutional Rights' in *Oxford Journal of Legal Studies*, **13** (1) (1993), pp. 18–51.

36 For an exaggerated, repetitive, self-indulgent, and often dazzling, series of essays which frequently make this point, see Stanley Fish, *Doing What Comes Naturally* (Durham, NC: Duke University Press, 1989).

37 See Cass Sunstein, *Legal Reasoning and Political Conflict* (Oxford: Oxford University Press).

38 See Ronald Dworkin, *Law's Empire* (Cambridge, MA: Harvard University Press, 1986); *Freedom's Law: The Moral Reading of the American Constitution* (Cambridge, MA: Harvard University Press, 1995).

39 Max Weber, *The Protestant Ethic and the Spirit of Capitalism* (London: Unwin, 1971), p. 25.

40 Ibid.

41 Max Weber, *Economy and Society*, vol. 2 (New York: Bedminster Press, 1968), p. 890.

42 Ibid., p. 891.

43 Ibid., p. 892.

44 Max Weber, *The Religion of China* (New York: Free Press, 1964), p. 102.

45 *The Decent Society* (Cambridge, MA: Harvard University Press, 1996), p. 283. Margalit has another illustration of the theory, with which many might find it possible to empathize: 'St. Paul believed that the human ideal for men is celibacy. But if someone has strong desires, he had better not remain a bachelor, trying to fornicate as little as possible and thus coming as close to the ideal even if he can never actually reach it. It would be better for him to get married.'

46 See Philippe Nonet and Philip Selznick, *Law and Society in Transition. Toward Responsive Law* (New York: Octagon Books, 1978), pp. 18–27, 'A Developmental Model'.

47 Selznick, *The Moral Commonwealth*, *op. cit.*, p. 335. As he writes elsewhere: 'there is or should be a dual focus on *baselines* and *flourishings*. We hold fast to the vital minimum even as we reach for the more subtle, more elaborated, more problematic ideal. Without protection of baseline values and procedures, the rule of law loses focus, obscured in a utopian plea for a world untainted by power or authority. This is the danger in radical criticisms of "liberal legalism". The criticisms are useful insofar as they show how the classical rule-of-law model undermines solidarity and delivers a cramped, impoverished justice. Such criticisms are misplaced,

however, insofar as they lose purchase on the need for elementary constraints on the abuse of power.

'There is nothing strange or exotic about the dual concern I recommend. It follows a familiar logic. In parenting and education, for example, we cannot act responsibly if we fail to address foundational needs for nurture, stimulation, and discipline, as well as elementary expectations with regard to learning and character. But we would fail as parents and educators if we did not encourage and support more complex virtues and higher competencies.' 'Legal Cultures and the Rule of Law' *op. cit.*, p. 34.

48 Campbell, *Ethical Positivism, op. cit.*, p. 9.

49 Campbell mentions some reasons summarily in ibid., p. 62 ff. However, of the reasons that matter to me, only a few are noted and even they are swiftly passed by rather than dealt with directly or in any depth (see p. 62, para. 2).

50 Weber, *Economy and Society*, vol. 2, *op. cit.*, p. 891.

51 For an excellent discussion of how the law filters into the world, see Marc Galanter, 'Justice in Many Rooms: Courts, Private Ordering, and Indigenous Law', *Journal of Legal Pluralism*, **19** (1981), pp. 1–47. As Galanter observes, '[t]he mainstream of legal scholarship has tended to look out from within the official legal order, abetting the pretensions of the official law to stand in a relationship of hierarchic control to other normative orderings in society. Social research on law has been characterized by a repeated rediscovery of the other hemisphere of the legal world. This has entailed recurrent rediscovery that law in modern society is plural rather than monolithic, that it is private as well as public in character and that the national (public, official) legal system is often a secondary rather than a primary locus of regulation' (p. 20).

52 A phrase from the seminal article by Sally Falk Moore, 'Law and Social Change: The Semi-autonomous Social Field as an Appropriate Subject of Study', in *Law as Process. An Anthropological Approach* (London: Routledge and Kegan Paul, 1978), pp. 54–81.

53 Eugene Bardach and Robert Kagan, *Going by the Book* (Philadelphia: Temple University Press, 1982).

54 Ibid., p. 100.

55 Carol Heimer, 'Legislating Responsibility', American Bar Foundation Working Paper No. 9711, p. 11.

56 Ibid., p. 13.

57 Bardach and Kagan, *Going by the Book, op. cit.*, p. 321.

58 See Geoffrey Brennan, 'Institutionalizing Accountability: Comments on the Evans, Niland and Braithwaite Papers', unpublished ms.

59 'The Routinization of Responsiveness: Regulatory Compliance and the Construction of Organizational Routines', American Bar Foundation Working Paper No. 9801, pp. 6, 7.

60 John Braithwaite and Valerie Braithwaite, 'The Politics of Legalism: Rules versus Standards in Nursing-Home Regulation', *Social and Legal Studies*, **4** (1995), pp. 336–7.

61 Campbell, *Ethical Positivism, op. cit.*, p. 6.

62 I have sought to make this general point at some length in '*The Concept of Law* and Social Theory', *Oxford Journal of Legal Studies*, 2(2) (1982), pp. 155–80.

63 Selznick, *The Moral Commonwealth, op. cit.*, pp. 436–7.

64 (1992) 175 CLR, 1.

65 *Wik Peoples* v. *Queensland* (1996) 187 CLR 1.

66 (1949) 62 *Harvard Law Review*, pp. 616–45.

67 Selznick, *The Moral Commonwealth, op. cit.*, p. 474.

4 Feminist Perspectives on Ethical Positivism

NICOLA LACEY[1]

In this chapter I shall address the affinities and points of conflict between feminist approaches to legal theory and the account of 'ethical positivism' provided by Tom Campbell in his book, *The Legal Theory of Ethical Positivism*.[2] As Campbell notes, for much feminist and critical legal theory, legal positivism represents the arch-enemy: it is characterized (or perhaps caricatured) as a formalistic approach which disguises the sexual politics of law and legal reasoning behind a quasi-scientific, purportedly value-neutral framework.[3] Campbell's claim is that this typecasting of legal positivism – if it is just at all – does not apply to the legal theory of ethical positivism. In order to assess this claim, I need to start with some conceptual ground-clearing. After offering a characterization of feminist legal theory, I shall attempt to unpick the various strands of its objections to legal positivism before going on to consider how far, if at all, each of these objections holds good as against ethical positivism. Finally, I shall identify a number of difficulties which remain to be confronted by the doctrine of ethical positivism – difficulties which are not exclusively revealed by feminist thought, but rather by a range of methods deriving from sociology and recent social theory on which feminists, among other (loosely speaking) 'critical' scholars, have drawn. In constructing this analysis I hope not only to provide a sympathetic critical assessment of Campbell's theory, but also to clarify the ambitions of feminist legal theory and its relationship with what might generally be thought of as 'mainstream' jurisprudence and political theory.

Feminist Legal Theory

I need to begin by saying something about what I mean by 'feminist legal theory'. There are two questions here. First, what do I mean by 'feminist *legal theory*' as opposed to 'feminist criticism of particular laws'? The two are, of course, rather different. One does not need to have a feminist theory of law to hold that, for example, the law of rape operates in objectionable ways from a feminist point of view. Feminist legal theory makes the more radical argument that there is something not merely about particular laws or sets of laws, but rather, and more generally, about the very structure or method of modern law, which is gendered. To most lawyers this is a far more counterintuitive claim than that of sexist bias in particular laws. It is, however, central to any strong feminist theory of law.

But this is to say only something very vague about what makes a 'legal theory' *feminist*. It is crucial to acknowledge from the outset – and this is an inevitable difficulty with the kind of enterprise which I am undertaking in this chapter – that to refer to 'feminist legal theory' is to gather together a set of heterogeneous approaches. In the face of this significant diversity, I shall simply set out from an inclusive conception of feminist legal theory as proceeding from two foundational claims and as characterized by a particular methodological orientation. First, at an analytic and indeed sociological level, and on the basis of a wide range of research in a number of disciplines, feminist legal theorists take sex/gender to be one important social structure or discourse. Feminists hence claim that sex/gender characterizes the shape of law as one important social institution. Analytically, therefore, feminist legal theory aspires to provide a more sophisticated conception of law than can theories which ignore the influence of sex/gender. Second, at a normative or political level, feminist legal theorists claim that the ways in which sex/gender has shaped the legal realm are presumptively politically and ethically problematic, in that sex/gender is an axis not merely of differentiation but also of discrimination, domination or oppression. Normatively, therefore, feminist legal theory aspires to produce both a reasoned critique of current legal arrangements and – in some versions – a positive version of how law might be constructed in ways which move towards ideals of sex equality or gender justice. Although not all feminist legal theorists endorse a utopian project, the critical reconstruction of ideas of equality, justice and rights has been one of the most persistent preoccupations of feminist legal and political thought.[4] Finally, at a methodological level, feminist legal theorists are almost universally committed to a social constructionist stance: in other words, to the idea that the power and meaning of sex/gender is a product not of nature but of culture. Feminist legal theorists are hence of the view that gender relations are, in principle, open to revision through the modification of powerful social institutions such as law.

Feminism and Positivism

Even this brief account provides grounds for a certain degree of bemusement about the common feminist antipathy to positivism understood as the separation of law and morality. At first sight, there is nothing in legal positivism which cuts either way on the first, analytic/sociological claim; nor, secondly, would a rigorous positivist separation of the identification of law from its moral assessment rule out either feminist critique or feminist reformism. Indeed, what we might call the 'contentlessness' of legal positivism – its view of law as a sociopolitical construct which can be filled with more or less any regulatory, coordinating or expressive substance – seems generally sympathetic to feminist ideas. The idea that positive law cannot *in principle* be reconstructed in terms more acceptable from the point of view of feminist ethics seem an odd form of what we might call 'legal essentialism'. How, then, are we to account for feminist theorists' general lack of engagement with contemporary legal positivism,[5] let alone for their tendency to hold positivism up as the archetype of everything which feminist legal scholarship rejects?

In order to explain this stance, we need to look more closely both at genres of feminist legal theory and at the various strands of legal positivism. Within the broad conception of feminist theory which I have sketched, it is worth distinguishing two main schools of feminist legal thought. The first, which might be called 'liberal feminism', like mainstream legal theory, is both committed to the ideals of gender neutrality and equality before the law and assumes that they are, in principle, able to be achieved. Its focus is primarily instrumental, seeing law as a tool of feminist strategy, and the impact of law as a basis for feminist critique. The second approach, which I shall label 'difference feminism', is shaped by an analysis of the limits of liberal feminism;[6] it is sceptical about the possibility of neutrality and, in some of its forms, even rejects neutrality as an ideal. It has an implicit commitment to a more complex idea of equality which accommodates and values, whilst not fixing, women's specificity 'as women'; and it has a focus on the symbolic and dynamic aspects of law rather than just on its instrumental aspects.[7] Clearly, there is no real tension between liberal feminism and legal positivism. However, difference feminism demands not only that we analyse the sexual politics of current legal arrangements, but also that we amend or even think beyond certain aspects of the epistemological and political framework which informs most positivist legal theory. In what follows I shall therefore concentrate on the implications of this more radical approach to feminist legal theory – difference feminism – for the tenets of positivist legal scholarship and theory. In so doing, I do not mean to imply that I find all aspects of difference feminism persuasive. What I do maintain is that difference feminism poses a challenge to the framework of conventional legal scholarship which is of sufficient intellectual power to demand a meticulous and reasoned response.

The Feminist Challenge to Positivist Legal Scholarship

Over the last 15 years, a number of important intellectual movements such as 'law in context' 'socio-legal studies' and 'critical legal studies' have begun to reshape the approach of legal scholarship. Notwithstanding their influence, the orientation of most legal research (and indeed of legal education) remains broadly positivist. By this I mean simply that it assumes the existence of a relatively discrete social phenomenon – law – and sees itself as imparting both knowledge of particular laws and techniques through which we can broaden and use this knowledge in intellectual and practical contexts. Furthermore, in so far as law texts reach beyond the description and analysis of law, they tend to do so by contextualizing that analysis within a set of broadly liberal ideas which are thought to inform legal arrangements in modern societies such as Australia and Britain. I therefore want to single out a number of assumptions common to positivistic and liberal legal scholarship which are the target of feminist critique of the sex/gender bias of law and legal method. These various points are closely interwoven, but it is useful to separate them out in order to prepare the ground for our analysis of their implications for the legal theory of ethical positivism.

The Neutral Framework of Legal Reasoning

The first target of feminist critique is positivism's assumption of the neutrality of the framework of legal reasoning. A central tenet of both positivist scholarship and the liberal ideal of the rule of law is that laws set up standards which may be applied in a neutral manner to formally equal parties. The questions of inequality and power which may affect the capacity of those parties to engage effectively in legal reasoning has featured little in either mainstream legal theory or legal education. These questions have, on the other hand, always been central to critical (originally Marxist) legal theory, and they find an important place within feminist legal thought. In particular, the work of social psychologist Carol Gilligan[8] on varying ways of constructing moral problems, and the relationship of these variations to gender, has opened up a striking argument about the possible 'masculinity' of the very process of legal reasoning.

As is widely known, Gilligan's research was motivated by the 'finding' of psychological research that men reach, on average, a 'higher' level of moral development than do women. Gilligan set out to investigate the neutrality of the tests being applied: she also engaged in empirical research designed to illuminate the ways in which different people construct moral problems. Her research elicited two main approaches to moral reasoning. The first, which Gilligan calls the 'ethic of rights', proceeds in an essentially legalistic way: it formulates rules which structure the values at issue, works out a hierarchical ordering between the rules, and then applies the rules to the facts. The second, which Gilligan calls the 'ethic of care or responsibility', takes a more holistic approach to moral problems, exploring the context and relationships, as well as the values, involved, and producing a more complex, but less conclusive, analysis. The tests on which psychologists have conventionally assessed moral development were based on the ethic of rights: analyses proceeding from the ethic of care were hence deemed morally underdeveloped. It was therefore significant that Gilligan's fieldwork suggested that these two types were gender-related, in that girls tended to adopt the care perspective, whilst boys more often adopted the rights approach.

Gilligan's assertion of the relationship between the two models and gender is controversial. Nonetheless, her analytical distinction between the two ethics is of great potential significance for legal theory because of its implication that the distinctive structure of legal reasoning may systematically silence the voices of those who speak the language of relationships.[9] The rights model is, as I have already observed, reminiscent of law: it works from a clear hierarchy of sources which are reasoned through in a formally logical way. The more contextual, care or relationship-oriented model would, by contrast, be harder to capture by legal frameworks, within which holistic or relationally-oriented reasoning tends to sound 'woolly' or legally incompetent, or is rendered legally irrelevant by substantive and evidential rules – indeed, by the positivist insistence on the exclusive relevance of formal legal sources and technical modes of reasoning.

There are, however, several important problems with some of the arguments deriving from Gilligan's research.[10] In the first place, examples such as the foundational role of a 'duty of care' in generating rights in the modern law of torts appear to subvert the dichotomy between rights and care as legal/ethical frameworks.[11] Furthermore, the fact that the contours of the duty of care and its concomitant 'neighbour principle' are clearly susceptible of feminist critique serves as a reminder that a switch to the framework of 'care' is no guarantee either that women's interests will be properly considered or that sex/gender will be legally construed in progressive ways. Second, a different way of reading the implications for law of Gilligan's approach is that legal issues – indeed, the conceptualization of legal subjects themselves – should be recast in less formal and abstract terms. However, such a strategy of recontextualization may obscure the (sometimes damaging) ways in which legal subjects are already contextualized.[12] In the sentencing of offenders, or in the assumptions on which victims and defendants are treated in rape cases, for instance, we have some clear examples of effective contextualization which cuts in several political directions – most of them unappealing to feminists. In certain areas, legal reasoning may already be 'relational' in the sense espoused by many feminists, except that it privileges certain kinds of relationships – for example, proprietary, object relations.[13] A general call for 'contextualization' may also be based on naive assumptions about the power of such a strategy to generate real change, given surrounding power relations: as rape trials show all too clearly, the framework of legal doctrine is not the only formative context shaping the legal process.

Nonetheless, I would argue that Gilligan's work has been of crucial importance in directing our attention to the particular assumptions upon which legal subjects are conceived in the courtroom, in legislation and elsewhere. Recontextualization understood not as reformist strategy but rather as critique – in other words, the development of a critical analysis which unearths the logic, the substantive assumptions, underlying law's current contextualization of its subjects, and which can hence illuminate the interests and relationships which these arrangements privilege – is a central tool of the most persuasive feminist legal theory. The question therefore arises as to whether legal positivism can accommodate such a critique. At the very least, it has to be admitted that the critique poses questions in which legal positivists have shown remarkably little interest. More radically, it seems that positivists could not develop such an interest without substantially modifying the *analytic* presupposition that legal reasoning is neutral. This connects with a point which I shall take up in more detail in later parts of this chapter: that of whether we can attain an adequate understanding of the dynamics of legal decision-making by focusing on law as exclusively a system of rules.

Law's Autonomy and Discreteness

Feminists also question law's autonomy and discreteness. It is a standard assumption of positivist legal scholarship that law is a relatively autonomous social practice, discrete from politics, ethics and religion. An extreme expression of this assumption is found in the conception of legal science elaborated in Hans Kelsen's 'pure' theory of law,[14] but weaker versions inform the entire positivist tradition. Indeed, this is what sets up one of positivism's recurring problems – namely, the question of foundations, of the boundaries between the legal and the non-legal, of the source of legal authority, and the relationship between law and justice.[15]

This mainstream assumption, like the idea that legal method is discrete or distinctive, is challenged by feminist legal theory. Feminist theory seeks to reveal the ways in which law reflects, reproduces, expresses, constructs and reinforces power relations along sexually patterned lines. In so doing, it questions law's claims to autonomy and represents law as a continuous practice into which deeper social, political and economic forces constantly seep. Hence the ideals of the rule of law call for modification and, in some versions, are reinterpreted as ideologies rather than ideals, let alone realities. As E.P. Thompson's reminder of the real, yet limited, impact of the rule of law serves to illustrate, there are strong continuities here between the feminist and the Marxist traditions in legal thought.[16]

Law's Neutrality and Objectivity

Feminist scholarship has raised questions about law's pretension to objectivity. As I have already mentioned, difference feminism has questioned the very idea of gender neutrality, of gender equality before the law, in a sexually patterned world. Furthermore, feminist legal theory questions law's claims to be enunciating truths, its pretension to neutral or objective judgement, and its constitution of a field of discrete and unassailable knowledge.

This argument takes a number of forms in contemporary feminist legal theory. One derives from the Foucauldian critique of feminist writers such as Carol Smart.[17] The argument is that law, by policing is own boundaries via its substantive rules and rules of evidence, constitutes itself as self-contained – as a self-reproducing system.[18] There is hence – as systems theory argues in some detail – a certain 'truth' to this aspect of law. But by standing back so as to cast light on the point of view from which law's truth is being constructed, we can undermine law's claims to objectivity. Another example is Catharine MacKinnon's well-known epistemological argument.[19] In MacKinnon's view, law constructs knowledge which claims objectivity, but objectivity expresses a male point of view. Hence 'objective' standards in civil and criminal law – the 'reasonable person' – in fact represent a position which is specific in not only gender but also class, ethnic and other terms. The epistemological assertion of 'knowledge' or 'objectivity' disguises this process of construction, and writes sexually specific bodies out of the text of law. The project of feminism is to replace them. The difficult trick is to do so without fixing their shape and identity within received categories of masculine and feminine. Thus not all feminists endorse the idea of abandoning 'reasonableness' tests or the appeal to otherwise universal standards, and argue instead for a reinterpretation of what equality or universality requires.[20] Here, as we shall see later, lies another point of potential affinity between feminist and ethical positivism.

Law's Centrality

In stark contrast to not only a great deal of positivist legal scholarship but also much 'law and society' work, some feminist writers have questioned law's importance or centrality to the constitution of social relations and the struggle to change those relations. Clearly, feminist views diverge here. Catharine MacKinnon, for example, is optimistic about using law for radical purposes; indeed Campbell cites the campaign for anti-pornography ordinances mounted by MacKinnon and Andrea Dworkin as an instance of feminist ethical positivism.[21] But many other feminists – notably British feminist Carol Smart – have questioned the wisdom of placing great reliance on law and of putting law at the centre of our critical analysis. Perhaps this is partly a cultural difference: the British women's movement has typically been relatively anti-institutional and confrontational. Yet even in the USA and in Australia, where there are stronger traditions of reformist legal activism, feminists associated with critical legal studies have been notably cautious about claims advanced in some critical legal scholarship[22] about law's central role in constituting social relations. Feminists have thus tended further towards a classical Marxist orientation on this question than have their non-feminist critical counterparts. In terms of analytic focus, however, this has led feminists to address a range of social institutions – the family, sexuality, the political realm, bureaucracies – well beyond the Marxist terrain of political economy. Feminist writers continue to be ambivalent about whether and how law ought to be deployed as a tool of feminist action, practice and strategy.[23] To the extent that feminist critique identifies law as implicated in the construction of existing gender relations, how far can it be used to change them, and do strategic attempts to use law risk the danger of reaffirming the power of a social institution which is structurally biased against women's interests?

Law as a System of Enacted Norms or Rules

Feminist legal theory typically reaches beyond a conception of law as a system of norms or rules derived from statutes, constitutions and cases – and beyond 'standard' legal officials, such as judges – to encompass other practices which are legally relevant or 'quasi-legal'. For example, the Oslo School of Women's Law had its main focus on administrative and regulatory bodies such as social welfare agencies and the medical system.[24] This reorientation is born of a very basic socio-legal insight: that the power and social meaning of law are determined not only at its legislative, doctrinal and judicial levels but also by a myriad non-legal, or partially legal, decisions about its interpretation and enforcement.

In some of its versions this institutional refocusing is informed by Michel Foucault's reconceptualization of power – a reconceptualization which has important implications for law.[25] Foucault distinguished between sovereignty power – power as a property or possession – juridical power and disciplinary power – the relational power which inheres in particular practices and which flows unseen throughout the 'social body'. His argument was that the later modern world was gradually seeing the growth of subtle, intangible, disciplinary power, at the expense of both the old sovereignty and the modern juridical power. Foucault was therefore inclined to think that law was waning in importance as a form of social governance. Carol Smart, however, has used his argument about power in relation to law in a different way by arguing that law itself embodies disciplinary power. For one of the distinguishing features of disciplinary power is its subtly normalizing effect and, as soon as we look beyond a narrow vision of law as a system of rules backed up by sanctions, we begin to see that one of law's functions is precisely to distribute its subjects with disciplinary precision around a mean or norm.

For example, the way in which legal rules and, crucially, their interpretation distribute social welfare benefits or allocate custody of children (on divorce or via adoption) reflects judgements about the right way to live; it expresses assumptions about 'normality'. A yet more spectacular example is that of the construction of gay and straight sexualities in criminal laws and in family and social welfare legislation. These 'normalizing' assumptions have a pervasive power which also structures the administration of laws – for example, of social welfare benefits and policing policies – at the bureaucratic level, generating phenomena such as reluctance to prosecute in 'domestic violence' cases, the oppressive policing of gay sexuality and the discriminatory administration of welfare benefits. Feminist (like other critical) analyses are interested here in not just legal doctrine but also legal discourse – in other words, how differently sexed legal subjects are constituted by, and inserted within, legal categories via the mediation of judicial, bureaucratic, police or lawyers' discourse. Feminist approaches therefore mount a fundamental challenge to the standard ways of conceptualizing law and the legal, and move to a broader understanding of legally relevant spheres of social practice.[26]

Law's Unity and Coherence

Feminists have questioned law's unity and coherence. Readers of both student texts and legal cases will be familiar with the very high importance attached by lawyers and legal commentators to the idea (or ideal) of law as a unitary and a coherent system of rules or norms. It is an idea which informs legal theory in a number of ways. Once again, Kelsen provides a spectacular example: his *Grundnorm* had to be hypothesized precisely because otherwise it would have been impossible to interpret law as a coherent, non-contradictory normative field of meaning. As a law student, one of the first things one is taught to do is to home in on contradictory or inconsistent arguments. The idea of coherence as the idea (or ideal) which lies at the heart of law finds its fullest expression in Ronald Dworkin's idea of 'law as integrity',[27] but it is also voiced in procedurally-oriented ethical and political theories – notably in critical theory of the Frankfurt School.[28]

Feminist scholarship, like much other critical legal theory, questions this belief in law's coherence and reconstructs the pretension to coherence as part of the ideology of both law and jurisprudence – as part of what helps represent law as authoritative, adjudication as democratically legitimate and so on. The critical analysis of contradictions, and the unearthing of what have been called 'dangerous supplements' and hidden agendas, takes place both at the level of doctrine and at that of discourse.[29]

To take some specific examples, the assertion within legal doctrine of particular questions or issues as within public or private spheres is contradictory, question-begging and underdetermined: sexuality, for example, is public for some purposes and private for others.[30] The idea of the legal subject as rational and as abstracted from its social context is undermined by exceptions such as defences in criminal law, shifts of timeframe in the casting of legal questions, and an arbitrary division of issues pertaining to conviction and those pertaining to sentence.[31] In contract law, one could cite shifts between a freedom of contract model and a model which views contract as a long-term relationship within which, for example, loss occasioned by the parties' general reliance upon the contractual relationship can be recognized and compensated.[32] Nor are these instances of incoherence confined to the doctrinal framework: they also mark the discourse through which human subjects are inserted into that structure. For example, the rational and controlled male of legal subjectivity is also the rape defendant who is vulnerable to feminine wiles and who is, on occasion, incapable of distinguishing 'yes' from 'no'. The unearthing of such contradictions is not just a matter of 'trashing': it forms part of an intellectual and political strategy – of exposing law's indeterminacy, of emphasizing its contingency, and of finding resources for its reconstruction in those doctrinal principles and discursive images which are less dominant yet which fracture and complicate the seamless web imagined by much legal scholarship.

Law's Rationality

Finally, feminist legal theory has questioned law's rationality. It has been argued that contradictions and indeterminacy in legal doctrine undermine law's supposed grounding in reason, just as the smuggling in of contextual and affective factors undermines law's apparent construction of the subject as rational, self-interested actor. Furthermore, in so far as law is successful in maintaining its self-image as a rational enterprise, this is because the emotional and affective aspects of legal practice are systematically repressed in jurisprudential and doctrinal representations. Once one reads cases and other legal texts not only for their formal meaning but also as rhetoric, one sees how values and techniques which are not acknowledged on the surface of legal doctrine are in fact crucial to the way in which cases are decided.[33] There is connection here with the arguments deriving from Gilligan's work which were rehearsed above. The link consists in the important question as to whether it is possible to accommodate within legal decision-making non-rational – emotive, affective, evaluative – factors while continuing to espouse, as an aspiration, the rationality of legal processes. Once again, the potential link with ethical positivism should be apparent.

Differentiating the Legal Theory of Ethical Positivism

These, then, are the principal ways in which feminist legal theory has challenged the tenets of positivist legal scholarship. But how, specifically, do they apply to Campbell's ethical positivism? Essentially, Campbell's theory is a political theory: it is a normative theory about the distribution of (broadly speaking) political power, albeit a normative theory which makes some important assumptions about the *possible* character of law and legal reasoning.[34] At risk of gross oversimplification, the argument is that, in democratic societies, there *ought* to be a separation of the legal from the political spheres, with the legislature specifying the content and rationale of laws with sufficient precision to enable impartial legal decision-makers to engage in what we might crudely call applicative rather than creative, non-evaluative rather than value-laden, interpretation. In Campbell's own words:

> ... a good legal system is, inter alia, one in which adjudicators use only empirical or, more broadly, morally neutral criteria in their identification *and interpretation* of laws, and one in which legislators enact laws which can be so identified *and interpreted*.[35]

The theory thus assumes (and gives some arguments for) the feasibility of law as a system of rules; it prefers legislative rules over a common law system. Notwithstanding its ethical eclecticism, it is in these important respects a theory of which Jeremy Bentham would have approved. Indeed, one might say that the nub of Campbell's argument, as of Bentham's, is that a legal positivist stance is a necessary component of any genuinely democratic politics.[36]

Does ethical positivism encounter the same objections as classical positivism from the point of view of difference feminism? Ethical positivism has one cardinal advantage over its earlier counterparts, such as H.L.A. Hart's concept of law as a system of rules.[37] This is quite simply the degree to which it is explicit about its normative stance. This allows Campbell to argue that ethical positivism is an attractive framework for feminism, because feminism's critique of positivism is directed to its descriptive adequacy rather than its normative appeal.

The explicit normative orientation of ethical positivism has two distinct advantages from a feminist point of view. First, it avoids the feminist argument about (at least part of) the unacknowledged politics of legal theory. Second, it deliberately opens up a space for feminist (and other) critique not only of particular laws but also of systematic failures to achieve the key aspirations of impartiality, rationality and accountability in the administration of justice. By reinterpreting internal claims to truth, objectivity, coherence and rationality rather as foundational *aspirations* of a modern legal order, the legal theory of ethical positivism distances itself from what has been criticized as the 'ideological' status of classical positivism.[38] In so doing, it clears the way for debate about whether the ideals in question are either desirable or reasonably practicable – a debate to which, of course, the feminist tradition in legal scholarship contributes.

There are other points of contact between feminism and ethical positivism, too. It is fair to say that feminist legal theorists have generally been slower to espouse a radical indeterminacy thesis in relation to legal interpretation than have some of their critical legal counterparts (particularly the Americans). This is largely because, as Campbell sees,[39] such a position threatens to cut the ground from under the critical movement itself. Although few, if any, feminist legal theorists would accept that rules straightforwardly determine outcomes, the orientation of feminist legal scholarship to detailed analyses of particular areas of legal regulation has generated insights into the ways in which specific legal arrangements, rules and doctrines do constrain decision-making in particular ways (and are hence worth changing). Moreover, in its explicit open-mindedness about the importance of law as a regulatory strategy,[40] ethical positivism may also have some affinities with feminists' reservations about a too-ready espousal of law either as a reformist tool or as an analytic focus for social theory. Many feminists would also find common cause with both Campbell's preference for relatively particular legislation and his trenchantly constructionist approach to rights.[41]

There is therefore much plausibility in Campbell's claim that ethical positivism works well as a model for instrumental feminist legal reformism. But can it accommodate the critique elaborated by difference feminism? Can the empirical and analytic aspects of the model of law and adjudication to which ethical positivism aspires (and which it assumes to be, in principle, achievable), provide a sufficiently rich and open framework to accommodate an analysis of the sexual politics of law? Does ethical positivism make explicit everything which a feminist would label 'political'?

Impartiality and Universality

As I hope will already be clear from my characterization of the feminist engagement with positivist legal theory, a number of difficulties remain to be confronted and debated. The first question has to do with ethical positivism's strong assumptions about the possible neutrality or universality of the framework of legal reasoning and about the nature of impartiality and objectivity as ideal features of the process and (in some sense) outcomes of judicial reasoning. Many feminists would certainly be sympathetic both to Campbell's reservations about the use to which Gilligan's work has been put in criticizing the adversarial model of rule-based legal reasoning and to his emphasis on the importance of social context to the conduct of judicial reasoning.[42] There is, however, room for doubt about the reliance which he places, in arguing for the plausibility of a generally (and genuinely) apolitical judicial role, on the availability of 'contextually evident meanings'.[43] For, as Campbell himself acknowledges, the pluralism of late modern societies entails the proliferation of subcommunities of meaning. In this context, it is not merely the theoretical discourse of postmodernism, to which Campbell quite often refers, but also the social conditions of postmodernity, which pose a challenge to the plausibility of his claims.[44] At the very least, it seems that diverse subcommunities of meaning would have to be properly represented both on the judicial bench and in other legally relevant fora if we were to have any confidence in the impartiality of legal reasoning.

In the view of many feminists, moreover, the difficulty about impartiality cannot necessarily be overcome merely by ensuring proportionate representation in decision-making fora. To see what further questions need to be placed on the agenda of legal and political theory, I want to consider three somewhat different feminist engagements with the theoretical underpinnings of the ideals of impartiality and universality. Each of these engagements stops short of a radical postmodernism which would decisively reject the aspirations and empirical assumptions of ethical positivism. They are approaches which espouse much of the critique of difference feminism yet which nonetheless imply that there is scope for a substantial dialogue with ethical positivism. As I shall try to show, however, they also imply that ethical positivism's conceptions of impartiality and neutrality in adjudication require more complex and wide-ranging argument than that provided by Campbell.

My first example is drawn from feminist philosopher Seyla Benhabib, whose work is located within the modernist tradition of discourse ethics. In a justly famous article, Benhabib argued that the key difficulty with liberalism lies not in its egoistic conception of the subject but rather in its abstract conception of moral and political reasoning. For Benhabib, the core of Gilligan's insight is that the 'concrete, embodied other', as differentiated from the 'generalized, abstract other', has been excluded from legal, moral and political reasoning.[45] For example, the thought experiment of a Rawlsian original position (as defended in his earlier work[46]) can generate neither universalizable conclusions nor a comprehensible notion of human individuation, for its ontological and epistemological bases are at odds with the moral and practical structure of the human condition. Its sublimation of concrete human selves into a single subject position needs to be replaced by a more substantially participatory community of discourse and debate (in the style of Habermas or, perhaps, the later Rawls[47]). Practical reasoning is inevitably situated in the concrete as well as aspiring to the universal; hence social decision-making must be located in a deliberative framework which recognizes human differences and particularities. When these are theorized out of the picture, the chance of genuine reciprocity also disappears, for perspectives can only genuinely be reversed when their distinctness is recognized. This leads Benhabib in the direction of 'an interactive universalism [which] acknowledges that every generalized other is also a concrete other'.[48] Benhabib's work is of particular interest because, while sympathetic to some of the key claims of difference feminism, she argues for a reinterpretation, rather than a rejection, of modern ideals such as universality and impartiality under conditions of postmodernity.

By contrast, feminist philosopher Iris Marion Young, while distancing herself from radical postmodernism, maintains that 'the ideal of impartiality legitimates hierarchical decisionmaking and allows the standpoint of the privileged to appear as universal'.[49] Young goes further than Benhabib in her diagnosis of the problems underlying modern conceptions of universality and impartiality. In her view, the reciprocity which underpins 'neutral' or 'just' decision-making is inevitably asymmetrical, for the simple reason that no human being can ever genuinely exchange positions with another: to assume such reversibility is, in her view, to repress difference and hence to destroy justice.[50] Nonetheless, her solution runs in a similar direction to that of Benhabib: the key issue is the development of a heterogeneous range of 'civic publics' which draw all social groups into political debate and in which that debate may aspire to the ideal of 'enlarge thinking' which Young borrows from Hannah Arendt. But these decision-making fora, in Young's view, need to be genuinely 'communicative' rather than merely deliberative, in that they must be capable of listening to claims couched not only in terms of rule-based argument but also within narratives and rhetoric. Like Nancy Fraser,[51] Young therefore insists that difference and particularly be written into the processes of public decision-making. Although neither Young nor Fraser considers the issue in any detail, it is apparent that their arguments have substantial implications for law as one form of practical deliberation.

Thirdly, in specifically legal theory, Drucilla Cornell, notwithstanding her continued interest in postmodernist and poststructuralist ideas, argues in her recent work that general standards of reasonableness and ideas of equality need to be maintained by what she calls ethical feminism.[52] In elaborating this argument, she avows the existence of some links between liberalism and deconstruction, between analytical and postmodern jurisprudence, which would be deeply sympathetic from Campbell's point of view.[53] But she asserts that ideals such as equality and impartiality can only be made meaningful if the social and psychic conditions necessary for legal subjects' to be able to think of themselves as individuals deserving of equal respect are fulfilled, and she maintains that these broader questions have been systematically obscured by most legal and political theory. In this respect, as I argued earlier, legal positivism proceeds on the basis of a set of assumptions which, from a feminist point of view, themselves call for critical analysis. Furthermore, the psychoanalytic dimension of Cornell's theory adds force to the arguments of Benhabib and, in particular, Young; if subjects are not transparent even to ourselves, then, *a fortiori*, the conditions under which reversibility of perspectives can be made meaningful will have to be formulated with care, to put it mildly.

Benhabib's, Young's and Cornell's various analyses of the limits or complexities of the moral ideas of impartiality or universality under conditions of difference raise a number of crucial questions for legal theory. These include matters such as the conceptualization of legal subjects; the social and psychological conditions under which real 'equality before the law' could pertain; the constitution of the judiciary; the nature of the legislative process; the conduct of trials; the diversification of decision-making fora and of modes of argument which can be heard in them (along with a vast range of questions about rules of evidence); the proper level of generality of legal reasoning and of legislative provisions; and the contextualization of legal rules. Readers familiar with the literature will recognize in this list many of the key issues which have preoccupied recent feminist legal theory. The analysis of such issues is not necessarily incompatible with Campbell's approach, but it has to be admitted that they play only a small part in his book. For example, although Campbell makes several references to the consistency of gender-specific or compensatory legal provisions with ethical positivism, just what would justify their adoption receives only brief attention, and the implications for the stance of legislative or judicial decision-makers is not addressed.

The tenets of ethical positivism may be consistent *in principle* with the feminist critique of the false objectivity and universality of legal processes. But feminists will continue to worry about the depth to which it has addressed the feasibility of attaining gender impartiality or the universality of legal rules – indeed, the very question of what these ideals would look like – in a society which remains organized along sex/gender lines to a significant degree. Indeed, many feminists will suggest that, notwithstanding its laudable aspiration to normative transparency, its sidelining of such issues implies that ethical positivism, like its predecessors, has an (albeit unintended) ideological dimension, in that it asserts (with unjustified confidence) the possibility of aspirations which play a key role in legitimizing modern law. Despite Campbell's insistence on the neutrality of ethical positivism in terms of the political and moral substance of law, the arguments which he advances for it are, at root, liberal arguments, and it is perhaps his (not fully acknowledged) espousal of a certain kind of liberalism which makes him less attentive to the complexities of universalism than feminists would wish a legal theorist to be.

Law's Autonomy

Doubtless, as Campbell implies, the existence of detailed legislation which was informed by feminist concerns would make a difference to the gender justice of the legal process. But this leads to a second difficulty: the assumption of autonomy. As we have seen, Campbell's analysis is based on the assumption that the legal not only *should* be, but *could* be, bracketed effectively from the political by an adequate practice of legislation and a separation of powers. In effect, ethical positivism asks us to place our faith in the idea that a more ambitious and thoughtful democratic–political practice could make a space for genuinely 'legal reasoning' which is non-political. It admits that there will be 'hard cases', but remains optimistic about keeping them within narrow bounds, and insists that they be confronted explicitly. As I have already argued, the shift of the argumentative fulcrum from the legal to the political process is generally sympathetic from a feminist point of view – indeed, it coheres with some of the most important feminist arguments.[54] But one does not have to be a subscriber to the radical indeterminacy thesis to wonder whether Campbell's analysis really moves us beyond the conundrum posed by H.L.A. Hart's *The Concept of Law*: if rules cannot be applied in a purely deductive way, even in 'easy' cases, what other factors are in play? The resort to articulated legislative intentions seems unlikely to resolve this dilemma. Moreover, aspiration to more detailed legislation could well lead to problems of complexity and technicality which would be counterproductive in terms of the time-honoured aspirations of codification.

Law as Rules: from Prescription to Practice?

Perhaps the largest distance between ethical positivists and difference feminists lies in ethical positivism's ideal of law as a system of rules or norms. Clearly, as Campbell argues, feminists could maintain their scepticism about whether this is the way current law really works while sharing the aspiration that it should be so reconstructed.[55] But 'ought' implies 'can', and there are good reasons to be sceptical about whether the power of law could ever be reduced to its operation as a system of rules. Here we begin to touch on some of the broader socio-theoretic themes on which difference feminism draws, and it is to these broader questions that I therefore turn to make a final assessment of the relationship between feminist and ethical positivist thought.

Ethical Positivism (De)limited?

In this final section, I want to raise four general socio-theoretic questions about the adequacy of ethical positivism as a framework for contemporary legal theory.

Conceiving the Political

The first question is concerned with ethical positivism's conception of the political. Like most contemporary political and legal theory, Campbell's account proceeds from a conception of the political which is closely identified with the nation-state. Political power is described as 'sovereign' power,[56] and the crucial issue for political theory is the distribution of this kind of power and the design of institutions to ensure its limitation, its legitimacy and the accountability of its holders. Specifically, it is the aspiration of ethical positivism to prevent, as far as possible, political power from spilling over into the legal sphere and, when it does so, to ensure the transparency of that blurring of boundaries.

One might be forgiven for wondering, in the light of the dramatic changes in the structure of political societies over the centuries, whether a theoretical framework which remains little changed as compared with the conceptions elaborated and defended by the thinkers of 200 or even 300 years ago – Locke, Hobbes, Rousseau and Bentham – is adequate to the task of political theory today. What may plausibly be regarded as political power has become fragmented and diffused in a number of directions. Most obviously, it has shifted to supranational and international bodies and to a variety of institutions of local governance or, indeed, to institutions which would have been regarded as 'private' even 20 years ago. The idea that we are seeing *political* power diffused through the policies of deregulation and privatization which have modified the governmental structure of many post-industrial countries in recent years, as well as the analysis of the economic power of bodies such as multinational corporations as *political* power, remain controversial. But one would expect political theory to have at least something to say about these kinds of changes in the sociopolitical structure of late modern societies. Furthermore, such changes are of direct relevance to law, as current debates about legal pluralism and the proliferation of local, transnational and international legalities testify.[57] It is therefore not only feminists who are exercised about the stability of lines drawn between public and private, political and personal. Although, at various points, Campbell engages in a critical discussion of alternative dispute resolution,[58] his book falls well short of any systematic description of how ethical positivism would respond to these sorts of change in the locus and distribution of political power. What is needed is not merely the 'democratic revivalism' which Deborah Cass[59] quite rightly attributes to ethical positivism, but also a reconsideration of our very ideas of democratic practice in the light of the critique articulated by the feminist political philosophies discussed in the previous section.

Power as Sovereignty

There is a second, conceptual as much as empirical, question about the notion of power and of the political deployed by ethical positivism. This is the notion of power as sovereignty, in the sense of a kind of property which can be lost and gained, redistributed, limited and controlled in relatively straightforward senses. While this is certainly one important way of understanding political power, the reception of Foucault's idea of disciplinary power, outlined earlier, has added a further way of interpreting the dynamics of the social and political world. As we have seen, feminists, among others, have argued that disciplinary power is one important aspect of the legal process. To the extent that this argument is persuasive, it must be the case that disciplinary power raises normative questions – questions about justification, legitimacy and accountability. Yet Campbell, in common with the vast majority of political theorists, simply ignores this aspect of law's power. The issue has been obscured by the fact that Foucault himself was famously uninterested in normative questions, and merely offered an analysis of power as discipline, along with a notoriously underdeveloped account of the capacity of such power to call forth human resistance. But to the extent that his analysis is empirically persuasive, it undoubtedly poses normative questions for political theorists. If disciplinary power is an integral aspect of law, in other words, a prescriptive legal theory must have something to say about it. And if the meaning of law cannot be determined by exercises of sovereignty power at the legislative level, can ethical positivism's assertion of the line between the political and the legal be maintained?

Between the Lines of Legal Reasoning

A third question arising from recent work in legal theory concerns whether ethical positivism's account of the (ideal) nature of adjudication is plausible. One important strand of the 'postmodern' legal theory to which Campbell refers has been the articulation and analysis of what is going on, as it were, between the articulated lines of judicial reasoning.[60] The theories advanced are almost as numerous as the theorists, but three important examples would be the analysis of legal reasoning as a form of rhetoric,[61] as a practice which needs to be analysed in semiotic terms [62] and, most recently, as structured by psychoanalytic dynamics.[63] Clearly, the ethical positivist might dismiss these analyses as irrelevant by arguing that he or she is merely defending the *idea* of transparent, consistently rule-based legal reasoning. But – as in the case of disciplinary power – to the extent that psychoanalytic forces are an inevitable part of adjudication, or to the degree that legal reasoning has inevitably rhetorical effects, these theories will not be so easy to 'banish to another discipline'. Although this is not something to which Campbell devotes any detailed analysis, his focus is generally upon what we could call the instrumental, as opposed to the symbolic or expressive, aspects of law and legal power. To the extent that he addresses the latter, he assumes that they can be separated clearly from the former.[64] Although a full defence of this position is beyond the scope of this chapter, I would hazard the suggestion that this compartmentalization is unpersuasive and runs against the grain of some of the most interesting developments in contemporary legal theory. As current debates about Aboriginal land rights in Australia illustrate very clearly, the symbolic aspects of law's power raise normative questions of legitimacy and justification, analytic and empirical questions about how law works, and practical questions about the conduct of the legislative and adjudicative processes.

The Legal and the Socio-Legal; the Analytical and the Sociological

Finally, and perhaps most directly, I want to suggest that an engagement with feminist legal theory gives pause for thought about ethical positivism's insistence that the sociology of law can be bracketed from analytical (normative) jurisprudence.[65] As Campbell acknowledges, this is an issue on which some positivists – notably those who, like Neil MacCormick and Ota Weinberger, espouse an 'institutional positivism'[66] – take a different view. Campbell's view of institutional positivism seems to be that it is useful in bolstering the case for the feasibility of law as a system of impartially administered rules, but that it blurs internal (legal) and external (sociological) visions of legal reasoning. Yet one of the most important insights of feminist and socio-legal scholarship has been that internal and external visions can only be compartmentalized at the expense of obscuring the theorist's view of the *modus operandi* and social power of law. This is because we cannot hope to understand the meaning and significance of legal arrangements unless we know something about the extra-legal assumptions which shape, first, the practices which precede the coming of any particular case to trial and, second, the exercise of judicial discretion. In the second case, I assume that Campbell would want to argue that judicial discretion should only be informed by extra-legal assumptions in a limited number of cases, and that these assumptions should always be articulated. Whether or not this is a plausible response partly depends on the view taken of the kinds of legal theory mentioned in the previous section. But even at a basic socio-legal level, the judicial interpretation of facts – sexual history evidence in rape cases being a prime example – suggests that the line between the legal and the extra-legal will be very difficult to maintain. Although I cannot take this argument further here, I am convinced that an adequate legal theory needs to keep firmly in view a dual conception of law as simultaneously a social practice and a body of doctrine, and to keep under scrutiny the ways in which the boundaries between these two aspects are managed in the practices of both legal theorists and the whole range of actors in the legal process.

Moving to the pre-judicial stage, I want to use some criminal law examples to illustrate the interaction between the internal and external visions by focusing on the impact of the enforcement process on the exercise of (doctrinal) legal power. Domestic violence is probably the classic example here, as it is such a stark case of conduct which is obviously covered by existing legislation yet which continues routinely to be marginalized in enforcement practice. (It is important to note, of course, that systematic selection at the enforcement stage may well shape judicial conceptions of the kind of conduct towards which a relevant piece of legislation is directed.) If we want to follow through on the ideals of ethical positivism, this suggests that we have to think about impartiality, consistency and fairness at the enforcement stage as much as at the trial stage. Admittedly, this argument is more straightforward with regulatory than with coordinating rules, but some such arguments might well apply there, too – as in, for example, the impact of unequal access to legal advice and the courts on the meaning of formally equal rules of civil law for differently situated citizens.

In either case, are ethical positivism's ideals realistic? A certain realism about the possibilities here is engendered by the famous example of the German requirement that all *prima facie* criminal offences be prosecuted – a requirement which empirical research has conclusively established to be honoured in the breach rather than in the observance. This is, from a 'critical' perspective, a classic case of consistency and formal equality as ideology; the rule of law is asserted at the level of legal rules but subverted – necessarily, perhaps – at the level of executive practice. In general, it is my contention that socio-legal scholarship has far broader implications for what analytical jurisprudence takes to be its proper terrain than is generally noticed and, in this respect, the legal theory of ethical positivism is not substantially different from its ancestors.

Conclusion

By analogy with the much debated relationship between Marxism and feminism, we could therefore suggest that the relation between feminism and ethical positivism is not so much an unhappy marriage as a loose coupling. Ethical positivism's explicitly normative position, its thoroughgoing constructionism in relation to law and legal concepts such as rights, its bias towards particularity and towards the legislative enunciation of legal standards are all sympathetic from a feminist perspective. Moreover, its avowal of the malleability of law leaves a space open for a feminist stream of political theory which would in turn feed into legal criticism, reformism and even utopianism. Difference feminists who believe that their critique nonetheless leaves space for both a reformulation of some of the key liberal ideals and a commitment to legal reform will see much to commend the aspirations of ethical positivism.[67] Yet in its basic conception of the respective terrain of the legal and the political, and in its relatively narrow conceptions of legal and political power, ethical positivism reveals its grounding in a tradition of analytical jurisprudence and political theory which has been all too willing to banish the insights of other branches of theoretically informed legal scholarship – socio-legal studies, the sociology of law, law and literature, law and economics, feminist, critical and postmodern legal theory – firmly to another discipline. Such theoretical separatism may inhibit ethical positivism's own capacity to address the serious questions which have been raised about the feasibility of attaining its ideals. In this chapter, I hope to have made the case for at least beginning a dialogue between occupants of the different worlds of contemporary legal theory. The normative transparency and intellectual integrity of ethical positivism equips it well to contribute to such a debate.

Notes

1 I should like to thank Anne Barron, with whom I had a very helpful discussion on the argument of the latter part of this chapter. Thanks also to the participants at the Workshop on Judicial Activism and Judicial Review in Australian Democracy held in Canberra in July 1998, and in particular to my respondent Helen Stacy, for their thought-provoking responses to an earlier version; and to Tom Campbell for organizing a forum which was genuinely open to the conversation across theoretical traditions envisaged at the end of the chapter. The analysis of feminist legal theory with which the chapter opens is largely drawn from the introduction to my *Unspeakable Subjects* (Hart Publishing, 1998).

2 Tom Campbell, *The Legal Theory of Ethical Positivism* (Aldershot: Dartmouth, 1996).

3 Ibid., pp. 63–4, 78, 87.

4 For further discussion, see Nicola Lacey, *Unspeakable Subjects: Feminist Essays in Legal and Social Theory* (Oxford: Hart Publishing, 1998), ch. 8.

5 Two outstanding exceptions to this general tendency are the Australian theorists Margaret Davies on *Asking the Law Question* (North Ryde NSW: Law Book Company, 1994) and *Delimiting the Law* (London: Pluto Press, 1996) and Valerie Kerruish, *Jurisprudence as Ideology* (London: Routledge, 1992).

6 See Margaret Thornton, *The Liberal Promise* (Oxford: Oxford University Press, 1990).

7 For more detailed discussion, see Lacey, *Unspeakable Subjects, op. cit.*, chs 6 and 7.

8 See Carol Gilligan, *In a Different Voice* (Cambridge, MA: Harvard University Press, 1982).

9 For a thoughtful analysis of the implications of an ethic of care for politics and law, see Selma Sevenhuijsen, *Citizenship and the Ethics of Care* (London: Routledge, 1998).

10 For a useful discussion, see Mary Jo Frug, *Postmodern Legal Feminism* (London: Routledge, 1992), ch. 3.

11 I am grateful to Neil MacCormick for pointing this out in discussion, and for the characteristic good humour with which he tolerated my mistaken memory that the point had been raised by one of the female participants!

12 See, further, Lacey, *Unspeakable Subjects op. cit.*, ch. 7.

13 For further discussion see Jennifer Nedelsky, 'Rights as Relationship', *Review of Constitutional Studies* (1993), p. 1; Luce Irigaray, *J'aime à toi* (Paris: Grasset, 1992); see also Lacey, *Unspeakable Subjects, op. cit.*, chs 4 and 8.

14 See Hans Kelsen, *The Pure Theory of Law* (Berkeley: University of California Press, 1967).

15 For an extended analysis of this problem, see Margaret Davies, *Delimiting the Law* (London: Pluto Press, 1996).

16 See E.P. Thompson, *Whigs and Hunters* (Harmondsworth: Penguin, 1975) pp. 259–65; Hugh Collins, *Marxism and Law* (Oxford: Clarendon Press, 1982).

17 See Carol Smart, *Feminism and the Power of Law* (London: Routledge, 1989), drawing on Michel Foucault, *The Archaeology of Knowledge* (London: Tavistock, 1972) and *Discipline and Punish* (Harmondsworth: Penguin, 1977).

18 Cf. the arguments of autopoietic theory: see Gunther Teubner, *Law as an Autopoietic System* (Oxford: Basil Blackwell, 1993).

19 See Catharine A. MacKinnon, *Toward a Feminist Theory of the State* (Cambridge, MA: Harvard University Press, 1989).

20 See, for example, Drucilla Cornell, *The Imaginary Domain* (New York: Routledge, 1995) ch. 1; for further discussion, see Lacey, *Unspeakable Subjects, op. cit.*, chs 4–7.

21 See MacKinnon, *Feminist Theory, op. cit.*, ch. 11: Catharine A. MacKinnon and Andrea Dworkin, *In Harm's Way* (Cambridge, MA: Harvard University Press, 1998); Campbell, *Ethical Positivism, op. cit.*, pp. 250–55.

22 See, for example, Roberto M. Unger, 'The Critical Legal Studies Movement in America', *Harvard Law Review*, **96** (1983), p. 561.

23 See, in particular, Smart, *Feminism, op. cit.*, ch. 1; Anne Bottomley and Joanne Conaghan (eds), *Feminist Theory and Legal Strategy* (Oxford: Basil Blackwell, 1993).

24 Tove Stang Dahl, *Women's Law* (Oslo: Norwegian University Press, 1986).

25 See Foucault, *The Archaeology of Knowledge* and *Discipline and Punish, op. cit.* and Smart, *Feminism, op. cit.*; for further discussion, see Lacey, *Unspeakable Subjects, op. cit.*, chs 3 and 5.

26 See Lacey, *Unspeakable Subjects, op. cit.*, ch. 8.

27 Ronald Dworkin, *Law's Empire* (London: Fontana, 1986).

28 Jürgen Habermas, *Faktizität und Geltung* (Frankfurt am Main: Suhrkamp Verlag, 1992).

29 Peter Fitzpatrick (ed.), *Dangerous Supplements* (London: Pluto Press, 1991).

30 See Frances Olsen, 'The Family and the Market', *Harvard Law Review*, **96** (1983), p. 1497.

31 See Mark Kelman, 'Interpretive Construction in the Substantive Criminal Law', *Stanford Law Review* (1981).

32 See Hugh Collins, *The Law of Contract*, 3rd edn (London: Butterworths, 1997).

33 See, for example, Frug, *Postmodern Legal Feminism, op. cit.*

34 For an astute analysis of the various different strands of Campbell's argument and of their relation to one another, see John Gardner's review of *Legal Theory of Ethical Positivism* in *King's College Law Journal*, **9** (1998–99), pp. 180–7. In essence, Gardner's argument is that Campbell fails to substantiate a link between the legal and the moral/political aspects of his theory. Gardner's conclusion resonates with my argument in this chapter, which suggests that while there are some affinities between Campbell's normative position and feminism, his conception of legal reasoning remains at odds with a difference feminist view of law.

35 Campbell, *Ethical Positivism, op. cit.*, p. 85 (emphasis added).

36 On the political base of Bentham's positivism, see Nicola Lacey, 'Bentham as Proto-Feminist?', *Current Legal Problems* (1998), p. 441.

37 H.L.A. Hart, *The Concept of Law*, 2nd edn (Oxford: Clarendon Press, 1994).

38 See Roger Cotterrell, *The Politics of Jurisprudence* (London: Butterworths, 1989) and *Law's Community* (Oxford: Clarendon Press, 1995); see also Valerie Kerruish, *Jurisprudence, op. cit.*

39 Campbell, *Ethical Positivism, op. cit.*, p. 62.

40 Ibid., p. 255.

41 Ibid., pp. 189ff; 166, 168.

42 Ibid., pp. 63–4.

43 Ibid., p. 133; see also pp. 135–6.

44 In employing the useful shorthand of 'postmodernity', I do not mean to marginalize the very important institutional and cultural differences between sociopolitical orders in the late twentieth century; indeed the variations in social, political and economic culture, even between geographically proximate countries at similar stages of post-industrial development, indicates the need for a comparative approach to questions of social reform: see Nicola Lacey and Lucia Zedner, 'Discourses of Community in Criminal Justice, *Journal of Law and Society*, **93** (1995); on the difficulties of disentangling 'agency', 'culture' and 'structure' in our assessment of institutional reform possibilities in different countries, see Martin Krygier, 'Is There Constitutionalism After Communism?', *International Journal of Sociology*, **17** (1997). However, it is undoubtedly the case that broad historical shifts in forces which transcend the boundaries of nation-states are significant for law and democracy, and it is these broad shifts to which the idea of 'postmodernity' is useful in alerting us. On the implications of changing culture and social structure for law and legal science, see Tim Murphy, *The Oldest Social Science?* (Oxford: Clarendon Press, 1997).

45 Seyla Benhabib, 'The Generalised and the Concrete Other' in S. Benhabib and D. Cornell (eds), *Feminism as Critique* (Cambridge: Polity Press, 1987) p. 77; also in Benhabib, *Situating the Self* (Cambridge: Polity Press, 1992) p. 148. See also the Introduction to, and Chapter 7 of, *Situating the Self*.

46 John Rawls, *A Theory of Justice* (Cambridge, MA: Harvard University Press, 1971).

47 Jürgen Habermas, *The Theory of Communicative Action* (1984), Volume 1: *Reason and the Rationalisation of Society* (1987), Volume II: *Lifeworld and System: A Critique of Functionalist Reason*, trans. T. McCarthy (Cambridge: Polity Press); John Rawls, *Political Liberalism* (New York: Columbia University Press, 1993).

48 Benhabib, 'The Generalised and Concrete Other', *op. cit.*, p. 92.

49 Iris Marion Young, *Justice and the Politics of Difference* (Princeton, NJ: Princeton University Press, 1990) p. 116; see generally Chapter 4.

50 Iris Marion Young, *Intersecting Voices: Dilemmas of Gender, Political Philosophy and Policy* (Princeton, NJ: Princeton University Press, 1997) chs 2 and 3.

51 Nancy Fraser, *Justice Interruptus* (London: Routledge, 1997).

52 Cornell, *The Imaginary Domain, op. cit.*

[53] See also Drucilla Cornell, *The Philosophy of the Limit* (New York: Routledge, 1992), pp. 2–9.

[54] See, for example, Young, *Justice, op. cit.*, and *Intersecting Voices, op. cit.*; Benhabib, *Situating the Self, op. cit.*

[55] See Campbell, *Ethical Positivism, op. cit.*, p. 78.

[56] See, for example, ibid., pp. 2, 5.

[57] See, for example, Boaventura de Sousa Santos, *Toward a New Common Sense* (London: Routledge, 1995); Gunther Teubner, 'The King's Many Bodies', *Law and Society Review* (1997).

[58] Campbell, *Ethical Positivism, op. cit.*, pp. 9, 255–7.

[59] Ibid.

[60] This is, of course, a preoccupation which such legal theory shares with several of its predecessors, and most notably with legal realism.

[61] See for example Peter Goodrich, *Legal Discourse* (London: Macmillan, 1987), *Reading the Law* (Oxford: Blackwell, 1986); *Languages of Law* (London: Butterworths, 1990); Costas Douzinas, Ronnie Warrington and Sean McVeigh, *Postmodern Jurisprudence* (London: Routledge, 1991); Costas Douzinas and Ronnie Warrington, *Justice Miscarried* (Hemel Hempstead: Harvester, 1994).

[62] Bernard Jackson, *Semiotics and Legal Theory* (London: Routledge, 1985).

[63] See Peter Goodrich, *Oedipus Lex* (Berkeley: University of California Press, 1995).

[64] Campbell, *Ethical Positivism, op. cit.*, p. 118.

[65] Ibid., pp. 78–85, 108, 111, 244. As will be apparent from what follows, I am more sympathetic to MacCormick's and Weinberger's attempt to theorize law as a social practice and hence to locate positivism as partly within the social sciences than is Campbell, although I think that this attempt poses greater difficulties for the separation thesis than they acknowledge. For further discussion of the links between different genres of legal theory, see Lacey, *op. cit.*, ch. 8. In 'All We Like Sheep', *Canadian Journal of Law and Jurisprudence* (1999 forthcoming) Jeremy Waldron provides a persuasive reading of Hart's *The Concept of Law* which is of particular relevance to Campbell's stance *vis à vis* 'institutional positivism'. Waldron emphasizes the sociological aspects of Hart's defence of positivism and in particular his (underdeveloped) assertion of a structural relationship between the potential moral advantages and disadvantages of a positivist system of law.

[66] Neil MacCormick and Ota Weinberger, *An Institutional Theory of Law: New Approaches to Legal Positivism* (Dordrecht and Lancaster: Reidel, 1986); see also Ota Weinberger, *Law, Institution and Legal Politics* (Dordrecht and Boston: Kluwer, 1991), particularly ch. VII.

[67] For a more detailed analysis of the scope for dialogue between feminist and positivist legal theory, see my 'Bentham as Proto-Feminist?', *op. cit.*

5 Legal Separatism and the Concept of the Person

MARGARET DAVIES

Preface: Who are We Anyway?

> The law is who we are, we are also the law. The law is everywhere, we breathe it, we eat it, we sing it, we live it.[1]

... so affirms Irene Watson, an indigenous woman from southern Australia, who is also educated in Anglo-Australian law. The power of this statement, and the surprise which it offers to a Western reader such as myself, is the clear assertion that 'we are also the law'. *We* are the law. It is possible perhaps to glimpse here a conception of the law in which the law is not separate from the human subject; it is, rather, of the individual. Such a law would be inseparable from the social and moral identity of the person – which subsists *through* the culture and the law.

Such a conception of the manifestation of law in the human person is almost unthinkable to the modern Western mind, which considers *the* law to exist outside of individually autonomous beings. In modern Anglo-Australian law, for example, the moral person is *subject* to the law but our identity is regarded as separate from the law, and independent from it in many important respects. We (the Western we) are *not* the law: a police officer is not the law, a judge is not the law, a member of parliament is not the law – even though each office is sometimes colloquially referred to in this way. The various ideas associated with the notion of the 'rule of law' are supposed to ensure the distinctness of law from any individual, and therefore the protection of each subject from non-legal exercises of power.[2] Most importantly, the law is certainly not us: we are essentially ourselves, and the law is just something imposed upon us in order to regulate our interactions.

The notion of the separate law does not offer an understanding of law which is neutral as between different values, moralities, and cultures, but is rather – in its very *form* – embedded within a culture which assumes autonomous pre-legal individuals. Positivism is a philosophy which advocates that the legal and the non-legal worlds are, or ought to be, separate on a factual institutional level, or – in the work of Hans Kelsen – ought to be separated at the conceptual level. I will return to these variations in positivism later, for the moment only noting that the common thread is some kind of faith in the existence or ideal of a separate legal domain. Normally, it is the relationship between law and the moral, social and political dimensions of our existences which is given most attention in the defence or criticism of positivism. However, one of the multitude of things from which law is separate in positivist thought is the human being (as distinct from the legal person), or perhaps more precisely, personal identity in its social and moral manifestations. Whatever else it may or may not be conceptually or practically, the law is not me and I am not the law. I may have various interactions or relationships with the law, but it is ultimately separable and different from my being: the individual and the law stand opposed, because the self is a pre-legal self, which finds external constraint in the law.

Even to speak of THE law, as if there is only one, and as if its basic identity is self-evident, perpetuates a sense of fixity in the concept of law as well as a continuing exclusion of any law which is incommensurable with the Western concept of law. We may ask, whose law is THE law? If this question makes any sense at all – that is, if it is *capable* of having any meaning – it is because the law which we take to be the one law constituting the nation, and which is nonetheless regarded as separate from our physical, moral and social beings, is not the only law, and is not as separate as it is conventionally understood to be. To ask 'Whose law is this?' implies a link of some sort between a person or a group (and therefore its individual members) and the law, and it also implies that there may be other laws, even within the area of coverage of the (purportedly singular) law.

This chapter is primarily about several issues arising from the separatist mentality which is apparent in the Western attitude to law. First, it asks how the relationship between human persons and the law can be understood. This question is posed primarily within the context of the positivist tradition in which THE law is thought to have an institutionalized existence which is (or ought to be) structurally and conceptually separate from less certain questions of morality, culture or personal identity. To this end, positive law also distinguishes between the legal person, which performs a technical function as holder of (variable) rights and responsibilities, and the human being, or social and moral person.[3] Second, what are the political consequences of this legal separatism? In asking such a question, I am principally interested in offering arguments which counteract the prescriptive positivist argument that law ought to strive for a separate institutional existence.

In the following discussion I have tried to follow, with some clarity, the distinction between the legal 'person' who is a construct of law, and the 'individual', 'human being', 'subject', or 'social/moral person' who is conceptualized as being prior to, or outside, the law. However, my ultimate aim is to show the fictional and ideological nature of this distinction and to illustrate that it breaks down in certain ways. An added complication is that postmodern theory tends to use primarily the terminology of the 'subject' – which is a position constructed within a particular framework. One is a subject of law,[4] of language, of culture, of moral systems, of the state and so on. The 'subject' is therefore not the same as the 'individual' or the 'human being', which is a more naturalized entity. However, as my primary concern is with the separation of law (including law's person) from non-legal personal identity, in the interests of simplicity I have tended to conflate these terms.

Law's Other Person

These introductory comments are not offered as an exposition of an indigenous concept of law or even as suggesting grounds for a comparative legal theory, although I do believe such theory has been somewhat undervalued in Western legal philosophy.[5] Rather, my intention is simply to highlight one of the basic cultural presuppositions of modern Western law – namely, its separation from the social and moral individual. It is a rather obvious point, but one worth constantly remembering, that there is more than one possible understanding of law and that there is nothing *inevitable* about the concept of law which predominates in Western culture. Whether that concept is descriptively accurate, or prescriptively desirable, for Western culture is a different matter, which I will come to later. But the fact that a concept is not inevitable is an important starting point which, to my way of thinking, leads us not to take our law as a given, but rather to reflect upon its founding assumptions: where does this law meet its cultural limits, and what are the consequences of the concept for the interrelationship between various aspects of our Western society?[6] I take the view that recognition of such conceptual difference leads first to introspection rather than (pre)judgement of the other: therefore instead of asserting that a legal understanding which does not reflect a certain formal structure of law is 'primitive' or 'pre-legal',[7] I begin (and end) by reflecting upon the cultural context and presuppositions of the liberal, positivist, Western understanding of law. It is my view that such self-reflection is integral to the process of understanding, and communicating with, any group conventionally cast as 'other'.

I do not wish to embark upon an exhaustive internal analysis of the forms of legal positivism, but a short and simplified summary of the different types of claim represented by positivist thought is necessary before proceeding. Clearly, positivism has several different strands,[8] each of which have in common a broad focus on the separation or separability of law from non-law, and a characterization of law as imposed or posited within legal institutional structures. However, the nature and significance of the focus on separation varies in different positivist approaches. In Anglo-American jurisprudential circles, positivism has tended towards the empirical or descriptive, while the continental tradition – particularly in the work of Hans Kelsen – has been conceptual.[9] Tom Campbell's ethical or prescriptive positivism, while reviving the reformist tendencies of the earliest English positivists, represents an important reorientation of positivist thought away from the epistemology of law and towards politics and ethics.

Within the Anglo-American tradition, much positivist thought has taken the form of an attempt to understand law as a particular kind of *social* phenomenon, describing law as essentially separate from its non-legal outside, emphasizing the distinctly legal character of certain institutions, doctrines and processes through the notion of a specific legal source.[10] While the approach within this tradition has not been solely empirical, it does present a view of actual law which emphasizes the distinctness of legal systems: whether or not such theory has set out primarily to describe existing legal systems in general terms, it has attempted to portray law as it is, and therefore attempts to be *true* of actual law.[11] Just as importantly, a description of law as separate still underpins legal practice, legal education and law-making. Conceptual positivism, as espoused most famously by Hans Kelsen, regards law as conceptually and analytically separate: in other words, law is a construct of thinking which is conceptually distinct from other phenomena. Thus Kelsen insists that legal 'science' involves the attempt to understand and describe law as a separate ideational construct.[12] In contrast to these classical versions of positivist thought, which focus on understanding the truth of law as a social fact or concept, 'prescriptive positivism', as recently and thoroughly expounded by Tom Campbell in *The Legal Theory of Ethical Positivism*, advances the position that, for ethical reasons, the positivist ideal ought to be defended and, as far as possible, realized. Prescriptive positivism represents a departure from mainstream positivism insofar as it openly defends the existence of an ethico-political basis for the idea of law as a system. Thus, in general terms, positivism takes the view that law is actually separate – at least to some degree – or that it ought to be separate from a non-legal outside. I will return to the critique of these positions later.

Especially within the ever-expanding critical tradition, positivism is frequently associated with the political theory of liberalism. The association is, as Campbell points out,[13] historical but not necessary – at least as far as positivism is concerned. Positivism developed and gathered strength within the context of liberal political thought, but it can live without many of the central liberal world-views. Consider, for instance, one of the great hallmarks of liberalism – the distinction made in traditional liberal political thought between the public and private areas of human existence. The division is made slightly different in different contexts,[14] but essentially the public is the realm of law, of regulation, of the state and of political participation, while the private is the realm of the individual and her or his particular social, familial, religious and cultural affiliations. The community and the market exist in a somewhat indeterminate space between the extremes of public and private. The traditional liberal view has been that the 'private' should remain as unregulated as possible[15] and that the sphere of law ought to be confined to the 'public' and to the regulation of any 'private' activities with which the interests of individuals can, or do, come into conflict. In this sense, the liberal approach may be said to presuppose the possibility of a separable and positive law: only if law is *capable* of being conceptualized as separable from the status of the individual can it be regarded as politically desirable that it retreat in this way to a limited domain. With its focus on the freedom and equality of individuals, liberal thought relies on the positivist dissociation of law from individual identity and status.

However, the distinction in positivism between law and non-law need not be drawn along the liberal lines of public and private. It is perfectly compatible with classical positivism that law intrude into any aspect of 'private' life, or retreat completely from it, the only question being whether a norm satisfies the formal and institutional requirements of 'law'. Rather than public and private, positivism distinguishes between law and non-law, arguing for the conceptual, though not the political or practical, limits of law. However, although positivism is compatible with any possible degree of interference in the 'private' sphere, its emphasis on the institutional and conceptual limits of law ensures that, at some point, it does assume a pre-legal subject and a separable practice of law – that is, an individual whose identity is not imbued with law, and a law whose identity is not inextricably bound up with non-legal 'laws'.[16] Therefore, although it is true that positivism is not absolutely committed to all aspects of liberal philosophy, it does reflect a similar, but not identical, division between a transcendent and distinct law, and the everyday social life of communities and individuals. Positivism may not, of necessity, support the politics of individualism,[17] but it does insist on a distinction between personal identity and law. For positivism, law is not limited in its content or application; rather, it is limited in its conceptual and institutional existence. I should note at this point that the feminist arguments which illustrate the mutually constitutive nature of public and private apply equally well to the positivist separation of the human individual from law.[18]

Clearly, in several senses, positive law is not separate from the social individual, since it is inevitably such beings who constitute, litigate, decide and administer it. Law is nothing more than a creation of people, and can obviously be destroyed by them. Saying this, however, does not reveal any integral link between law and personal identity – the law of the positivists is a creation of groups of people, which then becomes higher and distinct, leaving the identity of the individual as it was. Similarly, the human being may be said to enter into positive law through the artificial category of legal personality – a category which, as far as humans are concerned, builds on a perceived substratum of natural and/or moral personality however that is understood at different moments in history.[19] Nevertheless, the category of legal personality according to positivist law is not *necessarily* connected to human beings in their social lives, but is, rather, a fiction which expresses a set of legal roles and relationships. There is no legal reason why a tree or a cow could not have some form of legal personality,[20] but we have, at present, decided to limit personality to entities such as 'natural' persons, corporations, ships and states. The category of legal personality, and the varying incidents which accompany it, is a formal mechanism allowing humans to enter the law as a subject of law: at the same time, a distinction is maintained between the legal person – which is an abstract formal category – and the natural, social, physical person.[21] Juristically, therefore, we still tend to assume that our personal identity is an entity which exists in some tension with the formal structures of law.

This is not to say that the idea of non-separation between individual status or identity and the law is completely incomprehensible in Western thinking. The gradual incorporation of liberal and positivist values into Western law has resulted in a dissociation of the law from the human subject, but this has not always been the norm – certainly there are some precedents in the notion of a religious law which defines one's life and which, in some parts of the world, may still be enshrined in state law to varying degrees. In feudal systems the status of a person was defined by her or his position in a sociopolitical hierarchy which was inseparable from the legal distribution of personal powers and responsibilities.[22] Neither religious law nor feudal law seems to me to be quite the same as the concept of indigenous law which Watson expresses[23] – a notion which suggests a seamlessness between the person, the law, the land and the culture.

Notions of law which do not distinguish between the pre-legal identity of the autonomous subject and a transcendent and delimited law seem foreign and unevolved in some way – religious, historical, primitive or superstitious. Positive law has traditionally been defined in contrast to these *other* notions of law.[24] Indeed, some of the defining moment of positivist thought reveal a strong theoretical need to draw a clear line of demarcation between the proper, modern, scientific, rational understanding of law and such underdeveloped others. For instance, Bentham's criticisms of the notion of customary law, as evidenced in the common law of England, turn on the failure of such law to achieve an objective existence separate from the arbitrary preferences of judges: 'Caligula published his laws in small characters: but still he published them: he hung them up high, but still he hung them up. English judges neither hang up their laws, nor publish them.'[25] Unlike customary law, positive law is published and objectified; it is not intrinsic. Along similar lines, Hart distinguishes between modern law and custom or primitive law by deploying his concepts of secondary rules and the rule of recognition, which remove the process of legal change from the everyday life and practices of the community, placing it in some distinct institutional mechanism.[26] And Austin immediately characterizes *proper* laws as commands or posited rules, by definition separating the structure and content of laws from questions of being and of community standards: a law is 'a rule laid down for the guidance of an intelligent being by an intelligent being having power over him'.[27]

Positivism advances some compelling justifications for separating law from individual persons. It is the separation of law from the individual and from the realm of personal preference, prejudice, and relationships, which is said to encourage the impartiality of law and its dissociation from personal power. In this way, positivism allegedly supports the notion of equality under the law, it promotes clarity about the identity and content of law, and it ideally enables 'legal' decisions to be made according to law alone.[28] Most persuasively, the separation of law from questions of morality are said to leave a person free to choose whether or not to act in conformity with law.[29] My actions may be *influenced* by law, but if I determine that the ethically appropriate action would constitute a transgression of positive law, this choice is clearly open to me. Surely I cannot have such a clear perception of the moral fragility of law *unless* it is distinct to some degree from whatever ethical decisions I happen to make? And surely promoting the greatest possible conceptual separation of law from my own morality and identity will enhance my freedom in this respect? Or will it?

In certain respects, there is much that is commendable about these arguments, but I think they are misguided because they rely on a partial understanding of the domain of law, the nature of social and legal power and the situatedness of persons within a cultural and 'legal' normative web.[30] Although there is a sense in which we can understand law to be separate, either as a fact, as an ideational construct or as an ideal, such knowledge is not produced in a politically innocent fashion. Nor can it ever be said to be absolute, but is rather a story which is told about law which excludes other possible narratives, and which has a (usually unacknowledged) ideological function. The admirable idea behind prescriptive positivism is that a political theory ought to be built into the theory of law, therefore hopefully avoiding the criticism that positivism erases and disguises its political foundations: however, what remains concealed in prescriptive positivism, as I will argue shortly, is the question of the power relations embedded in legal form. The issue of power is not something which can be articulated merely at the level of overt political power or policy, but, rather, raises the spectre of entrenched social power – the power of exclusion and the politics of any knowledge, such as that presupposed by the call for neutral identification of law as law.

(In)separable Law: Critiques of Positivism

Objections to positivism have taken a number of different forms: positivism is said to rely upon a discredited and naive model of interpretation,[31] it is said to erase the political dimension inherent in legal decision-making,[32] it reinforces social hierarchies (in particular the male/female hierarchy) while defending the neutrality of law; it tends to reduce law to a self-defining system while neglecting consideration of the coercive basis of law;[33] and it alienates people from their communities by channelling relationships through a formal and abstract system of rights and responsibilities.[34] Many of these criticisms, and several others, are articulated very persuasively by Nicola Lacey in Chapter 4 of this volume.

The remainder of this chapter focuses upon the critique of positivism, emphasizing the question of the relationship of law to the individual human subject. While drawing heavily on the growing tradition of critique of positive and mainstream accounts of law, I also try to add to this tradition and to clarify the types of claim which are being made. Some of the arguments apply more to the descriptive and conceptual tradition in positivism, although some are directly concerned with prescriptive positivism. One of the difficulties with any such critical project is that it pits one culture of legal philosophy against another: I see an object as red; you see it as green.[35] We each think the other is deluded and misunderstand the subtleties of our respective positions. A struggle to control meaning is taking place but, unfortunately, we don't even know if we are at war, or on the same side. We can never even be certain of the stakes. Perhaps all that can be hoped for are more negotiations.

Bearing this reservation in mind, the arguments can be condensed as follows: first, that any separation of law from non-law is not a question of fact or aspiration but a political process. It is not that law 'is' separate, or 'ought to be' separate, but that law is produced as separate on an ongoing basis. Law is *held apart* from non-law; it is performed or constructed as a distinct entity. The separation of law is neither a matter of 'is' nor 'ought' but a performance which condenses 'is' and 'ought' into the one fictional moment. Second, this does not mean that law actually becomes separate. The separation of law is only ever conditional, and only operable at a certain ideational level. The separateness of law is a fiction, and is ideological in the sense of supplying a self-fulfilling cover story for itself. Therefore it is necessary to look behind and beyond this story. Third, in various ways, law is inextricable from its non-legal outside and always will be. And if the distinct identity of law is a myth, then so too is the idea of the law as distinguishable from the individual. Moreover, insofar as prescriptive positivism relies on the possibility of non-political knowledge it fails to overcome the problem of inherent (as opposed to explicit) power. Fourth, in any case, there are some very compelling reasons which can be advanced against the prescriptive positivist aspiration of a separate legal order. I will explain all of these angles of the argument in more detail later.

It is crucial to realize that the objections to positivism which I raise are not only indicative of problems with the content of any law which may be laid down in a regime of positive law. Clearly, there are many questions of content or procedure which could be dealt with differently and more sensitively. However, these are not simply matters which can be resolved by positive law becoming more adept at identifying and correcting the oppressive implications of its own doctrines. It is more a problem of the very *form* of law in the positivist conception. Positivism cannot overcome this objection, because it goes to the heart of the theory and the practice of positivism which is based upon the separability and unity of law.

What is Law?

> Before the law, the man is a subject of the law in appearing before it. This is obvious, but since he is *before* it because he cannot enter it, he is

> also *outside the law* (an outlaw). He is neither under the law nor in the law. He is both a subject of the law and an outlaw.[36]

As I have indicated, despite the variety of possible positivist approaches, and the distinct criticisms which may be offered of each, there is a theme common to all, which is the claim to some sort of separateness or separation between law and non-law. It is this theme which is at the core of my criticism of positivism, and I therefore focus upon that aspect. I will begin by considering whether the law *is* separate or can become separate, and conclude with some ideas about why separation ought to be rejected as both an understanding, and an aspiration, of law.

The question, however, is not really whether law is distinct, but *in what sense* it is distinct. We behave and speak as if law is a distinct ideational and institutional entity: I go to my office in a *Law* School, teach students about 'legal' doctrines, and regularly ask them to evaluate 'the law' according to their own values. Clearly, there is a sense in which we assume that law has a function and existence which is distinct from our spiritual beliefs, our health care, whatever we might do to ensure mental well-being, and our literary tradition (for example).

On another level, and looking more closely at the operation of law, it is only too obvious that law is completely inextricable from the social, moral, economic and political arenas. In the first place, obviously the content of positive law reflects social and political interests – a fact which does not undermine positivism at all since, although positive law is not unconnected with morality, it is not *necessarily* connected.

However, beyond this, the *processes* of law are imbued with human choice – particularly in the interpretation and application of law – meaning that certain social values which are not formally part of the law influence its operation. If this is taken as a claim that sometimes judges are biased or that sometimes legal rules operate in a discriminatory fashion, then it only counters positivism insofar as positivism assumes or argues that current legal standards are neutral and are applied impartially. The claim of mere bias in judging or in rules implies a departure from, *and therefore the existence of,* a standard which is not prejudicial, and towards which we could aspire in our understanding and formulation of law. Campbell's prescriptive positivism aims to eliminate as much choice as is practicably possible, thereby achieving a degree of neutrality in the process of interpreting and applying law.

But the problem goes much further than the question of bias. If the claim that legal processes are imbued with human choice is understood to mean that cognition of law is necessarily political, because the form of objective knowledge replicates and produces oppressive mechanisms,[37] then prescriptive positivism is aspiring towards an impossible goal. It is not possible to have *both* objective knowledge and application of rules *and* to achieve a just social ordering, because the process of objectification in knowledge takes away local and individual knowledge, reduces the (legal) world to a single and unified order and privileges the class, the gender, the race and the culture which already operates on the assumption of objectivity and neutrality.[38] 'Truth' is a product of discourse and power,[39] not a pregiven or neutral object. In fact, the law which assumes a disjuncture between itself and the human being or moral subject mirrors the Western notion of objective or scientific knowledge, which assumes a disjuncture between subject and object – a separation which is always itself a politically charged construct.

Therefore the separation of 'is' from 'ought' on which positivism relies is dubious in several relevant respects. Positivism depends on the possibility of pure description which is separate and distinct from any prescription. Descriptive positivism relies on this possibility because not to do so would make a mockery of the very idea of a 'descriptive' theory. Prescriptive positivist thought ultimately depends on the possibility of neutral identification and cognition of the rules or doctrines which comprise the law. Tom Campbell's 'separability thesis' takes the view that 'adjudicators need not have reference to moral (or economic or political or private preference) criteria in their determination of law'.[40] Because, in both cases, what is at stake is the description of categories, rather than of individual or specific objects, the description, cognition or identification of law carries with it a prescriptive element which cannot be separated in the fashion envisaged by Austin and others. For instance, to *describe* law as consisting of primary rules, secondary rules and a basic rule implies a norm. Such a description is not simply an abstraction from a group of objects which are self-evidently law. This description selects and extracts some such objects, excluding others, drawing a boundary and implying a norm or standard for the identification of law.

These critiques of the possibility of neutrality and objectivity seem fundamental to me, but there are many more arguments which can be mustered against the positivist emphasis on separation or separability. For instance, language is not capable of the precision required for the formulation of rules which are sufficiently determinate. There may be clear cases and hard cases, but the determination of what is clear and what is penumbral is itself a decision which takes place within a conventional, not a natural, context. In other words, any central–penumbral distinction is not itself politically innocent or neutral, but relies on a discursive framework which conditions what is to be regarded as obvious or commonsensical. Moreover, a consideration of the history and current institutional framework of law clearly illustrates that it is a construct within a political context from which it cannot be freed, or from the outside which shapes it.[41] Finally, law is not conceptually distinct from other social practices: law does not simply exist as law. Rather, the identification of law is a process which occurs through the exclusion of non-law, meaning that the distinction is always fragile, deconstructible and in process.[42]

Therefore, in contrast to positivist concepts of separate law as an institutional fact or aspiration, postmodern and feminist accounts of law view the notion of the separate legal domain as a *construction* of language, discourse and of socially validated systems of power. *De*construction of the positivist approach is therefore based on the practical and conceptual inextricability of law from its social others. Such approaches illustrate that law is not, and cannot, conceivably have a separate existence, and that the ideology of separation is an ongoing act of force which maintains existing political structures.

Importantly for my specific topic here, feminist and postmodern accounts also emphasize the construction of identities and subjectivities under the law – although, in this context, 'the law' refers just as frequently to the laws of language, culture or the psyche as to positive institutionalized laws.[43] One of the enduring contradictions exposed by contemporary theory relating to the subject (of 'discourse'[44]) is that identity is constructed as unconstructed. The independent social subject is in fact dependent – on the laws which structure both our social interactions and our methods of understanding our environment.

Even assuming that there can be some kind of distinction between legal and non-legal norms,[45] we also see this structure of produced autonomy, and the undecidability between the person subjected to law yet standing in opposition to it, repeated in relation to the positive law.[46] The human person is constituted as a free agent partly by his or her social separation from law, while the concept of a separate and objectifiable law is justified and supported by the presumption of an otherwise free person who, being different from law, is able to make the rational decision in its favour. The relationship between law and the human subject who comes into contact with it is explained in some detail by Peter Fitzpatrick: law and the individual subject are no longer regarded as interdependent, but are counterposed and mutually constitutive.

> There is a certain persistent opposition between law and the subject. Once upon a time, so we are told, a person was bound by their position within an encompassing system of laws, whether human, natural, or divine. A person's relations to all others were set within that system. But within modernity the subject is freed from such constraints.

> The subject is now outside of law but, in order to relate to other subjects, it now relies upon positive law – a law purged of contents once inextricably shared with morality and tradition.[47]

Fitzpatrick's complex reading of the relationship between law and the individual subject stresses the historical nature of the notion of law's transcendence and the mutually constitutive nature of the ends of the opposition. The human subject (that is, the legal person) is autonomous, is individual, is free, *because* it is left alone by the law; it obtains its positive character and content negatively. At the same time, law relies on the individual, 'self-responsible' subject to uphold its own transcendence, and to operate that which is excluded by a limited law.[48] Law and the individual are constructed as opposed and exterior to each other, but they are each constituted in terms of each other.

For reasons akin to those offered by Fitzpatrick, the distinction between a limited legal domain and the general social 'laws' which constitute our conditions of existence and identity is one which I reject as ultimately unjustifiable, even though it does tell a certain story about law and orders much of our thinking and behaviour in relation to it. I should make it clear that not only do I reject the idea that there is a bright line between law and non-law, but I reject also the notion that there are clear cases of law (and of non-law), with a penumbra of uncertain cases at the border. Although we do use the term 'law' as if this were the case, and although there is an institutional edifice built on the assumption of this distinction, the separation of law is a construct which is produced by language and systems of power.[49] Not only is law a social institution with a particular cultural heritage, it is also itself constituted in a multitude of ways, at every conceivable level of its existence, from the non-legal outside against which it is defined and which becomes irretrievably buried in its being. Moreover, the 'politics' of law are not only the overt policies which may become reflected in legal content and the hidden assumptions which inform certain doctrines, but also the politics of language, the politics embedded within Western society and the politics of separation.

Legal Ideology

> ... if I am in a car and I look at the scenery through the window, I can at will focus on the scenery or on the window pane. At one moment I grasp the presence of the glass and the distance of the landscape; at another, on the contrary, the transparence of the glass and the depth of the landscape but the result of this alternation is constant: the glass is

> at once present and empty to me, and the landscape unreal and full. The same thing occurs in the mythical signifier: its form is empty but present, its meaning absent but full.[50]

It is important to consider not only the ideological function served by law, but – as Valerie Kerruish has done – also that which is served by legal theories.[51] To state that positivism performs an *ideological* function is not necessarily a pejorative claim (and it is certainly not a claim uniquely applied to positivism)[52] and can be taken to mean several things. As Slavoj Zizek has succinctly explained, the term 'ideology' can be understood to denote several different types of relationship between a 'truth' and a political purpose.[53] It may be that all knowledge is ideological in some way, because all knowledge – while claiming to represent the state of things – performs a cultural and political function. However, different notions of ideology can still be useful in that they give us some idea of the various modes of the relationship between our 'truth' and its function.

In the first instance, then, there is the common concept of ideology as propaganda – a misrepresentation or partial representation of reality – or a complete fabrication – which serves an overtly political purpose.[54] For instance, in an early article, Hans Kelsen said that 'traditional legal science' had such an 'ideological colouring', characterizing ideology in the following terms:

> Ideology … covers up reality, by explaining it away if it wishes to defend it, by distorting it if it wishes to destroy it or replace it with a substitute. All ideology has its roots in willing and not in knowing; it springs from certain interests, or more correctly, from interests other than that of truth. In saying this, of course, nothing is implied as to the value or worth of these other interests.[55]

Such a use of the term, in opposing the will to truth, presupposes the existence of a knowledge which is non-ideological, neutral or objective – a belief which Kelsen clearly held very strongly at this point. Even if we do not believe in the existence of unconstructed or 'natural' knowledge, such a concept of ideology may still be useful in highlighting misrepresentations made in bad faith or relative ignorance and aimed at fulfilling an overt political end. However, this is not a claim I would necessarily direct against any legal theory.

Second, we can understand ideology as a process of naturalization of ideas and meanings which are not in fact natural, but rather produced by discursive conventions: 'ideology is "the perception that reifies the results of discursive procedures into properties of the 'thing itself'".'[56] To take a simple example, the perception that women are less 'rational' than men is currently understood as the result of the symbolic constructions of rationality, of gender difference and of socialisation processes which build on, and reinforce, these constructions. However, the idea that women are less than fully rational has frequently been naturalized – that is, considered as a natural property of women – with very powerful social consequences.

In this sense, Kelsen's own work can be said to rely on the ideology of science, which aims at simple description of objects. A positivism oriented towards the description of 'what law is' may account for what law looks like from a certain (privileged) subject position, in a particular (modern, Western) context and within the framework of a specific (liberal) politics, but it does not account for the fact that law may look quite different for a person or group who is by their social status, and not by choice, outside these positions or, even more strongly, whose 'law' is not THE (white/Western/male-dominated) law.[57] Descriptive positivism depends on the possibility of an objective knowledge of law and presents its understanding of law as a description of the properties of law itself, an understanding which roughly corresponds to the 'real' relationship between law and the individual. Such a view of law has the political effect of justifying law as it is, because it fails to foreground alternative knowledges of law, it naturalizes its own perception of law. Thus, while one possible description of law is that it actually does separate doctrine from individuals, another point of view could just as convincingly emphasize that in fact the doctrine, structure, and ideology of law reflect the 'law' of a particular person or social group.

Third, ideology is the operation by which a narrative about a social issue or institution becomes self-fulfilling and self-replicating:[58] Again, to take the example of gender, the identification of a (male or female) person as masculine or feminine within a symbolic system which creates this distinction along certain lines, strongly influences a person to perform, and through performance to become and to identify as, that gender.[59] The gender system is therefore reproduced through what Althusser called 'interpellation' of human beings as subjects[60] and by their performance of the norms of gender. The truth of the system becomes self-fulfilling.

Similarly, although the positivist story seems more or less 'true', this is primarily due to the fact that it is supported by the institutional power of the legal profession, the courts and the legal academy:[61] all these institutions are themselves reliant for their authority on the myth of transcendent and separable law which is therefore *assumed, lived, and performed* by legal officials rather than merely existing as a neutral social or institutional fact. The appeal to a 'description' of law masks the political and constructive undercurrent of the perspective. I should make it clear that my argument is not that descriptive positivism is simply 'false'.[62] It justifies and supports the notion that law has authority, objectivity and independence, encourages people to behave *as if* law actually is separate or separable, and erases its constructive function by professing a neutral description. We could call it factional, fictional and functional – which is a long way from being purely descriptive. Most importantly, I see positivism as integral to current methods of legal reproduction: to use the Althusserian explanation, we are all identified or 'interpellated' by the law as individuated legal subjects with an existence which is separate from law; we take on and perform this legal construction and, in so doing, re-create the law in its own image. Simple critique of positivist notions of separation or separability does not break the chain which relies as much on performance as it does on a theoretical appreciation of the nature of law.

A Law of Isolation and Exclusion

Prescriptive positivism is much more interesting than positivisms intended to represent a factual, institutional or ideal concept of law, especially insofar as it revives the strategic or political edge of the positivist tradition and acknowledges the political basis of a theory of law. Bentham and Austin clearly had strong reformist ideas, and prescriptive positivism is concerned with bringing out the political tradition in positivist thought.[63]

However, while uncompromisingly focused in its desire to minimize the possibility of arbitrary decision-making, and to clarify the grounds of law and the distinctness of law from its non-legal other, ethical or prescriptive positivism may not have paid sufficient attention to the oppressive potential of legal separatism. In my view it is also important to address the dangers of separation when practised by a powerful institution, in a context of social pluralism which incorporates intolerance of, and discrimination against, those who do not conform to predominant expectations. The separation of the law from the moral being in prescriptive positivist theory is intended to be *protective* of individual freedom and equality under a legal regime which is neutral as to the particular identity of the subject; our law is therefore said to be subject to debate and critique over its content, as well as its overall structure. However, the imposition of a positivist mentality on to a stratified and hierarchized society results in a reconsolidation of social power in the mechanisms of legitimate authority. If positivism *could* perform the prescriptive function for which it is apparently intended, legal power would act as an authoritative restraint on social or individual power. Instead, social power and legal power end up reinforcing each other. This is not necessarily an argument against prescriptive positivism *per se*, but rather an argument about the functional impact of positivism in a divided social context.

One way of thinking about the possible consequences of prescriptive positivism is to look more generally at the politics of separation – a topic which I have considered elsewhere in more detail.[64] In the West, the separatist mentality has usually been advocated as a way for marginalized or dispossessed groups of people to claim a space for themselves, to form an identity and a political voice, to control their own knowledges and destiny, and possibly even to form distinct self-determining political entities.[65] The crucial dimension of separatist ideals is that separation is a method of channelling power – taking the power of defining, identification, and determination away from the dominant group and rendering the dominant paradigms less powerful. Inevitably, those who fit squarely within the targeted group may feel threatened because of the potential disaggregation of their own power base. Even from within a particular group of people, where separatism might be seen as a possible option, it is frequently criticized for being divisive and exclusive – what good is feminist separation when it would require women to reject their own culture and alliances within it?[66] – for being impossible – can we really shed our conditioning and what would we replace it with anyway? – and, in some cases, for relying on problematic notions of purity.

Now, in some senses, the justifications for positivism mirror those made by marginalized peoples for political separation. In particular, a separate law clearly has the advantage of forming a distinct identity for itself by excluding certain others, and it channels social, legal and political power through established structures. However, in my view, the results of a separation practised by a powerful institution are quite different from the struggles of people who are excluded from access to social and political power.

In the first place, separation excludes: in privileging a particular narrative as 'law' positivism is predicated upon the exclusion of other narratives; in practice this means the exclusion of those who cannot adopt or understand the legal narrative or are not envisaged by it, and inclusion of those who do. Even if every human person formally has a legal voice, some voices are more easily heard by law because they arise in a language which it can recognize. Now, obviously we could say that this is a fault of law, and that it should listen more carefully or draw its lines differently, but the point is that the unification of law into a singular and distinct entity will inevitably, often invisibly, and not merely as a matter of overt political choice, delineate a particular cultural preference – at present, white, educated and masculine. Second, separation renders its competitors in the struggle for meaning less persuasive or even non-existent: positive law filters the everyday world, reduces the analysis of events and facts to a single truth and fails to perceive that there may not be a single reasonable reading of the 'facts'. The result, frequently remarked upon by those who feel undervalued or silenced by law, is that the stories told and heard by law are a one-dimensional misreading of actual social situations as perceived by their participants.[67] Finally, separation places formal blocks on access and knowledge and, although such blocks in positivist law may be dismantled by various means such as legal aid, plain language drafting and so on, it remains to be seen whether law will thereby become any more accessible to people in general.

In general terms then, I would say that, while eliminating the more obvious and open abuses of personal power, the positivist separation which is intended to equalize persons before the law in fact separates unequally, and I am sceptical about whether a more perfect realization of positivist ideals would improve this situation.

Conclusion: Theory and Power

> Each object is in reality a small virtual volcano. There is a continuity in the living: whereas theory entails a discontinuity, a cut, which is altogether the opposite of life. ... [Theory] is indispensable, at times, to make progress, but alone it is false. I resign myself to it as a dangerous aid. It is a prosthesis. All that advances is aerial, detached, uncatchable.[68]

The foregoing comments are not intended to be comprehensive and reduce a very complex theoretical picture. Rather than fully explain all the different claims of the anti-positivist positions, which would have involved entering into several theoretical traditions, I have chosen to summarize them, and situate them in relation to positivist thought. My perspective is offered in the spirit of further understanding the positivist mentality and the dangers contained within it. However, I would not advocate its complete abandonment or elimination. We need to remember that the positivist approach, even if it is based upon a series of foreclosures and exclusions, remains the framework for current Western understandings of law, and that arguments aiming at the elimination of social oppressions have historically taken place, and will continue to be framed, within this context. Like liberalism, positivism has even been strategically very useful for engineering social change, despite its limitations. Indeed, many purportedly anti-positivist approaches are potentially more dangerous and more stifling of individual and group difference.[69] This is not to say that the fictional construct of positivist law should always be adopted, simply that it may be strategically useful to do so in some instances. Some radical reconception of law which builds on the positivist foundation may yet provide a way forward, although such a reconception would not, I believe, itself be positivist, but would acknowledge a multiplicity of potential laws and of personalities under and outside the law.

Notes

1 I. Watson, 'Indigenous People's Law-Ways: Survival Against the Colonial State', *Australian Feminist Law Journal*, **8** (1997), p. 39.

2 S. Bottomley and S. Parker, *Law in Context*, 2nd edn (Sydney: Federation Press, 1994), pp. 46–53.

3 H. Kelsen, *The Pure Theory of Law* (Berkeley: University of California Press, 1967), pp. 171–4; A. Nekam, *The Personality Conception of the Legal Entity* (Cambridge, MA: Harvard University Press, 1938), ch. 2.

4 It is here that the terminology becomes extremely slippery: I would say, for instance, that the legal subject in postmodern theory denotes something different from the classical notion of the legal person. The former is the entity subjected to, and arising out of, legal discourse broadly conceived (the man 'before the law' in Kafka's tale) whereas the latter is a technical term performing a specifically legal function. Cf., for instance, J. Derrida, 'Before the Law', in Derek Attridge (ed.), *Acts of Literature/Jacques Derrida* (New York: Routledge, 1992), pp. 181–220 and H. Kelsen, *The Pure Theory of Law*, *op. cit.*, pp. 171–4.

5 For instance, the concept of a 'legal culture' is one which is common in comparative legal theory but less frequently used in mainstream Anglo-American legal theory: it is a useful term because it highlights the cultural dimension of law, which has not been a prominent part of Anglo-American jurisprudence. See M. Van Hoecke and M. Warrington, 'Legal Cultures, Legal Paradigms and Legal Doctrine: Towards a New Model for Comparative Law', *International and Comparative Law Quarterly*, **47** (1998), pp. 495–536; V. Grosswald Curran, 'Cultural Immersion, Difference and Categories in U.S. Comparative Law', *American Journal of Comparative Law*, **46** (1998), pp. 43–92.

6 Foucault said that the mysteries of the taxonomy of Borges' Chinese Encyclopaedia reveal the limitations of our thought, rather than the incoherence, irrationality, or illogical nature of the other systems of thought – 'the thing that ... is demonstrated as the exotic charm of another system of thought, is the limitation of our own, the stark impossibility of thinking *that*': M. Foucault, *The Order of Things* (London: Tavistock, 1980), p xv.

7 H.L.A. Hart, *The Concept of Law*, 2nd edn (Oxford: Clarendon Press, 1994), pp. 91–9.

8 Positivism could be characterized along different lines, and undoubtedly any attempt to categorize could be criticized, I take an approach which appears to me to be most obvious. I should also say that I take the position of one who does not follow or engage with the detail of positivist theory, but rather only its broad outline. This does not make me entirely an outsider, since all Western legal culture is imbued with positivist assumptions. However, it does mean that my evaluation is not completely centred on positivism but somewhat marginal, or even cross-cultural. A fuller account of positivist ideas is to be found in T. Campbell, *The Legal Theory of Ethical Positivism* (Aldershot: Dartmouth, 1996), pp. 78 ff.

9 H. Kelsen, *The Pure Theory of Law* , *op. cit.* H. Kelsen, *General Theory of Law and State* (New York: Russell and Russell, 1945); see also I. Stewart, 'The Critical Legal Science of Hans Kelsen', *Journal of Law and Society*, **17** (1990), pp. 273–308.

10 As Campbell says, 'the standard Legal Positivist analysis of law in terms of the general commands or rules emanating from a sovereign or other social source is routinely presented and understood primarily either as a truth about the meaning of "law" or as a key to the understanding of law as a social phenomenon': *Ethical Positivism, op. cit.*, p. 74.

11 J. Austin, *The Province of Jurisprudence Determined* (London: Weidenfield and Nicolson, 1954).

12 H. Kelsen, *The Pure Theory of Law, op. cit.*, p. 1.

13 '... Legal Positivism is not tied to the ideology of its origins. Law as a system of rules can serve collective as well as individual ends, and the individuals involved may be constituted in large measure by their social roles, group affiliations, and societal environment without undermining the assumptions of [legal positivism]': T. Campbell, *Ethical Positivism, op. cit.*, p. 5.

14 See M. Thornton, 'The Cartography of Public and Private', in M. Thornton (ed.), *Public and Private: Feminist Legal Debates* (Melbourne: Oxford University Press, 1995), pp. 2–16.

15 J.S. Mill, 'On Liberty', in J.S. Mill, *Utilitarianism* (London: Fontana, 1962); cf. I. Berlin, 'Two Concepts of Liberty', in *Four Essays on Liberty* (Oxford: Oxford University Press, 1969), pp. 118–72.

16 Bentham states this explicitly in imagining a pre-legal existence: 'As yet there is no law in the land. The legislator hath not yet entered upon his office. As yet he hath neither commanded nor prohibited any act. As yet all acts therefore are free: all persons as against the law are at liberty': J. Bentham, *The Limits of Jurisprudence Defined* (New York: Columbia University Press, 1945), p. 59.

17 Campbell, *Ethical Positivism, op. cit.*, p. 5.

18 See K. O'Donovan, *Sexual Divisions in Law* (London: Weidenfeld and Nicolson, 1985), ch. 1.

19 It would be generally true that the number of human beings who have the full complement of legal 'personality' characteristics has been expanding.

20 C. Stone, 'Should Trees Have Standing? – Towards Legal Rights for Natural Objects', *Southern California Law Review*, **45** (1972), p. 450; see also L. Fuller, *Legal Fictions* (Stanford University Press, 1967); A. Nekam, *The Personality Conception of the Legal Entity* (Cambridge, MA.: Harvard University Press, 1993).

21 In formulating a positivist understanding of the legal person, for instance, Kelsen rejects the notion that there is a right-holder outside the law (as in a theory which argues that there are natural rights which constrain and delimit legal rights). The legal person – both the juristic person (such as a corporation) and the physical person – are artificial constructs of law. Thus, 'The physical or juristic person who "has" obligations and rights as their holder, is these obligations and rights – a complex of legal obligations and rights whose totality is expressed figuratively in the concept "person": *The Pure Theory of Law, op. cit.*, p. 173. In this sense, the human being as a natural and social phenomenon and the legal person as a juristic construct are conceptually separate. See also I. Stewart 'The Critical Legal Science of Hans Kelsen', *op. cit.*, pp. 293–4.

22 See generally J.H. Baker, *An Introduction to English Legal History*, 3rd edn (London: Butterworths, 1994), ch. 26.

23 Watson, 'Indigenous People's Law-Ways', *op. cit.*

24 P. Fitzpatrick, *The Mythology of Modern Law* (London: Routledge, 1992); C. Douzinas and R. Warrington, *Postmodern Jurisprudence: The Law of Text in the Text of Law* (London: Routledge, 1991).

25 Bentham, *The Limits of Jurisprudence Defined, op. cit.*, p. 282.

26 Hart, *The Concept of Law, op. cit.*, pp. 91–9.

27 Austin, *The Province of Jurisprudence Determined, op. cit.*, p. 10.

28 Cf. Campbell, *Ethical Positivism, op. cit.*, pp. 78–91.

[29] ' ... modern Positivists take it to be a virtue of their theory that the sharp distinction between what law is and what law ought to be makes it a visibly open question whether citizens are morally bound to carry out their obligations': Campbell, *Ethical Positivism, op. cit.*, p. 98.

[30] Of course, all knowledge is incomplete, but I would say that, even within the framework of what is 'known' in legal theory, positivism has not sufficiently taken into account the views of the dissidents to its ideas. Campbell's work is, in this sense, possibly an important moment of transition.

[31] R. Dworkin, *Law's Empire* (London: Fontana, 1986). Dworkin's model of interpretation is itself highly questionable. See M. Davies, *Delimiting the Law: 'Postmodernism' and the Politics of Law* (London: Pluto, 1996), pp. 59–62.

[32] This is the argument that the process of identifying and applying law is inherently, and unavoidably, political, which is considered below. The criticism that legal policy is political doesn't really hit the mark (since it's obvious), although it is important to continue to demystify the continuing belief that law is actually neutral in some fundamental sense. Insofar as positivism reinforces such myths of neutrality, it is complicit in the widespread assumption that law actually is neutral regarding the distribution of power.

[33] J. Derrida, 'Force of Law: The "Mystical Foundation of Authority"', *Cardozo Law Review*, **11** (1990), p. 919; D. Cornell, 'The Violence of the Masquerade: Law Dressed Up as Justice', *Cardozo Law Review*, **11** (1990), p. 1047; M. Davies, 'Legitimate Fictions', in T. Cohen (ed.), *The Cambridge Companion to Derrida* (Cambridge: Cambridge University Press, 1999, forthcoming).

[34] For example, P. Gabel and D. Kennedy, 'Roll Over Beethoven', *Stanford Law Review*, **36** (1984), pp. 1–55; P. Gabel, 'The Phenomenology of Rights-Consciousness and the Pact of the Withdrawn Selves', *Texas Law Review*, **62** (1984), p. 1563; V. Kerruish, *Jurisprudence as Ideology* (London: Routledge, 1991), pp. 16–19.

[35] M. Detmold, 'Law and Difference: Reflections on Mabo's Case', *Sydney Law Review*, **15** (1993), pp. 159–67. Detmold's point is that community presupposes recognition of difference: therefore the red view cannot take over the green, and vice versa.

[36] J. Derrida, 'Before the Law', *op. cit.*, p. 204.

[37] 'Objective knowledge' is subject-independent knowledge of an object: that is, a knowledge in which the identity of the subject is irrelevant. See L. Code, 'Taking Subjectivity into Account', in L. Alcoff and E. Potter (eds), *Feminist Epistemologies* (New York: Routledge, 1993). See also D. Haraway, *Simians, Cyborgs, and Women: The Reinvention of Nature* (New York: Routledge, 1991), ch. 9.

[38] Sandra Harding attempts to reclaim the notion of objective knowledge, by arguing for a knowledge which is not so much objectification, but rather gives weight and subjectivity to the object or other as a 'resource': to 'enact or operationalize the directive of strong objectivity is to value the Other's perspective and to pass over in thought into the social condition that creates it – not to stay there, to "go native" or merge the self with the Other, but in order to look back at the self in all its cultural particularity from a more distant, critical, objectifying location': S. Harding, *Whose Science? Whose Knowledge*? (Ithaca, NY: Cornell University Press, 1991), p. 143.

[39] J-F. Lyotard, *The Postmodern Condition: A Report on Knowledge* (Manchester: Manchester University Press, 1984); M. Foucault, *Power/Knowledge: Selected Interviews and Other Writings* (Brighton: Harvester, 1980).

[40] Campbell, *Ethical Positivism, op. cit.*, p. 84. Campbell goes on to say that the separability thesis 'enables us to state neatly the essence of Ethical Positivism as the view that a good legal system is, inter alia, one in which adjudicators use empirical or, more broadly, morally neutral criteria in their identification and interpretation of laws, and one in which legislators enact laws which can be so identified and

interpreted'. On both scores – the ability to identify and interpret laws by reference to neutral criteria and the ability to create such laws – I believe the ideals of ethical positivism are unattainable.

41 See the brief discussion of Fitzpatrick, below.

42 This is a typically Derridean argument, which cannot be explained in the detail which it deserves. See, for instance, J. Derrida, *Positions* (Chicago: University of Chicago Press, 1981), translated and annotated by Alan Bass; Davies, 'Legitimate Fictions', *op. cit.*

43 See, for instance, Sarah Kofman, 'Descartes Entrapped', in E. Cadava *et al.* (eds), *Who Comes After the Subject?* (New York: Routledge, 1991); J. Butler, *Bodies that Matter*. I.M. Young, *Justice and the Politics of Difference* (Princeton, NJ: Princeton University Press, 1990), pp. 42–8.

44 The term' discourse' refers to systems of meaning within which we are constituted as subjects. Therefore it is possible to speak of legal discourse as a system extending beyond formal law, which comprises the norms through which legal meanings are created.

45 A distinction which I reject. See below.

46 C. Douzinas and R. Warrington, *Postmodern Jurisprudence, op. cit.*; Davies, *Delimiting the Law, op. cit.*

47 Fitzpatrick, *The Mythology of Modern Law, op. cit.*, p. 134.

48 Ibid., p. 135.

49 See Davies *Delimiting the Law, op. cit.*; See also Nicola Lacey, Chapter 4 in this volume.

50 R. Barthes, *Mythologies*, trans. Annette Lavers (London: Paladin, 1973), pp. 123–4.

51 Kerruish, *Jurisprudence as Ideology, op. cit.*

52 For instance, Kerruish distinguishes between a neutral and a negative sense of the concept of 'ideology': ibid., pp. 22–5.

53 S. Zizek, 'The Spectre of Ideology', in S. Zizek (ed.), *Mapping Ideology* (London: Verso, 1994), pp. 1–33. I have somewhat simplified Zizek's reading of the meanings of the scholarly critiques of ideology.

54 Ibid., p. 10. See also Kerruish, *Jurisprudence as Ideology, op. cit.*, p. 24.

55 H. Kelsen, 'The Pure Theory of Law: Its Method and Fundamental Concepts', *Law Quarterly Review*, **20** (1934), pp. 474–98 at p. 483.

56 Zizek, 'The Spectre of Ideology', *op. cit.*, p. 11, summarizing the understanding of ideology of Roland Barthes in *Mythologies, op. cit.*

57 Cf. Kerruish, *Jurisprudence as Ideology, op. cit.*, ch. 6.

58 Zizek, 'The Spectre of Ideology', *op. cit.*, p. 12. Zizek refers to Louis Althusser's 'Ideology, and Ideological State Apparatuses', in Zizek's *Mapping Ideology, op. cit.*, pp. 100–40, which is a classic reconstruction of Marxist theory on the relationship between (material) base and (ideological) superstructure.

59 J. Butler, *Gender Trouble: Feminism and the Subversion of Identity* (New York: Routledge, 1990); *Bodies That Matter: On the Discursive Limits of Sex* (New York: Routledge, 1993): *Excitable Speech: A Politics of the Performative* (New York: Routledge, 197), pp. 31–4.

60 Althusser, 'Ideology', *op. cit.*, pp. 128–36. At p. 130 Althusser states, for instance, that you and I are always-already subjects and, as such, constantly practise the rituals of ideological recognition which guarantee for us that we are indeed concrete, individual, distinguishable and (naturally) irreplaceable subjects. Thus, we are subjects by virtue of the fact that we practise and perform as subjects, and are hailed as subjects by others.

61 Cf. M. Foucault, 'Truth and Power' in Foucault, *Power/Knowledge, op. cit.*

62 Kerruish makes this point carefully: '... although our jurists' views of law are negatively ideological, they are not merely false or mere illusion. There is a basis in

social reality for their ideas of law': *Jurisprudence as Ideology, op. cit.*, p. 195. She argues that jurisprudence is 'negative' ideology because it neglects or forgets its basis in a particular 'standpoint'.

[63] Campbell very convincingly situates his approach within a context of positivist thinkers with strongly ethical or political motivations. See Campbell, *Ethical Positivism, op. cit.*, p. 74.

[64] M. Davies, 'Lesbian Separatism and Legal Positivism', *Canadian Journal of Law and Society*, **13** (1998), pp. 1–28. Since publishing this article, I have perhaps achieved a more subtle (and less hostile) understanding of positivism, but I think that the central arguments proposed are still effective.

[65] See, for example, Marilyn Frye, 'Some Reflections on Separatism and Power' in M. Frye, *The Politics of Reality: Essays in Feminist Theory* (Trumansberg: Crossing, 1993).

[66] M. Lugones, 'Hispaneando y Lesbiando: On Sarah Hoagland's *Lesbian Ethics*', *Hypatia*, **5** (1990), pp. 138, 143.

[67] An example which readily springs to mind is the way that the perspectives of battered women who kill are read as a 'syndrome', rather than as normal and understandable behaviour. See also R. Delgado, 'Storytelling for Oppositionists and Others: A Plea for Narrative', *Michigan Law Review*, **87** (1989), p. 2411; see also G.C. Spivak, 'Can the Subaltern Speak?', in C. Nelson and L. Grossberg (eds), *Marxism and the Interpretation of Culture* (Basingstoke: Macmillan, 1988), pp. 271–313.

[68] H. Cixous and M. Calle-Gruber, *Hélène Cixous, Rootprints: Memory and Life Writing*, trans. Eric Prenowitz (London: Routledge, 1994), p. 4.

[69] For instance, Dworkin's idea of law as 'integrity', and ultimately grounded in a rather singular notion of community values, does not acknowledge the real differences within any community, nor the fact that such differences are also frequently differences of power. Cf. Dworkin, *Law's Empire, op. cit.* Theories of natural law may also tend towards totalizing a concept of the good.

6 Positivism and Difference

HELEN STACY[1]

Introduction

Some of the most difficult legal and social issues arise from the problem posed by culture and difference. This may be difference arising from nationalism, or racial, ethnic and cultural movements, or gender and sexuality. They extend beyond the abstract and the academic to shape the immediate and the practical. This diversity poses a challenge for jurisprudence. The challenge for legal theory is to step outside the illusory, though comforting, paradigm of universalism in order to develop greater sensitivity to culture and difference.

In his 1996 book *The Legal Theory of Ethical Positivism*, Tom Campbell persuasively argues an aspirational case for a rule-based legal system that calls for ethical conduct from participants in legal conflict.[2] Acknowledging from the outset that we are operating today in 'a postmodern environment',[3] Campbell argues that positivism can go beyond its historical disconnection between law and morality. Rather, with 'an ethic of subordination of personal views to the morality of [one's legal] role',[4] Campbell invites us to see a rule-based legal system as morally significant in itself, as a 'vision of what a good legal system looks like and how it contributes to a just, effective and democratic polity'.[5]

Where does the approach of legal ethical positivism sit in the present cross-currents of legal and social theory? For much of the twentieth century jurisprudence in Western legal systems has been presented as a coherent philosophy of the system that underlies thinking and writing about law and legal adjudication. This view has built on the central characteristic of legal thought and legal reasoning of the previous three centuries – the idea that knowledge can be justified only if it rests upon unquestionable foundations. From this belief in epistemological foundations it has been assumed that the analytic approach of jurisprudence would support 'justice' and 'democracy' as the discernible and distinctive characteristics of (most) Western democratic economies. The mark of good legal scholarship from the pen of the judge and the barristers' argument has its basis in law as expressed in legislation and further explicated in precedent. Where precedent cannot directly supply the solution to a new social problem, recourse is had to general principles of proper conduct. These are found in the intentions of the long-dead men who created foundational legal documents, such as constitutions or commentaries, or sometimes more creatively in exercises of judicial discretion.

Since the 1960s this approach in Western jurisdictions to law as a distinctive and autonomous system has come under fire. Law is charged with being artificial and increasingly irrelevant to the realities of legal practice, the increasing complexity of life and the governance of the modern state. The traditional modern analysis of legal problems had assumed that law functioned autonomously of culture. Traditional analysis maintained that legal rules had an existence independent of the dynamics of class, race, age, religion and sexual orientation. This traditional view has been unsettled by two phenomena over the last three decades. First, the exposure of the cultural costs of colonialism in the post-colonial 1960s and 1970s has revealed the Western bias in 'human rights-talk'. Second, fundamental rights theories lost their epistemological clout (though not their political punch) as it became increasingly difficult to explain and justify which rights were 'fundamental' or 'universal', and why fundamental rights should overcome other rights or choices.[6] A noisy critique of legal institutions has thus arisen. It chastizes this century's jurisprudence for too confidently assuming that humanity possesses universal characteristics. Traditional jurisprudence, the noise accuses, is unable to provide a full analysis of the vast social, economic and cultural differences between people.

The ethical revision of analytical positivism provided by Campbell is a welcome development to the Hart–Fuller debates and the critical charge that analytical jurisprudence is both epistemologically and ontologically constricted. The debate about the ethics of law-making and legal adjudication at the close of the twentieth century poses this question: is law simply the will to power (compassionately exercised) or is there another way that sees law as an expression of ethical understanding of difference? Campbell wishes to emphasize the ethical prerequisites that make the separation between law and morality feasible, asserting that such separation is in itself an ethical undertaking. As he puts it:

> [Legal ethical positivism] depends both on the analytical thesis that law can be conceptually, argumentatively and operationally separated

> from morality and on the sociological thesis that actually legal systems can approximate to situations where their laws are administered in a rule-deferential manner.[7]

Under Campbell's legal ethical positivism, the role of judges is to act impartially through subjugating their own moral beliefs in applying the will of the people, as articulated through legislative enactments. Legal ethical positivism requires that the rules that the judge applies to the cases before him or her must have particular characteristics: they must have specificity, clarity and mutual consistency. Furthermore, the legal rule thus interpreted must be interpreted by the judge with some understanding of 'the situations to which the rule is intended to apply and the general nature of the political choice that was involved in its formulation or retention'.[8] There is, unsurprisingly, a clear preference for statute law over the common law in Campbell's reformulation of positivism, and an opposition to judicial discretion.

How might Campbell's ethical legal positivism fit into a world where the meaning of 'law' and 'morality' is ambulatory? Campbell argues that legal ethical positivism provides a framework 'in a postmodern environment'[9] that answers the critique of positivism offered by communitarian, socialist and feminist theories.[10] How does legal ethical positivism fit in the modern/postmodern world, where we have a new awareness of the porous effects of subjectivity and objectivity? What is the nature of modernity that Campbell suggests has been superseded by the postmodern environment, and what are the characteristics of modern legal reasoning and adjudication that postmodernism critiques? What is postmodernism in law? How might postmodern legal approaches coalesce with Campbell's project of defining adjudication which 'embodies rules of mutual convenience which aid social cooperation'[11] and contribute to a 'just, effective and democratic polity'?

These are, individually, limitless questions for exploration. This chapter will be confined to a selection only and leave other questions open. First, I describe some of the key assumptions of universality that have been attacked by critical legal studies, then by postmodernism, and now by what I have termed here 'the difference critique'. My descriptions of both are influenced by the view that modernity, as the Anglo-American tradition describes it, tends to overlook the impact of Continental philosophical influences that followed after Kant. This oversight in turn tends to obscure the sources and relevance of aspects of postmodern critique. Second, I look at Campbell's ethics of adjudication under his model of legal ethical pluralism, suggesting that it goes only part of the way towards dealing with difference in legal conflict. I raise here the possibility of adjudicating conflict with an even further heightened awareness of the intersubjective differences between legal parties to a dispute than Campbell's judge might possess. I ask how the modern/postmodern judge might deal better with conflict resolution across radically different lines of understanding and world views. Like Campbell, I raise these possibilities as aspirational.[12] Finally, I raise some of the problems that postmodernism poses for law. I suggest (though do not fully argue), that postmodernism can be read as a reformist stance that can advance legal thinking and adjudication. What is left unargued is the way in which postmodernism can justify its politics beyond the compassionate will to power that legal ethical positivism stakes out.

Modernity Moves to a 'Postmodern Environment'

How do the Postmoderns Describe Modernity?

Principles of legal reasoning in the West have developed from the constellation of political theory and jurisprudence that together make legal liberalism. Lawyers are educated to sympathize with the meta-discourses of modernity, the roots of the *polis* (Aristotle), the development of legal responsibility as the state's responsibility to police the negative rights of the individual (Rousseau[13]) and the nineteenth- and twentieth-century refinements to rights discourse (Bentham[14] to Hart[15] to Finnis[16]). These are the founding fathers of jurisprudence in Western liberal democracies or what is otherwise loosely known as 'the project of modernity' or 'the Enlightenment'. These terms describe the political and legal organization of the nation-state of the last several hundred years and rely on a foundational concept of human reason or 'rationality'.

During this period the legitimation of Western political and legal power altered from the monarch's will to representative democracy. Democracy carries the concepts of universal freedom and equality that, in England, came through Hobbes and Locke. From the German philosophical tradition, the philosophy of Kant[17] (the view of the transcendental subjects and objects of law) and Hegel[18] (the master–slave dialectic) have added to the theoretical basis of a confident assumption that justice would be achieved by political and legal systems guided by enlightened reason. Over this time, modernity has incorporated different views of political theory: liberalism, Marxism, socialism, pragmatism, realism, scepticism (and neo-liberalism, neo-Marxism, neo-pragmatism, and variations thereof). Despite their many differences, one of the goals of theorists and philosophers of modernity was to create and maintain legal institutions that would combine empirical knowledge ('the facts') with continuous certainty (precedent and 'the common law tradition'). This approach of reason within an analytic framework would, it was felt, produce a certain outcome to ensure the common good. By definition, legal rationality purports to exclude subjective bias in favour of reasoned objectivity.

Modern legal practitioners work at systematizing legal knowledge by using coherent and verifiable propositions about the nature of law and adjudication. The assumption within this conceptual framework is that a distinctively analytical legal method or theory will yield correct answers to problems that law must deal with. This traditional form of legal analysis rests upon cool, rational appraisals of all the available evidence, weighing and balancing the evidence with disinterest so as to identify the 'truth'. As long as this method is followed, the outcome can be relied upon as 'fair'. Certainty and predictability are the perceived benefits whereby citizens may confidently plan their actions *qua* the state and *qua* their fellow citizens. The safest form of attack on the legal conclusions reached relies on demonstrating a failure of lawyers and judges to look at all the evidence or a failure to scrupulously follow the analytical method.

Amidst this, legal modernity has also evolved the appositional idea that legal values are context-dependent. This arose in the nineteenth century from the sociological jurisprudence of that time and was influenced by Weber[19] and Durkheim.[20] In Europe during the 1930s, the Frankfurt School of critical social theory introduced 'praxis' – the outcome of constructing theory from empirical findings, principally from sociology but also from psychology, economics and psychoanalysis.[21] In the United States during the 1920s and 1930s, the Realist judges were influenced by Weber and Durkheim to bring a sociological perspective to legal adjudication. The Realists demonstrated a similar spirit of experimentation with previously rigidly held disciplinary boundaries and conceptual frameworks. Since the social ruptures deriving from the end of the Second World War, Western legal and political discourse has been increasingly influenced by the English-speaking world's focus on 'legal process' and 'fundamental rights'. The United States' pre-eminent role in global politics in the post-Second World War period has additionally ensured the infiltration of rights discourse into politics and law in both English-speaking and non-English-speaking Western jurisdictions.[22]

Jurisprudence, as it was perceived in Western jurisdictions until the 1960s, thus comprised a combination of two identifiable approaches. First, there was the scrutiny of the institutional relationship between courts and the legislature through the lens of democratic liberal theory. Second, an analysis of individual rights developed as a means of locating the systematic ways in which law produces and reproduces 'certainty', as well as maintaining broader democratic interests in the balancing act between the courts, the legislature and the administrative arms of government. Law has been regarded as a discipline that is autonomous from both the natural and social sciences, because legal reasoning and legal methods were thought to be sufficiently distinct from the methods of other disciplines.

Critical Legal Scholarship

In the 1960s spirit of equating modernity with patriarchal eschatology,[23] new schools of thought arose around legal identities excluded by patriarchy, such as those based on race, culture and gender. These new approaches to critical thought demonstrated a more significant point about the assumptions of Western legal thought: that legal identities are a construction, influenced by liberal values and history. These new schools of thought have laid the foundation for a jurisprudence based upon the dialectical relation between law and society and the complicated effects this has on individual agency and intentionality. This critique suggests that, if effective legal solutions to society's problems require a context-specific legal response, then legal decision-making cannot begin with an unshakeable assumption of the universality of human characteristics. This view remains, by and large, unacceptable to traditional jurisprudential thinkers who retain their commitment to the ideal of law as an autonomous, objective activity operating on a human identity that is relatively stable and fixed.

Critical legal studies sought to move beyond the idea of law as an autonomous discipline and to incorporate the insights of the social sciences.[24] The early critical legal studies movement of the 1970s revealed that the interpretive practices of law worked to reinstate or 'produce' the objective foundational theory for law. Rather, it was law's *own* claim to disinterested neutrality and objectivity that protected its reasoning and practices from the critique of exposure. New jurisprudential discourses of law and economics, women and the law, law and literature and indigenous peoples and the law have been a failure since then, emphasizing at every turn the heterogeneity of the juridic subject. This new body of scholarship employs interdisciplinary approaches to legal analysis to show how legal methodology is linked to social, economic, political and cultural contexts. Consequently, the bedrock jurisprudential assumption that law is a self-contained, autonomous system has been thoroughly questioned.[25] These new genres have asserted that law and, in particular, adjudication is unavoidably and always connected with political and moral values, notwithstanding legal liberalism's claims to objectivity and neutrality. As a result, critical legal scholars argue, law cannot be rendered coherent by a single comprehensive legal theory.

With its 'trashing' approach the early critical scholarship stripped away law's self-referential claim to objectivity to reveal other aspects that influence legal decision-making.[26] Nowadays, the suggestion that lawyers, judges and legal academics are influenced by ideology, biases and preferences that play a part in legal reasoning seems so self-evident as to be pedestrian, but when it was first made, traditional legal scholars perceived this critical claim as exemplifying a form of betrayal to traditional modes of legal thought. This scuffle demonstrated that Western liberal political theory, in working from a conception of the universalized human identity of the rational, self-interested economic legal subject, was simply maintaining a particular political tradition. It has shown that the apparently non-gendered human identity of the legal self is thoroughly gendered and operates largely to further the interests of men to the detriment of women. It has also shown that the language of racial equality in law is frequently a cloak for values that belong to the white or colonial majority, which are to the detriment of the non-white or colonized population.

Sociological jurisprudence and critical legal studies have thoroughly defused the idea of law as autonomous from social, economic, political and cultural contexts. However, despite the claims that these critiques have made, they have not adopted a radical *method* in order to make their claims. They have still assumed that it is possible to examine legal reasoning and legal practices from an external vantage point of the subject/object. This vantage point supposedly provides a place where the onlooker, unaffected by any allegiance to the status quo of traditional jurisprudence (or any status quo at all) may observe and expose particular legal values that operate under the guise of neutrality, such as the values of patriarchy, capitalism and racism. The search for new jurisprudential approaches for understanding law and adjudication has commonly struck the problem that it is often impossible to convey new insights within traditional legal concepts and in orthodox legal vocabulary. In attempting to point out the gendered nature of legal language to traditional legal scholars who regard legal language to be neutral, feminists have had to appeal to ideas and language that lie outside the conceptual framework and language of traditional legal reasoning. In order to expose the patriarchy embedded in legal language, legal reasoning and legal procedures, law's foundational claim to disinterested objectivity has been rebutted. The cross-disciplinary approach to law has demonstrated the ways in which legal reasoning and adjudication operate so as to always support law's own claim to objectivity.

Legal critique continues to evolve. Critical scholars of social theory draw attention to the random and unsystematic nature of our multicultural and multilingual world. In contrast to the picture of stability and predictability that modernity assumes, the difference critique instead points to the diversity of the human condition. It demonstrates how the theories and language of modernity have the effect of hiding and/or erasing cultural diversity. This erasure or hiding of difference occurs through the marginalization of difference or 'indifference to difference' through generalizations about human identity which ignore the subtlety and nuances of local and individual experience. Some of the means used to carry out this critique have been through the insights offered by linguistics and psychoanalysis. Language, whether spoken or written, is seen by these critical scholars as the vehicle whereby the effects of power, status and relationships with others are constituted. It is also the means whereby these factors have pre-conscious effects – meaning that language itself can be constitutive of effects on us and on others.

In law, this new critique has only recently emerged from the earlier broadening influence of critical legal studies. Affected by the anti-foundationalist stance of postmodernism coming from the humanities and social sciences generally and now most visibly located in the new discipline of cultural studies, legal critique is also questioning the paradox of one's ability to ever fully understand the 'other'. This view that an understanding of another's subjectivity is unattainable revolves around the unalterable difference that lies between people. 'Difference', as a mode of thought, sees the improbability of *any* claim to a vantage point that is somehow external to what is being viewed. This critique *on its own* does not seek to bring about social reform; that would be the simple exercise of the will to power and thus constitute a performative contradiction to the insight of unalterable difference. The difference critique in law rejects the foundational theories of analytic philosophy exemplified by Aristotle, Kant, Bentham and Hart, suggesting instead that these theories are inescapably part of the historical and social context of the times in which they were constructed. All they can ever claim to do, the difference critique suggests, is to offer a descriptive account of the dominant social practices and conventions of the society from which they spring.

Postmodernism, Law and the Difference Critique

As a critical and theoretical position, postmodernism in law derives from poststructuralism as a critique of the 'grand narrative' and of subject-centred reason. This criticizes the normalization of Enlightenment rationality that the critical legal studies movement claims as the framework for legal liberalism. Critical legal studies itself makes generalizations about modernity by describing Enlightenment rationality as mere liberal individualism. Postmodernism points out that this characterization is too simple. Postmodernism can be identified by its position that the scaffolding of modernity comes out of a *variety* of positions of the modern era. The Enlightenment is viewed as being as much a product of the Romantics as it is of rationalism;

Shelly, Goethe, Freud, Sade and Nietzsche all combine elements of both.[27] The postmodern critique of foundationalism takes its normative position from the critique of metaphysics offered by both Heidegger[28] and Nietzsche[29] (although to a different effect, Nietzsche emphasizing the will to power and Heidegger painting a primordial sense of crisis) and then extends this critique into an attack on the possibility of any external vantage point for making any normative assessment.

The tributaries of poststructuralism into the postmodernist current combine structuralism's critique of subject-centred thought with the insight of deconstruction – namely, that monological statements of truth are false or misleading or repressive. Deconstruction demonstrates that accepted truths involve a constant construction, as well as the constant tendency of those truths to break down and reveal their internal inconsistencies. Those who are labelled 'poststructuralists' or 'postmodernist' (although they refute the labels) draw from their refigurations of Kant, Hegel and Adorno. Michel Foucault,[30] Jacques Lacan[31] and Jacques Derrida[32] have each initiated a renewed analysis of the way in which our lives are structured by 'discourse' and how discourse structures relationships. This provides an understanding that the juridic subject is, at least in part, an amalgam of linguistic, semiotic and psychoanalytic effects, within social frameworks that 'discipline' his or her very thoughts.

With the advent of postmodernism, there is no longer an innocent 'subject' of discourse or political practice; we are all positioned within a far broader context. Dynamic social relations and social history inform our every encounter. It is within this recognition of structure and history (that is, *context*) that postmodern legal theory and practice seeks to locate the specific interests of different legal subjects. Law's engagement with what can be termed 'law's postmodern turn', or what has elsewhere been referred to as 'law's interpretative turn',[33] has suggested that legal language has the effect of positioning people as objects, rather than as speaking subjects, and that this placement as object predetermines a person's authority and legitimacy in the legal drama. More recently still, there have been some moves towards a reconstructive search for the possibilities of connections and alliances *across* differences.

Postmodernism strengthens critical legal studies by demonstrating how the binary oppositions of traditional law (win/lose, right/wrong, public/private, man/woman) work from a concept of individuality that wrongly assumes that there can be a single understanding of *all* people's experience. At the same time as the singularity of legal meaning is under question from the critique offered initially by the critical legal studies movement and now by postmodernism in law, the variety of the claims to 'difference' being made within the legal system has introduced a growing concept of pluralism around and within the previously singular meaning attached to the universal legal subject. Just as postmodernism points out the ways in which words, discourse and 'the text' work their own hegemony against *anyone*'s identity, the insight that words are only a by-product of the less obvious texts of our unconscious minds suggests that an understanding of the other may arise through first understanding the many subject positions that we each inhabit.

For example, postmodern legal feminism uncovers those forms of legal understanding which construct a fictional and homogeneous 'female' experience and identity – fictional because content is derived in opposition to, and in contradistinction with, men's norms and understandings.[34] The tools of genealogy and deconstruction that have come with the postmodern/poststructural critique have identified 'woman' and 'man' as largely a social construction and thus revealed sexism as no more than ideology. More recently, the debate over the sex/gender distinction has led to a complex reformulation of difference among *women* that is now reflected in feminist psychoanalytic approaches.[35] This latest move has emphasized the multifaceted nature of women's subordination within the justice system. It would seem that a political minority's means of staking out more productive territory as legal subjects may lie in an attitude of scepticism towards the 'naturalness' with which law sums up their singular subject status. When the forum for a claim is law, how might the legal subject be treated under the schema of ethical positivism as proposed by Campbell? Does the perspective of postmodernism and the difference critique offer something different? Do they necessarily reject Campbell's project, or are there some elements or compatibility?

Legal Adjudication

Legal Ethical Positivism

Campbell notes in *The Legal Theory of Ethical Positivism* that Austin did more than just provide an alternative account to Hobbes' view of laws as commands of the sovereign which were observed through fear of sanction.[36] Hart, in turn, converted Hobbes' commands to rules that were validated through their form and source – as long as these rules emanated from valid state power and were in the valid form, they were valid rules. Dworkin's extension to this is that law is more than Hart's rules and more than Austin's Radical Philosophy.[37] For Dworkin, law is reunited with morality in the form of interpretive acts of judges that apply the 'right' political and moral theories to the legal system in a construction of community as integrity. Moral philosophy, Dworkin tells us, is now an integral part of judicial activity. In a self-referential way, the judge always behaves morally when he (*sic*) locates in precedent the 'right' narrative about the community in which the legal conflict is present. This has the curious effect of removing any comparison between judicial activity and morality, because Dworkin's judge merely articulates a pre-existing community morality. Moreover, under Dworkin's schema, the judge can never act with something that might be called subjective or personal morality, because he (*sic*) is merely enunciating a community morality that already exists 'out there', embodied by *stare decis*. In a single swift move, judicial permanence is granted, while judicial discretion is removed. Dworkin sets up a guarantee of judicial popularity: there is no ability to criticize the judge for personal bias, because to do so would damn the community whose bias he articulates.

Into Dworkin's scenario of soft judicial acts, which (merely) speak for the community, 1980s and 1990s brought critical social and legal theory into law. This critique is both an understanding of the production of subjectivity in legal acts (whether legal speech or legal writing), and the suggestion that there be a break with the moral catastrophe of modernity that pretends to rope law together with what is thought to be 'objectivity'. That is, there is an understanding that the legal subject is, at least in part, the outcome of a variety of productions. The last section of *The Legal Theory of Ethical Positivism* accords an existence to class, gender and race, and the linguistic, semiotic and psychoanalytic effects of postmodernism. The aspect of modernity that clings to legal ethical positivism, as one might hope it would, is the desire that law generally, and specifically judges when adjudicating conflict, act on a basis that is more than simply relativism.

The ethically positivist judge under Campbell's formulation is guided by eight principles:

1 The judge should 'read... the rules in some appropriate register of the ordinary natural language of the society in which they ... apply'.
2 The judge should understand the legislation as expressing the outcome of making a political choice among other possible rules.
3 The judge must not 'tinker' with applying the rules so that they may more efficaciously achieve their intended political purpose.
4 Judges must not be influenced by their own subjective values.
5 Judges who have a personal interest in the case before them and 'utilising techniques to give scope for the appreciation of ... disparate points of view of those... directly involved' should be disqualified.
6 Recent legislation has greater authority over older legislation and over the common law.

7 Only certain types of rules should be modified in light of special circumstances, 'particularly cooperative and control rules'.
8 A judge may make an exception to the strict application of rules 'when the results are unexpected and clearly contrary to uncontroversial consensual values'.[38]

Of particular interest with regard to the matter of difference, Campbell points out that:

> The processes of interpretation in hard cases involve an extensive knowledge of the social and political context of the creation and continued use of the rule. And even in relatively easy cases judges have to be sufficiently aware of the social sources of moral and political bias and the ways in which these can affect the way rules are read and understood in order to avoid the danger of being affected by the values and assumptions of their own particular socioeconomic group.[39]

Although not using 'interpretation' in the 'characteristically postmodern... [sense] ... that all communications are of necessarily open and uncertain meaning',[40] Campbell does not advocate narrow individualistic theories *pace* Locke, but prefers instead: '...theories of meaning, which rely upon intersubjective agreement, sustained by shared cultural understandings'.[41] He notes that there needs to be some base level of shared understanding, and 'sufficient local agreement on meaning, rules and shared assumptions on the acquisition of knowledge to achieve effectual communication between legislators, judges and citizens'.[42] He adds to this that he adopts a sociological view of judicial interpretation – namely, that it is the judge's task to read legislative intent 'in terms of their literal or evident meanings as understood by participants in the relevant social meanings, as understood by participants in the relevant social situations'.[43]

If the ethically positivist judge is acting legitimately when applying the 'plain and simple' meaning of legislative enactments, does this mean that valid judicial adjudication derives fundamentally from allegiance to the community good as expressed in democratically obtained legal instruments? This would bear a similarity to Jürgen Habermas' reconstruction of legal rationality as an idealized form of democracy.[44] Or should the judge's decision come from the search for understanding the particularity of the legal conflict *within* the universal as expressed in the more general language of the statute?

The concept of judges as autonomous and neutrally disinterested in the moral beginnings and political endings of legal decisions ultimately rests on democracy's ability to locate one 'true' shared consensus of value that gain expression through legislation. This is becoming a harder claim to sustain, if it ever had any plausibility at all. It is becoming increasingly obvious (although, one could argue, through a more honest recognition of the facts, rather than from the facts themselves changing) that our society is divided along so many axes of social difference that legislation is unable to articulate a consensus that reflects a singular, or even loosely shared, choice of values. This inability to appeal to a stable meta-ethics or moral epistemology makes it difficult to sustain the idea of an interpretive practice in the sense that legal ethical positivism poses.

The tension can be illustrated: fundamental rights theorists who base their rights upon the Western literary canon have run foul of charges of elitism and anti-democratic practices in the post-colonial period. On one hand, this has led to specific critiques of legal performance by political minorities, such as the postmodern turn in both feminist legal theory and critical race theory. On the other hand, it has led to suggestions about how we might set up new preconditions for reaching consensus, such as Habermas' 'ideal speech situation' and his distinction between facticity and legitimacy.[45] Both these approaches have emphasized the structural and normative links between the legal regime and political, social, economic and cultural contexts. How, one asks (ethically), can we go back now and undo the recognition that these *a priori* links exist, and ask the ethical positivist judge to blind herself to her own situated identity and that of the parties to a legal dispute?

Postmodern Adjudication?

How might the postmodern judge view the approach of legal ethical positivism? What could the critique of difference mean for the postmodern judge in the practical sense of aiding adjudication? The postmodern suggestion that we 'announce our speaking position' (that is, declare our own values and context) must surely mean that legal adjudication itself must announce its own investment in an ethic of evaluation of conflicting values. The act of adjudication itself carries the normative stance of judgment in order to produce a single outcome from a field of multiple subjectivities. To declare a 'winner' as the outcome to legal conflict is an *a priori* ethical decision in favour of judgment. The activity of judgment is an *a prior* recognition of multiple subjectivities. Unlike Kant's court of reason, the postmodern insight is that judgement:

> Place[s] the law of the institution on trial in the court of ethics... the justice of the judgement will depend on law's answer to the unique and singular demands of the person who comes to the law... If there are criteria of justice,...they are criteria of doubt which precede calculation, rule of law, and they are only momentary....[46]

It is this intersection of universality and particularity that needs to be more clearly accounted for in legal ethical positivism if it is to have the capacity to work from a construct of difference rather than a construct of sameness.[47] This raises the question of what an appeal to law constitutes. Is it a removal from the determination of conflict *inter se*, where it is the minutely personal relations between the parties that create the outcome, or is it an appeal to law as the determination of the conflict *ex parte*, where the collective community affections provide another layer to the conflict between the parties? To speculate here on the way in which the role of the postmodern judge might differ from the ethically positivistic judge, one could suggest that the postmodern judge is required to see the intersubjective rationalities circulating between the parties as part of appreciating consensual communitarian affections as expressed in legislation. The ethically positivist judge, on the other hand, may be aware of the subjective, the intersubjective and the affective, but is bound to ignore the broader social or community morés on the subject except in so far as they are expressed in legislative enactment. The ethically positivist judge will not add the substrate of feeling and experience of the parties before the court. The ethically positivist judge therefore remains within Kant's Second Critique: he or she cannot rest upon corporeality but lives only in pure concepts. The postmodern judge however, includes the aesthetic order described in Kant's Third Critique that exists in pure feeling, or the validity of subjective attachment to experience. Costas and Douzinas suggest that:

> The task of judgement is both impossible and necessary, both risk and calculation, just and unjust. It is only the ceaseless capacity to raise the question of justice, to be open momentarily to the possibility of rethinking the law in each judgement, to doubt the existence of regulae or rules, to question the protocols and the procedures that can give justice and the subject of justice, the subject before the law, the possibility of being seen and their cause heard.[48]

Need this postmodern approach *necessarily* lie at distinct odds with legal ethical positivism wherein the judge acts objectively and on the plain and simple meaning of legislative enactments? Both the postmodern and the legal ethical judge acknowledges the ways in which context can shape the construction of facts and truth. In both forms of jurisprudence, competing claims to identify require judicial recognition of differing normative claims. For Campbell, these competing claims may be resolved by an appeal to law as an autonomous, objective activity that can line up the normative differences: 'Correct answers to legal questions require judges to access the underlying value choices....'[49] This suggestion that judges (merely) articulate the political and moral choices that lie behind legislation makes two assumptions: first, that the theory of representative democracy can adequately account for the social variety of values; and, second, that the value choices of society as they are articulated in legislation are up to the task of adequately dealing with the messy facts of social conflict.

The legal method that might come from the difference critique could begin with an acknowledgment that new legal practices may arise *simpliciter* through an intervention in the production and dissemination of meanings that characterize the postmodern approach. This uses the postmodern reading of legal practices and legal artefacts to search for the intelligibility of the reality of the legal subject. It thus acknowledges that 'reality' makes sense quite differently depending on the material social matrices of race, gender, sexuality and class.[50] This is a definitive move away from the premise of Kant, Hegel and Marx that 'knowledge' and 'experience' can be separated, while it accepts Marx's understanding that the legal subject can be 'decentred' through alienation from their subject status. It also accepts the young Hegel's dialectical approach that, through an interpolation of the 'O/other', we can better understand our own structures of understanding and interpretation. This suggests that, just as we occupy many social worlds at any one moment, so we move continuously along the spectrum of 'knowledge' and 'experience'. Thus legal method must be open to the 'knowledge' of narratives as they are based in subjective experience.

The difference approach includes narratives for two simple reasons.[51] First, narratives can be global. Example of global narratives are the narrative of democracy that is told within Western legal systems and the narrative of women as subordinated legal subjects (indeed, if there were a characteristic that might be deemed 'universal', it would be women's subordination across history and cultures). Second, comparisons among narratives can facilitate a form of cross-situational knowledge that provides an understanding of the forces at work behind the narratives. This enables law to ask new questions of the context of legal conflict. With the demise of metaphysical certainty, it is no longer feasible for lawyers to claim they work with 'nothing but the facts'. They can no longer claim that they are somehow free from any reliance on prior concepts such as ideas about causality, and understandings of where to look for empirical relationships. Rather, there needs to be a search for the narrative behind the facts as part of the theory upholding the view of the facts. The use of narratives demonstrates that the best theories are not simply assemblages of propositions, but analogical constructs comparing, contrasting, and identifying similarities among cases.[52]

What Does a Postmodern Approach to Law Add to our Understanding of Law?

The Political Problem

Postmodernism presents a political dilemma. The claim to a sense of self that is different from the legally universalized sense of self is a problematic one within the justice system. The claim to a range of subjectivities within any category of 'legal subject' is even more problematic as it emphasizes the difficulty of adjudicating conflicts that depend on the relativity of sense perceptions. The interpretive challenge posed by the difference critique to law is this: how can pluralism within the signifier 'juridic subject' be defended so as to respect the 'rights' of the vast diversity of peoples, without destroying the very framework of the legal institutions that we ask to hear and construe those rights? The challenge for the difference critique is to be politically effective when that requires an engagement with the very master discourse of law that proscribes such a narrow reading of legal identity.

In deconstructing the categories of gendered, social, cultural and economic relations in law, the difference critique provides useful insights into the way in which legal power works. But it is also crucial, for frankly political purposes, to mobilize the categories of legal identity that are the subject of deconstruction. The complex theorizing of postmodernism needs also to be informed by strategic concerns: every day, groups and individuals find themselves in situations which demand legal responses to their day-to-day concerns. Difference takes many forms, and while common beliefs or values can be clearly identified in a historical tradition that is shared by people, the need to evaluate differences in even that situation requires a theoretical justification. The search for 'common beliefs' must go beyond simply identifying a community that is grounded in a spatial proximity, or living under the umbrella of Western legal and political institutions, or in any other criteria of commonality. This emphasizes the need to develop methods that allow for connections across diversity, without thereby erasing the uniqueness of each voice. Juridical subjects need to be able to make a claim – a claim that is 'essential' (for here and now) – to legal protection that rests upon a certain level of constructed realism about their identity without thereby restricting that identity as they do so.

A postmodern approach that retains aspects of the liberal rights model for particular harms is a response to the modern/postmodern impasse.[53] First, it acknowledges that a postmodern pluralism must recognize that the passage from subjection to subjectivity cannot be effected merely by expanding existing versions of what it is to be a citizen. In other words, it acknowledges that increasing the categories of political identity does not necessarily increase political agency. Second, such a model of postmodern pluralism, tempered by aspects of liberal rights, addresses the concerns of some that the deconstruction of essential identity presents a threat to political agency just at a time when the loss of agency through 'the death of man' could potentially have troubling effects on areas of improved legal recognition of difference: women and people of colour want to keep their legal gains rather than surrender them to the argument that gender and race are (nothing more than) a social construction. One of the central concerns of 'difference' legal scholarship must be to preserve the *present* grounds on which legal subjects may make their claims before law as a 'right'. The twentieth century's legal gains for those who previously had little legal agency must not be lost through the postmodern 'loss of the subject' and 'loss of the body'. Read in this way, the difference critique is as much a political position as it is a different metaphysical approach to pluralism.

The History Question

It needs to be restated so that legal theorists do not overlook it: the ambits of our jurisprudential explorations are bounded by the limitations of our known world of legal conventions and categories. New facts and new information are 'tamed' within schemes of knowledge that we take as self-evident and beyond question. Judicial objectivity is one example of a convention that has only recently been undone. One of the ongoing challenges for jurisprudence is to go beyond the affirmation and reconstitution of the familiar legal categories to recognize other possibilities. This is the value of the highly contested debates surrounding 'difference' and 'otherness'. Difference has been with us for all of the Enlightenment, through colonial empire-building, through long-distance trade, through religion and through literature. The empirical occurrence of historical change and cross-cultural diversity has been with us far longer than the idea of modern nationalism. What is new is the contemporary expectation of cultural homogeneity that has increased within the nationalist ideal of the nineteenth, and particularly the twentieth, centuries.[54]

The corollary of an awareness of historical reality is to accept the unceasing changeability of our world – social, natural, political and legal. This unceasing contingency of different subject positions and subjective identities (what Arendt called 'natality'[55]) provides a canvass of navigating amongst the constant change, amidst the landmarks of tradition and differing inscriptions of ethical preferences. This form of engagement with the practical world is already deeply inscribed in the Enlightenment tradition. Kant was, after all, seeking to explore the limits of different forms of reason, knowledge and understanding; and this exploration continues in Hegel's and Habermas' neo-Kantianism. Indeed, Kant was the point of departure for Nietzsche and Heidegger, as he has been for Foucault and Derrida. Critical theory, as first suggested by Horkheimer and Adorno, was an attempt to move away from the traditionally abstract and universalizing approach of philosophy to an engagement with the historically concrete and empirical knowledge. Their Hegelianism included Marx's critique of history and reification and Weber's analysis of bureaucracy as the completion of instrumental rationality. At the heart of Horkheimer's and Adorno's critical theory law the Hegelian notion of immanence – the idea that an understanding of our categories of existing thought would allow us to transcend them so as to reveal both problems and previously unrecognized possibilities.[56]

The difference critique owes its existence as an idea to the modern as much as the postmodern. This means that, theoretically, as well as in hosts of empirical ways, there is an engagement with the features of modernity, even during the search for the transformative possibilities that lie beyond the categorical frameworks of the modern. Apart from recognizing that modernity provides the conditions of possibility to be even talking about 'difference', this suggests that to critique the normativities of modernity does not of itself preclude normative conclusions. The idea that an engagement with the troubled package called 'postmodernism' somehow necessarily involves a choice against modernism need not underlie legal attention to difference. This also means that 'difference' need not be constituted as 'other' to universality.

The Legitimation Question

From the late 1980s increasing awareness of the diversity of human existence has led to a loss of faith in legal neutrality. Human rights lawyers who sought to ground those rights in a stable moral epistemology find it difficult to shake off the charge of simply prioritizing one (notably Western) view of the 'good life'.[57] It is increasingly difficult for legal scholars to accept the idea of law as somehow objective and autonomous from its history and its particular cultural, social and economic contexts. The legal critique from the late 1980s has emphasized the view that language and culture always mediate one's reality. This has emphasized that what is deemed 'good' in law is always contingent on the perspective of the onlooker. This legal criticism aims to *embody* Kant's transcendental legal subject and situate him or her within a history, a time and a place. The idea is to locate the world and cultural values of the legal onlooker (the subject) in relation to the event (the object) that the subject is viewing.[58]

Together, critical legal studies and the difference critique have been able to highlight several important aspects of the contemporary Western legal system. First, they have demonstrated that law (like most disciplines) creates its own legitimization through reiterating its bases of legitimacy, and then normalizes that legitimization with the assistance of legal power. Second, they have demonstrated, through the analysis of language and culture, that legal language is the vehicle of law's reinscription of its own claim to legitimacy. The difference critique has demonstrated that a society's own cultural practices are the means of providing legitimation for legal, political, social and economic practices. Legitimacy does not derive from some external viewpoint or vantage place. Third, and perhaps most significantly, there is the continuing recognition that a great deal of the *ethical* aspirations of modern legal liberalism remains highly persuasive, flaws notwithstanding. Democracy, justice and equality retain their ethical appeal.[59] This appeal continues notwithstanding that the universalizing assumptions of legal institutions and processes are highly suspect. Despite the charges of nihilism frequently levelled at difference or postmodern scholars, there is an ongoing critical project to incorporate the 'best' ethical values of liberalism, albeit within a different epistemological framework to that of modernism.

Any location of ethics in law that also carries the insight about their constructedness begs several larger questions: where are those ethics to be found in each community, and how ought law to play its ethical role within an analytic of difference? Modernists argue that the fashion of postmodernism takes too many risks in its eclectic approach of a pastiche of many ideologies and empirical realities. According to this argument, the emphasis on human heterogeneity, or what is sometimes called 'radical Otherness', can only deliver a nihilistic deafness across intellectual lines. At this point, the controversy between the modernists and the postmodernists risks becoming so stark that there can be no practical responses to the insights of each. The postmodern breakdown of the boundary between law and society (a boundary that is central to the idea of autonomous law) has, at times, created a sense of embattled protectionism of the traditional modes of jurisprudence among traditional legal scholars. The modernist defence of Enlightenment universalism and rationality has, in turn, given rise to a caricature of the modernist – the resolutely positivistic lawyer, fearful that any questioning of the trickle-down effect of justice resulting from a Kantian-inspired jurisprudence of the separation of law and morality will bring calamitous social unrest. This is why it is refreshing to have the argument for legal ethical positivism put by Campbell; it is the wish to engage across lines of ethical, analytical and methodological difference that will bring a productive cooperation between legal thinkers and resultant law reform.

In law, the search for, and the construction of, substitute grounds for normative discourses of evaluation remains crucial. Postmodernism and the difference critique do not dispense with the requirement for legitimation. While it is necessary to dismantle law's present generalization of identity, there are risks attached to sliding down a particularism so extreme that there is no capacity to make evaluations *across* difference. Extreme particularization could merely result in a complete inability to place difference in relation to other phenomena. The more extreme form of the postmodern exaltation of differences does not provide a convincing framework for a system of justice which must resolve conflict. A complete lack of normative ethic to understand varying interests, opinions and values leaves no criteria at all for determining what the relevant effective subject matter of each legal conflict is to be. Given these difficulties of legitimation posed by extreme postmodernism, it is not surprising that analytical lawyers resist the ideas of 'difference' and 'radical Otherness' providing a jurisprudential framework. Why should we revert to simply accepting that communities legitimate themselves through their own declared difference to other communities, when the experience of genocide in the Balkans and some of the African states suggest that an appreciation of difference and radical Otherness might simply lead to more conflict? Even more dangerously still, extreme postmodernism may evoke a sense of nostalgia for the comfort of the (so-called) certainty afforded by the old narrative of legal liberalism. Nostalgia runs the risk that it may return us to the fiction of the universalized subject.

These concerns suggest a problem with a reading of difference as absolute relativism. Absolute relativism means that there can be no location of even a provisional 'truth'. More problematically, it precludes any meaningful communication about the construction of a more subtle and nuanced meaning of 'justice'. Just as postmodernism's 'death of the subject' risks losing women's' bodies at the historical point when women have some capacity to press their political and legal claim for bodily protection, so too there are some dangers inherent in pressing the contingency of the social antagonisms that mark each adjudicative moment. Not only does identity fragmentation place a supplicant before law in a precarious legal and political position; it may also set up a situation whereby each of the fragments is attributed with a closed and fully constituted identity – the new identity may, through stasis, become as equally inappropriate to empirical change as the old identity. Jurisprudence will have made no advance at all if the notion of a unified, homogenous, white male subject is simply replaced by a complete fragmentation and then a new reformulation of the meaning of 'legal subject' that becomes a new form of stasis.

Postmodern Pastiche

Just as in traditional and analytical jurisprudence, critical legal scholars and difference scholars disagree amongst themselves about the objectives and methods of their criticism. On the one hand, they point out the artificiality of the modernist's leanings towards universality, noting that the assumptions of homogeneity of individual identities that lie at the heart of modern law is (and has always been) a construct – a paradigm of its own. On the other hand, it would be incorrect to label the difference critique as signalling a new epoch that has somehow arrived after the demise of modernity. Modernity, after all, is also signified by the constant collision of difference. Difference has been perceived between societies since at least the colonial period that began in the seventeenth century. Today we see it in indigenous people's demands for justice in many constitutional jurisdictions.

The insights of Lyotard,[60] Derrida and Foucault have played a significant role in framing the difference critique. Derrida has warned of the 'violence of the masquerade' of language attempting to impose a single vision of reality or set of standards on the diverse experiments of thought and life. For Lyotard, an understanding of modernity comes from understanding the operation of language strategies that lead to institutional and bureaucratic constraints. Law, like science as described by Lyotard, becomes just one more game in a world in which 'all we can do is gaze in wonderment at the diversity of discursive species'. Foucault demonstrated the ways in which elites exercise their power in order to pathologize human behaviour and thus extend control over those who seem to be different from the 'rest of us'.

However, taking any one of the difference scholars on their own does not necessarily offer any real grip on the problems of analysing transformations of legal power and legal structures that can bring practical action. While these individual critiques all hold important insights, we are still left with a critique of the very worst of modernity. Even the more culturally specific account of 'historical tradition' as a basis for differentiating competing ethical claims in Richard Rorty's approach does not provide a normative justification for accepting one account of what is ethically appropriate over another.[61] There is growing pressure on the difference critique (from both modernists and those who might roughly be described as 'postmodern') to move beyond its critique of modernity and sketch some reconstructive options.

This, in turn, suggests that legal theorizing from within the 'difference' critique needs to traverse at least three distinct discourses. One discourse criticizes truth claims *per se*, arguing (along with Foucault) that truth is a production of knowledge and power. However, there is a problem with adopting this discourse on its own: locating truth or adjudicating difference becomes internally impossible. Truth disappears into power and thereby removes any criteria by which legitimate power may be distinguished from illegitimate power. There needs to be a supplement that provides some framework for the context of difference among people. The second discourse is one which locates truth claims within a linguistic community, arguing (along with Rorty) that incommensurate values within any community should be managed practically by living in mutual tolerance. Again, without a supplement, this discourse is limiting; it becomes an arbitrary appeal to liberal values that overemphasizes the role of state borders in identity creation, and simultaneously underemphasizes the differences that exist between people within spatially defined communities. These two discourses need to supplement one another, and in turn be supplemented by a third discourse.

The third discourse is one which seeks to identify criteria for law to make critical judgments about the evaluation of difference. To be meaningful, this discourse needs to allow for critical judgments to be arguable across the lines of ideological and cultural difference. This third discourse can be defensible, both politically *and* theoretically, if the criteria for the evaluation is just as identifiable (even if it is not as agreeable) to those who are not part of the dominant tradition, as to those who operate from within the tradition. The implication of this third discourse is that there must first exist a flourishing discourse of democracy and public life. This last aspect is crucial; people who are different to one another cannot simultaneously give an account to others of how they have entered into their identity, together with an account of how they wish to be in the future, if they do not have the structures and the discourse through which they can reliably convey their desires to others outside their realm of experience.

Avoiding Nihilism

The criticism of postmodern and poststructural approaches for their lack of definitive 'solutions' to adjudicate difference in law fails to appreciate some of the more subtle messages about rationality formation in the approaches, as well as the reformist politics that some postmodern scholars promote. A postmodern perspective of scepticism towards the project of equality does not imply a comprehensive rejection of modern liberal rationality nor its necessary replacement by an abyss of undefined and indefinable postmodern utopianism, despair or nihilism. Critical legal theory's function is to consider 'difference' without surrendering more formal ethical commitments to justice. In many ways, postmodernism is simply a return to the Kantian premise of the distinction between law and morality; 'justice' stands in for those ethical concerns that may not arise in law's *structural* capacity. Rather, justice is an extra, contingent on a particular legislature or judge's desire to locate or create a just approach or outcome between juridical subjects.

Not only do we need more than a very general view of 'society', we also need an empirical account of difference that can guide legal reforms to methods of adjudicating conflict in cases of radical difference. While it provides an account of historical and cultural situatedness and a sense of critical judgement, my suggestion is that the difference critique drawn from (at least) three different critical perspectives can accommodate an intellectual inclination towards cohesion as an outcome of legal process. It shares this with the liberal project, just as it acknowledges that a theoretical perspective can be a useful framework for understanding mechanisms of power in society and in searching for possibilities of change. Where the difference critique, as I have drawn it, strays from the liberal approach is in its utilization of the postmodern suspicion of certainty underlying language and subjectivity. Difference scholarship recognizes that each act of adjudication is an imperfect endeavour to capture individuals' subjective experience.

Conclusion

It has become increasingly difficult to accept the idea that an objective, autonomous legal approach is capable of providing 'solutions' for contemporary social problems. Technology has brought an increasing awareness of the 'global community'. People are more aware of the amount of diversity that exists both globally and within their own local and national community. More particularly, the tensions in Europe since the end of the Cold War have violently demonstrated the *lack* of social homogeneity that was once taken for granted. Indeed, as the awareness of heterogeneity increases, it seems that society can only become more ethnically, racially and economically divided. Increasingly, it seems that 'justice' cannot be guaranteed by recourse to universalized notions of human needs and wants. The appeal of law to universal values to resolve the tensions surrounding those divisions is revealed as legal artifice. Law is a creation of political, economic and social forces, which find their expression in historically contingent benchmarks of good behaviour.

Law is confronted with two needs: first, to better understand its own normative basis and recognize that law too often becomes the imposition of a single vision of identity or single set of standards;

second, to move beyond this one-dimensional construct of human identity in order to make evaluations across difference without resorting to either particularism or totalization. This calls for a reading of postmodernism that is more than pure critique and more than *reportage* of an epochal rupture. Law's adjudicative function means that there still needs to be a distinction between legitimate and illegitimate claims to power. There is a need to retain the encompassing idea of the criteria of adjudication. Additionally, there is a strong case for improving and/or creating legal and social structures that first potentiate discourse between positions of difference (*pace* Habermas) and the ongoing project of a normative approach to difference *per se.*

While law as a modernist enterprise is marked by universalism, sameness and ethnocentrism, the roots of the liberal social project also contain the political aspirations of equality, justice and liberation as normative constructs. An enterprise whereby we locate the compatibilities of different intellectual traditions, and search for the seams which may allow a dialogue across lines of differences – even a strained one – has great appeal. Rather than choose between modernity and postmodernity (which would be to concede to simple dualistic oppositions), it is more fruitful to locate ways that admit difference without turning to radical relativism. This requires a degree of rationalism, but shies away from the excessive formalism and abstract universalism that Hegel criticized in Kant's moral philosophy. The tension between universality and difference posed by modernism and postmodernism is, in some ways, reminiscent of the Hegelian dialectic of the master and the slave. This suggests that there has not been an epochal rupture so much as a fragmentation along the spectrum of difference.

The critical analysis of traditional jurisprudence has suggested that the traditional conceptual framework of law cannot be relied on to deliver justice. It needs the supplement of 'difference' to provide a metaphysical platform for a broader notion of justice. 'Justice' should be more characterized by an ability to constantly adapt legal solutions to keep pace with the apparently infinite variability of social circumstances. In many ways, the difference critique suggests a radical revision of the common law at its most creative. It moves well beyond Dworkin's seamless web, surfing worlds of thought beyond traditional law. This critical scholarship has been, and continues to be, controversial. Not all legal academics, and certainly very few lawyers, have a deep (or even passing) understanding of the waves of criticism directed towards the assumptions of universal human values and behaviour emanating from the humanities and the social sciences over the last decades.

It is important, both theoretically and practically, that those who work in the law more consciously confront the connections and the disconnections between 'justice' and 'difference', because of the empirical reality that people do not live in just one social world. The modern epistemology of consciousness is premised upon an idea of universalized human identity. In fact, people inhabit multiple worlds simultaneously. Assumptions about a stable and consistent social environment, of monolinguality and religious orthodoxy are, in reality, the exception and not the rule. A legal epistemology of consciousness that works off a single collectively or categorical framework cannot provide an account of multilinguality, variation and syncretism.

The challenge of issues of difference is a challenge of retheorizing our approaches in ways that transcend the superficial legal approaches of affirming difference through legislation that names difference and forbids its use as a category of identity that leads to legal disadvantage. It calls for an understanding of how we have come to create categories and how we have come to make sense of difference. An understanding of difference, and the organization of that difference into categorical taxonomies, tells us also that we have not exhausted the range of possibilities of categorization. The place of a postmodern jurisprudence is therefore not only to point out the universalistic tendencies of the Western jurisprudential tradition, but to explore ways of increasing our intellectual freedom without the constraints of our categories of thought occluding the transformative possibilities of what could be.

This is a weaker reading than the readings of strong postmodernism that are offered by some,[62] but a stronger reading of the postmodern environment than that given by Campbell. The reading of difference offered here assumes that there cannot be a complete break with knowledge and law or with tradition in general, quite simply because the modern and postmodern coexist. The demise of metaphysics that follows from a strong reading of postmodernism is potentially flawed in two respects. First, it leaves law as unknowable. We cannot reform what we cannot claim to know. Second, the deconstruction of jurisprudence itself involves a reconstruction of the history of law.[63] An awareness of the constructed nature of legal identity can lead to new categories of legal identity: it gives an opportunity to step outside the familiar ways of seeing things. To seize these opportunities in the desire of openness need not mean entry into a radical disorganization of reality in which there can be no claims or bearings to guide legal adjudication. The difference critique can offer an 'epistemic gain' in modern law by marking a middle ground between the foundationalism of orthodox law on the one hand, and the extreme relativism of some postmodernists on the other.[64] We need to go further than a simple argument for cultural relativism in framing a conception of legal methodology that engages with 'otherness'.

Implicit in this view of humanity as multiplicity is the idea that each individual inhabits multiple worlds simultaneously. Each person's horizon of experience is likely to comprise connections between many categories. Each individual is, in a sense, multilingual; a categorical framework or a single collectivity cannot fix him or her. We arrive at a position of recognizing that an appeal to a putatively universal experience/humanity is false, just as an appeal to only immediate experience gives us no standpoint from which to recognize misrecognition. A better approach is to see that there is a multiplicity of identities and a host of complexities and contradictions within individual and collective identities. This would allow us to recognize how particularity and generality, inclusion and exclusion of categories operate. Recognition of these complexities does not displace the recognition of struggles for individual and collective identities. Rather, it gives us a different place from which to start.

Notes

1 Thanks go to my colleagues Haig Patapan and Bryan Horrigan for their comments on an earlier draft of this paper.

2 T. Campbell, *The Legal Theory of Ethical Positivism* (Aldershot: Dartmouth, 1996).

3 Ibid., p. xi.

4 Ibid., p. 4.

5 Ibid., p. 2.

6 R. Gewirth, *Human Rights: Essays on Justification and Applications* (Chicago: University of Chicago Press, 1982); J. Hutchinson and P. Monahan (eds), *The Rule of Law: Ideal Or Ideology?* (Vancouver: Carswell, 1987); M. Tushnet, 'Critical Legal Studies: A Political History', *Yale Law Journal*, **100** (1992), p. 1515; R. Unger, *Knowledge and Politics* (New York: Free Press, 1975); R. Unger, 'Critical Legal Studies Movement', *Harvard Law Review*, **96**(3), (1983), p. 561.

7 Campbell, *Ethical Positivism, op. cit.*, p. 6.

8 Ibid., p. 7.

9 Ibid.

10 Ibid., p. 10.

11 Ibid., p. 5.

12 Ibid., p. 2.

13 J. Rousseau, 'The Social Contract', in E. Baker (ed.), *Social Contract: Essays by Locke, Hume and Rousseau* (New York: Oxford University Press, 1962).

14 J. Bentham, 'Anarchical Fallacies', in A. Melden (ed.), *Human Rights* (London: Wadsworth, 1970); J. Bentham, *An Introduction to the Principles of Morals and Legislation* (Oxford: Clarendon Press, 1970); P. Kelly, *Utilitarianism and Distributive Justice: Jeremy Bentham and the Civil Law* (Oxford: Clarendon Press, 1990).

15 H.L.A. Hart, *The Concept of Law* (Oxford: Clarendon Press, 1961).

16 J. Finnis, *Natural Law and Natural Rights* (Oxford: Clarendon Press, 1980).

17 I. Kant, *Groundwork of the Metaphysic of Morals [The Moral Law]*, trans. H.J. Paton (London: Hutchinson, 1956).

18 G.W.F. Hegel, *Hegel's Phenomenology of Spirit*, trans. A.V. Miller (Oxford: Oxford University Press, 1979); G.W.F. Hegel, *The Phenomenology of the Mind*, trans. J.B. Baillie (London: Allen and Unwin, 1949); G.W.F. Hegel, *Philosophy of History*, trans.

J. Sirbee (Chicago: Encyclopedia Britannica, 1952); G.W.F. Hegel, *The Philosophy of the Right*, trans. J.M. Knox (London: Oxford University Press, 1967).

[19] M. Weber, *Economy and Society*, ed. F. Rothland and C. Wittich (Berkeley: University of California Press, 1978).

[20] E. Durkheim, *The Division of Labor in Society* (New York: Free Press, 1964).

[21] M. Horkheimer, *Eclipse of Reason* (New York: Oxford University Press, 1947); M. Horkheimer, 'Traditional and Critical Theory' in *Critical Theory* (New York: Continuum, 1982); M. Horkheimer, *Between Philosophy and Social Science: Selected Early Writings*, trans. S. Hunter *et al.* (Cambridge, MA: MIT Press, 1987); M. Horkheimer and T. Adorno, *Dialectic of Enlightenment* (New York: Herder and Herder, 1972); M. Jay, *The Dialectical Imagination: A History of the Frankfurt School and the Institute of Social Research 1923–1950* (Berkeley: University of California Press, 1974).

[22] Charter of the United Nations (1948); Universal Declaration of Human Rights (1948); International Convention on Economic, Social and Cultural Rights (1976); International Convention on Civil and Political Rights (1980).

[23] A lateral use of Patapan's description of critical legal scholarship as 'Christianity without the patriarchal eschatology'. See H. Patapan, 'Anti-Lawyers: Religion and the Critics of Law and State' (book review of David Saunders), *Griffith Law Review*, forthcoming.

[24] D. Kennedy, 'Form and Substance in Private Law Adjudication', *Harvard Law Review*, **89** (1976), p. 1655; D. Kennedy, 'The Structure of Blackstone's Commentaries', *Buffalo Law Review*, **28** (1978), p. 209; D. Kennedy, 'Cost-Benefit Analysis of Entitlement Problems: A Critique', *Stanford Law Review*, **33** (1981), p. 387; D. Kennedy, *Legal Education and the Reproduction of Hierarchy* (Cambridge, MA: Afar, 1983).

[25] G. Minda, *Postmodern Legal Movements* (New York: New York University Press, 1995), ch. 4.

[26] M. Kelman, 'Trashing', *Stanford Law Review*, **36** (1984), p. 293.

[27] D. Calhoun, *Critical Social Theory: Culture, History and the Challenge of Difference* (Oxford: Blackwell, 1995).

[28] M. Heidegger, *The Basic Problems of Phenomenology*, trans. A. Hofstadter (Bloomington: Indiana University Press, 1982); M. Heidegger, *What is Called Thinking?*, trans. F. Wieck and J. Gray (New York: Harper and Row, 1968).

[29] F. Nietzsche, *The Will to Power* (New York: Vintage Books, 1974); F. Nietzsche, *The Gay Science*, trans. W. Kaufman (New York: Random House, 1974).

[30] M. Foucault, *Discipline and Punish: The Birth of the Prison*, trans. A. Sheridan (Harmondsworth: Penguin, 1979); M. Foucault, *Power/Knowledge: Selected Interviews and Other Writings 1972–1977*, trans. C. Gordon (ed.) (Brighton: Harvester Press, 1980); M. Foucault, *The History of Sexuality*, 4 vols, trans. R. Hurley (New York, Pantheon, 1988).

[31] J. Lacan, *Ecrits*, trans. A. Sheridan (New York: Norton, 1977); J. Lacan, *The Four Fundamental Concepts of Psycho-Analysis*, Seminaire series XI, 1969 (London: Hogarth Press and the Institute of Psycho-Analysis, 1977); J. Lacan, 'Guiding Remarks for a Congress on Feminine Sexuality', in J. Mitchell and J. Rose (eds), *Feminine Sexuality* (London: Macmillan, 1982); J. Lacan, 'Intervention on the Transference', in Mitchell and Rose, *Feminine Sexuality, op. cit.*; J. Lacan, 'The Meaning of the Phallus', in Mitchell and Rose, *Feminine Sexuality, op. cit.*; J. Lacan, *The Seminar of Jacques Lacan. Book I: Freud's Papers on Technique, 1953–54* (Cambridge: Cambridge University Press, 1988); E. Grosz, *Jacques Lacan: A Feminist Introduction* (Sydney: Allen & Unwin, 1990); E. Ragland-Sullivan, *Jacques Lacan and the Philosophy of Psychoanalysis* (Chicago: University of Chicago Press, 1986); S. Zizek, *The Sublime Object of Ideology* (London: Verso, 1989).

[32] J. Derrida, 'Structure, Sign and Play in the Discourse of the Human Sciences', in R. Mackey and E. Donato (eds), *The Language of Criticism and the Sciences of Man* (Baltimore: Johns Hopkins University Press, 1970); J. Derrida, *Speech and Phenomena*

and Other Essays on Husserl's Theory of Signs, trans. and intro. D.B. Allison (Evanston: North Western University Press, 1973); J. Derrida, *Of Grammatology*, trans. G. Chakravorty-Spivak (Baltimore: Johns Hopkins University Press, 1976); J. Derrida, *Writings and Difference*, trans. A. Bass (Chicago: University of Chicago Press, 1978); J. Derrida, *Glas*, trans. J.P. Leavey jr and R. Rand (Lincoln: University of Nebraska Press, 1986); J. Derrida, *The Post Card: From Socrates to Freud and Beyond*, trans. A. Bass (Chicago: University of Chicago Press, 1987); J. Derrida, 'Force of Law: The "Mystical Foundations of Authority"', trans. E.D. Litowitz, *Cardozo Law Review*, 11 (1990), p. 919.

33 Minda, *Postmodern Legal Movements*, *op. cit.*

34 N. Fraser, *Justice Interruptus* (New York: Routledge, 1997); I.M. Young, 'Policy and Group Difference: A Critique of the Ideal of Universal Citizenship' in I.M. Young (1990), *Throwing Like a Girl and Other Essays in Feminist Philosophy and Social Theory* (Bloomington: Indiana University Press, 1990); I.M. Young, *Intersecting Voices* (Princeton, NJ: Princeton University Press, 1997).

35 D. Cornell, 'The Poststructuralist Challenge To The Ideal of Community', *Cardozo Law Review*, **8** (1987), p. 989; D. Cornell, *Beyond Accommodation* (New York: Routledge, 1991); D. Cornell, *The Philosophy of the Limit* (New York: Routledge, 1992); D. Cornell, *The Imaginary Domain* (New York, Routledge, 1996); D. Cornell, *At the Heart of Freedom* (Princeton, NJ: Princeton University Press, 1998).

36 Campbell, *Ethical Positivism*, *op. cit.*, p. 4.

37 R. Dworkin, *Taking Rights Seriously* (London, Duckworth, 1977); R. Dworkin, *Law's Empire* (Cambridge, MA: Belknap Press, 1986). See also B. Horrigan, 'Paradigm Shifts in Judicial Interpretation: Reframing Legal and Constitutional Reasoning', in C. Sampford and K. Preston (eds), *Interpreting Constitutions: Theories, Principles and Institutions* (Sydney: The Federation Press, 1996), pp. 40–48, 55; and B. Horrigan, 'Black Holes in Legal Education', unpublished paper on file with author. Horrigan notes that Dworkin's faults include approaching the law with liberal assumptions from the start (tilt 1), basing the approach on the positive law (tilt 2), extracting from that a construct called 'interpretation' of a particular kind (tilt 3), constructing that from the standpoint that it must be seen in its best rather than actual light (tilt 4), using that to assert a strategy for finding the one right answer within the seamless web of this distorted construct of a special form of interpretation (tilt 5), incorporating within that construct criteria of adjudication which arguably do not commensurate each other, much less than point to one right answer in all cases (in the special non-demonstrable sense in which Dworkin uses that term), while doing all of this within an overall framework which contrasts rights as trumps with collective goals about what is best for society – with all of the objections about incommensurability, hegemony, pluralism, consensus, utilitarian assumptions that this brings. Horrigan also notes that Dworkin argues that his concept of interpretation is expansive enough to allow some – though not all or even most of the claims of – postmodernism. In a highly particular reading of the methods of postmodern critique, Dworkin also disclaims the capacity of newer theories to stand outside the domain of evaluation in the way that he says they purport to do.

38 Campbell, *Legal Theory of Ethical Positivism*, *op. cit.* pp. 10–11.

39 Ibid., p. 126.

40 Ibid.

41 Ibid.

42 Ibid., p. 127.

43 Ibid., p. 129.

44 J. Habermas, *Between Facts and Norms: Contributions to a Discourse Theory of Law and Democracy*, trans. William Rehg (Cambridge, MIT Press, 1995).

45 J. Habermas, *The Theory of Communicative Action*, 2 vols (Boston: Beacon Press, 1984, 1985); *Between Facts and Norms*, *op. cit.*

46 C. Douzinas and R. Warrington with S. McVeigh, *Postmodern Jurisprudence: The Law of Texts and Texts of Law* (London: Routledge, 1991), pp. 22–3, citing C. Douzinas and R. Warrington, *Justice Miscarried: Ethics and Aesthetics in Law* (Hemel Hempstead: Harvester, 1994).

47 Campbell, *Ethical Positivism*, *op. cit.*, p. 110.

48 Minda, *Postmodern Legal Movements*, *op. cit.*, p. 76.

49 Campbell, *Ethical Positivism*, *op. cit.*, p. 3.

50 J. Leonard, *Legal Studies as Cultural Studies* (Albany: State University of New York Press, 1995), p. 3.

51 Fraser, *Justice Interruptus*, *op. cit.*

52 Calhoun, *Critical Social Theory*, *op. cit.*

53 This response could be called 'pragmatic' in the Dewyian sense, or 'neo-pragmatic' in the Rortyian sense, or quite simply in keeping with the common law tradition of 'common sense'. This is an argument beyond the scope of this chapter. I acknowledge that the reference to 'liberal rights' raised the question 'Which liberal rights?' That also is beyond the scope of this chapter.

54 Calhoun, *Critical Social Theory*, *op. cit.*

55 H. Arendt, *Between Past and Future* (New York: Penguin, 1977); See also: H. Arendt, *The Human Condition* (Chicago: University of Chicago Press, 1958); H. Arendt [1951]: *The Origins of Totalitarianism* (New York: Harcourt, 1973); H. Arendt, *Lectures on Kant's Political Philosophy* (Chicago: University of Chicago Press, 1982).

56 Radical social change, they considered, would therefore come from radical negativity; through critical theory would come the realization of the degree of negation that society was imposing upon the individual previously bounded by those repressive categories; Horkheimer and Adorno, *Dialectic*, *op. cit.*; T. Adorno, *Negative Dialectics* (New York: Continuum, 1973).

57 W. Kymlicka, 'Three Forms of Group-Differentiated Citizenship in Canada', in Seyla Benhabib (ed.), *Democracy and Difference* (Princeton: Princeton University Press, 1996); M. Minow, 'Rights and Cultural Difference', in A. Sarat and T. Kearns (eds), *Identities, Politics, and Rights* (Ann Arbor: University of Michigan Press, 1995); K. McClure, 'On the Subject of Rights: Pluralism, Plurality and Political Identity', in Chantal Mouffe (ed.), *Dimensions of Radical Democracy* (London: Verso, 1992).

58 M.F. Katz, 'After the Deconstruction: Law in the Age of Post-Structuralism', *University of Western Ontario Law Review*, **24** (1986), p. 51; G. Wickham, 'Cautious Postmodernism and Legal Truths', *Law in Context*, **7**(2) (1989), p. 39; P. Schlag, '"Lehors de texte, c'est moi": The Politics of Form and Domestication of Deconstruction', *Cardozo Law Review*, **11** (1990), p. 1631; A. Hunt (1990) 'Law Confronts Postmodernism', *McGill Law Journal*, **35** (1990), p. 507; M. Radin and E. Michelman, 'Pragmatist and Poststructuralist Critical Legal Practice', *University of Pennsylvania Law Review*, **139** (1991), p. 1019.

59 I use 'ethical' here in the sense of a philosophy of morals.

60 J-F. Lyotard, *The Postmodern Condition: A Report on Knowledge* (Manchester: Manchester University Press, 1984); J-F. Lyotard, *The Differend: Phrases in Dispute*, trans. G. Van Den Abbeele (Minneapolis: University of Minnesota Press, 1988).

61 R. Rorty, *Philosophy and the Mirror of Nature* (Princeton, NJ: Princeton University Press, 1980); R. Rorty, 'Postmodernist Bourgeois Liberalism', *Journal of Philosophy*, **80**(1) (1983), p. 583; R. Rorty, 'Habermas and Lyotard on Postmodernity', *Praxis International*, **6**(1) (1984), pp. 32–44; R. Rorty, *Contingency, Irony and Solidarity* (New York: Cambridge University Press, 1989); R. Rorty, 'Remarks on Deconstruction and Pragmatism', in Chantal Mouffe (ed.), *Deconstruction and Pragmatism* (New York: Routledge, 1996), pp. 13–18.

[62] The strongest reading of postmodernism most directly approaches Heidegger's pitting of the Kantian form of time against the history of Being.

[63] G. Rose, *Dialectic of Nihilism: Poststructuralism and the Law* (Oxford: Basil Blackwell, 1984), p. 1.

[64] Charles Taylor refers to 'epistemic gain' in his 'Excurses on Historical Exploration', in C. Taylor, *Sources of the Self* (Cambridge, MA: Harvard University Press, 1989).

7 Is Positivism Committed to Intentionalism?

NATALIE STOLJAR

Introduction

Not all positivists are committed to intentionalism – namely, the thesis that interpreters must rely on the intentions of law-makers when interpreting legal rules. For example, Frederick Schauer argues that it is not necessary to answer the 'central interpretive question' of positivism – how rules should be interpreted in doubtful cases – by relying on the author's intention. He says that 'The recourse to original intent cannot plausibly be taken as a linguistic necessity. Even those most wedded to an intentionalist theory of meaning [e.g. H.P. Grice] do not hold that the meaning of the term just is that intention'.[1] On the other hand, Larry Alexander argues from Joseph Raz's positivist theory of law to the conclusion that there is a 'prima facie case for making authorial intent the touchstone of legal interpretation'.[2] On Raz's theory, laws are the legal authorities' determinations about what ought to be done. Alexander argues that these determinations are the authorities' attempts to communicate what ought to be done, and such attempts to communicate (such legal texts) mean what their authors intend them to mean. A third positivist, Tom Campbell, seems to endorse Alexander's argument in the course of addressing what he calls the philosophical problem of positivism. He says that assuming that 'it makes sense to see law as a process of communication, [the task of adjudicators] is to discern the intentions of legislators in so far as they are expressed in the authorised text'.[3]

The debate over whether the interpretation of legal rules should be guided by speaker's or author's intentions can be characterized as a debate over whether, in controversial cases, interpretation should be guided by the speaker's meaning or by the conventional meaning of the words of the rule. There are two common kinds of controversial cases. The first is one in which the conventional meaning is clear, yet diverges from the speaker's meaning. For example, suppose that the conventional meaning of the word 'vehicle' is 'motorized people-mover on wheels'. If so, the rule 'No vehicles in the park' would permit bicycles but prohibit electric wheelchairs. However, if the legislators intended the rule to prohibit bicycles and permit electric wheelchairs, the author's meaning diverges from the conventional meaning. A second kind of controversial case is one in which the conventional meaning is vague. H.L.A. Hart observed that general terms, such as the word 'vehicle', are open-textured.[4] This means that circumstances will arise in which the application of the term is indeterminate. For example, assuming the above conventional meaning of the word 'vehicle', it is indeterminate whether the rule 'No vehicles in the park' prohibits or permits street performers on motorized unicycles. Motorized unicycles are neither clearly inside nor clearly outside the class of people-movers on wheels, and thus it is indeterminate whether the term 'vehicle' applies to them.

In both kinds of controversial case, intentionalists typically claim that *the* meaning of the rule of the speaker's or author's meaning. In cases in which conventional meaning and speaker's meaning diverge, the speaker's meaning is understood to have priority over conventional meaning and, in cases in which conventional meaning is vague, the speaker's meaning is understood to have priority over other possible methods of interpretation. For example, Alexander acknowledges that legal rules have a conventional or dictionary meaning, which may diverge from the speaker's meaning, but argues that the authorities' legal text is '*[t]heir* attempt to communicate what they have determined ought to be done, and *that* text's meaning is the [speaker's meaning] not [the dictionary meaning]'.[5]

In this chapter I focus on Alexander's argument that intentionalism follows from the position that laws are the legal authorities' determinations about what ought to be done. The argument relies on one basic idea: legal rules are *acts of communication* by the legal authorities. However, because this observation, as it stands, is too general to support the conclusion, I therefore distinguish three different ways of parlaying the idea into an argument for intentionalism. For each alternative, I defend Schauer's conclusion that there is no conceptual reason for adopting speaker's meaning as *the* meaning of legal rules. Thus, even if we endorse the positivist idea that laws are determinations of the legal authorities, intentionalism does not necessarily follow.

In the next section, I outline an interpretation of Alexander's argument, which relies on an analysis of communication. Intentionalism might follow from the observation that laws are acts of communication if we adopt an intentional analysis of communication such as the one defended by Grice. I then consider a second way of arguing for intentionalism that depends on the idea that acts of communication, and hence legal rules, are a kind of illocutionary act. The interpretation of illocutionary acts is partly governed by pragmatics – by how the rule is intended to be used by the speakers or authors – and hence not solely by semantics – namely, the sense and reference of the words of the rule.[6] If the meaning of illocutionary acts is partly a matter of pragmatics, it seems that the meaning of legal rules is determined in part by the intentions of the authors. Finally, I explore a variation of the argument that employs a conception of speaker's meaning. It says that the ideas and beliefs that speakers have in mind, and intend to convey to their audience, comprise the speaker's meaning of the utterance. Hence to say what a legal rule means is to identity the beliefs or ideas that the legal authorities had in mind when they passed the law.

The three arguments just outlined are conceptual arguments. The first claims that intentionalism follows from the concept of communication, the second that it follows from an analysis of the meaning of illocutionary acts, and the third that it follows from the concept of speaker's meaning. If I am right that none of these conceptual arguments for intentionalism succeed, and in the absence of further conceptual arguments, Schauer's conclusion is correct. However, his conclusion does not rule out the possibility of holding intentionalism for substantive normative reasons. A normative question, namely how *ought* we to interpret legal rules in general, or in a particular controversial case, may always be asked. If the answer to the normative question is that we ought to interpret the rule by relying on the conventional meaning, or on some other consideration if the conventional meaning is vague, then intentionalism is false.

Communication and Intention

Larry Alexander writes:

> All texts are attempts by their authors to communicate.... Legal texts are attempts by the authorities to communicate their determinations of what ought to be done by those they govern. Novels are attempts by novelists to communicate details of character and plot to readers. Scientific texts are attempts by scientists to communicate their scientific findings to their intended audience. And so on. If texts are attempts by their authors to communicate, then *texts mean what their authors intend them to mean.*[7]

Alexander says that intentionalism follows from the fact that legal rules are acts of communication. In this section, I characterize his argument as implicitly relying on an intentional analysis of communication. These analyses claim that a necessary condition for speech-acts to be acts of communication is that certain communicative intentions accompany them. I first outline H.P. Grice's intentional analysis of communication, then consider briefly whether we should endorse it. I argue that since there is a plausible non-intentional analysis of communication on offer, the fact that laws are acts of communication does not entail intentionalism.

In his famous article, 'Meaning', Grice provides both an analysis of speaker's meaning and an analysis of acts of communication.[8] Indeed, on this analysis, a speaker means something by an utterance if and only if his or her utterance counts as an act of communication. Grice claims that, in order to be a communicative act, an utterance must be accompanied by certain intentions: an intention to produce a belief or other response in the hearer; an intention that the hearer recognize that first intention; and an intention that the hearer's belief come about through the recognition of the first intention.[9] For example, consider the pair:

a Feeling faint, a child lets its mother see how pale it is (hoping that she may draw her own conclusions and help).
b Feeling faint, a child says to its mother 'I feel faint'.[10]

For Grice, (a) is not a communicative act because the child lacks the higher-order intention that the mother come to believe that the child feels faint through recognition of the child's intention that she believe it. Rather, the child intends that the mother's belief come about through her observation that the child is pale. Since the mother could have gained the belief that the child feels faint simply through her observation that the child is pale, rather than through any recognition of the child's intentions, this is not a communicative act in Grice's view. However, in (b) in which the child states 'I feel faint', Grice alleges that the mother's belief is intended by the child to be produced through recognition of the child's intention, and hence the utterance in (b) constitutes a communicative act.

Let us assume that Grice's analysis of communication can be patched up to address certain well-known counterexamples.[11] If such an intentional analysis is endorsed, Alexander's argument has some force. All acts of communication, and hence all legal rules, would of necessity be accompanied by certain intentions of the speaker or author. It is plausible that inferences about those intentions are required for interpreters to understand legal rules and, if so, intentionalism in some form would be true.

Should we accept an intentional analysis of communication? The answer is controversial. For example, Simon Blackburn concedes that it is plausible for the case of 'one-off predicaments' – that is, cases in which 'I need to get you to believe something, *p*, and I can rely on no shared language'.[12] But he argues that 'this is no longer true once we have habits of taking utterances one way or another'.[13] In such cases, 'the habit or convention supplants the need for such beliefs and such intentions'.[14] Thus there are two possible analyses of communication on offer: a Griceian intentional analysis, and a conventional analysis such as the one suggested by Blackburn. Let us call these kinds of analysis respectively 'the inferential model' and 'the code model'.[15] If the code model were correct, the status of legal rules as acts of communication would provide no grounds for intentionalism whatever. For communication to occur, it would be sufficient for an interpreter to decode the 'message' symbolized by the language of the legal rule. So long as interpreters and authors share linguistic conventions – for example, so long as both are English speakers – interpreters would be able to successfully decode a legal rule without making inferences about the author's intentions on the occasion of writing the rule.

Some argue, however, that there is a significant obstacle to adopting the code model – namely the requirement of 'mutual knowledge'. As Dan Sperber and Dierdre Wilson put it, for a speaker and hearer to converge on the same meaning of an utterance, and hence for communication to occur, it is necessary that 'every item of contextual information used in interpreting the utterance must not only be known by the speaker and hearer, but mutually known'.[16] The requirement is that the speaker know about the hearer's background assumptions, and the hearer know about the speaker's background assumptions, and the speaker know that the hearer know about the speaker's background assumptions, and so on ad infinitum. Sperber and Wilson claim that:

> Within the framework of the code model, mutual knowledge is a necessity. If the only way to communicate a message is by encoding and decoding it, and if inference plays a role in verbal communication, then the context in which an utterance is understood must be strictly limited to mutual knowledge. Otherwise inference cannot function as an effective aspect of decoding.[17]

The mutual knowledge hypothesis leads to both the philosophical problem of a regress and the psychological problem that no one in fact has such knowledge.[18] If it is indeed necessary to sustain the code model, then it would seem that the code model it untenable.

Let me briefly sketch two possible answers to the mutual knowledge problem. Suppose first that mutual knowledge is a genuine requirement. If it is, it affects *both* the code and inferential models. Even on Grice's analysis, successful communication requires a recognition by the hearer of an intention in the speaker to produce an effect in the hearer, or in short it requires the hearer to have beliefs about the speaker's beliefs about the hearer's beliefs, and so on.[19] Moreover, as Sperber and Wilson themselves go on to argue, the Griceian analysis has been amended to deal with certain counterexamples by introducing either higher and higher-order intentions or the mutual knowledge hypothesis itself.[20] The inferential model is not immune from the problems of regress and psychological implausibility that Sperber and Wilson attribute to the code model. The two models are in the same boat with respect to these problems. This suggests that there must be a solution to the problems of mutual knowledge – for example, Blackburn suggests 'shutting off the regress' by including the 'intention that all intentions be recognised' in the set of intentions required by Grice's analysis.[21] The point is that, since there *is* successful communication and by hypothesis mutual knowledge is required on both models to bring it about, mutual knowledge must somehow be achieved.

There is reason to think, however, that mutual knowledge is not a genuine requirement. Evans and McDowell point out that the mutual knowledge hypothesis, if adopted, would entail the counterintuitive conclusion that communication is a highly reflective process. Mutual knowledge requires that both hearers and speakers have complex sets of beliefs and intentions about the other's state of mind. Evans and McDowell argue that most ordinary communication – that is, conversation – is not like this. Rather, conversation and communication are habitual and occur in the absence of positive beliefs or intentions on the part of the hearer or speaker about the beliefs of the other. Their suggestion is that, for each speaker and hearer, 'it is not that there is a complex set of beliefs he must *have*, but rather that there is a series of beliefs each of which he must *lack*'.[22] Evans and McDowell use the analogy of monetary transactions such as the acceptance of coins as payment for goods. These transactions work quite well in the absence of positive beliefs about others' beliefs about the legitimacy of transactions. But such transactions would not operate successfully in a case in which a person disbelieved that others would accept coins as payment, and hence what is required is that persons lack such beliefs. In the linguistic case, what is required is that the speakers *lack* the belief that hearers do *not* share their beliefs about the meanings of the words expressed in order for the process of decoding to count as communication. So, either mutual knowledge is not after all a genuine requirement, or if it is a genuine requirement, there is some way in which it can be achieved. The code model is therefore an acceptable alternative to the inferential model.

According to the code model, interpreters do not have to make inferences about the authors' intentions to understand an act of communication, and hence the fact that legal rules are acts of communication does not entail intentionalism.

It is important to note, moreover, that even if the inferential model were true, it would not help intentionalist arguments that rely on the claim that legal rules are acts of communication. This is because adopting an intentional analysis leads to the counterintuitive result that legal rules are *not* acts of communication. Grice's analysis requires that for a speech-act to be an act of communication, the author or speaker must have a complex hierarchy of communicative intentions accompanying their utterance. Grice himself distinguishes between drawing a picture with the intentions required for communication and drawing a picture with the intention of producing a work of art.[23] Similar distinctions apply for works of literature. For example, the intentions behind particular works of literature may not be communicative intentions, but rather to express the author's feelings or emotions, explore the motives of characters, tell a story, contribute to public debate, protest, provoke a reaction, entertain or achieve public recognition. Similarly, legal texts could be intended to request, command, regulate, control, admonish, set an example, punish, express a moral view, state the law, persuade or deter certain behaviours by members of a society. It is an empirical matter whether legislators in a particular case of voting for a law have the required communicative intentions, as well as the intention to make law and any other intentions that accompany the act of voting for the law. Indeed, it is unlikely that they have – consciously or unconsciously – the complex set of intentions required on Grice's analysis. And assuming they do not, many legal rules will not be exclusively or primarily acts of communication, and may not be acts of communication at all. Thus, the acceptance of Grice's intentional analysis of communication comes at the expense of the intuition that acts of voting for laws are acts of communication performed by law-makers. Intentionalists are caught in a dilemma. Either the code model of communication is correct, in which case there is no reason to posit intentionalism; or the inferential model is correct, in which case the premise of their argument – that legal rules are communicative acts – is false.

Legal Rules as Illocutionary Acts

Intentionalists may have a way out of the dilemma, however. Suppose that communicative intentions are posited as theoretical constructs, implicit in the inferential model of communication. Even if there is no empirical evidence of their existence as conscious or unconscious mental states, they are deemed to accompany speech-acts such as the passing of laws. Hence the intuition that legal rules are acts of communication by law-makers is compatible with an intentional analysis of communication. The interpretation of communicative acts is a special case of the more general case of the interpretation of illocutionary acts, to which I now turn.

In this section, I characterize Alexander's argument as an instance of a general argument about the interpretation of speech-acts – particularly illocutionary acts. Some writers – Jeffrey Goldsworthy for example – suggest that the interpretation of legal rules is not a matter of semantics but of pragmatics: that is, of how the rule is used by its authors.[24] The array of different possible uses of utterances such as legal rules suggests that they can be different kinds of speech-act. In J.L. Austin's terms, they can be *locutionary* acts, which are 'roughly equivalent to uttering a certain sentence with a certain sense and reference';[25] they can be *illocutionary* acts, or acts whose performance itself constitutes doing something, such as marrying, protesting, promising or warning; and, finally, they can be *perlocutionary* acts, or acts whose performance achieves certain effects, such as persuading, convincing, deterring or misleading.[26]A speech-act of passing a law will typically have locutionary, illocutionary and perlocutionary force: it will be an utterance with a certain sense and reference; it will constitute the act of making law; and it will have the effects of, for example, regulating and controlling citizens.

Philosophers have advanced both intentional and non-intentional analyses of speech-acts. Austin himself endorses a non-intentional analysis.[27] In his original account of illocutionary acts, paradigm illocutionary acts such as uttering 'I do' in a marriage ceremony or 'I promise' have their force not due to intention, but rather due to institutional conventions. More recently, Jennifer Hornsby has also outlined a non-intentional analysis of illocutionary acts using a notion of reciprocity.[28] Since Hornsby takes all illocutionary acts to be acts of communication, her approach also amounts to a non-intentional analysis of acts of communication.

Since we are here assuming the inferential model for the sake of argument, let us set aside the non-intentional analysis of illocutionary acts and assume the truth of an intentional analysis. Does intentionalism follow from the existence of communicative and other illocutionary intentions? In general, it is plausible that to grasp the meaning of illocutionary acts is in part to grasp the illocutionary force of the act. It is often pointed out that, unless we understand that a string of sounds or marks is intended to be a statement in a particular language, the utterance has no meaning. Hence the intention to use the sounds or marks as a statement in a particular language is a necessary condition of the sounds or marks having meaning. Consider the illocutionary act of warning 'There's a bull in front of you!'.[29] In order to distinguish between the locutionary act of uttering 'There's a bull in front of you' and the illocutionary act of warning 'There's a bull in front of you!', the audience must grasp the illocutionary component of the act – that is, the component of warning. Similarly, part of the meaning of the utterance by a judge 'The death penalty constitutes cruel and unusual punishment' is given by its illocutionary component – that is, the fact that in producing the utterance the judge is also making law. Unless the audience grasps the illocutionary force of the act, it will fail to grasp that the act makes law and hence fails to grasp the meaning of the act.

Here, then, is a sketch of a possible argument for intentionalism:

1 If an intentional analysis of illocutionary acts is true, the illocutionary *intentions* are part of the meaning of the act.
2 In order to grasp the meaning of the act, one must grasp the illocutionary intentions.
3 Hence, if an intentional analysis of illocutionary acts is true, intentionalism is true.

Since communicative acts are kinds of illocutionary act, Alexander's argument for intentionalism from the premise that legal rules are communicative acts can be characterized as a special case of this argument. If legal rules are communicative acts, and hence illocutionary acts, authors have communicative intentions that are part of the meaning of the act. Hence any theory of legal interpretation must take account of the communicative intentions.

There are at least two possible responses to this argument. The first is to distinguish the standard speaker's meaning from the occasional speaker's meaning.[30] The standard speaker's meaning is that corresponding to the way in which an utterance is standardly intended to be used by speakers of a language. For example, the sentence 'Notre Dame is in Paris' is standardly intended to be used as an English-language sentence and the sentence 'There's a bull in front of you' is standardly intended to be used as a warning. On an intentional analysis of illocutionary acts, these intentions are part of the standard speaker's meaning of the speech-acts of uttering those sentences. In addition, there may be utterances of 'Notre Dame is in Paris' and 'There's a bull in front of you' in which the speaker's intentions, on that occasion, diverge from the standard intentions. Hence the occasional speaker's meaning may diverge from the standard speaker's meaning. In such cases, intentionalists such as Alexander will argue that the occasional speaker's meaning takes priority over the standard speaker's meaning because a legal rule is an author's attempt *on a particular occasion* to communicate what ought to be done. If it is the standard illocutionary intention that is part of the meaning, however, a speaker's intention on the occasion of utterance about how his or her words are to be used is not necessarily a component of the meaning of the illocutionary act. Thus, once we distinguish the occasional from the standard speaker's meaning, we see that intentionalism does not follow from the premise that illocutionary intentions are part of the meaning of a speech-act. It is true that standard intentions may be part of its meaning, but intentionalism is committed to occasional not standard intentions.

A second way of answering the intentionalist argument is to point out that illocutionary intentions (whether standard or occasional) are not the kinds of intention in dispute between intentionalist and non-intentionalist theories of interpretation. Illocutionary intentions are intentions that utterances be *used* in certain ways. Consider one of Andrei Marmor's examples, that of the sentence 'Do you know an honest politician?'. The illocutionary intention is that the utterance be used as either a genuine question, a sarcastic remark, an exclamation of despair and so on.[31] Now consider the intentions employed by intentionalists in constitutional interpretation. Gregory Bassham usefully divides such intentions into four categories: scope beliefs, counterfactual scope beliefs, semantic intentions and extratextual intentions.[32] For example, a scope belief is a belief about 'the specific legal *implications or effects of*... provisions' – for example 'whether Congress is authorized to incorporate a national bank within the meaning of the Necessary and Proper Clause'; and a semantic intention is an intention 'regarding the *meaning* of a constitutional provision' – for example 'whether an "establishment of religion" means "preferential treatment by the State of some Christian sects over others"'.[33] In general, such intentions are about the semantic meaning – the sense or reference – of the words of the Constitution. They are not illocutionary intentions, or intentions about how the provisions of the Constitution are to be used. In a possible debate between an intentionalist and a formalist over the interpretation of the 'Necessary and Proper Clause', an intentionalist might say that Congress is authorized to incorporate a national bank under the clause only if the framers believed that national banks come under the scope of the clause, while a formalist might say that Congress is so authorized only if the conventional meaning of the words of the clause apply to national banks. These different approaches may lead to disagreement, but there will be no disagreement over the illocutionary meaning of the clause. Both intentionalists and formalists will agree that grasping the illocutionary intention – that is, grasping that the clause *is intended to be used to make law* – is a necessary condition of engaging in the process of interpretation at all. Thus, even if we assume that the illocutionary meaning and hence the illocutionary intentions are part of the meaning of a speech-act, disputes over the semantic meaning of the speech-act will remain. It is only this kind of dispute that concerns intentionalists and non-intentionalists.

If these answers to the intentionalist argument are successful, the idea that legal rules are a certain type of speech-act whose meaning is, in part, the intention behind the act does not support intentionalism.[34] The sense in which such intentions are part of the meaning of the act is relevant to the interpretation of the act only in providing a necessary first step, which is usually tacitly assumed by interpreters in any case. Even after an interpreter has grasped the illocutionary force of an act, all the controversial interpretive questions remain.

Intentions and Speaker Meaning

It might be suggested that, so far, I have missed the point of the intentionalist argument. Perhaps intentionalism does not depend on a controversial analysis of communication or on the claim that illocutionary intentions are part of the meaning of legal rules. In the course of his argument, Alexander articulates the intentionalist intuition in a slightly different way. He says that the speaker's meaning is the 'author's intention to communicate *certain ideas*, such as, in the case of legal authorities, what ought to be done'.[35] This suggests that there is a third way of characterizing Alexander's argument for intentionalism: Since the speaker's meaning corresponds to the ideas that an author has in mind, the ideas that law-makers intend, mean or wish to convey through the articulation of a legal rule comprise its meaning. As Bassham has pointed out, law-makers typically have different kinds of ideas in mind about the legal rules they author. For example, in the case of the rule 'No vehicles in the park', they have beliefs about the appropriate application of the rule – for example, they might believe that the word 'vehicle' refers to bicycles and not electric wheelchairs – and they have beliefs about the semantic meaning of the words of the rule – for example, they might believe that the word 'vehicle' means 'motorized people-mover on wheels'. Is the speaker's meaning of a legal rule reducible to the ideas or beliefs that the law-makers intend to convey?

John Searle has convincingly disposed of this possibility in an objection to Grice's theory. Suppose an American soldier captured by Italians during the Second World War wishes his captors to believe that he is an German soldier. He intends to convey to them the idea that he is a German soldier. So he says the only German words he knows, '*Kennst du das Land wo die Zitronen blühen*?' to try to induce this belief. By hypothesis the American soldier has the nested intentions by Grice's analysis, yet it is implausible that what he *means* by the German sentence is 'I am a German soldier'.[36] Thus the idea he intends to convey (that is, the belief he intends to induce) is not the speaker's *meaning* of his utterance. As Searle observes, 'what we can mean is at least sometimes a function of what we are saying. Meaning is more than a matter of intention, it is also at least sometimes a matter of convention.'[37] The speaker's meaning cannot plausibly be analysed wholly in terms of the ideas or beliefs that speakers wish to convey.

Moreover, even if we assume that speaker's meaning is reducible to the ideas or beliefs that speakers wish to convey, there will be cases in which it is indeterminate whether the idea that a speaker wishes to convey is the conventional meaning or an idiosyncratic speaker's meaning which diverges from the conventional meaning. Searle and others have pointed out that, in order to mean something by a sentence, a speaker must intend to convey its conventional meaning.[38] This is because, in order to intend to do something, a speaker must believe that what they're intending to do is possible.[39] I cannot intend to square the circle (unless I am irrational or deluded) because I know that it is not possible to do so. Thus, a speaker cannot intend to communicate an idea and hence mean something by an utterance *p*, unless he or she believes that it is possible to do so – that is, unless he or she believes that the utterance has a conventional meaning which will be understood by the audience. In uttering *p* , a speaker will not only have certain ideas that he is wishing to convey using the expression *p*, but will also be intending to convey the conventional meaning of *p*. It follows that law-makers must intend to convey the conventional meaning of a legal rule *in addition* to any other ideas they have in mind – for instance ideas about the legal implications of a clause or the semantic meaning of a particular rule.

In non-controversial cases, the ideas which a law-maker has in mind and wishes to convey using a sentence will coincide with the conventional meaning of the sentence. However, in cases in which law-makers are mistaken about the conventional meaning of a rule, they will intend to convey (mistaken) ideas about what the rule means, in addition to intending to convey the conventional meaning. And in cases in which the conventional meaning is incomplete or vague, law-makers may intend to include certain applications of the word or rule and intend to exclude others in addition to intending to convey the conventional meaning. Therefore, in controversial cases requiring interpretation, there will be more than one idea that law-makers are wishing to convey. If we assume that the speaker's meaning is reducible to the ideas that a speaker wishes to convey, each of those ideas will constitute a speaker's meaning. In such a case the speaker will mean (without realizing it) different incompatible things, only one of which coincides with the conventional meaning. An intentionalist will usually assume that interpretation should be guided by the idiosyncratic speaker's meaning because it is those idiosyncratic ideas that correspond to the determinations of the particular legal authorities on the particular occasion. But there is no conceptual reason to adopt this conclusion, because, on a particular occasion, authors will *always* have the intention to convey the conventional meaning as well. The question of which speaker's meaning has priority in these kinds of cases can be resolved only by an extended normative argument.

The third characterization of Alexander's argument, therefore, suffers the same fate as the first two. Searle's counterexample exposes the flaw in the claim that the speaker's meaning is best analysed as the ideas that a speaker intends to convey on a particular occasion. But even if we allow this analysis of speaker's meaning for the sake of argument, in the controversial cases of interpretation that concern intentionalists, it will be indeterminate whether the meaning of a legal rule is the idiosyncratic author's meaning or the conventional meaning. Thus there is no conceptual reason to endorse the intentionalist position that the interpretation of legal rules in controversial cases should be guided by the idiosyncratic intentions of the legal authorities.

It may seem obvious that there is an argument for intentionalism implicit in positivism when one notices, as Larry Alexander does, that, according to positivism, legal rules are the legal authorities' attempts to communicate. It seems to follow from the idea of communication that interpreters must somehow latch on to what is going on in the speaker's mind at the time of the utterance. I have tried to show that this intuition is mistaken. When they are made precise, none of the possible arguments for intentionalism which I have discussed establish that interpreters must rely on the authors' intentions to capture the meaning of legal rules.

Notes

1 Frederick Schauer, *Playing by the Rules* (Oxford: Oxford University Press, 1991), p. 218.

2 Larry Alexander, 'All or Nothing at All? The Intentions of Authorities and the Authority of Intentions' in A. Marmor (ed.), *Law and Interpretation. Essays in Legal Philosophy* (Oxford: Oxford University Press, 1995), p. 365.

3 Tom Campbell, 'Democratic Aspects of Ethical Positivism', chapter 1 of this volume.

4 H.L.A. Hart, *The Concept of Law* (Oxford: Oxford University Press, 1961), p. 121 ff.

[5] Alexander, 'All or Nothing at All?', *op. cit.*

[6] For an argument that legal interpretation is a matter of pragmatics, not semantics, see J. Goldsworthy, 'Marmor on Meaning, Interpretation and Legislative Intention', *Legal Theory*, **1** (1995), p. 439 and J. Goldsworthy, 'Implications in Language, Law and the Constitution', in G. Lindell (ed.), *Future Directions in Australian Constitutional Law* (Sydney: Federation Press, 1994), p. 150. For a discussion of the role of pragmatics in interpretation, see A. Marmor, *Interpretation and Legal Theory* (Oxford: Oxford University Press, 1992), p. 24 ff.

[7] Alexander, 'All or Nothing at All?', *op. cit.*, p. 361.

[8] H.P. Grice, 'Meaning', *Philosophical Review*, **66** (1957), pp. 377–88. Reprinted in H.P. Grice, *Studies in the Way of Words* (Cambridge, MA: Harvard University Press, 1989), pp. 213–23. References to Grice are to the latter.

[9] Ibid., p. 219. See Scruton's exposition for an example of an analysis of Grice using these three intentions: R. Scruton, *Modern Philosophy* (London: Sinclair Stevenson, 1994), p. 254.

[10] Examples from Grice, 'Meaning', *op. cit.*, p. 218. Also see D.K. Lewis, *Convention* (Cambridge, MA: Harvard University Press, 1969), p. 153.

[11] D. Sperber and D. Wilson, *Relevance* (Cambridge, MA: MIT Press, 1996), p. 31; P.F. Strawson, 'Intention and Convention in Speech-Acts', *Philosophical Review*, **73** (1964), pp. 446–7; S. Blackburn, *Spreading the Word* (Oxford: Oxford University Press, 1984), 114 ff.

[12] Blackburn, *Spreading the Word, op. cit.*, p. 111.

[13] Ibid., p. 113.

[14] Ibid., p. 114.

[15] The terminology is from Sperber and Wilson, *Relevance, op. cit.*, ch. 1.

[16] Ibid., p. 18.

[17] Ibid.

[18] Ibid.

[19] This is pointed out by Gareth Evans and John McDowell in 'Introduction' in Evans and McDowell (eds), *Truth and Meaning: Essays in Semantics* (Oxford: Oxford University Press, 1976), p. xx.

[20] See the references cited in note 11, above.

[21] Blackburn, *Spreading the Word, op. cit.*, p. 116. Thanks to Richard Holton and Philip Pettit for discussion of this point.

[22] Evans and McDowell, 'Introduction', *op. cit.*, p. xxi. I am indebted to Richard Holton for pointing out the Evans and McDowell response.

[23] Grice, 'Meaning', *op. cit.*, p. 218.

[24] In order to avoid certain epistemic problems associated with endorsing speaker's meaning as a theory of interpretation, Goldsworthy develops a third conception of meaning which he calls 'utterance meaning'. This is an epistemically curtailed version of speaker's meaning, namely: 'what evidence, readily available to the intended audience, suggests that the speaker [or author] intended to communicate in making the utterance': J. Goldsworthy, 'Marmor on Meaning', *op. cit.*, p. 442.

[25] J.L. Austin, *How to Do Things With Words* (Oxford: Oxford University Press, 1962), p. 108.

[26] Ibid., e.g. pp. 107, 108, 114, 121. And see Hornsby's discussion: J. Hornsby, 'Illocution and Its Significance', in S.L. Tsohatzidis (ed.), *Foundations of Speech Act Theory* (London: Routledge, 1994), p. 189.

[27] Austin, *How to Do Things, op. cit.*

[28] Hornsby, 'Illocution', *op. cit.*, pp. 192–3.

[29] Ibid., p. 192.

[30] S.L. Tsohatzidis, 'Ways of Doing Things With Words. An Introduction', in Tsohatzidis, *Foundations, op. cit.*, pp. 1–25, 2–3.

[31] Marmor, *Interpretation, op. cit.*, p. 16.

[32] G. Bassham, *Original Intent and the Constitution. A Philosophical Study* (Lanham, MD: Rowman and Littlefield, 1992), p. 29.

[33] Ibid.

[34] Note that Searle argues that Grice's communicative intentions are perlocutionary, not illocutionary intentions. They are intentions to produce a belief in the hearer: J. Searle, *Speech Acts* (Cambridge: Cambridge University Press, 1969), p. 46. If this is right, the argument from communication is even weaker, as there is no reason to suppose that perlocutionary intentions are part of the meaning of speech-acts.

[35] Alexander, 'All or Nothing at All?', *op. cit.*, pp. 364–5 (emphasis added).

[36] Searle, *Speech Acts*, *op. cit.*, pp. 44–4.

[37] Ibid., p. 45.

[38] For Searle's objections to Grice see ibid., pp. 43 ff.

[39] Scruton, *Modern Philosophy*, *op. cit.*, p. 255; K. Donnellan, 'Putting Humpty Dumpty Together Again', *Philosophical Review*, 77 (1968), pp. 203–15.

8 A Perspectival Theory of Law

WALTER SINNOTT-ARMSTRONG[1]

When a debate rages for a long time among intelligent people, there is almost always some truth on all sides. There is also usually some misunderstanding between the opponents. This pattern recurs in the debate among legal positivists, legal realists and natural law theorists. That debate has raged for millennia. Each side contains some truth and some misunderstanding.

To show this, I will step back from details. I will not comment on the extensive literature or discuss actual cases. My goal is to understand the broad motivations behind the main positions in the traditional debate. These positions will be characterized in general terms that abstract from variations within each tradition. Nevertheless, I hope to illuminate the basic issues at stake and to gesture in the general direction of a new approach.

Definitions versus Prescription

What is the traditional debate about? Many things. Parts of the debate concern semantic definitions and epistemic criteria. A *semantic* definition of law gives necessary and sufficient conditions for something to be a law or against the law. *Epistemic* criteria for law give tests that people can use to determine (or justify claims about) what is a law or against the law. Semantic definitions and epistemic criteria are often conflated in the traditional debate, which creates some confusions. It is also important to distinguish *a* law from *the* law, since an action could be said to violate a law without being against the law. My main topic will be with the semantic definition of the law, although I will sometimes write about epistemic criteria and about what is a law in order to capture certain aspects of the traditional debate. *Legal positivists* claim that the general definition of the law can be morally neutral in the sense that it need not refer to what is or is believed to be morally right or wrong, good or bad, and so on. *Natural law theorists* deny that any such morally neutral definitions can be adequate. This definitional dispute is over what is called *the separability thesis*.[2]

Legal positivists and natural law theorists also disagree with *legal realists* who claim that the law can be identified by looking at judges' decisions in particular cases without looking at any general rules, including those passed by legislators as well as the general moral rules emphasized by natural law theorists. Legal positivists and natural law theorists both insist that the law cannot be determined independently of general rules.

The debate among these three positions is not prescriptive, since it concerns what the law is and not what it ought to be. These views do not tell us which laws and critical decisions are good or bad but only which rules count as laws and which acts are against the law.

Still, legal positivism also has its prescriptive or normative side. Legal positivists often claim that laws should be written by legislators in such a way that judges can identify them and apply them to cases without depending on their own beliefs about what is morally right or wrong, good or bad, and that judges should then identify laws and decide cases in this way.[3] This claim is not about what law is or about how laws are in fact written, since positivists admit that many laws are not written in this way and that no law has to be written this way in order to be a law. Instead, this positivist claim is about how laws should be written and how legal cases should be decided. Of course, some natural law theorists make competing prescriptive claims about how laws should be written and how cases should be decided – namely, in accordance with natural law. So do some legal realists, who claim that judges should decide particular cases without too much, if any, regard for the general rules passed by legislators.

There is, then, one debate about the definitional issue of how to identify the law and a separate debate about the prescriptive issue of how laws should be written and how cases should be decided. Opponents in both debates are called positivists, realists, and natural law theorists, but it is perfectly coherent to be a positivist in one debate and a realist or natural law theorist in the other debate.[4] Confusion can result unless we separate the definitional debate from the prescriptive debate.

To ensure this separation, I will address these issues in different chapters. The definitional issue will be the topic of this chapter. When I refer to legal positivism, legal realism and natural law theory in this chapter, I have in mind the definitional versions of those theories. I will address the prescriptive theories in Chapter 13 of this volume.

It is tempting to skip the definitional issue and go straight to the hotter topic of how judges should act. That would be a mistake. The definition of the law might not seem very interesting for its own sake, but it is an essential preliminary to the prescriptive issue. If one does not know what the law is, then one cannot say anything precise and systematic about what the law ought to be. On a more practical level, people often decide what to do by determining what the law is, and they often criticize others for disobeying the law or for not applying the law when that is their job. In such contexts, the term 'law' is used as a tool for changing other people's behaviour, so it should come as no surprise that people fight over the right to use the word in the way they want. Each of these uses of the phrase 'the law' presupposes some view of the nature of the law, so they cannot be adequately justified or understood without first clarifying the definition of the law.

Kinds of Definitions

Although it is more usual to contrast prescription with description, I have chosen to contrast prescription with definition. The reason for this is that, in my view, the definitional debate is not purely descriptive because of the kind of definition that is at issue.

Different kinds of definition serve different goals and meet different standards.[5] Some definitions are lexical or *dictionary* definitions. Definitions of this kind report how common English speakers actually use the defined word. Such reports need to be justified by empirical research in linguistics or by introspection by speakers of the language.

It is doubtful whether any legal positivists, legal realists or natural law theorists intended their claims to provide such a dictionary definition of the word 'law'. They did not do empirical research on actual language use; nor did they usually base their theories on introspection. They also intended their theories to apply where English is not spoken. Most importantly, common English speakers are pretty loose with what they call 'law', so any descriptive definition would have to be very vague. I suspect that linguistic research would favour legal positivists, but it would fail to resolve the issues that fuel the traditional debate. So that debate is not really about dictionary definitions.

A second kind of definition is *stipulative*. A stipulative definition merely tells how someone intends to use the defined word, so it would be irrelevant to do empirical research about how other people use that word. The traditional debate cannot be about purely stipulative definitions. If legal positivists' definitions of law were purely stipulative, there would be no point in arguing for them, criticizing them or responding to criticisms, other than by saying 'That is how I use the word'. The same goes for legal realists and natural law theorists.

Between dictionaries and stipulation lie *precising* definitions. The goal of a precising definition is to specify a precise use within the vague limits of common language in order to serve some practical purpose. For example, linguists who want to define the word 'city' might ask hundreds of people which areas they would call a city. Or one might just stipulate, 'By "city", I mean a densely populated area of more than 50,000 people...'. Such stipulation is fine in a friendly contest to see who can name the most cities in Asia (as long as both contestants agree to the stipulation), but in other contexts a definition of a city might have important implications – for example, by affecting the distribution of funds if a law provides federal support for public transportation in all cities. When the definition has such effects, it needs to be justified at the very least to people who live in areas that are deprived of funds by the definition.

Of course, it would be very misleading to define a city as any area with more than ten people, or to require cities to have over 10 million people. Precising definitions usually must lie somewhere within the loose limits of common language. Still, many alternative definitions lie within those loose limits, so any choice of a particular precising definition needs to be justified in contrast with the other remaining possibilities. Such choices cannot be justified by showing that one alternative is the true accurate one. There is no way to determine truth or accuracy when each alternative lies within common language. The only way to justify such a definition is to show that the definition best fulfils the relevant interests.

This pragmatic test still will not pick out a single best precising definition without presupposing that certain interests are relevant and others are not, since different definitions can serve different interests. An official might need to distribute public transportation funds to cities, whereas an academic might want to study crime trends in cities. Each will favour, and be justified in adopting, the precising definition that best serves his or her interests. Relative to those particular interests, one definition may be demonstrably better than the other. Nonetheless, when different people have such different interests, they might be justified in adopting different precising definitions.[6]

A fourth kind of definition may be seen as a kind of precising definition, but still needs to be distinguished separately. A *theoretical* definition also specifies a precise use within the vague limits of common language in order to serve some purpose, but here the purpose is theoretical rather than practical. The goal is to construct the best theory and capture what is important about the defined thing. The above precising definition of a city does not purport to say what really is important about a city or to construct a theory about the true nature of cities. In contrast, when chemists define water as H_2O, they often do claim to capture what water really is. The purpose of this definition is to allow chemists to construct general theories about how water interacts with other chemicals, when it boils and so on. If water were defined not in terms of hydrogen and oxygen in general but, instead, in terms of the most common isotopes of hydrogen and oxygen, then the definition would not be as useful for theoretical purposes, since generalizations about how water forms compounds with other chemicals would not be as simple and powerful, insofar as H_2O with other isotopes of hydrogen and oxygen are covered by almost all of the same generalizations. That is how chemists justify their definition of water as H_2O without mentioning isotopes: it captures what is important about water for the theoretical purposes of chemistry.

Now, which of these four kinds of definition is at stake in the traditional debates about how to define the law? Since I have already argued that the proposed definitions are neither stipulative nor dictionary definitions, they must be either precising or theoretical definitions. The issue then becomes whether the purposes of the traditional debaters were practical or theoretical. Did legal positivists, for example, give their definitions in order to construct theories to help us understand how law actually operates (as with the theoretical definition of water) or were they trying to serve practical purposes (as with the precising definition of a city)? The answer is that they were doing both. Some legal positivists might have been purely theoretical, but most had political goals mixed in with their theoretical goals. They often argue for their definitions and against other definitions of law by pointing to the practical, political effects of adopting those definitions.[7] This makes their definitions of law practical in a way that chemical definitions of water are not. Admittedly, even chemists have practical goals in mind, insofar as they have an eye to uses of their theories to aid society or to make them money. However, chemists do not usually directly cite these practical uses to justify their theoretical claims. In contrast, legal positivists do often justify their definitions by citing effects of using those definitions or the alternatives. The same goes for legal realists and natural law theorists. These traditional positions still differ from the precising definition of a city, because nobody would claim that a precising definition of a city tells us what a city really is, and the traditional position also purport to discover what the law really is. To that extent, the traditional debate is about theoretical definitions. But, since such theoretical purposes are usually mixed in some proportion with practical purposes, the traditional positions about law seem to seek some mixture of a precising definition and a theoretical definition.[8]

This goal determines the tests to use in deciding among the traditional definitions. Both precising and theoretical definitions need to fall within common language, but that does not settle the debate. Common English speech about law is notoriously loose and even inconsistent. It might rule out a few definitions, but it still allows some competing definitions of the law by legal positivists, legal realists and natural law theorists. The only way to justify one such definition over another, then, is to show how one definition better serves the relevant interests of, or better captures what is important about, the law.

Social Institutions

Sometimes it might seem that a single precising or theoretical definition could capture all that is really important about the thing defined. For example, the standard definition of water as H_2O might seem to capture what is important about water: modern chemistry shows how fruitful this definition of water is. Nevertheless, the limits of what counts as water will be different when one orders a drink in a restaurant, since in such circumstances water often comes with ice, carbonation, fluoride and even flavouring. Although some scientists might respond that what restaurants serve is not really, or purely, water, professional organizations and courts might need to decide what to allow restaurants to serve in response to a request for plain water. Clearly, the interests that are relevant in this context are just as legitimate as the interests of chemical experimenters. There might, then, be one definition of water for the purpose of drinking and another for the purpose of chemistry.

Besides, even if each natural kind did take a single precising or theoretical definition, other such definitions need not be so singular. This is especially obvious with social institutions. Different people participate in social institutions for different reasons. Once they enter the institution, they play different roles. These different reasons and roles will give them different interests and will cause them to see different aspects of the institution as most important.

For example, what exactly is a church? The janitor might say that it is a building, and fund-raisers might say that they are going to build a new church. However, after the new building is finished, members who go to church mainly for social reasons will say that they still go to the same church (St Peter's), since the clergy and congregation did not change with the building. Still others focus on doctrines that are believed or taught. If the doctrines changed radically, some would say that they still go to the same church, but theologians and the national organization might say that it is now a different church. Even among those who emphasize doctrines, there can be disputes if, say, only 10 per cent of the doctrines change. Those who see this 10 per cent as important enough will call it a new church, while others will call it the same old church if they attach more importance to the stable 90 per cent of the doctrines. If a philosopher were to ask, 'Is it *really* the same church?' or 'What is the church *really*?', we would not expect agreement. Different people define the church differently, because they have different interests and play different roles, so they take different perspectives on the church and see different aspects of it as important. It is difficult to see how anyone could show that one perspective is the right one or that certain aspects are the important ones for every purpose.

These disputes about what is important in a church will lead to different views on the rules of the church. Suppose the congregation and priest claim to be Catholics, but the clear majority of the congregation do not oppose either contraception or sodomy, the priest opposes contraception but not sodomy, and the Pope claims that nobody can be a true Catholic without opposing both. If one sees formal institutional structures as important, one might say that this church has rules against both contraception and homosexual sodomy, even though these rules are neither followed by the congregation nor enforced by the priest. However, if one focuses on social relations within the congregation, one might say that this church has neither rule, despite what the priest and the Pope say.

Similar points could be made about other social institutions and about other concepts that interact with social institutions. Because social institutions include many people who become involved for many reasons, different people will usually take different perspectives on most large social institutions. These institutions, then, cannot be understood without taking into consideration all the different perspectives of those who participant in them.

Perspectives on Law

Law is another social institution where different people play different roles and, hence, have different interests. One's role can limit the kinds of reason that one may cite to justify a decision.[9] One's role can also affect one's interests, both by creating or destroying one's interest in something or by making something seem, or be, more important than when one is not in that role. Such collections and orderings of reasons and interests are what I mean by different *perspectives* on law taken by people in different roles.[10]

There are numerous intertwined roles and levels within any modern legal system, but I will simplify the discussion here by focusing on three main roles: those of legislators, judges and private persons. Admittedly, legislators and judges have private lives, too; and legislators sometimes act as judges, such as in impeachment trials in the United States or when the Law Lords decide a case in Great Britain. When I describe a particular role (such as judges), I describe people insofar as they occupy that role (such as judges *qua* judges). This is not to deny that a single individual can take different roles and perspectives on law at different times. I also do not deny the great variety in the jobs of legislators and judges at different levels and the even greater diversity in the lives of private persons. Thus, much of what I say will be oversimplified. Still, there are some common interests that keep my crude trichotomy from being too crude. I will discuss some other roles and the interactions among roles later, but I will begin with the three principal roles and perspectives on law.

My goal is to show that each of these three perspectives is expressed in one of the three classic definitions of law. The roles and perspectives are prior to the definitions of law, both in the sense that the definitions came later historically (even if certain political ideas caused those roles to be created) and also in the sense that the roles could exist without anyone explicitly formulating the definitions of law. Certain definitions then become, and remain, popular because they capture what is important from a certain perspective.

Legislators and Legal Positivism

Consider the perspective of a legislator. Legislators write laws. Actually, their clerks write the laws but the legislators still choose to support the laws that their clerks wrote, and then what legislators choose to support (or oppose) is the words in those laws. House bill no. 123 is a set of words. When this set of words is brought to the floor of the house, opponents propose amendments, which are additional or alternative words. The opposing sides argue about which words are better. Then they vote on the amendment and, if it passes, on Amended House Bill no. 123. What they vote for, or against, is a set of words. Given the nature of this legislative task, it is no surprise that legislators see laws as consisting of the words that they passed.

Of course, the legislators took those words to have certain meanings. A law about commercial banks is not a law about river banks. So it is not just the words but also their meanings, and possibly also the speakers' meanings, that constitute a law from the legislators' perspective. If legislators pass a bill whose words do not mean what they took those words to mean, then it is not clear what the law is from their perspective, just as it is not clear what I say when I misuse words. In any case, the crucial point here is that, even if words and meanings are part of a bill that passes, that bill is not changed by what other people, including judges, do later.

Admittedly, legislators support laws in order to achieve certain purposes. They hope that passing a law will have a certain effect on society. But legislators do not vote on those unstated purposes. If they had to vote on specific reasons for laws, majority support would be rare. When a law which they passed does not serve their purposes as they hoped, legislators will be disappointed; but they cannot claim that the law which they passed was not enforced. For example, if legislators vote to allow capital punishment because they think that this law will deter murder, but this law does not achieve this outcome, then the law still allows capital punishment (assuming it is constitutional).

The point is not that judges may not consider legislative purposes when they interpret laws passed by legislatures. That is a prescriptive issue about how judges should reach decisions. The point, for now, is just that its purpose is not part of a law that legislators pass. Admittedly, legislators often know that judges will consider legislative purposes in deciding cases, and this knowledge might affect how legislators write laws and which laws they pass. But legislators cannot be concerned solely with how judges will interpret laws, because their laws reach a wider audience, including private citizens. Moreover, what they vote on is still the words, and not any prediction about how judges will interpret those words.

Similarly, legislators know that individual laws will be applied in light of the rest of the legal system, and they use this knowledge in deciding which laws to support. A background of procedural laws must also be in place before anyone can be a legislator and before a vote can be taken. Nonetheless, what legislators choose to support or oppose is the single law that is before them at a certain time. Suppose a legislator votes for Bill no. 123, because he or she thinks that Bill no. 124 will pass the following day, and that these two laws will work together well, even though he or she would not vote for Bill no. 123 alone. The following day, House Bill no. 124 fails to pass, but the vote on House Bill no. 123 still holds, and that bill is still a law.

There are, then, two distinctive features on the legislative perspective on laws. First, legislators pass laws one by one, not as groups. Second, what they pass is a set of words with certain meanings. As a result, legislators tend to talk as if a law is a set of words passed at a particular time.

This perspective on law is reflected in definitions of law by legal positivists. There are many versions of legal positivism, but my argument applies to the movement as a whole. I will use Austin and Hart as examples. Austin followed Bentham, whose main goal was to figure out which laws maximize utility and then to get those laws passed. So it should be no surprise that Bentham and Austin view law from that legislative perspective. Austin then defines a positive law as a general command (or sanctioned expression of desire) by a human sovereign.[11] The crucial point here is that laws are commands or expressions, according to Austin. That means that they are words or uses of words on particular occasions, just as I said a legislator would claim.

More recent versions of positivism are more subtle and inclusive. Hart, for example, does allow as laws some rules that are not passed by sovereigns or legislation, but nonetheless constantly assumes that the laws passed by legislatures consist of the words that they voted on. His central discussion of open texture in 'the language of the rule'[12] would be misguided if law did not consist of language. Also, when Hart debates with Lon Fuller about the rule 'No vehicles in the park', Hart stresses the words in the rule, along with their meanings, in contrast with the purposes for which the rule was passed.[13] Even when discussing precedents, Hart emphasizes the words in judicial opinions rather than the principles that are implicit behind those precedents. This is one of Dworkin's main complaints against Hart.[14]

Thus, both traditional and recent versions of legal positivism are suited to capture those aspects of law that are important to legislators, given their peculiar role and interests. In that sense, legal positivism views law from the perspective of legislators.[15] Whether legal positivism can also capture other perspectives on law can be determined only after we describe those other perspectives.

Judges and Natural Law Theory

Judges have a different job from legislators in that they decide particular cases. This different role creates different concerns.

When judges decide a case, they do not consider only a single law: they need to consider all of the relevant statutes and constitutional clauses as well as judicial precedents. They must do this not just because statutes might conflict among themselves and with the Constitution, if any but because, even when there is no conflict, they need to consider rules of evidence and other procedural rules. They also need to determine whether any precedent restricts or reinterprets the statute. This makes a judge's job very different from that of a legislator. Legislators vote on bills one by one, whereas judges decide on whether the whole system of laws, or the law as a whole, allows a criminal conviction or civil damages.

Judges, then, have two jobs. First, they must reach decisions. To refuse to reach a decision would be to decide in favour of the defendant, so judges usually aren't allowed to refuse to decide a case (or even to postpone a decision for very long) just because the case is hard.[16] Moreover, judges must base their decisions on the law. Their job is to apply the law, not to impose their own moral beliefs on everyone else.[17]

Judges need to do both jobs in a range of cases over which they have little control. Whereas legislators can decide which bills to consider, judges typically cannot decide which cases come before their courts. The cases that do reach the court are rarely simple, since few people waste time on cases when the outcome is obvious.

It is difficult for judges to do both their jobs in the hard cases that come to court. When precedents, statutes or constitutional clauses conflict without clear rankings, or when they are too vague to dictate a single decision, the judge cannot decide the case on the basis of any of the sources of law alone. This means that he or she has no choice but to look beyond the explicit words in precedents, statutes and constitutions. Sometimes judges look for broader moral principles that somehow underlie the explicit words in precedents, statutes and constitutions, but evaluative claims are needed to show that a certain moral principle is implicit. The appeal to values is obvious when one argues that a broad right is implicit because it provides the *best* way to justify rights that are explicitly listed.[18] An appeal to values is also needed to argue that an implicit right is necessary for an explicit right to be secure or meaningful, since the necessity in question is not logical but is, rather, a matter of the best available or only acceptable means of adequately securing the explicit right.[19] Thus, judges cannot determine which moral principles are implicit without relying on their own moral beliefs. Sometimes judges admit this: sometimes they even refer directly to what is fair or just, and say that their job is to do justice.[20] Such decisions and claims are controversial, since many critics believe that judges should never base legal decisions on moral beliefs. But that is the prescriptive issue. Even if judges *should* not use such grounds, they often *do*; and they cannot avoid doing so in practice at least in some hard cases.

When judges use their moral beliefs to reach decisions, they cannot see themselves as applying the law unless they also see those moral principles as part of the law. Moreover, the judge will have to see those principles as having been part of the law, even before the decision, since otherwise the decision would seem retroactive and unfair.[21] Thus, judges will not be able to see themselves as accomplishing their dual job of deciding every case on the basis of the law unless they view the law as including moral principles.

A critic might respond that judges could (and possibly should) base their decisions on empirical beliefs about the original intent or about moral principles of legislators or of the majority instead of on the judges' own moral principles. However, even if original intent can be determined in some cases, there will be many others where no original intent can be found, or none that is sufficiently clear to dictate a single decision. It is also not obvious why original intent must always be followed when it is determinate.[22] These same arguments can be extended to show why the moral beliefs of contemporary society also cannot always be used to ground judicial decisions. One might respond that laws should be written so that judges never have to face such problems. However, nobody has ever done that or shown how to do that. It seems practically inevitable that there will be some cases where judges must reach decisions but cannot base these on anything other than their own moral principles. If their job is to apply the law, then they cannot see themselves as doing their job unless they perceive those implicit moral principles as part of the law.

In any case, this is the view of judges. Even if laws really do run out, so judges have strong discretion, and then judges really do go beyond explicit laws and use their own moral beliefs, judges still do not admit this in their official capacity. Judges never announce from the bench that their decisions are not based on the law for the good reason that such an admission would undermine respect for the legal system and create resentment in trial losers. Thus, judges talk as if they base every decision only on the law, and as if implicit moral principles are part of the law.[23]

The same tendency occurs when laws are extremely bad. One classic example is a law that requires that all blue-eyed babies be killed. Suppose this morally horrendous law is not rendered legally invalid by anything in the pre-existing precedents, statutes or Constitution in this jurisdiction. Many judges will want to refuse to apply this law but, at the same time, will also want to do their job, or at least say publicly that they are doing their job, which is to apply the law. These conflicting pressures will give judges a strong reason to announce that the blue-eyed baby law is legally invalid. Their real reason for this is that they see this law as immoral, even if they are not willing to admit publicly that this is their reason. Thus, judges will tend to talk as if morality restricts what is the law.

This feature of judges' linguistic usage is most easily captured by natural law theory. I doubt that many judges today would go so far as to adopt natural law theory in the crude forms of Cicero and Aquinas.[24] Nevertheless, more recent natural law theories do seem to try to capture the perspective of judges. This point could be illustrated with Lon Fuller,[25] but my main example will be Ronald Dworkin.[26]

Dworkin's views have changed over the years, but in one recent major work he writes:

> According to law as integrity, propositions of law are true if they figure in or follow from the principles of justice, fairness, and procedural due process that provide the best constructive interpretation of the community's legal practice.[27]

He goes on to propose two dimensions on which to test which constructive interpretation is best: An interpretation must, first, fit the precedents or past judicial decisions. When two interpretations both fit well enough, the best interpretation, and thereby the law, is determined by 'his more substantive political convictions about the relative moral value of the two interpretations'.[28] This second dimension is what makes Dworkin's account a version of natural law theory. Furthermore, it is clear that by 'his' convictions, Dworkin refers to the judge's convictions. Legislators do not normally interpret prior laws, much less 'the community's legal practice' as a whole. Fit with precedents does not constrict legislators. Of course, Dworkin realizes, and even emphasizes, that 'judges are in a very different position than legislators'.[29] My point is just that his whole theory is addressed to judges and would be pointless, at best, if addressed to legislators.

Many objections to Dworkin's theory seem to overlook this perspective. Critics say that the task of judges is to apply the law, but Dworkin licenses judges to base their decisions on implicit moral principles rather than on the law. This charge seems right insofar as law is defined from the perspective of legislators, so that law includes only the words and meanings of bills passed by legislatures. Dworkin does say that judges must, may, and should go beyond that kind of law in reaching judicial decisions. However, it is not so clear that – or even why – the job of judges is simply to apply law as defined in that legislative way. If the job of judges is instead to apply the law as defined from the perspective of judges, and if Dworkin's theory accurately reflects that judicial perspective, then Dworkin's theory does not license judges to base their decisions on anything other than the law. Legislators might not like Dworkin's theory for licensing judges to apply the law as judges see it, but that only confirms that Dworkin's theory, like other natural law theories, reflects the distinctive perspective of judges on the law.

Private Persons and Legal Realists

Most people are neither judges nor legislators. They are private persons. They are private insofar as they have no special status in making or applying the law. They are (legal) persons insofar as the law applies to them – that is, restricts and protects them. The perspective of private persons on the law is different from that of legislators and judges. Most private persons are woefully ignorant of the particular words in the laws passed by legislators. They also do not know the precedents that figure so prominently in judges' decisions. What they do know is that judges can send them to prison and take money or their home or children away from them. From the perspective of private persons, then, what is important about law is whatever determines whether they lose liberty, money, possessions, or family, as well as whether people who harm them will be punished or forced to pay damages.

All of the above is determined by judges' particular decisions. Suppose legislators pass a rule that is then questioned through the courts and eventually overturned as unconstitutional. That rule will not affect the lives of most private persons, except insofar as they are uncertain about whether it will be overturned. Similarly, if a rule passed by a legislature seems to apply to a particular case, but judges decide not to apply it to that case, then the parties in that case are not affected by the rule, except insofar as the parties wasted time because they did not know whether the courts would apply it. So what is ultimately important to private persons is how rules affect their lives outside courtrooms – and that depends primarily on particular judicial decisions.

Admittedly, private persons often cite laws as reasons for them to do or not to do something, even when they know that they will not get in trouble for breaking the law. Private persons also often cite laws to criticize official actions when they think that officials are not following or applying the law, even if they know that those officials will get away with such misbehaviour. Nonetheless, whereas not all private persons do, or need to, engage in this use of the law, all private persons are concerned about their lives, freedom, possessions and family. Even those private persons who do cite laws as reasons why they, or officials, ought to behave in some way, they still care *more* about their personal goods and, hence, about how officials actually behave. In these respects, such personal concerns are more central or essential to the private person's perspective.

It should also be recognized that laws can have effects when they are not applied. Even if nobody ever robs a bank, so that the law against bank robbers is never applied in any court, that law still affects people's lives if some people would rob banks in the absence of such a law. Moreover, laws can symbolize ideals and thereby affect society's values, which in turn affects private persons' lives. Law operates in many ways. Nonetheless, most private persons are most concerned about how the law affects them when they are prosecuted for crimes or are potential victims of crimes, when they sue or are sued, when officials decide whether their tax deductions are allowed, and so on. Most private persons view these decisions by officials as the most important element of the law.

To capture this perspective or set of concerns, it is natural to define law in terms of decisions by officials. This is what legal realists do. Karl Llewellyn writes, 'What these officials do about disputes is, to my mind, the law itself' and 'The main thing is what officials are going to *do*'.[30] This perspective is also captured by Oliver Wendell Holmes when he writes:

> ... a legal duty so called is nothing but a prediction that if a man does or omits certain things he will be made to suffer in this or that way by the judgment of the court; – and so of a legal right.[31]

While there are significant differences among these definitions by legal realists, all such definitions try to capture what is important about law from the perspective of private persons who care mainly about whether their liberty or property will be taken or protected by courts.

A similar point was made long ago again by Holmes, who said:

> If you want to know the law and nothing else, you must look at it as a bad man, who cares only for the material consequences which such knowledge enables him to predict, not as a good one, who finds his reasons for conduct, whether inside the law or outside of it, in the vaguer sanctions of conscience.[32]

In contrast, I do not want to say that private persons who are concerned for material consequences are 'bad' people. Nor are people who follow law for its own sake always good. When the law is evil, there can be much good in refusing to follow the law for its own sake. And there might be nothing morally wrong with taking a questionable tax deduction simply because one knows that it will be allowed by a tax inspector or a judge. Many private persons do follow the law even when they know they will not suffer if they disobey, but they are not necessarily better people. That depends on what the law is.

Moreover, victims of crimes are not bad, but they also care mainly about whether officials enforce laws. When women are beaten or raped, but the aggressors are not pursued by police, prosecutors or judges, then these victims often complain that the law does not protect them, and has to be changed. Such people will be little concerned about any rules on the statute books against what these aggressors do, if those rules are not enforced. What primarily concerns them is what judge and the police do to stop the crimes.

To such private persons, then, what is most important about the law is captured by legal realist definitions of law in terms of particular decisions by legal officials. However, such definitions of law by legal realists would be rejected as unhelpful or worse by legislators and judges. To tell a judge that the law is whatever he or she decides will be of no use in reaching one decision as opposed to another. To tell legislators that the law is whatever judges decide will in effect tell them that it does not matter whether or not they pass House Bill no. 123, or how that bill is worded. So, although definitions of law by legal realists do not capture the perspectives of legislators and judges, they do capture what they try to capture, which is just the perspective of private persons.[33]

Other Perspectives on Law

In addition to legislators, judges and private persons, many other people are involved in the legal system. One prominent group is lawyers. Do lawyers have their own distinctive perspective on law? I think not – for the following reasons. Lawyers are caught in the middle between their clients and judges. When their clients ask for advice, lawyers take the perspective of their clients, who are private persons. But when lawyers present arguments to judges, they have to take the perspective of judges in order to convince those judges. Thus, some parts of a lawyer's task are carried out from the perspective of private persons and others from the perspective of judges. Perhaps this dual role explains why these perspectives are often confused in articles about the nature of law by lawyers (and by law professors who train lawyers).

Police are also caught in the middle. Legislators pass laws that, in effect, order police to pursue certain types of crime. But police officers know that they are wasting their time if they cannot secure convictions in courts from judges. As a result, sometimes the police take the perspective of the legislators who are their bosses, and sometimes that of judges who decide the cases that the police bring to court.

One could also say that the executive branch is caught between legislators and private persons insofar as they are supposed to administer the laws of legislators with respect to private persons. This would yield a neat diagram:

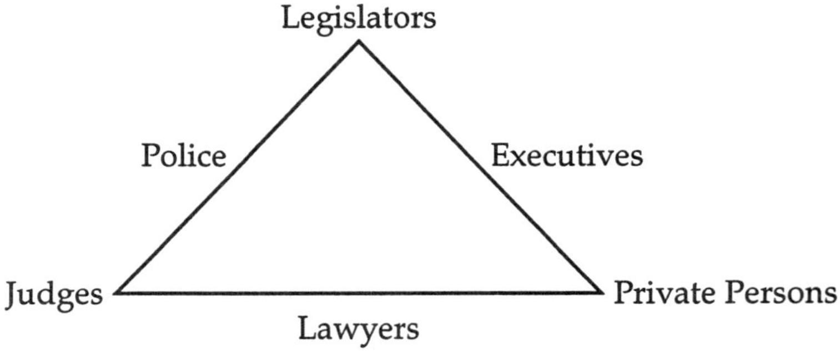

Unfortunately, this diagram is too simple, since executives are also concerned about facing judges in court, the police deal with private persons every day, and lawyers often confer with legislators. So we need to be careful not to let this simple diagram obscure the more complex reality.

Furthermore, many other perspectives are taken on law. When law students studying for a bar exam ask what the law is, their concern is to pass that exam, regardless of whether their answers help them later when they practise law. Law publishers also ask what the law is, with slightly different concerns. And state government officials have a somewhat different perspective on federal law. The notion of a private person also covers a very wide and diverse group, so different racial, sexual and economic groups view the law somewhat differently. I do not want to deny or disparage any of these complexities. There are perspectives within the perspectives that I discuss. In picking out the three main perspectives, all I intend to do is focus on certain abstract common concerns because these reflect the abstract theories of law in the traditional debate.

These three perspectives (along with the others on the diagram) also seem special because they are essentially legal and essential to law. They are essentially legal, because they are defined by legal rules. Judges and legislators are made judges and legislators by means of laws. So are private persons, since a private person is someone to whom the law applies, and the law itself determines those to whom it applies.[34]

The three main perspectives are also essential to law in the sense that every legal system must have legislators, judges and private persons. In contrast, legal systems can easily exist without bar exams or racial differences. Other cultures and legal systems might not have roles corresponding exactly to my descriptions of legislators, judges and lawyers, but there are limits, because we would not call something a legal system if it differed too much from paradigm modern legal systems.

Despite these complexities, the crucial point here is that many other perspectives on law can be understood in terms of how they interact with the main three perspectives (those of legislators, judges and private persons) that are reflected in the main three theories (legal positivism, natural law theory and legal realism). Perhaps that explains why these three theories of the nature of law have remained the dominant triad for so long.

Applications

The differences among these perspectives could be illustrated by many examples, but I will discuss only two.[35] My first example is speed limits. I have chosen this apparently trivial example so that strong emotions will not cloud the conceptual issues. However, speed limits are not as trivial as they might seem, since they are among the first laws encountered by teenagers, and thereby play a role in formulating many people's attitudes towards the law in general, even as adults.

Imagine the following scenarios which is not too distant from what actually happens in many jurisdictions from the United States to Australia. The road sign says, 'Speed limit 65 mph'. The legislature's purpose in imposing this limit was to reduce traffic accidents, in the belief that most drivers cannot drive safely at higher speeds. Nonetheless, the average speed where such signs are posted is 70 mph. Police radar is accurate only to plus or minor seven mph, and no admissible evidence is more accurate. As a result, any competent lawyer could successfully defend a client who is caught driving at 72 mph or less. The relevant legal system includes a right to competent counsel. Partly because of this, the police have a written public policy of not stopping anyone who is driving at under 75 mph. They always follow this policy in actual practice.

In such circumstances, how fast can one drive without breaking the law? Most people will answer that the speed limit is 65 mph, because the sign says, 'Speed limit 65 mph'. Most of my students start with this perspective, as do some of the friends whom I polled informally. It is also the perspective of legislators. When legislators decide whether to make the speed limit 55 or 65 mph, they are deciding which number to write in the law books and on the road signs. Rules of evidence and police practice are relevant to their choice, as is their goal of preventing accidents and unsafe driving. Nonetheless, even safe drivers are said to break the law if they drive faster than 65 mph. From this perspective, then, the law is whatever number legislators pick to post on signs. The reason is that legislators make the law, and that number is what they pick.

Judges, in contrast, are concerned to apply the law as a whole to particular situations, so they cannot look only at the road sign. As any legal scholar knows, that sign gets its legal force from the system of laws. That larger system includes other rules regarding evidence and competent counsel that creates a legal right not to be convicted or fined for driving at any speed up to 72 mph. What judges need to decide is which defendants to convict and fine, not which number to post on signs. From the judges' perspective, then, there is reason to see the real speed limit as 72 mph.[36]

Finally, suppose that a driver is in a hurry, like most people these days. Luckily, his lawyer happens to be sitting in the car with him, so he asks her, 'How fast may I drive legally?'. His lawyer could say, 'The speed limit is 65 mph' or 'There is no legal way for you to be fined if you drive up to 72 mph'. However, both these statements would overlook a very relevant fact: the public policy of police not to stop anyone below 75 mph. Since the lawyer knows this policy, and also knows that the driver's main concern is to avoid being fined, the lawyer's best advice would be, 'You may drive up to 75 mph without worrying about the law'.[37] One might object that the law is still 65 mph even if the police do not stop cars travelling at less than 75 mph. However, what is written on the sign does not matter to such a driver, as long as the police policy stays at 75 mph. If the sign is changed to 60 mph, but the police policy remains the same, then the driver would not care about the sign. The driver also would not care about legal possibility of being find for travelling at 73 mph if he or she knows that he or she will never be stopped at that speed. What matters is the public policy that police officers always follow. If this policy were changed without notice, a driver caught driving at 73 mph would have a legitimate complaint insofar as he acted on a public policy of legal officials (in contrast with a hunch that a friend on the police force would let him off). Police officers are legal officials just as much as legislators and judges, so their publicly announced policies create legitimate expectations. From the perspective of private persons, then, there is reason to say that the speed limit is 75 mph. Indeed, this is just what was said by some of my friends whom I polled.

My second example is more emotive. Suppose that a legislature passes a statute that assigns a seven- to ten-year sentence for coerced sex within marriage, and another statute requires more than one witness as evidence before any conviction under the first statute. Other laws forbid self-incrimination and forbid police from coming on to anyone's private property without notification before the time of entry in respect of any family matter. Illegally obtained evidence is excluded from trials, and defendants have a right to competent counsel.

In this jurisdiction John and Jane are married and live on a large, isolated farm in a house that is a mile from the closest border of the property. John is sole owner of the farm. One evening in the house, Jane tells John that she is too tired for sex, but John threatens to kill Jane is she refuses to have sex with him. Since Jane takes John's threat seriously, she agrees to have sex with him. Then Jane reports the incident to the police the following morning.

Under these circumstances, does John's act violate the law? It might seem clear that it does. John coerced his wife into sex. The first-mentioned legislative statute forbids this very kind of act. That is the end of the story for anyone who looks at law from the legislative perspective, such as a legal positivist. So legislators and positivists would say that John's act violates the law.

However, if this particular case ever gets to court, then the judge must find John not guilty and must treat him as not guilty in every way. This result is ensured by the other statutes that requires a second witness, forbid self-incrimination, limit police entry, exclude illegally obtained evidence and guarantee competent counsel. More generally, there is no realistic way for a court ever to convict John for this kind of act in these circumstances.[38] As long as John can never be found guilty, he must never be treated as guilty by any legal official. To that extent, in these circumstances, John's act does not seem to violate the law. The same kind of act is still illegal for others, and for John, in other circumstances, but the current law as a whole allows John to do what he has done in his home. Or, at least, a judge cannot say officially that John violated the law.

Of course, Jane will complain. She will say that the law as it stands does not protect her, so the law should be changed to make it possible to convict John and others in similar circumstances. Other women and men will agree. The reason why the law has to be changed is that John's act does not violate the current law as a whole. Or, at least, that is how it will look from the perspective of private persons who are concerned with whether the law will punish others who harm them, and not with 'paper rules' such as the words passed by legislators passed in the unenforceable statute against marital rape.

If the police find that they cannot enforce this marital rape statute because of the other laws, they make it clear that they will not waste their resources trying to prosecute husbands who violate this law, and wives like Jane will have even stronger reasons to complain that the law does not protect them or forbid what husbands like John do. Suppose one statute says that all women have a right to obtain an abortion, but another statute prohibits abortion clinics anywhere in the state, or the police publicly announce that they will not stop protesters who prevent any women from entering any abortion clinic. Then women will complain that the legal right supposedly granted by the first statute is hollow at best. Similarly, Jane could argue that the law as a whole gives her no real legal right not to be raped by her husband. Such indictments of the law reflect the fact that what is most important about law to private persons is not the words that legislatures pass but the actual decisions made by other legal officials.

Conclusion

These illustrations, along with the preceding arguments, suggest that legislators, judges and private persons take distinct perspectives on law and that these three perspectives are captured by the traditional definitions of law by legal positivists, natural law theorists and legal realists, respectively.

Can all these perspectives be combined into a single definition of law? I do not see how. Theoretical definitions are supposed to include all, and only those, features that are important or essential to the defined thing. If a theoretical definition of law includes only what is important to legislators, then it will not include some features that are important to judges and private persons. And if a theoretical definition of law includes all that is important to legislators, then it will include some features that are not important to judges or private persons. One might try to formulate a definition in unspecific terms that all parties can accept because they would be able to fill in details according to their own concerns,[39] but such a schematic definition would fail to specify which aspects of law are important and therefore fail to satisfy any of the parties in the traditional debate. In the absence of any other approach, it seems that no single coherent theoretical definition can capture all and only what is important from all three perspectives.

The same problem arises for other theoretical and precising definitions. There seems to be no way to formulate a unified definition of a church to satisfy the perspectives of priests and also of their congregations and janitors. There might be no single definition of water for chemists and restaurateurs and no single definition of a city that would work for federal officials distributing highway funds as well as for sociologists studying crime patterns in cities. Similarly, it does not seem possible to provide a single unified definition of law that would capture the concerns of legislators as well as those of judges and private persons.

What about legal theorists? I am not thinking of practical law professors who see their job as training future lawyers, judges or legislators, but rather of academics who want to understand the phenomenon of law as a whole, while remaining neutral among the interests and perspectives of legislators, judges and private persons.[40] The only way to do this is to describe the three perspectives on law and specify the features of law that are important from each perspective, without claiming that any of these features really is important or essential to law. This neutral description will not result in a single coherent definition of law, but it could mention every feature of law that is important to anyone, specify whom each feature is important to, and explain why and how each aspect is important to those to whom it is important.

If all this is accomplished, then it is not clear what would be gained by adding a general definition of the thing on which all of these perspectives are taken. Some legal theorists may still long for a single coherent definition, but why? A formal definition would not tell us anything new about law once we have a comprehensive description of law from every perspective. Even if a definition might add something, that something might just be beyond our grasp, in which case our only realistic alternative is the perspectival approach.

Objections

This argument may be crude, general, and incomplete, but I cannot go into more detail here now. My only hope is that these brief remarks at least point in a new direction that might be more illuminating than arguing about which traditional definition of law is the right one. In order to fan that hope, I will try to head off a few initial objections that might make some readers despair, too early, of ever developing any complete, defensible perspectival theory of law.

Do I Overlook a Priority?

Some traditionalists will object that, although many perspectives may be taken on law, one perspective is primary in that it somehow makes one theoretical or precising definition the correct one. For example, some legal positivists will probably argue that, since all legitimate political authority and power come from the people, the legislative perspective is more basic than the others, thereby making some corresponding positivist definition of law more basic.[41] A perspectival theorist might deny that the legislature really is more basic. If authority comes from the people, why isn't the private citizen's perspective primary? But I want to avoid that normative issue.

My response is that, even if the legislature is more basic in some sense, that does not make other perspectives and definitions inaccurate or incorrect. My topic here is definitional versions of legal positivism, legal realism and natural law theory. These claims about the nature of law might each capture part of that multifaceted phenomenon, even if one fact is more basic or has more value than the others. The foundation of a building might be more basic or important in some way, but one still cannot define or describe the building solely in terms of its foundation. To say that the legislative perspective is more basic is presumably to make a normative claim about the relative importance of different branches of government. That normative claim does not show any inaccuracy in descriptions of the other facets that can be seen only from other perspectives. If none of the other perspectives can be dismissed as illegitimate, then each of these other perspectives needs to be captured by any legal theorist who wants to remain neutral among all legitimate perspectives. That is what my perspectival theory aims to do.

Do I Conflate Separate Issues?

Other critics might charge that I confuse indefinite with definite articles, since there is *a* law against driving at 66 mph, even if this act is not against *the* law. Some might go further and say that driving at 66 mph is against the law, even if judicial practice and police policy is not to enforce the law in this case. They will claim that I confuse the law with its enforcement. I plead not guilty. My topic is the law, so I do not mind admitting that there is a law against driving at 66 mph. I might even admit that legislators talk about *a* law, while judges talk about *the* law. If different linguistic forms are used from different perspectives, those perspectives are still distinct and must all be captured by any completely adequate theory of law as a whole.

I draw the line, however, when it comes to separating the law from its enforcement. To assume that the law should be defined independently of its enforcement is to assume that the law is what the legislature passes, regardless of what judges and police officers do. But what these other legal officials do is important to many people. The point of a precising or theoretical definition is to capture what is important about the defined thing, so a definition of the law that did not include enforcement policies would be inadequate insofar as it did not reflect the concerns and perspectives of these people. This does not mean that there is anything wrong with the legislative perspective. All it means is that there is more to the law than can be seen from the legislative perspective, or from any single perspective alone.

Do I Trivialize the Debate?

Still other opponents might argue that I trivialize the traditional debate by allowing everyone to determine the law from their own perspective. If judges and legislators can each decide what law is, how can legislators criticize judges for failing to apply the laws that they, as legislators, have passed? Are they even talking about the same thing?

Trivialization is an endemic problem for definitional theories. And I admit that this debate about the definition of law is less important (at least directly) than the other debate among positivists, realists and natural law theorists – namely, the prescriptive debate about how legislators and judges ought to do their jobs. Still, I do not think that the definitional debate is trivial, much less that my view makes it trivial in the alleged sense.

My view is not like the well-known story of three blind people who feel different parts of an elephant and consequently each describe it differently. My thesis holds for fully-sighted people who can, and do, see every aspect of the law. Another difference is that elephants might be definable in terms of internal features, such as genetic structure, that cause and explain the felt features such as the trunk, tail, and legs, but law is not a natural phenomenon and has no such universal internal structure to define it. As with elephants, there are paradigm cases of the law that enable different theories to be about a common subject matter. However, unlike natural kinds, there need be no internal features of those paradigm cases that could be used to define what the law is.

For similar reasons, my view is different from Wittgenstein's famous discussion of a duck-rabbit drawing.[42] There is no physical drawing to see differently in the case of law. Moreover, different practical purposes underlie different views of law but not different views of the duck-rabbit. In my view, this practical conflict prevents the debates about law from becoming trivial.[43]

Perspectivalism also might seem to trivialize the debate by giving judges the right to decide what law is. My perspectival theory implies no such thing. On my view, it is perfectly legitimate for legislators to complain that judges are not following the law when judges do not follow what is law from the legislative perspective as captured in some version of legal positivism. However, it is also perfectly legitimate for judges to respond that they are, indeed, following what is the law from the judicial perspective as captured by some version of natural law theory. When legislators and judges argue in this way, they are each expressing their own legitimate perspectives. That does not mean that they have nothing to argue about. They are each trying to get the others to see the law from their perspective or even to show that their definition better captures what is really important or most important about the law. Each definition does capture what is important about the law to the person who is speaking, but they still disagree about whether this is, or should be, what is important or most important to the other people. That is the topic of the traditional debate in my view, even if the traditional debate was not framed explicitly in those terms.

Do I Contradict Myself?

Yet more critics might suppose that my theory implies that, in the circumstances outlined earlier, driving at 66 mph both violates and does not violate the law. This might be a contradiction, but I never assert or imply this. What I do assert is that a legislator may say the former and a judge may say the latter. However, neither person may make both statements at once. The whole point of a perspectival theory is that there is no single perspective or definition that incorporates the perspectives of both the legislator and the judge. Since one simply cannot view the phenomenon from both sides simultaneously, one is never in a position to make both of the contradictory statements. A perspectival legal theorist can describe both perspectives, but a theorist does not take or make statements from either perspective, since such a theorist tries to remain neutral among all perspectives. So a perspectival theorist is also not committed to any contradictory statements.

Compare a perspectival theory of cities according to which an official distributing highway funds may say that Burlington, which has 60,000 inhabitants, is *not* a city (because the best definition for these purposes require a city to have 80,000 inhabitants), but a sociologist studying crime trends may say that Burlington *is* a city (because the best definition for these purposes requires a city to have only 50,000 people). This perspectival theory does not take the perspective of either the official or the sociologist, so it does not imply either of the statements that seem to be contradictory. Moreover, the statements by the official and the sociologist are not really contradictory. Nor are statements by a chemist and a restaurateur who deny and affirm that a certain glass contains only water. Similarly, there is no real contradiction when a perspectival theory of law implies that legislators may say that driving at 66 mph does violate the law, and judges may say that driving at 66 mph does not violate the law. The difference in perspectives, concerns, and hence definitions, keeps these statements from being logically incompatible.

Am I too Relativistic?

A final group of critics will complain that my perspectival theory is a form of perspectivism, which is just a fancy name for relativism, so it is subject to all the well-known problems of relativism. However, the kind of perspectivism that I endorse does not imply wholesale relativism about anything.

A more radical form of perspectivism is endorsed by Friedrich Nietzsche when he states:

> There is *only* a perspective seeing, *only* a perspective 'knowing'; and the *more* affects we allow to speak about one thing, the *more* eyes, different eyes, we can use to observe one thing, the more complete will our 'concept' of this thing, our 'objectivity' be.[44]

Nietzsche applies this claim to all things. Admittedly on some days I am rather inclined to accept Nietzsche's general claim, but that confession is irrelevant here. My claim here is only that precising and theoretical definitions of social institutions are perspectival in the sense that their adequacy and justification depend on one's perspective. My claim applies only to precising or theoretical definitions and only to social institutions, so it is much more limited than Nietzsche's. That is why I prefer to describe my theory as perspectival rather than as fully-fledged perspectivism.

The limited scope of my theory makes it immune from most of the standard arguments against relativism. I am not saying that anything goes, or even that anything goes in precising and theoretical definitions of the law. Some such definitions of law can be rejected as incorrect, because they fail to capture any legitimate perspective on law. Relativism would follow if the only standard of legitimacy for a perspective were the concerns of that very perspective itself. However, each of my three main perspectives recognizes the legitimacy of the other perspectives.[45] Legislators know that they need people in the roles of judges and private persons, and vice versa. Moreover, as I argued, these three perspectives are essential to law and are essentially legal. That gives them a special legitimacy and primacy that cannot be claimed by all other perspectives – and also limits which theories and definitions of law are acceptable.

Nonetheless, even after rejecting some perspectives and definitions, my point is that several definitions of law remain and have an equal claim to define what is important about the law. These legitimate claims cannot all be recognized as equal in any single definition. This means that if you want your theory of law to remain neutral among all legitimate claims and concerns, as I do, then you have no choice but to adopt some perspectival theory of law.

Notes

1 I am grateful to the Australian Research Council for financial support and to several participants, especially Chin-Liew Ten, Fred Schauer and Tom Campbell, for helpful comments.

2 Tom Campbell formulates the conceptual separability thesis as 'the view that law and morality *can* be separated (in that, for instance, legal decisions need not draw on moral premises)': *The Legal Theory of Ethical Positivism* (Aldershot: Dartmouth, 1996, p. 3, cf. p. 69). In contrast, the descriptive separation thesis is 'the claim that law and morals actually are separate' (p. 3). Legal positivism is often and here defined so as to include the separability thesis, but not necessarily the separation thesis. Natural Law Theories are often and here defined so as to deny the separability thesis. On the separation thesis, see Frederick Schauer, 'Legal Positivism and the Contingent Autonomy of Law', Chapter 9 in this volume.

3 This is called the prescriptive separation thesis by Tom Campbell, *Ethical Positivism*, *op. cit.*, pp. 2–3, 71 and 85.

4 For example, David Brink, 'Legal Positivism and Natural Law Reconsidered', *The Monist*, 68(3) (July 1985), pp. 364–88.

5 The following discussion of definitions draws on Robert Fogelin and Walter Sinnott-Armstrong, *Understanding Arguments*, 5th edn (Fort Worth: Harcourt, 1996), pp. 329–31.

6 Similar points could be made about precising definitions of death in medicine and in criminal law, of insanity in criminal law and in civil commitment, of blindness in insurance and in restrictions on school bus drivers, and so on.

7 See, for example, Neil MacCormick, 'A Moralistic Case for A-Moralistic Law', *Valparaiso University Law Review*, **20** (1985), pp. 1 ff.

8 Brian Bix gives further arguments for a similar conclusion in 'Conceptual Questions and Jurisprudence', *Legal Theory*, **1**(4) (December 1995), pp. 465–79.

9 This limiting role of roles is emphasized by Joseph Raz when he discusses exclusionary reasons. I agree that roles can limit reasons and interests, but that is not all there is to roles.

10 In *The Concept of Law* (Oxford: Clarendon Press, 1961), pp. 86–8 (pp. 89–91 in the 2nd edn, 1994), H.L.A. Hart also talks about internal and external points of view on law, but what Hart means by a point of view is somewhat different from what I mean by a perspective, and he does not tie points of view to specific roles as I do.

11 John Austin, *The Province of Jurisprudence Determined* (London; Weidenfeld and Nicolson, 1955), pp. 13–14. Originally published in 1832.

12 Hart, *The Concept of Law, op. cit.*, pp. 121–32.

13 See H.L.A. Hart, 'Positivism and the Separation of Law and Morals' and Lon Fuller, 'Positivism and Fidelity to Law – A Reply to Professor Hart', both in *Harvard Law Review*, **71** (1958), pp. 593 ff. and 630 ff. respectively.

14 Ronald Dworkin, 'The Model of Rules I', reprinted in *Taking Rights Seriously* (Cambridge, MA: Harvard University Press, 1978), pp. 14–45.

15 Tom Campbell might seem to deny this when he writes, 'Legal Positivism can, however, be taken as a citizen's, as contrasted with a social scientist's, theory of law, a theory about the way lawyers, and in particular judges, should identify and understand law': (*Ethical Positivism, op. cit.*, pp. 78–9). However, Campbell might just be saying that legal positivism is a view of law that captures the legislative perspective on how other people (citizens, lawyers and judges) should view the legislature's pronouncements.

16 A legal system could allow judges to postpone decisions in certain kinds of case until the legislature provides more specific directives, but to apply these directives to the case in advance would involve admitted retroactivity. This might explain why this option is usually not available.

17 I am referring here to a common understanding of the judges' job. I am not assuming any particular definition of the law. This is crucial, since it would be circular for me to presuppose any definition of law in my descriptions of the three main roles or perspectives.

18 This seems to be the argument for a right to privacy in *Griswold* v. *Connecticut* 381 US 479 (1965).

19 For example, in *NAACP* v. *Alabama* 357 US 449 (1958), the US Supreme Court held that an implicit right to keep membership lists private underlies explicit rights to assemble and associate, because people could not associate without too much personal risk if all membership lists were public. This argument depends on value judgements about how much risk is too much.

20 Although this might merely mean that they avoid dashing expectations that are legitimate because they are based on law, that is not all there is to justice for most judges who consider that their job is to do justice. This perspective of doing justice is very attractive to those judges who do not want to see themselves as mere servants of the legislature.

21 As emphasized by Dworkin, 'The Model of Rules I', *op. cit.*, pp. 30 and 44. C.L. Ten has pointed out that a trial loser's prior expectations could not be legitimate because they are based on law when law is determinate or lacking, but it still seems unfair to take the loser's freedom or money without clear warning, and

judges normally would, and should, not publicly admit to doing so. See C.L. Ten, 'Perspectives and Roles', *Australian Journal of Legal Philosophy*, **24** (1999), pp. 57–63.

[22] For more problems with original intent, see Paul Brest, 'The Misconceived Quest for the Original Understanding', *Boston University Law Review*, **60** (1980), pp. 204 ff.; also Ronald Dworkin, 'The Forum of Principle' in *A Matter of Principle* (Cambridge, MA: Harvard University Press, 1985), pp. 33–71.

[23] Judges in continental Europe reportedly claim to follow statutes without injecting any of their own values. As Deborah Cass has pointed out (personal communication), Australian judges also often describe their own method in positivistic terms, although they usually soon add undermining qualifications. My point is that judges' actual practice often belies such positivistic self-descriptions which are nonetheless justified speech acts, whether or not they are self-serving or self-deluded.

[24] But see Clarence Thomas, 'The Higher Law Background of the Privileges and Immunities Clause of the Fourteenth Amendment', *Harvard Journal of Law and Public Policy*, **12** (1989), pp. 63–70 at p. 68: 'The higher law background ... provides the only firm basis for just, wise, and constitutional decisions.'

[25] See Frederick Schauer, 'Fuller's Internal Point of View', *Law and Philosophy*, **13** (1994), pp. 285–312 at p. 301: 'the same focus on defining law for the purpose of guiding the activities of lawyers and judges exists throughout much of the rest of the Fuller corpus.'

[26] Dworkin is sometimes described as holding a third theory of law distinct from both legal positivism and natural law theory, but he himself allows his theory to be described as a natural law theory in 'Natural Law Revisited', *University of Florida Law Review*, **34** (1982), pp. 165 ff.

[27] Ronald Dworkin, *Law's Empire* (Cambridge, MA: Harvard University Press, 1986), p. 225.

[28] Ibid., p. 248.

[29] Ibid., p. 244. Dworkin emphasizes the difference between legislators and judges in his rights thesis in his 'Hard Cases', reprinted in *Taking Rights Seriously*, *op. cit.*

[30] Karl Llewellyn, *The Bramble Bush: Some Lectures on Law and its Study* (New York; Columbia University School of Law, 1930).

[31] Oliver Wendell Holmes, 'The Path of the Law', *Harvard Law Review*, **10**(8) (25 March 1897), pp. 457–78 at p. 458.

[32] Ibid., p. 459.

[33] Cf. H.L.A. Hart, 'It is plain and has often been remarked that whatever truth there may be in [rule-skepticism's contention that rules are predictions of courts' decisions], it can at best apply to the statements of law ventured by private individuals or their advisers. It cannot apply to the courts' own statements of a legal rule': *The Concept of Law*, *op. cit.*, p. 143. The same could be said of that recent offshoot of legal realism called critical legal studies.

[34] Citizens are also made citizens by the law, but even illegal aliens are private persons insofar as they are governed and protected by the law.

[35] Another illuminating illustration is dead laws that were passed long ago and never repealed, but are no longer enforced. One reported example in Memphis requires all motor vehicles to sound their horns before every intersection. When legislators find such rules on the books, they sometime repeal them. These legislators must view dead laws as laws, since otherwise they would not bother to repeal them. In contrast, judges would probably refuse to find anyone guilty of violating such laws. And, if private persons were asked whether it is still against the law for a motor vehicle to go through an intersection without sounding its horn, most people in Memphis would deny this, even if they were aware of the dead law. So judges and private persons do not view such dead laws as laws or as part of the law, despite what legislators do and should do.

[36] The situation is actually slightly more complex than this, since someone might confess to driving at 66 mph, and then maybe that person could legally be convicted. For the sake of argument, I will assume that all convictions must be based on radar or other less accurate evidence. Another complication is that one might be arrested for driving at 69 mph if the radar shows one's speed to be seven mph faster than that. For the sake of argument, I will assume that the radar always registers one's speed accurately, although this cannot be proven in court.

[37] I do not disagree with Tom Campbell when he writes, 'While it is the lawyer's duty to advise the client in terms of what he may and may not do legally, this does not mean concentrating on how closely a person can get to breaking the law in the pursuit of his personal objectives without actually violating or going beyond the law': *Ethical Positivism, op. cit.*, p. 106. I agree because not all clients want to know how far they can go without getting in trouble and, even when they do, a lawyer might not have a *duty* to *concentrate* on these limits. Still, when a client clearly wants to know the limits, it would be less than ideal for the lawyer to withhold information about these limits among other considerations.

[38] I assume that it is physically impossible for the police to get from the border to the house quick enough to catch John in the act if they give prior notice, and that no friend will conspire with Jane to catch John. If any critic comes up with a practical way to convict John, then I will modify the example to include additional laws or facts that make that conviction impossible.

[39] That is what H.L.A. Hart seems to be trying to do when he formulates his 'soft positivism' so as to be acceptable to everyone – even Dworkin. But Hart still fails to capture the perspective of private persons and legal realists. Another example might be Neil MacCormick's institutional theory of law.

[40] Some might argue that no neutral perspective is possible, since everyone, including philosophers, have particular interests. I am not so pessimistic. Philosophers do have interests, or else philosophy would not be interesting; but philosophical definitions still can be neutral among the interests of legislators, judges and private persons, just as referees can have interests but still be neutral between the teams competing in a game.

[41] Campbell suggests such a response when he writes, 'From the viewpoint of Ethical Positivism, discussions of interpretation which start with the judicial role, particularly in appellate courts, start in the wrong place. Kelsen notwithstanding, the base relationship in law is between the sovereign law makers and the legal subject': *Ethical Positivism, op. cit.*, p. 133.

[42] Ludwig Wittgenstein, *Philosophical Investigations*, trans. G.E.M. Anscombe (New York: Macmillan, 1953), p. 194.

[43] Thus, my view of law is closest to W.B. Gallie's view of art, democracy and a Christian life in his 'Essentially Contested Concepts', *Proceedings of the Aristotelian Society*, **56** (1955–56), pp. 167–98.

[44] Friedrich Nietzsche, *On the Genealogy of Morals*, trans. Walter Kaufman, in *Basic Writings of Nietzsche* (New York; The Modern Library, 1966), Third Essay, Section 12.

[45] This is not true of the three theories. Legal positivists claim to have the whole truth and also claim that the other theories are not only partial but are false. Legal realists and natural law theorists return the favour. These claims to completeness are not legitimate in my view, despite the legitimacy of the perspectives that those theories capture.

9 Legal Positivism and the Contingent Autonomy of Law

FREDERICK SCHAUER[1]

Debates about judicial review, judicial activism and the role of the judiciary within a constitutional regime typically revolve around questions of legitimacy. In the United States, where judicial review is not spelled out explicitly in the Constitution,[2] these questions are especially salient. Even though it has been close to two centuries since judicial power to invalidate an Act of Congress was asserted by Chief Justice Marshall in *Marbury* v. *Madison*,[3] the fact that that power rests on so thin a textual mandate has served to keep the issue of the legitimacy of judicial review in the forefront of political debate and academic constitutional theory. Because American federal judges hold office for life,[4] because many acts of constitutional interpretation have the effect of negating the decisions of bodies more responsive to the electorate than the judiciary, and because these acts rest on an implied power, what Alexander Bickel called the 'counter-majoritarian difficulty'[5] has always loomed large on the agenda of the American constitutional theorist and constitutional practitioner. And when particular judicial decisions have only a tenuous connection with the constitutional text or the intentions of its drafters, as with decisions during the 1930s about economic liberty[6] and decisions during the 1970s about personal privacy,[7] or the run up against the deep-seated beliefs of a vast majority of the public, as with decisions protecting the right to burn the American flag[8] or denying states the ability to sponsor prayer in public schools[9] or granting powerful rights to those who are charged with or suspected of criminal activity,[10] the debates about the legitimacy of judicial review become even more heated and even more important.

Although these debates about the legitimacy of judicial review and the legitimacy of so-called 'judicial activism' have generally been useful, they have come at a cost. Part of this cost (although only part of it) is that debates about the legitimacy of judicial review have often pushed aside debates about judicial review and institutional design, with the concomitant questions about the comparative advantages, if any, of the courts, as to certain issues, and the comparative advantages, if any, of other bodies as to other issues. Although debates about institutional design – independent of the debates about legitimacy – have not been totally absent from the American constitutional scene, only a small part of that scene has been filled with questions that focus directly on what courts *do*, and whether what they do, when they do it and how they do it might be better suited to some tasks than others, questions of legitimacy in a political or philosophical sense aside.

My goal here is to try to look at this latter question through the lens of some of the traditional issues of classical legal theory. More specifically, I want to offer my interpretation of the tradition of legal positivism that directly addresses the question whether the institutions of law do things differently, and draw on different sources than other decision-making institutions likely to exist within a society. According to my interpretation the most important question that legal positivism has posed is that of legal autonomy – whether law is, in some interesting sense, different from other social and political institutions.[12] In recent years, however, some legal theorists, including some for whom the defence of legal positivism is a central part of their intellectual agenda, have lost sight of this question.[13] In so doing, they have lost the ability to ask the question that is central to thinking about the role of legal institutions within a constitutional culture. What, if anything, do legal institutions do that other institutions do not? Putting this question back on the agenda, and relating it to issues concerning the role of the courts under a Constitution, is the primary focus of this chapter.

Two Concepts of Positivism

What *is* legal positivism? The term is notoriously indeterminate, sometimes serving – especially in the United States – as a catch-all of jurisprudential abuse with little content.[14] Indeed, some years ago a prominent legal theorist urged that the term had become such an ambiguous pejorative that it would be best to abandon it in its entirety,[15] and things have not gotten any better since then.

Yet abandoning the term 'legal positivism' would be an unfortunate strategy since legal positivism and the tradition it represents mark two important concepts, both of which can be illuminated by seeing legal positivism in light of its oppositions. First, and of greatest historical importance, is legal positivism as the negation of natural law. But second, and of much greater contemporary importance, is legal positivism as the negation of normatively undifferentiated decision-making – the form of decision-making in which the decision-maker has available the full array of socially accepted norms. In this latter sense, legal positivism is about law as a limited domain.

I want to argue that the latter conception is more important to us than the former, but to do so it will first be necessary to take up the question of natural law, for in order to understand the first version of legal positivism, we must seek to understand the version of natural law theory to which it stands opposed.

In its more common usage, the term 'natural law' has virtually no connection with issues about law as an institution. For many people, 'natural law' is but one way of expressing the idea that there are certain values, norms, goods or whatever that are antecedent both to human creation and to the institutions created by human beings.[16] For some, the concept is closely connected to the idea of natural *rights*, such that to believe in natural law is to reject most forms of consequentialism. For others, natural law is the term that includes any non-relativist and non-subjectivist meta-ethics, such that even utilitarianism and other forms of consequentialism could be described as natural law perspectives. For some, the origins of natural law are divine and, for others, they are secular. But the important point here is that the word 'law' in this usage, which according to John Finnis may even best characterize the views of Aquinas,[17] is simply about the idea of objective moral command and has nothing to do with the idea of *law* in its institutional sense and thus nothing to do with the questions that are central to the enterprise we call legal philosophy.[18]

For our purposes here, however, the conception of natural law that is of interest is the one that can be found in Cicero,[19] in Blackstone,[20] in the standard (although not Finnis's) interpretation of Aquinas and in the procedural version of natural law offered by Lon Fuller.[21] For all these thinkers, as well as for many others, morality is a necessary condition of legality in the institutional sense, and thus it is a central claim of this version of natural law that immoral law is simply not law at all, largely because of the idea that law, in its institutional sense, shares an ontology with morality itself.

Because this conception of natural law is about a conception of law that aligns law with morality on an ontological level, and thus sees the impossibility of immoral *law* as an impossibility which is antecedent to human decision, the central claim of this version of natural law is that, properly speaking, morality is a necessary condition for legality in all possible legal systems in all possible worlds.[22] In this view, immoral law is not law in all places and at all times, not because of any social or human choice, but simply because of what is implicit in the very concept of law itself.

If this is the central natural law claim, and if this is a *conceptual* claim about the concept of law and not an empirical claim about certain legal systems in certain societies, then that claim can be falsified by showing that there is at least one possible legal system in one possible world in which morality is not a necessary condition of legality. Even if every legal system we know of is one in which morality is considered a necessary condition for legality, the natural law claim, say theorists such as Jules Coleman,[23] Wil Waluchow[24] and Philip Soper,[25] would be false so long as there remained the *possibility* that this could not be so. Since the natural law claim, these theorists and others maintain, is one about natural necessity at the conceptual level and not about actual legal, linguistic, political or institutional cultures, it is a claim that can be denied, or shown to be false, at that same conceptual level, independent of what actual legal systems in actual worlds have in fact done.

My aim here is not to arbitrate the dispute between classical natural law theory and what Coleman calls 'negative legal positivism', what Waluchow calls 'inclusive legal positivism', and what Brian Leiter calls 'soft positivism',[26] simply because this dispute, or this conception of positivism, does not seem to address very many of the interesting questions that we might wish to ask.[27] As H.L.A. Hart noted on the opening page of *The Concept of Law*, the 'What is law?' question is best thought of as a way of articulating a particular question about law that has some specific significance to the way in which we live.[28] Given that few people subscribe to the view that law, in the institutional sense, has a natural morality itself, the claim that such a view is false, which is the central claim of Coleman and others, is plausibly adjudged as true but unimportant. It may be interesting to show that Cicero and Blackstone were wrong in their views about the natural ontology of law *qua* law, but such a demonstration does not address any of the questions or issues that seem important in contemporary terms.

This is not true, however, about the conception of legal positivism that Ronald Dworkin takes up in *Taking Rights Seriously*[29] and *Law's Empire*,[30] and I want to suggest here that, even though Dworkin may be wrong in his claims about the falsity of legal positivism and perhaps even wrong in his claims about Hart's version of positivism, the version of legal positivism that he tackles is one that highlights a much more important question about the contingent nature of law in modern societies. In other words, I want to argue that Dworkin's conception of legal positivism is the right one, even if he is wrong to deny its (empirical) existence.

As I have argued at greater length elsewhere,[31] Dworkin's (small) stable of cases are perfectly designed to make a particular point about a particular conception of legal positivism. In his treatment of *Riggs*

v. *Palmer*,[32] he recognized that the case of the murdering heir was not a hard one in the strictly legal sense, but an easy one. According to the governing law at the time – the law recognized by the rule of recognition – the grandson should have inherited from the grandfather he killed, because the Statute of Wills, which was plainly recognized as law by the rule of recognition, plainly governed the transaction and plainly contained no exception for heirs who had themselves unlawfully accelerated their legacy in the way in which Elmer had. Yet, of course, Elmer did not inherit, and that was because the New York Court of Appeals set aside the clear indications of the rule clearly recognized by the rule of recognition in the service of a *principle* – in this case, the principle that no man may profit from his own wrong. If the rules recognized by the rule of recognition could be set aside for a principle, then what, Dworkin implicitly asks, is the point of saying that law consists of the rules recognized by the rule of recognition? If those rules can be set aside, then positivism, as the claim that law consists of the rules recognized by the rule of recognition, is false.

But as Neil MacCormick and others have correctly argued,[33] Dworkin's argument as an argument against positivism presupposes that principles, such as the principle that determined the outcome in *Riggs* v. *Palmer*, cannot be part of what is recognized by the rule of recognition, and that presupposition is simply false. MacCormick demonstrates persuasively that nothing about the *idea* of a rule of recognition – a source-based determination of what is to count as law – is inconsistent with the recognition of legal principles as well as legal rules, and that, in fact, most modern legal systems have routinely recognized legal principles, such as the principle that no man may profit from his own wrong. If Dworkin's claim against positivism rests on the claim that positivism cannot coexist with legal principles, then Dworkin's attack on positivism must fail.

But Dworkin has another arrow left in his quiver, and it is represented by the outcome in *Henningsen* v. *Bloomfield Motors, Inc.*[34] As with *Riggs*, the result that would have been indicated by the legal rule – in this case, the rule that people are bound to the waivers of warranty which they sign – was set aside by the court in the service of a principle – that under conditions of unequal bargaining power unconscionable waivers should not be enforced. But, unlike the principle that determined the outcome in *Riggs*, the principle that determined the outcome in *Henningsen* was not one that could have been found in the pre-existing corpus of the law, and was not one that could have been identified by a rule of recognition.

For Dworkin this is the final nail in the positivist coffin. For if the rules recognized by the rule of recognition can be set aside not only by *legal* principles, but also by the full undifferentiated array of socially recognized norms, than the idea of a *legal* rule of recognition is pointless. If judges – the prototypical legal officials – are empowered to make decisions according to the legal rules recognized by the legal rule of recognition and according to any other social norm, then positivism might not be technically wrong, but it would say nothing interesting about law as we know it. Dworkin's claim, therefore, can be seen as the claim that law is, in no interesting way, *autonomous*, and thus there is no important work done either by particular rules of recognition or by the idea of the rule of recognition itself.

As I have argued elsewhere, Dworkin is probably empirically wrong in his claims, since the legal rules recognized by the rule of recognition appear to have a presumptive, if not absolute, priority in decision-making within courts and other legal domains.[35] Thus the conception of positivism that Dworkin takes to be descriptively false is probably descriptively true as a presumption, even though that presumption can be overridden. But my concern here is not with whether Dworkin is right or wrong, nor with rehearsing arguments I have made elsewhere. I am concerned with the conception of positivism that Dworkin takes as his target and with Dworkin's implicit claim that this is the conception of positivism that best addresses the problems of today. And on this Dworkin seems most probably correct.

If Dworkin is right, then law exists merely as one component of an undifferentiated normative domain, with legal officials such as judges free to make their decisions from the full universe of norms within this array.[36] And if Dworkin is right, then such notions as 'existing law' become essentially meaningless. But if Dworkin is wrong, then pedigreed legal norms – an array of norms that is not extensionally equivalent to the full universe of a society's social norms – has a certain dominance or salience in legal decision-making. Nevertheless, whether he is right or wrong, the idea that positivism claims the existence of this extensionally disequivalent and rule of recognition-recognized set of legal norms is a concept that does address an important contemporary concern.

Note that morality *qua* morality has largely dropped out of this analysis. Although the traditional debates about natural law and positivism discussed the conceptual distinction between law and morality, a conception of positivism that focuses on the autonomy of law – on law as a *limited domain* – is now concerned about the distinction not between law and morality, but between law and everything else, where everything else includes, but is not limited to, morality. Moreover, the claim is no longer conceptual, but descriptive or empirical. The claim that Dworkin sets out to rebut is the descriptive claim that a rule of recognition (or, following Brian Simpson,[37] a set of practices of recognition that might not be expressible in the form of a rule) identifies a subset of a society's accepted norms, at least partly because of their source, designates them as law and limits the extent to which legal decision-makers may rely on other norms outside this set. This is the claim that Dworkin labels positivism and which he mistakenly assumes to be false with respect to the United States and England, but it is also the claim that puts at centre stage the question whether legal officials are doing anything different from what other officials do. If positivism in this sense is true for a society, we can understand why that society has autonomous or differentiated legal institutions, such as lawyers, law schools, bar examinations and specialist legal publishers. But if positivism in this sense – the limited domain sense of positivism – is false, then institutions whose existence appears to presuppose such a limited domain find it much more difficult to justify their existence.

Limited Domain Positivism and the Question of Judicial Review

The connection between all of this and the question of judicial review should now be relatively clear. Suppose that positivism in this limited domain sense is largely false,[38] and that judges in some society make their decisions not only on the basis of the norms that one might find collected in traditional law books, but on the basis of the full array of legal, moral, cultural, social and political norms recognized by a society at some point. If this is so, then how can be explain and justify the practice of judicial review?

Although the question I have just asked may seem merely rhetorical, it is not designed as such. Rather, it is intended to focus the inquiry on what, if anything, distinguishes legal institutions from other institutions and what such a distinction might mean for a number of significant institutional design issues. Thus, we might try to focus our attention on the ways in which legal institutions differ from other decision-making institutions, if indeed there are any differences at all.

Thus, even if legal positivism in my sense – that is, legal positivism as an extensionally differentiated set of norms – proves to be false for some society at some time, legal institutions, and courts in particular, might be distinguished by their methods of operation – a distinction we might call *procedural differentiation*. This means that, even if courts drew on all the same sources as legislatures, executive agencies and other governmental decision-makers, it might nevertheless be the case that numerous features of the way in which courts operate – the giving of reasons,[39] the consolidation of potentially numerous positions into, generally, only two positions,[40] the requirement of notice and hearing for affected parties[41] and so on – might result not only in different methods of operation but also different decisions in at least some cases.

Alternatively, legal institutions might be distinguished by virtue of *informational differentiation.* Even if courts used the same norms as other decision-making institutions, they might apply these norms to different data because of some distinct way in which they obtained their information. If, for example, courts found it especially difficult, because of their structure, to obtain empirical data, we might see different methods of dealing with data in court than we see elsewhere; consequently, we might also see different outcomes on account of this comparative inability to access the kinds of information that routinely forms part of the decision-making process in other institutions.

Furthermore, there is also the possibility that law distinguishes itself by its forms of reasoning. If this is so, legal institutions might be different, even if the array of norms, the array of data and the procedures are held constant, because of what I will term *methodological differentiation.* To the extent that there is something unique about legal reasoning- and this, of course, is highly contestable – [43] then legal institutions might claim once again to be different and, as a result of this difference, might have a comparative advantage over other kinds of institutions, each with their own distinctive forms of reasoning, in making certain kinds of decision or in dealing with certain kinds of controversy.[44]

Along with these three possibilities, there is also that of what I will now call *normative differentiation,* which is my primary concern in this chapter. As legal positivism has traditionally claimed (although in less of a descriptive and more of a conceptual manner than both Dworkin and I want to maintain), there are socially accepted norms that are not legally accepted and legally accepted norms that are not socially accepted, and this extensional differentiation in norm sets is central to what makes law, as law, autonomous. This differentiation is the central idea of the distinction between law and morality, it is the central idea of Hart's rule of recognition,[45] it is the central idea in Raz's sources thesis[46] and it is largely why the claims of positivism have proved so interesting to so many theorists for so long.

To me, however, the interest in this claim increases when we turn to questions of institutional design, and to questions about whether and when a society should allocate to its legal system decisions of a certain kind. Suppose that the tradition of legal positivism is correct in supposing that there is something different about the legal system. The question then arises (although it is not one that the legal positivism tradition has addressed) of what this system should be assigned to do in a complex society in which different kinds of decisions are assigned to different kinds of institution.[47] If the heart of a legal system *is* as Hart, Raz and many others have claimed it is, then what does this say about the tasks that should be assigned to that system, and is this a system that should be making decisions about *this* topic or that one?

One instantiation of this question is that of judicial review, in the narrower sense, or judicial activism, in the broader sense. If legal institutions are different – and, according to my argument here, the claim that legal institutions *are* different is the central claim of legal positivism – then what does this phenomenon of differentiation say about the kinds of decision that those differentiated legal institutions should be assigned to make? Is it possible that the virtues of judicial review lie in procedural differentiation, with the possible consequence that the comparative immunity from majoritarian forces is not only judicial review's greatest problem but also its greatest advantage? But is it also possible that one of the chief vices of judicial review lies in informational differentiation? If many of the decisions that are made in a regime of judicial review and judicial activism are fundamentally, policy decisions, are there reasons to believe that courts, because of the information they receive and the way in which they receive it, will be less well suited to this task than would a number of other institutions?[48]

We could ask many other similar questions, but it is not my purpose here to ask all of them, and certainly not my goal to answer any of them. Rather, it is to demonstrate that the best useful contemporary understanding of the legal positivist tradition – even if the best useful contemporary understanding of legal positivism is not the best in historical or exegetical terms – is the one that is implicit in Dworkin's foil. This is the understanding of legal positivism that focuses on normative differentiation and on law as a limited normative domain and which therefore best serves the goal of thinking of law and legal institutions as part of a larger strategy of institutional design. For Dworkin, the task is to describe and justify a system in which judicial review, for all of the continuing debate about its legitimacy in a moral and political sense, is a fact of legal and political life. But in societies in which judicial review and judicial activism is a question and not an answer, one way of addressing this question is by focusing on the ways, if any, in which law is different from other decision-making institutions that may exist in the society. That is the question that legal positivism is uniquely situated to address, and that, in the final analysis, explains the relevance of the legal positivist tradition to questions about judicial review and judicial activism.

Notes

1 This chapter is based on a paper prepared for the Workshop on Judicial Activism and Judicial Review in Australian Democracy, Australian National University, Canberra, Australia, 10–15 July 1998. I am grateful for the support of the Research School of Social Sciences, Australian National University, and to the Joan Shorenstein Center on the Press, Politics and Public Policy, Harvard University.

2 Article III of the US Constitution establishes the Supreme Court and gives it jurisdiction over all cases and controversies arising under the Constitution, laws and treaties of the United States. Nothing in the Constitution deals explicitly with the power to determine whether Acts of Congress, or Acts of the Executive or Acts of the states, violate the Constitution. William W. Van Alstyne, 'A Critical Guide to *Marbury* v. *Madison*', *Duke Law Journal*, (1969), pp. 1 ff.

3 US (1 Cranch) 137 (1803).

4 In the majority of states, however, the judges are elected. Election procedures and terms vary widely among the states.

5 Alexander Bickel, *The Least Dangerous Branch: The Supreme Court at the Bar of Politics* (Indianapolis: Bobbs-Merrill, 1962).

6 For example, *Nebbia* v. *New York*, 291 US 502 (1934); *New State Ice Co.* v. *Liebmann*, 285 US 262 (1932).

7 For example, *Carey* v. *Population Services International* 431 US 678 (1977); *Roe* v. *Wade*, 410 US 113 (1973).

8 *Texas* v. *Johnson*, 491 US 397 (1989); *United States* v. *Eichman*, 496 US 310 (1990).

9 *Abington School Dist.* v. *Schempp*, 374 US 203 (1963); *Engel* v. *Vitale*, 370 US 421 (1962). See also *Lee* v. *Weisman*, 505 US 577 (1992); *Wallace* v. *Jaffree*, 472 US 38 (1985); *Edwards* v. *Aguillard*, 482 US 578 (1987); *Stone* v. *Graham*, 449 US 39 (1980).

10 *Miranda* v. *Arizona*, 384 US 436 (1966); *Mapp* v. *Ohio*, 367 US 643 (1961). See also *Arizona* v. *Hicks*, 480 US 321 (1987).

11 See *Romer* v. *Evans*, 116 S. Ct. 1620 (1996); John Hart Ely, *Democracy and Distrust* (Cambridge, MA: Harvard University Press, 1980); Symposium, 'Constitutional Adjudication and Democratic Theory', *New York University Law Review*, **56** (1981), pp. 259–582.

12 See Robert P. George (ed.), *The Autonomy of Law: Essays on Legal Positivism* (Oxford: Clarendon Press, 1996); Frederick Schauer and Virginia J. Wise, 'Legal Positivism as Legal Information', *Cornell Law Review*, **82** (1997), pp. 1080 ff.

13 See Wil Waluchow, *Inclusive Legal Positivism* (Oxford: Clarendon Press, 1994); Jules L. Coleman, 'Negative and Positive Positivism', *Journal of Legal Studies*, **11** (1982), pp. 139 ff. For critique, see Frederick Schauer, 'Positivism Through Thick and Thin', in Brian Bix (ed.), *Analyzing Law: New Essays in Legal Theory* (Oxford: Clarendon Press, 1998), pp. 65 ff.

14 See Frederick Schauer, 'Positivism as Pariah', in Robert George (ed.), *The Autonomy of Law: Essays on Legal Positivism* (Oxford: Clarendon Press, 1996); Robert S. Summers, 'Legal Philosophy Today – An Introduction', in Robert S. Summers (ed.), *Essays in Legal Philosophy* (Oxford: Basil Blackwell, 1970), pp. 1 ff.

15 Robert Summers, 'Introduction', in *Essays in Legal Philosophy* (Oxford: Basil Blackwell, 1968).

16 See Robert P. George (ed.), *Natural Law Theory: Contemporary Essays* (Oxford: Clarendon Press, 1992).

17 John Finnis, *Natural Law and Natural Rights* (Oxford: Clarendon Press, 1980).

18 In the United States there is a minor political party called the Natural Law Party, but I have no reason to believe it is interested in questions of the philosophy of law.

19 Cicero, *De Republica de Legibus* (London: W. Heinemann, 1952) trans. C.W. Keyes.
20 William Blackstone, *Commentaries on the Laws of England*, vol. 1, p. 41.
21 Lon L. Fuller, *The Morality of Law*, rev. edn (New Haven: Yale University Press, 1969).
22 See Jules L. Coleman, 'Rules and Social Facts', *Harvard Journal of Law and Public Policy*, **14** (1991), pp. 703 ff.
23 Jules L. Coleman, 'Negative and Positive Positivism', *Journal of Legal Studies*, **11** (1982), pp. 139–64.
24 W.J. Waluchow, *Inclusive Legal Positivism* (Oxford: Clarendon Press, 1994).
25 Philip Soper, *A Theory of Law* (Cambridge, MA: Harvard University Press, 1984).
26 Brian Leiter, 'Realism, Hard Positivism, and Conceptual Analysis', *Legal Theory*, (1999 forthcoming).
27 For a similar critique, see Jeremy Waldron, 'The Irrelevance of Moral Objectivity', in Robert P. George (ed.), *Natural Law Theory: Contemporary Essays* (Oxford: Clarendon Press, 1992), pp. 159 ff.
28 H.L.A. Hart, *The Concept of Law* (Oxford: Clarendon Press, 1961), p. 1.
29 Ronald Dworkin, *Taking Rights Seriously* (Cambridge, MA: Harvard University Press, 1977).
30 Ronald Dworkin, *Law's Empire* (Cambridge, MA: Harvard University Press, 1986).
31 Frederick Schauer, *Playing By the Rules: A Philosophical Examination of Rule-Based Decision-Making in Law and in Life* (Oxford: Clarendon Press, 1991); Frederick Schauer, 'Formalism', *Yale Law Journal*, **87** (1989), pp. 509–42.
32 115 NY 506, 22 NE 188 (1889).
33 Neil MacCormick, *Legal Reasoning and Legal Theory* (Oxford: Clarendon Press, 1978); Philip Soper, 'Legal Theory and the Obligation of the Judge: The Hart/Dworkin Dispute', *Michigan Law Review*, **75** (1977), pp. 511 ff.
34 32 NJ 258, 161 A.2d 69 (1960).
35 Frederick Schauer, *Playing By the Rules: A Philosophical Examination of Rule-Based Decision-Making in Law and in Life* (Oxford: Clarendon Press, 1991); Frederick Schauer, 'Formalism', *Yale Law Journal*, **97** (1988), pp. 509 ff.; Frederick Schauer, 'The Jurisprudence of Reasons', *Michigan Law Review*, **85** (1987), pp. 847 ff.
36 'Full universe' is contestable as a matter of Dworkinian exegesis, since Dworkin is notoriously slippery about the data that are the raw material for his interpretive methodology. The discussion of *Henningsen* and other cases suggests that Dworkin believes that all socially accepted principles (but not policies) are available for legal interpretation, but at other points he appears to suggest that the products of legislatures, courts and administrative agencies have a particular dominance. See Gerald J. Postema, '"Protestant" Interpretation and Social Practices', *Law and Philosophy*, **6** (1987), pp. 283–308; Stephen R. Perry in 'Legal Theory', in Andrei Marmor (ed.), *Law and Interpretation: Essays in Legal Theory* (Oxford: Clarendon Press, 1995), pp. 97–135, n. 57 at p. 120. But, even under the narrower understanding, it is Dworkin's goal to press on the legal institutions/political institutions distinction, and thus on the law/politics distinction, at least within the domain of principles. This, as I argue here, is the central question that modern legal positivism ought to address, and I believe does address in some of its manifestations.
37 Simpson, 'The Common Law and Legal Theory', in R.S. Summers (ed.), *Oxford Essays in Jurisprudence*, 2nd series (Oxford: Oxford University Press, 1973).
38 As should be apparent from the foregoing discussion, my conception of legal positivism as claiming a limited domain of recognized sources is an empirical and not a conceptual claim. To put it bluntly, it addresses the more interesting question of what is the case about actual legal systems rather than the less interesting

question of what must be true about all legal systems in all possible worlds. Moreover, the empirical claim can be true to a greater or lesser extent, rather than simply true or false.

[39] See Frederick Schauer, 'Giving Reasons', *Stanford Law Review*, **47** (1995), pp. 63 ff.

[40] See Robert Nagel, 'How Useful is Judicial Review in Free Speech Cases?', *Cornell Law Review*, **69** (1984), pp. 302 ff.

[41] This is, of course, a major component – *audi alteram partem* – of the idea of natural justice. See D. Benjafield, *Principles of Australian Administrative Law* (Sydney, Butterworths, 1971).

[42] On the possibility that law's informational autonomy is in decline, largely because of the influence of technology, see Frederick Schauer and Virginia Wise, 'Legal Positivism as Legal Information', *Cornell Law Review*, **82** (1997), pp. 1080–110.

[43] In various ways, denying claims about the distinctiveness of legal reasoning has been central to the agendas of both legal realism and the critical legal studies movement.

[44] It is possible that Dworkin's distinction between policy and principle, and his view that courts should stick to the latter and not the former, is a form of methodological differentiation. It is also possible, however, that, whatever the normative merits of the policy/principle distinction, Dworkin's claims for its descriptive accuracy are false, with courts using policy as well as principle to set aside the indications of positivistically pedigreed legal rules. This is the claim that is central to Melvin Eisenberg, *The Nature of the Common Law* (Cambridge, MA: Harvard University Press, 1984), and if he is descriptively right then Eisenberg's implicit attack on legal positivism is even more telling than is Dworkin's.

[45] H.L.A. Hart, *The Concept of Law* (Oxford: Clarendon Press, 1961).

[46] Joseph Raz, *The Authority of Law* (Oxford: Clarendon Press, 1979).

[47] Interestingly, this *is* a question that pervades much of Lon Fuller's later work. For an extensive analysis, with appropriate references to Fuller's published and unpublished work, see Kenneth I. Winston, 'Legislators and Liberty', *Law and Philosophy*, **13** (1994), pp. 389 ff.

[48] See Frederick Schauer, 'Principles, Institutions, and the First Amendment', *Harvard Law Review*, **112** (1998), pp. 84 ff.; Frederick Schauer, 'Too Hard: Unconstitutional Conditions and the Chimera of Constitutional Consistency', *Denver University Law Review*, **72** (1995), pp. 989 ff.

PART II
ASSEMBLIES VERSUS COURTS IN DEMOCRATIC THEORY AND PRACTICE

10 The Philosophical Foundations of Parliamentary Sovereignty[1]

JEFFREY GOLDSWORTHY

Parliamentary Sovereignty and Legal Philosophy

The doctrine of parliamentary sovereignty has long been regarded as the most fundamental element of the British Constitution. It is said that parliament is able to make or unmake any law whatsoever, and the courts have no authority to declare statutes invalid for violating either moral or legal rights of any kind. A similar doctrine has traditionally been thought to apply to the power of parliaments in New Zealand and Australia, although in the latter case only in a heavily qualified form. In Australia, it is said that state and national parliaments are bound by the express and implied provisions included in various written constitutions, but not by moral rights or common law principles, and therefore that, within their respective constitutional boundaries, they are as sovereign as the British Parliament.[2]

Until recently there had been little doubt about the legal correctness of the doctrine of parliamentary sovereignty. Indeed, it has been an unquestioned assumption of British constitutional thought for at least several centuries. But today, it is increasingly being challenged by judges and academic lawyers in Britain, New Zealand and Australia. If a majority of judges ever find these challenges persuasive and repudiate the doctrine, the controversy over judicial activism will rise to an unprecedented pitch. Judicial repudiation of other traditional legal principles does not fundamentally threaten the powers of elected politicians, who retain legislative power to control or even reverse, the judges' decisions. But when judges question the doctrine of parliamentary sovereignty they pose a much more serious threat to the powers of the other branches of government.

What is at stake is the location of ultimate decision-making authority – the right to the 'final word' – in a legal system. If the judges were to repudiate the doctrine of parliamentary sovereignty, by refusing to allow parliament to infringe unwritten rights, they would be claiming that ultimate authority for themselves. In settling disagreements about what fundamental rights people have, and whether particular legislation is consistent with them, the judges' word rather than parliament's would be final. Since almost all serious moral and political controversies in contemporary Western societies can be understood as disagreements about rights, this would involve a massive transfer of political power from parliaments to judges. Moreover, it would be a transfer of power initiated by the judges, to protect rights chosen by them, rather than one brought about democratically by parliamentary enactment or popular referendum. It is no wonder that the elected branches of government regard that prospect with apprehension.

It is easy to understand why someone might regard the doctrine of parliamentary sovereignty as undesirable, and advocate its demise by a constitutional reform such as the adoption of a Bill of Rights. But my interest is with critics who argue that no such reform is needed, because the doctrine is not currently part of the law. How can they make such a claim? As one of them admits, 'it is hard to question … [the] doctrine without appearing to lose touch with practical reality. Until very recently, it was almost unthinkable that the courts would ever refuse to apply an Act of Parliament.'[3] How can the most senior officials of British government, including judges, have been so wrong for so long about the foundations of the legal system they administer?

Legal questions are usually answered on the basis of unchallenged assumptions about the foundations of the legal system. When those assumptions are questioned, it can be difficult to know where to turn for answers. What could possibly constitute the foundations of a legal system other than the actual practices and beliefs of the people who administer it? To answer that question, it is necessary to consult recent philosophical reflection on the nature of law and our knowledge of it.

Law as the Foundation of Law-making Authority

Until relatively recently, legal philosophy in Britain was dominated by the Hobbesian theory that, at the foundation of every legal system, there is a sovereign law-maker who is the creator of all law and whose power is therefore above the law. In Britain, the king in parliament appeared to fit the definition of a sovereign law-maker. But this theory did not fit the facts. Critics such as H.L.A. Hart have pointed out that in many legal systems, there is no sovereign law-maker in the Hobbesian sense of the term. At the foundations of all these legal systems are rules, rather than sovereign law-makers (in the Hobbesian sense of the term).[4]

Fundamental legal rules can come into existence either by express agreement among the members of a community, or at least the most powerful of them, as in the case of the adoption of a written Constitution, or by the gradual development of customs, as in the case of rules of succession governing traditional monarchical systems. In both cases, the continued existence of such laws depends on their being accepted as binding, at least by people who are able to force others to comply with them. To accept that such a law is binding is to have what Hart called the 'internal point of view' towards the law: it is to believe that there are good reasons for insisting that it be obeyed, and for criticizing those who fail to obey it.

Hart argued that, for a legal system to exist, its most fundamental laws must be accepted as binding by its most senior officials, and the system as a whole must be generally obeyed, for whatever reason, by those subject to it. Indeed, the most fundamental laws of any legal system simply are whatever laws are accepted as binding, and routinely applied in administering the system, by its most senior officials. The most important of these laws is a 'rule of recognition', which specifies the criteria that determine which other laws should be recognized as members of the system or, in other words, as valid laws. While the existence, as valid laws, of all the other laws of the system depends on their satisfying those criteria, the existence of the rule of recognition itself depends on its being accepted as binding by the most senior officials of the system, and on their decisions being generally obeyed by everyone else.[5]

According to Hart, the content of the rule of recognition, in any legal system, is entirely a matter of fact. It is whatever rule that system's most senior officials, and especially its judges, do in fact accept and apply in identifying valid laws of the system, irrespective of its merits from the perspective of political morality. That we might regard as morally repugnant the rule of recognition actually accepted and applied by the most senior officials of some legal system cannot alter the fact that it is a fundamental law of that system. In Britain, the most senior legal officials, including judges, have for a very long time recognized as legally valid whatever statutes parliament has enacted and have often said that they are bound to do so. The case for regarding the sovereignty of parliament as a central component of the British rule of recognition seems clear-cut, as Hart himself apparently believed.[6] Fear that parliament might one day grossly abuse its authority might be a good reason to change the rule, but that is a different matter.

The Common Law as the Foundation of Law-making Authority

According to Hart's theory, parliament's sovereignty is established by fundamental law. It is often argued that this fundamental law must be common law, and therefore that it can legitimately be modified or overruled by the judges.[7] This argument proceeds by a process of elimination. The doctrine was not, and logically could not have been, originally established by statute. Any parliament which enacted a statute purporting to confer sovereign power on itself would be begging the question, since the validity of that statute would depend on the very power it purported to confer.[8] But '[i]f the powers do not come from statute, then they must be part of the common law, for our legal system knows no sources of law other than these two'.[9] For this reason, Britain has been said to have a 'common law constitution'.[10]

The common law is declared by the judges, and is now generally believed to be subject to change according to judgments about justice that are necessarily made by the judges. They can modify or overrule even well-settled doctrines of the common law if they are persuaded that those doctrines were either unjust all along or have become incompatible with contemporary circumstances or values. It has been argued that they must also be able to change even fundamental doctrines of a constitutional nature. 'As a constitutional framework,' says Trevor Allan, 'the common law is self-evidently adaptable to new insights and fresh demands ... [and] must be developed with imagination to meet the needs of modern constitutionalism.'[11] He recommends that the judges modify or abandon the doctrine of parliamentary sovereignty. As he summarizes the whole argument:

> [L]egislation obtains its force from the doctrine of parliamentary sovereignty, which is itself a creature of the common law and whose detailed content and limits are therefore matters of judicial law-making. (It could hardly, without circularity, be a doctrine based on statutory authority.) Parliament is sovereign because the judges acknowledge its legal and political supremacy.[12]

Professor Wade has even suggested that 'in this one fundamental matter it is the judges who are sovereign'.[13]

Now, it is true that parliament did not, and could not, confer sovereign authority on itself by statute. But it does not follow that its sovereignty is a doctrine of common law – at least, not in the modern sense of 'common law'. The term 'common law' is now somewhat ambiguous. Until relatively recently, it meant customary law, which judges discovered and enunciated but did not make, whereas today it usually means judge-made law. There is nothing wrong with describing the doctrine of parliamentary sovereignty as a matter of common law in the old sense of the term. It is indeed a creature of custom, which gradually evolved from the sovereignty of the king in the Middle Ages. But it is quite wrong to describe it as a matter of common law in the modern sense of a law made by judges.

It is seldom noted that the doctrine of parliamentary sovereignty cannot have been established by judicial law-making for much the same reason that it cannot have been established by statute. The argument that it is a product of judicial law-making rests on two premises: that every law not created by statute is a matter of common law, and that the common law is judge-made law. But if these premises were both correct, then the judges' authority to make the common law, which was not created by statute, would itself be a matter of common law and therefore something made by the judges. That would mean that the judges originally conferred law-making authority on themselves, which is just as question-begging as the discredited idea that parliament originally conferred law-making authority on itself.

The source of these logical difficulties is the Hobbesian assumption that every law, including those which confer authority on parliament and the judges, must originally have been deliberately made by someone, and if it was not parliament, then it must have been the judges. That assumption leads to the questionable conclusion that either parliament or the judges originally conferred legal authority on themselves. But the truth is that the judges are no more qualified than parliament to be regarded as a Hobbesian sovereign, ultimately responsible for the creation of all law. The authority of either parliament or the judges, or both, must be based on laws that neither was solely responsible for creating. Those more fundamental laws are what H.L.A. Hart called the 'secondary rules' of the legal system, including rules of recognition, change and adjudication. A necessary condition for the existence of such rules is a consensus among the most senior officials of the legal system, in all three branches of government, legislative, executive and judicial. This avoids the question-begging that is implicit in any one branch of government purporting to confer law-making authority on itself. Parliament's sovereignty was not created by the judges alone, and its continued existence depends only partly, and not solely, on their willingness to accept it.

A common mistake in the interpretation of Hart's theory is to understand the rule of recognition as a rule constituted by the practices and convictions of the judiciary alone.[14] This is clearly not what Hart meant in the first edition of *The Concept of Law*. In describing the rule of recognition, he continually referred to its being constituted by the practices of legal officials in general: it 'rests simply on the fact that it is accepted and used as such a rule in *the judicial and other official* operations of a [legal] system whose rules are generally obeyed'.[15] The reason why Hart insisted that no legal system can exist unless its officials adopt the internal point of view towards its most fundamental rules, and particularly its rule of recognition, is that 'the characteristic unity and continuity of a legal system' depends on the acceptance of 'common standards of legal validity'.[16] He pointed out that, if only some judges accepted the sovereignty of parliament and they made no criticisms of those who did not, ordinary citizens would sooner or later be faced with contradictory legal directives, causing the legal system to disintegrate into chaos. But this reasoning extends to all of the most senior officials of the system: the same disastrous consequences would flow from a rift between the judiciary as a whole and the other branches of government. Hart explicitly acknowledged this point when discussing events in South Africa during the 1950s. At that time, 'the legislature acted on a different view of its legal competence and powers from that taken by the courts, and enacted measures which the courts declared invalid'. The legislature then established a special appellate 'court' to overrule the regular courts, but the latter declared that this too was invalid. As Hart concluded:

> ... [h]ad this process not been stopped ... we should have had an endless oscillation between two views of the competence of the legislature and so of the criteria of valid law. The normal conditions of official, and especially of judicial, harmony, under which alone it is possible to identify the system's rule of recognition, would have been suspended.[17]

It follows that parliamentary sovereignty can plausibly be described as a common law doctrine only in the old sense of that term, meaning a custom that the courts have recognized, but did not create, and therefore cannot unilaterally change. But, because its nature and status are so different from those of all other common law doctrines, as we understand them today, it might help prevent confusion if it were not described as a common law doctrine at all. As George Winterton has argued, it 'is, in fact, *sui generis*, a unique hybrid of law and political fact deriving its authority from acceptance by the people and by the principal institutions of the state, especially parliament and the judiciary'.[18]

It does not follow that the doctrine of parliamentary sovereignty cannot be changed. There are many examples of fundamental legal rules changing as a result of official consensus changing. Of course, a change in a fundamental legal rule has to start somewhere: someone has to initiate the requisite change in the official consensus that constitutes it. Parliament can do so, by enacting legislation such as the Australia Act 1986 (UK and Cth), which served Australia's remaining constitutional links with the UK, or the European Communities Act 1972 (UK). Such legislation will be effective provided that the courts are willing to accept it. Alternatively, the courts can initiate change, provided that the other branches of government are willing to accept it. There is nothing necessarily wrong with one group of officials attempting to initiate change in the fundamental rules of their legal system, but great caution is needed. If significant numbers of other officials are unlikely to agree with the proposed change, the result may be conflict endangering the stability of the system. A unilateral rejection by British courts of the doctrine of parliamentary sovereignty is unlikely to be meekly accepted by the other branches of government. Instead, they are likely to condemn it as an illegitimate attempt to alter the currently accepted balance of power in favour of the courts. By unsettling what has, for centuries, been regarded as settled, the courts would risk conflict with the other branches of government that might dangerously destabilize the legal system.

Legal Principles as the Foundation of Law-making Authority

Hart's theory of law, so effective in its criticisms of the Hobbesian theory, has itself been powerfully criticized by Ronald Dworkin. Hart argued that legal rules, rather than sovereigns, constitute the foundations of legal systems. Dworkin argues that legal principles, rather than rules, do so. His theory has been argued to cast doubt on the doctrine of parliamentary sovereignty.[19]

Dworkin argues that if relevant legal rules do not provide a clear answer to a legal dispute (which is therefore, by definition, a 'hard case'), judges look 'behind' the rules to the principles that underlie and justify them. For example, they resolve ambiguities in rules by reference to the principle that the rules are supposed to serve. The law includes not only rules but also their underlying principles and, in addition, more abstract principles which in turn underlie them, provided that all these rules and principles fit together in a coherent whole. If a particular principle or rule is incompatible with deeper principles, it must be rejected as a mistake. This is what happens when judges overrule common law rules laid down in earlier cases: they do not radically change the law, but merely correct an error in the application of deeper legal principles. The deepest principles that underlie a legal system determine its own distinctive 'institutional morality' which may differ from objective or true morality (assuming that there is such a thing). According to Dworkin, judges are legally bound to ascertain and apply the law's institutional morality. They do so by 'interpreting' the statutes and judicial decisions that are assumed to be legally binding, in order to identify the morally best set of deep principles that is consistent with most of them.[20]

Trevor Allan argues that Dworkin's theory applies to the most fundamental rules of the legal system, including what Hart calls the rule of recognition. A rule of recognition is not an arbitrary axiom. It is accepted by legal officials because they believe that it serves deeper principles. For example, judges obey statutes because they believe that they are required to do so by principles of democracy, justice, the rule of law and, most fundamentally, the principle of equal citizenship.[21] The rule of recognition cannot be the ultimate foundation of the legal system, because those principles are also part of the system and more fundamental than the rule.

> In short, the fundamental rule that accords legal validity to Acts of Parliament is not itself the foundation of the legal order, beyond which the lawyer is forbidden to look. That fundamental rule derives its legal validity from the underlying moral or political theory to which it belongs.[22]

Allan argues that the doctrine of parliamentary sovereignty cannot really be a fundamental element of the British legal system because it is not consistent with the principles that justify judicial obedience to statutes. Those principles are consistent with parliament having very great, but not unlimited, law-making authority. For example, the principle of democracy could not possibly justify judicial obedience to a statute which undermined democracy.[23] For the same reason, Allan implicitly denies that even the people themselves, voting in referenda, could possess a legally unlimited authority to make laws: the judges would be justified in preventing them from violating the most fundamental principles of the law.[24]

This is a more sophisticated version of the theory that parliament's authority is a matter of common law whose interpretation is the responsibility of the courts. On Allan's view, parliament's authority ultimately derives from deeper principles which are indistinguishable from the deepest principles of the common law. The law is a matter of reason, rather than arbitrary will, because it is grounded in these principles. It is the responsibility of the judges to ascertain and apply the law and, therefore, its deepest principles. They must reject as erroneous any particular rule or principle that is inconsistent with those deepest principles, and the doctrine of parliamentary sovereignty is such a rule.

Political Principles as the Foundation of Law-making Authority

Dworkin's theory must be shown to fit the facts, rather than the facts distorted to fit the theory. It cannot be an *a priori* truth that every legal rule in every legal system is subordinate to deeper legal principles that are judicially enforceable. Insofar as it is true of particular categories of legal rules, it is a contingent truth which, in any legal system, depends on the practices of legal officials. Dworkin himself presented his theory initially as a description, and subsequently as an 'interpretation', of how judges in common law legal systems do in fact decide hard cases, and claimed that it is confirmed by the way they themselves describe their reasoning.[25] His theory is plausible as a description or interpretation of the common law because, in applying and changing it, judges speak and act as if they are guided by fundamental principles. But it is less plausible in the case of the doctrine of parliamentary sovereignty, which is not a matter of common law in the modern sense of the term, and which has not traditionally been treated by judges as subordinate to deeper principles.

Whether parliament's legislative authority is subordinate to deeper legal principles must be determined, not by *a priori* reasoning, but by the practices and attitudes of British legal officials. This is a necessary consequence of the nature and function of law. Principles of morality are not self-executing. They only have practical consequences when someone identifies, interprets and acts on them. People notoriously disagree about what the most fundamental principles of morality are, and what they require people to do in specific circumstances. The most important function of a legal system is to enable people to cooperate with one another despite those disagreements, not (*per impossibile*) by achieving unanimity but by authoritatively deciding how they should behave even if they continue to disagree. To serve this function a legal system must include officials who are accepted as having authority to make such decisions.[26] In modern societies their authority is law-making authority, because translating abstract principles of morality into concrete prescriptions is what law-making is all about. Ideally, all members of the community – citizens and officials alike – would accept the authority of their law-makers, and would have good reasons for doing so. But as Hart showed, it is possible for a legal system to exist, and maintain order effectively, even if only its most senior officials, for bad reasons, do so, as long as they can compel the rest of the community to obey them.

It is important to be clear about what is required for a legal system to exist and maintain order effectively. It is not necessary that its law-makers have *de jure*, or morally legitimate, authority. But it is necessary that they have some measure of *de facto* authority, which is authority that is believed to be morally legitimate. Hart's thesis is that, at the very least, they must have *de facto* authority among the other senior officials of the system, including its judges. Having this kind of *de facto* authority to make laws is a necessary, even if not sufficient, condition for having *legal* authority to make them.[27] Someone may have morally legitimate authority to tell other people what they must do but cannot have legal authority to make laws unless senior legal officials, at the very least, accept that he or she has it.

Unless they are irrational, legal officials, like citizens, accept the authority of their law-makers only because they believe that there are good reasons – sound principles of political morality – for doing so. Those principles determine the existence of *de jure*, or morally legitimate, authority. But for the reason just explained, they do not by themselves establish the *de facto* authority that is required for a legal system to exist. The main problem for which law is necessary is to resolve chronic disagreements about what moral principles require, and those disagreements can extend to the question of who should be recognized as having morally legitimate authority to resolve them. Although a legal system is needed to settle disagreements about moral principles, it can do so only if there is sufficient agreement about some of them (at least among people powerful enough to coerce dissenters) to maintain its *de facto* authority to do so. This means that a legal system cannot be based on principles of political morality alone. It requires extensive agreement, at least among senior legal officials, as to how disagreements about those principles should be resolved. Significantly, even a judicial system cannot function effectively unless some judges have a *de facto* decision-making authority superior to that of others. If judges disagree about the law, practical necessity dictates that some of them accept the opinions of others as authoritative. Thus, the judges of lower courts must accept the decisions of higher courts as authoritative and, within the highest court, dissenting judges must accept the decisions of a majority as authoritative, even if they correctly believe those decisions to be wrong.

Legal officials, including judges, accept that other officials have legitimate authority to make certain kinds of decision, because they believe that there are principles of political morality that justify their doing so. If they could be persuaded otherwise, they would transfer their allegiance. This is demonstrated by the way in which rules of recognition change as the political allegiance of legal officials changes.[28] To this extent, it is correct to say that law is necessarily based on principles of political morality or, to put it another way, on 'reason'.[29] But it is more accurate to say that it is necessarily based on the beliefs of senior legal officials about principles of political morality – on *their* reason, rather than reason *per se*. Moreover, it is not based exclusively on the moral beliefs, or reason, of judges. As Hart pointed out, a rule of recognition is necessarily constituted by a general consensus among the most senior legislative, executive and judicial officials of a legal system and not by the beliefs and values of any single group of them. This is because, without such a consensus, a viable legal system can be neither established nor maintained.

It does not follow from the fact that a legal system is necessarily based on legal officials' beliefs about principles of political morality that those principles should be regarded as legal principles. For at least two reasons, it may be reasonable, or even necessary, to distinguish between the law and the principles of political morality that motivate legal officials to participate in its creation and enforcement.

First, it is possible for fundamental legal rules to be accepted by different officials for different reasons. A legal system based on such rules can function effectively so long as disagreements among officials about underlying principles do not undermine their acceptance of the rules. When officials believe that different and incompatible principles justify the most fundamental rules of law, it seems inapt to describe them as legal principles because, then, the law would be incoherent. As far as possible, those principles are best ignored by the legal system because, once introduced into legal debate, they may spark destabilizing disputes among officials. Such a system rests on what has been called an 'incompletely theorized agreement' – an agreement that is sufficient for practical purposes, but might be jeopardized by any attempt to achieve a deeper agreement about underlying principles.[30]

Second, even if all legal officials subscribe to the same underlying principles, they may lack the essential qualities that characterize law. Our concept of law excludes norms, such as customary or moral norms, that are neither enforced by the courts nor incorporated in a formally enacted legal instrument. The principles of political morality that underlie a legal system may fail to qualify as legal principles on this ground.

Although the moral authority of all legal institutions is necessarily limited by principles of political morality, it is impossible to provide legal mechanisms for the enforcement of all such limits. There cannot be an infinite regress of limits together with legal institutions charged with enforcing them. At some point, some institution, charged with enforcing limits to some other institution's authority, must be trusted voluntarily to comply with the limits to its own authority. There is no logical or natural necessity that the judiciary must be the institution that is trusted with ultimate authority to interpret and enforce underlying principles of political morality. They may have such as authority but only if other senior officials agree, or can be persuaded to agree, that they do. The existence of fundamental rules allocating decision-making authority requires a consensus among senior legal officials. If they disagree fundamentally about that allocation, there is no lawful way of settling their disagreement. For example, the immediate trigger of the English Civil War in 1642 was a dispute between the two Houses of Parliament and the King, concerning their respective constitutional powers. Neither the King nor the two Houses would have accepted that the judges had authority to resolve their dispute, since both claimed to possess an authority superior to that of the judges. The King regarded them as his servants, bound to enforce his laws, while the two Houses regarded inferior courts as subjects to their own superior jurisdiction. Because there were no lawful means of authoritatively resolving the disagreement, subjects had to make a moral choice as to whom to support in a civil war.[31]

Underlying principles that are not judicially enforceable could possibly be regarded as legal if they were incorporated in a formally enacted legal instrument such as an unenforceable Bill of Rights. But in countries without a Bill of Rights purporting to limit legislative powers, such as Britain, New Zealand and Australia, it is confusing to describe the principles that motivate official allegiance to the legal system as legal, rather than political, principles. It is confusing because, given the usual close relationship between our concept of law and judicial enforcement, it may erroneously suggest that the principles *must* be judicially enforceable, after all.

The Argument from Extreme Cases

By far the most popular argument against the doctrine of parliamentary sovereignty is that no-one could possibly be obligated to obey, and therefore parliament could not possibly have authority to enact, a statute that is blatantly and egregiously unjust or undemocratic. Trevor Allan resorts to improbable, extreme examples. He insists that the courts could not be justified in obeying a 'wicked' statute, which 'seriously contradicted the fundamental tenets of our political morality', such as one requiring all blue-eyed babies to be killed, depriving a large section of the population of the right to vote, or authorizing officials to inflict punishment for whatever reason they should choose.[32]

One difficulty with this argument is that, although it may show that it is unreasonable for officials to believe that parliament has unlimited law-making authority, it does not overcome the fact that they do so. That fact is sufficient to establish that, as a matter of law, parliament has unlimited authority, even if in this respect the law is unreasonable. This difficulty can be surmounted if it can be shown that legal officials cannot really mean what they say. I myself once constructed an argument of this kind:

> [I]t is not clear that British judges do in fact accept the rule of unlimited Parliamentary sovereignty. They may say they do, but they may be mistaken: they may be misinterpreting their own practices. Consider the blue-eyed babies Act [requiring that all blue-eyed babies be killed]. Judicial endorsements of the rule of unlimited Parliamentary sovereignty imply that were such an Act to be passed, the judges would be bound to enforce it. But would they in fact believe themselves bound to do so? More importantly for our purposes, do they now believe that they would be bound to do so? If, as we are surely entitled to assume, they are reasonable people, the answer to both questions must be no. If so, then the rule of unlimited Parliamentary sovereignty must be either a mistake, or an exaggeration of a more qualified truth.... But whatever the reason for their misrepresenting it, the rule which judges really accept is surely the rule on which they are actually prepared to act, rather than the rule on which they merely say or imply that they are prepared to act. Thus, it can be argued that the alleged rule of unlimited Parliamentary sovereignty is a misinterpretation of the traditional deference of British judges to Parliament. That deference must really be based on Parliament's having vast, but not unlimited, authority. For them to accept this, and consequently modify their conception of Parliament's sovereignty, would constitute not a change in their practice, but an improvement in their understanding of it.[33]

The fatal flaw in this argument is that it treats moral and legal authority, and moral and legal obligation, as equivalents. It would indeed be unreasonable to believe that a morally fallible legislature could have an unlimited moral authority to enact laws and that people would therefore have a moral obligation to obey whatever laws it might enact, no matter how undemocratic or unjust they might be. If legal authority to enact laws were the same as moral authority, then it would also be unreasonable to believe that such a legislature could have an unlimited legal authority to enact laws. But there are good reasons for distinguishing between moral and legal authority, and between moral and legal obligation. They are reasons for thinking that a morally fallible legislature could have an unlimited legal authority, despite having only a limited moral authority, to enact laws. It follows that the doctrine of parliamentary sovereignty is not, as many critics have suggested, irrational and therefore something that legal officials cannot really accept.[34]

It is not a logical or practical necessity that parliament should have ultimate legal authority to decide what the law should be. But it is a practical necessity that, with respect to any particular question, *some* institutions have it. Otherwise, the decisions of legal institutions would be no more than recommendations as to what the law is and could not resolve disagreements between people with passionately opposed views. In the seventeenth century, this was often put in terms of obedience. As one author put it: Appeals must not be infinite,

> There must be some supreme power, in whose final determination (be it *right*, or be it *wrong*) all inferiors must acquiesce and submit, otherwise, no controversies could be decided; nay, there could be no government, nothing but disorder and confusion in the world.[35]

This goes too far. What is necessary is that, on any legal question, there must be an ultimate authority whose decisions are accepted as authoritatively determining the law, even if they are disobeyed because they are unjust.

If the judges rather than parliament had this ultimate authority, we would be in the same predicament. Their decisions would have to be accepted as lawful even by people who, rightly or wrongly, believe them to be unjust. And because judges, like legislators, are morally fallible, we would still face the danger of occasional, possibly egregious, injustice.[36] In other words, if it is useful to ask whether a statute requiring that blue-eyed babies be killed could possibly be valid, it is equally useful to ask whether a judicial decision that a blue-eyed baby be killed could possibly be valid. And if a negative answer to the former question justifies judges having authority to invalidate statutes, a negative answer to the latter question must justify officials, other than judges, having authority to invalidate judicial decisions. But who might they be, and to whom would we turn if *they* declared that blue-eyed babies must be killed? Such reasoning produces either a vicious circle, or an infinite regress, of authority to overrule egregiously unjust decisions. In practice, the chain of legal authority, and the availability of legal methods of overruling egregiously unjust decisions, must at some point come to an end.

It is certainly arguable that judges are less likely than a legislature to reach outrageously unjust decisions, although this depends on answering very difficult factual and normative questions.[37] The answer to those questions can vary from one country to another, depending on culture, social structure and political organization. That the doctrine of parliamentary sovereignty facilitated massive injustice in South Africa, for example, is not a good reason for concluding it should be repudiated in Britain.[38] In South Africa it may have impeded the ability of judges to obstruct an unrepresentative and unjust legislature, but it does not follow that judges should be encouraged to obstruct representative and generally just legislatures.[39] Moreover, there are important considerations in addition to the comparative quality of legislative and judicial decisions. Justice itself is widely believed to require that every member of the community have an equal right to participate in public decision-making – a consideration that favours parliament rather than the judges.[40] To recognise parliament as having ultimate legal authority is therefore not obviously unreasonable.

At this point, critics might object that no matter who has ultimate legal authority, it cannot be absolute, for the very reason we have mentioned – the danger of occasional, egregious, injustice. People can be bound to obey laws (or judicial decisions) that they believe are unjust, but only up to a point. Officially sanctioned injustice can be so extreme that the reasons in favour of obedience are overridden. In a sufficiently extreme case, people might be morally entitled, or even obligated, to resort to violence rather than suffer or permit such injustice. Furthermore, legal officials, such as judges, might be morally bound to support them.

But this does not prove that judges necessarily possess legal authority to invalidate legislation on a routine basis. What judges are morally entitled, or even bound, to do in an extraordinary emergency may differ from what they are legally authorized to do. It does not follow from the fact that judges must decide for themselves whether or not they can enforce a statute with a clear conscience that, if they decide they cannot do so, they have authority to hold that the statute is legally invalid. If it did, it would also follow that bailiffs, police officers and prison warders have authority to declare that judicial decisions are legally invalid. Judges no less than parliament rely on the cooperation of other officials for the enforcement of their decisions: they do not step down from the bench and physically enforce them. Bailiffs, police officers and prison warders must decide for themselves whether or not they can, in good conscience, enforce judicial decisions, but it does not follow that they have legal authority to decide that those decisions are legally invalid. The same is true of ordinary citizens. They must decide for themselves whether or not they ought morally to disobey statutes, judicial decisions or other directives of legal officials. But it does not follow that a citizen has any legal authority to declare those statutes, decisions or directives invalid.

No legal system could function effectively if judicial decisions concerning citizens' legal obligations were no more legally authoritative than the opinions of the citizens themselves. Consider a judicial decision regarded by a citizen as legally erroneous. If the citizen were legally justified in resisting it, then the judges would not be legally justified in ordering bailiffs or police officers to enforce it and, if they did so, those officials would be legally entitled to defy them and to defend the citizen. Moreover, in the absence of some higher, more authoritative, decision-maker, all concerned would have to be guided by their own judgements of the legal issues involved. Citizens' and officials' legal obligations would be as interminably debatable as their moral obligations, and there would potentially be as many equally authoritative opinions as there are citizens and officials – many of them inconsistent with one another. The law would be indistinguishable from anarchy: instead of their legal disagreements being authoritatively resolved by judges, citizens and officials would be left to fight them out in the streets.

The only way to avoid anarchy is for some legal officials to have an authority superior to that of other officials and citizens to decide what legally ought to be done. Subordinate officials and citizens may rightly believe a particular decision to be wrong – perhaps even so wrong that it morally ought not to be obeyed – but that cannot affect its legal authority. From their point of view, there is necessarily a conceptual difference between the requirements of law and those of morality. But if so, then it is possible for a legislature to have a decision-making authority superior to that of judges, in which case there is a conceptual difference between moral and legal requirements from the judges' point of view as well.

It might be argued that there is a difference between judges, on the one hand, and bailiffs, police officers and prison warders, on the other. Judges are recognized by law as having authority to decide what the law is, whereas those other officials are not. But to argue this is to concede that the crucial question is what legal authority particular officials have. Judges who are bound by the doctrine of parliamentary sovereignty do not have authority to decide that statutes are invalid on the ground that they are unjust or undemocratic. That judges might be morally bound to disobey a statute, in an extraordinary case, does not alter that fact. In deciding whether or not they are morally justified in obeying statutes, they merely do what every government official or employee must necessarily do.

Michael Detmold rightly insists that judging is a practical, rather than a theoretical, activity. Its object is not the advancement of knowledge of the law for its own sake, but the termination of disputes, by deciding what the disputants legally ought to have done and requiring them to rectify any wrongdoing.[41] But all legal officials, from the highest to the lowest, are engaged in practical, rather than theoretical, activities. Judges may order people to be imprisoned, but court bailiffs, police officers and prison warders carry out their orders. The practical nature of the judges' decisions does not prove that they necessarily have ultimate decision-making authority, any more than the practical nature of other legal officials' decisions proves that they have it.

The maxim 'hard cases make bad law' can be used to reinforce this argument. The meaning of the maxim is that legal rules should be framed with ordinary, rather than extraordinary, cases in mind because it is better to achieve satisfactory results in the vast majority of cases that are likely to arise, even at the cost of unsatisfactory decisions in a small number of very unlikely cases (the 'hard' cases), rather than vice versa.[42] It may not be possible to qualify a rule so that it achieves satisfactory results in those unlikely cases without damaging its results in other cases.

Consider a rule prohibiting police from torturing suspected criminals. In almost all conceivable cases such a rule is preferable to one that permits the torture of suspects. But a hard case might arise if the police captured a terrorist whom they knew had hidden a nuclear weapon, set to explode within an hour, in a major city. They might be morally justified in torturing him, in order to prevent the deaths of millions of innocent people. But it does not follow that the rule should be amended so that the police had the authority to torture suspects in emergency situations. Such an amendment would be extremely undesirable because of the risk that the police would interpret that authority too broadly and inflict torture when it was unjustified. That some action might be morally justified in an extraordinary situation does not entail that a legal rule authorizing that action is justified.[43]

For the same reason, judicial defiance of parliament might be morally legitimate in extraordinary cases, but not something that should be recognized as lawful. The consequences of the doctrine of parliamentary sovereignty are generally beneficial: democratic decision-making is facilitated, and reasonably just statutes are enacted. Unjust statutes are sometimes enacted, but they are rarely obviously and egregiously unjust. Occasional injustice is a price that must be paid for democracy, as indeed for any decision-making procedure, since none can be guaranteed never to produce unjust laws. It is possible to imagine 'hard cases' involving statutes so outrageously unjust that morally they ought not to be obeyed, even by judges. But it does not follow that the doctrine of parliamentary sovereignty ought to be abandoned and the judges authorized to invalidate outrageously unjust statutes, since they might interpret that authority too broadly and invalidate statutes that are not outrageously unjust. What judges would be morally entitled, or even bound, to do in extraordinary emergencies may differ from what they are legally authorized to do. Hard cases do not make good law.

In a healthy democratic society, cases of clear and extreme injustice are rare; in most cases, whether or not a law violates some basic right is open to reasonable arguments on both sides. The whole point of having a democracy is that, in these debatable cases, the opinion of the majority, rather than of an unelected elite, is supposed to prevail.[44] The price to be paid for giving judges authority to invalidate a few laws that are clearly unjust or undemocratic is that they must also be given authority to overrule the democratic process in a much larger number of cases where the requirements of justice or democracy are debatable. When the probability of the different dangers actually occurring is taken into account, that of excessive judicial interference with democratic decision-making might be higher than that of parliamentary tyranny.

An additional consideration is that it is unlikely that a judicial declaration of invalidity would be effective in extreme cases such as those imagined by Allan. As Lord Irvine has suggested, a government determined to enact evil laws could probably be defeated only on the political battle field, and not in the courts: it is 'romanticism to believe that judicial decision could hold back what would, in substance, be a revolution'.[45] A government and parliament prepared to flout minimum standards of justice or democracy are unlikely to have sufficient respect for the rule of law to meekly submit to judicial correction. They are more likely to use their powers to appoint, dismiss and threaten judges, in order to reduce them to submission. The argument from extreme cases is therefore open to the further objection that, in those cases, the proposed remedy of judicial invalidation would probably be useless anyway.

Allan is therefore wrong to say that the question is '[w]hether or not judicial allegiance to statute would be justified in extreme or unusual situations'.[46] If 'allegiance' means 'obedience', that is an easy question, and the answer is that it would not be justified. But it does not follow that the law should recognize that the courts have authority to invalidate statutes. Nor does it follow that the law already recognizes that they have such authority. The hard question, which Allen is really addressing, is whether judges should claim an authority that will threaten democratic decision-making in many cases that are likely to arise, in order to provide a remedy for extreme situations that are very unlikely to arise and which would probably be useless if they did.

It follows that the doctrine of parliamentary sovereignty is not irrational. Indeed, it is arguably perfectly consistent with Dworkin's theory of law, because there are moral principles capable of justifying, as well as explaining, the commitment of British legal officials to the doctrine. Arguably, the morally best political theory, of all those which 'fit' the institutional history of the British Constitution, fully supports the doctrine. If so, a theory such as Allan's can be criticized for failing not only Dworkin's 'dimension of fit' but also his 'dimension of morality'. It fails the latter if a legal system in which unelected judges have authority to invalidate statutes, on the basis of their own assessment of abstract and controversial principles of political morality, is morally inferior to a system in which a democratically elected legislature possesses the ultimate authority to decide what those principles require.

The Alleged Necessity of Judicially Enforceable Constitutional Rights

Why is it that the doctrine of parliamentary sovereignty has recently been subjected to these criticisms? I suspect that it is because the United States model of judicially enforceable constitutional rights has become so influential that many people now believe it to be not only desirable, but essential, for the preservation of human rights and democracy. It is not clear why this belief has lately become so prevalent, since there is little, if any, evidence that the United States is a more just and democratic society than other Western nations whose constitutions do not include such rights. As Robert Dahl has observed:

> No one has shown that countries like the Netherlands and New Zealand, which lack judicial review, or Norway and Sweden, where it is exercised rarely and in highly restrained fashion, or Switzerland, where it can be applied only to cantonal legislation, are less democratic than the United States, nor, I think, could one reasonably do so.[47]

The ultimate source of the assumption that judicial enforcement of fundamental principles is somehow necessary in any society committed to democracy and human rights is an influential contemporary understanding of the ideals of 'constitutionalism' and 'the rule of law'. For many people, these concepts require legislative power to be subject to constitutional limits enforceable by an independent judiciary. Trevor Allan, for example, insists that it is 'ultimately impossible to reconcile the rule of law with the unlimited sovereignty of Parliament ... An insistence on there being a source of ultimate political authority, which is free from all legal restraint ... is incompatible with constitutionalism.'[48]

But it is question-begging to assume that a Constitution such as Britain's, so deeply rooted in tradition, or others derived from it, necessarily conform to contemporary understanding of *a priori* principles, especially when those understandings are inspired by the United States model of government which was a radical departure from British tradition.[49] Moreover, if 'the rule of law' required that the authority of every legal institution be subject to legal limits enforceable by some other legal institution, it would be a chimerical ideal which could never be realized in practice. As we have seen, in any legal system, at least one institution must ultimately be trusted to adhere to whatever principles are believed to limit its authority. Moreover, those principles must be highly abstract and flexible in application, in order to ensure that government can respond appropriately to all the exigencies of changing circumstances. That is why a judicially enforceable Bill of Rights consists of very abstract and flexible principles of political morality whose interpretation is ultimately indistinguishable from moral and political philosophy. It is not immediately clear why a judiciary, charged with weighing up and applying abstract moral principle to concrete cases, is any more subject to 'the rule of law' than is a sovereign legislature which is responsible for translating the same principles into legislation.

Judicial review of the validity of legislation is neither an essential prerequisite for the protection of human rights and democracy nor, therefore, a necessary element of any legal system dedicated to those principles.[50] It is certainly possible to argue that it would improve the protection of human rights and democracy. The question for countries such as the United Kingdom, Australia and New Zealand is whether or not it would be desirable for that reason. That question is currently being debated by those who favour, and those who oppose, the formal adoption of a written Bill of Rights. The arguments in this chapter are not intended to resolve that debate. They are intended merely to defend the orthodox understanding that the doctrine of parliamentary sovereignty is currently part of the constitutional law of all three countries – albeit in a heavily modified form in Australia. If it were not, there would be no need to debate the merits of a Bill of Rights: the judges would already have authority to invalidate legislation that they regard as inconsistent with fundamental rights. Since they do not already have that authority, proponents of judicial review must persuade us that they ought to.

Notes

1 This is a shortened version of the final chapter of my book, *The Sovereignty of Parliament, History and Philosophy* (Oxford: Clarendon Press, 1999) and is published here with the permission of Oxford University Press.

2 J. Goldsworthy, 'The Constitutional Protection of Human Rights in Australia', in G. Craven (ed.), *Australian Federation: Towards the Second Century* (Melbourne: Melbourne University Press, 1992), p. 152.

3 T.R.S. Allan, *Law, Liberty, and Justice: The Legal Foundations of British Constitutionalism* (Oxford: Clarendon Press, 1993), p. 16.

4 H.L.A. Hart, *The Concept of Law* (Oxford: Clarendon Press, 1961), ch. 4.

5 Ibid., chs 5 and 6. The qualification 'most senior' is my own, not Hart's. Low-level government employees are more like ordinary citizens, in terms of their relationship to the most fundamental rules of the legal system.

6 Ibid., pp. 144–8.

7 The claim that it is a common law rule is ubiquitous. But see, in particular,

M.J. Detmold, *The Australian Commonwealth: A Fundamental Analysis of Its Constitution* (Sydney: Law Books, 1985), pp. 229–30, and Allan, *Law, Liberty and Justice, op. cit.*, p. 10.

8 P.J. Fitzgerald (ed.), *Salmond on Jurisprudence*, 12th edn (London: Sweet and Maxwell, 1966), p. 111.

9 C. Munro, *Studies in Constitutional Law* (London: Butterworths, 1987), p. 103.

10 Allan, *Law, Liberty and Justice, op. cit.*, p. 4; see also T.R.S. Allan, 'The Common Law as Constitution: Fundamental Rights and First Principles', in C. Saunders (ed.), *Courts of Final Jurisdiction: The Mason Court in Australia* (Sydney: Federation Press, 1996), p. 146.

11 Allan, *Law, Liberty and Justice, op. cit.*, p. 10.

12 Ibid.

13 Sir William Wade, *Constitutional Fundamentals*, 2nd (London: Stevens, 1989), p. 33.

14 Neil McCormick has cautioned against this mistake in his *Legal Reasoning and Legal Theory* (Oxford: Clarendon Press, 1978), p. 56.

15 Hart, *The Concept of Law, op. cit.*, p. 117, emphasis added, and 109–14 *passim*.

16 Ibid., p. 113.

17 Ibid., pp. 118–19.

18 G. Winterton, 'Constitutionally Entrenched Common Law Rights: Sacrificing Means to Ends?', in C. Sampford (ed.), *Interpreting Constitutions: Theories, Principles and Institutions* (Sydney: Federation Press, 1996), p. 136.

19 Allan, *Law, Liberty and Justice, op. cit.*, esp. at pp. 130–34, but also at pp. 7–12, 44–7 and 292–90.

20 R. Dworkin, *Taking Rights Seriously* (Cambridge, MA: Harvard University Press, 1977), esp. chs 2–4, and *Law's Empire* (Cambridge, MA: Harvard University Press, 1986), esp. chs 6 and 7.

21 On equality, see Allan, 'The Common Law', *op. cit.*, pp. 151–2 and 165, and *Law, Liberty and Justice, op. cit.*, p. 290.

22 Allan, *Law, Liberty and Justice, op. cit.*, pp. 265–6.

23 Ibid., p. 282.

24 Allan, 'The Common Law', *op. cit.*, pp. 158, 159 and 164.

25 Dworkin, *Taking Rights Seriously, op. cit.*, p. 123, *Law's Empire, op. cit.*, esp. chs 1, 3 and 7. For the way in which judges themselves describe the process, see *Taking Rights Seriously, op. cit.*, pp. 86–7, 112 and 115–16.

26 This coordinating function of law is emphasized in much recent jurisprudential literature. See, for example, J. Finnis, *Natural Law and Natural Rights* (Oxford: Clarendon Press, 1980), pp. 245–52 and G. Postema, 'Coordination and Convention at the Foundations of Law', *Journal of Legal Studies*, **11** (1982), p. 165.

27 This should be accepted even by those who believe that having *de jure* authority is also a necessary condition for having legal authority (which I deny).

28 Allan, *Law, Liberty and Justice, op. cit.*, pp. 279 and 280–81.

29 Both Detmold and Allan speak of the common law being ultimately a matter of 'reason'. M. Detmold, 'Law as Practical Reason', *Cambridge Law Journal* (1989), p. 436, *passim*; Allan, *Law, Liberty and Justice, op. cit.*, p. 15.

30 C. Sunstein, *Legal Reasoning and Political Conflict* (New York: Oxford University Press, 1996).

31 P. Hunton, *A Treatise of Monarchy* (1643), extracted in D. Wootton, *Divine Right and Democracy* (Harmondsworth: Penguin, 1986), p. 175, esp. at pp. 209–21.

32 Allan, *Law, Liberty and Justice, op. cit.*, pp. 130, 282, and 285 respectively.

33 J. Goldsworthy, 'The Self-Destruction of Legal Positivism', *Oxford Journal of Legal Studies*, **10** (1990), p. 449, esp. at pp. 482–3.

34 For the suggestion that it is irrational, see Allan, 'The Common Law', *op. cit.*, pp. 156–160.

35 *The Royal Apology: Or, An Answer To the Rebels' Plea* (London, T.B. for Robert Clavel, 1684), pp. 35–6.

36 Anyone who doubts this should read the infamous judgment of the US Supreme Court in the 'Dred Scott' case: *Scott* v. *Sandford* (1857) 60 US (19 How.), 393.

37 See Goldsworthy, 'Constitutional Protection', *op. cit.* n. 1, pp. 167–9.

38 The case of South Africa is discussed in D. Dyzenhaus, *Hard Cases in Wicked Legal Systems: South African Law in the Perspective of Legal Philosophy* (Oxford: Clarendon Press, 1991).

39 See J. Bakan, 'Some Hard Questions About the Hard Cases Question', *University of Toronto Law Journal*, **42** (1992), p. 504.

40 J. Waldron forcefully makes this point in 'A Rights Based Critique of Constitutional Rights', *Oxford Journal of Legal Studies*, **13** (1993), p. 18.

41 This is the most fundamental point made in all of Detmold's jurisprudential writings: see esp. 'Law As Practical Reason', *Cambridge Law Journal*, **48** (1989), pp. 436–71.

42 In this context, the term 'hard cases' does not have the same meaning that it has in the debate between Hart and Dworkin.

43 Michael Detmold draws this distinction very clearly in his *The Unity of Law and Morality: A Refutation of Legal Positivism* (London: Routledge and Kegan Paul, 1984), pp. 217–18.

44 For a very powerful argument to this effect, see Waldron, 'A Rights-Based Critique', *op. cit.*, n. 39.

45 Lord Irvine of Lairg, 'Judges and Decision-Makers: The Theory and Practice of *Wednesbury* Review, *Public Law* (1996), pp. 59, 77.

46 Allan, *Law, Liberty and Justice, op. cit.*, p. 286.

47 R. Dahl, *Democracy and its Critics* (New Haven, CT: Yale University Press, 1989), pp. 189–91, emphasis added.

48 Allan, *Law, Liberty and Justice, op. cit.*, p. 16.

49 On the question-begging nature of this aspect of Allan's argument, see George Winterton, 'Constitutionally Entrenched Common Law Rights', *op. cit.*, n. 17, pp. 136–7.

50 It may be a practical necessity in some legal systems committed to that protection, but it is not in all of them. Whether or not it is depends on the culture, social structure and political organization within which each legal system operates.

11 Legislation by Assembly

JEREMY WALDRON

Introduction

In discussions of judicial activism it is as important to understand the institutions that surround our courts as it is to understand the courts themselves and the nature of judicial reasoning. This is because accusations of activism often presuppose that a judge is doing something in law or politics that ought to be done by some other agency of government and, in many cases, the institutional differences between the two are supposed to explain why.[1] When we are discussing judicial activism in modern constitutional law it is particularly important to understand *legislatures* – what they are, how they work, and what is the basis of their legitimacy – because the issue raised is often that something has been decided by the courts in a way that involves an inappropriate encroachment on the tasks of congress or parliament. For this reason, we need theories about legislatures and theories about courts. Fortunately, there is no shortage so far as theories about courts are concerned. But there is very little available to us in the way of a philosophically adequate theory of legislatures.[2] In this chapter, then, I will not say very much on the topic of adjudication (except for a few remarks about statutory interpretation at the very end). I am eager, instead, to take up the task of enhancing our theoretical understanding of legislatures and particularly (as my title indicates) our understanding of legislation by large representative assemblies.

Does Size Matter?

Philosophy works best when we question the obvious. Although obvious questions may appear to have obvious answers, our task is to ask what explains the obviousness.[3] Legal and political philosophy are no exception from this general remit, and I want to begin by asking a question about the following obvious point.

Everywhere, legislatures – parliaments and congresses – have significantly more members than the decision-making membership of either the highest courts in a given system or the highest authority in the executive. In Australia, for example, the Federal Parliament has a total of about 200 members, whereas the High Court sits in panels of five, and (depending on how you count) the Australian executive consists of either the head of state alone or the prime minister with a small cabinet of 20. In the United States the Supreme Court consists of nine justices, the executive comprises the president (with, again, a cabinet of about 20), while the federal legislature (House plus Senate) has a membership of 535. In Great Britain, the prime minister's cabinet seats about 20. The House of Lords sits as a court with panels of five. The British Parliament, by contrast, has a membership of about 1900, if you include everyone in both houses including (at the time of writing)[4] earls, bishops, dukes, marquesses and barons. In the House of Commons alone, there are 659 members.

True, the courts and the executive in all these countries have subordinate courts and agencies arrayed under them, as well as large staffs. But then so, of course, do the parliamentarians. The numerical difference that interests me is displayed in the highest levels of the branches of government we are considering. The highest court comprises nine or ten, sometimes as few as five; the executive comprises twenty odd, with the president or prime minister as *primus inter pares*. The legislature, on the other hand, has hundreds of members at the highest level, all of whom are entitled to regard one another as equals (at least so far as each chamber is concerned). Thus, for example, in the British House of Lords, considered as a legislative chamber, there are various distinctions between government, opposition and independent peers, there are distinctions of noble rank, there are differences between life peers and the congenital variety, and there are important political differences between back-benchers, front-benchers and cross-benchers. Nevertheless, despite all of these differences, each of the 1200 plus members of the House of Lords has equal authority in a vote to enact a bill. By contrast, when the House of Lords is sitting as a court, in a matter whose outcome may be equally important for the law, final authority is distributed among a number of judges.

Political scientists often remind us that real legislative power is vested in a much smaller number of people than the full membership of parliament or congress. They emphasize the power of the executive in Westminster-style systems where the parliament very seldom fails to enact any bill proposed by the executive and very seldom enacts any bill *not* proposed by the executive. Equally, in the USA, they point to the power of committees as the effective legislative power.[5] This might suggest that the disparity of numbers to which I have called your attention is more a matter of what Walter Bagehot called a 'dignified' characteristic of constitutional custom than an 'effective' aspect of constitutional reality.[6] In some countries that is no doubt true: for example, the Chinese legislature has 2900 members, but I doubt that real legislative power is distributed equally in that assembly. Nevertheless, in the end this debunking gambit will not do. For I have no doubt that if the very same political scientists were called on to advise an East European country on the reconstruction of its Constitution, they would say, among other things, that the country should have a structure of courts with a high court sitting in panels of five or so, that it should have a small and decisive executive body of about 20 ministers or secretaries of state, and that it should have a legislative chamber of some hundreds of members to enact and amend its laws. And this insistence – on a parliament of some hundreds of members – would be seen not just as a quaint concession to antiquarianism, like the restoration of a Hohenzollern to the throne of Romania, but, rather, a more or less *obvious* feature of working constitutional structure. We have a sort of a *constitutional instinct* that the law-making branch, located above all the other branches of government, should consist of large numbers of people. We take it for granted that if there is explicit law-making or law reform to be done in society, it should be done in or under the authority of, a large representative assembly. The challenge, then, is to explain this constitutional instinct – to run it to earth, so to speak – and then to see whether there is anything about the explanation that helps in our further resolution of the problems that arise when we regard enacted legislation – statutes and statutory texts – as things to be interpreted as authoritative sources of law.

The explanation that springs immediately to mind, of course, is the idea of *democracy*: legislation is supposed to have democratic legitimacy, and that is why it is important for the legislature to be a large body. By itself, that won't do as an explanation, for two reasons. First, it begs the question of why *law-making* – alone among the tasks and functions of government – requires this sort of democratic legitimacy. Second, it neglects the point that democratic credentials come in all shapes and sizes. In the United States President Clinton has democratic credentials in the sense that more people voted for him as the sole occupant of his office than for any other candidate (although this is complicated by the electoral college system). So we haven't yet got a contrast on democratic grounds. We haven't yet explained why democratic values are mapped on to hundreds of representatives for the legislative function and mapped on to very small numbers of representatives (maybe just one) for the highest executive function. If it were simply a matter of democracy, why would we be so uneasy about legislation by the decree of a single elected and electorally accountable individual? An appeal to the value of *participation* won't do either. Although it, of course, is true that more citizens participate in law-making when you have a 500-member assembly than if you have a one-person legislature, the difference between the fraction of the citizenry participating in a one-person legislature and the fraction participating in a 500-person legislature is minuscule when (as in the United States) the denominator is a background population of more than a quarter of a billion.

The notion of *representation* looks like a more promising answer: the idea is that it is important for law-making to take place in an inclusive representational context. But even with this explanation we still have work to do. We have to be able to show that the Hobbesian concept of representation (where a large group may be said to be represented by one man)[7] is out of place in this context. So we must ask again: why is it important, specifically with regard to *legislation*, that the people of a society be represented by *people* rather than that they be represented – as Hobbes suggested – by just one person? Why is it important for explicit law-making, as opposed to the other functions of government, that action be taken in the name of large numbers by large numbers of people?

I don't want to mislead you: I do think that something like representation is the key here. But it is important to explore the idea in detail and to take the long way round – partly because representation itself is a concept whose complexity and difficulty in political theory is belied by the ease with which it rolls off the democratically educated tongue[8] and partly because if we start to plumb the depths of this notion, rather than repeating mantras about inclusiveness, we might get a better grip on the discomfort that people feel about judicial activism and judicial law-making. I suspect that this discomfort is not so much an uneasiness about judges as such, but an uneasiness about an apparent slight to what I have called our constitutional instinct about legislation and large numbers. It is important therefore to get to the bottom of it.

The task of developing an adequate account of our instinct for legislative assemblies faces two large philosophical complications. The first consists in a very clear consensus, in the canon of Western political theory, that the size of a legislative assembly is an obstacle rather than an advantage for law-making.

Take, for example, Thomas Hobbes. Hobbes conceded that a sovereign legislature *might* be a democratic assembly,[9] but he was pretty adamant that such a set-up would be imprudent or inadvisable because, among other reasons, 'a Monarch cannot disagree with himselfe

... but an Assembly may; and that to such a height, as may produce a Civill Warre'.[10] Or consider Jean-Jacques Rousseau, in many ways the apostle of participatory democracy. Even Rousseau acknowledged that the mass of ordinary people are going to have a terribly hard time in plenary session, to set an agenda for themselves or organize a body of laws. He introduced the mythic figure of 'the Law-giver' specifically to reintroduce the single-mindedness that he thought necessary for an adequate system of laws. Even though the Law-giver would not himself have legislative authority, as an agenda-setter, he would have a single-mindedness that would enable him to cut through what would otherwise be huge coordination problems arising when a large diverse group of opinionated people come together to legislate, each with various bright ideas about law, policy and justice.[11]

Consider also the Marquis de Condorcet, who was famous for showing – in what we now call his 'Jury Theorem'[12] – that the larger the decisional body the greater the probability of its coming up with the right answer to any question posed to it, provided, of course, that the average competence of the individual members is greater than 0.5.[13] What is less well known is that Condorcet also maintained – this time as an empirical rather than an arithmetical matter – that the larger the legislative assembly, the lower the likelihood that the average competence of the individual members would be above 0.5! So while there was an arithmetical tendency in one direction, there was also a kind of sociological tendency in the other direction which didn't exactly neatly cancel out the Jury Theorem but insisted nevertheless that the more people you add to the legislature the lower the average level of competence. And very quickly, Condorcet thought, that competence would drop below the coin-tossing level.[14]

On a slightly different tack, James Madison, in *The Federalist* argued that the framers of a constitution should keep the legislature *as small as possible*, consistent with minimally adequate representation, because the larger the group the more likely the sceptre of reason would be wrested away by the mob. For Madison it was not just a matter of individual competence, it was about the sheer dynamics of groups. Had every citizen in Athens been a Socrates, said Madison, every Athenian assembly would have been a mob.[15] Similarly, English thinkers, from Blackstone to Bagehot, have been worried by the potential for legal and political chaos or paralysis when an assembly of hundreds turns its hydra-headed attention to legislation. Walter Bagehot reminded us of the saying, in England, that a big meeting never does anything. Yet, here we are, he said, in our parliamentary system, governed by a big meeting. How is something coherent supposed to emerge from this diverse babbling assemblage of hundreds of opinionated people?[16] (About the only outsider in this theoretical consensus is John Locke, who wrote in the 1680s that, while it was of course possible to have a single-person legislature, it was very inadvisable and that, really, people should never regard themselves as truly free 'till the Legislature was placed in collective Bodies of Men, call them Senate, Parliament or what you please'.[17])

So we have an almost complete theoretical consensus pointing in the opposite direction from what I have called our constitutional instinct. That makes the task of theorizing the instinct unpromising, to say the least.

A second difficulty, more germane perhaps to the 'legal positivism' side of our discussions in this book, is a consensus among legal philosophers that the issue of legislative size *really does not matter* from an analytical point of view. It is seen by philosophers as something beneath the notice of general jurisprudence. Who cares whether the laws are made by a Saudi king or a Burmese junta or an English parliament? Most positivists think it important that there should *be* a legislature,[18] but they are not particularly interested in what it is, who it comprises or how it works. What matters for the purposes of (say) the positivist 'sources thesis'[19] is that there be rule-generating institutions, that they have determinate procedures and that there be a rule of recognition to identify their output. From the point of view of modern positivist theory, the legislature may safely be regarded as an institutional black box:[20] the deliberations and procedures of the institution may be politically interesting, but it is 'pre-legal' process and 'pre-legal' reasoning, of little interest to a legal scholar or certainly to a legal philosopher.[21]

This theoretical indifference to structure has a long pedigree in positivist jurisprudence. It is true that both Jeremy Bentham's and John Austin's work gesture towards the idea – which, of course, was the political reality in their contemporary England – that a legislature might be a large and numerous body. Nevertheless the style and presentation of the idea of legislative sovereignty remained firmly individualistic in both these theories. Thus, although Bentham said neutrally that we identify a *sovereign* whenever we notice 'any person *or assemblage of persons* to whose will an entire political community are (no matter on what account) supposed to be in a disposition to pay obedience: and that in preference to the will of any other person',[22] that phrase – 'assemblage of persons' – was almost his only concession to the point. For the rest of his jurisprudence, and in much of his political philosophy, the sovereign was almost always referred to as '*he*' (and for once, refreshingly, it is the number not the gender of the pronoun that preoccupies us).[23] I am not saying that Bentham was uninterested in legislative assemblies – on the contrary, he can claim to have founded the peculiar English obsession with the shape and furniture of parliamentary chambers. But he saw no consequences for jurisprudence in the assembly aspect of legislation. And the same seems to be true of recent positivist theory. Even H.L.A. Hart – whose jurisprudence alone among the English positivists is able to provide a conceptual account of rule-governed structure at the centre of legislative sovereignty – is as happy talking about the legislator as an individual as he is talking about the legislature as an assembly. For although Hart refers sometimes to the Queen-in-Parliament, most of the points he makes could as easily be made – and, indeed, many of them *were* made – with reference to a personal legislator called Rex.[24]

So I am working against consensus on two fronts. The legal philosophers say that the size and structure of a legislature does not matter in jurisprudence; I suspect it does. And the political theorists, for the most part, say that to the extent that size matters, smaller is better; whereas I think there is something affirmatively important in the idea of law-making by a large assembly. The view, then, which I want to defend is that the size of a legislative assembly really does make a difference – a difference that is relevant for analytical jurisprudence and certainly for constitutional law. I want to show in particular that it makes a difference to our understanding of the *concept* of law, to our understanding of the *authority* of law and to our understanding of the proper basis for *legal interpretation*.

The Concept of Law

Let us begin with the concept of law. Once upon a time there was an adage, central to Roman and early medieval jurisprudence, '*Quod principi placuit vigorem legis habet*' ('Whatever pleases the prince has the force of law'). It conveyed a very sovereign- and sovereignty-oriented notion of law, with the prince or king or emperor conceived as inherent law-maker, and law understood as his command or, literally, as the prince's pleasure. It's an old idea, which is why I quote it in Latin, but it is not without current influence: we find important traces of it in the concepts of sovereignty that are still deployed even nowadays in philosophical jurisprudence. We find a sense of it also in the almost intuitive conviction that law only really exists in a society constituted as a centralized order with an overwhelmingly powerful authority at its head. (That is why the idea of international law still strikes us as tenuous.)

In medieval jurisprudence, '*Quod principi placuit ...*' expressed the notion of law as essentially the law of the king or the law of his kingdom, *lex regni*. But it was never an unopposed conception. It always stood in strong antithesis to a somewhat different conception of law – the notion of *lex terrae* (the law of the land). By *lex terrae*, medieval jurists did not just mean land law or property law (although that was an important part of it), they meant law as held in common among the more important inhabitants of the land – law as something which structured and articulated the relations of relatively independent centres of power and authority on the ground. The law that bound a villein to his manor was *lex terrae* as so were the laws that bound the barons to their king and him to them, as well as the laws of inheritance, allegiance, service, markets, criminal justice and so on. And law understood in this way often prevailed over the sovereignty concept. It was a remarkable element in the success of the baronial faction in England in 1215, for example, that in the famous provision of Magna Carta which held that '[n]o free man is to be taken and imprisoned, or disseised, or outlawed, or exiled, or by any means distrained, nor will we proceed against him, ... except by the judgment of a court of his peers', the charter added the phrase 'according to the law of the land' ('*vel per legem terrae*') rather than King John's own favoured formulation, '*vel per legem regni*'.[25]

Lex terrae, the law of the land, was understood as law held among the inhabitants of the land. But although it contrasted with the imperiousness of '*Quod principi placuit*...', it was not a democratic idea. If anything, it was feudal in conception and there was certainly no question of all the serfs going off to vote for representatives or participate in a referendum on law reform. Nevertheless, *lex terrae* did embody the idea that the land was configured politically and juridically, as well as topographically, as a plurality of places, interests and authorities, and as a plurality of power centres, linked juridically by oath or compact and dynamically by council and bargaining. It conceived of a law-governed society as a place where structures of legal authority were held *among* this plurality of power centres rather than as something dominating or superseding them or something from which they derived a purely dependent authority. I don't mean this to convey an immemorial vision of customary society in Merrie England. On the contrary, *lex terrae* was quite dynamic in many ways and open to legal change, even on such fundamental matters as inheritance.[26] But it was pervaded by the idea that legal change not only must be responsive to the diversity of interests in the kingdom, as a king like John might purport to be responsive to the diversity of interests in England, but it must be also be enacted in the context of *actual deliberation, council and bargaining* among those power centres. The many centres of power and authority in the land were not just to be treated as objects of concern and regal solicitude; they demanded respect for themselves as active sources of juridical intelligence.

Although, as I said, this was not a democratic idea, nevertheless, as the Cambridge legal historian Walter Ullmann has argued, it was a framework on which later ideas about representation, voice, and democracy might quite easily be woven. The leading idea was that what was in the interests of the kingdom could be determined only by those who were substantially affected – that is, only by *their own* insight into *their own* needs and wants. In the regal conception of '*Quod principi placuit...*', it was the king's understanding of the interests of the community that was all-important. In the conception of *lex terrae*, by contrast, the idea took hold that, in legislation the principal elements of the kingdom – of which there were many – were entitled to speak for themselves. Once that was accepted, then broader ideas of representation in law-making found, as Ullmann put it, an 'easy and unimpeded ... inlet',[27] and the steady growth of the English tradition that eventually included the commons in parliamentary legislation begins to become intelligible.

I believe that there is an important connection between this conception of law, as essentially law of the land and not simply *lex regni*, and the idea of law-making by a representative assembly. If I am right, then I think one of the failings of the positivist school is that it has not asked whether there is anything useful to jurisprudence in this idea of law as held among a people or among a plurality of power centres, as opposed to law laid down from on high by a sovereign and his judges.

From our point of view, the form of law most evidently connected with *lex terrae* is custom or customary law. This we may understand as the notion of law welling up in the normative consciousness of the people of a locality or the people of a society generally, or in the practices of a specialized group such as the community of merchants in a given set of markets. Custom need not presuppose unanimity or even strong social homogeneity. It may comprise normative practices that some are comfortable with, even while others wish they were otherwise. But it is, above all, the idea of the emergence of law from below, and of evolution and legal change through experimentation on the ground. As such, customary law is law conceived of as answerable to the variety of interests and experiences that exist and occur in the community. A custom survives as law (when it does) because it has become familiar and turned out to be acceptable as a norm over a period of years to most of the people whose interactions have been organized under its auspices.

Now we all know that, in the traditional positivist view (by which I mean the view of theorists like Thomas Hobbes, Jeremy Bentham, and John Austin), customary law was conceptualized reductively within the model of sovereign law. The legal positivists attempted to redescribe customary law as a version (sometimes an unsatisfactory version) of law laid down from on high – as Bentham put it, 'a miscellaneous branch of statute law ill-expressed and ill-defined'.[28] Custom was viewed as a source of law only in the sense that the sovereign or his agents – the judges – might recognize a given practice and tacitly command that it be followed. Even though the custom might have had a sociological existence apart from such recognition, it had a *juridical* existence only in virtue of this tacit adoption by the sovereign.[29] So custom was conceived reductively in the image of '*Quod principi placuit*...'.

But we are also well aware of the modern critique of that reduction, particularly in the early chapters of *The Concept of Law*. H.L.A. Hart saw the early positivists' attempt to reconceive all law in the Procrustean image of the sovereign command as one of their defects.[30] That awareness (of Hart's critique) is worth hanging on to. Since the single sovereign as law-maker is a model that already has failed reductivist pretensions in jurisprudence, we should proceed with caution in an area where, once again, it seems to be trying to reduce all models of law to a single abstract image, or to pretend that differences within that range of abstraction do not matter. I am not saying that it is necessarily ill-advised to assimilate assembly legislation to legislation by one ruler for the purposes of legal philosophy. But there is certainly room for misgiving, once we notice that the traditional sovereign model is one that has already tried and failed to render importantly diverse sources of law into its own image. My hunch, then, is that it may be as much of a mistake to assimilate legislation by assembly to legislation by a single sovereign, as it is to assimilate customary law to enacted law. Maybe our legal positivism needs a mature, non-reductive theory of diverse sources of law. Certainly we need a theory that is capable of distinguishing law-making by judges from law-making by legislatures. What I am suggesting is that we should also contemplate the possibility that the theory of law-making by large assemblies may be different from the theory of law-making by single enlightened individuals.

It may occur to readers that I am playing a little bit fast and loose with Hart's theory, accepting his refutation of the reduction of custom to sovereign command while condemning him for not attaching greater significance to articulate legislative structure. But Hart is a case on the cusp in this regard. There can be no doubt that his jurisprudence is an improvement on the old positivist model of law as sovereign command; and his theory of secondary rules is indispensable for the sort of structural analysis of the sources of law that I would like to undertake. But, in my view, Hart's model still falls well short of any interesting articulation of the idea of *lex terrae*, the law of the land. To the extent that he does approach that idea, it is more in terms of his account of 'primitive' or pre-legal society – a society whose practices consist of a simple set of primary rules.[31] That certainly looks like the sort of thing I have been talking about. However, in Hart's model, that form of primitive or proto-law is superseded by secondary rules (and by first-order rules recognized by secondary rules) which do not have any necessary independent social presence of their own. A Hartian legal system may still be understood under the auspices of the social practice conception of rules, but the crucial practices no longer subsist among the people in all their diversity; rather, they subsist among a core of officials, sufficiently strong and well-organized that they can coerce anyone in the society who is not initially a participant in their practices.[32] And although it is true that corps of officials might have their own diversity, including their own diverse reasons for participating in the secondary rules, there is nevertheless a strong sense in which Hart's conception of the secondary rules remains a kind of a sovereign conception, inasmuch as it insists that the secondary rules are practices existing mainly among a specialist elite of officials.[33] In that sense Hart's theory has a tendency – although I do not believe it was an unmitigated tendency – to view the law in rather statist terms.

In addition, Hart's approach can easily lead us to underestimate the distinctive role of both legislative assemblies and those secondary rules of change and recognition that constitute and empower legislative assemblies, even in a society otherwise dominated by a state. As I have said several times, Hart furnished modern jurisprudence with the tools it needed to comprehend legislative complexity, but the example he set was one in which the detailed deployment of these tools was taken to be unnecessary. It was not thought philosophically important for us to relate the reception, interpretation and application of the rules recognized by the rule of recognition to the structural circumstances of their genesis. There was no attempt to analyse the ambivalent relation between a large representative legislative assembly drawn from among the people, on the one hand, and the rather more cohesive organization of the state and the state's officials (including judges) with their distinctive *esprit de corps*, on the other. Thus one of the failings of modern legal positivism is that, by orienting itself unambiguously to the state and to state agencies such as courts, it has lost sight of the tension between government and law-makers, where the latter are understood as a special assembly of those who are supposed to be subject to the laws.

Legislated Custom?

I have a second medieval story to tell: this time it is from the sunny centre of medieval jurisprudence, not its damp northwestern margins. In the thirteenth and fourteenth centuries, the cities of Northern Italy were engaged fairly regularly in what we would call *legislating* – making laws on matters such as weights and measures, market rules, common commercial law, family succession, political arrangements and so on. Their civic assemblies legislated rather well on all accounts, but there was a jurisprudential problem. Theoretically the legislative activity of these cities seems to have been anomalous because the only prevailing legal theory of explicit law-making at the time was the doctrine we have already discussed: '*Quod principi placuit, legis vigorem habet*' ('What pleases the prince has the force of law'). In the context of medieval Italy 'the prince' meant the Holy Roman Emperor (to be found, usually, somewhere in Germany), and the trouble was that the emperor's attitude to cities like Pisa, Milan and Bologna ranged from complete indifference to active and militarized hostility so far as their aspirations for autonomy were concerned. To the extent that the emperor was indifferent, '*Quod principi placuit...*' was at best a fiction associated with their law-making, but to the extent that he was an authority against whom some of these cities were in open revolt, he could hardly be deemed to have given his imprimatur to their legislative activity. As long as the traditional Roman law doctrine about law-making was interpreted literally, the cities had, in Quentin Skinner's words 'no possibility of vindicating any *de jure* independence from the Empire, while the Emperors were assured of the strongest possible legal support in their campaigns to subjugate the cities'.[34]

There were all sorts of jurisprudential attempts to square this circle. In the kingdoms of Northern Europe, it was maintained that the king is emperor in his own land – '*Rex in regno suo est Imperator*' – and that was the basis of his sovereign authority to legislate. (How useful such conceptions were against baronial opposition in the name of *lex terrae* is, as we saw in previous section, quite another matter.) But such doctrines could hardly be applied to self-governing cities. Even in those cities which were ruled by single individuals, there was no question of the local tyrant regarding himself as the *princeps* for the juridical purposes of '*Quod principi placuit, vigorem legis habet*'. And certainly doctrines evolved for theocratic monarchy had little or no application to cities that retained republican forms of government, with law-making by civic assembly, rather than by anything remotely resembling regal fiat. Other possible solutions were limited in their scope. No-one denied that a corporation or a collegial body such as a university was entitled to legislate for its own internal affairs. But such legislation was limited in its application to those who were members of the body in question, whereas it was undeniable that the cities were exercising something more like territorial sovereignty – that is, the right to enact laws that would bind anyone who came within their walls or traded in their markets.

An early fourteenth-century jurist, Bartolus of Sassoferrato – in Quentin Skinner's view, 'perhaps the most original jurist of the Middle Ages'[35] – came up with an intriguing solution to this difficulty about civic legislation. The key to Bartolus's contribution to jurisprudence – what made him in the eyes of Romanists a *Post*glossator – lay in his recognition that, when the theory of Roman law appeared to contradict stable and well-established facts, it was sometimes the theory, not the facts, that ought to be modified. The cities legislate, they legislate competently, and their law-making appears to be accepted by those over whom they claim authority. If jurisprudential doctrine denies that such a legislative capacity is possible because only the emperor is sovereign, then jurisprudential doctrine must be adapted to reality.

Bartolus began by reminding his contemporaries that the requirement of the emperor's imprimatur never applied to custom or customary law; it was always understood that a people were entitled to give themselves customs as a community. So, said Bartolus, why can't we regard legislation as a *fast-track* development of custom? It is true that custom rests on the venerable principle of tacit consent but, Bartolus suggested, if you screw up your eyes tight enough and are prepared to be a little bit generous, maybe explicit consent can do as much work in authorizing legislation as tacit consent does in the traditional theory of custom. Now, of course, from our point of view, Bartolus has things exactly the wrong way around. We privilege *explicit* consent in our accounts of political obligation, and it is tacit consent that is seen as the unsatisfactory poor cousin.[36] But the background assumption in Bartolus's account is more thoughtful than it looks: tacit consent exhibited consistently in conduct over (say) ten years might have a bit more substance to it than a single impulsive verbalization of consent at a particular moment.[37] (A further important difference may be that tacit consent is oriented in the medieval account towards legitimacy rather than political obligation; the question is not 'What obligates the people to obey the laws?' but rather 'What entitles the city – as against the emperor – to legislate?') At any rate, Bartolus argued that if the basis of legitimate custom is (tacit) consent, then a legislative assembly may be seen as a form of fast-track custom emergence, with its own deliberations taking the place of the experience which generates custom, and with its voting procedures taking the place of the rough majoritarianism that characterizes the general acceptability of a customary norm over a period of time. Thus, he maintained that statute law enacted by a civic assembly might have the same standing and the same power – '*paris potentiae*' was the slogan he used – as the customs of that city.[38]

I find this a stimulating idea, not least because it seems to work in exactly the opposite direction from the reductivism we considered at the end of the previous section. There we criticized the Bentham/Austin attempt to reduce customary law to statute law. Now we are considering an attempt to understand statute law on the model of customary law. But there is this important difference: the Bentham/ Austin reduction purports to be indifferent to the structure and size of the legislature, whereas the Bartolus line of argument makes no sense if we are talking about statutes enacted by a single law-maker. The detailed analogy with custom – deliberation as experience, voting as an equivalent of broad acceptability – simply will not work unless we are talking about legislation enacted by a large assembly representing and articulating roughly the variety of interests and experiences in the community that any custom would have to confront as it developed, grew, became familiar and secured popular acceptance. We are therefore well on the way to giving some substance to our hunch at the end of the previous section that there might well be differences between legislation by one man and legislation by an assembly which are as significant for legal theory as the differences between statute and custom as sources of law.

Size, Respect and Authority

I said I would deal, secondly, with legislation by assembly in relation to *legal authority*. Is there a connection between the issue of numbers – the size or perhaps the diversity of a legislative assembly – and the authority which law claims against even the most recalcitrant citizen?

One obvious response is to ask: are we likely to get better laws when they are enacted by assemblies than when they are enacted by a small group of enlightened individuals? (To ask this question is to invoke the conception of authority developed by Joseph Raz: if, as an individual, I compare the two institutional alternatives to following my own sense of the reasons that apply to my conduct, do I do even better by following the assembly's resolutions than by following the resolutions of an enlightened legislator?[39]) The first of the philosophical difficulties I mentioned earlier – the consensus in the canon of political theory that large legislatures are an obstacle to good lawmaking – warns us not to expect an affirmative answer. Still, if one wanted to persevere, one might explore something along the lines of the argument about the wisdom of the multitude in Book 3 of Aristotle's *Politics*. Aristotle acknowledged that there are likely to be a few individuals in each society who are more knowledgeable and more enlightened than anybody else. Nonetheless, he claimed, the many, when they pool their knowledge, might be much smarter than the few wisest among them.

> For the many, of whom each individual is not a good man, when they meet together may be better than the few good, if regarded not indi-

> vidually but collectively, just as a feast to which many contribute is better than a dinner provided out of a single purse. For each individual among the many has a share of excellence and practical wisdom, and when they met together, just as they become in a manner one man, who has many feet, and hands, and senses, so too with regard to their character and thought. Hence the many are better judges than a single man of music and poetry; for some understand one part, and some another, and among them they understand the whole.[40]

Tom has experience of one aspect of the matter on which the assembly is purporting to legislate, Dick has experience of another, Harry of another and so on. They can bring these diverse experiences together in deliberation, rather in the way in which Aristotle himself (in his own method in the *Ethics*) brought together diverse little scraps of material and insight from hither and yon – proverbs, common views, fragments of others' philosophies – and synthesized something remarkable out of them.[41]

The argument is an interesting one. In the end, however, I do not think that the authority advantages of legislation by assembly are located exactly on this issue of the relative *wisdom* of the law-makers. The gain for the authority of law has more to do with the issue of plurality and disagreement; it has more to do with *fair* representation than with wise decision-making.

I would like to invoke here an idea that I have used in other writings – that of 'the *circumstances* of politics', as something analogous to what John Rawls calls the circumstances of justice.[42] In Rawls's account, the circumstances of justice are those aspects of the human condition, such as moderate scarcity and the limited altruism of individuals, which make justice both possible and necessary.[43] We may say, along similar lines, that the felt need among the members of a certain group for a common decision on some matter, together with disagreement about what that decision should be, are *the circumstances of politics*. For example, there are various views in society about property, welfare, education and race relations. We disagree very strongly about what the common settlement on these matters should be, but we strongly prefer that there *be* a common settlement rather than that each faction try to enforce its particular views as best it can.

Given these circumstances, people should not be surprised to find themselves from time to time under a legal obligation to participate in a scheme that they themselves regard as undesirable or even unjust. That is more or less bound to happen, given that it is the function of law to sustain a collective settlement in circumstances of disagreement. In modern legal philosophy we tend to think that the law is in crisis when it conflicts with the firm and conscientious moral convictions of the individual citizen. But the premise on which I am proceeding – that the point of law is to enable us to act *in the face* of disagreement – indicates that instances like these should not be regarded as limiting cases for law's authority. If moderate scarcity is one of the circumstances of justice, then inevitably not everybody will get everything they want; the inevitability of somebody being frustrated is placed therefore in the core of our theory of distributive justice, rather than on its margins or in second-best theory. Similarly, we should regard disagreement with a law on the grounds of its injustice as something likely to be found in the core of our theory of legal authority, not on its margins or in the repository of second-best theory so far as legislative authority is concerned. There would, certainly, be a crisis for legality if the extent of the perceived injustice of a given law were, in some people's view, sufficient to undermine the first circumstance of politics – namely, the sense that any agreement on this matter would be better than none. There might be an extent of injustice such that people will say, 'No. We would rather have no agreement at all than settle on something we disagree with *that* much'. But, short of that crisis, ordinary disagreement is part of the normal background to law, and I want to argue that the issue of legal authority is to be resolved not by disposing of such disagreement but by taking explicit account of it in the way we make our laws.[44]

So far as legislation is concerned, questions of legal authority are posed in the following form: can a reasonable response be made to the citizen who proposes to act on a firmly and conscientiously held view of his own about justice or public policy which is contrary to the view about justice or public policy embodied in a statute? The first thing we can do, of course, is point to the circumstances of politics: we remind the challenger that we do need a common settlement on this matter. Second, we should remind the challenger that we are also committed, particularly in modern politics, to the idea that a social settlement be adopted only after careful consideration of all the conflicting alternatives. Indeed, we should say, our ideas of political deliberation goes even further than this. It is not only that the alternatives should be considered in the way that (say) Frederick the Great might 'consider' alternative views before enacting one of them, or in the way that we academics 'take possible objections into account' as we draft our papers. The alternatives must be not only regarded but *respected*, by being actively *represented* in the law-making process. This is not just for John Stuart Mill-type reasons – the argument in *On Liberty* about the importance of dissenting views being represented in *propria persona*, rather than in the watered-down form that they tend to take in someone else's representation of them.[45] The views do need to be represented by their own advocates, in order to give them a full and vigorous hearing. But the point I am making is this: law may properly elicit allegiance only from those that the law respects; and that you respect a person not just by taking their interests and views into account, but by taking *them* into account as active intelligences and consciences.

The same point can be phrased in terms of respect for right-bearers. When we talk about rights, we emphasize in the first instance how important it is for the state and the law to recognize that I, as a citizen, have a life of my own to live. Human rights are tokens of that respect. Equally, however, it is important for the law, particularly in its secondary aspects,[46] to respect each right-bearer as an active *thinker* of laws – an active *intelligence* likely to have its own bright ideas about what we should do around here. Law has to stake its claim to authority among not only a diversity of interests but also among a diversity of law-*thinkers*. And it will be in a better position to do this if it has emerged as law in the heat of debate among such rival thinkers of law.[47]

There is a tendency to associate legislation with a certain level of noise, invective and adversarial politics, and it is sometimes difficult to relate that to the idea of authority. Surely, one might say, authority is a matter of *gravitas* – ideally, the black-robed, leather-bound, ponderous deliberation of a court. In response to that image, however, we should remember Machiavelli's advice (in the *Discourses*) not to be fooled into thinking that calmness and solemnity are necessarily the mark of a good policy, and noise and conflict a symptom of political pathology. 'Good laws', said Machiavelli, may arise 'from those tumults that many inconsiderately damn.' And he continued:

> To me it appears that those who damn the tumults between the nobles and the plebs blame those things that were the first cause of keeping Rome free, and that they consider the noises and the cries that would arise in such tumults more than the good effects that they engendered.[48]

We should look, he said, at what conflict and tumult and large numbers can accomplish for liberty, and not be too easily disconcerted by the noisy or unsavoury atmosphere of the popular assembly.

Let me return, then, to the point about the circumstances of politics, as the context in which challenges to law's authority have to be assessed. It is important to be able to say to the challenger not only that, of course, some people are bound to disagree with law and that that is simply the circumstance in which law operates, but also that those disagreements were aired as forcefully and as fiercely as possible at the time the law was enacted, in a fair process of deliberation, and that choice was made among them on a basis that was fair to all the citizens – that is, all the potential law-thinkers in the community.

(One has to flesh this out, of course, with an account of the fairness of majority voting among equals in the circumstances of politics.[49]) If we can say something like that, then it seems to me that we have a better answer to the person who challenges a statute on moral grounds than by investing all our energies in trying to show that he or she is more likely than the legislature to be mistaken in his or her reasoning.

So the issue of authority does share an important connection with the representation within the legislature of all the importantly diverse views in the community (that is, of all the views that might subsequently form the basis of a challenge to the authority of the law). It is not enough to have one person trying to represent diverse views in his or her own mind; they should be present *in propria persona*, each arguing its case as forcefully as it can. And certainly it is not enough to have law emerging from political conflict in the rather shamefaced way that happens in a court decision, with judges doing their best to conceal the fact that their decision represents just one rival view among others. That's not the way to *respect* one's moral or ideological adversaries. For all its black robes and leather-bound splendour, the character of the judicial process is not something one can credibly invoke as the basis for a respectful response to a good-faith challenge to the morality of a legal decision. By contrast, an appeal to the procedures of a legislative assembly, with all the principal views in the community actively represented by their most forceful advocates, *is* a respectful response to the challenge. For one can say, 'We had to decide on one view among all the alternatives, and we gave each of the alternatives the fairest hearing and the fairest prospect of victory that was possible consistent with equal respect for them all'.

Legislative Interpretation

There are many people who refuse to regard work as jurisprudentially interesting unless it eventually comes down to something that affects the way judges reason. Personally, I think that the points I have been making *are* important for the way in which we think about courts, inasmuch as the legitimacy of judicial review often depends on a rather mindless denigration of the modern process of legislation by assembly. US jurisprudence, especially, is devoted almost unanimously to the denigration of legislation by assembly as deal-making, log-rolling, pork-barrelling, Arrovian cycling – *anything*, except dignified law-making. In US jurisprudence nobody would dream of adopting the same sort of rose-tinted view of the legislature as they do every day for the courts.[50] Here, I have been trying to develop an attractive and realistic ideal of the legislative assembly which we can then place alongside our normative picture of the courts in order to assess their rival claims as respectable sources of law.

This brings me to my third point: the effect that all this might have on theories of legislative interpretation. The particular issue I want to address is the issue of appeal to legislative history as a basis for ascertaining legislative intent. (I mean the sort of practice that was only recently legitimized in England by the House of Lords in the case of *Pepper* v. *Hart*,[51] but which has long been endemic in the USA, where attorneys will spend hours pouring over the legislative records trying to find some favourable scrap of comment by some legislator, often inserted into the record precisely for that purpose by the legislator in question.[52] It is often assumed that people who believe strongly in the legitimacy of legislatures must also believe in the legitimacy of this way of resolving interpretive disputes. I want to show that, although such appeals to legislative history *might* make sense if we were talking about a single legislative sovereign,[53] such an approach is much less plausible when we are talking about a legislative assembly. And this is not merely because of the technical difficulties of concocting a single intention out of an assembly of people with rival and diverse views;[54] it is also because of fundamental issues about validity and recognition in the context of law-making by a deliberative assembly.

Let me begin the argument with some rather abstract remarks about recognition. In modern jurisprudence we are familiar with the concept of *a rule of recognition*, as a crucial type of secondary rule, from H.L.A. Hart's book *The Concept of Law*. Hart suggested that, if a society develops procedures for changing the rules of conduct upheld in that society, then it will also need to introduce or develop a second-order rule which enables its members (or at least some effective subset of its members) to distinguish between those rules or purported rules which currently have the society's imprimatur and those which do not. A rule of recognition, Hart said:

> ... will specify some features or features possession of which by a suggested rule is taken as a conclusive affirmative indication that it is a rule of the group to be supported by the social pressure that it [i.e. the group] exerts.[55]

A crude rule of recognition might specify a list somewhere carved on some public monument, and it may stipulate that if a putative rule is not on that list, it does not count, for the time being, as one of the rules of the group. A more sophisticated rule of recognition might refer us to the certified record of legislative enactments such as an official gazette or to the official law reports.

But although Hart's work made us familiar with the part played by the rule of recognition in a legal system, he did not invent the idea nor was he the first to see its importance. The idea of a rule of recognition plays a role also in Thomas Hobbes's philosophy of law, written some 300 years previously.[56] Like Hart, Hobbes distinguished between the judgement a person might make concerning the morality of a rule and the judgement he might make concerning its legal validity. For Hobbes, the importance of this distinction lay in the social value of having a single legal framework even in the midst of moral disagreement: people who disagree about right and wrong, just and unjust, can nevertheless agree on the need to organize social life on the basis of one set of determinate answers to those questions, even if many of them individually judge those determinate answers to be in themselves unwise or morally incorrect. That the measure one thinks wicked is nevertheless *a valid law* is a judgement that alerts a person disposed to disobey the measure (for example, on moral grounds) to the dangers of unilateral and uncoordinated action in a context of disagreement.[57]

This also provides the basis of Hobbes' conception of the importance of a secondary rule of recognition in relation to law-making. The business of legislating addresses the problem of competition between rival views and interests. Different people hold, and are willing to fight for, rival definitions of justice and the common good (whether because their particular definition advances their material interests or simply because they are, in some other fashion, attached to a particular definition). That is the context that makes legislation necessary, but it is also the context that makes secondary rules, like rules of recognition, necessary. We need a rule of recognition on Hobbes's account, not just because there is uncertainty as to what the law is but also because there is disagreement in the community as to what ought to be taken as law. Says Hobbes:

> Nor is it enough the Law be written and published; but also that there be manifest signs, that it proceedeth from the will of the Soveraign. For private men, when they have or think they have force enough to secure their unjust designes, and convoy them safely to their ambitious ends, may publish for Lawes what they please without, or against the Legislative Authority. There is therefore requisite, not only a Declaration of the Law, but also sufficient signes of the Author, and Authority.[58]

Such signs, Hobbes says, will depend on accessible criteria of validity such as 'publique Registers, publique Counsels, publique Ministers, and publique Seals'.[59] On this account, the apparatus of legal recognition is oriented to a compelling and substantive political end – that of ensuring that, when someone faces what purports to be a legal demand, he or she can ascertain whether that demand really *is* playing the role which Hobbesian law and Hobbesian legal validity aspire to play so far as the diminution of social conflict is concerned. In other words, there has to be some way of distinguishing real legislation from forged legislation – real laws from fake laws. If someone rides into my village and announces 'It is now the law that we all have to worship as Presbyterians', I am going to insist on examining the authenticity of the 'statutory text' that he is waving. If I recognize it as authentic, then I will understand that we are settling on Presbyterian forms of worship in order to put an end to our otherwise internecine religious conflicts. But if the person who made the announcement cannot produce authentication, then his 'proclamation' of what the law is will have to be dismissed as another stratagem in the religious wars, not (as a law would be) a way of ending them.

The general point illustrated by Hobbes's discussion is that one's account of rules of recognition is necessarily connected to one's account of what ultimately matters about the law-making process. For Hobbes what ultimately matters in law-making is univocality, determinacy, decisiveness and the resolution of social conflict; without these, he thinks, we are no better off with law than we would be without it. What one needs to know, therefore, in the way of recognition, is that the purported law really does have the features of univocality, determinacy and so on associated with Hobbesian sovereignty. If everyone is announcing laws on their our own authority without reference to a sovereign, we might as well have no law at all so far as the Hobbesian theory is concerned. The state of nature would simply reproduce itself as a war of rival pseudo-laws and we would be back where we began, before there was any authoritative law-making at all.

In modern democracies, which are no less riven by moral and ideological disagreement, we take a slightly different approach as to what matters in law-making. Certainly univocality and determinacy matter to us more or less in the way they mattered to Hobbes: we too value legal certainty. But it also matters to us that legislation should emerge from a process that is genuinely *deliberative* – that is, a process distinguished not just by its Hobbesian decisiveness but also by the engagement in formal deliberation of all the views that might reasonably be thought competitive with whatever legislative proposal is under consideration. If there are rival proposals, then they should contend in an explicit form for this coveted status of legality, and there should be a fiery and open debate. We believe that such views should confront one another directly and explicitly (as a matter of respect for the intelligence of those who hold them) and that laws should be crafted in the heat of the debate that results. As I have insisted throughout this chapter, modern legislatures are structured to secure this process, with rules about representation, parties, hearings, debates, amendments and, above all, rules about voting.

Now, as I stated earlier, Hart's jurisprudence has the virtue that it has the capacity to account for the normative, rule-governed character of this structuring. What is less apparent from Hart's account – what one wishes he had developed further – is the connection between (1) this structuring function of secondary rules, (2) the recognition function of secondary rules, and (3) the moral authority that valid law *qua* law is conceived to have in the community. In *Leviathan*, the connections between the Hobbesian versions of (1), (2) and (3) is fairly clear:

1 structuring is a matter of decision procedure and decisiveness;
2 recognition is a matter of ensuring that the univocality of that decisiveness is not undermined by the attempts of various competing forces in society to give spurious legal effect to their own particular views; and
3 validity is the assurance that a person has, in regard to a set of rules, that compliance with *those rules* really can make a decisive difference to the otherwise intractable problem of social order.

In Hart's theory, by contrast, the connection between (1) and (2) is left largely unexplained: we are told nothing except that (1) and (2) address separate problems of a pre-legal society – namely, rigidity and uncertainty. Moreover any connection between them and (3) is positively denied.[60] Now Hart justifies that denial partly in the interests of conceptual pragmatic clarity: he insists that the source and validity of a law is one thing and its claim on us is another.[61] But it would perhaps have been clearer and more helpful to distinguish between the claims that law has on us *qua* law, and the final all-things-considered claim that law has on us in relation to its justice, righteousness and general desirability.[62] Certainly, the *final* claim that law has on us is conditional, and any account of that claim – certainly any account that Hart would offer – will be a hesitant and uneasy one. But there might be something to say, nonetheless, about the moral importance of legal validity – what it contributes, at least *prima facie*, to social order – not just about the distinctiveness of the concept. And I suspect that that something ought to be connected with Hart's version of (1) and (2), and with the version of his theory, which he failed to supply, of the intimate connection between them.

With all this in mind, let us return now to the issue of legislative history. I indicated earlier that there are various reasons for being suspicious of appeals to legislative history in statutory interpretation. The issue can usefully be presented partly as one of recognition.

What exactly is to be recognized – by the rule of recognition – as a part of the legislation? What are we to take as the 'outer limits', so to speak, of the statute we have to interpret? Does it stop short at the edge of the enacted text or does it also include other parts of the deliberative record?

One problem with according authority to other parts of the deliberative record is that it blurs the line between deliberation and enactment. In its ideal form, deliberation is understood to involve a whole array of contributions from various representatives, many of which will stand in a dialectical relation to whatever is eventually enacted. Some of the contributions will be in direct opposition to the proposed bills; some will be expressions of lukewarm support, or rebuttal of particular objections; others may support the measure with an enthusiasm that goes somewhat beyond its terms. Even among the wholehearted supporters, some will be inclined to spin the understanding of the bill one way and others will be inclined to spin it in a slightly different direction. Of this array of contributions to the legislative debate, the traditional rule has been that the only ones with legal authority are those in the text that was actually put to a vote.[63] So far as that rule is concerned, we have a determinate procedure for sorting, as it were, the wheat from the chaff: there are rules that tell us:

1 how to identify (what are the authoritative marks of) the motion under discussion;
2 what processes to watch for, so far as amendments to the motion are concerned;
3 what is to count as the common text in a multistage or multicameral process of legislation; and
4 what is the decision procedure for voting.

There are no such rules with respect to all the things said in deliberation. If legislators B and C disagree about the correctness or the authority of something said by legislator A about the statute, there are no rules – apart from the ones I have mentioned, which are focused on the text of the statute – for resolving the disagreement. Furthermore, there are no rules alerting any other legislator to the significance of what legislator A might be saying or trying to read into the record. After all, the one advantage of explicit procedural rules is that they alert the members of the assembly to the various points in their proceedings that might matter so far as the subsequent authority and interpretation of their handiwork is concerned.[64] So there is always going to be a problem of authority in representing a particular contribution as a part of the legislation, or as canonically pertinent to its interpretation. A person faced with such a representation is being required, in effect, to accept something as law (or as canonically relevant to the interpretation of law)[65] despite the fact that it has not been marked as law and is not a rule recognizable as law (against a background of disagreement) for the purposes for which we think marking and recognizing something as law is important.

We do value deliberation in our processes of legal change. But it is surely a necessary implication of that value – and important in direct proportion to the importance of energetic and adversarial deliberation – that *not everything which is said in legislative debate can have legislative authority*. Accordingly, we value the integrity of a deliberative politics that ends in a formal procedure such as voting, so that there is a fair and ascertainable basis for determining *which*, among the various contributions that have been made in debate, are to count a part of the law and which are not. Our notion of validity, oriented as it is to the explicit process of enactment, is supposed to provide us with a bright line that secures for us a legislative process that is both deliberative and decisive. It is arguable, then, that appeals to extratextual evidence of legislative intent muddy the waters, so far as the recognition of law is concerned, in exactly the way (though perhaps for better motives) that Hobbes's 'private men' try to muddy the waters and who, 'when they have or think they have force enough to secure their unjust designes,... may publish for Lawes what they please without, or against the Legislative Authority'.[66]

Notes

1 See the discussion of institutional interrelationships in Henry M. Hart and Albert M. Sacks, *The Legal Process: Basic Problems in the Making and Application of Law*, ed. William N. Eskridge and Philip P. Frickey (Westbury, NY: Foundation Press, 1994), pp. 158–67.

2 For the difference between theories of legislation and theories of legislatures, see Jeremy Waldron, *Law and Disagreement* (Oxford: Clarendon Press, 1998), ch. 2, esp. pp. 21–4.

3 See Jeremy Waldron, 'What Pluto Would Allow', in Ian Shapiro and Judith Wagner DeCew (eds), *Nomos XXXVII: Theory and Practice* (New York: New York University Press, 1995), pp. 138, esp. pp. 170–1.

4 The current proposal to eliminate hereditary peers from legislative authority in the House of Lords will reduce the numbers significantly (unless an equivalent number of life peers is appointed).

5 See generally Nelson, Polsby, *Congress and the Presidency*, 3rd edn (Englewood Cliffs, NJ: Prentice Hall, 1976), p. 131.

6 See Walter Bagehot, *The English Constitution* (London: Oxford University Press, 1928), p. 4.

7 Thomas Hobbes, *Leviathan*, ed. Richard Tuck (Cambridge: Cambridge University Press, 1988), ch. 16, pp. 114–15.

8 See Hanna Fenichel Pitkin, *The Concept of Representation* (Berkeley: University of California Press, 1972).

[9] In a sense, Hobbes regarded democracy as the *ur*-form of government: 'The first in order of time of these three sorts [of government] is democracy, and it must be so of necessity, because an aristocracy and a monarchy, require nomination of persons agreed upon; which agreement in a great multitude of men must consist in the consent of the major part; and where the votes of the major part involve the votes of the rest, there is actually a democracy: Thomas Hobbes, *De Corpore Politico*, ed. J.C.A. Gaskin (Oxford: Oxford University Press, 1994), ch. 21, pp. 118–19.

[10] Hobbes, *Leviathan, op. cit.*, ch. 19, p. 132.

[11] Jean-Jacques Rousseau, *The Social Contract*, trans. Maurice Cranston (Harmondsworth: Penguin Books, 1968), bk. II, chs 6–7, pp. 83–8.

[12] See Marquis de Condorcet, 'Essay on the Application of Mathematics to the Theory of Decision-Making', in Keith Michael Baker (ed.), *Condorcet: Selected Writings* (Indianapolis: Bobbs-Merrill, 1976).

[13] For an outline, see Waldron, *Law and Disagreement, op. cit.*, n. 43, p. 135.

[14] Ibid., p. 49. See also David Estlund, Jeremy Waldron, Bernard Grofman and Scott Feld, 'Democratic Theory and the Public Interest: Condorcet and Rousseau Revisited', *American Political Science Review*, **83** (1989), pp. 1317–40.

[15] James Madison, Alexander Hamilton and John Jay, *The Federalist Papers*, ed. Isaac Kramnick (Harmondsworth: Penguin Books, 1987), Numbers LV and LVII, pp. 336 and 351.

[16] Bagehot, *The English Constitution, op. cit.*, pp. 122–3. A similar point by Blackstone is discussed in David Lieberman, *The Province of Legislation Determined: Legal Theory in Eighteenth Century Britain* (Cambridge: Cambridge University Press, 1989), p. 62. See also John Stuart Mill, *Considerations on Representative Government* (Buffalo, NY: Prometheus Books, 1991), ch. V, p. 109.

[17] John Locke, *Two Treatises of Government*, ed. Peter Laslett (Cambridge: Cambridge University Press, 1988), II, ch. vii, sect. 94, pp. 329–30.

[18] For doubts even about this, see Joseph Raz, *Practical Reason and Norms*, 2nd edn (Princeton, NJ: Princeton University Press, 1990), pp. 129–48. See also the discussion in Waldron, *Law and Disagreement, op. cit.*, pp. 34–5.

[19] See Joseph Raz, *The Authority of Law: Essays on Law and Morality* (Oxford: Clarendon Press, 1979), p. 47.

[20] For this general point, see Waldron, *Law and Disagreement, op. cit.*, pp. 42–8.

[21] This is Joseph Raz's way of putting the point, in conversation with the author.

[22] Jeremy Bentham, *Of Laws in General* ed. H.L.A. Hart (London: Athlone Press, 1970), p. 18, emphasis added. Austin's language is similar: 'Every positive law, or every law simply and strictly so called, is set by a sovereign person, or a sovereign body of person, to a member or members of the independent political society wherein that person or body is sovereign or supreme': John Austin, *Lectures on Jurisprudence*, 5th edn, ed. R. Campbell (London: J. Murray, 1885), Lecture VI.

[23] In Jeremy Bentham's *Introduction to the Principles of Morals and Legislation*, ed. J.H. Burns and H.L.A. Hart (London: Methuen, 1982), the implicit recipient of Bentham's advice almost always appears in the text as 'the legislator', with scarcely a reference to the pluralistic possibility. And this despite Bentham's insistence that he was talking about those who actually make laws, not just the monarchs who sign them: 'I speak here of those who frame laws, not of these who touch them with a sceptre' (ibid., p. 238n).

[24] See H.L.A. Hart, *The Concept of Law*, 2nd edn (Oxford: Clarendon Press, 1994), pp. 52–61.

[25] Magna Carta, *c*. 39. See also Walter Ullmann, *Principles of Government and Politics in the Middle Ages* (London: Methuen, 1961), pp. 163–4.

[26] I have in mind examples such as the Assembly at Merton (1234–35), which discussed whether the principle of legitimation by a subsequent marriage was to be adopted in England, and in which the barons resolved '*nolumus mutare leges Angliae*'.

See Walter Ullmann, *Jurisprudence in the Middle Ages* (London: Variorum Reprints, 1980), I, p. 62.

[27] Ullmann, *Principles of Government*, *op. cit.*, p. 190.

[28] Bentham, *Of Laws in General*, *op. cit.*, p. 235.

[29] For some discussion of important differences between Bentham, on the one hand, and Hobbes and Austin, on the other, so far as the reduction of custom to posited law is concerned, see Jeremy Waldron, 'Custom Redeemed by Statute', *Current Legal Problems*, **51** (1998), pp. 93–114.

[30] Hart, *The Concept of Law*, *op. cit.*, pp. 45–9.

[31] Ibid., p. 91.

[32] See ibid., pp. 94–8, 112–17, and 200–2.

[33] See Jeremy Waldron, 'All We Like Sheep', *Canadian Journal of Law and Jurisprudence* (1999, forthcoming).

[34] Quentin Skinner, *The Foundations of Modern Political Thought*, Vol. 1: *The Renaissance* (Cambridge: Cambridge University Press, 1978), pp. 7–8.

[35] Ibid., p. 9. See also Ullmann, *Principles of Government*, *op. cit.*, p. 266, for the reputation of Bartolus as *princeps juristorum*. (Bartolus lived from 1314 to 1357.)

[36] See A. John Simmons, *Moral Principles and Political Obligation* (Princeton, NJ: Princeton University Press, 1979), chs 3–4.

[37] For a helpful discussion, see Joseph Canning, *The Political Thought of Baldus de Ubaldis* (Cambridge: Cambridge University Press, 1988), p. 100.

[38] See Ullmann, *Principles of Government*, *op. cit.*, p. 283.

[39] See Joseph Raz, *The Morality of Freedom* (Oxford: Clarendon Press, 1986), chs. 2–4, esp. p. 53 for what Raz calls *the normal justification thesis*: '[T]he normal way to establish that a person has authority over another person involves showing that the alleged subject is likely better to comply with reasons which apply to him (other than the alleged authoritative directives) if he accepts the directives as authoritatively binding and tries to follow them, rather than by trying to follow the reasons which apply to him directly.'

[40] Aristotle, *The Politics*, ed. Stephen Everson (Cambridge: Cambridge University Press, 1988), p. 66 (bk. III, ch. xi, 1281a43).

[41] See Aristotle, *Nichomachean Ethics*, trans. H. Rackham (London: Heinemann, 1934), p. 377 (bk. VII, ch. 1, 1145b1). See also the discussion in Jeremy Waldron, 'The Wisdom of the Multitude: Some Reflections on bk. III, ch. 11 of Aristotle's *Politics*', *Political Theory*, **23** (1995), esp. pp. 570–1.

[42] See Jeremy Waldron, 'The Circumstances of Integrity', *Legal Theory*, **3** (1997), esp. pp. 2–3, and also Waldron, *Law and Disagreement*, *op. cit.*, pp. 101–3.

[43] John Rawls, *A Theory of Justice* (Cambridge, MA: Harvard University Press, 1971), pp. 126 ff.

[44] See Waldron, 'Circumstances of Integrity', *op. cit.*, pp. 21–2.

[45] See John Stuart Mill, *On Liberty* (Indianapolis: Bobbs Merrill, 1956), Ch. 2, p. 45: 'Nor is it enough that [a deliberator] should hear the arguments of adversaries from his own teachers, presented as they state them, and accompanied by what they offer as refutations. This is not the way to do justice to the arguments, or bring them into real contact with his own mind. He must be able to hear them from persons who actually believe them; who defend them in earnest, and do their very utmost for them.'

[46] Using Hart's sense of 'secondary': *The Concept of Law*, *op. cit.*, pp. 94 ff.

[47] For right-bearers as right-*thinkers*, see Waldron, *Law and Disagreement*, *op. cit.*, pp. 221–31 and 249–52.

[48] Nicolà Machiavelli, *Discourses on Livy*, trans. Harvey C. Mansfield and Nathan Tarcov (Chicago: University of Chicago Press, 1996), bk. I, ch. 4, p. 16.

[49] See Jeremy Waldron, 'Legislation, Authority and Voting', *Georgetown Law*

Review, **84** (1996), p. 2185, esp. pp. 2206 ff. See also Waldron, *Law and Disagreement, op. cit.*, 111 ff.

[50] For a particularly forceful statement of this point, see Roberto Mangabeira Unger, *What Should Legal Analysis Become?* (London: Verso, 1996), pp. 72–3.

[51] *Pepper* v. *Hart* 3 WLR [1992].

[52] See Antonin Scalia, *A Matter of Interpretation: Federal Courts and the Law* (Princeton: Princeton University Press, 1997), p. 34: 'One of the routine tasks of the Washington lawyer-lobbyist is to draft language that sympathetic legislators can recite in a prewritten "floor debate" – or, even better, insert into a committee report.'

[53] Cf. Andrei Marmor, *Interpretation and Legal Theory* (Oxford: Clarendon Press, 1992). But even in the case of the single law-maker, we would still face the problem of deciding which mental states exactly – hopes, expectations, wishes, counterfactual wishes, etc. – of the legislators we were trying to plumb: see Ronald Dworkin, *Law's Empire* (Cambridge, MA: Harvard University Press, 1986), pp. 321–33.

[54] See ibid., p. 320. See also Kenneth A. Shepsle, 'Congress is a "They," Not an "It": Legislative Intent as Oxymoron', *International Review of Law and Economics*, **12** (1992), p. 239.

[55] Hart, *The Concept of Law, op. cit.*, p. 94.

[56] To cite Hobbes as an antecedent is not to diminish Hart's contribution; but I believe that if we think about rules of recognition in a Hobbesian light we get a better and more interesting view of the contribution that this idea makes in legal and political theory.

[57] See generally, Hobbes, *Leviathan, op. cit.*, chs 17–26.

[58] Ibid., ch. 26, p. 189.

[59] Hobbes went on to describe these registers, seals, etc. as the means 'by which all laws are sufficiently verified, verified, I say, not authorized, for the verification is but the testimony and the record, not the authority of the law' (ibid.). (I read this as pointing to the distinction between rules of legal change and rules of recognition. Compare the endnote on this issue in Hart, *The Concept of Law, op. cit.*, p. 294.)

[60] Hart, *The Concept of Law, op. cit.*, pp. 92 ff.

[61] Ibid., pp. 200–12. See also Waldron, 'All We Like Sheep', *op. cit.*

[62] Cf. Dworkin, *Law's Empire, op. cit.*, pp. 108–13.

[63] See Jeremy Waldron, 'The Dignity of Legislation', *Maryland Law Review*, **54** (1995), p. 633 at pp. 651–65. See also Waldron, *Law and Disagreement, op. cit.*, pp. 75–87.

[64] But see also Dworkin, *Law's Empire, op. cit.*, pp. 342–3 for the possibility of informal rules in this regard.

[65] See also the distinction between 'permissive' and 'mandatory' legal sources in Hart, *The Concept of Law, op. cit.*, p. 294. I am grateful to Leslie Green for drawing this passage to my attention.

[66] Hobbes, *Leviathan, op. cit.*, ch. 26, p. 189.

12 Defining Judicial Restraint

JOHN DALEY[1]

Introduction

'Judicial restraint' and 'judicial activism' are time-honoured legal terms. In the last few years, they have become common political currency in debates over the Australian High Court. But the limited literature which attempts to define these terms explicitly is not particularly satisfactory. I provide a more rigorous definition for 'judicial restraint', at least in the context of constitutional decisions. This definition will then lead to a definition of 'judicial activism'.

My conclusion is that restraint in constitutional cases is a distinctive disposition towards the judicial role. It adheres to two propositions:

1 Judges should make decisions in constitutional cases on the basis of previously posited rules so as to facilitate self-direction;
2 Judges should avoid exercising functions other than deciding on their own role and enforcing posited rules so as to facilitate self-direction.

Judicial restraint is not a simplistic claim that judges should *never* make law; rather it is a complex claim that they should *avoid* doing so except in so far as it is necessary to apply previously posited rules.

My method for defining restraint is to take a number of doctrines which have been identified as doctrines of judicial restraint. I then identify what they have in common. This process – which might be described as 'interpretation' or 'reflective equilibrium' – may result in a limited redefinition of which legal doctrines are truly doctrines of restraint, and hence to a refinement of my definition of restraint itself. I seek to show that my definition, in contrast with other definitions of restraint, identifies more clearly what doctrines of restraint have in common.

Lawyers often speak of 'conservative' judges. But they do not use the adjective in its usual political sense. 'Conservative' (or 'restrained') judges may have quite left-wing opinions about the redistribution of wealth or the need for state intervention. Judges are 'conservative' because of their attitudes to the judicial process and the appropriate role of judges within it. 'Restraint', therefore, is different from conventional political categories. Furthermore, the concept of restraint appears to have some coherence. Lawyers will often make accurate predictions of a judge's decision on the basis of their *judicial*, rather than their *political*, conservatism. Judges who subscribe firmly to some of the doctrines of restraint usually subscribe firmly to the others.[2]

To some extent my project of definition is descriptive: what do restrained judges do? It turns out that restraint is more complex than merely an assertion that judges should 'do their job'. On my definition, restrained judges make predictable decisions when faced with some classes of choices which are otherwise underdetermined. Because my definition prescribes outcomes, it provides a basis for evaluating claims that the Australian High Court has, or has not, been more activist in recent years.

However, as I show, it is impossible to define what restrained judges do without asking: how are restrained judges' decisions justified? As often happens when describing justifications, this part of the project must consider the coherence of the justifications and thus the justifiability of judicial restraint itself. My investigation reveals more complexity than conventional appeals to the courts' lack of democratic legitimacy. Ultimately, my definition goes some way towards answering claims that judicial restraint is unjustified.

Doctrines of Restraint

A doctrine of judicial restraint is a legal doctrine to which judges explicitly appeal in judgments as a justification for a particular decision. Abraham gives the most extensive list, identifying 16 doctrines of restraint.[3] He does not claim that 'restrained' judges always follow every doctrine, nor does he claim that 'activist' judges never resort to them. The claim is one of degree: restrained judges are more likely to appeal to doctrines of restraint, and are less willing to consider creating or applying exceptions to them. However, activist judges may deny that some, or all, of the doctrines are a valid basis for any decision at all. The first 16 items on the following list follow Abraham, albeit slightly reordered to clarify my subsequent analysis.

Matter

Judges should only decide a legal question if at least two parties disagree over that question and the relevant law applies to the parties. In Australian terminology there must be a 'matter'; in the United States there must be a 'case or controversy'.[4] The doctrine is an umbrella for other doctrines of judicial restraint, including that a court should refuse to provide an 'advisory opinion', refuse to decide moot questions, refuse to decide cases which are not yet ripe, and refuse to decide constitutional questions when interpretation of the statute makes the constitutional question moot. As I will show, each of these doctrines, like other doctrines of restraint, is not absolute. Rather, it is a question of more or less. The more restrained judge is less ready to find that there is a matter; the more activist judge is more ready to do so.

Advisory Opinions

Judges should refuse to provide an 'advisory opinion'.[5] This requirement is an element of the first doctrine, that judges should only decide if there is a 'matter'. Before proceeding to the merits, restrained judges look for a more concrete relationship between the applicant's situation and the orders sought.

Mootness

Judges should only decide live issues: they should not decide a legal question if its outcome is moot for the parties. Restrained judges require the applicant's interest to fall within more conventional legal categories of interest, and require more certainty that the court's order will affect the applicant. Mootness is sometimes distinguished from ripeness. Both doctrines refuse to consider the issue because any remedy will not affect the litigants. Whereas a case is moot if the interaction between the litigants is now completed so that the court's remedy will be irrelevant to the respondent, a case is not ripe if the litigants must interact in the future before it is clear that the court's intervention will affect the respondent. Again mootness and ripeness are elements of the requirement that there be a 'matter'.

Judicial Parsimony

Judges should not decide a constitutional issue if resolving a question of statutory construction makes the constitutional point moot.

Exhaustion of Other Remedies

Judges should not consider a case until the applicant has exhausted other remedies, such as internal administrative review and applications to courts lower in the judicial hierarchy. This may be considered an element of the doctrine that cases should not be determined until they are ripe. Activist judges are more prepared to relax this rule on the basis that other remedies would not be effective, or that exhausting other remedies would serve no purpose in the instant case.

Standing

Judges should strictly apply the rules of standing: unless the applicant has a close personal interest in the outcome, judges should refuse to proceed to the legal merits of a case.[6] Standing is sometimes described as the requirement that the law have greater effect on the applicant than the general public. This formula is misleading. An applicant has standing if, for example, there is a prosecution against the applicant, even though the terms of the law apply equally to all persons. The real test is one of close personal interest in the outcome. More restrained judges require the applicant to have a more clearly defined personal interest, more readily distinguishable from the interests of the general public.

Benefit/Burden

Judges should not consider the constitutionality of a statute if the applicant has already accepted its benefits. This doctrine has no obvious counterpart in Australian jurisprudence. Presumably restrained judges are more ready to find that a statute provides a 'benefit', and are more ready to find that an appellant's conduct amounts to an acceptance of that benefit.

Substantialness

Judges should not consider constitutional issues which are not substantial – that is, the doctrine of *de minimis* applies to constitutional law. Activist judges are more likely to find that a minor constitutional infringement, in fact, has a substantial impact.

Questions of Fact

Judges should only review questions of law and refuse to review questions of fact decided by an administrator or a first-instance judge (although, of course, the fact/law distinction is notoriously elusive).

Restrained judges are more prepared to characterize a question as one of fact, not law, and less prepared to relax the doctrine in the particular case. The doctrine's application also depends on the context. Whereas the Australian High Court generally refuses to grant special leave to cases which turn on a question of fact, the Court will not refuse to consider a constitutional challenge merely because the application of the Constitution turns on a question of fact.[7] Nevertheless, it may be a doctrine of restraint in constitutional cases to prefer an interpretation which means that the case at bar and future cases turn on legal, rather than factual, questions.[8]

Precedent

Judges should apply precedent strictly, at the level of generality identified as significant in the original precedent.[9] Restrained judges are less likely to create new exceptions to existing precedential rules, and less likely to apply existing rule to new situations not within the ambit of the original rule.[10]

Political Questions

Judges should avoid deciding 'political questions' which involve particular classes of issues better determined by other branches of government. Although this doctrine is well-developed in the United States, it is less formalized in Australia.[11] Restrained judges interpret the political questions doctrine so as to cover a broader class of cases, and are more ready to find that particular facts fall within one of those classes.

Presumption of Constitutionality

Judges should presume a statute constitutionally valid unless there is a 'clear' argument to the contrary. Restrained judges are less likely to find a contrary argument 'clear'. The High Court has all but universally rejected this approach.[12] Ironically, its most forceful Australian proponent, Murphy J, is usually regarded as one of the more activist judges in the Court's history.

Presumption of Legitimate Motives

Judges should presume that legislative and executive motives were legitimate unless there is clear evidence to the contrary.[13] Restrained judges are more likely to place a benign interpretation on legislative and executive actions.

Severability

Judges should presume that any invalid provision is severable from the remainder of the statute. Restrained judges are more prepared to hold that an invalid provision is not essential to the efficacy of the remainder of the statute.

Avoidance of Purely Political Assessments

Judges should avoid making decisions *purely* on the basis of their own political assessment.[14] Abraham does not explain how he distinguishes between this doctrine and the next.

Avoidance of Purely Policy Assessments

Judges should avoid making decisions *purely* on the basis of their own policy judgements.

A number of other doctrines are commonly cited as being part of judicial restraint. Abraham does not explain whether he has any reason for omitting them from his list.

Textualism

Judges should decide by applying the 'plain meaning' of a relevant legal text (archetypally the Constitution) rather than deciding on the basis of the 'purposes' of the provision.[15] Given the complex linguistic issues raised by 'plain meaning', a brief excursus is necessary.

Fuller claimed that a rule cannot be applied without reference to its purpose.[16] However, the whole point of an entrenched rule is that it can be applied distinctly from its justification.[17] But posited rule and justification are not rigidly divided. The referent of a word is influenced by what justifications for the act described are plausible in the circumstances. For example, 'paint the window' and 'break the window' refer to two different actions, as do 'paint the window for the blackout' and 'break the window where the wood is rotten'.[18] My understanding of 'window' in each command is guided both by how 'window' has been used in that language in the past and by what meaning of 'window' is plausible given everything I know about the context. A meaning is plausible because it describes an act either which I have experienced, or which is justified, or which I think that others might consider justified.[19]

Thus, understanding language involves me in balancing my knowledge of what is justified, what others think justified and how words are commonly used. One can vary the relative weight given to pragmatic (that is, contextual) considerations on the one hand and a text's lexical and syntactical meaning on the other.[20] A restrained judge will be more ready to interpret words accepting to their more common usages and will be less ready to interpret words by reference to what he or she thinks is justified. In Dworkin's terms,[21] we might say that, in interpreting a legal text, a restrained judge gives less weight to justification, and greater weight to 'fit' with existing linguistic practices.

Deference to Administrative Decisions

Judges should defer to any plausible interpretation of a statute by an agency where that interpretation is within the agency's sphere of expertise. This doctrine is sometimes cited as one of judicial restraint.[22] Like the presumption of constitutionality above, the doctrine is well-developed in the United States, but not accepted in Australia.[23] Australian judges have only applied the more limited doctrine of questions of fact – namely, that a judge should not overrule an administrator's factual conclusions merely because, in the judge's opinion, a different conclusion would be preferable.

Decision According to an Articulated Rule

Justice Scalia argued that judges should try to decide uncertain cases by articulating a dispositive rule rather than as the result of a conclusion 'in all the circumstances', which does not explain which of those circumstances is crucial.[24] At least some commentators would not consider this a doctrine of judicial restraint. Indeed, Sunstein claimed the opposite: that a restrained judge *avoids* articulating the decisive rule by giving an 'incompletely theorized' judgment.[25]

Restrictive Interpretation of Individual Rights

It is sometimes thought that a restrictive interpretation of constitutional individual rights is a doctrine of restraint. It may be, however, that this is merely a particular case of the restrained judge's preference to avoid judgments based on considerations of policy – that is, what is morally justified.

Remedies Requiring Supervision

O'Hair claims that it is a doctrine of judicial restraint to avoid ordering a remedy which would require continued judicial supervision.[26] Again, this doctrine is missing from many other lists.[27]

What Doctrines Imply for a Definition

Various scholars accept various permutations of these doctrines of restraint. Canon, for example, includes within judicial restraint the doctrines of legislative deference, respect for precedent, textualism, avoidance of substantive policy decisions and deference to the decisions of agencies and individuals.[28] Similarly, Australian judges have not adopted all the doctrines of restraint. It may be thought that this picking and choosing between doctrines of restraint indicates that restraint is an arbitrary category. On the other hand, the marginal status of certain doctrines may be explained if they only fit the definition partially.

Approaches of Restraint

What, if anything, unifies these apparently disparate doctrines? Why are *these* legal doctrines identified as doctrines of restraint, but not any number of other legal rules? Posner identified three approaches which may lie behind the doctrines of restraint:[29]

1 **Deference.** Judges should avoid contradicting the decisions of other branches of government.[30]
2 **Reticence.** Judges should avoid making moral (and perhaps political, social and economic) choices.[31]
3 **Prudence.** Judges should avoid making decisions which will impair their capacity to make other decisions.

Deference

One approach of judicial restraint is to attempt to preserve the decisions of authorities other than the courts. Some versions limit this approach to preserving the decisions of other branches of government. Other versions extend the approach to preserving the decisions of the Constitution's authors (that is, either textualism or orginalism) and the decisions of other courts (that is, precedents).

Posner ultimately preferred to define restraint as deference to the decisions of federal and state legislatures and executives.[32] Galligan adopted a similar definition of activism as 'control or influence by the judiciary over political or administrative institutions, processes or outcomes'.[33] As a definition, it has the limited virtue of being readily measurable: it is reasonably easy to discern whether a court's order supplants the decision of a legislature by invalidating legislation or by quashing an executive decision.[34]

The deferential approach necessarily implies a narrow construction of individual constitutional rights. An expansive interpretation of individual legal rights is often seen as the hallmark of activism.[35] However, the deferential approach may not necessarily be hostile to individual rights more broadly conceived. As *Lochner* shows, legislation which infringes the rights of some may establish different rights for others.[36]

This definition of restraint applies readily to administrative law and to constitutional litigation over individual rights – which is central to the constitutional history of the United States. It is more difficult to apply to federal constitutional litigation – which is central to the constitutional history of Australia. In constitutional litigation between federal and state governments, *any* decision must frustrate the action of at least one government. For example, the High Court upheld the Commonwealth legislation in the *Uniform Tax Cases*[37] and thereby effectively declared pre-existing state legislation imposing income tax inoperative. Similarly, in *Re Residential Tenancies Tribunal (NSW); ex p Defence Housing Authority*[38] the Court upheld the validity of state legislation regulating residential tenancies and invalidated Commonwealth executive action in breach of it. It makes little sense to characterize such decisions as judicial activism. On Galligan's definition of activism as control over government decisions, *any* judicial decision in a federal dispute would be activist.

Posner excluded textualism, originalism or a strict adherence to precedent from the deferential approach, claiming that the approach would otherwise becomes self-contradictory.[39] A choice between invalidating legislation in accordance with precedent or upholding the legislation contrary to precedent would inevitably lead to a decision that is both activist and restrained.[40] Similarly, textualism would conflict with deference to the legislature if invalidity were clearly required by the constitutional text.[41] However, an approach may be coherent even though it generates contradictory considerations in *some* cases. Posner's own, more limited, approach of restraint results in contradictory considerations in a federal-state dispute.[42] An approach is incoherent only if it leads to contradictory considerations in *every* case. Posner did not – and could not – show that an approach deferential to government decision, constitutional text and original intent *always* results in contradiction. Restraint may coherently dictate both deference, and the priority to be given, to government, constitutional text, original intent and precedent.[43]

By contrast, one can limit the class of authorities to which judges defer even more narrowly than does Posner. Tribe confines restraint to judicial refusal to decide on the substantive validity of Constitutional amendments.[44] This, however, defines judicial restraint as a category so narrow that it is all but empty.[45] Certainly, it will rarely result in any of the doctrines of judicial restraint outlined above.

How does a deferential approach result in the doctrines of restraint already discussed? The 'gatekeeping' requirements – that there be a matter, that the applicant have standing, and that the remedy sought will not require supervision – all generally favour governments.

In constitutional litigation governments are usually respondents behind the gates. Deference to administrative fact-finding and legislative motives, the political questions doctrine and ready severability will obviously favour governments over private litigants. However, it is not obvious why it is desirable to defer to governments when these doctrines apply, and not otherwise. Further explanations are required to show why the deferential approach does not also justify much greater limitations on judicial review.

Textualism and respect for precedent are not necessarily implied by deference to government decisions. It is not obvious that these different aspects of restraint have a common justification. If textualism and respect for precedent are part of judicial restraint, then justifications must be found not only for the authority of the legislature, but also for the authority of constitution-makers and previous courts.

Likewise, the avoidance of purely policy or political decisions is not implied by an approach deferential to government. Avoiding policy considerations may not always favour governments. For example, legislation preventing a shout of 'fire' in a cinema would be struck down as infringing a constitutional guarantee of free speech if the court were to refuse to consider the policy objectives lying behind the constitutional text.

Nor does an approach deferential to government suggest that courts should decide according to an articulated rule. However, as noted already, the inclusion of this doctrine as a doctrine of restraint is questionable.

In summary, deference to the legislature and executive explains some, but not all, of the doctrines of restraint. It is not obvious what justifications are shared by doctrines manifesting deference to legislature and executive, and doctrines such as textualism and respect for precedent. Nor does a deferential approach explain why courts would defer to the legislature when a doctrine of restraint applies, but not otherwise.

Reticence

Other writers have seen the true core of judicial restraint as 'the proposition that judges should not be making policy decisions'.[46] Most claim that judges should avoid 'moral' reasons, while others counsel avoidance of 'policy', 'political',[47] or 'non-accessible'[48] reasons, or 'polycentric' considerations.[49] Although he would not characterize it as an approach of 'restraint', Dworkin's distinction between judicially cognizable 'principles' and judicially irrelevant 'policies'[50] is another attempt to mark a set of reasons which judges should ignore.

The highest hurdle for the reticent approach is to explain why judges should make some moral decisions – in particular the moral choice to adopt a reticent approach and the moral choice to apply legislation in most cases – and yet avoid making other moral decisions.[51] I explain below how this objection might be met, and how the approach might otherwise be justified.[52]

Does a reticent approach generate the doctrines of restraint? Whilst it clearly indicates a preference for text and precedent, it is less clear that it implies gatekeeping doctrines of standing and the like. These doctrines may be the result of the *justifications* of a reticent approach, but they are not obviously implied by the simple formulation of the reticent approach commonly stated in the literature. A more complex formulation of the proper judicial role, and the reasons for it, is required to explain the doctrines of restraint.

Prudence

As Posner notes, there are two different versions of prudential restraint. 'Political prudential restraint' urges that judges avoid making decisions which would incur political reprisals outweighing the virtue of the original decision. 'Functional prudential restraint' urges that judges avoid making decisions which would result in an increase in the courts' workload so that the courts are incapable of dealing with future cases adequately. Both approaches claim that the doctrines of restraint are applied selectively, not according to their terms, but according to whether some external factor *in the particular case* makes it desirable for courts to avoid intervention. Prudential restraint is ultimately a legal realist claim: that the reasons given by a court do not actually determine the decision. Compare this with the deferential and reticent approaches which would apply the doctrines of restraint to every applicable case on the basis that applicable doctrines of restraint further the approach in every case.

Political prudential restraint Political prudential restraint claims that judges do not, and perhaps should not, make decisions which would incur political reprisals which would interfere with the judiciary's ability to make other decisions.[53] Political prudential restraint does not assert that the doctrines of judicial restraint are applied consistently; rather, a judge will manifest restraint only to avoid political controversy.[54]

Bickel presents a more subtle version of this thesis. He claims that the doctrines of restraint may be used to defer judicial decision on the constitutional merits so as to encourage ordinary political and legislative processes to frame an appropriate and wise decision.[55] In this respect, Bickel's thesis is similar to a reticent approach. However, at other points Bickel suggests that the doctrines of restraint are and should be used to defer a judicial decision on the constitutional merits in order to minimize consequent social unrest,[56] or to prepare the public and to ensure ultimate popular agreement with a later substantive constitutional decision.[57] Although Bickel claims to be advocating the rigorous application of doctrines of judicial restraint, closer analysis suggests that his argument supported selective application according to whether the outcome in the particular case would preserve and enhance the Court's authority.[58]

Despite claims that the argument is 'undemonstrable' and speculative,[59] there is some evidence that the US Supreme Court has occasionally used an approach of political prudential restraint.[60]

Justifying political prudential restraint is more difficult. First, the approach may be unjustified it if defers the application of principled rules which embody substantively just outcomes.[61] However, that consideration is not conclusive. On a consequentialist approach, it is at least arguable that preserving judicial authority for other cases may justify an undesirable outcome in a particular case. Second, if one denies Bickel's claims that a political prudential approach would apply the doctrines of political restraint whenever they are applicable, the analysis is open to the objection common to all realist analyses: it fails to take seriously the reasons which judges themselves provide for their decisions. Bickel's analysis is not always guilty of this flaw, although it may be a fair way to characterize some of his arguments.[62] Finally, the prudential approach must explain why, despite the assumptions of the approach, judges should decide cases at all.[63]

The beauty of Bickel's prudential approach is that it captures many of the doctrines of judicial restraint. Like Posner's deferential approach, however, it does not explain textualism or respect for precedent. And as already noted, the prudential approach may not justify applying the doctrines of judicial restraint on their terms to every case. This may not be a serious flaw: the doctrines may be merely overinclusive rules which are the best rule-based approximations to achieving the prudential aims of the approach. Nevertheless, it would be preferable to find an explanation of restraint which justifies, in every applicable case, the application of the doctrines of judicial restraint according to their terms.

Functional prudential restraint Functional prudential restraint considers the implications of a substantive decision for the courts' workload.[64] It is a version of the traditional 'floodgates' argument: by creating new substantive rights, the courts may increase their own workload to the point where they cannot deal adequately with future cases. However, this approach explains fewer of the doctrines of restraint than political prudential restraint, and suffers from the same flaws as that approach. And, although it would justify a respect for precedent, it would not necessarily be served by textualism.[65]

Restraint can be defined more inclusively as a combination of all these approaches of deference, reticence and prudence.[66] But what do the various components of this *smorgasbord* approach have in common other than the label 'restraint'? My suggestion will be that there is a more coherent way to define the term.

Scepticism about Restraint

Even more cynically (or perhaps 'realistically') some claim that a judge only invokes doctrines of restraint if the ultimate court order will result in policy consequences of which the judge approves.[67] However, *some* correlation between the application of a doctrine and a particular policy outcome does not demonstrate that *all* applications of the doctrine are motivated by that policy outcome. Those applications which do not correlate with policy outcomes require other explanations and a fully developed theory of judicial restraint.[68]

Proportion

Finally, Santow J attempts to define restraint as 'the avoidance of excess'.[69] However, the concept, so defined, has little meaning. Despite his criticisms of the reasoning in *Theophanous*, Santow J thought that it was nevertheless a 'restrained' decision because it was consistent with the High Court's general approach in other cases curbing executive power in favour of the individual and the public right to information. This would define restraint as *any* approach to judging except capriciousness. This definition should be adopted only after concluding that no other concept of restraint can be rigorously constructed.

Principles of Restraint

The deferential, reticent and prudential approaches to judicial restraint each attempt to unify restraint in terms of outcomes rather than justifications. They describe judicial behaviour rather than underlying justifications. However, restraint manifests itself in judicial decisions which, it is claimed, are part of a coherent and normatively justified philosophy. It is therefore likely that the common element in doctrines of judicial restraint is their underlying justification. Furthermore, the doctrines of restraint are limited. They do not imply that judges should never decide. A theory of restraint must also articulate what judges *should* do.

I will suggest that restraint can be successfully defined in terms of two interlocking principles and the justifications behind them, and this suggestion will occupy much of the rest of this chapter. Such a definition must simultaneously fulfil both normative and descriptive criteria. Normatively, the justifications on which it relies must be coherent and at least plausible. Descriptively, the principles and their justifications must explain most, if not all, of the doctrines of restraint.

A definition of restraint must start with an account of the judicial role. Judges are free-willed individuals with the ability to make moral choices about their own actions. Any coherent normative theory of judging must accept that judges have a moral choice about their own role. The theory must explain why judges should choose to decide cases at all, and then explain why they should choose to decide them in a particular way.

Of course, judges may claim that their role is defined by a posited rule. But, even so, it is a judge's choice to define his or her role according to the rule. No rule can be its own justification. A normative theory which claims that the judicial role should be defined, in whole or in part, by rule must ultimately accept that the judge could define his or her role otherwise, and explain why the judge should choose not to do so.

The first task for judicial restraint, therefore, is to define the role of judges. Judicial restraint claims:

Principle 1

Judges should make decisions in constitutional cases on the basis of posited rules which facilitate self-direction.

This principle is accepted by most, if not all, theories of judging. It is difficult to imagine a judge or a jurisprude who claims that judges should *never* decide according to posited rules.

Judicial restraint is distinctive because it denies that there is any other justification for judicial authority. Judicial restraint also claims:

Principle 2

Judges should avoid exercising functions other than deciding on their own role and enforcing posited rules which facilitate self-direction.

This second principle is far more controversial than the first, and gives judicial restraint a distinctive character which separates it from other theories of adjudication. Furthermore, the justifications for the second principle are more complex than for the first. They depend on the indeterminacy of many moral questions, as well as judgements about the relative competence of the judiciary and other institutions.

My thesis is that these two principles encapsulate most of the consequences of the norms for the judicial role accepted by restrained judges.

Before outlining the possible justifications for these principles of restraint, it would be well to counter some threshold objections to them.

Incoherency in the Principles of Restraint

The second principle has been attacked as arbitrarily involving some moral choices, but excluding others. How can a judge consistently make the moral choice that it is desirable to decide according to rules and yet claim that it is undesirable for the judiciary to make other moral choices?[70]

The attack on judicial restraint assumes that the moral choice about the judicial role is equivalent to other moral choices made by judges. There are four possible rejoinders. First, perhaps some moral questions have a different nature from others. Rawls attempted to distinguish the Right from the Good using this strategy. He claimed that one could distinguish between moral questions by determining whether people located behind a veil of ignorance would agree upon the answers. The reaction to Rawls' work suggests that many will be unpersuaded about this strategy. Second, it may be possible to make a sensible judgement about the likelihood that a norm is correct separately from selecting the correct norm. Perhaps moral judgements can be like scientific judgements which specify both the observed measurement and the probability and extent of error. So it may be that, whilst judges have a high degree of certainty in the proposition that they should enforce rules, they have less certainty about the answers to other moral questions. Third, some moral questions may admit of only one right answer, whilst others involve incommensurables and have no single morally right answer.[71] On this view, a judge might claim that there exist definitive answers to some moral questions – such as the desirability of judicial decision according to rules – whilst asserting that other questions lack such answers. Fourth, perhaps a moral choice to adopt a particular institutional role is distinct from other moral choices. Campbell argues that the judicial role is defined not by the judge but by the judge's society.[72] A person's choice to take on a judicial role is then seen as 'ethical' rather than 'moral' so that the choice to become a judge, and the choice about what that role involves, is distinct from other moral choices. But even this theory must explain why an individual would adopt this role and then not seek to change it, particularly when judges have real opportunities to redefine their judicial role explicitly. And this leads back to the original puzzle: why should individuals make this moral choice and yet seek to define (or not to redefine) their role as avoiding other moral choices?

Demonstrating that any of these arguments is *plausible* is beyond the scope of this chapter. Only detailed investigation of the justifications for the second principle can demonstrate that any of these arguments is even *applicable* to judicial restraint. Nevertheless, liberalism is built on a similar distinction between types of moral question;[73] it is at least plausible that judicial restraint may be supported successfully in a similar way.

Conflicts Between the Principles of Restraint

The principles of restraint sometimes conflict with each other. Enforcing a rule may involve not merely applying the rule to particular facts, but making a moral choice. This is obviously the case when the rule uses words which lack more or less accepted concrete referents and invokes a moral concept such as 'just' or 'reasonable' whose application to particular cases is underdetermined by rules or linguistic convention.

The principles of restraint also conflict if a rule is ambiguous in its application to specific facts. Enforcing an ambiguous rule or set of rules necessarily involves a moral choice about what is relatively important. For example, s.51(20) of the Australian Constitution provides that the Commonwealth Parliament may make laws 'with respect to ... trading or financial corporations'. Is a corporation to be characterized as a 'trading' corporation because its original purpose was trading, because its activities are *predominantly* trading or because its activities are *substantially* trading?[74] Resolving this question ultimately requires a judgement about the purpose of the provision. Where a text is semantically ambiguous, its application requires a choice between alternative meanings and thus a judgement about the point of the provision. This necessarily involves moral judgements about which ends are valuable. Making this choice would breach the second principle of restraint. But failure to choose would amount to a refusal to apply the provision at all, breaching the first principle of judicial restraint.

However if restrained judge does follow the first principle, and chooses between ambiguous meanings, the second principle of restraint may provide a basis for choosing. For example, the judge may choose a rule which will itself provide linguistic grounds to dispose of future cases. The judge may deliberately avoid choosing a rule whose application is more likely to raise further non-linguistic questions. For example, the High Court's choice to interpret s.92 of the Australian Constitution as only prohibiting discrimination against goods and services from out of state and partly motivated by a desire to avoid the moral choices which turned out to be entailed by the previous interpretation which imposed a more general prohibition subject to a general exception of 'reasonable regulation'.[75] Restrained judges do not deny that there are sometimes 'gaps' in the law, nor do they deny that *sometimes* judges should make moral choices; they merely claim that the number of moral choices involved should be minimized.

Textual ambiguity is one instance amongst several where the principle that judges should apply posited laws conflicts with the principle that judges should not exercise other functions, such as making moral choices. The principles of judicial restraint do not prescribe answers to conflicts between themselves. Constitutional rules which require moral choices, particularly constitutional rights, may be enforced literally, thereby invoking more moral choices, or they may be interpreted less literally and read down, thereby minimizing the moral choices which judges must make. Either approach would be consistent with one of the principles of restraint, but not the other.

However, the principles of restraint and their justifications may highlight the considerations relevant to resolving these conflicts. For example, restrained judges may be less willing to interpret text literally if the rules governing a sphere of conduct are necessarily very ambiguous. It is then relatively less important to enforce such rules for they are, in any case, incapable of providing much guidance to individual action.

The existence of conflicts between the various principles of restraint does not demonstrate that they are incoherent or inevitably indeterminate.[76] Although the principles are ambiguous in situations where they conflict, there are other situations where the principles provide unambiguous guidance for decision. In these circumstances the principles of judicial restraint may suggest very different answers from those generated by other theories of constitutional interpretation. For example, some normative theories claim that judges should interpret constitutional provisions so as to promote a political theory either deduced in the abstract or inferred from existing posited rules.[77] This involves the judiciary in functions other than enforcing rules and does not promote the enforcement of posited rules. Unsurprisingly then, such judicial philosophies are contrary to judicial restraint.

The principles of restraint also explain why judicial law-making is considered legitimate only if it is 'interstitial'.[78] If a case falls between existing laws, or is governed ambiguously by an existing law, then the application of the posited law requires the judge to decide how the laws mesh together, or what the existing law means. To the extent that the judge makes law, the judge does so as a necessary step in applying and enforcing posited rules. On the other hand, changing a posited rule, however morally desirable it may appear, is not a necessary incident of applying and enforcing posited rules.

Justifying Restraint

The two principles of judicial restraint, therefore, are not internally incoherent. Are there good reasons to adopt them? Two types of argument support the principles of restraint: first, the various justifications for rule-following; and, second, arguments about relative institutional capacity and competence.

Enforcing Rules

The first principle of restraint is often uncontroversial. It is accepted by all judges, if not by everyone else, that judges should *sometimes* decide according to posited rules. The justifications for the first principle must explain why it is desirable for judges always to follow posited rules, without picking and choosing between what judges perceive to be bad rules, so that the decision may differ from the judges' unfettered views about what would be the right action in the circumstances.

Schauer and Campbell have provided more detailed discussions of the reasons for coercive regimes to make decisions by following rules rather than by making judgments in each individual case.[79] In brief, possible arguments for rule-following include:

- **Autonomy**. By making the actions of other people and of government more predictable,[80] rules promote the capacity of individuals to plan and execute their own autonomous lives.[81] Alternatively this idea may be captured as the 'liberty advantage' of rules.[82]
- **Coordination**. By making the actions of other people and of government more predictable, rules provide a means to coordinate conduct towards goals achieved in concert.[83]
- **Psychological security**. By making the actions of other people and of government more predictable, rules provide individuals with the psychological security that government and others will not arbitrarily and unforeseeably interfere with them.[84]
- **Minimization**. By delimiting the considerations for resolving disputes, rules both enable individuals to avoid disputes and

provide a more efficient method for resolving disputes which do arise.[85]

- **Impartiality**. By limiting and specifying relevant considerations, rules reduce the scope for a decision-maker to choose criteria for decision arbitrarily and thereby unconsciously or consciously decide on the basis of morally irrelevant criteria, such as personal favouritism.[86]
- **Fairness**. By limiting and specifying relevant considerations, rules ensure that decisions are made consistently by different adjudicators and at different times.[87] However, consistency is not a virtue if decisions are made on an incorrect basis.[88]
- **Efficiency**. By limiting and specifying relevant considerations, rules decrease the cost of decision-making.[89]
- **Socialization**. By requiring uniform conduct, rules provide a means for individuals to identify with each other and so to bond in a community.[90]
- **Moral form**. Because rules are general in form, they are more likely to attain the Kantian ideal of embodying a universalized moral judgement.[91]
- **Focused deliberation**. Because, in form, rules focus on particular considerations, rule-makers are compelled to consider which issues should be determinative for decisions; the form of rules thus promotes deliberative decision-making.[92]
- **Allocation of jurisdiction**. Rules are a means for rule creators, rather than rule appliers, to make decisions. This may be desirable, first, because it is quicker (and therefore cheaper) to identify the relevant considerations once in a rule rather than every time a decision is made.[93] Second, the rule-maker may make morally or factually better choices about the determinative considerations,[94] because he may have more time, more expertise, better access to information or be less susceptible to emotion or partiality. Finally, the rule-maker may have more legitimacy than the decision-maker to make these choices. The rule-maker may facilitate greater public participation because members of the public are more involved in selecting its personnel, or in the decision-making process itself.[95] These considerations for institutional choice are discussed further below.[96]
- **Defining relevant issues**. Rules can also allocate jurisdiction directly by preventing a particular decision-maker from making certain types of decision or by restricting the decision-maker's authority to a limited range of decisions. The creation of such jurisdictional rules is again justified on the basis that decisions are better made by some institution other than the particular decision-maker, and that self-direction and cooperation require

clarity as to who has jurisdiction to make specific types of decision.

The applicability and importance of the various justifications for rule-following will vary depending on the field of activity and the character of the particular society. Judicial restraint relies solely on the first ground for following legal rules – namely, that they promote self-direction. Courts are required both to declare authoritatively the application of rules in particular circumstances and to provide confidence that other arms of government will apply posited rules to individuals according to their terms. Conversely, the first principle of restraint implies that rules should not be judicially enforced when individual self-direction is not promoted. This might be defensible because other justifications for rule-following are not particularly cogent. Alternatively, it may be that other rationales for rule-following are not significantly promoted by judicial intervention. For example, it does not matter if a rule-promoting coordination is breached, provided that worthwhile coordination is achieved in other ways and provided that no individual's conduct is directly affected.[97]

Whatever the advantages of decision according to rule, they must be balanced against the costs. Applying a rule may exclude relevant considerations so that a decision-maker would make better decisions unfettered by the rule. The extent of this disadvantage depends on:

- how often an unfettered decision would differ from the application of the rule

and

- how often, and to what extent, an unfettered decision would be a morally preferable result to the application of the rule.

Nevertheless, some disadvantages as a result of applying the rule does not necessarily justify abandoning the other advantages of rule-following already described. Enforcing rules is justified whenever the advantages of rule-following outweigh the disadvantages.

Avoiding Functions Other than Rule Enforcement

The second principle of restraint is that judges should avoid exercising functions other than enforcing rules. It is difficult to provide a simple justification for such a negative assumption. Other possible judicial functions may be rejected because of institutional comparisons – arguments that those functions would be better exercised by institutions other than the judiciary. Such arguments of institutional choice must do more than show that the judiciary would perform a function well or poorly. Even if judges exercise a function badly, it may be desirable that the function be performed, and no institution would perform it better than the judiciary. Similarly, even if judges exercise a function well, another institution might do even better.

An institution may be preferred for making a class of decisions because:

- it is more likely to assess the relevant facts correctly
- it is more likely to assess the relevant moral considerations correctly
- it has greater legitimacy to make that decision
- it can decide at lower costs

or

- its decisions minimize collateral damage to other institutions or capacities.

These institutional choice arguments, and their application to public institutions, require some elaboration.

Factual assessment A court may be more likely to assess facts correctly because it will be less tainted by irrelevant bias, or because it ensures the exclusion of irrelevant consideration or because its processes encourage the collation and presentation of all the relevant evidence. It may, on the other hand, be less likely to assess facts correctly because, for example, the parties and the court do not have ready access to relevant information or because relevant information can only be collected informally in a way which severely compromises the independence – and therefore the legitimacy – of courts (see 'collateral institutional damage', p. 303 below).

The judiciary may also make a less accurate assessment of the facts because adjudication concentrates on the parties to litigation and excludes other interests. The legitimacy of courts often depends on their role in settling disputes: this legitimacy would be compromised if the court considered unrepresented interests.

The problems of gathering information are particularly acute in constitutional cases where it may be difficult for the parties to collect relevant data or where disparate lobby groups with little access to the courts have the best available information. Although constitutional courts have evolved techniques such as the 'Brandeis brief', the problems remain.[98]

Moral assessment A court may be more likely to assess relevant moral considerations correctly because of the normal requirement to articulate reasons. Errors in moral reasoning are more likely to be exposed through the process of writing reasons than through the legislative process in which assumptions and norms often remain unspoken.

A court may also be thought more likely to reason correctly because, unlike the legislature, it is not biased towards the interests of the majority. Although such bias is predicted by social choice theory,[99] enactment by majority legislatures of anti-discrimination law and social security safety nets suggests that the practice of legislatures does not always agree with the theory.

Moral problems may shade into factual problems. The best course of action often depends on precise factual knowledge and, in particular, on foreseeing the social consequences of a particular rule. Arguably, the US Supreme Court does not have an enviable record in this regard.[100] Whether one characterizes these issues as 'factual' or 'moral' is irrelevant for present purposes: in either case they involve choices not guided by the application of rules using linguistic criteria.

Judicial moral evaluations are also suspect if the moral problems cannot be fully answered by practical reasoning. Some options may not be comparable – or at least 'on a par' – so that there is no sufficient reason to decide between them. In these circumstances any superior capacity for moral reasoning possessed by the judiciary would then be to no avail. Moreover, even if the existence of such a lack of comparability is not accepted,[101] a method for *discovering* the right answer must still be defined. Judicial moral evaluations are equally suspect if discerning the correct moral answer is so difficult that the court is no more likely to find it than any other body. There is little escape from the problem – be it epistemic or ontological – that it is difficult to provide sure answers to many controversial value choices.[102]

Irrespective of philosophy, therefore, some issues require difficult value choices which cannot be solved by practical reasoning. As an institution, the judiciary may have some advantages: it is more likely to make decisions free of bias; and its deliberative reasoned process ensures consideration of whatever reasons are available. On the other hand, judges tend to have an homogeneous background which emphasizes some values – particularly fair process and individual liberty – in ways which are not entirely rational. Lacking day-to-day contact with a broad spectrum of society, judges may have relatively little appreciation of some important values.

Legitimacy An institution's legitimacy may stem from a number of sources. One justification for legitimacy is that the institution is more expert, and so its decisions are more likely than the individual's own choice to reflect the dependent reasons – that is, those reasons which apply directly to an individual.[103] On this view, the judiciary's legitimacy relative to other institutions depends on its capacity relative to other institutions to make accurate factual, technical and moral judgements – a problem I have already discussed.

Another source of legitimacy is that an institution's authority is needed to solve coordination problems. Some human goods can only be attained through cooperative action. Authority ensures that people cooperate even when, as is all but inevitable, they are not unanimous.[104] An institution's ability to ensure coordination depends on many factors: the detail of the directives it gives; how often it can give directives; how easily its directives can be adjusted to changing or unforeseen circumstances; how readily people can ascertain applicable directives; and how easily it is to identify people who do not conform with directives. The subject matter may affect the relative importance of these factors and thus which institution is better able to provide coordination. For example, legislative directives may be appropriate to set the rules of the road, but inappropriate to designate the temporary closure of streets to enable new pipes to be laid.

Decisions may also be legitimate because they peacefully resolve the conflicts between the choices of individuals in society. *Some* decision is justified because it ultimately promotes social cooperation, even if it is not the best decision which either or both parties could have reached. Although the judiciary's ability to resolve conflicts between individuals' choices is the normal justification for the existence of adjudication, other institutions – legislatures, executives and even the market – are also capable of this. For instance, legislation can lay down new rules, executives can exercise discretions favouring one individual over another and markets can make the success of choices dependent on the willingness to pay.

An institution may also be legitimate to the extent that it reflects the preferences of individuals. The fundamental assumption of liberty is that it is *prima facie* valuable for the preferences of individuals to be implemented where possible. An institution may be legitimate because it helps individuals achieve their preferences. However, no institution can implement the preferences of all citizens because some people prefer that the preferences of others *not* be fulfilled and because unanimity so rarely occurs in practice. The best that can be done is to implement the preferences of more, rather than fewer, people. A representative democracy is only an imperfect instrument for this end. Representatives do not always implement, or act upon, the preferences of their electors; and representatives may not always be elected by the preferences of a majority. Nevertheless, a democratic legislature may be *more likely* than most institutions to reflect the preferences of more individuals. Of course, this may not always be the case. In some circumstances legislatures may be more vulnerable to interest groups and thus implement popular preferences less well than legal institutions.

Finally, an institution may have legitimacy because it gives an opportunity for individuals to participate in its decision-making processes. It may be inherently valuable for individuals not merely to have their preferences implemented, but to participate in decisions about whether they will be implemented.[105] Again, no institution can achieve this ideal, but some may come closer than others. For example, a court may provide greater participation because it ensures that a person can present their own argument, which will be properly considered; on the other hand, a legislature may provide more opportunity for participation to those whose interests are only peripherally affected and who would not be allowed, or who would not be able to afford, to participate in court proceedings.

Arguments for a restrained judicial role are sometimes put briefly in the form that judges 'are not elected' or that judges 'lack democratic legitimacy'. These are ultimately appeals to either or both of the preceding two arguments. The expanded argument is that democratic institutions are more likely than courts to reflect individual preferences, and/or are more likely to provide opportunities for participation. However, as the preceding discussion illustrates, these features are not the only foundations for legitimacy.

Each of these justifications of legitimacy may be more or less applicable to a particular situation. No institution has more legitimacy in all situations. The relative legitimacy of each institution in the circumstances must be compared – and rather than being absolutely applicable to an institution, the justifications for the legitimacy of an institution will themselves usually be a matter of degree.

Cost The costs of reaching decisions are an important criterion for institutional choice. Transaction costs can distort markets away from the theoretically optimal decision. It is less well recognized that similar problems beset the legislature, executive and judiciary.[106] For example, people cannot further their interests through the legislative process without investing, often at significant cost, in acquiring information.[107] Costs may be incurred in identifying one's interest, in acquiring information about how to further that interest and in the process of furthering the interest through publicity and lobbying. The costs of participating in the judicial process are notorious and may significantly distort the ultimate outcomes of judicial decision-making.

Institutional comparisons must consider not only the direct costs to participants but also the costs to society at large. The time invested in deciding issues – whatever the institution – may be significant. And where the institution has limited time, the true cost of decision-making includes the costs of lost opportunities to look at other issues. For example, an ultimate appellate court can only consider a limited number of cases: considering (say) extra cases about the ambit of a parliament's power to regulate industrial relations may result in the court not considering extra cases about the bounds of an individual's freedom of speech.[108]

Collateral institutional damage A final issue for institutional choice is that an institution's performance of one function may damage the ability of that institution, or another institution, to carry out other functions. This attitude is legally expressed in the doctrine of separation of powers. The theory is that performance of 'non-judicial' functions – such as investigation for a criminal prosecution – impairs the judiciary's ability to carry out its 'judicial' function of applying the law to the relevant case. It is also claimed that it may impair public confidence in the judiciary's ability to do so, thereby reducing public adherence to law.

The argument is not limited to impairment of the judiciary's functions. It has also been argued that if judges are involved in making too many moral choices, thereby removing them from the public agenda, then public participation in the legislative process – and its effectiveness – is decreased.[109]

Partial reform Institutional choice should also consider the techniques which institutions can use to make law. Legislatures can change the interacting parts of an area of law simultaneously. By contrast, judicial law-making is case-by-case. According to classical theory, if an improvement to the law requires two simultaneous changes, each of which alone would be regressive, the judiciary would be unable to effect change. Courts are caught by the 'dilemma of partial reform'.[110]

The importance of this problem should not be exaggerated. It may not be common for one part of a desirable new scheme to be undesirable on its own. Courts in fact do change one part of the law and indicate *in dicta* that the coordinate rules will also be changed when they arise for decision.

Conclusion Restrained judges avoid making choices other than on the basis of applying rules. They may do this because they think that, relative to other institutions, the judiciary will make worse factual decisions, make worse moral decisions, coordinate less, fail to reflect legitimate preferences, fail to promote popular involvement in decision-making, cost more, inflict damage on other processes and/or be incapable of comprehensive reform. Restrained judges do not necessarily subscribe to all of these views. Further work beyond this chapter's scope might reveal how different views on these institutional questions nuance attitudes to judicial restraint.

In any case, the weight of these justifications for restraint will vary with circumstances – which explains why no judge is as restrained as possible all the time. Furthermore, their application will vary with the society. For example in a society where the rule of law has been weak for a generation, judges may be more concentrated to create public confidence in rules, than to second-guess legislatures; judges in a society with a history of legislative abuses may be correspondingly more confident with their own judgments.[111]

Matching Principles and Doctrines of Restraint

How do the doctrines of restraint reflect the principles that:

- judges should make decisions governing many areas of human activity on the basis of posited rules which facilitate self-direction, and
- judges should not exercise functions other than deciding their own role and enforcing posited rules which facilitate self-direction?

A strict approach to standing, the requirement that there be a matter, and associated doctrines of ripeness, mootness, parsimony and the exhaustion of other remedies are regarded as typical doctrines of judicial restraint. These doctrines are entailed by the principles of restraint. Judicial restraint assumes that the sole legitimate purpose of judging is to ensure compliance with rules by both state and individual so as to facilitate self-direction. If the applicant lacks standing, or the case is not yet ripe, or a case can be decided on non-constitutional grounds, then by definition the applicant's conduct does not depend on whether the constitutional rule is followed. The doctrine that one who accepts the benefit of a statute cannot then challenge its constitutionality is similarly justified. Such an applicant has succeeded in ordering his or her life despite the failure to comply with constitutional rules.

The refusal to review questions of fact is not obviously implied by the principles of restraint. Its justifications probably lie in the desirability of ensuring finality to litigation and in the relative expertise of trial and appellate judges. Perhaps those appellate judges who doubt their own capacity relative to the legislature are also more likely to doubt their own capacity relative to another judge or administrator. But the connection is not a necessary one.

A strict approach to precedent is clearly implied by the principles of restraint. Such an approach both makes the outcome of applying existing rules more certain and avoids the moral choices required in deciding whether to extend a precedent or make exceptions to it.

The political questions doctrine deals with situations in which the principle of avoiding non-rulebound considerations completely overrides the principle of applying rules. Most of the Australian applications of the political questions doctrine concern rules governing the basic sources of authority. Judicial intervention over whether (for example) parliament was legitimately dissolved will ultimately create *greater* uncertainty over the application of rules than simply acquiescing in a possibly unlawful transfer of *de facto* authority. In cases concerning basic sources of authority a judicial order may result in there being *no* legislative authority. Thus, these cases raise special problems for the first principle: there is no point in applying constitutional rules (which outline legislative power) if that will result in no body at all being able to exercise legislative power. Unsurprisingly, therefore, in these situations the second principle of restraint entirely overrides the first.

The presumption of constitutionality illustrates a significant difference between the principles of restraint and a deferential approach. The first principle of restraint requires that constitutional rules be applied according to their terms. It contradicts the deferential approach which would defer to the legislature concerning the correct application of those rules. It is interesting that the presumption of constitutionality has taken hold in the United States but not in Australia. Judicial deference to administrative decisions raises similar considerations and is similarly applied in the United States, but not in Australia.

Severability serves the first principle of restraint by ensuring that, as far as possible, statutory rules are applied.

Textualism serves the first principle – that the primary aim of governance according to rules is to facilitate self-direction. A rule only facilitates self-direction if it has a source-based text which is more certain guide to action than the rule's underlying justification. A judge who accepts the first principle of restraint is therefore implicitly committed to a primarily textualist approach to interpretation.

A narrow interpretation of constitutional rights flows from the second principle – that judges have neither the authority nor the expertise to do anything other than enforce rules. As constitutional rights are rarely spelt out in exhaustive detail, their interpretation often requires the court to make difficult moral choices, unaided by the text. If the scope of the constitutional right is narrowed, fewer moral choices arise for the judiciary. The narrow interpretation of constitutional rights is a specific case of the more general phenomenon of judges interpreting constitutional text so as to minimize the decisions which depend on moral choices or economic evaluations. Of course, this is not a strictly textual approach to interpretation and, in this way, the second principle of restraint conflicts with the first. Consequently, a restrictive approach to the interpretation of explicit constitutional rights is not always regarded as a doctrine of restraint.

Originalism is sometimes claimed to be a doctrine of restraint, particularly in the United States. However, it is not readily explained by the principles of restraint and, indeed, may appear to contradict it. If legal rules aim primarily to guide individuals by their very terms, this aim is undermined if the rules are in fact interpreted not merely in light of their text but on the basis of the opinion of some other body such as the Constitution's authors. Originalism will only serve the justifications for the first principle of restraint if it increases certainty. This will only be so if the original intent is reasonably certain in its application, and some of the judges who advocate originalism do indeed justify it on exactly this basis.[112] Alternatively, originalism may reflect a preference for the decisions of the constitutional drafters over the decisions of the judiciary. Scepticism about both these justifications may explain why originalism has never been unequivocally accepted in Australian constitutional interpretation.

The preference for a decision on the basis of an articulated rule rather than as an 'all things considered' judgment acknowledges that, in interpreting rules, judges face ambiguities and, in resolving those ambiguities, may create precedents which reduce future uncertainty. Doing so serves the first principle of restraint. By contrast, a decision on the basis of 'all the circumstances' does not. However, a judgment in 'all the circumstances' only requires the judge to make a more limited moral judgement because it imposes no real limits on future decisions. By making a more limited moral decision, it adheres more closely to the second principle of restraint. This conflict between the principles of restraint perhaps explains why the preference for deciding on the basis of an articulated rule is not always regarded as a doctrine of restraint.[113]

Related Issues

Judicial Restraint and Judicial Activism

What are the alternatives to judicial restraint? If I have identified the essence of restraint correctly, then unrestrained judges will refuse to adhere to one or both of the principles.

First, an unrestrained judge might simply deny that the primary purpose of judging is to enforce posited rules so as to facilitate self-direction. Instead it might be thought that the judiciary's primary function is to resolve disputes. Of course, the one case may well entail both functions, but differences may arise between them. A judge devoted primarily to resolving disputes would not be so concerned with the basis on which the dispute is resolved; by contrast a judge devoted to enforcing rules would not be so concerned with resolving a dispute if the application of rules provides no solution. A judge devoted primarily to resolving disputes would still take a strict approach to doctrines such as avoiding advisory opinions (when by definition there is no dispute), but would be less inclined to textualism, precedent, ignoring political questions and the like.

Those sceptical that legal materials often provide determinate technical answers would come to similar conclusions. For example, Stone thought that legal materials seldom provide unique logical answers, and that judges have a significant leeway of choice in most cases.[114] Consequently, he concluded that talk of judicial restraint is misplaced.[115] Such sceptics would deny that the primary aim of judges is to decide according to posited rules.

Alternatively, an unrestrained judge might deny that judges should *avoid* making moral and other judgements not on the basis of posited rules. Such a judge would not actively seek to do so, but if required by posited rules to make moral judgements, would do so with the full plenitude that the posited rules required. Except to the extent that doctrines of restraint are themselves embodied in posited rules, such a judge would have a relatively less restrictive attitude towards gatekeeping mechanisms.

Finally, an unrestrained judge might positively *seek* to make moral judgements, irrespective of posited rules. Depending on the depth of this conviction, such a judge would be prepared to breach any or all of the doctrines of restraint in order to make the world a better place. The basis for this view might be a radically different justification for judicial review. For example, if judicial review were justified principally on the basis that it safeguards basic liberties (a more tenable view where the Constitution contains a Bill of Rights), or because it provides reasoned judgements, then the second principle of restraint would be actively denied. On this view, applying most, if not all, the doctrines of restraint would be undesirable.

This brief outline suggests that there may be a middle way between activism and restraint. This middle way is followed by judges who do not avoid moral judgements in the pursuit of posited rules, as distinct from those who interpret posited rules in order to *increase* or *decrease* the scope for moral judgements.

Constitutional Modification of Restraint

It is possible to have legislative or constitutional provisions modifying some of the doctrines of restraint. For example, the Supreme Court Act (Canada), s.53 provides that the Supreme Court may give advisory opinions.[116] However, the analysis of restraint would suggest that an otherwise restrained judge committed to textualism may try to restrict the ambit of constitutional provisions modifying the other doctrines of restraint or construe the Constitution so as to invalidate provisions which attempt to do so.

Judicial Restraint and Private Law

My analysis has been directed primarily to constitutional review. To some extent it will also be relevant to judgments in private law. However, the justifications involved may be different because private law judgments are subject to legislative overruling. Private law decisions are also distinct from constitutional decisions because, whereas some private law decisions derive their authority purely from precedent, all federal constitutional decisions claim their authority from the constitutional text.

Conclusion

I have identified the two principles of restraint as follows:

1 judges should make constitutional decisions on the basis of posited rules; and
2 judges should avoid exercising functions other than deciding on their own role and enforcing posited rules.

These principles not only have justifications which are at least plausible, but they also seem to explain most of the doctrines of restraint. Most of the doctrines which are not universally accepted as doctrines of restraint embody conflicts between the principles, which explains their marginality.

A more rigorous definition of restraint provides a basis for evaluating claims that the Australian High Court was more activist over the last decade or so than it might have been. There are two ways of demonstrating this claim. First, one could demonstrate that, in applying posited constitutional rules, the Court had opportunities to avoid moral questions and yet deliberately embraced them. Or, second, one could show that the Court failed to apply posited rules for reasons other than avoiding moral judgements. The justifications outlined for restraint indicate the grounds on which these choices might be criticized or defended. Without a rigorous definition, accusations of 'activism' can be little more than a bare feeling that the outcome is undesirable.

A rigorous definition of restraint also provides more shape to debates over whether the High Court 'makes law'. During the 1990s an Australian industry dedicated itself to demonstrating that judges do make law.[117] This is a puzzling enterprise. Certainly Dixon never claimed that judges never make law.[118] As Dworkin admitted, theorists 'have had little luck in caging and exhibiting mechanical jurisprudents (all specimens captured – even Blackstone and Joseph Beale – have had to be released after careful reading of their texts)'.[119] The real question is whether judges have failed to apply posited rules or have been overly keen to impose their own political and moral values. Whether or not these charges are justified, a discussion in terms of restraint and activism would helpfully clarify the debate as one about *when* and *how* judges should make law.

Notes

[1] Earlier drafts of this chapter have benefited from the perceptive criticisms of Nick Barber, Tom Campbell, John Finnis, Joseph Raz, the Graduate Political Theory Seminar at Oxford University and the participants in the Workshop on Judicial Activism and Judicial Review in Australian Democracy held in July 1998 at the Australian National University. Those problems which remain, or which have subsequently been created, are my own responsibility. I am grateful for the financial support of the Commonwealth Scholarship Commission and the Old Members of University College, Oxford.

[2] This claim is empirical. It fits my general impression of Australian High Court judgments, but demonstrating the correlation is beyond the scope of this chapter.

[3] Henry J. Abraham, *The Judicial Process*, 7th edn (New York: Oxford University Press, 1998), pp. 385–410, although, as noted below, some of these doctrines overlap. Robin Brian O'Hair, *The Bankruptcy of Judicial Restraint and Judicial Activism* (University of Queensland, Faculty of Law: unpublished PhD thesis, 1986), p. 423 gives another lengthy list which differs in minor respects, as does Christopher Wolfe, *Judicial Activism* (Pacific Grove: Brooks/Cole, 1991), pp. 2–5. Shorter lists appear in Charles M. Lamb, 'Judicial Restraint on the Supreme Court', in Stephen C. Halpern and Charles M. Lamb (eds), *Supreme Court Activism and Restraint* (Lexington, MA: Lexington Books, 1982), pp. 7–36 at p. 8, and J. Clifford Wallace, 'The Jurisprudence of Judicial Restraint', *George Washington Law Review*, **50**(1) (1981), pp. 9–12.

[4] *Commonwealth Constitution*, ss. 75–78; *United States Constitution*, Art III, s. 2. In this section I provide a brief, but by no means comprehensive, introduction to relevant Australian law and literature; for US law see Abraham, *The Judicial Process*, *op. cit.*, pp. 385–410.

[5] See John Williams, 'Rethinking Advisory Opinions', *Public Law Review*, **7** (1996), p. 205.

[6] See Henry Burmester, 'Locus Standi in Constitutional Litigation', in H.P. Lee and George Winterton (eds), *Australian Constitutional Perspectives* (Sydney: Law Book Company, 1992), p. 148.

[7] See Susan Kenny, 'Constitutional Fact Ascertainment', *Public Law Review*, **1** (1990), p. 134.

[8] *Cole* v. *Whitfield* (1988) 165 CLR 360 contradicted this aspect of the doctrine: the Court abandoned a legal test (however unworkable) which evaluated the legislation on its face in favour of a test whose application almost invariably turns on a relatively complex set of facts.

[9] See also Lewis F. Powell, 'Stare Decisis and Judicial Restrain', *Washington and Lee Law Review*, **7** (1990), p. 281.

[10] Neil MacCormick, *Legal Reasoning and Legal Theory*, rev. edn (Oxford: Clarendon Press, 1994), pp. 213–16; but cf. scepticism that precedent ever significantly constraints judicial decisions in Julius Stone, *Legal System and Lawyers' Reasonings* (London: Stevens & Sons, 1964), pp. 267–80.

[11] Geoffrey Lindell, 'The Justiciability of Political Questions', in H.P. Lee and G. Winterton (eds), *Australian Constitutional Perspectives* (Sydney: Law Book Co, 1992), p. 180.

[12] Henry Burmester, 'The Presumption of Constitutionality', *Federal Law Review*, **13** (1983), p. 277.

[13] A recent example is *Kruger* v. *Commonwealth* (1997) 190 CLR 1 at 85–8 per Toohey J, at 144 per McHugh J.

[14] L. Zines, 'The High Court and the Constitution: The Search for Objective Criteria' in Alice Erh-Soon Tay and Eugene Kamenka (eds), *Law-making in Australia* (London: Edward Arnold, 1978), p. 207 describes the Australian High Court's attempts between 1920 and 1978 to choose interpretations which would avoid future decisions involving political or policy judgments.

[15] For example, Bradley C. Canon, 'A Framework for the Analysis of Judicial Activism' in Halpern and Lamb, *Supreme Court Activism*, *op. cit.*, p. 385 at pp. 386–7; Lamb, 'Judicial Restraint', *op. cit.*, p. 8; Wallace, 'The Jurisprudence of Judicial Restraint' *op. cit.*, pp. 11–12; James E. Wyszynski, 'In Praise of Judicial Restraint', *Detroit College of Law Review*, **117** (1989), p. 120; and, although he disclaims the term, Grover Rees, 'Cathedrals without Walls: A View from the Outside', *Texas Law Review*, **61** (1982), p. 347.

[16] Lon L. Fuller, *The Morality of Law*, rev. edn (New Haven, CT: Yale University Press, 1969), pp. 81–91, 264–89.

[17] Frederick Schauer, *Playing by the Rules* (Oxford: Clarendon Press, 1991), pp. 53–62.

[18] John R. Taylor, *Linguistic Categorization*, 2nd edn (Oxford: Clarendon Press, 1995), pp. 264–89.

[19] See *Mannai Investment* v. *Eagle Star* (1997) 3 All ER 352 at 377–85 per Lord Hoffman.

[20] For a further discussion of how context may or may not ensure that a textual rule is unambiguous in a given situation, see Brian Bix, *Law, Language and Legal Determinacy* (Oxford: Clarendon Press, 1993), pp. 63–76; but affirming that context is not everything, see Andrei Marmor, *Interpretation and Legal Theory* (Oxford: Clarendon Press, 1992), pp. 146–58.

[21] Ronald Dworkin, *Law's Empire* (Cambridge, MA: Harvard University Press, 1986), pp. 338–40, 350–4.

[22] Wysznyski, 'In Praise of Judicial Restraint', *op. cit.*, pp. 150–1; Canon, 'A Framework' *op. cit.*, pp. 386–7.

[23] Mark Leeming, 'Courts, Tribunals and the Separation of Powers in Australia and Canada', *Public Law Review*, **8** (1997), p. 143 and p. 144.

[24] Antonin Scalia, 'The Rule of Law as a Law of Rules', *University of Chicago Law Review*, **56** (1989), p. 1175.

[25] Cass R. Sunstein, *Legal Reasoning and Political Conflict* (New York: Oxford University Press, 1996), pp. 35–61.

[26] O'Hair, *The Bankruptcy of Judicial Restraint*, *op. cit.*, pp. 761–7.

[27] The majority judgment was sceptical that the doctrine remains part of Australian law in *Patrick Stevedores* v. *MUA* (1998) 153 ALR 643 at 670; but cf. the dissenting judgment of Callinan J at 704–9.

[28] Canon, 'A Framework', *op. cit.*, pp. 386–7.

[29] Richard A. Posner, *The Federal Courts* (Cambridge, MA: Harvard University Press, 1996), pp. 314–34.

[30] Posner refers to judges who avoid contradicting the decisions of other branches

of government as 'self-restrained'. This term is inappropriate for the current project of attempting to define restraint.

31 Posner, *The Federal Courts, op. cit.*, at p. 314 refers to judges who avoid making moral choices as 'deferential'. This term is inappropriate because often a judge who avoids making a moral choice does not 'defer' to anyone.

32 Ibid., pp. 318–20. Michael Paulsen, 'The Many Faces of "Judicial Restraint"', *Public Interest Law Review*, **3** (1993), pp. 3–24 also adopts this definition. Dworkin, *Law's Empire, op. cit.*, at p. 369 defines 'passivism' in this way.

33 B. Galligan, 'Judicial Activism in Australia' in Kenneth M. Holland (ed.), *Judicial Activism in Comparative Perspective* (London: Macmillan, 1991), p. 70.

34 Hence Gregory A. Caldeira and Donald J. McCrone, 'Of Time and Judicial Activism', in Halpern and Lamb, *Supreme Court Activism, op. cit.*, pp. 103–27 which analyses the 'activist periods' in the US Supreme Court's history according to the number of cases in which either state or federal legislation was ruled invalid.

35 Marvin Schick, 'Judicial Activism on the Supreme Court' in Halpern and Lamb, *Supreme Court Activism, op. cit.*, pp. 37–55 at p. 46; Michael Kirby, 'Judicial Activism', *Western Australian Law Review*, **27** (1997), p. 12.

36 Nevertheless, common discourse about rights *does* emphasize the interests (the 'rights') of an identifiable, and therefore potentially litigating, individual over the interests of people unidentifiable at the time of the litigation. There is no analytical reason to characterize only one set of interests as 'rights', or *a priori* to value one over the other.

37 *South Australia* v. *Commonwealth* (1942) 65 CLR 373; *Victoria* v. *Commonwealth* (1957) 99 CLR 575.

38 (1997) 146 ALR 495.

39 Posner, *The Federal Courts, op. cit.*, pp. 328–31.

40 For example, in *Cole* v. *Whitfield* (1988) 165 CLR 360, the High Court overturned a long line of precedent but upheld the validity of legislation which restricted business conduct.

41 Again in *Cole* v. *Whitfield*, ibid., the Court upheld legislation, contrary to the plain meaning of the constitutional injunction that trade between the States be 'absolutely free'. On its face, this text would seem to invalidate *any* government restriction of interstate trade, even if it were 'reasonable regulation' or 'appropriate and adapted' to a legitimate purpose.

42 See the examples in notes 37–8.

43 But see Paulsen, 'The Many Faces of "Judicial Restraint"', *op. cit.*, suggesting that various restrained judges differently prioritize deference to these authorities.

44 Laurence H. Tribe, 'A Constitution We Are Amending', *Harvard Law Review*, **7** (1983), p. 433.

45 Walter Dellinger, 'Constitutional Politics', *Harvard Law Review*, **97** (1983), p. 446.

46 Mikfa Abner, 'A Reply', *Duke Law Journal*, (1987), p. 380 at p. 385. See also Tom D. Campbell, *The Legal Theory of Ethical Positivism* (Aldershot: Dartmouth, 1996), pp. 112, 176–7; Kirby, 'Judicial Activism', *op. cit.*, pp. 1–4, although cf. at p. 12; J. Skelly Wright, 'The Judicial Right and the Rhetoric of Restraint', *Hastings Constitutional Law Quarterly*, **14** (1987), p. 487 at pp. 491–2; Wyszynski, 'In Praise of Judicial Restraint', *op. cit.*, p. 121. See also Julius Stone, *Social Dimensions of Law and Justice* (London: Steven & Sons, 1966), pp. 667–70, although he argues that, because legal sources are usually indeterminate, it is incoherent to advocate restraint.

47 Abner, 'A Reply', *op. cit.*, p. 385; Abraham, *The Judicial Process, op. cit.*, pp. 408–9.

48 Kent Greenawalt, *Private Consciences and Public Reasons* (New York: Oxford University Press, 1995), pp. 141–50.

49 Lon L. Fuller, 'Forms and Limits of Adjudication', *Harvard Law Review*, **92** (1978), p. 353; but cf. J.W.F. Allison, 'Fuller's Analysis of Polycentric Disputes and

the Limits of Adjudication', *Cambridge Law Journal*, **53** (1994), p. 367 querying whether this category can be satisfactorily defined.

[50] Ronald Dworkin, *Taking Rights Seriously* (London: Duckworth, 1977), pp. 77, 97–100, 297–327. However, the cogency of this distinction has been criticized: see, for example, Lawrence Alexander and Michael Bayles, 'Hercules or Proteus?', *Social Theory & Practice*, **5** (1980), p. 267 at pp. 286–93; Joseph Raz, 'Legal Principle and the Limits of Law', *Yale Law Journal*, **81** (1972), p. 823.

[51] For example, Dworkin, *Law's Empire*, *op. cit.*, pp. 372–3; Sotirios A. Barber, *On What the Constitution Means* (Baltimore: Johns Hopkins University Press, 1984), p. 218.

[52] See pp. 292–3 below.

[53] John P. Roche, 'Judicial Self-Restraint', *American Political Science Review*, **49** (1955), p. 762, particularly at pp. 771–2.

[54] David Novak, 'Economic Activism and Restraint' in Halpern and Lamb, *Supreme Court Activism*, *op. cit.*, pp. 95–6.

[55] Alexander M. Bickel, *The Least Dangerous Branch*, 2nd edn (New Haven, CT: Yale University Press, 1986), p. 156 (citing birth control decisions before *Griswold* v. *Connecticut* (1965) 381 US 479); a similar approach is advocated in John P. Stevens, 'Judicial Restraint', *San Diego Law Review*, **22** (1985), p. 437, and Sunstein, *Legal Reasoning*, *op. cit.*

[56] Bickel, *The Least Dangerous Branch*, *op. cit.*, p. 174 (citing the Supreme Court's dismissal of challenge to anti-miscegenation statute), and pp. 196–7 (citing the Supreme Court's refusal of jurisdiction in early challenges to electoral district malapportionment).

[57] Ibid., pp. 238–43 (citing the Supreme Court's stand against segregation, and suggesting that the Court might, in a similar way, have been preparing the ground to invalidate capital punishment – a prophecy still unfulfilled).

[58] Gerald Gunther, 'The Subtle Vices of the "Passive Virtues"', *Columbia Review*, **64** (1964), p. 1 at pp. 13–16.

[59] Wayne McCormack, 'The Justiciability Myth and the Rule of Law', *Hastings Constitutional Law Quarterly*, **14** (1987), p. 595 at pp. 631–2.

[60] For example, Anthony Champagne and Stuart S. Nagel, 'The Advocates of Restraint' in Halpern and Lamb, *Supreme Court Activism*, *op. cit.*, pp. 303–18 at pp. 310–11; Posner, *The Federal Courts*, *op. cit.*, p. 314.

[61] Gunther, 'The Subtle Vices' *op. cit.*, at pp. 24–5.

[62] Ibid., pp. 22–4.

[63] Ibid., pp. 13–16.

[64] Posner, *The Federal Courts*, *op. cit.*, p. 315.

[65] For example, Christopher E. Smith and Avis Alexandria Jones, 'The Rehnquist Court's Activism', *Connecticut Law Review*, **26** (1993), p. 53 show how respect for the legislative text of the federal *habeas corpus* statutes was contradicted by functional prudential restraint.

[66] See Posner, *The Federal Courts*, *op. cit.*

[67] Novak, 'Economic Activism', *op. cit.*, pp. 95–6, Harold J. Spaeth and Stuart H. Teger, 'Activism and Restraint' in Halpern and Lamb, *Supreme Court Activism*, *op. cit.*, pp. 277–301 at pp. 295–6 provide some statistical evidence that US Supreme Court decisions on standing correlate with substantive views on the relative value of individual freedom and government restriction and, at pp. 285–6 show that judicial decisions on deference to state legislation correlate with whether the legislation was favourable to business or labour.

[68] Although Brian Galligan, *Politics of the High Court* (Brisbane: University of Queensland Press, 1987), pp. 231–2 alleges that the High Court has protected liberal values and private enterprise against socialist challenges, he does not show that

decisions concerning doctrines of restraint were in fact driven by such considerations.

[69] G.F.K. Santow, 'Aspects of Judicial Restraint', *Australian Bar Review*, **13** (1995), p. 116 at p. 145.

[70] Dworkin, *Law's Empire*, *op. cit.*, pp. 372–3 and S.A. Barber, *On What the Constitution Means* (Baltimore: Johns Hopkins University Press, 1984), p. 218 attack restraint on this basis.

[71] Whether 'incomparability' may be a better term, and whether incommensurability exists, are beyond my scope: see generally Ruth Chang (ed.), *Incommensurability, Incomparability, and Practical Reason* (Cambridge, MA: Harvard University Press, 1997).

[72] Tom Campbell, *The Legal Theory of Ethical Positivism* (Aldershot: Dartmouth, 1996), pp. 3–4, 95–123.

[73] In particular, liberalism assumes that tolerance is a higher-order moral norm than other moral norms.

[74] See *R* v. *Federal Court of Australia; Ex p WA National Football League (Adamson's Case)* (1979) 143 CLR 190; *Commonwealth* v. *Tasmania (Tasmanian Dam Case)* (1983) 158 CLR 1.

[75] *Cole* v. *Whitfield* (1988) 165 CLR 360 at 403–4. Ironically the previous interpretation had itself been justified on the basis that constitutionality should depend on the legislation's necessary legal effect and not its ultimate social or economic effect: *Hughes and Vale* v. *New South Wales (No 1)* (1954) 93 CLR 1 at 22.

[76] See p. 287 above.

[77] For example, Dworkin, *Law's Empire*, *op. cit.*, pp. 379–99.

[78] This classification of different types of judicial law-making is based on John Bell, *Policy Arguments in Judicial Decisions* (Oxford: Clarendon Press, 1983).

[79] Schauer, *Playing by the Rules*, *op. cit.*, pp. 135–66; Campbell, *Ethical Positivism*, *op. cit.*, pp. 49–65.

[80] A rule will only increase predictability if it restricts the number of considerations relevant to the decision, thereby either reducing the range of equally correct decisions, or reducing the possibility of erroneous decisions (Schauer, *Playing by the Rules*, *op. cit.*, pp. 137–44). Rules do not always restrict the number of considerations. A rule may use a term so vague that its application invokes even more considerations than those relevant without the rule. Nor do fewer considerations always make decisions more predictable. If an additional consideration is only relevant when other considerations are equal, than the additional consideration increases predictability. But a consideration is only likely to have such a limited effect if its influence is itself governed by a rule.

[81] John Finnis, *Natural Law and Natural Rights* (Oxford: Clarendon Press, 1980), pp. 272–3.

[82] Campbell, *Ethical Positivism*, *op. cit.*, p. 59.

[83] Schauer, *Playing by the Rules*, *op. cit.*, pp. 162–6.

[84] Campbell, *Ethical Positivism*, *op. cit.*, p. 53.

[85] Ibid., p. 53.

[86] Ibid., p. 54.

[87] Ibid., pp. 54–6.

[88] Schauer, *Playing by the Rules*, *op. cit.*, pp. 135–7.

[89] Campbell, *Ethical Positivism*, *op. cit.*, p. 57.

[90] Ibid., pp. 56–7.

[91] Ibid., pp. 59–61. A judge can also make decisions on the basis of universalized moral judgements. However, the judge can equally make each decision 'in all the circumstances'. By contrast, a legislator who does not supervise each application of the rule *necessarily* makes universal moral judgements.

[92] Ibid., p. 60.

93 Schauer, *Playing by the Rules*, *op. cit.*, pp. 145–8.
94 Ibid., pp. 149–55.
95 Ibid., pp. 158–62; Campbell, *Ethical Positivism*, *op. cit.*, p. 61.
96 See pp. 298–304.
97 More complex issues arise if government is federal and the coordination of governments is itself facilitated by judicial enforcement of constitutional rules. Consequently, in federal systems governments doctrines of restraint may apply differently to litigants who are governments rather than individuals.
98 Kenny, 'Constitutional Fact Ascertainment', *op. cit.*
99 For example, William H. Riker and Barry R. Weingast, 'Constitutional Regulation of Legislative Choice', *Virginia Law Review*, **74** (1988), p. 373.
100 L.R. BeVier, 'Judicial Restraint: An Argument from Institutional Design', *Harvard Journal of Law and Public Policy*, **17**(1) (1994), p. 7.
101 For example, Dworkin, *Taking Rights Seriously*, *op. cit.*, pp. 279–90; Dworkin, *A Matter of Principle* (Oxford: Clarendon Press, 1985), pp. 119–45.
102 Bix, *Law, Language and Legal Determinacy*, *op. cit.*, pp. 77–132.
103 Joseph Raz, *The Morality of Freedom* (Oxford: Clarendon Press, 1986), pp. 23–105.
104 Finnis, *Natural Law*, *op. cit.*, at pp. 231–54.
105 Such an idea lies behind some theories of citizenship and deliberative democracy: see, for example, Cass R. Sunstein, *The Partial Constitution* (Cambridge, MA: Harvard University Press, 1993), pp. 135–6.
106 Neil K. Komesar, *Imperfect Alternatives* (Chicago: University of Chicago Press, 1994), pp. 29–34.
107 Ibid., pp. 69–73.
108 See the examples in Posner, *The Federal Courts*, *op. cit.*, pp. 315–18.
109 For example, Robin West, 'The Aspirational Constitution', *North Western University Law*, **88** (1993), p. 241.
110 Raz, *Authority of Law*, *op. cit.*, pp. 194–7.
111 I am grateful to Martin Krygier for pressing this point.
112 Antonin Scalia, 'Originalism: The Lesser Evil', *Cincinnati Law Review*, **57** (1989), p. 849.
113 See p. 285 above.
114 Stone, *Legal System*, *op. cit.*, pp. 316–23.
115 Stone, *Social Dimensions*, *op. cit.*, pp. 667–70.
116 See Peter W. Hogg, *Constitutional Law of Canada*, 3rd edn (Scarborough: Carsewell, 1992), pp. 214–19.
117 The literature is voluminous. See, for example, Anthony Mason, 'The Role of the Courts at the Turn of the Century', *Journal of Judicial Administration*, **3** (1993), p. 156 at pp. 163–4; Louise Bygrave, 'Judicial Decisions and Policy', *Australian Journal of Public Administration*, **57** (1998), p. 68 and many of the subsequent articles in the same issue.
118 See Daryl Dawson, 'Do Judges Make Law? Too Much?', *Judicial Review*, **3**(1) (1996), p. 1 at p. 2.
119 Dworkin, *Taking Rights Seriously*, *op. cit.*, pp. 15–16.

13 A Patchwork Quilt Theory of Constitutional Interpretation

WALTER SINNOTT-ARMSTRONG[1]

Both the Warren Court in the United States and the Mason Court in Australia declared many important legislative statutes unconstitutional. Whenever judges do this, they frustrate and antagonize a majority, including legislators and citizens who worked long and hard to pass those statutes, or who planned their lives around those statutes. Such judicial decisions are particularly problematic when they depend on moral beliefs of the judges, since then they raise a difficult question: why should the statute's constitutionality be determined by the moral beliefs of such a small number of judges rather than by the moral beliefs of the much larger number of legislators and citizens?

Many legal theorists answer that it should not, so judges should never base their legal decisions, even in part, on their own moral beliefs. This is an *extreme* prescriptive separation thesis, and one which is held by Robert Bork in the United States.[2] A more *moderate* prescriptive separation thesis is held by Tom Campbell in Australia, who claims, 'no legal system *ought* to permit morally explicit or other controversial standards being used to establish the existence of law or determine its implications'.[3] While Campbell's thesis allows judges to use moral standards that are not controversial,[4] it is still universal insofar as it says that judges should *never* use moral standards that are controversial, making this moderate thesis far from weak. This moderate prescriptive separation thesis is central to Campbell's legal theory of ethical positivism,[5] as well as to most traditional forms of prescriptive legal positivism.[6]

In opposition, prescriptive legal realists argue that as the job of judges is to do justice, they should not worry too much about the rules laid down by legislators when following these rules would, in their opinion, be unjust.[7] The principal aim of constitutional rights is to protect individuals and minorities against majority oppression and, it is argued, the majority could not be sufficiently constrained if judges were bound to follow rules laid down by the legislature and could not use their own moral beliefs. On this view, then, judges should use their own moral beliefs whenever this is needed to achieve justice.

I will argue that both of these extreme views are too simple. Allowing judges to use their own moral beliefs has both benefits and costs, which need to be weighed against each other. There is no reason to believe that the benefits and costs will be the same in all circumstances or that the balance will always tip the same direction.[8] Consequently, the only adequate solution is to give up the search for a blanket theory that prescribes a single method of adjudication to cover all areas of law.

Instead of a blanket theory, I will propose a patchwork quilt theory that requires judges not to use any of their own moral beliefs in some circumstances, but then requires judges to use some of their own moral beliefs in other circumstances, even if those moral beliefs are controversial. This patchwork quilt approach would be easy to support by pointing to vast differences among different countries, some of which have much less reliable judges and face much greater dangers. Even within established modern democracies, such as Australia and the United States, it would be easy to argue for a patchwork quilt theory by citing important differences among different areas of law, from parking laws to constitutions. But my patches are smaller. I will try to show relevant variations within the smaller classes of cases involving different constitutional clauses and even a single constitutional clause.[9]

Moral Language in Laws

First, I need to clarify the issue. Many commentators contrast judges using their own moral beliefs with judges following the plain meanings of the words in the law. This is a false dichotomy. The words of the law often direct judges to use their own moral beliefs, especially when the law contains moral language. For example, the US Constitution prohibits unreasonable searches and seizures, excessive bail, and cruel and unusual punishment. It also requires due process and just compensation. Other phrases, including 'freedom of speech' and 'equal protection', are implicitly moral. There is some, but less, moral language in the Australian Constitution. Outside constitutional law, there are limits on 'unconscionable' contracts and so on.

To apply such moral language, judges have to use *some* moral standards of what is 'due' or 'just' or 'cruel' and the like. This raises a crucial question, namely: *whose* moral standards should judges use? *Originalists* tell judges to use only the original legislators' moral standards, as revealed by the words they chose or by other documents relevant to original intention or purpose. *Contemporists* claim that judges should use contemporary standards of decency or of morality.[10] But both originalism and contemporism conflict with the actual texts of most constitutions. The usual moral clauses do not require 'what we (the framers or ratifiers) consider just compensation' or 'what contemporary society considers just compensation'. Nor do these clauses forbid 'what we (the framers or ratifiers) consider cruel punishment' or 'what contemporary society considers cruel punishment'. Instead, standard moral clauses require what *is* just compensation, and they prohibit what *is* cruel punishment. To apply the literal meanings of these clauses, then, judges must determine what really is just compensation or cruel punishment. If a punishment is cruel, but judges, believing that it is not cruel, decide that it is constitutional, then they are wrong and they do not do as the clause demands. However, at least they will have followed the right method insofar as they used their beliefs about what is cruel and what is not, and not their beliefs about what the ratifiers or contemporary society regarded as cruel. The only way for judges to try to apply such moral clauses is to use their own beliefs about morality. In this way, such moral clauses seem to direct judges to do exactly what the prescriptive separation thesis tells them not to do.[11]

To avoid this dilemma some defenders of the prescriptive separation thesis say that legislators should never use such moral clauses in laws. However, such moral clauses are practically impossible to avoid in the real world. Legislators are notoriously unable to predict all of the different kinds of case that will arise under a law. When they can predict cases, they often still cannot agree on how to decide those specific cases, despite their agreement on general principles. Because of these limitations, legislators are often unable to devise a formula or list of specific kinds of case to be required or prohibited. They cannot refer to 'what we think' because the legislature does not yet think anything definite about the future cases. They cannot refer to 'contemporary standards' when the aim is to limit the majority. The only option, then, is to write statutes and constitutional clauses in specific moral language. The point and effect of such language is to authorize judges to decide the cases that the legislators did not foresee or agree on. This delegation of authority might be seen as a 'second-best approach',[12] but it is unavoidable, common, within the authority of the legislature and often supported by good reasons.

Nonetheless, we still need to determine how judges should adjudicate cases when faced with such moral clauses. Judges could try to use original or contemporary moral standards rather than their own moral beliefs in as many cases as possible. This would not work in cases where original and contemporary standards are too conflicting and too indeterminate, but then judges could always let majority legislation stand until a legislature changes it. By using such methods, judges *could* minimize the degree to which they base legal decisions on their own moral beliefs.

The question is whether this minimization is *desirable* in a legal system. To that question, my answer is a resolute 'sometimes'. Of course, it is easy to say 'sometimes'. The difficult task is to specify when. So I need to ask when judges should use their moral beliefs.

Reasons for Non-moral Rules

My most basic answer refers to consequences. The usefulness of a method depends on the consequences of applying it. So, in constitutional law, judges should use their moral beliefs when – and only when – and to the extent that doing so will lead to the best decisions. Controversies will rage over which decisions are best, but here I will assume that the best decisions are those that make society best in terms of both utility and fairness. This assumption will allow me to focus on another set of controversies. Even if we agree about which decisions are best, we still need to determine when these best decisions are more likely to result from judges using their own moral beliefs.

To determine that, I will compare two extreme methods of adjudication. The first, which I will call *the moral case method*, is for judges to use their own best judgement of what is morally right or wrong in the particular case before them, even when their moral beliefs are controversial. The second method of adjudication, which I will call *the non-moral rule method*, is for judges to apply the standards of the original legislators or of contemporary society, even when the judges think that those other people's moral standards are wrong.[13]

When these different methods of adjudication are built into different legal systems, each method and each resulting system has some advantages and some disadvantages. These costs and benefits have been discussed very helpfully both by Fred Schauer and by Tom Campbell.[14] However, I do not agree with all of the reasons for rules that have been given, so I want to begin by dismissing two bad reasons for the non-moral rule method of adjudication.

One common mistake is to think that allowing judges to use their own moral beliefs would undermine the impartiality that is essential to good judging. If judges put more weight on their own moral beliefs than on those of other citizens and legislators, then how can they be impartial? The non-moral rule method is supposed to ensure this kind of impartiality.

This supposed reason for rules, however, rests on a confusion of *neutrality* with *impartiality*.[15] Consider a basketball referee who calls fouls loosely so that the game will go faster. This referee uses his own belief about the values of fast play to decide which fouls to call, so he is not neutral among values. Moreover, the value he places on fast play might actually help one of the teams. Nonetheless, the referee can still be impartial between the teams who are playing, so long as he does not adopt this method of calling fouls because of which team it will help or harm. Similarly, judges can also be impartial between the parties in a lawsuit, even when they are not neutral among values, because their decisions are based on their moral beliefs about freedom, equality and so on. So long as they remain impartial in this way, judges can still do their jobs well even when they base legal decisions on their own moral beliefs.

Basketball might not seem analogous to constitutional cases when one party argues for freedom and the other argues for equality. However, even if the judges decides for freedom over equality, or vice versa, this decision need not be based on any preference for one of the parties over the other. The judge is impartial in the required way so long as he or she would have decided the same way if each party had been in the position of the other and had given the arguments of the other side.

A related common, but mistaken, claim is that judges who use their own moral beliefs violate the principle of universalizability, because they are not following rules, and universalizability requires rules.[16] This argument apparently does not depend on contingent features of the circumstances, so it would be very strong if it worked. But that is why it fails. Universalizability is not an advantage for the non-moral rule method unless the moral case method violates universalizability. It does not – or, at least, it need not. When legislators delegate authority to judges to decide which punishments are cruel, for example, judges can often give reasons for counting a punishment as cruel, and they can apply those reasons universally. Even when judges do not give reasons, they might make the same decisions in all relevantly similar cases. When judges base their decisions on their own moral beliefs rather than on beliefs of the legislature, their moral beliefs and acts might be just as universalizable as the legislators' moral beliefs. So the non-moral rule method of adjudication has no real advantage on grounds of either impartiality or universalizability.

Many other common misconceptions also lead to some to overestimate the justifications for the non-moral rule method.[17] Avoiding these mistakes is important. However, instead of trying to ward off all of the bad reasons for rules, I will now try to be more constructive by turning to good reasons for them.

These good reasons, in contrast with the two just criticized, are contingent. The circumstances affect when these reasons hold and also how strong they are. This means that we need empirical investigations to determine when the non-moral rule method has these advantages. I have no hard empirical evidence, so I will have to make do, for now, with a few tentative speculations.

The first advantages of rules is *efficiency*. If judges are to decide on a case-by-case basis, they will have to look at each case in great detail. Suppose, for example, that judges are told simply to declare someone eligible to run for a legislature when that person is mature enough. In these circumstances judges will have to look at each candidate carefully, which will take a lot of time and attention. However, they can avoid this effort if they have a clear rule to follow. That is why the US Constitution simply specifies a certain number of years of age that is required to be eligible to run for each office. Such clauses tell judges which detail is important – namely, age. The Constitution as a whole then tells judges which other properties, if any, are also required, enabling them to determine eligibility simply be looking at birth records and other relevant documents, so that very few cases come to court.

Determinate rules applied non-morally do not, however, always increase efficiency. To be effective, such rules have to be made too complex, but moral judgements are easy to make, then it might be more efficient to have a simple, but vague, rule that cannot be applied without judges using their own moral beliefs. However, where determinate rules need not be too complex, and where moral judgement is difficult, then the non-moral rule method of adjudication *does* increase efficiency.

The importance of efficiency also varies. We want judges to take their time, at the expense of efficiency, before they sentence someone to prison or death. In contrast, efficiency assumes a greater importance when a certain type of case frequently arises, when the details of each case are hard to determine, when there is not much at stake relative to the court costs, and when court dockets are already crowded, so that courts can use their time to better effect. Standard cost-benefit analysis, thus, shows that the circumstances affect the absolute and relative importance of efficiency.

The second reason for the non-moral rule method is a certain kind of *equity* or fairness. If different judges decide each case separately and use different moral beliefs, then different people who did exactly the same thing will receive different treatments. One person might be fined heavily, while another might not, if judges are told simply to make fines appropriate. The non-moral rule method prevents this kind of inequity. If judges must fine everyone $100, even if a judge thinks that $100 is too much or too little in a particular case, then everyone will be fined the same amount for the same offence.

Of course, because different legislatures can also pass different statutes in different locations and at different times, a similar kind of inequity can be introduced by legislative rules. The non-moral rule method will leave judges and others with no way to correct those legislative inequities, although it does at least prevent judges from introducing additional inequities.

This kind of equity is more important where relative position is crucial. If judges impose heavy fines on one business but not on another, then the latter will suffer in competition. Other goods, in contrast, do not depend for their value on how much others have. If one person is allowed to commit suicide, but another is not, their relative position in itself does not make either one any better or worse off. When such a non-comparative good is at stake, this kind of inequity does not matter so much. So, again, the importance of this kind of inequity varies with the kind of case.

The third reason for the non-moral rule method is *predictability*.[18] If judges decide on a case-by-case basis, it will be difficult for law-abiding citizens to know what to do to avoid losses in court. For example, if judges are told simply to allow affirmative action programmes when they are fair, then schools will not know which kinds of programmes to construct in order to avoid the expense and confusion of lawsuits and of reconstructing the whole programme when a court finds that it is not fair. It will be much easier for schools to plan if judges follow clear rules in deciding the constitutionality of affirmative action programmes without using their own moral beliefs.

Predictability is not, however, always increased by determinate rules applied non-morally. If determinate rules are very complex, but moral beliefs are uncontroversial, then citizens and lawyers might be able to predict official action more easily if there is a simple but vague rule that cannot be applied without judges using their own moral beliefs. Still, where determinate rules need not be too complex, and moral judgement is controversial, then the non-moral rule method of adjudication does increase predictability.

The importance of predictability also varies, since many aspects of our lives do not require, or even benefit from, planning. Spontaneity often invigorates. Nevertheless, predictability becomes important when people make long-term plans and expensive preparations. This is especially true in matters of economics, where businesses must plan capital expenditures years in advance. Predictability also becomes important in any area where personal choices do, or might, affect people's lives far into the future. The more important and distant are the effects of one's choices, the more important predictability becomes.

The fourth reason for the non-moral rule method is the danger of *judicial error*. If judges decide each case on its own moral merits, then they will make mistakes. They will decide a case in one way because they honestly think that that decision is best, when that decision really is not best. In contrast, if judges follow the non-moral rule method, then judges will introduce fewer errors. They might misinterpret or misapply the moral standards of legislators, but at least they will not add mistakes because their own moral beliefs are wrong. In this way, the non-moral rule method reduces the possible sources of error.

This does not prove that the non-moral rule method will always reduce errors in the legal system as a whole. Legislators also make mistakes, and following the non-moral rule method of this reason for the non-moral rule method depends on the relative risk of judicial errors as opposed to legislative errors that judges would otherwise correct. It also depends on the relative number, seriousness and difficulty of correcting those errors.

These relative dangers vary because of differences between the positions of judges and legislators. Compared with legislators, judges receive a great deal of information about particular cases, they are usually trained in legal reasoning, they must publicly state their reasons for their decisions, they are not as subject to political pressures and lobbying, and they supposedly do not look after a certain group's interests or make deals. On the other hand, judges also receive less information about society in general, they usually do not hear directly from third parties who will be affected by their decisions (except in *amicus* briefs), they make decisions in smaller and less diverse groups, and they are usually chosen with less public scrutiny.

These factors make judges more likely than legislators to make mistakes on certain kinds of cases. Which kinds of case depends on many details and has to be determined by empirical investigation, so here I can only venture a few speculations. It seems that judges will be *more* error-prone than legislators on issues of social policy, except where social policies are likely to be distorted by corruption, short-term interests and disproportionately powerful lobbying groups. In contrast, their relative resources make judges *less* prone to error than legislators in cases of minority rights, at least where minority rights should override or limit majority goals. We should not overestimate the tendency of judges to protect minority rights, since that tendency depends on the dominant culture among judges who can be just as biased as legislators.[19] We should also not underestimate the ability and tendency of legislatures to represent minority interests, at least where the cost is not too high. However, a minority in society is not a minority in court, but just one of the two parties before the court. This makes a difference. There are many cases where discrete and insular minorities that are despised by the majority have been protected by courts in the United States as well as Australia.[20]

This is a reason to insist on the non-moral rule method in many (but not all) cases of social policy, but also to defend just as strongly the moral case method in many (but not all) cases of underprivileged minority rights – at least in countries such as the United States and Australia.[21] More generally, the risk of judicial error is a stronger reason for the non-moral rule method in areas where there is reason to distrust judges, if there is also reason to have more faith in the legislature.

The fifth reason for the non-moral rule method concerns the *allocation* of power in democracies. The moral case method gives judges a great deal of power. Even if judges' decisions are not errors, their power can be objectionable if judges are not in the right position to make this kind of decision. There is something wrong with the right decision made in the wrong way.

The main complaint against judges making certain decisions is that those in the highest courts are usually not elected. This makes it inappropriate to give them power to decide issues that ought to be resolved democratically according to intuition or some background theory. For example, it seems inappropriate for judges to determine most tax rates, even when they do hit on the best tax rate. On the other hand, when underprivileged minorities suffer from legislation by the majority, there seems to be less reason to restrict judges to moral beliefs of the majority, because this will severely limit minority protections. Political theorists disagree about exactly when an issue ought to be decided democratically, but almost everyone agrees that elections are appropriate for some issues, and that the moral case method of adjudication is appropriate for other issues.

Thus, each of these five reasons for the non-moral rule method of adjudication has different force in different circumstances. Their forces vary with the country (which might be stable or not, and might have a more or less trustworthy judiciary), with levels of courts (such as trials, appeals and a Supreme or High Court), and with different areas of law (such as criminal, civil and constitutional). None of this should be surprising. Consequences depend on circumstances.

What is more often overlooked is that these justifications for the non-moral rule method have different forces in different areas within constitutional law. Constitutional law is often seen as a unified subject, but different parts of the Constitution vary in ways that are important in determining the best method of adjudication. My patchwork quilt theory concludes that judges ought to use different methods of adjudication in these different areas of constitutional law.[22]

I cannot argue for this thesis in all of the different areas of constitutional law. There are too many. Instead of trying to be comprehensive, I will illustrate some variations by contrasting a few cases. What I say about these cases will be sketchy and inconclusive. Nonetheless, I hope that my few comments here will seem sufficiently plausible to suggest that the justifications for the non-moral rule method apply with great force to some cases, but with much less force to other cases within constitutional law.

Capital Punishment

My first example is capital punishment. In *Gregg* v. *Georgia*,[23] Justices Brennan and Marshall argued in dissent that the death penalty violates the Eighth Amendment of the United States Constitution, which prohibits 'cruel and unusual punishment'.[24] Their arguments had to depend on their own moral beliefs, since it is very doubtful that capital punishment is cruel according to the moral beliefs of the original ratifiers or of the contemporary majority.[25]

The arguments by Brennan and Marshall would be acceptable to those who argue that judges should apply the Eighth Amendment to cases by using their own moral views about what is cruel. Brennan and Marshall were criticized, however, by commentators who held that judges ought to be restricted to the moral beliefs of the original ratifiers or of contemporary society. So, did Brennan and Marshall use the right method in this case? My patchwork quilt theory implies that we cannot determine which method is right until we ask another question: how important are the reasons for the non-moral rule method of adjudication in deciding the constitutionality of capital punishment?

The first reason is *efficiency*. Capital cases arise frequently and require a great deal of attention. However, the issue of constitutionality is not about particular capital case but about whether statutes that prescribe capital punishment should be allowed. That issue does not arise very often, and the value of the court's time pales in comparison with the value of the lives at stake. So efficiency does not seem very important in such cases.

The second reason for the non-moral rule method is to avoid *inequity*. There is some unfairness if one murderer gets capital punishment but another similar murderer gets life imprisonment. However, we often accept different punishments for similar crimes as long as each punishment is adequate and not excessive. In addition, the executed murderer would not be any better off if the other murderer were also executed. Relative position does not matter much in this area. Besides, this kind of inequity would not be avoided if judges followed the moral beliefs of the original legislators or of the contemporary majority and allowed capital punishment, since even then some murderers would get capital punishment and others would not. So inequity does not provide a strong reason to follow the non-moral rule method in this case.[26]

The third reason for the non-moral rule method concerns *predictability*. This also does not seem very important here, since nothing very bad would happen if the Supreme Court occasionally changed its mind about the constitutionality of capital punishment, and nobody could predict what they would decide next. Murderers rarely rely on judicial decisions when they decide whether or not to murder. Legislators sometimes rely on judicial decisions when they vote for or against a capital punishment statute, but the losses are not great if they rely incorrectly. So predictability does not matter much in this case.

The fourth reason for the non-moral rule method is the risk of *judicial error*. It would be horrible if an innocent person were executed. However, the issue here is not particular cases but the constitutionality of capital punishment. On that issue, judicial errors are not very important. Suppose that judges declare capital punishment to be unconstitutional when it is not. Murderers still get life imprisonment, which is a harsh punishment, so the majority's will is not frustrated much, and the murder rate will not go up much, if at all (although new evidence might change this assessment). Conversely, suppose judges declare capital punishment to be constitutional when it is not. If it really is cruel, then few legislatures will allow it, and few juries will impose it. Indeed, in the United States, it is actually carried out in a notoriously small percentage of murder convictions. The mistake of allowing it is still important to those who are executed, but the rest of society is not affected much by these few executions. So, either way, judicial errors about the constitutionality of capital punishment are not disasters for society.

The final reason for the non-moral method is *allocation of power*. Many issues should be decided democratically, but the question of whether a punishment is cruel seems to be exactly the kind of issue that should not be decided by legislatures. The main point of the Eighth Amendment was to protect unpopular individuals and groups against the kinds of excess that elected legislators are prone to adopt in times of great public anger or fear. If judges should not have power in this kind of case, then it is hard to see any role at all for judicial review of legislatures.

Every one of these claims is controversial and questionable. Still, if most of this is right, then there is little reason not to allow judges to use their own moral beliefs in deciding which punishments are cruel under the Eighth Amendment. This does not determine whether or not capital punishment is unconstitutional. My point is only about method: judges may and should decide this issue by consulting their own moral beliefs about cruelty and not only by applying the moral beliefs of the original ratifiers or of contemporary society. That is enough to refute any strong or moderate version of the prescriptive separation thesis.

Flag-burning

The story is very different with laws against flag-burning in the United States. Opponents of these laws claimed that they violate the First Amendment to the United States Constitution, which prohibits any law 'abridging the freedom of speech'. Defenders of such laws claim that flag-burning is conduct rather than speech and that the flag is so important as a symbol that we need to protect it. The issue reached the Supreme Court in *Texas* v. *Johnson*.[27]

This case cannot be decided without using *some* moral beliefs. Flag-burning is both conduct and an expression of political ideas, so judges need to decide which aspect of flag-burning is most important to determine whether or not to count it as speech. If it is speech, then judges need to decide whether flag-burning (unlike perjury) is the kind of speech that deserves legal protection, and whether legal prohibitions on flag-burning serve a compelling state interest with no less intrusive means.[28] That depends on how important the flag is as a symbol of the country, how much harm flag-burning causes, and whether other ways of expressing the same beliefs would be forceful enough. These decisions require some moral beliefs.

But whose moral beliefs? Chief Justice Rehnquist claimed to base his dissent on what is 'regarded as evil and profoundly offensive to the majority of people', as shown by many historical sources and poems. But he also went on to claim that flag-burning 'is "no essential part of any exposition of ideas, and [is] of such slight social value as a step to truth that any benefit that may be derived from [it] is clearly outweighed" by the public interest in avoiding a probable breach of the peace'.[29] At this point Rehnquist's argument seems to depend crucially on his own moral beliefs.

Whatever Rehnquist's basis actually was, the main question here is whether judges *ought* to decide this case on the basis of their own moral beliefs or, instead, on the basis of the moral beliefs of the original ratifiers or of contemporary society. My patchwork theory implies that we should settle this question by asking another: how important are the reasons for judges to follow the non-moral rule method in this particular case or other cases like it?

The first reason for following the non-moral rule method is *efficiency*. There is a lot of talk and political protest in the United States (as well as in Australia). Some is useful. Some is dangerous. If judges had to determine the moral status of each protest individually, they would be very busy. Moreover, the particular form of a protest usually does not matter much. The burning of flags offends many, but other ways of expressing the same ideas would have had almost the same effects. Thus, there is little to be gained and much efficiency to be lost by asking judges to determine the moral status of each particular protest.

The second reason for the non-moral rule method is *equity*. Speech is an area where much depends on one's relative position. If one political group cannot speak out, but their opponents can, then their opponents will probably win the election or have a greater influence on the government. This makes it very important for judges not to prevent some political speech and allow other political speech when there is no relevant difference. The only way to avoid such inequity is for judges to follow the non-moral rule method rather than to decide each case separately.

The third reason for the non-moral rule method is *predictability*. If judges could use their own moral beliefs to determine whether each protest should be protected, then, since protesters could not predict particular judges' moral beliefs, they also could not predict whether their protests would land them in jail. This would have a 'chilling effect'. Many people would be too scared to participate in any political protest, including the many beneficial protests. Protesters would worry not only about the immediate future but also about decades to come, if they thought that their form of protest could become illegal in the future, and then they might suffer retroactively, as in the McCarthy era. Fears of such long-term dangers would stifle much beneficial protest if judicial decisions on speech were not predictable far into the future. That is a strong reason to want determinate rules to restrict judges as well as legislators, and to want those rules to be very difficult to change.

The fourth reason for the non-moral rule method is the danger of *errors by judges*. If judges use their moral beliefs in each case to decide which protests deserve constitutional protection, then they might make two kinds of error. They might protect protests that should not be protected with the consequence that bystanders and the country might be harmed. But it is hard to see how such harms are caused by flag-burning or by any other non-violent political protests. On the other hand, judges might fail to protect protests that should be protected. That would bring the chilling effect just discussed. Of course, legislative error can be serious in the same way if legislators prevent useful protests, but that does not show that judicial error is not also serious, since speech is often stifled by officials other than legislators. Both judicial and legislative errors can be reduced by a constitutional protection of political protest applied with the non-moral rule method of adjudication.

The final consideration is *allocation of power*. Here, I must admit that judges do seem to be the natural people to limit political protest if anyone does. We can't trust the majority or the legislature, since they would be too tempted to silence their critics or rivals. But this does not mean that judges should decide which political protests can be limited. The other possibility is that there should be entrenched constitutional rules that judges must follow without consulting their moral beliefs about the particular case.

Thus, the reasons for the non-moral rule method of adjudication seem very strong in the case of flag-burning. Similar reason would apply to most other forms of political protest. It seems to be too inefficient, inequitable, unpredictable and dangerous to let judges use their own moral beliefs to decide in each case whether or not a particular form of protest should be protected.

Australian Capital Television

My argument so far might seem to suggest that the prescriptive separation thesis fails in criminal law but holds in laws about free speech. That would be too simple. The patches in my quilt are smaller than that, because some areas of free speech are crucially different from restrictions on political protests.

This point can be illustrated by the *Australian Capital Television* or *ACTV* case in Australia.[30] I will not say whether that decision or its method was correct, but will, instead, confine myself to pointing out some differences between this and the flag-burning case. These differences show why one cannot infer the right method in one case from the right method in the other case.

The statute at stake in the *ACTV* case was the Political Broadcasts Act.[31] The negative part of this Act banned political advertisements on radio or television during an election period. The positive part of the Act established a system of free time for candidates, 90 per cent of which went to parties in proportion to the votes they received in a previous election. The purpose of this complex statute was to take pressure off political parties to raise money and to reduce the influence of uninformative image making in electronic media.

This statute was claimed to violate a constitutional guarantee of freedom of speech or communication. This right was never explicitly stated in the Australian Constitution, but it was supposed to be implied at several places. This implication could not be derived without the judges using their own moral beliefs, which they clearly did. For example, Chief Justice Mason held that the Act needed but lacked a 'compelling justification', and that protection of speech has 'paramount weight' compared with competing public interests.[32]

This decision was, and is, very controversial, but my point is only about method: there are differences between this case and the flag-burning case that are important in determining the appropriate method of adjudication.

First, there seems to be less need for *efficiency* in the *ACTV* case. What is at issue here is a general scheme rather than a set of protests by individuals, so judges need not worry that their dockets will fill up if they overturn this Political Broadcasts Act. To claim the general power of judicial review using implied constitutional rights would greatly increase the cases before the High Court, as would claiming the authority to review all restrictions on communication. My claim is only about applying this authority, if such there be, to the Political Broadcasts Act in this case.

Furthermore, the decision did not increase *inequities* due to different judges using different moral beliefs. Some might argue that the Political Broadcasts Act would have removed unfairness between rich and poor political candidates and parties. However, even if this other kind of unfairness is allowed, it is not introduced by the fact that judges used their own moral beliefs.

Moreover, unlike political protests, people and candidates do not usually construct their lives and political careers around predictions about which kinds of political advertisement will be allowed (although the Political Broadcasts Act would have helped politicians spend less time raising money). Besides, legislators could change the rules as often as judges. So *predictability* does not strongly favour the non-moral rule method in this case.

The fourth reason for non-moral rules is the risk of *errors by judges*. Here there is a real problem. The best restrictions on political advertisements are those that provide maximum information and the best effects on government and on society. But which restrictions are those? These large-scale social questions are not the kind of questions that judges are normally trained to answer. That lack of training increases the risk that judges will make mistakes.

Nonetheless, the crucial issue here is the *relative* risk of trusting legislators instead of judges. Legislators are tempted to favour restrictions that promote their own political success. Indeed, the main argument against the Political Broadcasts Act was its tendency to favour parties in power. Not only does the negative part of the Act forbid new groups from advertising, its positive part ensures that smaller parliamentary groups cannot buy more advertisements as their popularity and contributions increase. This means that the groups in power, and the distribution of power among them, will be protected by this statute. Moreover, if judges cannot use their moral beliefs against this statute, it is not clear how they could stop ever more dangerous restrictions on political speech in the future.[33]

The final issue is the *allocation* of power. Defenders of the Political Broadcasts Act might argue that, ultimately, it is the majority, not a few judges, who should decide which kind of government to have. The problem, of course, is that the majority usually favours the legislators in power, even when they harm minorities. Since it is only unelected officials, such as judges, who can weigh minority rights impartially without fearing political repercussions, it does seem natural to give judges the power to determine which restrictions on political advertisement are justified.

The point is not that the ACTV decision was correct. I do not want to commit myself to any view about whether the judges should have been allowed to use their moral beliefs in this case. Moreover, even if they should have been allowed, Australian laws might have forbidden the judges to use their own moral beliefs.[34] And even if they were legally allowed to use their own moral beliefs, the justices might have used the wrong moral beliefs, if the Political Broadcasts Act promoted democracy rather than interfering with it. In any case, my claim is only that, because of the differences between the *ACTV* case and the flag-burning case, even if the non-moral rule method were used in the flag-burning case, that doe not imply that the same method should be used in the *ACTV* case. If not, then the patches on my quilt covers smaller areas than single constitutional amendments.

When

I have said that 'sometimes' the non-moral rule method should be used. Now it is time to say 'when'. Fortunately, my five factors and three examples suggest an answer. If we face a new kind of case, what we need to do is consider all the reasons for the non-moral rule method and determine how strong they are in this new area. When the reasons are strong, judges should exercise restraint and avoid basing their decisions on their own moral beliefs. When the reasons for the non-moral rule method are not strong, judges should use their own moral beliefs about which decision is morally right (at least when they are not clearly forbidden). Similar lines of thought can determine not only when judges should use their own moral beliefs but also which moral beliefs and how these moral beliefs should be used in each kind of case. This will leave many gradations in how many moral beliefs should be used in how many ways, but these can be justified by corresponding gradations in the reasons for the non-moral rule method.

Thus, the five reasons for the non-moral rule method give a pattern to my quilt. Less metaphorically, they provide a meta-method – that is, a second-order method for choosing a first-order method of adjudication in a given case. Much more needs to be done to clarify each of the reasons for the non-moral rule method. Maybe, for example, my list should be shortened or lengthened. Nonetheless, even if I need to reweave my particular patchwork quilt, my main point is that we need to shift our focus to these issues of meta-method instead of the fruitless arguments about which method of adjudication is right in all cases.

Even with its meta-method, this quilt theory obviously cannot be applied mechanically. Judges need judgement. But these considerations do suggest one way to give guidance to judges who sincerely want to figure out which method is best in a case. What we need is a way to classify kinds of case and a method for measuring the relative strengths of the reasons for rules in each. This will aid us in formulating guidelines to help judges decide which method to use in which cases. These guidelines will also help the rest of us understand what is going on. Judges sometimes use their moral beliefs and sometimes insist on not using them in what often seems an arbitrary way. My quilt theory provides a rationale for this common, but otherwise baffling, practice. It thereby both explains what judges have been doing all along and also helps them improve their practice.

Practical problems still remain: how can we make judges use the right method? One answer is that not all judges are power-hungry. Some are conscientious in the sense that they honestly want to judge in the right way. They can be convinced to use the right method and meta-method simply by being convinced that these are the right methods. I think that there are more conscientious judges than many cynics suppose.

Other judges are very concerned with reputation or the esteem in which they are held by certain communities – often the legal community but sometimes also newspaper editors and the public. These judges can be convinced to use the right method and meta-method by convincing these communities that these are the right methods, and then convincing the judges that these communities believe this.

Unfortunately, other judges are less scrupulous. They use whichever method and meta-method suit their current political goals or even self-interest. If there are enough unscrupulous judges in a country, then the legislature might need to pass explicit secondary rules of adjudication that require judges to use certain methods to decide certain kinds of case.[35] My meta-method could be adapted to help the legislature formulate such secondary laws of adjudication. These laws would have at least symbolic force. If need be, they could be enforced by threats of harm to reputation, of overturning contrary decisions, or even of impeachment by the legislature, since such laws would make it illegal for judges to use the wrong method.

Such legislative restrictions on the judiciary might not be a practical or political possibility in many countries. If not, it is not clear what anyone can do except try to make the judges more scrupulous and then try to convince them that certain methods are the right ones. In that case, the first step is to determine what the right methods are in which cases. That is what I have tried to begin doing here, although much work remains to be done.

Notes

1 I am grateful to James Boyle, Tom Campbell, Neil MacCormick and Fred Schauer for helpful comments on this chapter.

2 Robert Bork, *The Tempting of America* (New York: Macmillan, 1990).

3 Tom Campbell, *The Legal Theory of Ethical Positivism* (Aldershot: Dartmouth, 1996), p. 71. Campbell seems closer to Bork's extreme thesis when he writes, 'a good legal system is, inter alia, one in which adjudicators use only empirical or, more broadly, morally neutral criteria in their identification and interpretation of laws, and one in which legislators enact laws which can be so identified and interpreted' (p. 85). A weaker statement of his thesis occurs on p. 3: 'the identification and application of law ought to be kept as separate as possible from the moral judgments which go into the making of law.' At other places, such as p. 2, Campbell claims only a 'presumption' in favour of separation, without specifying limits on when the presumption is overridden. These weaker versions are compatible with allowing judges to use their own values in very many cases – at least if there is no better alternative. If this is all Campbell claims, then maybe we do not disagree so much after all. That would be great, but I will still direct my arguments against the moderate thesis in the text.

4 It is not clear what Campbell means by 'controversial'. Is a moral standard controversial when it would be rejected by 10 per cent of society? Or 30 per cent? Or 50 per cent? I will assume that a moral standard is controversial unless it is clearly supported by a majority of society, since one of the main objections to judges using controversial standards in that this steals power from the majority.

5 The term 'ethical positivism' might seem to suggest positivism about ethics, so I prefer to call this view 'prescriptive legal positivism' or just 'legal positivism' when the context makes it clear that the prescriptive version is at issue. Nothing substantive hangs on this terminology, as far as I can see.

6 The traditional debate among legal positivists, legal realists and natural law theorists is actually many debates. Sometimes these antagonists debate about the nature or definition of law. See my 'A Perspectival Theory of Law', chapter 8 in this volume. Sometimes their debate is descriptive. See Frederick Schauer, 'Legal Positivism and the Contingent Autonomy of Law', chapter 9, this volume. At other times, however, the debate is about how legislators should write laws and how judges should decide cases. This latter, prescriptive debate will be my topic in this chapter.

7 For example, Jerome Frank, *Law and the Modern Mind* (New York: Brentano's, 1930), ch. 14 argues that overemphasis on rules 'promotes judicial self-delusion and produces that ineffectual suppression of the judge's personality which leads to the indirect, unobserved and harmful effects of his personality on judicial decisions'. Legal realists do admit that rules can be indirectly important.

[8] Campbell seems to agree when he writes, 'The question of whether the benefits of rules outweigh their harmfulness depends on context and purpose and cannot in general be prejudged': *Ethical Positivism, op. cit.*, p. 62. He does not seem to notice that such admissions refute his moderate, but universal, prescriptive separation thesis.

[9] My project is somewhat similar to that of John Hart Ely who argued in *Democracy and Distrust* (Cambridge, MA: Harvard University Press, 1980) that judges should use their moral beliefs in some kinds of case (to guard the process of democracy) but not in others (substantive moral issues). However, my quilt has different patches than his.

[10] Campbell, *Ethical Positivism., op. cit.*, pp. 151 and 223 mentions this method but admits its limitations.

[11] See Ronald Dworkin, *Taking Rights Seriously* (Cambridge, MA: Harvard University Press, 1978), pp. 131–49; also David Brink, 'Legal Theory, Legal Interpretation, and Judicial Powers', *Philosophy and Public Affairs*, **17** (1988), pp. 105–48. Legislators probably assume that judges share their moral beliefs. That might be why they are willing to delegate authority to judges. But they still do delegate even if this assumption turns out to be false.

[12] Campbell, *Ethical Positivism, op. cit.*, p. 150. J.L. Austin saw all judge-make law as valid when the sovereign delegated law-making authority by silence. Thus, my more modest claim that legislators delegate such authority in some cases by using moral language has impeccable positivist credentials.

[13] My dichotomy might seem to run together two distinct issues: cases versus rules and moral versus non-moral. However, as Fred Schauer argued in *Playing by the Rules* (Oxford: Clarendon Press, 1991), the functions of a rule is to remove certain considerations from the purview of a decision-maker. I am interested here in rule that restrict judges from using their own moral beliefs in deciding particular cases.

[14] Schauer, *Playing by the Rules, op. cit.*, ch. 7, and Campbell, *Ethical Positivism, op. cit.*, pp. 50–61 and 108–10. My list of good reasons for rules is closer to Fred Schauer's more restrained list.

[15] This point derives from Bernard Gert, *Morality* (New York: Oxford University Press, 1998), ch. 6, but it also fits Campbell's own definitions of impartiality in *Ethical Positivism, op. cit.*, pp. 97 and 110–11.

[16] This argument might seem to be suggested by Tom Campbell when he discusses the moral form advantage of rules in *Ethical Positivism, op. cit.*, p. 60. However, I suspect that what Campbell means is closer to what I call equity below.

[17] For example, Schauer in *Playing by the Rules, op. cit.*, pp 155–8 argues that stability in itself is no virtue.

[18] Schauer in ibid., p. 137 ff. refers to this reason as reliance rather than reliability, because he claims that reliability is of no use unless people actually rely on it. To the contrary, I think that reliability has benefits even in the absence of actual reliance, because reliability gives people the ability to plan, and abilities are valuable even when they are not exercised. Moreover, reliance in the absence of reliability can create obvious problems. That is why I do not see reliance as the reason for rules. I then refer to predictability instead of reliability because a person gains nothing if a process is reliable but the person does not know the way in which it is reliable and thus cannot predict what it will do. Similar reasons show why stability in and of itself is not valuable if it cannot be predicted. So predictability is the basic value in this group of related notions.

[19] Authorizing judicial value judgments is not *completely* safe. However, the relevant question is whether it is *more* safe than the alternatives. That depends on the circumstances. So my argument is premised on my assessment of the dangers mainly in the United States – an assessment that is admittedly speculative, controversial and open to revision.

[20] Consider Chinese immigrants in *Yick Wo* v. *Hopkins* (1886), Nazis in Skokie (*Collin* v. *Smith* (1978)), and many criminals, such as in *Miranda* v. *Arizona* (1966) and *Enmund* v. *Florida* (1982).

[21] Compare Dworkin's argument for his rights thesis that judges should base decisions on principle, but not on policy, in his *Taking Rights Seriously, op. cit.*, pp. 82–90.

[22] Here I am concerned with the conditions under which a method is right, not with what we ought to tell judges. Hence, my arguments will leave open the possibility that, even though we know that judges sometimes should use their own moral beliefs, we ought to publicly tell judges 'Never use your own moral beliefs', because telling them 'Never' is the strategy most likely to result in their using their moral beliefs only in those cases where they should. As Aristotle said, sometimes we need to aim past the mean in order to counteract a known tendency to hit short of the mean.

[23] *Gregg* v. *Georgia* 423 US 153 (1976).

[24] Capital punishment has also been questioned under the equal protection clause of the Fourteenth Amendment but, for simplicity, I will focus on the moral term 'cruel' in the Eighth Amendment.

[25] Even if the original ratifiers denied that capital punishment is cruel, they might have failed to see this implication of their own standards of cruelty, just as they failed to see the implications for slavery of their belief that 'all men are created equal'. Also, capital punishment might be cruel now, even though it was not cruel then, because different alternatives are available at the different times. It is also not completely clear what contemporary society thinks, since there is some evidence for the Marshall hypothesis that American citizens today tend to oppose capital punishment when they know more about it. I ignore these complications in the text, because they do not seem to be the real basis for the claims of Brennan and Marshall.

[26] Fairness between races (and sexes?) does matter a lot, but that issue concerns the Fourteenth rather than the Eighth amendment.

[27] *Texas* v. *Johnson* 109 S.Ct. 2533 (1989).

[28] This is the test of strict scrutiny, which shows that constitutional rights in the United States are not absolute, and which gives judges the power to decide when such rights are overridden.

[29] *Texas* v. *Johnson* 109 S.Ct. 2533 (1989), quoting *Chaplinsky* v. *New Hampshire* 315 US 568 at 571–2 (1942).

[30] *Australian Capital Television Pty. Ltd* v. *The Commonwealth of Australia* 177 CLR 106 (1992).

[31] The Political Broadcasts and Political Disclosures Act of 1991 (Cth).

[32] *ACTV* v. *The Commonwealth* 177 CLR 106 at 143 (1992).

[33] There would be a serious problem if a judge allowed or prohibited a kind of advertisement because of a moral belief that one particular candidate is better. However, my claim is not that judges can use whatever moral beliefs they want, but only that they can use *some* moral beliefs. What is wrong with using moral beliefs about particular candidates is that it undermines the kind of impartiality that is required for good judging.

[34] Even when judges should be authorized to use their own moral beliefs, they might not actually be so authorized. Clear words in the Constitution might not leave room for certain judicial moral beliefs even when their using such beliefs would otherwise be appropriate. For example, judges should not use their moral beliefs to determine when citizens are eligible for political offices if the Constitution specifies a certain age as the only requirement. In such ways, the words in the Constitution, or in statutes, can place limits on when and how judges should use their own moral beliefs in reaching legal decisions.

[35] Cf. H.L.A. Hart, *The Concept of Law* (Oxford: Clarendon Press, 1961), pp. 96–9.

14 Citizenship, Race and Adjudication[1]

MARGARET THORNTON

Citizenship provides a valuable framework for rethinking the changing status of subordinated peoples in a post-colonial context. It is neither encumbered by the language of the victim nor, in the Australian context, by what has been pejoratively termed the 'black armband view of history'.[2] Furthermore, the universality of citizenship within liberal theory assumes that there is an equal apportionment of rights and responsibilities between all citizens. Universal discourse has a negative side, however, for it enables the erasure of difference. In recent years, feminist, critical race and postmodern scholars, among others, have been increasingly inclined to challenge the classic concepts of modernity, including the assumed universality of 'the citizen', to show that they are in fact partial. The result, as Margaret Somers puts it, is the recognition that '[c]itizenship is a "contested truth" – its meaning politically and historically constructed'.[3]

I am interested in civil society as a key site where this 'contested truth' is played out, and I proposed to focus on the way in which both adjudication and the initiation of litigation operate as key sites of meaning. First, the analysis challenges the conventional understanding of the 'activist judge' in liberal democratic thought, suggesting that judges are perennially, not selectively, active in the constitution of social norms. Second, I consider the initiation of litigation as a means by which active citizens are produced. The two strands of inquiry are illustrated by going behind the universalistic façade of citizenship to explore the contradictions in the context of race and Aboriginality in Australia.

Active Citizenship

Despite the universalizing tendencies of liberal legalism, the philosophical critique of differential citizenship is not new. Kant acknowledged the existence of differential citizenship by drawing a distinction between active and passive citizens.[4] He identified the attributes of a citizen as *freedom* (obedience to a law predicted on a person's consent to it), *equality* (between citizens) and *independence* (based on the exercise of autonomous choice). These three concepts also underpin that of civil personality and allow citizens to pursue their rights juridically. Kant identifies enfranchisement as the mark of being a citizen. However, in separating citizens into those who are *active* and those who are *passive*, he acknowledges that 'the concept of a passive citizen seems to contradict the concept of a citizen as such'.[5] That is, how can one be free, independent *and passive*? Women and 'others' are not similarly situated to 'benchmark men' – that is, those who are white, able-bodied, heterosexual, middle class and who espouse a mainstream religion and a right-of-centre politics. Hence, an ontological fissure is immediately apparent within the supposed universal carapace of citizenship. Kant relegates all women, minors and men without agency, such as domestic servants and apprentices, to the passive category: they are all 'mere underlings [*Handlanger*] of the commonwealth' because they lack 'civil independence'. However, Kant's passive–active dichotomy is not fixed, for it is possible to move from the passive category to the active one. In the late eighteenth century, however, this proviso was undoubtedly intended to apply only to those who approximated the benchmark men of the time, who were able to alter their status – from apprentice to journeyman, for example – not to women, and certainly not to married women.[6]

Marshall, in his now classic formulation, accepts the basic Kantian concept of civil citizenship as fulfilling the first step in his tripartite schema, which he distinguishes from the political and social elements.[7] In order to secure freedom, there must be liberty of the person, freedom of speech, thought and faith, the right to own property, the right to conclude valid contracts and the right to justice. In Marshall's progressivist schema, he associates civil citizenship with the eighteenth century, political citizenship (involving the struggle for the universal franchise) with the nineteenth century and social citizenship (involving the struggle for social and economic rights) with the twentieth century.

The arena of civil society emerged as an identifiable metaphysical space and as a corollary of civil citizenship during the eighteenth century. Civil society was not only the locus of freedom, but a source of empowerment against an authoritarian state. Until its recent revival, the language of civil society had all but disappeared but, somewhat ironically, the conservative turn taken by contemporary Western states has engendered a renaissance.[8] The political trend has been to contract the public sphere by reducing expenditure on education, health and welfare services, by privatizing public goods and by limiting accountability and public access to information. As the language of economic rationality, efficiency, flexibility, commodification and globalization has replaced the language of civility, it would seem that the possibility of realizing Marshall's third stage of citizenship, social citizenship, has receded. Social citizenship cannot be realized without a robust public sphere. The linguistic shift in favour of civil society may constitute evidence of a longing for a reconstituted public sphere. Nevertheless, the gendered and raced character of civil society in the past suggests that we should not look to the past without first removing our rose-tinted spectacles.

Despite the fact that the concept of civil citizenship is the oldest strand of modern citizenship, it has received remarkably little scrutiny compared with political and social citizenship within liberal theory. It tends to be unproblematically assumed that all citizens are rights-bearing and free to choose whether to exercise the rights that are the hallmark of civil citizenship; this is the problem with universality. I propose to focus on the process of civil litigation, rather than on the substantive rights themselves. In this context, the judicial role is usually under the spotlight only if the rights that are recognized are perceived to be politically radical, particularly in the context of constitutional adjudication. Radical interpretations attract the soubriquet, an 'activist judge' or an 'activist court'.[9] An excessively narrow construction of a legislative or constitutional text might elicit some minor tut-tutting within the ranks of the relevant legal hermeneutic community, but narrowness is likely to be viewed as being in accord with strict legalism, a strand of positivism in which judges defer unquestioningly to the legislature – or at least claim to do so.[10] Conservatism is believed to convey an appearance of neutrality and *non*-activism. Little attention is paid to the fact that, in the process of deferring to the legislature, judges actively produce knowledge that shapes the social construction of race and gender. Indeed, I suggest that adjudication is a key site where differential citizens are produced. However, I am not confining myself to the adjudicative role alone, for the act of initiating civil litigation may be imbricated with adjudication in distinctive ways.

I do not wish to suggest that formal litigation, with its competitive and adversarial characteristics, is necessarily the best way to resolve disputes, but that the act of asserting a legal right is an important symbol of active citizenship. By pursuing rights, such as those arising from group harms, through publicly funded courts, women and subordinated peoples are challenging the passive conceptualizations of citizenship conventionally assigned to them. The narrative of citizenship, closely intertwined, as it is, with property, has been structured so as either to exclude or to render marginal those who are not benchmark men. Women, Aboriginal people and 'others' who have been excluded from property ownership, as well as from education and enfranchisement, have sought to rewrite this narrative through the liberatory struggles of the nineteenth and twentieth centuries in order to revise the conventional understandings of citizenship. This entails moving beyond ossified narratives of subordination to a positive and more active conceptualization. Property is not only fundamental within the free enterprise and individualistic norms of capitalism, but land, or 'real' property, is also central to the non-materialistic norms of traditional Aboriginal society which stress a spiritual connectedness with land and which shape a person's identity. Claims to land have been at the forefront of civil actions by Aboriginal people but are deeply resisted by the mainstream. Even though authorized by legislation, native title claims are seen as dissonant acts which give rise to vociferous claims for amendment or repeal of the enabling legislation.[11]

Within the Western liberal tradition, property is accepted as the backbone of liberal society and as an essential prerequisite to the realization of freedom. As Vogel points out, prominent political thinkers, including Pufendorf, Montesquieu and Rousseau, believed that the preservation of civil society depended on the harmonious transmission of property along family lineages.[12] The property qualification for enfranchisement, the retention of which was hotly contested in the nineteenth century, further attests to the nexus between property, class and citizenship. The basis of this property right was, according to Locke, the right of each person to own (his) own body.[13] Locke is, of course, alluding to the middle-class Englishman, the paradigmatic active citizen, for the rights of 'passive' citizens over their own bodies remains debatable. This is still apparent in the case of women and the struggle for reproductive rights in most jurisdictions. Until recently, the limitations on Aboriginal people, regarding the civil rights to travel, work and associate, also illustrate the importance of the precondition.

The assertion of rights is assumed to be the prerogative of benchmark man who epitomizes active citizenship; he is the paradigmatic rights-bearing citizen. Women and 'others', who share most of benchmark man's identifying characteristics, may be able to occupy the subject positions of active citizens selectively. Benchmark man, or his corporatized or transnational equivalent, has historically dominated our civil courts where he has been able to acquire political capital. A monopoly over property has facilitated access to the courts, including the ability to pay for high levels of advocacy. Responsibility for the 'winner's' costs increases the risk of litigation for those without property. Legal aid is rarely available for civil cases which set out to test the ambit of a right, for they are high-risk ventures.

The ability to afford the cost of access to justice, in conjunction with the possession of property and full employment, is a further distinguishing sign of active citizenship.[14] The liberal presumption of formal equality before the law disguises procedural inequities, as well as the identity of *who* comes to law. Freedom, independence and equality remain inextricably intertwined with property, whiteness and masculinity, despite the liberatory movements of the nineteenth and twentieth centuries. The domination of civil courts by benchmark men, and by corporations controlled by benchmark men, means that their success in litigation ensures that they are the invariable authors of jurisprudence, just as history is authored by the victors of wars.[15] The result has been to erase the voices of poor and subordinated peoples, as well as women, from the meaning of active citizenship. The assignation of women to the caring responsibilities of the private sphere has underpinned the construction of liberal citizenship in masculinist terms so that benchmark men alone have been free to contribute actively to the life of the polity.[16]

Habermas challenges the way in which the citizenship monologues of benchmark men are equated with the universal by stressing the importance of communication.[17] For Habermas, the idea of a 'communicative ethic' is a necessary constituent element of civil society in a democratic polity. Within this ethic resides the mutuality of citizenship, without which democracy is impoverished.[18] While adjudication may not have been the form of communication that Habermas had in mind, it represents a crucial and authoritative discourse within civil society, which should not be overlooked. If the voices of particular social constituents are consistently absent from judicial discourse there can be no communication and no mutuality. Juridical asymmetry which privileges the voices of benchmark men is suggestive of oligarchy – plutocracy, in particular – not democracy, and certainly not ethical democracy. Justice, as well as active citizenship, is predicated on a dialogic sensibility.

In addition to the idea of dialogue between diverse constituents, including benchmark men and racialized 'others', active citizenship also includes psychological and subliminal dimensions. For example, one must acknowledge the role of courage in resistance and in initiating litigation in order to effect the transition from passive to active citizenship. In the American context, Holloway Sparks has written perceptively about the role of dissident practices and political courage, as illustrated by the action of Rosa Parks who went to gaol rather than give up her seat to a white man on an Alabama bus.[19] In Australia, the struggle by Aboriginal people has produced heroic individuals, such as Eddie Mabo, who have been prepared to lend their names to litigation on behalf of the collective good.[20]

Accordingly, rather than focus on the polity as the conventional location of the citizen, I am seeking to move the site of interest to the initiation, and, resolution, of litigation in order to develop a contemporary and more nuanced understanding of what it means to be a citizen. Because my analysis is to be illustrated by reference to the constitution of Aboriginal citizenship in Australia, I need to begin with the second of these two elements – namely, the adjudicative element or the outcome of litigation – because, in contradistinction to the initiation of litigation, the judicial construction of identity is not contingent on citizenship.

The Judicial Construction of Citizenship

Kant exhorts respect for the independence of colonized peoples but does not consider whether this would suffice to endow them with passive citizenship status within colonizing polities. He repudiates colonization by conquest,[21] and avers that conquest should not result in loss of civil freedom and land for those subjugated. In the case of a settlement, it may take place only by contract, not by force, and may not take advantage of the 'ignorance of those inhabitants with respect of ceding their lands',[22] particularly when they depend on large tracts for their sustenance.[23] It is apparent that Kant's dichotomous citizenship schema does not take account of indigenous people – a criticism that can be levelled at liberal theory generally.

The formal citizenship status of benchmark men in Australia – Kant's active citizens by virtue of property and enfranchisement – remained ambivalent until as recently as 1948.[24] That is, even privileged white colonials (who became Australians after Federation in 1901) remained British subjects for more than 150 years after white settlement. Apart from this formal diminution in status, they enjoyed the full panoply of citizenship rights within the colonial polities.

I have found scant evidence of Aboriginal people asserting civil rights before the twentieth century.[25] Indeed, it was generally believed that they could not.[26] Perhaps, this is unsurprising since apparently they were not even regarded as passive citizens, but as sub-citizens. The acceptance of the common humanness of the colonial British subject and the racialized 'other' did cause some blurring of the boundary following increased interaction in the early days of white settlement, so that 'Aboriginal people came to be treated as if they were British subjects for some purposes'.[27] Nevertheless, this recognition of common humanness and a sense of belonging to the same community did not suffice to qualify Aboriginal people as citizens, even in the passive sense. Under colonial rule their formal status was that of 'indigenous subjects'.[28]

While there may have been a dearth of civil cases involving Aboriginal people in the nineteenth century, there was no shortage of criminal cases. Criminality is not dependent on citizenship. Indeed, the abrogation of civil rights through legislative, executive and judicial fiat served to normalize the colonial conjunction of indigeneity and criminality. The authoritative texts of criminal law have played a key role in subordinating Aboriginal people and marking them as 'others' to white people. That is, wildness and irrationality were stressed in order to enhance the superiority, rationality and normativity of the European settlers. For example, the language of the courtroom, the paradigmatic site of neutrality and authority, frequently referred to indigenous peoples as 'uncivilised aboriginals', 'primitive natives', 'half-castes', and 'lubras'. Demeaning language together with the use of pejorative Europeanized nicknames, such as 'Devil Devil *alias* Bumblefoot',[29] 'a black, named *Ugly*',[30] and 'Neddy Monkey',[31] rather than Aboriginal names, illustrate the way otherness was constructed in the colonial judicial context.[32]

This norm and 'other' binarism was also played out many times by counterposing Christianity with heathenism so that civil citizenship came to be linked with monotheism – Christianity in particular. A striking illustration of the normative use of religious tests is the way in which Aboriginal people were deemed incompetent to give evidence because they lacked a 'belief in a superior Being, the avenger of falsehood, which the Law required to sanction an oath'.[33] Nevertheless, if an Aboriginal person made certain statements to a competent (white, preferably male) witness, that person could be called upon to repeat them.[34] Mediated through the oath of the white Christian man, Truth was attainable. The incompetence of 'untutored aboriginals' lingered on from the beginning of British settlement but, in order to increase the conviction rate, legislative provision was subsequently made in the states and territories for an 'incompetent person' to promise to tell the truth or to give unsworn evidence.[35]

The selective admissibility of the evidence of Aboriginal people led to other anomalies. A white wife could not be compelled to give evidence against her husband on the basis that the indivisibility of marriage would be undermined but, in the case of an Aboriginal person, the absence of a Christian ceremony of marriage gave rise to a presumption that there was no marriage at all:

> The Court cannot take judicial notice of the religious ceremonies and rites of these people, and cannot, without evidence of their marriage ceremonies, assume the fact of marriage.... To assume, because this person described herself as a 'lubra,' and as married, that she was the prisoner's wife within the meaning of the Act, is assuming too much....[36]

The refusal to recognize Aboriginal marriage contrasts with the attitude adopted towards the Scottish law of marriage in which the only requirement was a contract *per verba de presenti*. This ritual was judicially recognized as it preserved the common law of 'civilized' Europe and was not deemed in any way to be the same as a similar practice found among 'uncivilized' people:

> We may recognise a marriage in a civilised country, but we can hardly do the same in the case of the marriages of these aborigines, who have no laws of which we can take cognizance.[37]

The constant denial of the competency of Aboriginal people to give evidence in a court is a form of judicial activism through which judges create new norms rather than defer to those embedded in legislation.[38] The dualistic construction of competence facilitated subsequent social and legal binarisms, including those entrenched within discriminatory and paternalistic legislation. Via the medium of authoritative legal texts, judicial activism helped reify the subordination of Aboriginal people. Anglo-Australian courts have effectively policed the boundaries of citizenship throughout the 200-year history of white settlement, including determining who is or is not an Aboriginal person. Rather than a neutral hermeneutic site, therefore, adjudication has played an active role in the construction of the conjunction of Aboriginality and subjection.

Out of Subjection

Aboriginal identity politics inevitably has its roots in the history of suffering and oppression. The concept of *ressentiment* is useful to invoke here – a concept that has been coined to highlight the collective sense of victimhood and the correlative desire and energy to ameliorate past harms.[39] Nevertheless, as suggested at the outset, victim discourse is problematic in the context of citizenship. Identifying the group through common harms can entrench the notion of victimhood that the group is seeking to overcome, which is antipathetic to the idea of full citizenship. The group's occupation of the moral high ground impels it to reaffirm its victim status as 'other' to the privileged norm at the same time that it challenges the assignation to otherness. I am conscious of this paradox in considering the initiation of civil litigation as a positive act, for the assertion of a legal right may also necessitate assuming the trappings of a victim.

The rebellion against passivity and protectionism by Aboriginal people, together with demands for reparation and reconciliation after 200 years, is also bound to incur resistance. Dissidence by 'others' necessarily threatens the line separating them from the normativity of benchmark men. Adherence to the norm can no longer be claimed if the line between it and the 'other' appears to be dissolving. Furthermore, wrongs that involve property are invariably strongly contested. Foucault's important insight regarding the circulatory nature of power[40] is borne out in the ensuing struggle. As the initiative is seized by one 'side', the other 'side' marshals its forces and resists, or retaliates, and so it goes on. Through active manifestations of citizenship, identity is actively created and re-created.[41] Thus, victimhood is moderated by struggle, strength and courage. The result is not a neutralized and anodyne notion of identity but one that is dynamics and variegated. Through the dialectical re-creation of identity, citizenship can be understood anew, not just as a bland universal, devoid of variation, as conventionally imagined by law and liberal theory, but as a site of action, of performance.

During the early years of white settlement, there was a focus on the control and suppression of the supposed wildness and dangerousness associated with Aboriginal people. During the protectionist era, which emerged at the beginning of the twentieth century, when white women were engaged in active citizenship struggles, Aboriginal people were increasingly constructed as childlike and dependent, requiring the consent of a guardian or protector for all decisions they sought to make, including freedom of movement and association.[42] Infractions were treated harshly, usually be incarceration. Aboriginal people were segregated, and fraternization could constitute an offence.[43] The criminalization of acts such as a white husband visiting his Aboriginal wife on a reserve without a permit underpins the spirit of *de jure* and *de facto* segregationist policies.[44] Indeed, white law for Aboriginal people came to be understood largely in its negative, punitive and criminal sense.

The struggle for civil rights on the part of Aboriginal people began with returned Aboriginal servicemen in 1919.[45] The dualistic models of race began to be supplemented by an assimilationist model which 'let in' to the community of citizens select Aboriginal people who most resembled their benchmark comparators. While assimilationist policies have been attacked as racist because they deny the legitimacy of the identity of the other, the assertion of legal rights is also predicated on norms of comparability, analogous reasoning and assimilation. Even more elemental is the fact that the identification of a violation of rights is predicated on having both a sophisticated knowledge of English and some appreciation of law as a remedial instrument in civil society – both of which require a modicum of formal education. The education received by Aboriginal children until the 1960s was minimal, with girls being trained for domestic service and boys for work on cattle stations.[46] This model of education can be understood as training for subordination, not for the pursuit of rights, independence and agency in accordance with the precepts of universality and equality that underpin active citizenship.

Growing out of the paternalism of protectionist policies was the somewhat contradictory official aim of 'training for full citizenship, so that Aboriginal people might ultimately be assimilated into the general community'.[47] This process involved the erasure of the differences that law had entrenched over 150 years. The removal of children from their families is the most notorious practice in the assimilationist arsenal, the high point of which was attained during the 1950s and 1960s.[48] Such disempowering practices detracted from the possibility of attaining full citizenship.

Wardship for Aboriginal adults was also clearly contrary to the basic norms of citizenship as it resulted in a denial of all civil rights. An administrator could assign wardship status to thousands of Aboriginal persons with a stroke of the pen.[49] The restrictions of wardship are both underscored and challenged in a case involving the distinguished Aboriginal artist, Albert Namatjira, who received a three-month gaol sentence (reduced from six months) for supplying alcohol to an Aboriginal person.[50] In this case, we see the courageous and dissident act of an Aboriginal person who challenged passivity by appealing against a conviction after he himself had been accorded the same formal citizenship status as white people.[51] Appealing against the imposition of a criminal conviction for a summary offence 'all the way to the High Court' laid the groundwork for the initiation of civil litigation. However, the pervasiveness of the disabling narrative of Aboriginal dependency within legal discourse made it difficult to move instantaneously to the acceptance of positive representations. The prohibition on the provision of alcohol to Aboriginal people, but not to whites, together with multifarious restrictions under the guise of welfare, highlights the ambiguities.[52]

An Aboriginal person could appeal against the declaration of wardship, in which case a tribunal was authorized to determine, as a matter of fact, whether the appellant should be 'let in' to the community of citizens or not. Evidence had to be adduced to show that 'the appellant was well worth award wages as an employee and in general was well qualified for citizenship'.[53] In the case of *Dingle*, the tribunal accepted that the appellant and his wife were:

> ... honest and courteous people with decent principles, and they and the children, although accustomed to simple bush living quarters, maintain good standards of hygiene, personal cleanliness and neatness of attire. She [Miss Desailly] also described the appellant, despite his illiteracy, as intelligent with a clear understanding of money and

> its value, and said that he was orderly in his general behaviour and personal associations with various native friends.[54]

Despite the fact that the appeal was heard in the very year (1962) that Aboriginal people were collectively enfranchised,[55] and well after they were deemed to be Australian citizens by virtue of birth (1948), the judge constructed a citizenship position that remained on the margins. While an illiterate white person may also be confined to passive fringe-dweller status, he or she is unlikely to be confronted by an affirmative obligation to argue to be 'let in' to the formal community of citizens. Birth, in conjunction with whiteness, confers the panoply of citizen rights without regard to personal habits, standards of dress or level of education.

As advances were made in the political and legislative arena, the initiation of civil litigation began to occur, but *stare decisis* was invoked to maintain the status quo. Beneath the cloak of technocracy, judicial activism subtly guarded the line between the benchmark norm and the Aboriginal other in order to retain a passive conceptualization of citizenship. Yet the trajectory of social change never follows a straightforward linear path, and the negative reception that litigants received may partly explain why so few civil cases were initiated, even after the formal changes of the 1960s.[56]

In 1965 a married couple issued a write of *habeas corpus* for the recovery of their children who had been brought up by foster parents.[57] The parents were unsuccessful, and their evidence was treated dismissively by the judge:

> Both applicants were self-contradictory and evasive in evidence of having made six-monthly visits to Bathurst Island during that period. The applicant mother was no less unconvincing in superfluous and unsolicited repetitions of assertions of love for the children, her accompanying demeanour comprising constant and transparently over-acted use of an unfolded and neatly pressed handkerchief to wipe both eyes, neither of which showed any sign of a tear. I am unable to accept the testimony of the applicants in these respects.[58]

Although the children had been born to the parents when they were in-patients in a leprosaurium, the harshness of the judge's words in describing a mother who had been officially deprived of her four teenage children reveals the active role of the law in sanctioning and legitimating state violence against Aboriginal people.[59] Such decisions served to diminish the active citizenship status of the children, as well as that of the applicant parents.

Assimilationist strategies have officially fallen out of favour since the early 1970s, and difference has been acknowledged and even celebrated. However, strategies such as anti-discrimination legislation, which provide an avenue of recourse for complaints of discrimination, possess an assimilationist core, as proof depends on comparability with a racialized (white) norm. The individualized focus of civil rights, which Marshall suggests harmonized the individualistic phase of capitalism,[60] has limited the systemic nature of racially discriminatory harms by conveying the impression that the wrong was no more than an aberrant and isolated instance.[61] Furthermore, the overwhelming preponderance of complaints heard by the Human Rights and Equal Opportunity Commission under the Racial Discrimination Act 1975 (Cwlth) have dealt with the questions of access to drinking in hotels, thereby adding a twentieth-century gloss to the otherness of Aboriginal people.[62] To date, remarkably few complaints have dealt with the more positive dimensions of contemporary life, such as employment, confirming that the realization of Marshall's concept of social citizenship remains illusory. Perhaps, most perplexing in the context of discussing active citizenship is the paradox inherent in the assertion of a right.[63] That is, the negative language of being discriminated *against* requires a complainant seeking a remedy to occupy the subject position of a victim in order to make out a persuasive case.

Towards Full Citizenship

Enfranchisement occurred as early as 1894 for Aboriginal women in South Australia, although this may have been unintentional because of the undifferentiated reference to 'women' in the Act,[64] but it was not until 1962 that all Aboriginal people were enfranchised. Despite the manipulation of the vote that occurred in the early years of enfranchisement,[65] the *right* to vote remains an important symbol of citizenship. Significant activity has flowed from the act of enfranchisement and from the 1967 referendum.[66] Both enfranchisement and the referendum represented high political moments which encouraged the assertion of rights by Aboriginal people, particularly in the promotion of group rights. Not only do we see the exercise of rights within civil society as a focus of active citizenship, but we see how their assertion is a precondition to reimagining citizen identity.

The referendum signalled a more respectful stance in relation to Aboriginal people on the part of courts in criminal cases. In criticizing the practices of the police involved in an interrogation, White J stated: 'Ajax was not given the usual legal protection of the *ordinary citizen*.'[67] Here, without labouring the point, is a clear judicial statement that comparable treatment, rather than different, inferior or special, is expected for Aboriginal people. This case followed the development of the Anunga Rules in which judges of the Supreme

Court of the Northern Territory developed a set of guidelines to be followed by police officers in interrogating Aboriginal persons. The guidelines are noted for their emphasis on courtesy and care in the formulation of questions, having regard to the fact that English is not the first language of many Aboriginal people. The Rules represent a positive example of judicial activism in the changing conceptualization of Aboriginal citizenship that was beginning to take place.

One of the early civil cases was *Milirrpum* v. *Nabalco*,[68] a land rights case. Although Blackburn J held that common law did not recognize the formal interests of indigenous peoples to land, the case represented a watershed because it foreshadowed a protracted struggle over land. 'Aboriginal land rights' became a symbol of active citizenship, illustrating the symbiosis between civil society and the polity in the way that the initiation of litigation produces political capital. Out of the struggle, state and territory legislation was enacted, giving rise in turn to numerous legal actions. In *Coe* v. *The Commonwealth*,[69] an action was instituted on behalf of the 'Aboriginal community and nation' against the UK government, as well as the Commonwealth of Australia. Although the High Court action dealt only with the right to amend the statement of claim, the substantive claim challenged the proclamations of sovereignty, made on behalf of the British Crown, that Aboriginal 'ownership rights' were extinguished. While the finding of Gibbs CJ that the claims were 'absurd and vexatious' may have been strictly *obiter*, the application to amend was dismissed.

Coe was to be vindicated, at least in part, by the High Court in *Mabo* v. *Queensland (No. 2)*,[70] which recognized Aboriginal proprietary interests in land, or what the Court termed 'native title'. The judgment is remarkable in Australian legal history for the passionate concern shown by the majority judges for substantive justice, marking a sharp break with the formalism typical of most constitutional cases. As Motha points out in a perceptive essay, *Mabo* was much more than a dispute over land:[71] it compares with the 1967 referendum as another high political moment of the history of relations between indigenous and non-indigenous people. The decision was widely attacked as an improper exercise of judicial activism because the High Court had allegedly failed to display adequate deference to the Constitution. Perhaps even more contentious was *Wik Peoples* v. *Queensland*[72] which held that native title was not extinguished by pastoral leases made under statute and that coexistence continued during the life of a lease, extinguishment occurring only in the case of inconsistency. The 'activism' of the court was again widely denounced. Aboriginal land rights are potentially far more threatening to dominant landed interests than conventional civil rights, because of the collective nature of the interest asserted. The substantive alterations to the common law were also dramatic, particularly the demise of the myth of *terra nullius* and the revisioning of Australian legal history, which sought to take account of Aboriginal perspectives.[73] While I do not espouse a simple progressivist thesis of social change, the generation of political capital through a communicative ethic does mean that a reversion to passivity for Aboriginal people is unlikely. Communicative speech does have to be assertive to resound throughout civil society and the polity. Legal speech carries with it the requisite degree of authority.[74]

While the 'creation' of 'native title' represents a brave reimagining of legal history at one level, scrutiny reveals that mixed messages nevertheless continue to emerge from adjudicative sites. The legalization of complex disputes can result in an excessive focus on the procedural and the technical so that justice is rendered peripheral.[75] Indeed, the land acquired through litigation in the post-*Mabo* period has been minimal and has had little effect on the quality of life; poverty and the incarceration rate continue to be major problems. Furthermore, the running of such cases has generated a veritable legal industry adding millions of dollars to the cost of legal claims.[76]

There is also a problem appertaining to the meaning of Aboriginality emerging from the new adjudicative mode. For example, it can be averred that ostensibly positive concepts such as 'native' title are resonant of the difference, peculiarity and wildness of the 'other', counterposed against the normative notions of property-holding found in the Anglo-Australian legal system, for the emergence of a new binarism (or a variation of the old one) can be discerned: *we* have seisin, legal interests and indefeasibility, while *they* have native title, equitable interests and defeasibility. The normative understanding of Lockean property precepts has shaped and marginalized the specificity of Aboriginal land interests, including traditional usufructuary rights.

Motha also draws attention to the paradox for equal citizenship in the recognition of difference,[77] because universalism can be understood as a 'totalitarian gesture which results in the annihilation of the "other"'.[78] The conundrum posed by the tension between universality and particularism in the construction of equality has been conceptualized by feminist scholars as the sameness–difference debate.[79] On the one hand, there is a desire to be treated the *same* as benchmark men in similar circumstances while, on the other hand, there is a recognition that the failure to take cultural and biological differences into account can result in inequality. A similar constellation of ambiguities besets the citizenship and race debate which means that closure in the meaning of citizenship can never be attained: to universalize is to deny the distinctiveness of the other; to emphasize the other is to dichotomize, essentialize and hierarchize. Justice nevertheless requires ethical communication in which the voices of others are heeded by benchmark men, including judges. This argument returns us to the starting point and the 'contested truth' of citizenship.

Conclusion

I have considered the ways in which civil litigation operates to produce citizens who accord with the Kantian passive–active binarism and have illustrated the thesis in relation to Aboriginal people in Australia. In the early years of the colony, Aboriginal people, far from being passive 'citizens', were non-citizens. The judicial fiction of *terra nullius* contributed to this status. When acknowledged in the context of criminalization, Aboriginal people were deemed to be uncivilized and beyond the pale – a view that was legitimated with the aid of the authoritative voice of law.

The initiation of civil actions may be understood as a crucial site of contest, in tandem with legislative action, in the transition from passive to active citizenship. Vital fragments of the moving picture, which represent the role played by adjudication, have frequently been omitted as a result of exclusive concentration on the *polis*, the paradigmatic site of the universal. I have sought to remove the universalizing carapace and backlight the adjudicative role in order to show that activist judges are not necessarily radical. Indeed, in the case of race relations in Australia, it can be seen that the seemingly neutral voice of the judiciary occludes the many and varied ways in which the racial binarism of the benchmark norm and the Aboriginal 'other' are subtly reconfigured and reaffirmed. Adjudication is one of the 'variable ways in which citizenship formation develops within relational settings of contested but patterned relations among people and institutions'.[80] The changing nature of 'contested but patterned relations' from indigenous subjects to passive citizens – citizens without rights – has been illustrated through the adjudicative and litigious lenses.

I have also sought to capture the more recent phase of contest, located in a virtual space between passivity and activism, as Aboriginal people struggled to be accepted as full citizens – or citizens *with* rights. As they slough off dependency in favour of self-determination, new incarnations of citizenship are being imagined. The variegated nature of the struggle challenges the appropriateness of the Kantian passive–active binarism in a post-colonial and multicultural context. The rigid and closed concepts of classical liberal citizenship fail to capture the narrative of struggle and change that characterizes Aboriginal citizenship. As Kymlicka has argued, minority rights are in fact central to the very future of liberalism itself.[81] Civil citizenship, far from representing the elementary first stage of citizenship, as Marshall suggested in his tripartite taxonomy, is much more complicated when citizens other than benchmark men are taken into account. A focus on the racialized or sexualized 'other' cautions against the temptation to espouse progressivism. The complexities of rights are then also apparent, particularly when conceptualized in collective terms. It can be seen that judges, far from being the mechanical arbiters of texts, are engaged in an active hermeneutic process that enables them to play a key political role in the constitution of citizens. I have sought to show that the meaning of citizenship transcends the fixed universals of the polity assigned to it by liberal theory and that civil society is a crucial site where active citizenship is constituted.

Notes

1 Thanks are extended to Jan Doust for research assistance.

2 The historian, Henry Reynolds, points out that recent disquiet about Australia's treatment of Aboriginal people is not a new sentiment, for it echoes a concern of humanitarian reformers since the 1820s. See Henry Reynolds, *This Whispering in Our Hearts* (Sydney: Allen & Unwin, 1998), p. 248.

3 Margaret R. Somers, 'Rights, Relationality, and Membership: Rethinking the Making and Meaning of Citizenship', *Law and Social Inquiry*, **19** (1994), pp. 63–12, 65.

4 Immanuel Kant, *The Metaphysics of Morals*, trans. Mary Gregor (Cambridge: Cambridge University Press, 1991), §46, p. 126. See also Dennis F. Thompson, *The Democratic Citizen: Social Science and Democratic Theory in the Twentieth Century* (Cambridge: Cambridge University Press, 1970).

5 Ibid.

6 I have considered the issue of women and citizenship at greater length in 'Embodying the Citizen' in M. Thornton (ed.), *Public and Private: Feminist Legal Debates* (Melbourne: Oxford University Press, 1995); 'Historicising Citizenship: Remembering Broken Promises', *Melbourne University Law Review*, **20** (1996), pp. 1072–86; 'The Judicial Gendering of Citizenship: A Look at Property Interests during Marriage', *Journal of Law and Society*, **24** (1997), pp. 486–503.

7 T.H. Marshall, *Citizenship and Social Class and Other Essays* (Cambridge: Cambridge University Press, 1950). Marshall's conceptualization as a product of successive stages of development in the transition from feudalism to capitalism has been trenchantly critiqued by Somers, 'Rights, Relationality, and Membership', *op. cit*. She argues that Marshall's developmental schema is predicated on the fiction that the market is self-regulating and autonomous, rather than intimately connected to politics.

8 Nicholas R. Fyfe, 'Law and Order Policy and the Spaces of Citizenship in Contemporary Britain', *Political Geography*, **14** (1995), pp. 177–89.

9 For discussion, see Ronald Dworkin, *Law's Empire* (London: Fontana, 1986), pp. 369 ff.

10 The *ex cathedra* view of Sir Owen Dixon, a former Chief Justice of the Australian High Court, is exemplary: 'There is no other safe guide to judicial decisions in great conflicts than a strict and complete legalism.' Owen Dixon, *Jesting Pilate*

(Sydney: Law Book, 1965), p. 158. As Tom Campbell points out, however, '[N]o actual legal system comes close to the positivist ideal…'. See Tom D. Campbell, *The Legal Theory of Ethical Positivism* (Aldershot: Dartmouth, 1996), p. 125.

11 The extraordinary political phenomenon of the One Nation Party which marked late Twentieth Century Australia secured support with a policy based, in part, on a platform of anti-Aboriginality which averred that White Australians were treated less favourably than Aboriginal people as a result of land rights. See, for example, Pauline Hanson's One Nation Press Release, 1 October 1997; Pauline Hanson, Speech to Australian Senate, Second Reading, *Appropriation Bill (No 1)*, 2 June 1998.

12 Ursula Vogel, 'Marriage and the Boundaries of Citizenship', in Bart von Steenbergen (ed.), *The Condition of Citizenship* (London: Sage, 1994), pp. 80–1.

13 John Locke, *Second Treatise of Government* (1690), ed. C.B. Macpherson (Indianopolis: Hackett Publishing, 1980), §27.

14 Jocelyn Pixley has addressed the implications for citizenship of permanently high levels of unemployment in post-industrial societies. See Jocelyn Pixley, *Citizenship and Employment: Investigating Post-Industrial Options* (Cambridge: Cambridge University Press, 1993).

15 Cf. Richard Devlin, 'Nomos and Thanatos (Part A). The Killing Fields: Modern Law and Legal Theory', *Dalhousie Law Journal*, **12** (1989–90), pp. 298–348, at p. 316.

16 Carole Pateman, *The Sexual Contract* (Cambridge: Polity Press, 1988), esp. pp. 154 ff.

17 Jürgen Habermas, *The Structural Transformation of the Public Sphere: An Inquiry into a Category of Bourgeois Society*, trans. Thomas Burger with Frederick Lawrence (Cambridge: Polity Press, 1989).

18 Cf. Iris Marion Young, *Intersecting Voices: Dilemmas of Gender, Political Philosophy, and Policy* (Princeton: Princeton University Press, 1997), pp. 60–74.

19 Holloway Sparks, 'Dissident Citizenship: Democratic Theory, Political Courage, and Activist Women' in *Citizenship in Feminism: Identity, Action and Locale*, (special edn.) *Hypatia*, **12** (1997), pp. 74–110.

20 *Mabo* v. *Queensland (No. 2)* (1992) 107 ALR 1.

21 Kant, *Second Treatise*, *op. cit.*, §15, pp. 86–7.

22 Ibid., §62, p. 159.

23 Kant's views are of particular interest since he was writing at the very time that White settlement was occurring in Australia. The *Groundwork of the Metaphysics of Morals* (1785) was followed by *The Metaphysics of Morals* (1979).

24 Nationality and Citizenship Act 1948 (Cwlth).

25 A rare example is found in *Ex parte West* (1821) 2 Legge 1475 (NSWSC) which reports that 'Tommy', an Aboriginal boy, was released by a squatter on a writ of *habeas corpus*, after being stolen from his parents. The judge described the act as an 'outrage'. However, it is unclear from the report as to who actually initiated the action.

26 *R* v. *Murrell* (1836) 1 Legge 72.

27 Nicolas Peterson and Will Sanders, 'Introduction' in Nicolas Peterson and Will Sanders (eds), *Citizenship and Indigenous Australians: Changing Conceptions and Possibilities* (Cambridge: Cambridge University Press, 1998), pp. 1–32, at p. 4.

28 Ibid., p. 7.

29 *R* v. *Devil Devil*, 3 June 1825 (NSW SC), *Sydney Gazette*, 9 June 1825, http://www.austlii.edu.au/au/special/nswsc/pre1900/1825/182531NSWSC.html.

30 *Regina* v. *Mogar* (1850) *Legge* 652 (NSWSC). For a consideration of naming practices following the arrival of Europeans, see Marilyn Wood, 'Nineteenth Century Bureaucratic Constructions of Indigenous Identities in New South Wales' in Peterson and Sanders, *Citizenship*, *op. cit.*

31 *R* v. *Neddy Monkey* (1861) 1 Wyatt & Webb 40 (Vic SC).

32 For what has become the classic work on the construction of the 'other', see Edward Said, *Orientalism: Western Conceptions of the Orient* (Harmondsworth: Penguin, 1978). See also Peter Fitzpatrick, *The Mythology of Modern Law* (London and New York: Routledge, 1992).

33 *R* v. *Fitzpatrick and Colville* [1824] 8 NSWSC, *Sydney Gazette*, 14 June 1824, p. 2, col. 1 ([AustlII] Supreme Court of New South Wales pre 1900). A variation of this Christian–heathen binarism can be seen relatively recently in Papua and New Guinea in a new phase of colonialism in which Australia assumed the role of colonizer with all the colonial trappings of superiority *vis-à-vis* the indigenous people. In *The Queen* v. *Madobi* (1963) 6 FLR 1, the dying declaration of a 'a native of Papua and New Guinea' was held to be inadmissible (contrary to the accepted evidentiary rule) on the basis that the Christian would be bound to speak the truth when about to face [his] Maker. The deceased apparently believed that he would spend the hereafter on a neighbouring uninhabited island.

34 Ibid.

35 For a discussion of the history, see *Da Costa* v. *The Queen* (1968) 118 CLR 186, per Windeyer J. This case reveals that the issue of competence for Aboriginal people continued to be contested right up until the time of the 1967 referendum.

36 *R* v. *Neddy Monkey* (1861) 1 Wyatt & Webb 40 (Vic SC), 41.

37 *R* v. *Cobby* (1883) 4 NSWR 355, 356. In fact, Aboriginal customary law continued to operate within indigenous communities but it could always be overridden by Anglo-Australian law.

38 It is doubtful whether Campbell's theory of ethical positivism would be able to address linguistic subtleties of the kind illustrated, which incrementally contributed to the construction of indigenous people as sub-citizens. In the absence of any legislative guidance, or shared meaning within the relevant hermeneutic community, it would appear to invest the judge with a greater degree of individual agency than Campbell would find acceptable. See Campbell, *Ethical Positivism, op. cit.*

39 Wendy Brown, *States of Injury: Power and Freedom in Late Modernity* (Princeton, NJ: Princeton University Press, 1995); Susan Bickford, 'Anti-Anti-Identity Politics: Feminism, Democracy, and the Complexities of Citizenship', *Hypatia*, **12** (1997), pp. 111–31.

40 Michel Foucault, *Power/Knowledge: Selected Interviews and Other Writings 1972–1977*, ed. Colin Gordon, trans. Gordon *et al.* (Brighton: Harvester Wheatsheaf, 1980), p. 98.

41 Bickford, 'Anti-Anti-Identity Politics', *op. cit.*, p. 122.

42 For an account of the extensive power with which 'protectors' were invested, see John Chesterman and Brian Galligan, *Citizens Without Rights: Aborigines and Australian Citizenship* (Cambridge: Cambridge University Press, 1997).

43 Aborigines Act 1905 (WA), s. 36 made it an offence to be within five chains of an Aboriginal camp.

44 As late as 1963, that is, after the formal enfranchisement of Aboriginal people, a Victorian judge held that such regulations were not unreasonable on their face. *Ogilvie* v. *Lowe* [1963] VR 225, per Sholl J.

45 Alastair Davidson, *From Subject to Citizen: Australian Citizenship in the Twentieth Century* (Cambridge: Cambridge University Press, 1997), pp. 191 ff.

46 Many examples are recounted in Human Rights and Equal Opportunity Commission (HREOC), *Bringing them Home: Report of the National Inquiry into the Separation of Aboriginal and Torres Strait Islander Children from Their Families* (Sydney: Human Rights and Equal Opportunity Commission, 1997). See also Sally Morgan, *My Place* (Fremantle: Fremantle Arts Centre Press, 1987).

47 The annual report of the Aborigines Welfare Board for the year ended 30 June

1946, quoted in *Williams* v. *Minister for Aboriginal Lands Rights Act 1983*, NSW Unreported Judgments, http://online.butterworths.com.au.

48 HREOC, *Bringing them Home*, *op. cit.*

49 Welfare Ordinance 1953 (NT) s 14(1). See also *Re Appeal by Arthur Dingle* (1962) 3 FLR 226 (Wards Appeal Tribunal).

50 *Namatjira* v. *Raabe* (1959) 100 CLR 664. Cf. *Dowling* v. *Bowie* (1952) 86 CLR 136.

51 While Aboriginal people could be exempted from the jurisdiction of protective legislation and have the privileges of citizenship bestowed upon them, the conditions to be satisfied were more stringent than for white people. For example, Davidson recounts the story of an Aboriginal woman who had a child out of wedlock and was stripped of citizenship rights. See Davidson, *From Subject to Citizen*, *op. cit.*, p. 210.

52 Aboriginal people were ineligible for state welfare benefits on par with other citizens for many years. As Peterson points out, however, social rights can make Aboriginal people economically passive. See Nicolas Peterson, 'Welfare Colonialism and Citizenship: Politics, Economics and Agency' in Peterson and Sanders, *Citizenship*, *op. cit.*, pp. 101–17 at p. 112. On the other hand, some of the welfare schemes devised for indigenous people have been creative and employment-generating. See Will Sanders, 'Citizenship and the Community Development Employment Projects Scheme: Equal Rights, Difference and Appropriateness' in Peterson and Sanders, *Citizenship*, *op. cit.*, pp. 141–53.

53 *Dingle*, *op. cit.*, p. 233.

54 Ibid., p. 232.

55 Prior to this date, the formal enfranchisement status of Aboriginal people was confused. Only Queensland and Western Australian Aborigines were formally excluded from the Commonwealth Franchise Act of 1902, but few were in fact eligible to vote because their names did not appear on electoral roles and they were often discouraged from voting. For details, see Chesterman and Galligan, *Citizens Without Rights*, *op. cit.*, pp. 157 ff.

56 Colin Tatz is one of the few commentators on Aboriginal race relations to focus on the underutilization of civil law, which he conceptualizes as positive law or, following Illich, a 'convivial yet powerful weapon'. See, for example, Colin Tatz, 'Aborigines and Civil Law in Peter Hans and Bryan Keon-Cohen (eds), *Aborigines and the Law: Essays in Memory of Elizabeth Eggleston* (Sydney: George Allen & Unwin, 1984).

57 *R* v. *Silvester Pilimapitjimiri* (1965) *NT Judgments* 776 (SC Darwin).

58 Ibid., at 777.

59 Pilimapitjimiri's case is in sharp contradistinction to Tommy's case a century earlier. See note 25 above.

60 Marshall, *Citizenship and Social Class*, *op. cit.*, p. 43.

61 I have demonstrated how liberal legalism individualizes systemic social harms in the handling of complaints of discrimination. See Margaret Thornton, *The Liberal Promise: Anti-Discrimination Legislation in Australia* (Melbourne: Oxford University Press, 1990).

62 Margaret Thornton, 'Revisiting Race', in Race Discrimination Commissioner, *Racial Discrimination Act 1975: A Review* (Sydney: Human Rights and Equal Opportunity Commission, 1995), pp. 88–100. The disproportionate focus on the issue of freedom of access to hotels has to be understood in light of the policy of the protectionist period when not only was service denied to most Aboriginal people, but it was a criminal offence to supply liquor to an Aboriginal person or to possess alcohol on a reserve. In the Northern Territory, a minimum penalty for a first offence of supplying alcohol to a ward attracted a prison term of six months with hard labour. See, for example, *Camfoo* v. *McEvoy* (1962) 3 FLR 81.

[63] Cf. Kristin Bumiller, *The Civil Rights Society: The Social Construction of Victims* (Baltimore/London: Johns Hopkins University Press, 1988).

[64] White Australian women were federally enfranchised in 1902, but Aboriginal enfranchisement was dependent on state enfranchisement. See Commonwealth Franchise Act 1902 (Cwlth).

[65] Davidson, *From Subject to Citizen, op. cit.*, pp. 196–9.

[66] Constitution s. 51 (xxvi) was amended to allow the Commonwealth to make laws with respect to race that did not exclude Aboriginal people. See Bain Attwood and Andrew Markus, 'Representation Matters: The 1967 Referendum and Citizenship', in Peterson and Sanders, *Citizenship, op. cit.*, pp. 118–40.

[67] *The Queen* v. *Ajax* (1977) 17 SASR 88, 92, emphasis added.

[68] *Milirrpum* v. *Nabalco* (1971) 17 FLR 141 (NTSC).

[69] *Coe* v. *Commonwealth* (1979) 53 ALJR 403.

[70] *Mabo, op. cit.*

[71] Stewart Motha, 'Encountering the Epistemic Limit of the Recognition of "Difference"', *Griffith Law Review*, **7** (1998), pp. 79–96.

[72] *Wik Peoples* v. *Queensland* (1996) 141 ALR 129.

[73] See, for example, Lee Godden, '*Wik*: Legal Memory and History', (1997) *Griffith Law Review*, **6** (1997), pp. 122–43; Peter Rush, 'An Altered Jurisdiction: Corporeal Traces of Law', *Griffith Law Review*, **6** (1997), pp. 144–68.

[74] Of course, it is not the only factor of relevance as political activism, education, sport and other activities of civil society all generate active discourses. Stokes discusses how Aboriginal people developed several distinct identity discourses through their political activism. See Geoffrey Stokes, 'Citizenship and Aboriginality: Two Conceptions of Identity in Aboriginal Political Thought', in Geoffrey Stokes (ed.), *The Politics of Identity in Australia* (Cambridge: Cambridge University Press, 1997), pp. 158–71.

[75] *Kruger* v. *The Commonwealth* (1997) 71 ALJR 991 is exemplary. In this case, the plaintiffs were former 'stolen children' whose case was transmuted into a dispute about the ambit of the Territories power (Australian Constitution, s. 122). See also *Kartinyeri* v. *The Commonwealth* [1998] HCA 22 (1 April 1998) which explores the ambit of race power (Australian Constitution, s. 51 (xxvi)) apropos the dispute over construction of the Hindmarsh Island Bridge and the alleged fabrication of secret women's business. For discussion of the contextual issues, see Diane Bell, *Ngarrindjeri Wurruwarrin: A World that Is, Was and Will Be* (Melbourne: Spinifex, 1998).

[76] As an illustration, the legal costs of the trial in *Yorta Yorta Aboriginal Community* v. *State of Victoria* [1998] 1606 FCA (18 December 1998) have been estimated at approximately AU$16.5 million ($2.5 million for the Aboriginal claimants and $14 million for the non-claimant parties, who initially numbered 500). The claimants are appealing to the Full Bench of the Federal Court. A High Court challenge and a rehearing (with the possibility of further appeals) are not unlikely (discussion with Wayne Atkinson, one of the Yorta Yorta claimants, 14 January, 1999).

[77] Motha, '*Mabo*', *op. cit.*, p. 84.

[78] Ibid., p. 87, following Max Horkheimer and Theodor W. Adorno, *The Dialectic of Enlightenment*, trans. John Cumming (London: Allen Lane, 1972, orig. 1944).

[79] Catharine A. MacKinnon, *Toward a Feminist Theory of the State* (Cambridge, MA: Harvard University Press, 1989), esp. pp. 216–23.

[80] Somers, 'Rights, Relationality, and Membership', *op. cit.*, p. 73.

[81] Will Kymlicka, *Multicultural Citizenship: A Liberal Theory of Minority Rights* (New York: Oxford University Press, 1995), p. 194 *et passim*.

15 The Vice of Judicial Activism

ARTHUR GLASS[1]

A modern democracy requires judges to settle disputes, but there is always the worry that judicial decision-makers will overreach themselves in carrying out this role. This is a much greater possibility in the common law world for, in this legal tradition, while judges often have no canonical texts to defer to and draw upon in making their decisions, they have to justify their decisions publicly, at length, and these justifications will themselves be treated as authoritative legal texts. Those who suspect judicial overreaching speak with suspicious hostility of 'activism'.

Professor Campbell harbours such suspicions. He explains the vice of activism as follows. Courts may fail to apply law in accordance with its plain and stipulated meaning ('negative judicial activism') or they may make a decision or formulate a rule which is not warranted by existing authoritative legal texts ('positive judicial activism').[2] Such activity is triply offensive. It is undemocratic (judges are unelected officials), it is inefficient (as, generally speaking, courts do not have the knowledge to make good law) and it undermines 'rule governance' by introducing elements of arbitrariness into the legal system.

Judicial creativity, of course, cannot be wholly eliminated. It is an ineradicable feature of any modern legal system. Nor does Campbell say otherwise. For as he, and others well understand, 'rules do not apply themselves'. Someone has to do this work and that someone (the judge) has to decide both which rules to apply and just what these chosen rules mean in the circumstances of the case. Alternatively, the rules may prove deficient; they may be poorly drafted, or internally inconsistent or fail to cover the situation at hand. As we shall see, it is part of Campbell's account that legal rules should not be in this state. They should be drafted as clearly as possible and be as extensive as the situation requires. The model for good law is law authored by a parliament which weighs the relevant concerns (the interests, values and rights) and puts this legislative judgement succinctly into legal form. An ideal parliament would survey the legal rules as a whole and oversee their interaction. But the world being what it is, these goals will never be realized in full.[3] Nonetheless this is Campbell's regulative ideal.

Ethical positivism is the name Professor Campbell gives to his account of legal positivism. What is distinctive about this approach is its normative concerns. It seeks to improve legal practice rather than analyse the character of its basic concepts. Much of its message is directed at the legislature. Make law in the form of clear rules. To do otherwise defeats 'rule governance' and the values which this goal serves – basically, the values of personal freedom, equality of treatment and respect for others, associated in our tradition with the demands of individual autonomy. But ethical positivism also speaks to judges, offering them an 'ethics of adjudication'.[4] What this ethics amounts to is conveniently summarized by Campbell as the basic positivist principle of adjudication:

> ... apply a pre-existent rule in accordance with the plain and stipulated meaning of the authorised text in relation to the intended audience in the context of the legal enterprise, positivistically conceived.[5]

To 'positivistically conceive' of the legal enterprise is to understand the virtues of rule governance.[6] Law in the form of statutory rules has the clarity to guide behaviour, and law made directly by a democratically elected parliament, or at least overseen by parliament, has the legitimacy to demand the respect of the people. Implicit within this account is the assumption that a clear enough distinction can be drawn between law-making on the one hand and law-finding and law application on the other.[7]

In responding to the problem of 'activism', ethical positivism asks judges to discipline themselves.[8] Self-control here calls for a proper understanding of the techniques and methods through which judges find and apply the law and, bearing in mind the risks of the job, an appropriate attitude of deference towards the law-maker. If the message can be reduced to one point, it is that judges should be slow to apply law other than in accordance with its clear terms.

In this chapter I criticize Professor Campbell's account of 'activism' on two counts. First, I question whether he has properly described the problem. To make this point I first draw together his more detailed remarks on rule application and then discuss some possible criticisms of this account before focusing on what I see as its main defect – the basic assumptions underlying his analysis.

The second criticism is of a different kind. Implicit in Campbell's account is the not unfamiliar idea that legislative power and judicial power should be kept distinct. Summoning up the doctrine of separation of powers immediately discloses an absence in Campbell's discussion of activism – namely, that he is unconcerned with the administrative branch of government. Yet here are our main group of law appliers. And even if the focus remains on the courts, an important part of judicial work in a modern democracy involves the court's supervision of administration action.[9] The final two sections argue that what we expect of our courts in this area is not well understood within the terms provided by ethical positivism.

Judges and Rules

In settling legal disputes judges have to find the relevant law, interpret its meaning and apply it to the matter at hand. Campbell gives an elaborate account of how this should happen.

1 As far as is possible, each rule should be in a form that lends itself to positivist adjudication. It should be clear and succinct (to the extent that this is consistent with its objectives) and compatible with other relevant legal rules.[10] The requirement of clarity and specificity extends to the policy objectives which motivate the rules.[11] And there is also the suggestion, less developed, that the legal criteria incorporate questions of fact, as far as this can be done.[12] In these ways the space for subjective beliefs and interests to operate is greatly reduced.
2 Judges should be aware of the possibilities and the risks of current legal methodology. Rule application calls for the identification and interpretation of possible relevant rules. Campbell says little about rule identification: as the emphasis is on how things should be, it is assumed that the law-maker has minimized this problem.[13] The rules of recognition – the rules which formally separate the legal from the non-legal material – have been formulated as clearly as these can be in the circumstances.

   As for interpretation, this is discussed only in general terms. Campbell recommends 'bounded interpretation' (interpretation which limits itself to plausible readings of a specific text) over 'comprehensive' or 'innovative interpretation'. These latter types of interpretation are seen as far too free-wheeling for legal analysis. 'Comprehensive interpretation' is an approach which overemphasizes the role of the interpreter. It is described as an approach in which 'meaning is given, rather than derived from what is written or spoken'.[14] 'Innovative interpretation', for its part, is, well, just too innovative![15]
3 More concrete guidance for judges is given by Campbell when he

moves on to discuss such familiar legal techniques as the plain meaning rule, purposive interpretation and the argument for coherence. What he says about these matters is eminently sensible. The plain meaning rule should have priority among the methods of statutory interpretation as this approach best promotes 'rule governance'. However if giving the words of the legal text their 'evident contextual meaning' would lead to an absurdity, there is good reason to avoid this consequence. This much can be found in any handbook of statutory interpretation. Campbell adds, shrewdly, that this escape route from plain meaning can be abused and because of this, judges should not seek out ambiguity. The use of contexts other than plain meaning is relevant only if there are a number of equally plausible rival readings.[16]

Similar points are made with regard to purposive interpretation. Such an approach is helpful if used to disclose the political choice made by the law-maker. Knowing this may help the law applier understand just what the particular rule requires and, without this knowledge, a positivist approach could well degenerate into an unworldly formalism.[17] But, again, there are dangers. A purposive approach can easily lead to an attitude which pays too little regard to the actual words used by the law-maker. Like any approach which is too context-dependent it loses sight of the point of having rules in the first place – their exclusionary force.[18] Because of this risk judges should not speculate about what ends the law-maker had in mind. They should stay with the goals publicly stated and defended during the law-making process. 'Rational reconstruction' of legislation – stating now, at the time of decision, what a reasonable law-maker would have had in mind at the time of enactment – is to be avoided.[19]

As for the argument for coherence, the larger context of the legal corpus may be relevant for working out the meaning of a particular provision but, again, there are risks associated with this strategy, for it can lead to a downgrading of the clear meaning of the specific provision.[20] The right balance between plain meaning and overall coherence, according to Campbell, will favour current statements as to the meaning of the specific provision over overall coherence.[21]

4 When there is no applicable rule, the judge is directed to 'activism' as the second-best approach. Here it is expected that the judge will work with more material than the existing legal rules and draw overtly on the full range of factors available to the law-maker. The model proposed is one of delegated legislation.[22]

One difficulty here is that not all gaps in the law demand to be filled with new law. An apparent silence may in fact be an area of social life purposely left unregulated. Here Campbell notes the role performed in legal analysis by 'closure rules'. But, again, the methodology generates choices. A rule which states that if somebody is not clearly prohibited it is permitted is an appropriate approach to take to criminal law, but not to other areas of law. It seems out of place in private law, for instance, or even in public law if the emphasis is on state activity rather than individual conduct. In other words, 'closure rules' are important but rarely decisive of the issue, since a judgement as to their applicability comes at the end of the reasoning process, not at the beginning.

5 Overall, judges should develop the qualities of deference and restraint. The basic message for the courts is, avoid 'activism' as far as possible. Exercise restraint when the possibility of law creation arises.

Rules, Purposes and Gaps

It might be said that all this is rather familiar. But such a remark would not do justice to the detail of Campbell's argument and the measured way in which he builds his position. And even if his account draws on the work of others – Raz, MacCormick, Schauer – that alone does not make ethical positivism any less useful an approach.

What of claim 1 above that legal rules should be clear and specific? The basic model of law here is statute law, or regulations, for this type of law has both the form and the specificity of content to allow 'rule governance' to work.[23] One point that comes to mind is to contest the possibility or desirability of always setting out our law with a high degree of specificity. There is no reason to think that all of our social goals are best pursued if we regulate in this way. But, to this, Campbell has an answer. To the extent that we currently have law in less specific form, we should change it – but only so far as this is appropriate for the subject matter at hand. If it turns out that general standards, rather than specific rules, are more suitable for regulating certain areas of social life then so be it. However, at some stage, this response may wear thin, for it is so much part of Campbell's argument that effective government calls for specific rules that it is not compatible ultimately with a large-scale abandonment of rules for standards. Moreover, he frequently makes this very point.

One could quibble with some of the detail of Campbell's discussion of legal methods. The purposive approach cannot, in my view, be so easily cabined. Often the purposes publicly stated at the time of enactment will not deal with the problem conclusively, if at all.[24] For what now arises for decision is a new problem, and any discussion of the argument for coherence should take up such ideas as Dworkin's 'local priority',[25] Hoy's 'competing contexts'[26] or Günther's distinction between norm justification and norm application.[27] But on the principal points Campbell is right. Tensions exist among the traditional approaches to statutory interpretation and this should be openly acknowledged; courts should stay with the plain meaning of the statutory text, unless there is good reason not to; and judges should be wary of these 'good reasons' for, like the serpent in the Garden of Eden, these could lead them astray.

As for the gaps in the law (point 4 above), how should these be described? Are they more properly thought of as an area beyond the present rules or, rather, as spaces which exist *within* the present rules? Campbell aligns himself with the Hart/Raz position on this. Rules run out. And when they do, it is better to openly concede this point and fashion an appropriate legal rule from other material. It was on this very issue, of course, that Ronald Dworkin distinguished his approach from orthodox positivism.[28] As with so much in these debates, it is a matter of which account better accords with how we think courts should operate.[29] If it was put to Campbell that his approach may well give up too quickly on *legal* values, he would probably argue that such a tendency can be resisted. And, presumably, he would agree that any judicial fashioning of new law should consider legal values, along with the relevant social interests.

Campbell's account is a plausible discussion of those matters which it addresses. For my part, I would have more to say about interpretation since I find a hermeneutic approach indispensable in that it discloses the regulative assumptions structuring legal analysis.[30] Moreover, I agree with Dworkin on the question of how best to understand legal gaps. To my mind, he well describes both how judges presently understand their work and how we would like them to understand it. But, as I have indicated, I don't think that these differences amount to much when the issue is *concrete* guidance for decision-makers. Finally, I agree with Campbell that a proper approach must emphasize the importance of textual meaning. But it would be an odd account of judging which did not give primacy to this approach.

My criticism of Campbell is not that his remarks are wrong but that they are, to some extent, misdirected. This comes about, I think, because of the way in which he initially sets up the problem of 'activism'.

The Structure of 'Activism'

Campbell is concerned with a particular type of adjudication. As a *normative* account which stresses the importance of specific rules, it has no interest in case analysis or in legal reasoning which involves a large degree of discretion. For in a legal system 'positivistically conceived' there should be as little of these practices as possible. Consequently, Campbell's 'ethics of adjudication' is in fact an ethics of statutory interpretation.

Because of this, the emphasis is on the application of rules which have a concise canonical form. 'Activism' is seen as failing to apply a rule at hand in accordance with its meaning, or applying a rule which has no warrant in the existing legal materials.[31] However, understood in these terms, an account of 'activism' is unlikely to be of much assistance. Few judges will knowingly fail to apply a rule in accordance with its meaning, or rely on a rule which has no legal warrant as they see it. The problem will be the prior one of working out this meaning or of evaluating the strength of the legal warrant claimed.

Campbell further clarifies 'activism' in contrast to what he sees as the legitimate process of 'concretization' – the process of applying a general norm to the particular thing.[32] But the distinction between 'activism' and 'concretization' cannot be made convincingly, at least in such general terms, because 'concretization' will inevitably concern the *meaning* of the general norm. For the norm now either does, or does not, extend to the case at hand and, when adjudication raises the issue of meaning, this is never done in the abstract. A rule's meaning is always considered in the context of the rules applicability to *particular things*. This is well exemplified in discussions of the inseparability of questions of law and questions of fact – inseparable, that is, when these matters are considered in the abstract.[33]

Campbell's great worry is judicial subjectivity. How can rules be applied without recourse to the moral opinion of judges?[34] This concern is exacerbated, of course, when combined with the problem of pluralism – that, on many important matters, the community and the judges do not speak with one voice. Campbell's examples are the disagreements that exist concerning abortion and euthanasia.[35] But these issues are hardly the subject matter of many cases, and the chapters in *The Legal Approach to Ethical Positivism* which exemplify Campbell's approach deal with free speech – not an unimportant topic, but one in which it is easy to show, at a general level, the diversity of views underlying our commitment to this value.

Rarely does a case generate a direct choice between important social values. Most legal work is more mundane, and this makes the problem of judicial subjectivity both more complicated and more intractable. Judges may share an identifiable common outlook, as often maintained in leftist critiques of the law, but, like the rest of us, they are also individuals with singular life experiences. This personal outlook will give rise to an interest in any particular case (conscious or unconscious) to view the matter before the court in a certain way. But this interest will rarely be as simple as the wish to promote X as an important social goal. For one thing, the judge will often be committed to a number of interests in play that pull in different directions. Furthermore, as a reading of the law is necessary to decide the issue at hand, its effect on larger social goals will often be intangible, if not negligible. I exemplify these points below.

Because of his concentration on statutory interpretation and his conception of judicial subjectivity, Campbell is kept from two important aspects of the topic – namely, what motivates judges to 'activism' in the first place and the concepts developed within legal practice which militate against this. Without understanding what pushes judges to activism it appears only as judicial self-aggrandisement or as the judiciary protecting vested interests against legislative change. Such explanations figure heavily in Campbell's account. And without taking up the particular concepts generated within legal practice to deal with 'activism', the response to it can only be the negative – don't do it. To argue for these points I need a particular example and, for this, I propose to use judicial review of administrative decisions in the context of Australian migration law.

Judicial Review of Migration Decisions

I take up this area of law for three reasons. First, it is a domain of law whose form is in line with Campbell's recommendations for specificity. Australian migration law is now a thicket of detailed rules and the grounds for judicial review of migration decisions are themselves structured and restricted by legislation.[36] Second, judicial review of administrative action is an area in which it is often said that the courts work hand-in-hand with the law-maker rather than against it. For it can be claimed, with a degree of plausibility, that both of these arms of government have an interest (as do the people) in keeping the executive within the law. Executive power is ultimately authorized by the law-maker and must be prevented from exceeding these limits. Judicial review is not the only way of controlling executive discretion but it is an important way. Third, this is an area in which a number of concepts used by the courts (the law/fact distinction, the jurisdictional error/non-jurisdictional error distinction, procedural fairness and so on) are notoriously unstable.

Judicial review of migration decisions in Australia is in the hands of the Federal Court. A survey of this Court's work over the past few years reveals that it has dealt with at least five different types of problems:

1 *The validity, or misuse, of material* relied on in the decision-making process. This includes such issues as: the validity of specific regulations (criteria for a visa class apparently placed in an inappropriate schedule,[37] regulations apparently discriminatory);[38] improper use of policy documents; the failure of the Department of Immigration to authorize certain tests which were relied on in the administrative decision.[39]
2 *The meaning of legal terms* used in migration law. The Court ruled, for instance, that: the term 'spouse' only applies to persons of the opposite sex;[40] that the 'daily care and control' of a dependent child does not require the physical presence of the parent;[41] that 'orphan' extends to someone who has living adopted parents;[42] and that 'trade' means any skilled non-professional work.[43]
3 *Bias* in the decision-maker. Has the decision-maker prejudged the case?[44] Was the decision-maker overzealous in his efforts to discredit the applicant's case?[45]
4 *Procedural justice*. Was the applicant given sufficient opportunity to respond to adverse material?[46] Should the decision-maker have provided advice?[47] Should confidential material have been disclosed?[48] Should deficiencies in the applicant's case have been pointed out?[49] Should the decision-making body have carried out its own investigations into the matter at issue?[50]
5 *Proper justification* for the decision. Was the reasoning adequately disclosed?[51] Was the evidence properly evaluated?[52] Was the correct standard of proof used?[53]

At one level, all these grounds are alike. They have the review court asking: did the decision under review involve an error of law? That, after all, is the basic distinction at work in this areas. The court's job is to supervise the legality of the decision, not its correctness. Judicial review is called for, not merits review.[54] Types 1 and 2 appear to fit this classification. Type 1 deals with the power of the executive. Actions beyond power are unlawful, and it is the court's role to provide a remedy in these circumstances. Type 2 is about the meaning of the law. Again, declaring the meaning of legal terms is a task we ordinarily associate with courts.[55]

Types 2, 4 and 5, on the other hand, appear to be different. The court here is not directly concerned with the lawfulness of the original decision, as this term is generally understood. What is at issue is rather its fairness or reliability. Of course, the goals of fairness or reliability can be put as legal obligations, and, unless the administrative decision-maker is under a legal obligation to provide procedural fairness or to justify its decisions in a certain way, there is no basis for complaint to a review court. But, usually in cases involving state power, and clearly in the Australian migration context, these requirements are legal obligations. What is at stake is not the existence of these obligations but their content – what a fair process amounts to in the circumstances, or what a proper justification of a decision would look like.

In other words, a consideration of the work of review courts shows that we expect these courts to judge administrative agencies against a number of basic norms. These standards must be in legal form. But saying this conceals their diversity. We want the review court to ensure that the administrative body applied valid law, correctly understood, but we also want it to check whether the administrative decision-maker adopted proper procedures, both because people should be treated fairly (this is an end valuable for its own sake) and because following these procedures will increase the likelihood of achieving a reliable decision.

The relevance of these matters for Campbell's account is as follows. First, it is not easy to see how the issues raised by problem types 3, 4 and 5 could be put into the form of specific legal rules. The law-maker can guide the Court by making use of existing legal categories. For example, the present grounds of review in this area rely on the distinction between actual bias and apprehended bias and make use of the established concepts of the 'rules of natural justice' and '(Wednesbury) unreasonableness'[56] – but issues of procedural justice and proper justification for the decision do not seem amenable to further specification. Or, expressed better, whatever specification is offered will never deal adequately with the complex web of ideas underpinning these norms.[57] Nor do they appear reducible to empirical questions – Campbell's other suggestion, it will be recalled, for providing greater precision to adjudication.

Second, although judges undoubtedly have their own views about migration policy – how many migrants should be admitted, through what programmes, from what countries and so on – it is difficult to see these extra-legal beliefs as motivating particular decisions. For one thing, judicial decisions are too particular to have any effect on these larger issues. Migration decisions rarely deal with classes of applicants and the result of successful judicial intervention is not the grant of a visa, but a reconsideration of the matter by the executive. For another, there are numerous other interests which will come into play, including institutional concerns as to the proper division of labour between the courts, parliament and the executive, as well as the very matters that animate Campbell's account – the need to promote democratic law-making and the need for rule governance. Unbridled executive discretion threatens these two interests. In addition, there is concern that administrative decision-making in this area is at times woefully inadequate, as well as a belief that the court has special responsibilities in this area because applicants are drawn, by and large, from a particularly vulnerable group.

Third, when the court evaluates the executive's procedures or reasoning, the standards it brings to bear upon this evaluation themselves encourage restraint. Take the requirement imposed on the executive to make inquiries. This calls for *reasonable* inquiries *in the circumstances of the case,* not all inquiries that a court might conceivably make.[58] In other words, the requirement that the decision be properly justified brings into play a number of considerations which work to restrict the supervisory role of the review court.[59] The court is told not to treat imprecise formulations as obvious errors of law, not to impose standards too rigorous for the type of decision-making involved, to be aware of the advantages of the original decision-maker who both sees the witnesses and has the knowledge which comes from experience in a specialist area, and that the weight to be given to the evidence is a matter for the original decision-maker.[60]

One approach to these standards – *reasonable* inquiry or *reasonable* justification – is to point to their malleability. Surely they are too subjective to guide the work of the courts? Thus their real role is ideological; they help conceal what is essentially an assertion of judicial will. These are important arguments which are not easily dealt with. But this sceptical approach is not available to Campbell. For implicit within his 'ethics of adjudication' is the claim that legal methods are followable. For example, he argues that it makes sense to call upon judges to apply the plain meaning rule, but not if this would lead to an absurdity, or if the plain meaning is out of step with the rule's purpose, or if this meaning is seriously inconsistent with other legal rules. If advice like this can be effective, then standards such as the executive must make reasonable inquiries, or must provide a reasonable justification, can also have an effect, in the sense that these concepts provide a useable framework for debating and evaluating these questions. This is especially true when it is remembered that these norms are not applied in the abstract, but are fleshed out by the factual circumstances of the case under review.

Conclusion

The 'ethics of adjudication' is said to be a workable framework for a rule-centred approach to law-making and application.[61] However, the above example highlights three inadequacies. First, any discussion of 'activism' should address that other branch of government – the administration – more frequently in the law application business. How can administrative discretion be kept in check? Campbell's response is to have as little administrative discretion as possible.[62] But some small degree of it seems inevitable in a modern state. An important response to this problem involves the courts. But an approach to judicial activism which sees it only as a danger to be avoided will have the effect of *increasing* administrative activism.[63] Presumably that is why judicial review of administrative action has led the courts well beyond the model of rule application recommended by Campbell.

The brief survey of Australian migration cases shows that we have a number of expectations with regard to migration decisions. We want them to be legal, accountable, honest, impartial, reliable, involve the participation of the applicants, follow proper procedures and be appropriately justified. And we expect the review court to oversee all of these matters. (One might imagine that Campbell would favour less, rather than more, supervision by the courts but it is inconceivable that he would want no supervision.) What we demand of our courts here is not adequately understood in the terms provided by ethical positivism. It is not a matter of pointing out that proper methods of interpreting statutes for these matters cannot be reduced to precise rules, but nor is it a matter of pointing to the open-ended nature of the court's work and treating it all as a matter of discretion. For the crucial question concerns *the level of intensity* of this supervision.

The norms through which judicial review operate are effective at this level. They help guide the court to an appropriate level of scrutiny in each case. The basic idea of judicial review is that executive decisions should be reconsidered when they have *significantly* departed from the standards of procedural fairness appropriate to the decision-maker under review. It is the context of the actual decision which allows this question of significant departure to be considered with a degree of objectivity.[64] And the availability of types or examples, both positive and negative, provide further context for rational decision-making.[65]

Just to be clear about this, I acknowledge that judicial review of administrative action raises difficult issues as to the court's legitimacy and competency, in this area, for at times judicial review is undoubtedly an impediment to effective administration, both because of its unpredictability and because of its inability to deal with 'polycentric' disputes.[66] That is why restraint is called for. My point is not that judicial review is always appropriate, but that it might be. And neither its rightness or wrongness can be well understood in an account which treats all intervention outside the application of clear rules as an aberration.

Can this example be generalized to other areas of law? Other areas will not have the demand for activism arising within the problem of activism itself – the call for judicial activism to keep in check administrative activism. But they will have other interests at work which can be linked back to the values underlying ethical positivism –

personal freedom, equality of treatment and respect for others. Judges will be drawn towards 'activism' in order to safeguard these values. Only a specific account of these matters will establish whether such interventions are justified.[67]

Notes

1 I thank my colleagues Martin Krygier and Robert Shelly for their comments on an earlier draft of this chapter. The mistakes, if there are any, are my own.

2 Tom Campbell, 'Democratic Aspects of Ethical Positivism', (chapter 1, this volume). I do not offer a rival definition of 'activism' as my point is that none can be given in general terms. But as I continue to use the word I should indicate that, by it, I mean no more than a judicial decision not *obviously* rendered within the framework of the existing legal order. Since I believe such decisions to be both inevitable and common, the term is not necessarily negative.

3 Tom Campbell, *The Legal Theory of Ethical Positivism* (Aldershot: Dartmouth, 1996), p. 125.

4 Ibid., pp. 108 ff.

5 Campbell, 'Democratic Aspects', *op. cit.*, p. 9; see also Campbell, *Ethical Positivism, op. cit.*, pp. 109, 110.

6 Campbell, *Ethical Positivism, op. cit.*, pp. 2, 118.

7 Ibid., pp. 116, 121.

8 Ibid., p. 96.

9 There is of course much in *The Legal Theory of Ethical Positivism* about *constitutional* review, for it is in this context that the issue of judicial activism/restraint is most often raised. But there is no discussion of judicial review of administrative action.

10 Campbell, *Ethical Positivism, op. cit.*, pp. 117, 219.

11 Ibid., pp. 217, 227 f.

12 Ibid., pp. 225, 236.

13 Ibid., p. 148.

14 Ibid., p. 130.

15 The opponent here is Ronald Dworkin.

16 Campbell, *Ethical Positivism, op. cit.*, p. 135.

17 Ibid., p. 85, 147.

18 Ibid., p. 45. The way rules work to exclude reasons otherwise relevant from practical deliberation.

19 Ibid., p. 143.

20 Ibid., p. 128.

21 Ibid., p. 91. Favouring coherence over the specific provision can work to 'dilute legal change' (p. 115).

22 Ibid., pp. 91, 116, 129. Although the risks associated with this approach are acknowledged: ibid., pp. 151, 152.

23 Ibid., p. 8.

24 For a different account of the role of author's meaning in statutory interpretation see A. Glass, 'The Author of Common Law Texts', *Ratio Jurio* **8** (1995), pp. 91–103.

25 Ronald Dworkin, *Law's Empire* (London: Fontana, 1986) pp. 250 ff, 402.

26 David Hoy, 'Dworkin's Constructive Optimism v Deconstructive Nihilism', *Law and Philosophy*, **6** (1987), pp. 321–56 at p. 346.

27 This is conveniently discussed by Jüngen Habermas in *Between Facts and Norms* (Cambridge, MA: MIT Press, 1996) pp. 219–21.

28 Ronald Dworkin, *Taking Rights Seriously* (London: Duckworth, 1978) pp. 86–7.

29 For elaboration of this point see M. Krygier and A. Glass, 'Shaky Premises: Values, Attitudes and the Law', *Sydney Law Review*, **17** (1995), p. 385.

30 A. Glass, 'Interpretive Practices in Law and Literary Criticism', *Australian Journal of Law and Society*, **7** (1991), pp. 16–26.

31 Campbell, 'Democratic Aspects', *op. cit.*

32 Ibid., fn. 16.

33 On this see Neil MacCormick, *Legal Reasoning and Legal Theory* (Oxford: Clarendon Press, 1978), pp. 93 ff; Etienne Mureinik, 'The Application Of Rules: Law Or Fact?', *Law Quarterly Review*, **98** (1982), pp. 587–620. And generally on 'concretization', Habermas, *Between Facts and Norms, op. cit.*, pp. 199, 218.

34 Campbell, *Ethical Positivism, op. cit.*, pp. 72, 81, 85, 86, 88, 132, 189, 219.

35 Ibid., p. 152.

36 Migration Act 1958, Part 8.

37 *Ramos* v. *Minister*, Federal Court of Australia, Hely J, 30/11/98.

38 *De Silva* v. *Ruddock* (1998) 159 ALR 55.

39 *Din* v. *Minister* (1997) 147 ALR 673.

40 *Rohner* v. *Minister* (1998) 157 ALR 24.

41 *Ha* v. *Minister*, Federal Court of Australia, Davies J, 21/8.96, unreported.

42 *Phung* v. *Minister* (1997) 49 ALD 566.

43 *Pillay* v. *Minister* (1997) 47 ALD 12.

44 *Eshetu* v. *Minister* (1997) 145 ALR 621, *Ferati* v. *Minister*, Federal Court of Australia, Heerey J. 23/12/98.

45 *Sun Zhan Qui* v. *Minister* (1998) 151 ALR 505.

46 *Cho* v. *Minister*, Federal Court of Australia, Madgwick J, 22/12/98, unreported.

47 *Hamilton* v. *Minister* (1994) 53 FCR 349.

48 *Gilson* v. *Minister*, Federal Court of Australia, Lehane J, 21/7/97, unreported.

49 *Horvath* v. *Minister* (1994) 35 ALD 422.

50 *Singh* v. *Minister* (1996) 35 ALD 425.

51 Again, in Australian migration law there is no question as at times whether decision-makers have to give reasons. They have to. *Muralidharan* v. *Minister* (1996) 136 ALR 84, *Kandiah* v. *Minister*, Federal Court of Australia, Finn J, 3/9/98.

52 *Elmi* v. *Minister* (Federal Court of Australia, Emmett J, 30 September 1998.

53 *Epeabaka* v. *Minister* (1999) FCA 1.

54 M. Aronson and B. Dyer, *Judicial Review of Administrative Action* (Sydney: Law Book 1996), pp. 16 f, pp. 186 ff.

55 As to whether the court should at times defer to the agency's understanding of the law is an issue I do not pursue.

56 See Migration Act 1958, s. 476(1)(f) and s. 476(2). Just how effective these specifications are has been the subject of frequent litigation. See the case law summarized in *Eshetu* v. *Minister* (1997) 145 ALR 621, before the High Court at the time of writing.

57 Habermas, *Between Facts and Norms, op. cit.*, p. 198.

58 *Sun Zhan Qui* v. *Minister for Immigration* (1998) 151 ALR 505, among other examples. Reasonable inquiries is thought of as a judgment which weighs up – how important was the inquiry for deciding the issue, what other evidence was available, how easy was it to for the administrative decision-maker to make the inquiry, etc.?

59 *Wu Shan Liang* v. *Minister for Immigration* (1996) 185 CLR 259, especially at 272, 291–293.

60 Ibid.

61 Campbell, *Ethical Positivism, op. cit.*, p. 244.

62 Ibid., pp. 9, 60.

[63] In his discussion of *Liversidge* v. *Anderson* (1942) AC 206 and the *Capital Television* case (1992) 177 CLR 106 (*Ethical Positivism, op. cit.*, 144, 183) Campbell avoids this issue by treating legislative power and executive power as one.

[64] See the earlier discussion on p. 365.

[65] Developing this point is beyond the scope of this chapter but see Habermas, *Between Facts and Norms, op. cit.*, pp. 220 f.

[66] Carol Harlow and Richard Rawlings, *Law and Administration*, 2nd edn (London: Butterworths, 1997), chs 16, 17, among many discussions.

[67] On the judiciary's role in establishing the rational acceptability of norms see Habermas, *Between Facts and Norms, op. cit.*, ch. 5.

16 The Role of Law and the Role of Lawyers

TIM DARE

Introduction

One notable feature of Tom Campbell's *The Legal Theory of Ethical Positivism* is the inclusion of a discussion of lawyer's ethics.[1] Although legal ethics has received increasing attention over the past decade or so, few authors have treated the subject within the context of a more general study of the philosophy of law.[2] Campbell does so. Put very broadly, *The Legal Theory of Ethical Positivism* is concerned to remind us that the positivist insistence on the distinction between law and morality is itself a moral view. Broadly, the moral arguments which Campbell offers in support of the positivist distinction concern the role of law. His treatment of legal ethics is essentially an application of this general strategy to the more detailed questions addressed in the legal ethics debate. He suggests that the foundational moral arguments on which ethical positivism rests have significant implications for the ethical obligations of lawyers. Insofar as those values support a model of law as a sophisticated set of rules, they also support a conception of the lawyer's role as 'contributing to accurate rule implementation...'.[3]

Although I shall say nothing more about Campbell's discussion of legal ethics, I regard this chapter as at least sympathetic to his approach to legal ethics. My aim is to defend a modified form of what has become known as the 'standard conception of the lawyer's role', according to which lawyers owe special duties to their clients, the effect of which is to render permissible, or even mandatory, acts which would otherwise be morally impermissible. The conception is colourfully evoked by Macaulay's famous question as to '[w]hether it be right that a man should, with a wig on his head and a band around his neck do for a guinea what, without these appendages, he would think it wicked and infamous to do for an empire'.[4]

'The standard conception' has become a somewhat ironic epithet. If numbers count, the standard view now is that the conception cannot be right. It has passed from orthodoxy to fair game, replaced by a new orthodoxy that it 'must be abandoned, to be replaced by a conception that better allows the lawyer to bring his full moral sensibilities to play in his professional role'.[5] But I do not think we should abandon the standard conception. I believe that it is essentially the right way to conceive of lawyers' ethical obligations. My defence of the conception begins with an appeal to the function of law. The point of the institution which supports a given role will feature significantly in any justification of that role and its role obligations. The nature of the lawyer's role and the role obligations it imposes, depends on the function of the role within the institution of which it is a part, and hence upon the function of that institution. I will suggest that the fundamental function of the institutions of law in modern constitutional democracies is to mediate between the range of views to be found in such communities on fundamental questions such as what constitutes human flourishing, what basic goals are intrinsically most worthy of pursuit, and what is the best way for individuals to live their lives. The law allows the advocates of very different views on these matters to live together, despite their differences. The nature of the roles occupied lawyers within the institutions of law is settled largely by this mediating function of law. We will go on to examine the principles which make up the standard conception of law in light of this account of law and legal roles. For the most part, I will suggest, the approach supports the standard conception. We will see, however, that the appeal to the point of law gives us reason to reject readings of the conception as requiring lawyers to 'hyper-zealously' pursue every advantage obtainable for their clients through the law. That is, I appeal to the role of law, to defend a moderate version of the standard conception.

The Standard Conception and the Role of Law

Law and Reasonable Pluralism

We begin, then, with an account of the function of law. The institutions of law in Western democracies no doubt serve many functions: they are dispute resolution devices; they supply answers to coordination problems (they tell us, for instance, which side of the road to drive on); they secure the provision of certain public goods, such as health care and roads; they allow conduct which would simply not be possible other than in institutional contexts (just as one cannot 'hit a six' or 'hit a home-run' without the institutions of cricket or baseball, nor can one 'incorporate a company' without the institution of company law); they facilitate planning by treating certain kinds of undertaking or arrangement as enforceable; they identify certain forms of conduct as required or prohibited; and lend the power of the state to better ensure compliance.

This is no doubt an incomplete list of the functions of the institutions of Western law. Yet, even in this abbreviated form, it may seem so diverse as to render impossible a compelling appeal to law's function: how can one appeal meaningfully to 'the function of law' when it has so many functions? The answer is that a common and general function lies behind these more specific ones. John Rawls' recent work is suggestive. It is based upon the premise that the citizens of modern democracies are, and will, remain sharply divided over fundamental questions such as what constitutes human flourishing, what basic goals are intrinsically most worthy of pursuit and what is the best way for individuals to live their lives. This 'plurality of conceptions of the good', Rawls concludes, is inevitable; it is 'the natural outcome of the activities of human reason under enduring free institutions'.[6]

Not all views about these fundamental matters count as reasonable. But even with Nazis and lunatics to one side, a plurality of reasonable views remains. In modern times, the claim goes, we have come to recognize a multiplicity of ways in which a fulfilled life can be lived, without seeing a hierarchy among them which we feel justified in enforcing. We have been forced to acknowledge that even where we believe that we have discerned the superiority of some ways of life over others, reasonable people may not share our view. Pluralism and reasonable disagreement are ineliminable features of the political landscape in modern constitutional democracies.

The challenge for such communities is to find a way that 'there may exist over time a secure stable and just society among free and equal citizens profoundly divided by reasonable though incompatible religious, philosophical and moral doctrine'.[7] A central part of the liberal answer to this question has been the adoption of a certain kind of neutrality as a political ideal. The members of a pluralist community, the idea goes, will often be able to agree on the structure of neutral institutions and practices even where they cannot agree on the right outcome of a policy question as a substantive matter. Although it is unlikely that they will ever reach agreement on the substantive political questions which motivate their disagreement, each may accept, as fair, a system which allows every view to be expressed, which allows representatives of every view to stand for office, which gives every person a vote, which allocates seats to representatives of the various positions in proportion to the percentage of votes cast in favour of that position and so on. Procedures such as these are intended to ensure that all reasonable views are taken equally seriously and that none is preferred by the very structure of the procedures. Of course, such practices cannot guarantee outcomes that will suit all the reasonable views. Often there will be no such universally acceptable outcome. There simply is no resolution of the abortion debate which will seem substantively correct to every reasonable disputant. The hope of liberalism, however, is that even those whose substantive preferences do not win the day on this or that occasion will have cause to accept as fair the decisions of these institutions because they accept the procedures by which they were reached.

The institutions and practices to which a procedural understanding of neutrality give rise allow the creation of stable and just communities, despite the presence of a widespread diversity of conflicting, and perhaps even incommensurable, conceptions of the good. They do so by mediating between this diversity of substantive views and concrete decisions which communities must take. Joseph Raz, speaking of the practice of normally proceeding through the mediation of rules, makes the point when he writes that:

> ... the practice allows the creation of a pluralistic culture. For it enables people to unite in support of some 'low or medium level' generalisations despite profound disagreements concerning their ultimate foundations, which some seek in religion, others in Marxism or in Liberalism, etc.[8]

How do procedures or rules mediate in this way? We can give only a partial answer here.

First, different, and perhaps even incompatible, views about how we should live often support common rules 'since different premises may lead to the same conclusions'.[9] We are familiar with social and political alliances that seem strange at first glance. Feminists and conservatives, for example, find themselves unlikely political bedfellows in the debate over censorship. Although they hold dramatically different views on the justification of censorship, they (often) agree that pornography ought to be restricted or prohibited. Thus we have procedural consensus without substantive consensus.

Second, even where we do not have a fortuitous convergence of different views on common institutional responses, the procedural approach allows the advocates of diverse views to cooperate without abandoning their own views or embracing the views of others. Suppose we disagree about some option which will affect our future common action and that it has become obvious that each has given the other all the reasons they can imagine for favouring their view over the other. Our continued membership in a common community will sometimes require us to find a way of going on, of deciding what to do, despite our disagreement as to what ought to be done. Perhaps we toss a coin and you win. The toss changes the situation significantly. If our discussion really was exhaustive, you could not give me any more reasons in favour of your view. After the toss, however, you can give me a new reason – namely, the fact that the decision procedure we accepted has selected your preference. The normative force of *this* reason, however, does not depend on my thinking that you were right about the substantive matter. I can accept it as a reason for action while continuing to hold on to my own view of what, from a substantive perspective, ought to have been done.

Of course, we do not settle our political disputes by the toss of a coin. The decision-making procedures which are the focus of the actual accommodations between competing conceptions of the good in our community are enormously complex. Instead of the straightforward coin-tossing procedure, we have a set of procedures which include those for selecting governments, for making and interpreting law, for determining ownership of goods and so on. As Kurt Baier writes:

> Although there seems to be no consensus on a conception of justice [in Western constitutional democracies], there is a consensus on something else, namely, on the procedures for making and interpreting law and, where that agreement is insufficiently deep to end disagreement, on the selection of persons whose adjudication is accepted as authoritative.[10]

Adherents of the various and diverse conceptions of the good which are represented in our communities cannot be expected to agree on any single conception of the good. They can agree, however, on the form of procedures which will give them, if not what they want, at least what they need. Although we do not, and will not, agree on fundamental matters such as what constitutes human flourishing, what basic goals are intrinsically most worthy of pursuit and what is the best way for individuals to live their lives, we can agree on procedures which respect the diversity of views represented in the community, and which issue decisions with which we can live.

This section has addressed the role of law in pluralist communities. It began with the observation that the nature of roles and role obligations depended on the nature and function of the institutions of which they were a part. I have suggested that the institutions of law are designed and intended to mediate between the diverse range of views of what ought to be done and particular decisions about what is to be done – that is, the general function which lies behind the more specific tasks performed by the institutions of law – behind decisions about what public goods are to be secured, about which option is to be rendered salient to solve coordination problems, and about which sorts of undertakings will receive the protection of law. These and the other specific tasks listed earlier are addressed by the institutions of law in order to allow people who have different views about such matters to coexist despite their ongoing substantive disagreements. This means that the role of the institutions of law is to allow 'there to exist over time a stable and just society among free and equal citizens profoundly divided by reasonable religious, philosophical and moral views'.[11]

The Role of Law and the Lawyer's Role

We began with the claim that one important strand in the justification of role and role obligations relied on the function of the institutions of which they were a part. I have argued that the fundamental function of law in Western democracies is to mediate between reasonable, but inconsistent, views of what we should do as a community. Our aim now is to draw the appropriate conclusions about lawyers' roles and role obligations from this account of the function of law. To show this derivation properly we need to give close attention to the specific features of the lawyer's professional ethical obligations, such as the duty to maintain confidences and the duty to avoid conflicts of interest. In this chapter, however, we will work at a much broader and cruder level, seeking merely to outline the derivation of the more general principles which make up the standard conception – the principles of neutrality, non-accountability and partisanship.

The principle of neutrality Some of these derivations are obvious. According to the principle of neutrality, the lawyer must not allow his or her own view of the moral merits of the client's objectives or character to affect the diligence or zealousness with which he or she pursues the client's lawful objectives. The principle is explained by appeal to the fact of reasonable pluralism. Given the fact of reasonable pluralism we do not order our communities by direct appeal to any particular view of the good. Instead, we seek the support and cooperation of the advocates of a diverse range of views by undertaking, in effect, to appeal to the determinations of decision procedures structured to take all reasonable views seriously. Lawyers who calibrate their professional efforts according to their own view of the good – or, indeed, according to any particular view of the good – not only 'privilege' the view they favour and disenfranchise the view of the client, they undercut the strategy by which we secure community between people profoundly divided by reasonable but incompatible views of the good. Where legal rights are established by the procedure, decisions about what is to be done are to be settled by appeal to those rights, not by appeal to particular views of the good, still less any particular individual's views of the good.

In short, the principle of neutrality recognizes that it is not the lawyers' responsibility to determine what we will do as a community, what rights we will allocate and to whom. The complexity of the procedures on which a pluralist community, such as ours, must rely means that lawyers do have tremendous power in this regard. Their legal expertise means they are better placed than any other group of citizens to work in, and with, our legal and political institutions. The principle of neutrality recognizes this power and its potential for abuse. It guards against the possibility that someone might be denied rights allocated by a legal system because its lawyers find those rights or their allocation to that person morally objectionable. Since legal representation is at least sometimes necessary to secure legal rights, the lawyer or the community of lawyers could render the person's claim to their lawful rights worthless by refusing to represent them at all or by making a less than zealous effort on behalf of an existing client. Given the function of law in pluralist communities, the principle of neutrality states an important and deeply moral obligation. It is a central part of an adequate legal ethics in such communities.

The principle of non-accountability Similarly, the appeal to pluralism explains the principle of non-accountability – the principle according to which lawyers are not to be judged by the moral status of their client's projects, even though the lawyer's assistance was necessary to the pursuit of those projects. If we recognize that there are many plausible views about which interests should receive legal protection, we have reason to leave decisions about which are to be protected to procedures which recognize the fact of reasonable pluralism and which constrain the influence of individuals who happen to find themselves positioned to act as gatekeepers to the realm of legal rights. If these procedures do serve this mediating role, then we cannot assume that lawyers identify or sympathize with particular rights or with their allocation to particular clients. Lawyers might have strong moral objections to a client's projects, but accept the importance of appealing to the procedurally allocated rights rather than to their own moral preferences. Furthermore, the appeal to pluralism gives us reason to hope that lawyers will not allocate their expertise in a way which will function as a *de facto* barrier to unpopular but protected views of the good. The principle of non-accountability removes one reason lawyers may have for refusing to act for clients whose moral views and legal goals do not accord with their own. In this guise the rule acts as a defence for those who do take on unpopular cases. They may plead the rule in response to the mistaken assumption that they would not have taken on the case if they did not endorse the goals of the client. Thus the rule removes a barrier to such clients obtaining representation necessary to avail themselves of legal rights.[12]

The principle of partisanship The derivation of the principle of partisanship, the remaining and most problematic strand of the standard conception, may seem less obvious. This principle calls upon lawyers to aggressively and single-mindedly pursue the client's interests all the way up to the limits of the law. How does the appeal to pluralism generate this duty? We can use David Luban as a focus for our discussion. He argues that the principle of partisanship cannot be justified by:

> ... [t]he argument ... that the best way to guarantee that an individual's legal rights are protected ... is to provide her with a zealous advocate who will further her interests.[13]

For current purposes, we can treat the rights argument referred to in this passage as equivalent to the appeal to pluralism. Read in this way, Luban's claim is that we cannot derive the principle of partisanship from the sorts of argument advanced in this chapter. But I think that his conclusion is based upon a common mischaracterization of the principle of partisanship which treats it as requiring lawyers to be more zealous than is actually necessary. I believe that Luban is right when he says that the more zealous version of the principle cannot be derived from the sorts of argument advanced in this chapter. But once the principle of partisanship is characterized in a more moderate form, its derivation from the appeal to pluralism is reasonably straightforward.

Mere zeal and hyper-zeal. What are these more and less moderate understandings of the principle of partisanship? According to one interpretation, the principle calls upon lawyers to exercise what we may call 'mere zeal'. The merely zealous lawyer is concerned solely with the legal interests of his client. He pursues those interests, 'without fear ... and without regard to any unpleasant consequences to himself or to any other person'. On this account, the interests various codes require lawyers to 'fearlessly uphold ... without regard for personal interests or concerns'[14] are those which are protected by law, not simply anything which happens to be in the client's interests, let alone anything in which the client happens to be interested.

It is often in our interest to have more than we are entitled to under law, and no doubt we are often interested in having more than our bare legal entitlement. But this is of no great concern to the merely zealous lawyer. His professional obligation is to zealously pursue the client's legal rights. He is to be partisan in the sense that he must bring all his professional skills to bear upon the task of securing *his* client's rights. But he is under no obligation to pursue interests which go beyond the law.

According to the alternative understanding, the principle of partisanship commits lawyers to what we may call hyper-zeal, where the hyper-zealous lawyer is concerned not merely to secure her client's legal rights, but to pursue any advantage obtainable for her client through the law. 'My legal rights', says Luban, 'are everything to which I am in fact legally entitled to, not everything the law can be made to give', but 'good' lawyers can almost always get me more than that to which I am legally entitled:

> Every lawyer knows tricks of the trade that can be used to do opponents out of their legal deserts – using delaying tactics for example, to make it too costly for an opponent without much money to prosecute a lengthy suit even though the law is on her side, or filing a nuisance claim carefully calculated to be cheaper to settle than defend.[15]

According to Luban and the tradition he draws from, the principle of partisanship *requires* lawyers to use these tricks to obtain for their clients all that the law can be made to give. The standard conception, he implies, calls upon lawyers to secure the goals of mere zeal – the defence of the client's rights – by adopting the tactics of hyper-zeal:

> The no-holds barred zealous advocate tries to get everything the law can give ..., and thereby does a better job of defending the client's legal rights than a less committed lawyer would do.[16]

But I think this is a mistake. I hope in the next few pages to show that the principle of partisanship requires lawyers to be merely zealous, and not to be hyper-zealous.

The derivation of mere zeal. I begin with the derivation of mere zeal. The duty of mere zeal seems to flow from the appeal to pluralism in fairly straightforward fashion. Those arguments postulate a set of procedures which mediate between the diversity of views of the good and decisions about what is to be done. Individuals often require lawyers if they are to obtain the benefit of the procedures around which their communities are formed. They require lawyers to take advantage of the mechanisms which will allow them to have their property distributed a certain way after their death, to secure money over their property, to advance a defence when they are charged with an offence and so on. The lawyers in these cases act on behalf of their clients. In effect, they do for the client things that the client would do for themselves if the legal system were not so complicated. If clients wish to avail themselves of the rights allocated to them under the legal system, their lawyers, insofar as they act on the client's behalf, must help them do so. That is what constitutes acting on the client's behalf with respect to the legal system.

Sometimes, of course, we feel uneasy about people who stand on their rights. Even if a client does have a legal right to avail himself of a statute of limitations, his decision to do so may show him to be callous and nasty.[17] But the appeal to pluralism shows that decisions about what is for the public good, about what sort of tax system we should have, about how long somebody can wait to seek a remedy in contract, about whether *this* defendant has *this* right and so on are things to be decided, not in private in the offices of particular lawyers but in the public arena of politics where everyone can have a say, or in the public domain of the courts where reasons must be given and opportunities exist for challenge and representation. The arguments show that it is not up to individual lawyers to decide what interests will receive legal protection, what legal rights will be allocated to whom. That is the function of the procedures which make communities such as ours possible. Lawyers who fail to exercise mere zeal, who take it upon themselves not to pursue legal entitlements available to their clients when their clients wish them to do so, privilege whatever moral view they are following in preference to that of their client and undercut the procedures which allow the advocates of a plurality of views to live in common community.

Furthermore, although we often admire people who sacrifice their own interests for the benefits of others, the moral quality of these sacrifices depends crucially on it being the rights-holder who makes the sacrifice. It is difficult to imagine the circumstances in which I act well by sacrificing some entitlement of yours, although there are many circumstances in which we think well of you for doing so. What is a virtuous act done by one person is a vice done by another. R.E. Ewin puts this point as follows:

> The client can, through the lawyer who is handling the negotiations, be generous, but for the lawyer to take it upon herself to act in that way without instructions from the client is for the lawyer to be 'generous' with what is someone else's, which is not to be generous at all. .... It is not simply that the lawyer *may* not be generous in that case; the lawyer *cannot* be generous.[18]

Lawyers who try to be generous by sacrificing their client's rights – whether by not merely zealously pursuing those rights or perhaps by simply not advising the client that the rights are available – display not the virtue of generosity, but instead a vice, 'something like arrogance'.[19]

The problem of hyper-zeal. We turn now to the problem of hyper-zeal. Luban suggests that the principle of partisanship commits lawyers to hyper-zealous advocacy, to pursuing not merely the client's legal rights but all that the law can be made to give. And, of course, his is not an idiosyncratic view. Lord Brougham's classic characterization of the advocate as bound to pursue the client's interests 'at all hazards and costs to other persons', without 'regard [to] the alarm, the torments, the destruction which he may bring others', even to the extent that 'it should be his unhappy fate to involve his country in confusion', surely takes us beyond mere zeal and into the realm of hyper-zeal.[20] In questioning Luban's linking of the standard conception and the principle of partisanship with the duty of hyper-zeal, then, we question a reading of the principle of partisanship which dates back at least to Brougham. Notwithstanding its pedigree, however, I do not think the attempt to pin a duty of hyper-zeal on the standard conception is warranted. Indeed, the appeal to pluralism allows us to see why lawyers do not have a duty of hyper-zealous advocacy.

Much of this discussion has been based on the idea that the lawyer's role is to allow clients to avail themselves of rights allocated to them by social institutions. If this is an accurate account of the lawyer's role, it seems to follow directly that it is not a lawyer's function to allow clients to satisfy interests beyond those allocated by law. Sometimes, of course, clients may wish to do so, and nothing thus far entails that it is the lawyer's function to prevent them.[21] But if we understand the lawyer as occupying a role in an institution, then we seem able to say at least that the demands that can be made on them must be demands to the 'resources' of the institutions of which they are a part. Lawyers occupy roles in an institution designed to allow pluralist communities by specifying what rights members of the community shall have. The role obligations are framed by reference to the point of that institution. Hence lawyers have no special responsibilities to allow their clients to avail themselves of resources or benefits which lie outside the law. The lawyer's responsibility is to further the interests of the client, insofar as the institutional rights and duties of the client allow. The institutional framing of the lawyer's responsibilities means that the lawyer is not required to do just anything that would further the client's interests.

Some cases are simple. It may be that my interests would be served if the witness who saw me rob the bank was bumped off. But it does not follow that my lawyer is thereby placed under a duty to bump off the witness. And notice that this is true not just because it is illegal to murder witnesses. The lawyer has the same moral and legal reasons as everyone else for refusing to advance my interest by bumping off the witness, plus a reason that only lawyers have: his role in an institution intended to ensure that I am able to avail himself of all the rights allocated to me by law. I cannot require my lawyer to satisfy my interest in having the witness bumped off, since that is not one of those rights. Put simply, the lawyer's responsibility is structured by the institutional rights of law. In his capacity as lawyer, he or she can, and should, respond to my request for help with these 'extra-legal' interests, by pointing out that that is not his job. His job is to act on the client's behalf, relative to the institutions of law.

Other cases seem more difficult – as evidenced by Luban mentioned earlier. Every lawyer, he said, knows tricks of the trade that can be used to do opponents out of their legal deserts

> ... using delayed tactics for example, to make it too costly for an opponent without much money to prosecute a lengthy suit even though the law is on her side, or filing a nuisance claim carefully calculated to be cheaper to settle than defend.[22]

And he adds some others:

> The rules of discovery, initiated to enable one side to find out crucial facts from the other, are used nowadays to delay trial or to impose added expenses on the other side; conversely, one might respond to an interrogatory by delivering to the discoverer tons of miscellaneous documents to run up their legal bills or to conceal a needle in a haystack. ... Similarly, rules barring lawyers from representations involving conflicts of interest are now regularly used by adversaries to drive up the other side's costs by having the counsel disqualified.[23]

Luban complains that the principle of partisanship requires lawyers to use such tricks if they can advance their client's interests by doing so. These cases may seem more difficult than that involving the inconvenient witness, since the lawyers involved in them could be acting perfectly legally. And, of course, it may be true that responding to the other side's interogatory with tons of miscellaneous documents is the best way of serving the client's interests: perhaps, for example, the client has a hopeless case. Nonetheless, although these cases are more difficult, the rights argument gives us a response. As Luban describes some of these cases, the lawyer 'indulges in overkill to obtain as legal rights benefits that in fact may not be legal rights'.[24] Under this description, the rights argument provides the lawyer with a response similar to that he would give were I to ask him to bump off the inconvenient witness. His responsibility is structured by the institutional rights of law and his job is to act on the client's behalf, *relative* to the institutions of law. It is not his job to pursue interests which are not protected by law.

We may also be able to develop this response a little by noting that an aspect of the role of helping clients to avail themselves of their legal rights is helping them ascertain what those rights are. And now we can respond that simply preventing a case coming before the decision procedures of our community by abusing the rules of discovery or conflict of interest, is not helping ascertain what rights a client may demand, even if it does further their interests. It is not doing the lawyer's job. Rather, it is preventing the job from being done. I have suggested that it is the role of lawyers to assist individuals to avail themselves of the rights allocated to them by their communities. This role does not generate obligations or permissions to avoid determinations of rights claims. Lawyers who abuse process of discovery – for instance, to prevent a case coming to court – quite simply do not perform that role. An understanding of the duty of zealous advocacy which portrays lawyers as being allowed, or obliged, to use every lawful tactic to prevent the legal system addressing a case is simply mistaken. Note why it is mistaken. It is wrong because it fails to see how the duties of lawyers are derived from a proper understanding of their roles. I am quite happy to concede that this may be a revision of the standard and well pedigreed understanding of the standard conception. If it is, then so be it: it is one which gives a proper place to the moral considerations which inform the lawyer's role, while holding on to the idea that such roles are subject to role-differentiated obligations.

The upshot is that Luban is right when he says that the rights argument does not support excesses of professional zeal. But since these *are* excesses, their failure to find support in the rights argument is a mark in that argument's favour. By the same token, the fact that the more moderate version of the principle of partisanship can be derived from the rights argument is a reason to suppose both that the principle, in this form, expresses a genuine obligation on lawyers in pluralist communities, and that the standard conception has long been misunderstood as requiring more than acceptable zeal from lawyers.

Mere zeal, hyper-zeal and abuse of process. I mentioned earlier lawyers who abuse the process of discovery. It is worth pursuing the example a little further, since the jurisdiction to prevent abuse of process seems to support the arguments just given for interpreting the duty of zeal as a duty of mere rather than hyper-zeal. The discussion in the last few sections has relied on two ideas: first, not every lawful advantage that can be obtained through the law is a legal entitlement; and, second, the duty of zealous advocacy requires lawyers to pursue only their client's legal entitlements. That is, the duty of zealous advocacy is a duty of mere rather than hyper-zeal. I have argued for the distinction between legal entitlements and other advantages available through the law by appeal to the function of law: lawyers are not required to pursue every advantage available to clients through the law, the argument goes, because their professional roles are structured by the function of the institution to which those roles belong, and the function of that institution is to determine and protect legal entitlements not to secure every possible lawful advantage. So much, I have argued, is consistent with a proper understanding of the standard conception of the lawyer's role.

The most obvious reason for thinking that the doctrine of abuse of process might be helpful in this context is the similarities between judicial formulations of the doctrine and its significance, and the argument advanced above which appealed to the function of law. Bluntly, the courts have given a *functional* account of abuse of process. An abuse in this context consists in 'a party using court proceedings and procedures for a purpose unrelated to the objectives which the court process is designed to achieve'.[25] 'The focus in such a suit is on the purpose for which the proceedings exist....'[26] We might equally say that the focus is on the *function* of the procedures. So in *Grainger* v. *Hill*,[27] the case which is the source of the tort of abuse of process, a writ of arrest was issued under a mortgage of a ship. The plaintiff's intention was not in fact to avail himself of his rights under the mortgage, but to bring pressure on the defendant to surrender the ship's register – something quite outside the mortgage. Tindal CJ said 'that the process of the law has been abused, to effect an object not within the scope of the process'.[28] Abuse of process consists in using legal procedures to pursue 'collateral advantages',[29] or for 'ulterior purposes'.[30]

My suggestion is that there is a useful analogy between these 'ulterior purposes' or 'collateral advantages' and the advantages available through the law which are other then legal entitlements. Of course, lawyers should not regard themselves as allowed, let alone required, to abuse the processes of the legal system, and just what will count as an abuse of process is to be determined by reference to the purpose or function of the procedures in question. The abuse of process jurisdiction requires lawyers to identify the proper object of legal proceedings, by reference to the function of those proceedings, and then to restrict their advocacy to the pursuit of those objects. This is essentially the same test, and the same outcome, as that recommended in the argument from the function of law given above. Thus the abuse of process jurisdiction is an illustration both of our ability to distinguish between legal entitlements and other advantages available through law, and of the use of that distinction to restrict legitimate advocacy. Lawyers may legitimately restrict themselves to merely zealous advocacy, where that is to say that they must zealously pursue their client's legal entitlements but need not zealously pursue every advantage – we might say every collateral advantage – that the law can be made to provide.

Thus, I propose an analogy between the functional argument for distinguishing between mere and hyper-zeal and the abuse of process jurisdiction. We can begin to explore this analogy by noting a very general respect in which the abuse of process jurisdiction echoes the functional account of the limits of legitimate advocacy. The echo becomes apparent when we consider the common recognition of the need for caution in the exercise of the jurisdiction. Sir John Donaldson MR gives the classic statement when he says that the jurisdiction 'falls to be exercised with care and discretion and only in clear cases', because '[i]t must never be forgotten that it is not for solicitors or counsel to impose a pre-trial screen through which a litigant must pass before he can put his complaint or defence before the court'.[31] To the same effect, the judge in a recent Australian case remarked on 'the tension' between the jurisdiction and:

> … the important right of a person to have a case conducted in the courts irrespective of the view which his or her legal adviser has formed about the case and its prospects of success. The courts must be open to any party who claims that he or she has been wronged and seeks to vindicate a right or to compel the enforcement of an obligation.[32]

In describing the tension in these terms, these judges indicate that the elements the abuse of process jurisdiction seeks to balance – crudely, the prevention of abuse on the one hand and the principle that lawyers may not act as gatekeepers to legal rights on the other – are the very ones which have structured the legal ethics debate itself. The two inquiries address essentially the same questions; they seek to balance the same elements.

The analogy and the claim as to its usefulness to the attempt to specify the ethical limits on advocacy are also supported by more detailed attention to the jurisdiction. We saw that the most challenging cases for the attempt to limit zealous advocacy seemed to be those in which lawyers were called upon to pursue *lawful*, but ethically objectionable, goals for their clients. I suggested that we might secure the appropriate limitation by appeal to the function of law. The abuse of process jurisdiction seems helpful here as well. For although the plaintiff in *Grainger* v. *Hill* wanted something to which he had no claim, the ulterior purpose or collateral advantage which lies behind an abuse of process need not itself be illegal or improper. The question is, rather, whether the purpose or advantage is a proper goal *of the particular proceedings*. In *Williams* v. *Spautz*,[33] for example, the respondent had been dismissed from his position as a university lecturer. Spautz immediately commenced proceedings against the university seeking a declaration that his dismissal was invalid. Over the next ten years, he also issued 'an extraordinary number of proceedings' – the majority being criminal prosecutions – against those whom believed to have had a role in his dismissal. Among the 30 plus criminal informations laid by Spautz were the three alleging criminal defamation against Williams and two others, which were the subject of the current case. The trial judge found, and the High Court agreed, that the 'predominant purpose of Dr. Spautz in instituting and maintaining the criminal proceedings ... was to exert pressure upon the University ... to ... agree to a favourable settlement of his wrongful dismissal case'.[34] The criminal proceedings were held to be an abuse of process, not because there was anything improper about Spautz's goal of seeking to have his dismissal reviewed,[35] or because there had been any improper conduct in the course of the proceedings, but because it was not proper for Spautz to use criminal defamation proceedings, designed and intended to determine whether an accused had committed an offence, for the ulterior purpose of convincing the university to reconsider his dismissal. The proceedings were an abuse of process because they were used for a purpose other than that for which they had been designed and intended, notwithstanding that the ulterior purpose was itself proper, or even that it was possible that Spautz might have won the criminal defamation cases had they been prosecuted to a conclusion. The abuse of process doctrine, then, supports the idea that appeal to the function of law may allow lawyers to decline to pursue every lawful advantage available under law.

Further, a recent abuse of process case has made clear that lawyers cannot shelter behind the wishes of their clients when accused of abuse of process. In *White Industries (Qld) Pty Ltd* v. *Flower & Hart (a firm)*,[36] the respondent law firm had acted for a plaintiff in earlier proceedings against White.[37] White won the earlier case and were awarded costs, but the plaintiff had gone into liquidation just before the end of the 150-day trial. White argued that the law firm's conduct of the matter was an abuse of process and that the firm should pay the award of costs. The Federal Court agreed. They found that Flower & Hart had issued proceedings against White on behalf of their client, alleging fraud, negligence and breach of the Trade Practices Act (which prohibits misleading or deceiving conduct in the course of trade) believing from the outset that their client could not win. The partner in charge of the case wrote to the client, suggesting the heads of proceeding, before continuing, 'I do not have to make clear that you could not win any litigation if put to the test'. Neither the firm nor the client were unduly bothered by this prognosis, since neither was interested in winning. The proceedings were brought not for the purpose of determining the allegations, but to gain a temporary bargaining stance and delay inevitable payment of money owed to White by the client. They were issued, therefore, for an ulterior purpose. The firm argued, among other things, that they had done no more than follow their client's instructions to 'to take every point, fight everything and make life difficult for White and its legal advisers'. Their client, they said, was an experienced litigant and wont 'to take a small prospect of success and convert it into an impregnable case...'.[38] But the Federal Court found that it was not a sufficient 'simply to say – he was doing what his client wanted'. Indeed, Goldberg J continued:

> The fact that Mr Herscu [the client] had a robust approach to litigation, did not believe anything was impossible and was unconcerned about entering litigation with limited prospects made it all the more important for Flower & Hart to have regard to the manner in which it institutioned and conducted proceedings on his behalf and on behalf of his companies and to be conscious of its duty to the court.[39]

White Industries is also relevant in another respect. I suggested earlier that we might strengthen the conclusion that the duty of zeal does not require or allow lawyers to pursue every possible lawful advantage available to clients, by noting that it was an aspect of the role of helping clients avail themselves of their legal rights to help them ascertain what those rights were. Given this, I suggested, the functional approach allowed us to conclude that simply preventing a case coming before the decision procedures of a community was not doing the lawyer's job. It was preventing the job being done. *White Industries* supports this contention. Goldberg J states:

> I do not consider that it is a legitimate purpose for the institution of a proceeding in this court that the purpose of the proceeding is to postpone, delay or put a barrier in front of a claim of another party and the payment of an amount due in respect of that claim. The purpose of the proceedings in a court of law is to vindicate a claimed right. ... It is not part of the legal processes of this Court that its process and procedures be used as an instrument of oppression so as to frustrate the bringing, and expeditious disposition of a legitimate claim.[40]

Critics of the standard conception maintain that existing limitations on zealous advocacy are insufficient to prevent lawyers acting unethically. The abuse of process jurisdiction is also helpful here.

Although the principle of partisanship is subject to 'the established constraints on professional behaviour', writes Luban, those concerned with the ethical conduct of lawyers should take no comfort from this limitation, since it 'still leaves plenty of latitude for practices that some may find unjust'.[41] We have already seen one response to this complaint. It was an implication of the earlier discussion of the role of law that whether practices should be allowed could not be settled by the fact that 'some may find' those practices unjust. Given that law mediates between reasonable, but inconsistent, views about what we should do as a community, some of the time, some of the people will inevitably find some of the legal accommodations unjust. So much follows from the earlier discussion of the role of law in pluralist communities. If we show the link between the abuse of process jurisdiction and the function of law, and support the claims for the significance of that link for the limits of legitimate advocacy, we may have produced another response to Luban's dismissal of existing constraints. If the jurisdiction to prevent abuse of process allows courts to restrict lawyers to merely zealous advocacy we will have shown it to be a more significant constraint on legal practice than Luban's dismissal allows.

Conclusion

I have been concerned in this paper to defend a version of the standard conception of the lawyer's role. The version differs from common interpretations in portraying lawyers as bound to exercise mere but not hyper-zeal on behalf of their clients. The defence has proceeded from an appeal to the role of law in pluralist communities. The fundamental function of the institutions of law in modern constitutional democracies, I have suggested, is to mediate between the range of views to be found in such communities on fundamental questions such as what constitutes human flourishing, what basic goals are intrinsically most worthy of pursuit and what is the best way for individuals to live their lives. The law allows the advocates of very different views on these matters to coexist despite their differences. Note that these are *moral* considerations. Hence, although the standard conception calls upon lawyers to neutrally represent their clients, the standard conception is not amoral; it is grounded in fundamental moral concerns. Those concerns show both why lawyers should maintain neutrality and where the boundaries of legitimate advocacy are to be found.

Notes

1 Tom Campbell, *The Legal Theory of Ethical Positivism* (Aldershot: Dartmouth, 1996), pp. 101–8.

2 Campbell rightly identifies William H. Simon as another author who treats legal ethics as an aspect of a more general jurisprudence. Campbell discusses Simon's article 'The Ideology of Advocacy: Procedural Justice and Professional Ethics', *Wisconsin Law Review*, **29** (1978), pp. 30–144. The themes introduced in this article are given a sustained treatment in Simon's recent book *The Practice of Justice: A Theory of Lawyer's Ethics* (Cambridge, MA: Harvard University Press, 1998).

3 Campbell, *Ethical Positivism*, *op. cit.*, p. 108.

4 Thomas Babbington Macaulay, 'Essay on Bacon' in David Salmon (ed.), *Macaulay's Essay on Bacon* (London: Longmans, Green and Co., 1904), p. 37.

5 Gerald Postema, 'Moral Responsibility in Professional Ethics', *New York University Law Review*, **55** (1980), pp. 63–89.

6 John Rawls, *Political Liberalism* (New York: Columbia University Press, 1993), p. xvi, emphasis added.

7 Ibid., p. xviii.

8 Joseph Raz, *The Morality of Freedom* (Oxford: Clarendon Press, 1986), p. 58.

9 John Rawls, 'The Idea of an Overlapping Consensus', *Oxford Journal of Legal Studies*, 7 (1981), pp. 1–25 at p. 9.

10 Kurt Baier, 'Justice and the Aims of Political Philosophy', *Ethics*, **99** (1989), pp. 771–90 at p. 775.

11 John Rawls, *Political Liberalism* (New York: Columbia University Press, 1993), p. xviii.

12 See *Rondel* v. *Worsley* [1969] 1 AC 191 (House of Lords).

13 David Luban, *Lawyers and Justice* (Princeton, NJ: Princeton University Press, 1988), p. 74.

14 Clause 6.6 International Code of Ethics, adopted Oslo July 1956, amended Mexico, 1964.

15 David Luban, *Lawyers and Justice*, *op. cit.*, p. 75.

16 Ibid., p. 75.

17 The classic illustration is *Zabella* v. *Pakel*, 42 F2d 452, 7th Cir. 1957.

18 R.E. Ewin, 'Personal Morality and Professional Ethics: The Lawyer's Duty of Zeal', *International Journal of Applied Philosophy*, **6** (1991), pp. 35–45 at p. 39.

19 R.E. Ewin, 'Personal morality', *op. cit.*, p. 39.

20 Lord Brougham, *The Trial of Queen Caroline*, 3 vols, ed. J. Nightingale (London: J Robins & Co. Albion Press, 1820–21).

21 Saying that 'it is not the function of the lawyer to allow clients to satisfy interests beyond those allocated by law' is not the same as saying 'it is the function of lawyers not to allow clients to satisfy interests beyond those allocated by law'. The positioning of the negation is important.

22 Luban, *Lawyers and Justice*, *op. cit.*, p. 75.

23 Ibid., p. 51.

24 Ibid., p. 77.

25 *White Industries (Qld) Pty Ltd* v. *Flower & Hart (a firm)* [1998] 806 FCA (14 July 1998), unreported, Federal Court of Australia per Goldberg J.

26 *Spautz* v. *Williams* [1983] 2 NSWLR 506, 539: approved in *Williams & Ors* v. *Spautz* (1991–1992) 74 CLR 509, 517, HCA.

27 (1838) 4 Bing. (NC) 212 [132 ER 769].

28 (1838) 4 Bing. (NC) 212, 221 [132 ER 769, 773].

29 *In Re Majory* [1955] Ch 600: '... court proceedings may not be used or threatened for the purpose of obtaining for the person so using or threatening them some

collateral advantage to himself, and not for the purpose for which such proceedings are properly designed and intended' per Lord Evershed MR at 623.

[30] *White Industries, op. cit., passim; Moevao* v. *Department of Labour* [1980] 1 NZLR 464, 482.

[31] *Orchard* v. *South Eastern Electricty Board* [1987] QB 565, 572 per Sir John Donaldson MR.

[32] *White Industries, op. cit.*

[33] *Williams & Ors* v. *Spautz* (1991–1992) 174 CLR 509.

[34] Ibid., 509, 516.

[35] Indeed, separate proceedings challenging the validity of the dismissal continued throughout the relevant period, no question being raised about their procedural legitimacy.

[36] *White Industries, op. cit.* The case is noteworthy if only because the barrister, Ian Callinan QC, strongly criticized in the judgment, had been appointed to the bench of the Australian High Court by the time of the decision.

[37] *Caboolture Park Shopping Centre Pty Ltd (In liquidation)* v. *White Industries (Qld) Pty Ltd* (1993) 45 FCR 224.

[38] *White Industries, op. cit.*, 8.

[39] Ibid., 73.

[40] Ibid.

[41] Luban, *Lawyers and Justice, op. cit.*, p. 156.

17 Judicial Activism and the Rule of Law in Australia

LESLIE ZINES

In the *Oxford Companion to the Supreme Court of the United States* 'judicial activism' is defined as 'the charge that judges are going beyond their appropriate powers and engaging in making law and not merely interpreting it'.[1] In describing judicial activism by the High Court of Australia I am not confining my attention to cases that came within that description. I have taken 'judicial activism' to be a neutral and descriptive phrase, rather than a purely pejorative one. In other words, I am including cases where the making of law might be regarded, in my view, as appropriate for the Court.

From about the 1950s until about the early 1980s it was not uncommon for the High Court of Australia to be criticized for being too legalistic, particularly in constitutional interpretation, for not having sufficient regard to social and political considerations, for not articulating the real factors that produced its decisions or for not being aware that the rules and principles the judges purported to rely on did not determine the cases.[2]

Two Chief Justices, however, rescued the word' legalism' from becoming purely dyslogistic by claiming that it would be unfortunate if the Court adopted any other approach in constitutional law. They claimed that a close adherence to legal reasoning maintained the confidence of all parties in federal conflicts and produced constitutional stability.[3] While academic lawyers often referred to the US Supreme Court as an appropriate model, many High Court judges regarded it as an example to be avoided.[4]

Since the mid-1980s, at any rate, the methods and attitude of the Court have changed and so has the nature of the criticism. Both the defenders and critics of the Court have accepted that it has produced many changes to what was earlier perceived as the law. This occurred in all areas of law, whether constitutional law, statutory interpretation or common law. Also, whereas once the High Court rarely examined cases outside Britain or Australia,[5] it now roams the world in its search for wisdom. It has become commonplace to have presented in argument and cited in judgments cases from the courts of, for example, Canada, New Zealand and the United States, the European Court of Human Rights, the European Court of Justice and the International Court. International law, whether in the form of treaties binding Australia or customary law, has been notable in the development of the common law, but also as an aid to statutory and constitutional interpretation.[6]

Many of the changes are the result of a conscious attempt to give greater consistency or coherence to various areas of common law. Old favourites on which many lawyers in Britain and Australia were weaned at Law School disappeared over a period of a few years, including *Rylands* v. *Fletcher* and the various classes of occupiers' liability, the distinction between money paid under a mistake of fact and mistake of law, and the doctrine of privity of contract in respect of insurance. Increased regard for those vulnerable to private power has resulted in a greater intrusion into commercial transactions of equitable principles and, particularly, the concept of unconscionability.[7] Although the latter caused some to deplore the fettering of freedom of contract, and some layers were a bit dazed at the speed with which familiar rules and principles were disappearing, the main complaints against the Court concerned other matters.

The notion of rights and freedoms has had a key role to play in many of the changes that have occurred over the past decade in many areas of law, including constitutional law. Yet Australia has nothing that could be called a bill or charter of rights. There are a few scattered and disconnected provisions, binding only on the Commonwealth and relating to trial by jury, just terms for the acquisition of property and freedom of religion.[8] Even if these were interpreted as liberally as possible they would have nothing like the impact of the constitutional guarantees in the United States, Canada, India or Europe.

Lionel Murphy, a Justice of the High Court from 1975 until his death in 1986, was the most rights-driven and loose interpreter of any judge in his attempt to find in the Constitution all the freedoms and guarantees that exist in those jurisdictions, but he was always alone in that regard.[9] The big changes came after his death and are associated with a period during which Sir Anthony Mason was Chief Justice – 1987 to 1995. It was probably the most activist period in Australian legal history.

What many would consider the most important decision of the period might be seen as reducing, rather than increasing, individual rights. It related to s. 92 of the Constitution, which provides, *inter alia*, that 'trade, commerce and intercourse among the States shall be absolutely free'. From at least the 1940s it had been interpreted to give individual traders the right to trade interstate, free from legislative or executive hindrance except for those regulations which were necessary in the interest of society, such as health and safety rules. In the hands of some judges this individual economic right resembled that derived in the United States from the Fifth and Fourteenth Amendments in the early twentieth century. One big difference was that it was confined to interstate trade and did not extend to all economic activity as in the United States, or to all those activities that are now within the reach of the commerce power. In 1988 the Court put an abrupt end to this development and held that s. 92 was designed merely to prevent laws discriminating against interstate trade and commerce with a protectionist purpose or effect.[10]

That case is also notable for the Court giving formal blessing, for the first time, to an examination of the history of the making of the Constitution and the debates of the Constitutional Conventions in the 1890s. There was some irony in this decision. Whereas 40 years before, the Court had used s. 92 to invalidate an attempt by the Commonwealth Government to nationalize the banks, it now seems that they could be nationalized when no one would dream of doing so. The effect of this decision was to increase the power of all governments in Australia; but other decisions attacked as being activist had the opposite effect.

In the absence of many individual rights and freedoms in the Constitution, most judicial attempts to find guarantees have resulted from inferences that certain limitations on governmental power were necessary for the preservation of constitutionally-created institutions. The principal institutions relied on by the Court are the federal judicature and representative government.

Freedoms Derived from Judicial Power

Chapter III of the Constitution deals with the judicature. Section 71, the first provision in that Chapter, declares that the judicial power of the Commonwealth shall be vested in the High Court of Australia, such courts as parliament creates and other courts (that is, state courts) which it invests with federal jurisdiction. From this seemingly simple provision an array of entrenched rights has emerged, and is still emerging with no sign of abatement. It has long been accepted that s. 71 ensures that only the courts mentioned can exercise federal judicial power and that parliament cannot vest a court with non-judicial power (such as industrial arbitration) unless incidental to its primary jurisdiction.[11]

It is then reasoned, from the separation of powers, that parliament cannot require or authorize courts to exercise their jurisdiction in a manner that is inconsistent with 'the nature of judicial power'. Deane J has referred to s. 71 as 'the Constitution's only general guarantee of due process'.[12] Broadly speaking, this would seem to ensure procedural fairness, but the notion allows much discretion for the court to determine what common law rules of procedure, pleading and evidence are so fundamental that to abolish or alter them would amount to the court trying cases by reference to methods that are not judicial. This is underlined by a statement by Deane J that the judicial chapter is based on an assumption of 'traditional procedures, remedies and methodology'.[13] This raises many unanswered questions as to whether a more inquisitorial system might be applied to some issues, whether oral argument is essential, what, if any, traditional remedies might be abolished, or whether the common law right of an accused to confront witnesses against him can be abolished or qualified.[14] Some rights of this nature are protected by express provisions in other constitutions, but not in Australia. They arise, say the courts, simply as a by-product of the separation of judicial power which in turn is a by-product of a provision vesting judicial power in courts.

Similarly, although there is no provision prohibiting bills of attainder as in the United States, it is clear that the separation of powers prevents such a law by the Commonwealth Parliament. This in turn raises difficulties of distinguishing a disguised attempt by parliament to punish persons from the imposition of harsh or unfair liabilities or duties on specified persons or groups. The issue is most acute where the legislation provides for compulsory detention outside traditional categories.[15]

One question on which judges were divided (and which is undecided) is whether a retrospective criminal law is an invalid exercise of judicial power by the legislature. In a challenge to war crimes legislation two judges (Deane and Gaudron JJ) expressed the view that it was and a third (Toohey J) said that it was except where, as in the instant case, it involved an act, such as murder, which was universally condemned.[16] If this view were accepted, it would be another instance of a constitutional guarantee that exists in other constitutions being implied in the Australian Constitution from a section that vests judicial power in the courts.

The Australian Constitution confers no right of an accused to counsel. The inability of an indigent accused to obtain counsel and the refusal of the state to provide one was not regarded as a reason for staying the trial. In 1979[17] Mason J had said that 'an accused in Australia does not have a right to present his case by counsel provided at public expense'. In 1992, however, the Court held that, while there was no such right, there was a common law right to a fair trial and, in most cases, representation by counsel was relevant to such a process. If followed that a court should exercise its power to stay proceedings where an indigent accused charged with a serious offence is unable to obtain legal representation, through no fault of his or her own.[18] Brennan J, in dissent, said that this was an unwarranted intrusion into the functions of the political arms of government. In fact, the case was adjourned to enable the Commonwealth and states to present arguments and to present factual, statistical and economic material as to the practical implications of acceding to the accused's submissions. Only the Commonwealth and South Australia intervened and, it was said:

> ... no argument was put to the court that recognition of such a right to the provision of counsel at the public expense would impose an unsustainable financial burden on government.

That did not stop the decision from being denounced as an unwarranted judicial interference. Recently, as a result of a substantial reduction in funds for legal aid by the Commonwealth, the Attorney-General called for the states to legislate to override the principle and said, in effect, that any judge could ensure a fair trial without counsel. This produced outrage among the judges and strong attacks on the Attorney-General by the Law Council of Australia.

There is, however, a question whether the *Dietrich* principle will be regarded as constitutionally entrenched in respect of federal crimes. Two judges, Deane and Gaudron JJ, said that it was.[19] It seems to me that if its basis is a fair trial there is plenty of argument, on present authority, that as a result of the separation of powers, the Commonwealth Parliament cannot require the judiciary to conduct an unfair trial.

While the Court was principally concerned with determining a common law principle, it ranged far and wide in the search for guidance. References were made to the Canadian decisions, under their Criminal Code, to the Convention on Civil and Political Rights, and to cases on the United States Constitution and the Canadian Charter.

For those who see the doctrine of the separation of judicial power in Australia as a great reservoir of procedural and substantive rights there seem to be one drawback. As it is derived from Chapter III of the Constitution it is confined to the exercise of *federal* jurisdiction. As criminal law is not within federal legislative authority unless incidental to other subjects, the impact of the rights is somewhat limited. No one has suggested that the separation of powers applies directly to the states. Recently, however, the Court took a step which could, if developed, promote a panoply of rights in respect of state judicial power. A

State Act was applied to only one named person, Gregory Wayne Kable, who had been convicted of the manslaughter of his wife. The Act was aimed at keeping him in detention because he had threatened to kill other people on his release. The Court was empowered to make orders of six months' duration that he be detained if satisfied that he was more likely than not to commit a serious act of violence and detention was appropriate to protect the community. The latter was declared to be the paramount consideration.

The Court, by majority, held the Act invalid because it was inconsistent with Chapter III. This time they relied on a provision which empowered parliament to invest any court of a state with federal jurisdiction (s. 77(iii)). The majority said that the Constitution prevented the states from giving to a state court, which exercised federal jurisdiction, functions that were 'incompatible' with the exercise of that jurisdiction. The act came within the category because it diminished public confidence in the integrity of the Court when exercising federal jurisdiction.[20]

Clearly, this case opens up the possibility of constitutional implications of procedural due process and so on being applied to state courts as they have all been vested with federal jurisdiction. If so, it will be inferred from a provision which simply empowers parliament to invest federal jurisdiction in state courts.

Rights and Freedoms Derived from Representative Government

Outside the circle of legal practitioners and academic lawyers, there has been little political or community reaction to the above cases, except for *Dietrich* in respect of legal aid. There was, however, a considerable amount of criticism of the High Court acting beyond its proper function as a result of a series of cases based on the concept of representative government, from which there was derived an implied freedom of communication on political and governmental matters.

This new freedom burst on the scene in two cases in 1992. In the first case[21] the Court held invalid a federal provision making it an offence to use words calculated to bring a member of a Commonwealth tribunal, the Industrial Relations Commission, into disrepute. Although the reasons varied, four judges[22] held that the provision infringed a freedom implied from the Constitution to discuss governmental and political matters. The provision, as interpreted, suppressed all criticism regardless of whether it was true or fair.

In the next case,[23] known as *The Political Advertising Case*, the Court was concerned with federal legislation prohibiting, with certain exceptions, the broadcasting of political advertising during an election period. It covered material in respect of all elections, whether Commonwealth, state, territory or local government. The excepted circumstances were the broadcasting of news, current affairs, political launches, talk-back radio and provisions for free broadcasts. The legislation was held wholly invalid by four judges (Mason CJ, Deane, Toohey and Gaudron JJ). Only one judge held it wholly valid (Dawson J). The majority based their decision on infringement of freedom of political communication relevant to a system of representative government implied in the Constitution.[24]

The *Political Advertising* decision was greeted with mixed reactions, extending from complaints of judicial usurpation of the democratic process to superlative praise.[25] A number of writers expressed the fear or hope that Australia might go down the same route as the United States in judicial interpretation of the First Amendment, without the necessity of adopting a bill of rights. By and large, however, the judges tried to distinguish what they were doing from the interpretation of a broad constitutional right of freedom of speech.

Mason CJ pointed out that there had been a rejection of a bill of rights by the founders and that, as a consequence, 'it is difficult, if not impossible, to establish a foundation for the implication of general guarantees of fundamental rights and freedoms'.[26] He added (I think rightly) that the framers saw the protection of the citizen arising from 'the common law in association with the doctrine of parliamentary supremacy'. The reasoning therefore rested not on the need for implying a bill of rights, but on the view that the Constitution provided for a system of representative government. The freedom of communication arose because it was seen as a necessary element of that governmental system. The Constitution does not use the terms 'representative government' or 'freedom of communication', so what was the Court relying on? The main provisions were ss. 7 and 24 which provide that senators and members of the House of Representatives, respectively, 'shall be directly chosen by the people'. Sections 62 and 64 provide for ministers and the Executive Council and ensure that, as a rule, ministers shall be members of parliament. Section 128 requires a combination of parliament and the people voting in a referendum to alter the Constitution.

Some of the judges inferred that, at any rate since the enactment of the Australia Act 1986, which formally ended UK legislative and executive power in Australia, that 'the people' were now 'sovereign'.[27] As members of parliament and the executive exercise power on behalf of the people they were, said the Chief Justice, 'accountable to the people for what they do and have a responsibility to take account of the views of the people'.[28] The approach of most of the Court was therefore to reason from the express provisions of the Constitution to a system of representative government (said to be part of the 'structure' of the Constitution) and to ask what was essential to the operation of that system.

Some who accepted the principle laid down criticized the Court for its balancing of the interests involved and for the actual decision. Brennan J, for example, accepted the implied freedom in relation to federal elections, but regarded the provisions as consistent with representative government and even helpful. The government justified the legislation on the basis that it was designed to prevent corruption that may come about as a result of the parties seeking large funds for television advertisements, to provide more equality and fairness for those who cannot afford the high cost of broadcasting, and to put a stop to the 'trivialization' of political debate that comes with very brief advertisements. The Court accepted these as worthy objects justifying some prohibitions on communication. In the result, the sticking point was that the free-time provisions were perceived to be discriminatory, favouring political parties represented in parliament and their candidates. The other candidates had only 10 per cent of the time prescribed, while non-candidates were excluded. In any case, the regime for allocating free time depended on executive discretion in making regulations and there were no specified criteria. There was no discussion, however (perhaps because there was no argument), as to whether any other system was practicable to achieve parliament's objects.

In any event, the Court seemed to distinguish judicial protection of the democratic process and the capacity of the people to choose and control their representatives from those restrictions on parliamentary power designed to protect the individual from parliament or society. In the manner of J.H. Ely[29] the judges distinguished between restrictions based on substantive values and those based on political processes and institutions. The difficulty, or impossibility, of making that distinction is well canvassed in the literature,[30] but it does indicate the object of the Court and the manner of its thinking even though the minimum freedoms and principles required for representative government will always be a matter of dispute, as will the necessary balancing of those freedoms with other pressing social interests using vague and slippery concepts such as 'proportionality' and the like.

In so far as ss. 7 and 24 were at the core of the Court's reasoning, they are confined to the Commonwealth system, and there are no equivalent provisions in the federal Constitution in respect of the states' organization of government. Nevertheless the communication about state political affairs came within the freedom because of the indivisibility of political communication for purposes of national affairs. The Chief Justice relied on the unlimited range of matters relevant to parliamentary debate and the continuing relations between the tiers of government, such as Commonwealth funding of other levels of government. Matters of local concern, it was said, had the potential to become matters of national significance. It was therefore said to be unrealistic to separate the different forms of communication about governmental affairs.[31]

In 1994 the Court examined, in the light of the implied freedom, the law of defamation in two cases – one involving a defamation suit by a federal member of parliament[32] and another concerning a suit by state members.[33] A majority of four (Mason CJ, Deane, Toohey and Gaudron JJ) held that the existing statutory and common law of defamation was inconsistent with the implied freedom in its application to communication on political matters. A joint judgment of three majority judges rejected the principle in *New York Times* v. *Sullivan*[34] on the ground that the placing of the onus of proving deliberate falsehood on the plaintiff paid too little regard to the protection of reputation. It also considered that there had been too great an expansion in the United States of those who were regarded as 'public figures'. It was held that the publication was not actionable if the defendant established that it was unaware of the falsity, did not publish it recklessly and the publication was reasonable in the circumstances. Deane J would have gone further (and further than *Sullivan*) by holding that the implied freedom precluded the application of state defamation laws for any statements about the official conduct or suitability for office of a member of parliament or other holder of high office.[35]

In April 1995 Mason CJ retired, Brennan J was made Chief Justice and the vacancy was filled by Gummow J of the Federal Court. That year the Court rejected an argument that s. 24 of the Constitution required that electorates have, so far as practicable, equal number of electors,[36] thus rejecting an American line of authority.[37] In the course of that case, McHugh J, who was in the minority in the defamation case, complained strongly that all the earlier decisions on the implied freedom rested on reasoning that did not interpret the text, but imported foreign matter from outside. He said that the majority had reasoned from a free-standing concept of representative government independently of the terms of the Constitution. He berated the Court for not following a principle enshrined since 1920[38] that it was not legitimate to construe the Constitution by reference to political principle or theories 'that are not anchored in the text of the Constitution or are not necessary implications from its structure'. He referred to the implication of representative democracy as involving 'top down' reasoning, taking that term from an article by Posner.[39] Like Brennan CJ he also rejected the notion that the Constitution changed common law rights and duties of individuals. Gummow J, in that case, seemed to indicate some sympathy for the views expressed by McHugh J. So far as the implied freedom cases were concerned it now looked as though there might be a four to three split for overruling them. To this end Dawson J encouraged the Victorian Solicitor-General to challenge them when the latter was not originally minded to do so.[40]

In *Lange* v. *Australian Broadcasting Corporation*,[41] another defamation case, the Court affirmed the principle of representative government at the federal level and the freedom of communication on public affairs in so far as it is an incident of that principle. This time the judgment was, very surprisingly, unanimous. There was more definite emphasis on basing the system of representative government on the express provisions of the Constitution, but that did not affect the decision very much. The Court accepted a statement from Birch, *Representative and Responsible Government* (at p. 17) that representative government required elections to parliament which 'must be free, with all this implies in the way of freedom of speech and political organization'.[42] This statement opens up, of course, a freedom of association.

The Court held that the implied freedom of communication on governmental matters was not to be interpreted as a positive right, but as a limitation invalidating laws, and it created an immunity from legal – particularly legislative – control. This statement seemed to deny an effect on the common law.

The freedom was interpreted quite broadly. It was not confined to election times. It extended to information relating to the executive government, including statutory authorities and public utilities obliged to report to parliament or to a minister. It was, of course, limited by a law satisfying a legitimate end if it is reasonably appropriate and adapted to achieving the object, having regard to the requirements of representative government.

In an apparent sideswipe at *Theophanous* the Court said that the issue in defamation was not, as in the United States, the creation of a 'constitutional privilege' against the enforcement of state common law. That is because, in Australia, there is a national common law formulated by the High Court as a national court of appeal.

Although, earlier the judgment had referred to the freedom as a limitation on legislative and executive power, the Court went on to say that the common law must conform to the Constitution. The protection of reputation must admit, as an exception, the constitutionally required freedom to discuss government and politics. In 1901 the balance struck by the common law might have been seen as consistent with freedom essential for representative government, but developments since then demanded a different balance.

In the upshot the Court remodelled the common law to make it consistent with the freedom. Statutes could expand the area of freedom of communication beyond that laid down, but could not diminish it. The Court in fact expanded the common law defence of qualified privilege so as to take it beyond that required by the Constitution. To that extent it is vulnerable to statutory alteration. The category of qualified privilege at common law was thus extended to cover communication on all matters of governmental affairs. Matters within the defence which might not be covered by constitutional protection were said to be those concerning the United Nations or state and territory matters which did not bear on the federal level of government.

While qualified privilege traditionally only required honesty of purpose, that was because it was restricted to publication to a limited number of persons. The extended privilege related to mass communication on political matters. There should, the Court said, in those circumstances be added a requirement of reasonableness of conduct. In most cases this would require (as in the 'constitutional defence' in *Theophanous*) the defendant to show that it was unaware of falsity of the publication and did not act recklessly. It was also said that conduct will not be reasonable if, in normal circumstances, the defendant has not sought a response from the person defamed and published that response.

It has been suggested by some that the approaches in *Theophanous* and *Lange* in respect of the relationship of the Constitution to the common law are very different. The argument is that *Lange* denied that the constitutional implication operated directly to alter the private rights of individuals *inter se* and, therefore, *Theophanous* was in effect overruled. Yet it was held that the common law must conform to constitutional requirements. I cannot see that there is any difference in result. In each case the defendant is guaranteed a defence by virtue of the Constitution.[43]

One major difference brought about by *Lange* is that it holds that some political matters related to the states and territories may not have a sufficient connection with the governmental system at the Commonwealth level to come within constitutional protection. The Court does, however, accept that many of those matters will, because of the factors referred to in the earlier cases. The present view, however, that there is a gap, is bound to produce arid legal arguments in future cases.

In the companion case of *Levy* v. *Victoria*[44] the plaintiff challenged a state law preventing him from entering an area at the beginning of the duck-shooting season. His purpose was to hold up dead ducks for the television cameras as a protest against the shooting of birds. He lost the case on the ground that, assuming his activities were constitutionally protected, the law was an appropriate means of achieving the object of public safety. It was made clear, however, that such a protest would come within the area of communication on governmental affairs. It was pointed out that the task of the Court was not to construe a constitutional term, such as 'speech', but to ask what relevance the conduct has to the working of representative government as required by the Constitution. Non-verbal conduct capable of communicating an idea about the government of the Commonwealth, and intended to do so, came within that freedom.

Constitutional Rights Derived from 'Fundamental Principles'

During this period, there were manifestations of 'activism' which were far less rooted in the terms and structure of the text than the cases I have dealt with, but which failed to receive majority support and are currently unlikely to do so.

As I mentioned earlier, Murphy J took as his starting point the concept of a free and democratic society and read into the Constitution a large number of disparate restrictions on the power of the Commonwealth and the states. These were said to come from the nature of Australian society. No one followed him, in that regard, while he was on the Court.

The first time a majority suggested that there *might* be restrictions on power that were not found in the express or implied provisions of the Constitution or other superior law was in *Union Steamship Co. of Australia Pty Ltd* v. *King*.[45] In that case the Court rejected the view expressed in the State Supreme Court that the phrase traditionally indicating plenary legislative power in the constitutions of former British dependencies – 'peace, order (or welfare) and good government' – was a substantive limitation on legislative power. The Court went on to say:

> Whether the exercise of that legislative power is subject to some restraints by reference to rights deeply rooted in our democratic system and the common law ... is another question which we need not explore.[46]

Earlier Sir Robin Cooke, President of the Court of Appeal of New Zealand, had suggested, in three cases, that there were some common law rights that might go so deep that even Parliament could not destroy them.[47] Deane and Toohey JJ pursued that approach in the High Court. They proclaimed it in *Leeth* v. *Commonwealth*[48] where they held that federal power, in the absence of an indication to the contrary, was limited by a common law doctrine of equality of the people.[49]

One powerful hurdle which Deane and Toohey JJ had to overcome was the provisions of the Constitution expressly prohibiting discrimination or requiring equality of a geographical nature in respect of specified matters.[50] Historically, there was a bigger hurdle. The framers had expressly rejected a provision guaranteeing, among other things, 'equal protection of the laws'. This led Sir Owen Dixon to say to an American audience that 'our Constitution makers refused to adopt any part of the Bill of Rights of 1791 and *a fortiori* they refused to accept the Fourteenth Amendment'.[51] Further, they had to admit that, in order to find the common law as the font of equality, it was necessary to put to one side the position of the Crown and the discriminatory treatment of women, which were placed in the category of 'some past anomalies'.

This doctrine of an overriding common law was further elaborated by Deane and Toohey JJ in *Nationwide News*, where they referred to the powers of the Commonwealth being subject to implications 'which flow from the fundamental rights and principles recognised by the common law at the time the Constitution was adopted ...'.[52] Such a principle, of course, would have greatly enlarged the Court's power. Which common law rights were fundamental would depend entirely on the values of the judges and their view of the community's values (which are usually the same). As John Doyle, now Chief Justice of South Australia, has pointed out, the descriptor 'common law' may give the impression of tradition and evolution, which may be incorrect. The view of Murphy, Deane and Toohey JJ would certainly lay the ground for a fully-fledged implied bill of rights – a massive transfer of power to the judges. Most of the judges have since rejected these views and, in particular, the principle that governmental power is limited by an implied guarantee of 'equality'.[53]

Native Title

The complaint that the High Court was engaged in judicial activism was loudest and most shrill in respect of those decisions that concerned the traditional land rights of Aboriginal people. Until 1992 the orthodox view was that, on the acquisition of sovereignty by the Crown, the Crown acquired the ownership of all the land in Australia. This was based on the principles set out in Blackstone's *Commentaries* relating to the three methods of acquiring sovereignty over other lands. They consisted of acquisition by conquest, cession and settlement. In the first two cases the common law provided for the preservation of existing property rights until, and unless, the new sovereign transferred it to itself or to others. In respect of acquisition by settlement (which was the case with Australia) the assumption was that the land was *terra nullius* – that is, that it belonged to no one. These common law rules were derived from international law.

The Supreme Court of New South Wales had laid down in 1847 that the Crown had absolute ownership of all land in Australia from the moment that British sovereignty was proclaimed.[54] Similarly, the Privy Council had declared in 1889 that New South Wales came within a category of acquisition comprising a 'colony which consisted of a tract of territory practically unoccupied, without settled inhabitants or settled law, at the time when it was peacefully annexed'.[55] This type of acquisition was distinguished from colonies with a system of law acquired by conquest or cession. Annexation of that type did not disturb existing property rights. In the case of Australia it was assumed that there was none to disturb.

In the late 1960s a claim was made to land in the Northern Territory by a tribe of Aborigines. For the first time a court heard evidence of Aboriginal laws and customs, including the relationship of the people to the land. Blackburn J of the Northern Territory Supreme Court found a 'subtle and elaborate system' of law, saying that, 'If ever a system could be called "a government of laws and not of men", it is that shown on the evidence before me'.[56] However, he felt obliged, on the basis of authority, to hold that, although earlier cases had been based on a misconception, the law was that New South Wales came within the category of a settled colony where the doctrine of *terra nullius* prevailed.

The decision which changed this was *Mabo (No 2)*[57] which, for the first time in over 200 years, recognized native title to land in Australia. The case began in 1982 with a claim in the High Court by Meriam people in respect of land on the Murray Islands in the Torres Strait, which were annexed to Queensland in 1879. Although the case was concerned with common law rules of property, it became enmeshed with constitutional law as a result of the enactment by the Queensland Parliament of the Queensland Coast Islands Declaratory Act 1985 which declared, retrospectively, that the islands were vested beneficially in the Crown freed from all other interests from the time of annexation, and that no compensation was to be payable by reason of annexation. The Act was, of course, enacted for the purpose of putting an end to the litigation. However, in *Mabo* v. *Queensland (No 1)*,[58] the Court held that, on the assumption that the plaintiffs could establish the land rights they claimed, the Act was inconsistent with the Racial Discrimination Act of the Commonwealth. On that basis it was inoperative by virtue of s. 109 of the Constitution which provides that any State Act that is inconsistent with a Commonwealth Act is, to the extent of the inconsistency, invalid.

The effect of this was that any finding that native interests existed by virtue of common law could not be overridden by state statutes. The Commonwealth Parliament could remove that legislative impediment by repealing or amending the Racial Discrimination Act.

However, while the states are not constitutionally bound to provide compensation for the acquisition of property, the Commonwealth is. The question therefore would arise as to whether an amendment to the Act for the purpose of enabling the states to extinguish native title would amount to a Commonwealth law with respect to the acquisition of property.

The Murray Islanders put forward as a secondary argument that they were to be distinguished from Aborigines because they were Melanesian cultivators of the soil. Gardening was their principal occupation and was an important element in their culture. Their traditional customs recognized individual and family rights of occupation of defined areas of land. This argument related to a decision of the Privy Council in 1919 in *Re Southern Rhodesia*[59] that, in estimating the rights of Aboriginal tribes, some were 'so low on the scale of social organization that their usages and conceptions of rights and duties are not to be reconciled with the institutions or the legal ideas of civilized society'. The authorities seemed to indicate that Australian Aborigines came within that category.

The Court, however, rejected a distinction between societies based on a scale of civilization. This was described by Brennan J as 'a discriminatory denigration of indigenous inhabitants, their social organization and customs'.[60] It was regarded as false in fact and unacceptable.

The Court, therefore, had to choose whether it would follow previous understanding or adopt new principles based on present-day views of the facts about Aboriginal society and current values condemning discrimination. In coming to its decision the Court was fortified by international law. The International Court of Justice in *Advisory Opinion on Western Sahara*[61] had condemned the theory of *terra nullius* in respect of inhabited land. The High Court, therefore, rejected it as part of the common law, and the earlier rule was declared to be unjust and discriminatory. Brennan J said: 'The expectations of the international community accord in this respect with the contemporary values of the Australian people.'[62] He added that 'international law is a legitimate and important influence on the development of the common law, especially when international law declares the existence of universal human rights'.

The conclusion was bolstered by the legal situation regarding indigenous land rights in the United States, Canada and New Zealand. That still left the question whether the demands of certainty and possible social and economic consequences made it desirable that the previous authorities be upheld. In deciding to the contrary, the majority were influenced by the fact that this was the first time that the issue had been squarely faced and argued in Australia in an appellate court. All the other cases in which pronouncements had been made did not directly determine the issue. In any case, the High Court had never, as a court, made any pronouncement on the matter.

In upholding common law recognition of native title, it was made clear that it was a fragile property right, subject to being extinguished by a valid grant by the Crown of an inconsistent title. To produce the necessary legal framework for the exercise of this authority, the Crown was held to have acquired on annexation not beneficial ownership of all the land in Australia, but merely the radical title. This refers to the common law notion, based on earlier feudal principles, that all estates in land are held by the Crown. The Crown could, subject to statutory rules, obtain beneficial ownership by appropriating land to itself. It could also dedicate or reserve land for public purposes – for example, for the building of a post office or court house – or grant it to others. As Brennan J put it, 'The radical title without more is merely a logical postulate required to support the doctrine of tenure ... and to support the plenary title of the Crown. ...'[63] While it seemed clear that a grant of freehold overrode native title, it was also said that the grant of a lease also extinguished that title. That is because the lessee acquires possession and the Crown acquires the reversion expectant on the expiry of the term.

The complaints of judicial activism included the following:

1 The Court had purported to rely on the expectations of the international community and the contemporary values of Australian society, yet the decision resulted in deep social divisions and protests. It was argued that the parliaments are in a better position to know what the current values are. As for other countries with indigenous title, it was stated that they were affected by treaties with Indians and Maoris. Australia has no such treaties.
2 The Court had produced uncertainty in the area of property law which, it was thought, had been settled for two centuries. If it was thought that this law was in any way unjust it should have been left to parliament to rectify, having regard to the consequences.
3 The Court should have confined itself to determining the rights of the people of the Murray Islands, whose lifestyle and mode of dealing with the land were very different from those of Australian Aborigines. The Court's reply to this argument was that to confine itself to the Murray Islands would require it to proceed on an assumption of different grades of society which it found unacceptable.
4 The Court's use of history was attacked by some as faulty. It was also accused of undermining the legitimacy of the nation.
5 Critics also pointed to emotive language used by some of the judges as evidence that the Court was simply changing the law in

accordance with its own values rather than acting as a judicial body applying the existing law. In the judgment of Deane and Gaudron JJ, they admit that they used emotive language not usually found in a judgment. They said:

> The acts and events by which the dispossession in legal theory was carried into effect constitute the darkest aspect of the history of this nation. The nation as a whole must remain diminished unless and until there is an acknowledgment and retreat from, those past injustices.

The mining industry in particular was at the forefront of attempts to have native title extinguished. Instead parliament passed the Native Title Act 1993 regulating claims for native title, setting up a tribunal for that purpose and giving Aboriginal people negotiating rights in respect of mineral exploration and mining. On the other hand, grants of land made by states after the Racial Discrimination Act and before a prescribed date were confirmed as valid. Subject to this and some other exceptions, the legislation was described by the Court as having removed the defeasibility of native title.[64]

The political turmoil resulting from the *Mabo* decision was intensified when the implications of it were further examined in *Wik Peoples* v. *Queensland*.[65] As mentioned earlier, statements in *Mabo* indicated that native title was extinguished by the grant by the Crown of a leasehold estate. The Wik people claimed that that was not the case in respect of a pastoral lease, which in Australia is a special form of interest created by statute and sometimes made subject to the usages and customs of Aboriginal people. By a majority of four to three (Toohey, Gaudron, Gummow and Kirby JJ; Brennan CJ, Dawson and McHugh JJ dissenting) it was held that a pastoral lease did not have the character of a leasehold interest at common law with its quality of exclusive possession. Comparison was made with the expression 'mining lease', which, it has been said, is really a sale by the Crown of its minerals for a price paid as royalties.[66] It was pointed out that pastoral leases covered vast areas, as large as many English counties and bigger than some nations.[67] The legislation was designed to give pastoralists some security for their pastoral activities, and the leases were for 'pastoral purposes only'.

Applying the principle that statutes should be interpreted so as not to abrogate fundamental rights, particularly property rights, it was held that nothing in the Act or the grant should be taken as excluding the indigenous people from the land (even though the legislature at the time would not have known of native title).

The decision was that the mere granting of a pastoral lease did not extinguish any native claim which the plaintiff might be able to establish. In so far as there was any inconsistency, the rights under the least prevailed. The decision was fairly orthodox in its reasoning. The issue was whether a pastoral lease was a 'lease' in the common law sense. The majority answered in the negative having regard to the historical events surrounding its creation, the terms of the statute and the lease and the rules of statutory construction. The effect of the case on private interests was, however, greater than *Mabo*. A large part of the area of the country is held under pastoral lease, and many farmers felt threatened. Some of this fear and uncertainty was caused by some mischievous comments of ministers who suggested that it was still uncertain whether Aboriginal title could be claimed on freehold land. As a result, word spread that suburban backyards were at risk. Apart from all that, however, the decision led to great uncertainties which, it was argued, could not wait for resolution by the normal common law method, on a case-to-case basis. Many pastoralists did not know which Aborigines might claim entry, where on the property they could go and what activities would be covered by native title. It also was not clear what activities were included in 'pastoral purposes'. The government then introduced a bill to cut back on Aboriginal rights, which was twice rejected by the Senate. A last-minute compromise with an independent senator enabled it to pass on the third attempt, after some amendments.

Whatever might be said of the implied freedom cases or *Mabo*, the reasoning of all the judges in *Wik* was quite orthodox. Yet the torrent of abuse following that decision was, if anything, even greater. The phrase 'judicial activism' has become common among Australian conservative politicians and commentators, one legal journalist even describing it as a 'swear word'. Although the Court has always been the subject of such criticism, it has become more vituperative in recent years.

To some extent, this may have occurred because the Court has been more open about its resort to values and policy judgements. Some, however, suggest that it has moved too far ahead of, or away from, public opinion. Still others say that it merely reflects a general lowering of respect and regard for Australian social, political and legal institutions. In any event, Australian judges (unlike American judges, who are used to it) have been dismayed by the reaction.

Notes

1 At p. 454.

2 For example, G. Evans, 'The Most Dangerous Branch' in D. Hambly and J. Goldring (eds), *Australian Lawyers and Social Change* (Sydney: Law Book Co., 1976) p. 13.

[3] Dixon CJ (1952) 85 Commonwealth Law Reports (hereafter CLR) xiv; Barwick CJ in *Attorney-General (Cth); Ex rel McKinley* v. *Commonwealth* (1975) 135 CLR 1 at 17.

[4] L. Zines, *The High Court and the Constitution*, 4th edn (Sydney: Butterworths, 1997), n. 4, p. 64.

[5] Except during the first 17 years, when American constitutional cases were often cited and followed.

[6] K. Walker, 'Treaties and the Internationalisation of Australian Law' in C. Saunders (eds), *Courts of Final Jurisdiction* (Sydney: Federation Press, 1996), pp. 204–35; A. Mason, *The Internationalisation of Domestic Law*, Law and Policy Papers No. 4 (Canberra: Centre for International and Public Law, ANU, 1996).

[7] L.J. Priestly, 'Influences on Judicial Law-making' in C. Saunders, *Courts of Final Jurisdiction, op. cit.*, pp. 99–101; I. Renard, 'Fair Dealing and Good Faith' in C. Saunders, *Counts of Final Jurisdiction, op. cit.*, pp. 71–80; A. Mason, 'The Place of Equity and Equitable Remedies in the Contemporary Common Law World', *Law Quarterly Review*, **110** (1994), p. 238.

[8] Sections 51 (xxxi), 80 and 116 of the Australian Constitution.

[9] G. Williams, 'Lionel Murphy and Democracy and Rights' in M. Coper and G. Williams (eds), *Justice Lionel Murphy: Influential or Merely Prescient?* (Leichardt, NSW: Federation Press, 1997), ch. 3; L. Zines, *Constitutional Change in the Commonwealth*, (Cambridge/New York: Cambridge University Press, 1991) pp. 45–6.

[10] *Cole* v. *Whitfield* (1988) 165 CLR 360.

[11] *Waterside Workers Federation* v. *J.W. Alexander Ltd* (1918) 25 CLR 434; *Boilermakers Case* (1956) 94 CLR 254 (High Court); (1957) 95 CLR 529 (Privy Council).

[12] *Re Tracey; Ex parte Ryan* (1989) 166 CLR 518 at 580.

[13] *Polyukovich* v. *Commonwealth* (1991) 172 CLR 501 at 607.

[14] F. Wheeler, 'The Doctrine of Separation of Powers and Constitutionally Entrenched Due Process in Australia', *Monash University Law Review*, **23** (1997), p. 248.

[15] *Chu Kheng Lim* v. *Minister for Immigration* (1992) 176 CLR 1; *Kruger* v. *Commonwealth* (1997) 146 Australian Law Reports (hereafter ALR) 126.

[16] *Polyukovich, op. cit.* Mason CJ, Dawson and McHugh JJ held to the contrary.

[17] *McInnes* v. *The Queen* (1979) 143 CLR 575 at 581.

[18] *Dietrich* v. *The Queen* (1992) 177 CLR 292.

[19] Ibid., Deane J at 408; Gaudron J at 436.

[20] *Kable* v. *DPP* (NSW) (1996) 138 ALR 577 (Toohey, Gaudron, McHugh and Gummow JJ; Brennan CJ and Dawson J dissenting). While the Act involved action under a State Act the matter came within federal jurisdiction because the Constitution was raised by way of defence. For the majority judges, other than Toohey J, however, it was enough that federal jurisdiction was vested in the Court.

[21] *Nationwide News Pty Ltd* v. *Wills* (1992) 177 CLR 1.

[22] Brennan, Deane, Toohey and Gaudron JJ.

[23] *Australian Capital Television Pty Ltd* v. *Commonwealth* (1992) 177 CLR 106.

[24] Brennan J accepted the implied freedom in respect of federal matters but regarded the legislation as consistent with it. McHugh J held the provisions relating to Commonwealth elections invalid because they impaired the right of electors in federal elections to choose their members of parliament under ss. 7 and 24 of the Constitution. Brennan and McHugh JJ held the provisions relating to state elections invalid on federal grounds.

[25] A series of articles on the decision is contained in *Sydney Law Review*, **16**, pp. 145–305.

[26] *Australian Capital Television Pty Ltd, op. cit.*, at 136.

[27] Ibid., at 137–8 per Mason CJ. See also Deane and Toohey JJ in *National News Pty Ltd* v. *Wills* (1992) 177 CLR at 70, Deane J in *Theophanous* v. *Herald and Weekly Times Ltd* (1994) 182 CLR at 180, McHugh and Gummow JJ in *McGinty* v. *Western Australia* (1996) 136 CLR 230 at 274–5.

28 *Australian Capital Television Pty Ltd* v. *Western Australia* (1996) 136 CLR 230 at 274–5.

29 J.H. Ely, *Democracy and Distrust: A Theory of Judicial Review* (Cambridge, MA: Harvard University Press, 1980).

30 For example, J. Waldron, 'A Rights-Based Critique of Constitutional Rights', *Oxford Journal of Legal Studies*, **13** (1993), p. 18.

31 *Australian Capital Television Pty Ltd*, *op. cit.*, at 1 [illegible]2, 168–9, 216.

32 *Theophanous*, *op. cit.*, at 104.

33 *Stephens* v. *West Australian Newspapers Ltd* (1994) 182 CLR 211.

34 *New York Times* v. *Sullivan* (1964) 376 United States Reports (hereafter US) 254.

35 To ensure a majority, however, he supported the answers of the other three majority judges.

36 *McGinty*, *op. cit.*, at 140.

37 *Westbury* v. *Sanders* (1964) 376 US 1. The High Court had earlier refused to follow American cases in *Attorney-General (Cth)*, *op. cit.*

38 *Engineers' Case* (1920) 28 CLR 129.

39 *McGinty*, *op. cit.*, at 230–5. The Posner article is R.A. Posner, 'Legal Reasoning from the Top Down and the Bottom Up: The Question of Unenumerated Constitutional Rights', *University of Chicago Law Review*, **59** (1992), pp. 381–432.

40 A. Blackshield and G. Williams, *Australian Constitutional Law and Theory* (Annandale, NSW: Federation Press, 1998), 2nd edn, p. 1118.

41 *Lange* v. *Australian Broadcasting Corporation* (1997) 145 ALR 96.

42 Ibid., at 106.

43 It is true, however, that the joint judgment in *Theophanous* said that the defamation law must be taken to have been altered in 1901. That was a quite unnecessary view. It was enough to say, as Deane J did in that case and the judgment in *Lange* did, that conditions had changed so that the earlier version of the law did not threaten representative government in 1901, but did so later.

44 *Lange*, *op. cit.*, at 248.

45 *Union Steamship Co. of Australia Pty Ltd* v. *King* (1988) 166 CLR 1.

46 Ibid., at 10.

47 L. Zines, *Constitutional Change in the Commonwealth*, *op. cit.*, n. 40, pp. 47–8.

48 *Leeth* v. *Commonwealth* (1992) 174 CLR 455.

49 Brennan J seemed to accept a principle of equality that may have been limited to preventing different federal laws in each State, because he did not refer to the common law. He relied only on the recital in the preamble that the people of the several States agreed to unite to a Federal Commonwealth. The argument in the case was limited to that form of equality. Mason CJ, Dawson and McHugh JJ rejected the concept as an implied guarantee. Gaudron J did not express a view, but rejected it in a later case: *Kruger* v. *Commonwealth* (1997) 146 ALR 126 at 195.

50 For example, s. 51(ii) and (iii), s. 88, s. 99.

51 O. Dixon, *Jesting Pilate* (Melbourne: Law Book Co., 1965), p. 102.

52 *Nationwide News Pty Ltd*, *op. cit.*, at 69.

53 *Kruger*, *op. cit.*, at 155 (Dawson J), 194 (Gaudron J), 218 (McHugh J), 226–8 (Gummow J).

54 *Attorney-General* v. *Brown* (1847) 1 Legge 312.

55 *Cooper* v. *Stuart* 14 Appeal Cases at 291.

56 *Millirrpum* v. *Nabalco Pty Ltd* (1971) 17 Federal Law Reports 141 at 267.

57 *Mabo* v. *Queensland (No. 2)* (1992) 175 CLR 1.

58 *Mabo* v. *Queensland (No. 1)* (1988) 166 CLR 186.

59 *Re Southern Rhodesia* [1919] Appeal Cases 211 at 233–4.

60 *Mabo (No. 2)*, *op. cit.*, at 40.

61 *Advising Opinion on Western Sahara* (1975) International Court of Justice Reports at 39.

[62] *Mabo (No. 2), op. cit.*, at 42.
[63] Ibid., at 50.
[64] *Western Australia* v. *Commonwealth* (1995) 183 CLR 373 at 457.
[65] *Wik Peoples* v. *Queensland* (1996) 187 CLR 6.
[66] Ibid., at 117.
[67] Ibid., at 244.

18 Judicial Activism and Judicial Review in the High Court of Australia

GEORGE WILLIAMS[1]

Introduction

The High Court of Australia has become the subject of vitriolic and uninformed criticism. From the handling down of *Wik Peoples* v. *Queensland*[2] on 23 December 1996, the High Court, under Chief Justice Sir Gerard Brennan, experienced perhaps its most difficult period since it was created in 1903. The judges were attacked as a 'pathetic ... self-appointed [group of] Kings and Queens', a group of 'basket-weavers' and even the purveyors of 'intellectual dishonesty'.[3] Less intemperate attacks on the High Court commonly charged that the Court had been 'activist'. In this context, 'activist' acquired a pejorative connotation and became a label applied to 'meddling judges' who had strayed beyond their judicial responsibilities into the legislative field of value judgment and social and economic policy.

Both the tenures of Chief Justice Sir Anthony Mason, from 1987 to 1995, and Chief Justice Sir Gerard Brennan, from 1995 to 1998, marked important periods of judicial creativity. Developments that might have taken many years, or even decades, were compressed into the span of only a few years. For example, in 1992 the High Court held that the Constitution embodies an implied freedom of political communication.[4] In 1995 this freedom was applied to craft a constitutional defence similar to *New York Times Co* v. *Sullivan*[5] against defamation actions brought by political figures.[6] In 1997, after retirements from the Court, the 1992 decision was reaffirmed, but the 1995 decision was effectively overruled and a new extended common law defence of qualified privilege put in its place.[7] Many other decisions also marked significant advantages or changes in the law. These were not confined to constitutional law, but occurred in areas such as criminal law,[8] family law,[9] restitution[10] and native title.[11]

Rapid development of the law was partly a product of the Court's own special leave procedures, which ensure that it deals with only the most important and problematic issues.[12] However, the pace and extent of change also demonstrated a willingness on the part of the Court's judges to acknowledge and apply a law-making role. For example, like his predecessors, Sir Anthony Mason applied policy considerations and even 'community values'.[13] However, unlike them, he admitted doing so. Mason, in his published writings and speeches,[14] and the Mason Court through its decisions, swept away the popular notion that the court was engaged in a purely legalistic endeavour that did not involve making law or recourse to policy factors. This established that the law-making process was not confined to parliament.

This chapter explores themes raised by this period of 'activism' or 'creativity' on the High Court and probes more deeply into some of the issues raised by Leslie Zines in Chapter 17 of this volume. The themes explored are: changing approaches and sources in the construction of constitutional rights; double standards evident in the Court's development of constitutional rights; and the direction taken by the contemporary High Court. The focus is on the Court's work in interpreting the Australian Constitution to protect human rights. Although the Constitution contains only a few scattered provisions that protect express civil and political and economic rights, and has only limited scope to recognize implied rights, this area has been one of the most controversial for the High Court.

Changing Approaches and Sources in the Construction of Constitutional Rights

For almost the entire twentieth century, the Australian High Court has not been receptive to the view that the Constitution, and thus the Court, has a role to play in fostering the human rights. While High Court judges have been confident and creative in determining the scope of Commonwealth power or in deriving implications from Australia's federal structure, they have been uneasy about applying the document as a protector of individual liberty (even where the document itself, as, for example, in s. 117 in protecting the rights of out-of-state residents, expressly takes this position). The lack of a bill of rights in the Constitution and the limited role seen for constitutional rights by the instrument's framers has influenced the judges of the High Court to the extent that they, with few exceptions, have seen almost no role for the Constitution to protect civil and political rights.

The High Court's traditional approach was expressed in the following statement of Knox CJ, Isaacs, Rich and Starke JJ in the *Engineers'* case,[15] which railed against the derivation from the Constitution of implications protective of rights:

> If it be conceivable that the representatives of the people of Australia as a whole would ever proceed to use their national powers to injure the people of Australia considered sectionally, it is certainly within the power of the people themselves to resent and reverse what may be done. No protection of this Court in such a case is necessary or proper.[16]

Even if later judges did not hold to this view, it nevertheless exerted a powerful force. The legalistic approach to interpretation applied by judges for much of the twentieth century limited their ability to apply doctrine or material that might suggest a different approach. As Sir Anthony Mason has suggested, 'Legalism, when coupled with the doctrine of *stare decisis*, has a subtle and formidable conservative influence'.[17] Where legalism masks the original values underpinning a decision, that decision may be reproduced even where those values no longer hold true. It is by this means that the approach set out in the *Engineers'* case has been fortified in many of the decisions on express civil and political rights.

Accordingly, while a unanimous Court in *R* v. *Public Vehicles Licensing Appeal Tribunal (Tas); Ex parte Australian National Airways Pty Ltd*[18] was prepared to state that the Commonwealth's legislative powers in s. 51 of the Constitution 'should be construed with all the generality which the words used admit', the Court leant towards a narrow literal interpretation of the express civil and political rights in the instrument. This latter approach has rarely been made explicit. Exceptions are the judgments of Gibbs, Mason and Wilson JJ in *Attorney-General (Vict); Ex rel Black* v. *Commonwealth (DOGS Case)*.[19] In rejecting a submission that the guarantee of freedom of religion in s. 116 of the Constitution should be broadly construed, Wilson J stated:

> The plaintiffs' plea for a broad construction overlooks the fact that we are dealing with a clause which does not grant power, but denies it. While it is true that a constitutional grant of plenary legislative power should be construed with all the generality which the words used will admit, carrying with it whatever is incidental to the subject matter of the power, the same is not true of a provision which proscribes power.[20]

The High Court has given only narrow and grudging scope to the Constitution's express civil and political rights, at least until recent times. There have been indications that the narrow approach to certain rights in the Constitution may be reversed. This began with the unanimous decision in *Street* v. *Queensland Bar Association*,[21] where a substantive interpretation was given to s. 117, which states:

> A subject of the Queen, resident in any State, shall not be subject in any other State to any disability or discrimination which would not be equally applicable to him if he were a subject of the Queen resident in such other State.

The result in the *DOGS* case had rested on a narrow view of the role of constitutional rights, whereas *Street* rested on the opposite, finding that such rights can play a prominent part in constitutional jurisprudence. In stark contrast to the approach articulated by Wilson J in the *DOGS* case, Deane and Toohey JJ argued for a broad construction of rights-based limitations on governmental power. Such sentiments have been echoed by other judges since *Street*, such as by Gaudron J in *Kruger* v. *Commonwealth*,[22] and played an important part in dissents by Murphy J in earlier cases.[23] Most powerfully, in interpreting s. 51 (xxxi) of the Constitution, which states that the Commonwealth can legislate for 'the acquisition of property on just terms', Kirby J argued in *Newcrest Mining (WA) Ltd* v. *Commonwealth*:

> There is one final consideration which reinforces the view to which I am driven by the foregoing reasons. Where the Constitution is ambiguous, this Court should adopt that meaning which conforms to the principles of fundamental rights rather than an interpretation which would involve a departure from such rights.[24]

Such statements represent a doctrinal change in the approach of the Court to constitutional rights, particularly express civil and political rights. However, apart from the decision in *Street*, it has yet to make an impact upon such rights. While *Street* showed that there had been a fundamental shift in approach, as echoed in subsequent judgments, it is not clear how far this will be carried. There remains considerable judicial reluctance to apply the Constitution in a way that recognizes an interventionalist role in protecting individual liberty.

The jurisprudence of the High Court has shifted so that some of its members are now finding that rights, like Commonwealth powers, should be broadly construed where a choice exists between a broad and a narrow construction. The reasons for this are complex and have not been articulated by the Court. Part of this explanation lies in the fact that the Court's focus and business is shifting from issues concerning Australian federalism to issues involving constitutional rights. Many of the large questions in Australian federalism, such as the ambit of the Commonwealth's 'external affairs' power in s. 51 (xxix), have been resolved or demand less of the Court's time than they did in previous decades.[25]

In addition, since the Second World War it has become increasingly recognized in international law, and in the domestic law of other nations, that the judiciary does have a central role to play in protecting rights. Such developments naturally seep into the High Court's work on Australian law through the use of precedent from other nations and less formally through the involvement of its judges, such as Kirby J, in international judicial colloquia.[26] Kirby J has been more supportive of this process – and in particular of the use of international law in constitutional interpretation – than any other High Court judge.[27] In *Newcrest* he found that 'international law is a legitimate and important influence on the development of the common law and constitutional law, especially when international law declares the existence of universal and fundamental rights'.[28] It remains to be seen whether this dictum gains general acceptance, and thus allows instruments such as the International Covenant on Civil and Political Rights 1966 and the International Covenant on Economic, Social and Cultural Rights 1966 to directly impact upon the interpretation of the Constitution. Even if such a principle does not gain wider support on the High Court, it is clear that the Court's development of constitutional rights in the 1980s and 1990s is broadly reflective of, and undoubtedly influenced by, international developments.

Another factor that has dissolved the antipathy of the modern High Court to the protection of individual freedoms by constitutional means is its increasing reliance on the decisions of courts in other constitutional systems. Despite the warning issued in the *Engineers'* case ('we conceive that American authorities, however illustrious the tribunals may be, are not a secure basis on which to build fundamentally with respect to our own Constitution'[29]), Australian judges have increasingly turned to decisions of nations such as the United States and Canada, where constitutional law plays an important role in the protection of human rights. Indeed, the constitutional jurisprudence of such nations is pervaded with the objective of protecting the individual from arbitrary governmental interference. Although the differences between these systems and the Australian Constitution has not led the High Court to apply such decisions uncritically,[30] in developing the implied freedom of political communication in decisions such as *Australian Capital Television Pty Ltd* v. *Commonwealth*[31] and *Theophanous* v. *Herald & Weekly Times Ltd*[32] such precedent has played an important role in enabling the High Court to explore the boundaries of the Australian Constitution.

Underpinning the narrow construction given to express civil and political rights was the High Court's long-running obsession with such provisions as limitations on Commonwealth power.[33] Thus, in *Australian Communist Party* v. *Commonwealth*[34] the High Court struck down the Communist Party Dissolution Act 1950 (Cth) not because it infringed a fundamental freedom implied from the Constitution but because the law could not be characterized as falling within a head of Commonwealth power. As has been suggested by Toohey J, extra-judicially while a member of the High Court, the 'preservation of liberty' achieved by the decision in the *Communist Party* case 'may be only a fortuitous by-product of that power-dividing process'.[35] The change in the Court's approach has meant that provisions such as s. 117 have now been seen as more than mere limitations on governmental power. This is particularly appropriate in the case of s. 117 which is expressed as a personal right. In *Street*, s. 117 was viewed not only as a restriction on what the Commonwealth can do, but also as a guarantee, or commitment, to individual liberty.[36] Such provisions are more easily given a substantive interpretation when they are viewed other than merely in relation to the power that they limit.

Double Standards and Implied Rights

The Australian Constitution lacks a bill of rights, and those express civil and political rights that it does contain have been, with the recent exception of s. 117,[37] interpreted almost out of existence. It is therefore not surprising that, in the context of ever increasing international recognition of human rights, the High Court looked to other avenues to foster civil liberties. One such avenue was the notion of deriving implications from the Constitution. Despite the rhetoric of the *Engineers'* case and its rejection of constitutional implications, the High Court has a long history of deriving implications from the Constitution. As Dixon J argued in *Melbourne Corporation* v. *Commonwealth*[38] in 1947, the 'efficacy of the system logically demands' that certain implications be given recognition. In that case Dixon J recognized as implied immunity of the states from Commonwealth laws. If an implication could provide the states with some immunity from Commonwealth laws – the very thing that the decision in the *Engineers'* case had railed against – it might be possible to use a similar approach to discover implications of human rights. As Mason CJ argued in one decision, 'there is no reason to limit the process of constitutional implication to that particular source'.[39]

The implied freedoms developed in the 1990s to protect human rights have a different foundation to the implied immunity of the states from Commonwealth laws. In *Melbourne Corporation*, Dixon J stated that the 'efficacy of the system logically demands', but which system? The 'system' he was referring to was the federal system created by the Constitution, which gave rise to an implied immunity that could be 'plainly seen in the very frame of the Constitution'.[40]

On the other hand, the implied freedom of political communication developed by the Court in more recent times is derived from the system of representative government enshrined in the Constitution. Other freedoms such as any implied freedom from retrospective criminal laws arises from the separation of judicial power achieved by Chapter III of the Constitution.

The Constitution creates a system of representative government. This is spelt out in many of its provisions. Most importantly, ss. 7 and 24 require, respectively, that the members of the Senate and the House of Representatives be 'directly chosen by the people'. This imperative recognizes a system of government based on democratic elections; parliamentarians are to be 'chosen' – that is, elected – by the 'people'. The implied freedom of political communication drawn by the High Court from this system of representative government, and ss. 7 and 24 in particular, has been carefully and critically scrutinized over several cases. Indeed, the significance of one recent decision on the implied freedom, *Lange* v. *Australian Broadcasting Corporation*,[41] lies in its development of the interpretive methodology underlying the freedom rather than in any expansion or contraction of the right. Earlier cases had also been concerned to ensure that the implied freedom was constitutionally viable. Thus, in *McGinty* v. *Western Australia*[42] the High Court sought to tie the freedom developed in *Nationwide News Pty Ltd* v. *Wills*[43] and *Australian Capital Television Pty Ltd* v. *Commonwealth*[44] more precisely to the text and structure of the Constitution.

Decisions such as *McGinty* emphasized the need for any implication of rights to be fully attributable to the language of the Constitution. In *McGinty*, McHugh J was critical of the idea that the implied freedom might be drawn from the system of representative democracy as if that system were a 'free-standing principle'.[45] By this, he was concerned to honour the commitment made by the majority in the *Engineers'* case that the Court would not derive implications from sources extrinsic to the Constitution. As Brennan J stated in *Queensland Electricity Commission* v. *Commonwealth*:

> Any implication affecting the specific powers granted by the Constitution must be drawn from the Constitution itself. It is impermissible to construe the terms of the Constitution by importing an implication from extrinsic sources.[46]

Accordingly, the scope of the implied freedom of political communication must be determined and bounded by the extent to which it is given recognition by the text of the Constitution. If it exists beyond that provided for by the text, the ambit of the implication will be uncertain and the legitimacy of the freedom called into question. As a consequence of the Court recognizing this, the implied freedom of political communication, as well as other freedoms that can be derived from the system of representative government, can now be clearly seen to be delineated by the Constitution.

Implications have also been derived from the separation of judicial power achieved by Chapter III of the Constitution. This separation entails two consequences. As Dixon J recognized in *Victorian Stevedoring and General Contracting Co Pty Ltd and Meakes* v. *Dignan*,[47] 'the Parliament is restrained both from reposing any power essentially judicial in any other organ or body, and from reposing any other than that judicial power in such tribunals'. Hence, the Constitution requires that:[48]

1 Only Chapter III courts (that is, courts created under s. 71 of the Constitution) be conferred with judicial power; and
2 Chapter III courts cannot be conferred with power other than judicial power, except where such other power is ancillary or incidental to the exercise of judicial power.

Important rights have been implied by the High Court from this foundation. However, the implication of rights from the separation of judicial power has not been subjected to the same interpretive rigour as have the implications from the system of representative government. The fidelity of modern judges to the interpretative scheme laid down in the *Engineers'* case and to the text of the Constitution has been a constant theme in cases on the implied freedom of political communication, such as in *Theophanous* v. *Herald & Weekly Times Ltd*.[49] On the other hand, this has not emerged as a concern in the derivation of rights from Chapter III. This is a strange omission. The debate over the place of the *Engineers'* case is at least as relevant in that context.

The High Court has not yet been able to soundly base rights derived from Chapter III in the text and structure of the Constitution. One reason for this is that the Court has not focused, as it has in the field of representative government, on one possible implied freedom, but has ranged over a number of possible implications. Several of these implications – such as the possibility that the federal parliament cannot enact a retrospective criminal law[50] – have yet to be resolved. Another example is the controversial suggestion in decisions such as *Leeth* v. *Commonwealth*[51] and *Kruger* v. *Commonwealth*[52] that the Constitution contains a guarantee that would require substantive, or perhaps only procedural, due process in the exercise of judicial power. By contrast, the High Court quickly recognized the existence of the implied freedom of political communication in *Nationwide News* and *Australian Capital Television*. It was then able to largely concentrate on the legitimacy and scope of the freedom rather than on whether the freedom even existed.

In *Kable* v. *Director of Public Prosecutions (NSW)*[53] an implication from the separation of judicial power did gain majority support. However, the implication in that case was not squarely based in the Constitution. The Community Protection Act 1994 (NSW) empowered the Supreme Court of New South Wales to make 'preventive detention orders' against Gregory Wayne Kable, who had apparently written letters threatening the safety of his children and his deceased wife's sister. Such orders would have enabled Kable to be imprisoned even though he had not been found guilty of a criminal offence. A majority of the High Court consisting of Toohey, Gaudron, McHugh and Gummow JJ, with Brennan CJ and Dawson J dissenting, found that the Act was invalid because it infringed the separation of judicial power achieved by the Commonwealth Constitution. The Act was invalid because 'it purports to vest functions in the Supreme Court of New South Wales that are incompatible with the exercise of the judicial power of the Commonwealth by the Supreme Court of that State'.[54]

A key element of the reasoning of the majority in *Kable* was that the incompatibility doctrine should be applied to determine whether the power to make 'preventive detention orders' could be vested in the State Supreme Court. That doctrine was applied to find that such a power was incompatible with the judicial function because the power 'comprise[d] the institutional impartiality of the Supreme Court'.[55] The incompatibility doctrine had been developed as an exception to the *persona designata* rule[56] – that is, the rule that a non-judicial power can be conferred upon judges of Chapter III courts by the federal parliament if such power is conferred on a judge not as a member of the court, but in his or her personal capacity. In this context, there was nothing to suggest that the incompatibility doctrine might operate as a limit upon the power of state parliaments to legislate for state Supreme Courts. Why then was the doctrine applied in *Kable*? It was one thing to find that the Commonwealth Constitution might limit the power of a state parliament to abolish the Supreme Court of that state (this clearly being an implication from provisions such as ss. 73 and 77(iii) but it was another thing to import the incompatibility doctrine as a general limitation on the power not only of the Commonwealth to exercise judicial power under Chapter III, but also the power of the New South Wales Parliament to exercise judicial power under a state Constitution. Significantly, the result in *Kable* could not be based on the New South Wales Constitution because it had been found in *Kable* and in earlier decisions[57] that the Constitution Act 1902 (NSW) did not embody a separation of judicial power. This gave the application of the incompatibility doctrine from the Commonwealth Constitution the appearance of being contrived.

The use of the incompatibility doctrine in *Kable* and in *Nicholas* v. *The Queen*[58] by McHugh and Kirby JJ does not sit well with the strong position taken by judges such as McHugh J in *McGinty* where he spoke strongly against the notion of guarantees based on a 'free-standing principle'. Yet it is difficult to describe the use of the incompatibility doctrine in *Kable*, by judges including McHugh J, as anything else. The doctrine was taken out of the context in which it was developed – that is, the *persona designata* rule – and applied as a broad-based limitation on state and federal power. This was achieved without grounding the doctrine in the text and structure of the Commonwealth Constitution.

The majority in *McGinty* found that the implied freedom of political communication must be directly implied from the text and structure of the Constitution. They criticized the idea that the freedom could be seen as an implication from an implication – in other words, that the freedom could be seen as an implication from the system of representative government which is itself an implication from the Constitution, including ss. 7 and 24. The argument – which is itself a problematic notion[59] – was that such second-order implications are too far removed from the text of the Constitution to be legitimate inferences.[60] The incompatibility doctrine as applied in *Kable* may be seen as an implication of at least the second order. It cannot, or at least so far has not been persuasively shown to, be based in Chapter III of the Constitution. Rather, it exists as an implication from the fact that the Constitution in some ways limits the states' power to legislate for, and about, their Supreme Courts, which is in turn clearly an implication from Chapter III, particularly ss. 73 and 77(iii). If the Court is to rely on the notion that implications cannot be drawn from implications in the field of representative government, this should be equally applied in analysing freedoms drawn from Chapter III of the Constitution.

The High Court has been concerned to construct a tight analytical framework for the derivation of rights from the system of representing government created by the Constitution. The reasoning applied in describing implications from Chapter III lacks this. As a result, the ambit and nature of implications drawn from this source remain unclear and extremely uncertain. Developments in the 1990s have left the High Court with much work to do. In pushing the frontiers of Chapter III of the Constitution, the Court has outpaced its own development of constitutional methodology. This also occurred for a time in the development of the implied freedom of political communication. As with that freedom, the High Court must now establish a sound approach to underpin new concepts such as due process and the incompatibility doctrine in order to retain the legitimacy of its decision-making. Decisions on concepts such as the incompatibility doctrine have yet to develop into a stable and predictable jurisprudence that is clearly founded in the text and structure of the Constitution.

It is important that the Court remedy this discrepancy by re-examining the basis on which it has approached freedoms derived from the separation of judicial power. Unless it does this, the development of notions such as due process in the exercise of judicial power may extend beyond the proper limits imposed by the Constitution and, at the same time, undermine the persuasiveness of High Court decision-making in this area. There are also greater dangers. As Kirby J remarked in *Kartinyeri* v. *Commonwealth*, 'judicial interpretation of the Constitution risks the loss of legitimacy if it shifts its ultimate focus of attention away from the text and structure of the document'.[61]

The decisions on implied constitutional rights demonstrate that there are deep influences at work that have contributed to the unsatisfactory nature of High Court interpretation. The interpretation of the Constitution and the rights therein will always be shaped by visions of the Constitution and the perceived role of the High Court. This is an inevitable component of constitutional interpretation by judges. What is unsatisfactory is that such influences have rarely been explicit. As a result, the field of express and implied rights is replete with double standards and unarticulated premises.

The failure to articulate the deep doctrines that have shaped constitutional interpretation of constitutional rights is an unfortunate consequence of the legalism that has pervaded constitutional interpretation for much of the twentieth century. Legalism appeals to the desire of the judiciary for controversy-free adjudication. Hence Sir Owen Dixon's statement on becoming Chief Justice of the High Court in 1952 that 'There is no other safe guide to judicial decisions in great conflicts than a strict and complete legalism'.[62] However, where the Court of the 1990s adopted a legalistic approach, as in decisions such as the *Wik* case, this has not protected the Court from public controversy. Beset by criticism and failing to achieve a consistent or coherent vision of constitutional rights, the Court must move beyond legalism to an approach that identifies the forces at work in the interpretation of constitutional freedoms. The Court has begun this process, but has a long way to do. This process must continue: confidence in the Court and the legitimacy of its constitutional jurisprudence depend on it.

Judicial Activism and the Contemporary High Court

Since early 1995 the High Court has seen five of its seven judges depart. Only Gaudron and McHugh JJ remain from the Mason Court. Over this period, the High Court has been less willing to explicitly acknowledge or embrace a law-making role than it was during the Mason era.[63] This shift might be partly a reaction to the high level of criticism levelled at the Court, but may also reflect the fact that, when first appointed to the High Court, judges are less likely be creative law-makers. Mason himself was far more willing to engage in law-making when he neared the end of his tenure of the Court, than he had during his first decade or more.[64]

Two 1998 High Court decisions illustrate the Court's more restrained approach to issues of human rights and constitutional interpretation. The first decision is *Kartinyeri* v. *Commonwealth*.[65] As enacted, s. 51 (xxvi) of the Constitution empowered parliament to make laws with respect to 'The people of any race, *other than the aboriginal race in any State*, for whom it is deemed necessary to make special laws'. A referendum held in 1967, which was supported by 89.34 per cent of voters and was carried overwhelmingly in every state,[66] deleted the words in italics. It also repealed s. 127 of the Constitution, which had provided: 'In reckoning the numbers of the people of the Commonwealth, or of a State or other part of the Commonwealth, aboriginal natives shall not be counted.' Although the 1967 changes to the constitutional text gave recognition to Aboriginal people and repealed the discriminatory s. 127, they did not actually grant Aboriginal people any rights. Indeed, it remained unclear whether the extension of the races power in s. 51 (xxvi) to Aboriginal people gave the federal parliament the power to legislate for the benefit *as well as the detriment of* Aboriginal people.[67] This issue was argued before the High Court in *Kartinyeri* v. *Commonwealth.*

The Court failed to resolve the ambit of the race's power in that case. In a legalistic decision that hinted at, but did not explore, the possible relevance of 'fundamental common law rights' and the 'rule of law',[68] Gummow and Hayne JJ suggested that s. 51 (xxvi) could be used to impose a detriment on Aboriginal people. On the other hand, Gaudron and Kirby JJ found that this would not be constitutionally permissible, while Brennan CJ and McHugh J did not decide the issue. The case was heard by only six judges, Callinan J having disqualified himself from deciding the matter.

The second decision is *Nicholas* v. *The Queen*,[69] in which a majority of the Court exercised caution in dealing with the separation of judicial power. The Court's earlier decision in *Ridgeway* v. *The Queen*[70] concerned heroin imported into Australia in breach of the Customs

Act 1901 (Cth) by law enforcement officers who sold it to Ridgeway in an attempt to entrap him. A majority of the High Court found that evidence of the importation of heroin should not have been admitted because, at common law, a judge has the discretion 'to exclude, on public policy grounds, all evidence of an offence or an element of an offence procured by unlawful conduct on the part of law enforcement officers'.[71] In response to *Ridgeway*, the federal parliament inserted a new Pt 1AB into the Crimes Act 1914 (Cth).[72] Part 1AB applied to 'controlled operations' in which law enforcement officers engage in what would otherwise be illegal conduct that 'is carried out for the purpose of obtaining evidence that may lead to the prosecution of a person for an offence against section 233B of the *Customs Act 1901* or an associated offence'.[73] The Part worked to exempt law enforcement officers from criminal liability so that the discretion identified in *Ridgeway* is not enlivened. Part 1AB also had a retrospective operation, s. 15X providing that in defined circumstances:

> In determining, for the purposes of a prosecution for an offence against section 233B of the *Customs Act 1901* or an associated offence, whether evidence that narcotic goods were imported into Australia in contravention of the *Customs Act 1901* should be admitted, the fact that a law enforcement officer committed an offence in importing the narcotic goods, or in aiding, abetting, counselling, procuring, or being in any way knowingly concerned in, their importation is to be disregarded.

This section excluded the fact of illegality on the part of law enforcement officers from the consideration of a trial judge in determining whether the *Ridgeway* discretion should be exercised in favour of an accused person. The issue in *Nicholas* was whether s. 15X was invalid for breaching the separation of judicial power achieved by Chapter III of the Constitution.

The High Court delivered seven separate judgments, highlighting the absence of conceptual coherence in this area. A majority of the High Court, Brennan CJ, Toohey, Gaudron, Gummow, and Hayne JJ, found that s. 15X was valid. McHugh and Kirby JJ dissented. The accused had made three submissions as to why s. 15X was invalid. First, s. 15X invalidly directs a court to exercise its discretionary power in a way which is inconsistent with the essential character of a court or with the nature of judicial power. Second, s. 15X usurps judicial power in applying to identifiable cases and being directed specifically to the accused in those cases rather than to the public generally. Third, the attempt to remove the discretion set out in *Ridgeway* invalidly undermines the integrity of the Court's processes and public confidence in the administration of justice. The second argument was rejected on the basis that s. 15X is concerned with the effect of illegality on the part of law enforcement officers and is not designed to 'secure the conviction of' any persons.[74] In contrast to a law such as a Bill of Attainder, s. 15X could be classified as an 'evidentiary provision'.[75] The third argument failed because the *Ridgeway* discretion was not devised by the High Court to protect the reputation of the courts. Moreover, Chapter III courts were bound to apply s. 15X because 'It is for the parliament to prescribe the law to be applied by a court and, if the law is otherwise valid, the court's opinion as to the justice, propriety or utility of the law is immaterial'.[76]

In relation to the first submission, the majority recognized that the Constitution prevents the Commonwealth from passing a law, such as s. 54R of the Migration Act found invalid in *Lim,* directing a Chapter III court as to its order or judgment in its exercise of judicial power. However, this left some scope for a parliament to shape the exercise of judicial power by a Chapter III court. As Brennan CJ stated, 'a law which merely prescribes a court's practice or procedure does not direct the exercise of the judicial power in finding facts, applying law or exercising an available discretion'.[77] Section 15X was found to be just such a law. It did not impede or otherwise affect the finding of facts or deal directly with issues of guilt or innocence. Instead, 'it removes the barrier which *Ridgeway* placed against tendering to the jury evidence of an illegal importation of narcotic goods where such an importation had in fact occurred'.[78] Hence, s. 15X was not inconsistent with the separation of judicial power but was instead conducive to the exercise of such power. Underpinning this conclusion was the finding that the Commonwealth could legislate to direct the exercise of judicial power by manipulating the rules of evidence in the form of s. 15X. Brennan CJ even found if the Commonwealth had gone further than s. 15X by passing a law declaring that evidence of an illegal importation should be admitted and denying any discretion in the trial judge to exclude such evidence, this would have been valid as 'a mere procedural law assisting in the court's finding of material facts'.[79]

The minority took a different view of s. 15X, finding that it was more than a rule of evidence or procedure. McHugh J found that s. 15X could not be compared with legislation that regulates the exercise of judicial discretion by requiring certain matters to be taken into account. He characterized s. 15X as 'a direction to a court exercising federal jurisdiction that it cannot have regard to a fact that is relevant and often critical in determining whether the court's processes are being demeaned'.[80] The effect was to 'hamper, and in some cases to prevent, such a court from protecting its processes and thereby maintaining public confidence in courts exercising the judicial power of the Commonwealth'.[81] This offended the separation of judicial power as conceived by McHugh J in *Kable*. Kirby J took a similar approach, finding that the 'high particularity' of the legislation ('Almost certainly, only five individuals are involved') and the 'unrepaired affront of condoning unexcused criminality' invoked 'the unavoidable obligation of the courts' to uphold the 'integrity of the judicial system'.[82]

The dissents of McHugh and Kirby JJ showed that the High Court possesses the tools to constitutionalize much of the criminal trial process. The incompatibility doctrine as developed in *Kable* could have enabled the Court to find that the federal parliament is incapable of legislating to undermine public confidence in the administration of criminal justice. A pessimistic view of the strength of public confidence would translate into a narrow view of parliament's capacity to control the exercise of the judicial process through, for example, changes to the rules of evidence. The majority decision in *Nicholas* demonstrated restraint in not taking this course. This took account not only of the potential width and uncertain boundaries of the incompatibility doctrine as developed in *Kable* but also the dangers, for the Court, of seeking to wrest control of the trial process from federal and states parliaments. This restraint still leaves the High Court with a powerful role in this area. While the Court will allow legislatures some leeway in developing rules of procedure and evidence, these might still be struck down where they render a trial by a Chapter III court 'unfair', such as, for example, in the extreme case of a legislature providing that an accused could not call evidence in support of his or her innocence. To require a Chapter III court to conduct an 'unfair' trial may be to require such a court to exercise judicial power in a way that is inconsistent with its nature.

Conclusion

The High Court has come to explicitly acknowledge its law-making role. This is particularly evident in its interpretation of the Constitution to protect fundamental rights. These changes have incurred a significant cost in that the tension between the High Court and the other arms of government has increased markedly. It is no coincidence that, at the same time as the decline of legalism and the rise of its rights jurisprudence, the High Court attracted increasing controversy and the legitimacy of its decision-making came under direct challenge, including from Australia's political leaders.

In more recent times, the Court has been less willing to creatively apply the Constitution or to embrace a law-making role. While the judicial role always offers considerable leeway for choice, legalism no longer offers the High Court a refuge from controversy and scrutiny. There is no turning back to prior eras of 'strict and complete legalism'. The Court will inevitably face difficult cases raising unresolved issues of law that will expose its reliance on matters of policy and value judgment. As a result, even in decisions such as the *Wik* case, where the Court adopted a legalistic or black-letter approach, it was not insulated from controversy and criticism.

Notes

1 Significant parts of this Chapter are based on my book *Human Rights under the Australian Constitution* (Oxford: Oxford University Press, 1999).

2 *Wik Peoples* v. *Queensland* (1996) 187 CLR 1.

3 Quoted in M. Kirby, 'Attacks on Judges – A Universal Phenomenon', *Australian Law Journal* **72** (1998), p. 599 at p. 601.

4 *Nationwide New Pty Ltd* v. *Wills* (1992) 177 CLR 1; *Australian Capital Television Pty Ltd* v. *Commonwealth* (1992) 177 CLR 106.

5 *New York Times Co* v. *Sullivan* 376 US 254 (1964).

6 *Theophanous* v. *Herald & Weekly Times Ltd* (1994) 182 CLR 104; *Stephens* v. *West Australian Newspapers Ltd* (1994) 182 CLR 211.

7 *Lange* v. *Australian Broadcasting Corporation* (1997) 189 CLR 520.

8 *Dietrich* v. *The Queen* (1992) 177 CLR 292.

9 *Secretary, Department of Health and Community Services* v. *JWB and SMB (Marion's* case*)* (1992) 175 CLR 218.

10 *David Securities Pty Limited* v. *Commonwealth Bank of Australia* (1992) 175 CLR 353.

11 *Mabo* v. *Queensland (No. 2)* (1992) 175 CLR 1; *Wik Peoples* v. *Queensland* (1996) 187 CLR 1.

12 See Judiciary Act 1903 (Cth), s 35A.

13 According to Sir Anthony Mason, 'The Role of a Constitutional Court in a Federation: A Comparison of the Australian and the United States Experience' *Federal Law Review*, **16** (1986), p. 1 at p. 5, 'it is impossible to interpret any instrument, let alone a constitution, divorced from values. To the extent they are taken into account, they should be acknowledged and should be accepted community values rather than mere personal values. The ever present danger is that "strict and complete legalism" will be a cloak for undisclosed and unidentified policy values.' See also G. Sturgess and P. Chubb, *Judging the World: Law and Politics in the World's Leading Courts* (London: Butterworths, 1988), p. 345.

14 See, for example, Sir Anthony Mason, 'The Role of a Constitutional Court in a Federation: A Comparison of the Australian and the United States Experience' *Federal Law Review*, **16** (1986), p. 1; Sir Anthony Mason, 'Should the High Court Consider Policy Implications when Making Judicial Decisions?' *Australian Journal of Public Administration*, **57** (1998), p. 77.

15 *Amalgamated Society of Engineers* v. *Adelaide Steamship Co Ltd* (1920) 28 CLR 129.

16 Ibid., at 151–2.

17 Mason, 'The Role of a Constitutional Court', *op. cit.*, p. 5.

18 *R* v. *Public Vehicles Licensing Appeal Tribunal (Tas); Ex parte Australian National Airways Pty Ltd* (1964) 113 CLR 207 at 225.

19 *Attorney-General (Vict); Ex rel Black* v. *Commonwealth (GODS* case*)* (1981) 146 CLR 559 at 603 per Gibbs J, at 614–15 per Mason J, 652–3 per Wilson J. cf. ibid. at 577 per Barwick CJ.

20 *Attorney-General (Vict)*, *op. cit.*, at 652–3.

21 *Street* v. *Queensland Bar Association* (1989) 168 CLR 461.

22 *Kruger* v. *Commonwealth* (1997) 190 CLR 1 at 123, 131.

23 See, for example, *R* v. *Pearson; Ex parte Sipka* (1983) 152 CLR 254 at 268, 274.

24 *Newcrest Mining (WA) Ltd* v. *Commonwealth* (1997) 190 CLR 513 at 657.

25 See, for example, in relation to s. 51 (xxix), *Victoria* v. *Commonwealth (Industrial Relations Act* case*)* (1996) 187 CLR 416.

26 See M. Kirby, 'The Australian Use of International Human Rights Norms: From Bangalore to Balliol – A View from the Antipodes', *University of New South Wales Law Journal*, **16** (1993), p. 363; M. Kirby, 'The Role of International Standards in Australian Courts' in P. Alston and M. Chiam (eds), *Treaty-Making and Australia: Globalisation versus Sovereignty* (Leichhardt, NSW: Federation Press, 1995), p. 81.

27 Cf., for example, the use of international law by Gummow and Hayne JJ and Kirby J in *Kartinyeri* v. *Commonwealth* [1998] HCA 22 at paras 95–9 and paras 166–7, respectively.

28 *Newcrest Mining, op. cit.*, at 657.

29 *Amalgamated Society of Engineers, op. cit.*, at 146 per Knox CJ, Isaacs, Rich and Starke JJ. See *West* v. *Commissioner of Taxation (NSW)* (1937) 56 CLR 657 at 679 per Dixon J in which the use of Canadian precedents is also cautioned against. See generally on the use made of United States precedents, P.E. von Nessen, 'The Use of American Precedents by the High Court of Australia, 1901–1987', *Adelaide Law Review*, **14** (1992), p. 181.

30 See the use of *New York Times Co* v. *Sullivan* 376 US 254 (1964) by the High Court in *Theophanous, op. cit*. Cf. the citation of Canadian decisions such as *Switzman* v. *Elbling* [1957] SCR 285 and *Reference re Alberta Statutes* [1938] SCR 100 by Brennan J in *Nationwide News, op. cit.* and Mason CJ in *Australian Capital Television, op. cit.*

31 *Australian Capital Television, op. cit.*

32 *Theophanous, op. cit.*

33 See S. McLeish, 'Making Sense of Religion and the Constitution: A Fresh Start for Section 116', *Monash University Law Review* **18** (1992), p. 207.

34 *Australian Communist Party* v. *Commonwealth* (1951) 83 CLR 1.

35 J. Toohey, 'A Government of Laws, and Not of Men?', *Public Law Review*, **4** (1993), p. 158 at p. 169.

36 See M. Coper, *Encounters with the Australian Constitution* (North Ryde, NSW: CCH, 1987), p. 372.

37 See *Street, op. cit.*

38 *Melbourne Corporation* v. *Commonwealth* (1947) 74 CLR 31 at 83.

39 *Australian Capital Television, op. cit.*, at 134.

40 *Melbourne Corporation, op. cit.*, at 83 per Dixon J.

41 *Lange, op. cit.*

42 *McGinty* v. *Western Australia*, (1996) 186 CLR 140.

43 *Nationwide News, op. cit.*

44 *Australian Capital Television, op. cit.*

45 *McGinty, op. cit.*, at 234.

46 *Queensland Electricity Commission* v. *Commonwealth* at 231.

47 *Victorian Stevedoring and General Contracting Co Pty Ltd and Meakes* v. *Dignan* at 98.

48 These principles have been restated many times. See, for example, *Gould* v. *Brown* (1998) 151 ALR 395 at 454–5 per Gummow J.

49 *Theophanous, op. cit.*

50 See *Polyukhovich* v. *Commonwealth (War Crimes Act* case*)* (1991) 172 CLR 501.

51 *Leeth* v. *Commonwealth* (1992) 174 CLR 455.

52 *Kruger, op. cit.*

53 *Kable* v. *Director of Public Prosecutions (NSW)* (1996) 189 CLR 51.

54 Ibid., at 109 per McHugh J.

55 Ibid., at 121 per McHugh J.

56 See *Grollo* v. *Palmer* (1995) 184 CLR 348.

57 *Clyne* v. *East* (1967) 68 SR (NSW) 385; *Building Construction Employees and Builders' Labourers Federation of New South Wales* v. *Minister for Industrial Relations* (1986) 7 NSWLR 372.

58 *Nicholas* v. *The Queen* (1998) 151 ALR 312.

59 The idea that a precise set of steps can be calculated in determining the means by which one concept is derived from another is problematic. Depending on the approach, it can be argued that one or more steps are involved in almost any process of implying one concept from another.

60 See generally N. Aroney, *Freedom of Speech in the Constitution* (St. Leonard's, NSW: Centre for Independent Studies, 1998).

61 *Kartinyeri* v. *Commonwealth* (1998) 152 ALR 540 at 584.

62 'Swearing in of Sir Owen Dixon as Chief Justice' (1951) 85 CLR xi at xiv.

63 A good example is the decision of the High Court in *Breen* v. *Williams* (1996) 186 CLR 71.

64 M. Kirby, 'A.F. Mason: From Trigwell to Teoh', *Melbourne University Law Review*, **20** (1996), p. 1087.

65 *Kartinyeri, op. cit.*

66 The 'yes' vote is sometimes cited as being 90.77 per cent. However, this figure excludes the fact that 1.58 per cent of votes cast were informal.

67 See A.R. Blackshield and G. Williams, *Australian Constitutional Law and Theory: Commentary and Materials*, 2nd edn (Annandale, NSW: Federation Press, 1998), pp. 164–76; M.J. Detmold, 'Original Intentions and the Race Power', *Public Law Review*, **8** (1997), p. 244; N. Pengelley, 'The Hindmarsh Island Bridge Act. Must Laws Based on the Race Power be for the "Benefit" of Aborigines and Torres Strait Islanders? And what has Bridge Building got to do with the Race Power Anyway?', *Sydney Law Review*, **20** (1998), p. 144; J. Williams and J. Bradsen, 'The Perils of Inclusion: The Constitution and the Race Power', *Adelaide Law Review*, **19** (1997), p. 95.

68 *Kartinyeri, op. cit.*, at 569.

69 *Nicholas, op. cit.*

70 *Ridgway* v. *The Queen* (1995) 184 CLR 19.

71 Ibid., at 33 per Mason CJ, Deane and Dawson JJ.

72 Crimes Amendment (Controlled Operations) Act 1996 (Cth).

73 Crimes Act 1914 (Cth), s. 15H.

74 *Nicholas, op. cit.*, at 323 per Brennan CJ.

75 Ibid., at 330 per Toohey J.

76 Ibid., at 326 per Brennan CJ.

77 Ibid., at 319.

78 Ibid., at 319 per Brennan CJ.

79 Ibid., at 322.

80 Ibid., at 348.

81 Ibid., at 349.

82 Ibid., at 378, 381–2.

Index